Galaxy Series

THRUST

FOCUS

VANGUARD

PERSPECTIVES

ACCENT: U.S.A.

COMPASS

Olive Stafford Niles   Reading Consultant, Connecticut State Department of Education. Lecturer in courses on the teaching of reading, American International College, Springfield, Massachusetts. Formerly, Director of Reading, Public Schools of Springfield, Massachusetts; Member of the Board of Directors, International Reading Association; Director: High School and College Reading Center, Boston University.

Elsie Katterjohn   Formerly, Reading Coordinator, Willowbrook High School, Villa Park, Illinois; Chairman of the Language Arts Department, Community High School, North Chicago, Illinois.

FOCUS

Editorial direction: **Leo B. Kneer**

Development: **Aloha S. Lawver**
with Donald Abramson,
Ellen Wettersten, and Harold Eaton

Design: **Robert Amft**

Scott, Foresman and Company

The authors and editors of *Focus* acknowledge with gratitude
the contributions to this anthology made by the teachers
listed below who tried out materials in classrooms and assessed the
effect of various selections on their students. Their students
helped, too, through their candid comments on the selections
they were asked to read.

Mrs. Virginia Briner
Daniel Webster Junior High School, Waukegan, Illinois

Dr. June S. Wilson
The University School, Ann Arbor, Michigan

Mrs. Sheila B. Feigelson
The University School, Ann Arbor, Michigan

Mrs. Florence Meaghan
Franklin Junior High School, Cedar Rapids, Iowa

Mr. Charles Olschefski
Pasteur Elementary School, Detroit, Michigan

Mrs. Margaret Petters
Daniel Webster Junior High School, Waukegan, Illinois

Mrs. Linda C. Roberts
Southern Junior High School, Louisville, Kentucky

Miss DeLite Sharp
Taft Junior High School, Cedar Rapids, Iowa

Mrs. Barbara H. Taylor
Barret Junior High School, Louisville, Kentucky

We also wish to express appreciation to Mr. Raymond Griffin,
formerly Principal of the Wadsworth Upper Grade Center,
Chicago, and to Mrs. Jeanne Connelly Junker, Principal of the
Bryn Mawr School, Chicago, who permitted us to try out
selections in classrooms in their schools.

CONTENTS

FOCUS

10 TURNING POINT

11 FLEXIBILITY

12 INVENTORY

ILLUSTRATIONS:

range (rānj), 1. dis extent: *a range of price* within certain limit 3. distance a gun c etc., of an object ai ing. 6. land for gr 8. wander; rove; ranged these plair happened on vaca about. 11. row 13. line of direc with the house. books by size. line on someon with the king. which certain

nce between certain limit

rom 5 cents to 25 dollars.

prices ranging from $5

shoot. 4. distance from

ed at. 5. a place to pract

ing. 7. of or on land fo

m. 9. wander over: B

Our talk ranged over

10. act of wandering

line of mountains.

n: The two barns are

. put in a row or

put in groups or cl

side: Loyal citizens

. rank, class, or or

nts or animals live

ging east anc

One of the four was twice a killer.
But he would go free—if no one else
lived to tell the story.

The Long, Cold Night

by Allan Vaughan Elston

THE SMOKE and stench of the room would have stifled a newcomer, but David, by now, was fairly used to it. The young cabin boy lay numbly in his upper bunk, listening to the talk of the four sailors.

"Come 'nother month, we sight sunlight," Kaspar guessed.

But Grotan, the shaggy giant, disagreed. "Ye're a mont' off, mate," he argued. "Call it the last week o' February, I say, and set yer sights from there."

The two men debated the date drearily, while Diker, a thin, rat-faced man, riffled the cards, staring hollowly at the fire and saying nothing. David lay wretchedly in his sleeping bag. By the light of an evil-smelling lamp, through a blue haze of smoke, he could see the four who were keeping vigil with him through the arctic night.[1]

Their hut was of planking, torn from

[1] **arctic night.** Within the Arctic Circle there are long periods during the fall and winter months when there is no sunlight. This period lasts for six months at the North Pole, but is shorter in places near the outer edge of the Arctic Circle.

the ship's wreckage on the beach. They had fuel aplenty from wreckwood and driftwood strewn along the beach, and a litter of other supplies salvaged from that part of the *Norwhaal* which had grounded not far offshore.

Three things had been most needed when the sea had delivered the five half-frozen survivors to this arctic beach: food, tools, clothing. In a calm at low tide, Grotan and Hale had ventured out on a raft to the grounded wreck. They had returned with salt beef, oil, bedding, and a sea chest. The chest was the only box of clothing left in that shambles of wrecked cabins. And here was a grim joke: the brass plate on the chest bore the name of the murdered mate.

They had also recovered one tool, an ax. From his upper bunk, David could see the ax leaning against a wall. It was a fire ax. The men had used it both as hammer and as blade to build this refuge. But the sight of the ax always frightened David. On the night before the arctic storm that proved fatal to the *Norwhaal* and most of her crew, that same ax had been employed for murder. Its sharp blade had laid low the *Norwhaal*'s mate.

There had been no known motive for the crime. Yet it was certain that guilt lay among the four who sat in this hut. At the instant of the crime, everyone except these four and the murdered mate had been assembled forward with Skipper Quayne.

With a shiver, David turned his eyes away from the ax. His dull gaze came to rest on a stout, iron-bound door of three-inch oak, intact with lock and hinges. This had once been the door of the *Norwhaal*'s brig on the afterdeck. For lack of another, it had been built into this hut. Now the same four men who had been locked in the brig of the *Norwhaal* on suspicion of murder found refuge behind that same massive door.

Grotan turned toward David. "What hour is it, lad?" His voice was soft, yet his water-blue eyes, set too close together, always filled the boy with vague distrust. In build Grotan was splendid. His long yellow mustaches and yellow beard gave him the look of a heroic viking.

"Twelve o'clock, sir," David said. He had the only timepiece among them.

"Noon," Hale murmured. He was so thin he reminded David of a skeleton.

"Midnight," Kaspar argued. He seldom agreed with anyone. "But wot's the difference?"

"Right you are, mate," Grotan said. "The only time as counts is whalin' time. That'll be June, or mebbe the ebb o' May.[2] They'll pick us up then, if we don't rot o' scurvy."

Hale turned his bony head to stare at Grotan. Hale was skin and bones. His eyes were like the sockets of a

---

[2] **ebb o' May,** decline of May, or end of May.

skull. This and his frightful paleness made him to David the least companionable of them all.

"She'll fetch plenty o' difference to the wrong 'un among us," Hale said sourly.

As David returned the watch to his pocket, his fingers touched a heavy brass key he kept hidden there. The skipper's last order came vividly back to him: "Take this key and let those men out of the brig!" Moments after the Captain's order, as David turned the key in the stout oak door, a gigantic island of ice, chisel-sharp, had sliced through the *Norwhaal* like a knife through cheese. The impact was at midship, where Captain and crew were huddled, waiting for a chance to lower the lifeboats. Only the four imprisoned men and David, their deliverer, had survived.

The boy tossed restlessly for a while longer. Then he crawled out of his sleeping bag. The two small hearthstones which he kept there to warm his feet were cold. So he took them down to the soft ash at the hearth's edge.

"Blast a short deck, I say!" Kaspar complained. He threw down his frayed cards and stood up. The men had been using a fifty-one-card deck found in the mate's chest.

"Lend a hand, Davy," Grotan purred. A bellow would have suited him better, David thought. "See if ye can turn up that missin' card."

"If it's anywhere," the boy said, "it's in the chest."

"Right he are. Stand away from the chest, bullies, while the lad takes another poke through it. It's the Jack o' Diamonds."

David searched through the chest without success. But at the bottom corner his eye fell upon a small black leather-bound book. He had noticed it before, but had given it no attention. Now a word of gilt lettering on the cover caused him to pick it up. It was a diary.

"Kept a log, did he?" snarled Diker.

Grotan's silky voice broke the silence: "Well, wot if he did keep a log? I know wot ye're thinkin'—that mebbe he named the bully wot done him in. But how could he?"

Kaspar blinked. "Yeah, how could he? He couldn't very well log that trick."

" 'At's right," Diker wheezed. "When 'at ax dropped him, he never moved again."

"Mebbe we better keep it," Grotan said calmly. "Hand it over, lad."

"Yes, sir." David held out the diary.

"Naw ye don't," Kaspar protested. "If one looks, we all looks." He snatched the book and they all crowded shoulder to shoulder with him.

It was an ordinary diary, briefly recording the weather day by day and little else. But then came a startling comment:

One of this new crew looks a little like Bart Shonts, who kept bar at a New Bedford waterfront grog shop. Won't report him to the skipper till I'm sure. If he is Shonts, New Bedford wants him for killing a longshoreman.

Kaspar licked his thumb and turned another page. For day on day during the voyage north, the mate made no further mention of Bart Shonts. Finally they came to the last entry. It was dated the night before the wreck—the night on which the mate had been killed with the ax. The final notation read:

Going to find out whether that man's Bart Shonts. He's down the aft passage right now, polishing brass and glass on the fire kit. I'll just drop by and sing out, "Hello, Shonts," and watch his face.

That was all. Yet instantly the motive of the crime became clear.

Diker squealed, "It weren't me! I didn't—"

"Ye say ye didn't, ye stinking rat!" Grotan cut in softly. "And so do I. But somebody did."

Hale said somberly, "Aye, somebody. Somebody as kept bar at New Bedford."

"And when we gets back to New Bedford," Kaspar shrilled, "they kin point the man out."

Grotan turned to David. "Well, lad, it's clear *ye* didn't do it. So ye're the right 'un to keep this book. When the whalin' fleet comes, turn it over. They kin take the four of us in irons to New Bedford, and hang whoever as turns out to be Shonts."

He handed the book to David. The boy looked from one man to another. Which one . . . ? It could have been Grotan himself. . . . Or the skull-faced Hale. Hale, from the first, had been haggard and nervous.

Or Diker! The chinless Diker with the red, rattish eyes. The eyes of a criminal, they might well be.

Or Kaspar? Not so likely Kaspar, David thought. Kaspar was stubborn and ill-tempered, but not repulsive like Diker. Nor so somberly mysterious as Hale. Nor with Grotan's suggestion of silky deceit.

Whichever it was, the man who had once used the ax might well use it again. David shuddered.

For long and terrible hours they sat silently in the glow of the hearth, each man hugging his own thoughts.

Often in the past the drone of the others' talk had lulled David to sleep. But now there was no talk. David could hear an occasional cracking of the ice pack offshore, but nothing more. It was a merciless sound, but not half so grim as the silence of the hut. That silence fairly screamed aloud the menacing presence of a murderer.

Hours later David awoke with a start. In the cold gloom he could see Kaspar's blocky form sagging in the hammock. A snore under his own bunk told him that Grotan was there. Neither Hale nor Diker was in sight, but the door was barred on the inside, so David knew that all the inmates were in bed. Yet some detail of the room was wrong.

It was the ax. Or rather the fact that the ax was gone.

Kaspar stirred in his hammock and growled, "What time is it, boy?"

David's voice, answering that it was five o'clock, aroused the others.

Diker climbed out. His eyes immediately sought the ax.

His voice came like the bark of a dog: "Who took it?"

"Took what?" Kaspar asked hoarsely. But he was already out of his hammock, staring at the place where the ax should be.

Hale came slipping like a ghost from his upper berth. "Aye, who took it? And what fer?"

Grotan was out now, towering above all of them.

"It's ye as took it, ye big bully bum!" Diker shrilled at Grotan. "It's hid in his bunk, I'll stake ye. He's bidin' a chance to blow down the whole blasted crew!"

Grotan's big hand pushed him to a sprawl. Then, facing Hale and Kaspar,

he said, "Aye, I'm the one as took it. Wot I'm not takin' is chances."

"Chances o' wot?" Hale asked. His question seemed false and flat.

"Chances o' murder, that's wot," Grotan said. His close-set eyes stared at Diker and his voice was dangerously soft. "So I walks out on the ice pack with that ax, and I drops it through a seal hole into the sea."

"He's a blasted liar! Search his bunk!" Diker screamed. He began clawing through the bedding on Grotan's bunk. He found nothing.

"The ax, so help me, is at the bottom of the sea," Grotan swore.

"Who elected *you* to take charge of that ax?" Kaspar bawled.

"Elected myself," Grotan said, and tamped tobacco in his clay pipe. "Why? Because I don't aim to get blowed down in my sleep. One o' ye three bullies is twice a killer. And sure to go scot-free if—"

Hale licked his thin lips. "If wot?"

"If he's the only man o' the crew alive at whalin' time," Grotan said.

The men bickered for hours while David looked on dully from his bunk.

At last he slept fitfully, dreaming strange and terrible dreams. When he awoke, the cabin was dark and the others were in bed.

He crawled down, lighted the lamp, and began to set out tins of salt beef on the chest. In a little while Grotan aroused himself and joined him. Grotan's lids were puffy and his face was swollen. Kneeling close by the boy, he whispered, "Davy, keep yer eye on Diker."

David could see Diker sleeping in the bunk under Hale's. Hale, he noticed, was wide awake, staring ghoulishly down at them.

Suddenly Hale's lips moved. David could read the soundless syllables formed there. They said, "Watch Grotan."

David shivered. How could he watch them all, through the stretch of this northern night?

The rattle of pans aroused Diker. David went to wake up Kaspar, but Kaspar did not hear his call or feel his touch. A green cord had been torn from the man's hammock and noosed tightly about his throat. Kaspar had been garroted in his sleep.

For sixty hours after they buried Kaspar in the snow, David did not shut an eye. Nor did Grotan. Nor Hale. Nor Diker. One of the three had killed Kaspar, and those three sat eyeing one another.

A grim witness, Death itself, had acquitted Kaspar. Of the remaining three, one indisputably was Shonts, easily convictable at New Bedford—*if* one single voice survived to tell the story.

But that one voice would not survive. Shonts planned to garrote them all, one by one, in their sleep. The answer was—no sleep.

With David up, Grotan, after sixty hours, risked a wink of sleep. But only a wink. Then he came out, haggard and shaggy, for a session of solitaire on the mate's chest. His voice asked strainedly, "Wot time is it, lad?"

David delved into his pocket. There he felt the brass key. It was the key to that oaken door, the brig door, and they did not know he had it. David kept that secret jealously. These men were in a brig and he, David, had the key. Constantly that thought recurred to his sick and weary mind. But what good was it? What use could he make of the key?

David drew forth the watch. "Eight o'clock," he said.

"Morning," Hale muttered.

"Night, mates," Grotan corrected.

"It's all night and it's all hell!" Diker shrieked.

"Hell for somebody, when we gets 'im to New Bedford," Grotan agreed.

By the end of the week a light was winking outside at each noontime. Winter dawn was breaking. And Hale was slowly going mad. Through long hours he would lie in bed sobbing, screaming sometimes, always complaining. It racked David's nerves. It wore out the patience of Grotan and of Diker until they cursed the sick man. Hale refused to eat. Time and again David took food to him, and was shrieked away.

Finally, when David took him a cup of hot tea the man seized his wrist and tried to bite it. David fell back in horror. He saw froth on Hale's lips. He called to Grotan.

They strapped Hale down, then. Forty hours later he died, mad and starved.

"It don't prove as he wasn't Shonts, lad," Grotan said, after Hale was buried in deep snow beside Kaspar. "But I doubt if he was, Davy. Watch Diker."

Then Diker slipped up and whispered, "Watch Grotan. If we both go sleepin' while he's up, we're done fer, boy."

David tried desperately to believe that all guilt was now dead with Hale. But he couldn't. He was far from trusting either of the two left with him. When drowsiness forced him to sleep, a horned imp who was Diker and a beast with the shaggy head of Grotan pranced through his dreams.

Drowsiness always won, and many

times David slept soundly—generally with both men awake, one to protect him against the other. But in the end David awoke from a deep sleep to find that Diker was also sleeping soundly, while Grotan sat smoking his clay pipe and playing solitaire on the mate's chest.

"I reckon that proves it, Davy, eh?" Grotan purred.

Yet even then David wasn't sure. More than a month must pass before they could hope for the whalers. More than a month was plenty of time for Shonts, if Shonts was still in this hut, to eliminate one man and a boy.

Twice more, in the next week, David emerged from his dreams to find Grotan awake and Diker asleep. Never once did he find them the other way.

One day, when light was half a day long, Diker complained that his gums hurt. The next morning he refused to leave his bunk. He was sick, he said.

Grotan came over for a look. "I was afeered o' that," he whispered to David. "He's down o' scurvy."

Diker weakened fast. The sweat of a fever bathed him, and his gums were swollen frightfully. His eyes became sockets, deep and black.

"Bad job it didn't happen afore he kilt Kaspar, lad," Grotan said. "But ye don't need to worry no more, Davy. Time he's up, if he ever gits up, the whalers'll be droppin' anchor offshore."

Yet David still wasn't sure. And now, instead of the crackling groans of the ice pack, he could hear constantly the swishing of waves. Day was chasing night out of the north.

Every hour Diker weakened. The snags of his yellow teeth loosened in his head. By then he was delirious. He shouted for the cabin boy and for Skip-

per Quayne. He begged Quayne to let him out of the brig. Shonts was in there with him, he swore, and Shonts was choking him with a cord.

"He'll be out all right, come mornin'," Grotan guessed. Diker *did* leave the brig next morning, dead of scurvy. They buried him in a deep snowdrift, well apart from Kaspar and Hale.

"We dassn't put him 'longside two honest seamen, Davy," Grotan decreed. "He's Shonts, I say. Ye know that for certain, don't ye?"

"Yes, sir." But David didn't know it at all.

"Hand over 'at mate's notebook, Davy." Grotan's voice was smoothly persuasive. "We'll log it all nice and shipshape."

David's numb hand took the mate's diary from his pocket and gave it to Grotan. On the first blank page, Grotan wrote:

Seaman Diker, ailius Shonts, kilt Seaman Kaspar then dyed of skurvy hisself Hail went crasy mad Seamon Grotan and cabin boy standing by to sight whaling craft.

"That logs it shipshape, Davy," Grotan said. Then, carelessly, he dropped the book into his own pocket.

A feeling grew over David that Shonts did not lie under snow, that Shonts stood alive and six-feet-three, wearing the smile of a great golden wolf. But if Grotan was Shonts, why did he spare David?

The hand of fear clutched David through every hour Grotan was awake. When Grotan slept, his dread almost left him, for Grotan snored. The snores were convincing. No fiend or murderer, David thought, could rest as easily as that.

One day while Grotan slept, David

made a discovery. As he was going through the mate's chest in search of a new wick for the oil lamp, he shook something out of an old sea boot. It was the missing card of the mate's playing deck—a Jack of Diamonds.

It was oddly disfigured. Someone, using a yellow pencil, had sketched upon this Knave of Diamonds a flowing beard and two long yellow mustaches, and had crowned him with a golden shock of hair.

The suggestion of this picture jolted David. Slowly a vision formed in his mind—a vision of the *Norwhaal*'s mate, playing solitaire with this deck, and wondering about the seaman who might be Shonts.

What would Shonts look like with a yellow beard? The mate's eye might have dropped to the Knave of Diamonds lying face up before him. And he might have picked up a yellow pencil and sketched mustaches, a shock of hair, and a beard on the face of the Knave.

For a moment David was certain. Grotan was Shonts! And, if so, David was doomed. Then it came to him that this card was in no way conclusive. Perhaps Kaspar or Hale or Diker had found the card, unmarked, and had used it to cast suspicion upon Grotan.

In a turmoil of conflicting doubts, David put the card in his inner pocket. He said nothing about it to Grotan.

There was another week, then, of terrifying vigil. Each noon Grotan climbed the mast on which their distress signal fluttered, and peered out to sea. He grew silent and fretful. The boy gave him a wide berth. Always he waited until the man was in bed and snoring before ascending to his own bunk.

One night while digging his warm stones from the ashes of the fire, David found a square of scorched leather there. It was half of the front leather cover belonging to the mate's diary.

David looked toward Grotan's bunk. The man lay there with his eyes closed, but it seemed to David that one of those eyelids quivered. Was Grotan really asleep? Had he observed David retrieving the scrap of leather?

The boy hastily concealed the scrap in his pocket. Then, in a tremble, he climbed to his bunk. He resolved not to sleep until he heard snores from Grotan.

When these came, he did sleep. It was the sudden stopping of those sounds which presently awakened him.

David did not open his eyes. He lay quite still, giving strained attention to the silence from the bunk below.

He heard Grotan get out of bed and cross the room in sock feet. The cat-like stealth of that tread petrified him. The boy opened his eyes.

Grotan had lighted the lamp, casting a shapeless shadow of himself on the wall opposite. The shadow moved, like the living silhouette of a monster. Not toward David's bunk, but toward the green-corded hammock which had been Kaspar's. The hands of the shadow reached out and broke off a length of cord. The hands slowly fashioned that cord into a noose—a noose like the one which had strangled Kaspar.

David screamed. He sat upright in his bunk.

Over there, by the hammock, stood Grotan. Guilt covered his face. One hand was behind him. "Wot's the matter, Davy?" he asked quickly. "Nightmare?"

The boy nodded frantically. The

man's eyes bored at him suspiciously. "Wot didja dream about, Davy?"

"About—Diker." The lie choked desperately from the boy's lips. He saw that Grotan half believed it. His eyes narrowed with an indecision which David fearfully understood. Should he deal with the boy now, Grotan was debating, or later?

"Well, skin down and dish out a mess o' rations."

The man stooped, put on his boots, and strode out of the hut.

When he was well gone, David came feverishly to life. He stumbled to the door—the stout, iron-bound door of three-inch oak—and slammed it shut. He dropped the oaken bar in place across the brackets.

When Grotan came back, he would have to crash in. That he could do, using a log to batter with, but it would take time. David climbed to an upper bunk and peered out through an air hole. He could see Grotan going up the hill toward the signal mast. He saw the man climb the mast and peer toward the sea.

Then he heard a hoarse shout. He saw Grotan slide to the ground, jump up and down, and wave his arms frantically toward the sea.

David slipped to the floor and ran to the seaward side of the hut. He climbed to the top of the woodpile and peered through another air hole. Out there, on the open sea, was a schooner. She was far offshore as yet, but her bowsprit was pointed this way.

David's legs felt like wisps of grass as he slid down to the floor. His first thought was to get out and run. Then he realized that he would be safer here, with that barred door between him and Grotan. Grotan, with no chopping tool, could hardly batter his way in during the brief time at his disposal.

So David left the door barred. Then he climbed again to the landward peephole and looked out. What he saw plunged him into panic. For Grotan, after all, *did* have a chopping tool. David was just in time to see him dig the ax out of a snowdrift.

Now Grotan was plunging like a mad beast toward the shack. When the door resisted his push, he uttered a low rumble of surprise. Then he lifted the ax and crashed it into the door. The blade bit deep. Back the ax went over his shoulder; down it came again, with a Titan's blow, on the door.

David, through the peephole, watched him swing those blows. He heard the splinter of oak. He slipped to the floor and stood with a fist pressed against his mouth.

The thuds of the ax now came in rhythmic sequence. David flinched at each blow as though it struck his heart. At five-second intervals, the blows came like drumbeats. Slowly but surely, Grotan was chopping his way through the door.

Then an inspiration came to David. If the descending ax, with all of Grotan's power behind it, should meet no resistance, then—

David quickly removed the oaken bar and laid it on the floor. The ax at this instant, he guessed, was poised over Grotan's shoulder. A crushing blow would come. David timed it with his own heartbeats.

With a sudden jerk, he pulled the door wide open. Empty space met that final chop of Grotan's. His great body came toppling in, and he sprawled face down on the floor.

In a flash David had the ax and was

outside with it. In the same flash a brass key came from his pocket. He slammed and locked the door.

Dropping the ax, he raced down the beach. Not far offshore he saw a whaler standing by to lower a boat.

David shouted in pitiful hysteria, jumping up and down, waving his frail arms. He saw the boat coming.

He collapsed in a faint, then. In a little while he heard voices. Rough men were grouped around him. One of them, in the uniform of a skipper, was kneeling by his side.

"What's your name, lad?"

"David Jones, sir," he said.

"And where might your crew be, lad?"

"He's locked in the brig, sir."

Then David, the cabin boy, handed the skipper a heavy brass key.

THE END

Talking it over

1. *a.* Of the five survivors of the wreck, how many are suspected of murder?

b. Why are these particular men under suspicion?

2. Why does the discovery of the mate's diary make it necessary for the killer to get rid of the other survivors?

3. *a.* Even after Hale and Diker die, why isn't David sure that Grotan is the murderer?

b. David finds the Knave of Diamonds playing card and the scorched cover of the diary. Why do these two things suggest who the murderer is?

Words in action

What does *bark* mean?

It depends, of course, on how the word is used. The bark on a tree is one thing; the bark of a dog is something else.

Below are groups of three sentences, all of which contain the same word. In two of the sentences the word has about the same meaning, but in the other the meaning is different. On your paper, after the number of the sentence group, write the letters of the two sentences in which the word in bold type has the same meaning. Be prepared to explain how you could tell.

1. *a.* The **deck** had been marked by a dishonest player.

b. The captain ordered all hands on **deck**.

c. Jim hid the **deck** in his desk when the teacher looked his way.

2. *a.* Grotan used a **log** to batter down the door.

b. The board of inquiry searched the **log** to determine how far the ship had traveled on December 4.

c. The pilot kept the plane's **log** up to date by recording all changes in speed and altitude.

3. *a.* The teakwood **chest** was filled with colorful souvenirs of the Orient.

b. The handles on the **chest** need polishing.

c. The caveman beat his **chest** and gave a triumphant shout.

4. *a.* "You **knave**!" the king shouted after the fleeing man.

b. No one realized that it was the **knave** Gambler Joe had slipped from his sleeve which won him the poker game.

c. This **knave** must be punished.

His first big break

Allan V. Elston had been writing for cheap magazines for ten years before any of his stories were accepted by an important national magazine. Then, in 1934, the *American Magazine* announced an experiment. Instead of publishing only stories written by well-known authors, they would have office boys paste a piece of black tape over the author's name on each manuscript sent in. The editors would select stories without knowing who had written them. Six stories were chosen in this way for the April 1935 issue. One of them was "The Long, Cold Night." After that, many of Mr. Elston's stories appeared in popular magazines.

The author also recalls an incident involving an eighth-grade boy who had been assigned to write a short story. The boy's story not only won praise from his teacher but was published in the school paper. Then someone recognized it as one of Mr. Elston's. The boy wrote to him saying he had been expelled for plagiarizing, but would be taken back if he wrote a full confession and apology to the author and received his forgiveness. Mr. Elston air mailed the "pardon" and the boy was reinstated at school.

Before he became a full-time writer, Mr. Elston was an engineer. He served in World War I and was a lieutenant colonel of Tank Destroyers in World War II. In recent years he has been writing what he calls "semi-historical western novels" at the rate of about two a year.

When Cholmondely got on the bus,
all the passengers
rushed for the door.

CHOLMONDELY
the Chimpanzee

by Gerald Durrell

WHEN Cholmondely,[1] the chimpanzee, joined the collection of animals I was making for zoos, he immediately became the uncrowned king of it, not only because of his size, but also because he was so remarkably intelligent.

Cholmondely had been the pet of a District Officer who, wanting to send the ape to the London zoo and hearing that I was collecting wild animals in that part of Africa and would shortly be returning to England, wrote and asked me if I would mind taking Cholmondely with me and handing him over to the zoo authorities. I wrote back to say that as I already had a large collection of monkeys, another chimpanzee would not make any difference, and so I would gladly escort Cholmondely back to England. I imagined that he would be quite a young chimp, perhaps two years old, and standing about two feet high. When he arrived I got a considerable shock.

A small van drew up outside the camp one morning and in the back of it was an enormous wooden crate. It was big enough, I thought, to house an elephant. I wondered what on earth could be inside, and when the driver told me that it contained Cholmondely

[1]**Cholmondely** (chum′lē)

I remember thinking how silly his owner was to send such a small chimpanzee in such a huge crate. I opened the door and looked inside and there sat Cholmondely. One glance at him and I realized that this was no baby chimpanzee but a fully grown one about eight or nine years old. Sitting hunched up in the dark crate, he looked as though he were about twice as big as me, and from the expression on his face I gathered that the trip had not been to his liking.

Before I could shut the door of the box, however, Cholmondely had extended a long, hairy arm, clasped my hand in his, and shaken it warmly. Then he turned round and gathered up a great length of chain (one end of which was fastened to a collar round his neck), draped it carefully over his arm, and stepped down out of the box. He stood there for a moment and, after surveying me carefully, examined the camp with great interest, whereupon he held out his hand, looking at me inquiringly. I took it in mine and we walked into the marquee together.

Cholmondely immediately seated himself on one of the chairs by the camp table, dropped his chain on the floor, and sat back and crossed his legs. He gazed around the tent for a few minutes with a rather supercilious expression on his face, and evidently deciding that it would do, he turned and looked at me inquiringly again. Ob-

viously, he wanted me to offer him something after his tiring journey. I had been warned before he arrived that he was a hardened tea drinker, and so I called out to the cook and told him to make a pot of tea. Then I went out and had a look in Cholmondely's crate, and in the bottom I found an enormous and very battered tin mug. When I returned to the tent with this, Cholmondely was quite overjoyed and even praised me for my cleverness in finding it, by uttering a few cheerful "hoo hoo" noises.

While we were waiting for the tea to arrive, I sat down opposite Cholmondely and lit a cigarette. To my surprise, he became very excited and held out his hand across the table to me. Wondering what he would do, I handed him the cigarette packet. He opened it, took out a cigarette, and put it between his lips. He then reached out his hand again and I gave him the matches. To my astonishment, he took one out of the box, struck it, lit his cigarette, and threw the box down on the table. Lying back in his chair he blew out clouds of smoke in the most professional manner. No one had told me that Cholmondely smoked. I wondered rather anxiously what other bad habits he might have which his master had not warned me about.

Just at that moment, the tea was brought in and Cholmondely greeted its appearance with loud and expressive hoots of joy. He watched me carefully while I half filled his mug with milk and then added the tea. I had been told that he had a very sweet tooth, so I put in six large spoons of sugar, an action which he greeted with grunts of satisfaction. He placed his cigarette on the table and seized the mug with both hands; then he stuck out his lower lip very carefully and dipped it into the tea to make sure it was not too hot. As it was a trifle warm, he sat there blowing on it vigorously until it was cool enough, and then he drank it all down without stopping once. When he had drained the last drops, he peered into the mug and scooped out all the sugar he could with his forefinger. After that, he tipped the mug up on his nose and sat with it like that for about five minutes until the very last of the sugar had trickled down into his mouth.

I had Cholmondely's big box placed some distance away from the marquee, and fixed the end of his chain to a large tree stump. He was too far away, I thought, to make a nuisance of himself but near enough to be able to watch everything that went on and to conduct long conversations with me in his "hoo hoo" language.

But on the day of his arrival he caused trouble almost as soon as I had fixed him to his tree stump. Outside the marquee were a lot of small, tame monkeys tied on long strings attached to stakes driven into the ground. They were about ten in number, and over them I had constructed a palm leaf roof as a shelter from the sun. As Cholmondely was examining his surroundings, he noticed these monkeys, some eating fruit and others lying asleep in the sun, and decided he would have a little underarm pitching practice.

I was working inside the marquee when all at once I heard the most terrific uproar going on outside. The monkeys were screaming and chattering with rage, and I rushed out to see what had happened. Cholmondely, apparently, had picked up a rock the size of a cabbage and hurled it at the smaller monkeys, luckily missing them all, but frightening them out of their wits. If one of them had been hit by such a big rock, it would have been killed instantly.

Just as I arrived on the scene, Cholmondely had picked up another stone and was swinging it backwards and forwards like a professional ball player, taking better aim. He was annoyed at having missed all the monkeys with his first shot. I grabbed a stick and hurried towards him, shouting. To my surprise, Cholmondely dropped the rock, put his arms over his head, and started to roll on the ground and scream.

In my haste, I had picked up a very small twig which could not hurt him at all, for his back was as broad and as hard as a table. I gave him two sharp cuts with this silly little twig and followed it up with a serious scolding. He sat there picking bits of leaf off his fur and looking very guilty.

With the aid of the Africans, I set to work and cleared away all the rocks and stones near his box, and, giving him another scolding, went back to my work. I hoped that this telling-off might have some effect on him, but when I looked out of the marquee some time later, I saw him digging in the earth, presumably in search of more ammunition.

Not long after his arrival at the camp, Cholmondely fell ill. For nearly two weeks he went off his food, refusing even the most tempting fruit and other delicacies, and even rejecting his daily ration of tea, a most unheard-of occurrence. All he had was a few sips of water every day, and gradually he grew thinner and thinner, his eyes sank into their sockets, and I really thought he was going to die. He lost all interest in life and sat hunched up in his box all day with his eyes closed. It was very

bad for him to spend all day moping in this fashion, so in the evenings, just before the sun went down, when it was cool, I used to make him come out for walks with me. These walks were only short, and we had to rest every few yards, for Cholmondely was weak with lack of food.

One evening, just before I took him out for a walk, I filled my pockets with a special kind of biscuit that he had been very fond of. We went slowly up to the top of a small hill just beyond the camp and then sat there to admire the view. As we rested, I took a biscuit out of my pocket and ate it, smacking my lips with enjoyment, but not offering any to Cholmondely. He looked very surprised, for he knew that I always shared my food with him when we were out together. I ate a second biscuit and he watched me closely to see if I enjoyed it as much as the first. When he saw that I did, he dipped his hand into my pocket, pulled out a biscuit, smelled it suspiciously, and then, to my delight, ate it up and started looking for another. I knew then that he was going to get better.

The next morning he drank a mugful of sweet tea and ate seventeen biscuits, and for three days lived entirely on this diet. After this his appetite returned with a rush, and for the next fortnight he ate twice as much as he had ever done before, and cost me a small fortune in bananas.

There were only two things that Cholmondely disliked. One of them was the Africans and the other, snakes. I think that when he was a baby some Africans must have teased him. Whatever the reason, he certainly got his revenge on more than one occasion. He would hide inside his box and wait until an African passed close by. Then he would rush out with all his hair standing on end, swinging his long arms and screaming in the most terrifying manner. Many a fat African woman carrying a basket of fruit on her head who chanced to pass too close to Cholmondely's box would have to drop her basket, pick up her skirts, and run for dear life, while Cholmondely danced victoriously at the end of his chain, hooting and showing all his teeth in a grin of delight.

With snakes, though, he was not nearly so brave. If he saw me handling one, he would get very agitated, wringing his hands and moaning with fear. If I put the reptile on the ground and it started to crawl toward him, he would run to the very end of his chain and scream loudly for help, throwing bits of stick and grass at the snake to try and stop it from coming any closer.

One night, I went to shut him up in his box as usual, and, to my surprise, he flatly refused to go into it. His bed of banana leaves was nicely made, and so I thought he was simply being naughty. But when I started to scold him, he took me by the hand, led me up to his box, and left me there while he retreated to the safety of the end of his chain and stood watching me anxiously. I realized there must be something inside the box which frightened him, and when I cautiously investigated I found a very small snake coiled up in the center of his bed. It was a harmless type, but Cholmondely, of course, could not tell the difference, and he was taking no chances.

Cholmondely was so quick at learning tricks and so willing to show off that when he arrived in England, he became quite famous and even made several appearances on television. He delighted the audiences by sitting on a chair, with a hat on, taking a cigarette and lighting it for himself, pouring out and drinking a glass of beer, and doing many other things.

I think he must have become rather swollen-headed with his success, for not long after this he managed to escape from the zoo and went wandering off by himself through Regent's Park, much to the horror of everyone he met. On reaching the main road, he found a bus standing there and promptly climbed aboard, for he loved being taken for a ride. The passengers, however, decided they would rather not travel by that particular bus if Cholmondely was going to use it as well, and they were all struggling to get out when some keepers arrived from the zoo and took Cholmondely in charge. He was marched back to his cage in disgrace, but if I know Cholmondely, he must have thought it worth any amount of scoldings just for the sight of all those people trying to get off the bus together and getting stuck in the door. Cholmondely had a great sense of humor.

THE END

⟳ Talking it over

1. *a.* About how big was Cholmondely? How do you know?

b. What incidents show that Cholmondely was something of a bully?

c. What incidents suggest that he was also somewhat cowardly?

2. Judging from Mr. Durrell's account of his experiences with Cholmon-

dely, how does he feel about collecting animals? Why does he do it?

⇄ Words in action

Do you know how to tell apes from monkeys? One way is to look for tails: monkeys have them, apes don't.

If you were to look up *tail* in an unabridged dictionary, you would find as many as 37 meanings listed. All of them have some relation to the familiar meaning of *tail*.

By using common sense, you should be able to answer the following questions. However, if you are not sure of an answer, check with a dictionary.

1. If you wanted to see whether the **tail light** of a car was out of order, would you go to the front or to the back of the car?

2. If Mary Ann wears her hair in a **pigtail,** is her hair long or short?

3. Where is the **tail** of a kite attached?

4. If a pilot landed his plane at the Chicago airport ahead of schedule, is it likely that he had a strong head wind or a strong **tail wind?** Why?

5. If you were being **tailed** by a detective, where would you expect to find him?

6. If only the **tail end** of a movie was exciting, which part interested you most?

7. If someone takes a quick look at something and **turns tail,** would you expect him to run toward it or away from it?

8. **Tailgating** is a bad habit of some motorists. Why is it dangerous?

Photo by W. Suschitzky

He owns a private zoo

The zoo nearest you is likely to have most of the well-known animals of the world. But if you want to see a footle (a green-furred monkey that fits comfortably into a teacup), you might have to travel to the island of Jersey in the English Channel.

Here, Gerald Durrell runs a full-fledged private zoo. Many of the 600 animals in his zoo are so unusual that little is known about them. Some are of species now threatened with extinction because their natural environment is being destroyed. Hairy frogs, flying squirrels, bushbabies, and Guiana dragons are only a few of the many animals visitors see.

Mr. Durrell's expeditions to collect animals have taken him to Africa, South America, Australia, and Southeast Asia. Some of his most popular books describing his adventures are *Three Tickets to Adventure, Island Zoo,* and *The New Noah,* from which "Cholmondely the Chimpanzee" is taken. This book also tells about Cuthbert, the mischievous bird, and Sarah Huggersack, the only anteater film star in the world.

*"May this hand
rot on my arm if I sign the
marriage contract!"*

SUNDAY COSTS 5 PESOS

A One-Act Comedy of Mexican Village Life
by Josephina Niggli

Fidel Duran (fē del′ dü rän′), *who is in love with Berta*
Berta Cantu (ber′ tä kän tü′)
Salome (sä′ lō mä) ⎱ *friends of Berta*
Tonia (tō′nyä) ⎰
Celestina Garcia (sä les tē′nä gär sē′ä)

A housed-in square in the town called *The Four Cornstalks (Las Cuatro Milpas)*[1] in northern Mexico. On the left of the square is the house of Tonia with a door and a stoop. At left center back is the house of Berta, which boasts not only a door but a barred window. At right center back is a square arch from which dangles an iron lantern. On the right side proper is the house of Salome. Tonia's house is pink, and Salome's is blue, while Berta's is content with being a sort of disappointed yellow. All three houses get their water from the well that is down left center.

It is early afternoon on a Sunday. All sensible people are sleeping, but through the arch comes Fidel Duran. His straw hat in his hand, his hair plastered to his head with water, he thinks he is a very handsome sight indeed as he pauses, takes a small mirror from his pocket, fixes his neck bandanna—a beautiful purple one with orange spots—and shyly knocks, then turns around with a broad grin on his face.

Berta opens her door. She is very pretty, but unfortunately she has a very high temper, possibly the result of her red hair. She wears a neat cotton dress and tennis shoes, blue ones. Her hands on her hips, she stands and glares at Fidel.

Berta: Oh, so it is you!

Fidel (*beaming on her*): A good afternoon to you, Berta.

Berta (*sniffing*): A good afternoon indeed, and I bothered by fools at this hour of the day.

Fidel (*in amazement*): Why, Berta, are you angry with me?

Berta (*questioning Heaven*): He asks me if I am angry with him. Saints in Heaven, has he no memory?

Fidel (*puzzled*): What have I done, Berta?

Berta (*sarcastically*): Nothing, Fidel,

---

[1] **Las Cuatro Milpas** (läs kwä′trō mēl′päs)

nothing. That is the trouble. But if you come to this house again I will show you the palm of my hand, as I'm showing it to you now. (*She slaps him, steps back inside the door, and slams it shut.*)

Fidel (*pounding on the door*): Open the door, Berta. Open the door! I must speak to you!

(*The door of Salome's house opens, and Salome herself comes out with a small pitcher and begins drawing water from the well. She is twenty-eight, and so many years of hunting a husband have left her with an acid tongue.*)

Salome: And this is supposed to be a quiet street.

Fidel (*who dislikes her*): You tend to your affairs, Salome, and I will tend to mine. (*He starts pounding again. He bleats like a young goat hunting for its mother.*) Berta, Berta.

Berta (*opens the door again*): I will not have such noises. Do you not realize that this is Sunday afternoon? Have you no thoughts for decent people who are trying to sleep?

Fidel: Have you no thoughts for me?

Berta: More than one. And none of them nice.

Salome: I would call this a lovers' quarrel.

Berta: Would you indeed! (*Glares at Fidel.*) I would call it the impertinence of a wicked man!

Fidel (*helplessly*): But what have I done?

Salome: She loved him yesterday, and she will love him tomorrow.

Berta (*runs down to Salome*): If I love him tomorrow, may I lose the use of my tongue, yes, and my eyes and ears, too.

Fidel (*swinging Berta to one side*): Is it fair, I ask you, for a woman to smile at a man one day, and slap his face the next? Is this the manner in which a promised bride should treat her future husband?

Salome (*grins and winks at him*): You could find yourself another bride.

Berta (*angrily*): We do not need your advice, Salome Molina. You and your long nose—sticking it in everyone's business.

Salome (*her eyes flashing*): Is this an insult to me? To me?

Berta: And who are you to be above insults?

Salome: I will not stay and listen to such words!

Berta: Did I ask you to leave the safety of your house?

Salome (*to Fidel*): She has not even common politeness. I am going! (*Crosses right.*)

Berta: We shall adore your absence.

Salome: If this were not Sunday, I would slap your face for you.

Berta (*taunting*): The great Salome Molina, afraid of a Sunday fine.

Fidel (*wanting to be helpful*): You can fight each other tomorrow. There is no fine for weekdays.

Salome: You stay out of this argument, Fidel Duran.

Fidel: If you do not leave us I will never find out why Berta is angry with me. (*Jumps toward her.*) Go away!

Salome (*jumps back, then tosses her head*): Very well. But the day will come when you will be glad of my company. (*She goes indignantly into her house.*)

Fidel (*turns to Berta*): Now, Berta.

Berta (*interrupting*): As for you, my fine rooster, go and play the bear to Celestina Garcia. She will appreciate you more than I.

Fidel (*with a guilty hand to his mouth*): So that is what it is.

Berta (*on the stoop of her own house*): That is all of it, and enough it is. Two times you walked around the plaza with the Celestina last night, and I sitting there on a bench having to watch you. (*Goes into the house.*)

Fidel (*speaking through the open door*): But it was a matter of business.

Berta (*enters with a broom and begins to sweep off the stoop*): Hah! Give me no such phrases. And all of my friends thinking, "Poor Berta, with such a sweetheart." Do you think I have no pride?

Fidel: But it is that you do not understand—

Berta: I understand enough to know that all is over between us.

Fidel: Berta, do not say that. I love you.

Berta: So you say. And yet you roll the eye at any passing chicken.

Fidel: Celestina is the daughter of Don Nimfo Garcia.

Berta: She can be the daughter of the president for all of me. When you marry her she will bring you a fine dowry, and there will be no more need of Fidel Duran trying to carve wooden doors.

Fidel (*his pride wounded*): Trying? But I have carved them. Did I not do a new pair for the saloon?

Berta: Aye, little doors—doors that amount to no more than that—(*She snaps her fingers.*) Not for you the great doors of a church.

Fidel: Why else do you think I was speaking with the Celestina?

Berta (*stops sweeping*): What new manner of excuse is this?

Fidel: That is why I came to speak with you. Sit down here on the step with me for a moment.

Berta (*scandalized*): And have Salome and Tonia say that I am a wicked, improper girl?

Fidel (*measuring a tiny space between his fingers*): Just for one little moment. They will see nothing.

Berta (*sitting down*): Let the words tumble out of your mouth, one, two three.

Fidel: Perhaps you do not know that the town of Topo Grande, not thirty kilometers from here, is building a new church.

Berta (*sniffs*): All the world knows that.

Fidel: But did you know that Don Nimfo is secretly giving the money for the building of that church?

Berta: Why?

Fidel: He offered the money to the Blessed Virgin of Topo Grande if his rooster won in the cockfight. It did win, so now he is building the church.

Berta (*not yet convinced*): How did you find out about this? Or has Don Nimfo suddenly looked upon you as a son, and revealed all his secrets to you?

Fidel: Last night on the plaza the Celestina happened to mention it. With a bit of flattery I soon gained the whole story from her.

Berta: So that is what you were talking about as you walked around the plaza? (*Stands.*) It must have taken a great deal of flattery to gain so much knowledge from her.

Fidel (*stands*): Do you not realize what it means? They will need someone to carve the new doors. (*He strikes a pleased attitude, expecting* *her to say, "But how wonderful, Fidel."*)

Berta (*knowing very well what Fidel expects, promptly turns away from him, her hand hiding a smile, as she says with innocent curiosity*): I wonder whom Don Nimfo will get? (*with the delight of discovery*) Perhaps the Brothers Ochoa from Monterrey.

Fidel (*crestfallen*): He might choose me.

Berta: You? Hah!

Fidel: And why not? Am I not the best wood carver in the valley?

Berta: So you say.

Fidel: It would take three years to carve those doors, and he would pay me every week. There would be enough to buy you a trousseau and enough left over for a house.

Berta: Did you tell all that to the Celestina?

Fidel: Of course not! Does a girl help a man buy a trousseau for another girl? That was why it had to appear as though I were rolling the eye at her. (*He is very much pleased with his brilliance.*)

Berta: Your success was more than perfect. Today all the world knows that the Celestina has won Berta's man.

Fidel: But all the world does not know that Fidel Duran, who is I, myself, will carve those doors so as to buy a trousseau and house for Berta, my queen.

Berta: Precisely. All the world does not know this great thing—(*flaring out at him*) And neither do I!

Fidel: Do you doubt me, pearl of my life?

Berta: Does the rabbit doubt the snake? Does the tree doubt the lightning? Do I doubt that you are a teller of tremendous lies? Speak not to me of cleverness. I know what my own eyes see, and I saw you flirting with the Celestina. Last night I saw you—and so did all the world!

Fidel (*beginning to grow angry*): So that is how you trust me, your intended husband.

Berta: I would rather trust a hungry fox.

Fidel: Let me speak plainly, my little dove. Because we are to be married is no reason for me to enter a monastery.

Berta: And who says that we are to be married?

Fidel (*taken aback*): Why—I said it.

Berta: Am I a dog to your heel that I must obey your every wish?

Fidel (*firmly*): You are my future wife.

Berta (*laughs loudly*): Am I indeed?

Fidel: Your mother has consented, and my father has spoken. The banns have been read in the church! (*Folds his arms with satisfaction.*)

Berta (*screaming*): Better to die without children than to be married to such as you.

Fidel (*screaming above her*): We shall be married within the month.

Berta: May this hand rot on my arm if I ever sign the marriage contract!

Fidel: Are you saying that you will not marry me?

Berta: With all my mouth I am saying it, and a good day to you. (*Steps inside the house and slams the door. Immediately opens it and sticks her head out.*) Tell that good news to that four-nosed shrew of a Celestina. (*Slams the door again.*)

(*Fidel puts on his hat and starts toward the archway, then runs down and pounds on Tonia's door, then runs across and pounds on Salome's. In a*

moment both girls come out. Tonia is younger and smaller in size than either Salome or Berta and has a distressing habit of whining.)

Salome: What is the meaning of this noise?

Tonia: Is something wrong?

Fidel: I call you both to witness what I say. May I drop dead if I am ever seen in this street again! (*He settles his hat more firmly on his head, and with as much dignity as he can muster, he strides out through the arch.*)

(*The girls stare after him, then at Berta's door, then at each other. Both shrug, then with one accord they run up and begin knocking on Berta's door.*)

Salome: Berta!

Tonia: Berta, come out!

(*Berta comes out of her house. She is obviously trying to keep from crying.*)

Salome: Has that fool of a sweetheart of yours lost his mind?

Tonia: What happened?

Berta (*crying in earnest*): This day is blacker than a crow's wing. Oh, Salome! (*She flings both arms about the girl's neck and begins to wail loudly.*)

(*Tonia and Salome stare at each other, and then Tonia pats Berta on the shoulder.*)

Tonia: Did you quarrel with Fidel?

Salome: Of course she quarrelled with him. Any fool could see that.

Berta: He will never come back to me. Never!

Tonia (*to Salome*): Did she say anything about the Celestina to him?

Salome (*to Berta*): You should have kept your mouth shut on the outside of your teeth.

Berta: A girl has her pride, and no Celestina is going to take any man of mine.

Tonia: But did she take him?

Berta (*angrily to Tonia*): You take your face away from here!

Salome: The only thing you can do now is to ask him to come back to you.

Tonia (*starting toward the archway*): I will go and get him.

Berta (*clutches at her*): I will wither on my legs before I ask him to come back. He would never let me forget that I had to beg him to marry me. (*Wails again.*) And now he will marry the Celestina.

Tonia (*begins to cry with her*): There are other men.

Berta: My heart is with Fidel. My life is ruined.

Salome (*thoughtfully*): If we could bring him back without his knowing Berta had sent for him—(*She sits on the edge of the well.*)

Tonia: Miracles only happen in the church.

Salome (*catches her knee and begins to rock back and forth*): What could we tell him? What could we tell him?

Tonia: You be careful, Salome, or you will fall in the well. Then we will all have to go into mourning, and Berta cannot get married at all if she is in mourning.

Salome (*snaps her fingers*): You could fall down the well, Berta! That would bring him back.

Berta (*firmly*): I will not fall down the well and drown for any man, not even Fidel.

Tonia: What good would bringing him back do if Berta were dead?

Salome: Now that is a difficulty. (*Begins to pace up and down at left.*) If you are dead, you cannot marry Fidel. If you are not dead, he will not come back. The only thing left for you is to die an old maid.

Tonia: That would be terrible.

Berta (*wailing*): My life is ruined. Completely ruined.

Salome (*with sudden determination*): Why? Why should it be?

Tonia (*with awe*): Salome has had a thought.

Berta: You do not know what a terrible thing it is to lose the man you love.

Salome: I am fixing up your life, not mine. Suppose—suppose you did fall in the well.

Berta: I tell you I will not do it.

Salome: Not really, but suppose he thought you did. What then?

Berta: You mean—pretend? But that is a sin! The priest would give me ten days' penance at confessional.

Salome (*flinging out her hands*): Ten days' penance or a life without a husband. Which do you choose?

Tonia: I will tell you. She chooses the husband. What do we do, Salome?

Salome: You run and find this carver of doors. Tell him that a great scandal has happened—that Berta has fallen in the well.

Tonia (*whose dramatic imagination has begun to work*): Because she could not live without him—

Berta: You tell him that and I will scratch out both your eyes!

Tonia: On Sunday?

Berta (*sullenly*): On any day.

Salome: Tell him that Berta has fallen in the well, and that you think she is dying.

Tonia: Is that all?

Berta: Is that not enough?

Salome (*entranced with the idea*): Oh, it will be a great scene, with Berta so pale in her bed, and Fidel kneeling in tears beside it.

Berta: I want you to know that I am a modest girl.

Salome (*irritated*): You can lie down on the floor, then. (*glaring at Tonia*) What are you standing there for? Run!

Tonia (*starts toward the archway, then comes back*): But—where will I go?

Salome: To the place where all men go with a broken heart—the saloon. Are you going to stand there all day? (*Tonia gives a little gasp and runs out through the arch.*)

Berta: I do not like this idea. If Fidel finds out it is a trick, he will be angrier than ever.

Salome: But if he does not find out the truth until after you are married—what difference will it make?

Berta: He might beat me.

Salome: Leave that worry until after you are married. (*inspecting Berta*) Now how will we make you look pale? Have you any flour? Corn meal might do.

Berta: No! No! I will not do it.

Salome: Now, Berta, be reasonable.

Berta: If I had really fallen down the well, it would be different. But I did not fall down it.

Salome: Do you not want Fidel to come back to you? Are you in love with him?

Berta: Yes, I do love him. And I will play no tricks on him. If he loves the Celestina better than he does me—(*with great generosity*) he can marry her.

Salome (*pleading with such idiocy*): But Tonia has gone down to get him. If he comes back and finds you alive —he will be angrier than ever.

Berta (*firmly*): This is your idea. You can get out of it the best way you can. But Fidel will not see me lying down on a bed, nor on a floor, nor any place else.

Salome: Then there is only one thing to do.

Berta: What is that?

Salome: You will go into the house, and I will tell him that you are too sick to see him.

Berta: That will be just as bad as the other.

Salome: How can it be? Then if he finds out it is a trick, he will blame me, and you can pretend you knew nothing of it. I do not care how angry he is. I do not want to marry him.

Berta (*with pleased excitement*): Then he could not be angry with me, could he? I mean if he thought I had nothing to do with it? And I would not have to do penance either, would I?

Salome: Not one day of penance. Tonia should have found him by now. (*Goes to the arch and peers through.*) Here they come—and Fidel is running half a block in front of her.

Berta (*joyously*): Then he does love me!

Salome: Into the house with you. You can watch through the window.

Berta (*on stoop*): Now, remember, if he gets angry, this was your idea.

Salome (*claps her hands*): And what a beautiful idea it is!

(*Berta disappears into the house. Salome looks about her, then dashes over to her own stoop, sits down, flings her shawl over her face, and begins to moan loudly, rocking back and forth. In a moment Fidel dashes through the arch and stops, out of breath, at seeing Salome.*)

Fidel (*gasping*): Berta!

Salome (*whose moaning grows louder*): Poor darling, poor darling. She was so young.

Fidel (*desperately*): She is—she is dead?

Salome (*wailing*): She will make such a beautiful corpse. Poor darling. Poor darling.

Tonia (*exhausted and out of breath, has reached the arch. Looks about her in astonishment*): Why, where is Berta? Did she go into the house?

Salome (*in normal tones*): Of course she went into the house, you fool. Did she not jump down the well? (*remembering Fidel*) Poor darling.

Tonia (*blankly*): Did she really jump down it? I thought she just fell in by accident.

Salome (*rising, grimly*): Are you telling this story—or am I? (*wailing*) Now she can never go to the plaza again.

(*Fidel looks helplessly from Tonia, who cannot quite get the details of the story straight, to Salome, who is having a beautiful time mourning.*)

Fidel: Where is she? I want to see her.

Tonia (*coming out of her trance*): She is right in here. Did you say she was on the bed or on the floor, Salome?

Salome (*getting between them and Berta's door*): You don't want to see her, Fidel. You know how people look after they've been drowned.

Tonia: But he was supposed to see her. That was why you sen—

Salome (*glaring at her*): Tonia, dear, suppose that you let me tell the story. After all, I was here and you were not.

Fidel (*exploding*): For the love of the saints, tell me! Is she dead?

Salome (*thinking this over*): Well—not exactly.

Fidel: You mean—you mean there is hope?

Salome: I would say there was great hope.

Fidel (*takes off his hat and mops his face*): What can I do? Oh, if I could only see her—

Salome: If you would go to the church and light a candle to Our Blessed Lady and ask her to forgive you for getting angry with Berta—perhaps things will arrange themselves.

Fidel: Do you think she will get well soon?

Salome: With a speed that will amaze you.

Fidel: I will go down and light the candle right now.

(*As he turns to leave, who should come through the archway but Celestina Garcia. She can match temper for temper with Berta any day, and right now she is on the warpath. Brushing past these three as though they did not exist, she goes up to Berta's door and pounds on it.*)

Celestina: I dare you to come out and call this Celestina Garcia a four-nosed shrew to her face.

Salome (*trying to push Fidel through the arch*): You had best run to the church.

Fidel (*pushing past her and going up to Celestina*): How dare you speak like that to a poor drowned soul?

Salome (*to Celestina*): Why do you not go away? We never needed you so little.

Celestina: So she is pretending to be drowned, eh? Is that her coward's excuse?

Berta (*through window*): Who dares to call Berta Cantu a coward?

Celestina: You know well enough who calls you, and I the daughter of Don Nimfo Garcia.

Tonia: Ai, Salome! And now Fidel will

know that Berta was not drowned at all.

Fidel (*who has been listening to this conversation with growing surprise and suspicion, now turns furiously toward Berta's house*): Not drowned, eh? So this was a trick to bring me back, eh? I am through with your tricks, you hear me? Through with them!

Berta (*through window*): You stay right there until I come out. (*She disappears from view.*)

Fidel (*turning to Salome*): I see your hand in this.

Salome: The more fool you to be taken in by a woman's tricks.

Celestina: What care I for tricks? No woman is going to call me names!

Berta (*coming through the door*): You keep silence, Celestina Garcia. I will deal with you in a minute. And as for you, Fidel Duran—

Fidel (*stormily*): As for me, I am finished with all women. The world will see me no more. I will enter a monastery and carve as many doors as I like. Do you hear me, Berta Cantu?

Berta (*putting both hands over her ears*): What do I care for your quack, quack, quack!

Fidel: Now she calls me a duck! Good afternoon to you! (*He stalks out with wounded dignity.*)

Celestina (*catching Berta by the shoulder and swinging her around*): I ask you again: Did you call me a four-nosed shrew?

Berta: I did, and I will repeat it with the greatest of pleasure. You are a four-nosed shrew and a three-eyed frog.

Celestina: I have always looked on you as my friend—you pink-toed cat!

Berta: And I have always trusted you —you sly robber of bridegrooms! (*She raises her hand to slap Celestina. Salome catches it.*)

Salome: This is Sunday, Berta! And Sunday costs five pesos.

Tonia: If you had to pay a fine for starting a fight on top of losing Fidel —ay, that would be terrible.

(*Berta and Celestina glare at each other, and then slowly begin to circle each other, spitting out their insults as they do so.*)

Celestina: It is my honor that is making me fight, or I would wait until tomorrow.

Berta: If I had five pesos to throw away, I would pull out your dangling tongue—leaving only the flapping roots.

Celestina: Ha! I make a nose at your words.

Berta: As for you—you eater of ugly-smelling cheese—

(*They jump at each other, but remember the penalty just in time and pull back. Again they begin to circle around, contenting themselves with making faces at each other. Salome suddenly clasps her hands.*)

Salome: You are both certain that you want to fight today?

Celestina: Why else do you think I came here?

Berta: These insults have gone too far to stop now.

Salome: The only thing that stands in the way is the five pesos for the Sunday fine.

Tonia: And five pesos is a lot of money.

Salome: Then the only thing to do is to play the fingers.

Celestina: What?

Berta: Eh?

Salome: Precisely. The one who loses strikes the first blow and pays the fine. Then you can fight as much as you like.

Tonia (*with awed admiration*): Ay, Salome, you have so many brains.

Celestina (*doubtfully*): It is a big risk.

Berta (*shrugging*): Perhaps you are afraid of taking a risk.

Celestina: I am not afraid of anything. But Tonia will have to be the judge. Salome is too clever.

Berta: Very well. But Salome has to stand behind you to see that you do not cheat. I would not trust you any more than I would a mouse near a piece of fresh bacon.

Celestina (*pulls back her clenched fist, then thinks better of it, and speaks with poor grace*): Very well.

(*Celestina and Berta stand facing each other. Tonia stands between them up on the stoop. Salome stands behind Celestina.*)

Tonia (*feeling a little nervous over this great honor of judging*): Both arms behind your backs. (*The girls link their arms behind them.*) Now, when I drop my hand, Berta will guess first as Celestina brings her fingers forward. The first girl to guess correctly twice wins. Are you ready? (*All nod.*) I am going to drop my arm.

Salome: Celestina, put out your fingers before Berta guesses. We will have no cheating.

Celestina (*sullenly*): Very well.

(*She puts out two fingers behind her, and Salome, seeing this, raises up her arm with two fingers extended, opening and closing them scissors fashion. Berta frowns a little as she looks up at the signal and Celestina, seeing this, swings around and looks at Salome who promptly grins warmly and pretends to*

be waving at Berta. Celestina glares at Salome and then turns to Berta.

Celestina (*sarcastically*): Let me guess first, Berta. Salome isn't ready yet.

Berta: Very well.

Celestina (*guessing as Berta swings her arm forward*): Three.

(*Berta triumphantly holds up one finger. Biting her lip, Celestina starts to swing forward her own arm. Salome, intent on signaling Berta, holds up her own five fingers spread wide, and does not notice until too late that Celestina has swung around to watch her.*)

Celestina (*screaming*): So I cheat, eh?

(*With that she gives Salome a resounding slap on the cheek. The next moment the two women are mixed up in a beautiful howling, grunting fight, while Tonia and Berta, wide-eyed, cling together and give the two women as much space as possible. Let it be understood that this is only a fight of kicking, hair-pulling, and scratching. There is no man involved, nor a point of honor. Rather a matter of angry pride. So the two are not attempting to mutilate each other. They are simply gaining satisfaction. The grand finale comes when Celestina knocks Salome to the ground and sits on her.*)

Celestina (*breathing hard*): There! That was worth five pesos.

Tonia: You have to pay it. And Don Nimfo will be angry with you.

Celestina (*pulling herself to her feet*): I am too tired to fight any more now, but I will be back next Tuesday, Berta, and then I will beat you up.

Berta (*sniffing*): If you can.

Celestina (*warningly*): And there is no fine on Tuesday.

Berta: Come any day you like. I will be ready for you.

Tonia (*to Celestina*): You should be ashamed to fight.

Celestina: Who are you to talk to me? (*Stamps her foot at Tonia, who jumps behind Berta.*) Good afternoon, my brave little rabbits!

(*She staggers out as straight as she can, but as she reaches the archway she feels a twinge of agony and is forced to limp. By this time Salome has gathered together what strength she has left, and she slowly stands up. Once erect, she looks at Berta and Tonia as though she were considering boiling in oil too good for them.*)

Salome (*with repressed fury*): My friends. My very good friends.

Tonia (*frightened*): Now, Salome—

Salome (*screaming*): Do not speak to me! Either of you! (*She manages to get to the door of her house.*) When I need help, do you give me aid? No! But just you wait—both of you!

Tonia: What are you going to do?

Salome: I am going to wait for a weekday, and then I am going to beat up both of you at once. One (*taking a deep breath*) with each hand! (*She nearly falls through the door of her house.*)

Berta (*with false bravado*): Who is afraid of her?

Tonia: I am. Salome is very strong. It is all your fault. If you had not gotten mad at Fidel, this would not have happened.

Berta (*snapping at her*): You leave Fidel out of this.

Tonia (*beginning to cry*): When Salome beats me up, that will be your fault too.

Berta: Stop crying!

Tonia: I am not a good fighter, but I can tell Fidel the truth about how you would not jump down the well to win him back.

Berta: You open your mouth to Fidel and I will push you in the well.

Tonia: You will not have strength enough to push a baby in the well when they get through with you.

Berta: Get out! Get out of here!

(*She stamps her foot at Tonia and the girl, frightened, gives a squeak and runs into her own house. Berta looks after her, then, beginning to sniffle, she goes over and sits on the well. She acts like a child who has been told that it is not proper for little girls to cry, and she is very much in need of a handkerchief. Just then Fidel sticks his head around the arch.*)

Fidel (*once more the plaintive goat*): Berta. (*Berta half jumps, then pretends not to hear him. Fidel enters cautiously, not taking his eyes off of Berta's stiff back. He moves around at the back, skirts Tonia's house, then works his way round to her.*) Berta.

Berta (*sniffling*): What is it?

Fidel (*circling the back of the well*): Are you crying, Berta?

Berta (*stubbornly*): No!

Fidel (*sitting beside her*): Yes, you are. I can see you crying.

Berta: If you can see, why do you ask, then?

Fidel: I am sorry we quarreled, Berta.

Berta: Are you?

Fidel: Are you sorry?

Berta: No!

Fidel: I was hoping you were, because —do you know whom I saw on the plaza?

Berta: Grandfather Devil.

Fidel: Don Nimfo himself.

Berta: Perhaps you saw the Celestina, too.

Fidel (*placatingly*): Now, Berta, you know I do not care if I never see the Celestina again. (*Pulls out a handkerchief and extends it to her.*) Here, wipe your face with this.

Berta: I have a handkerchief of my own. (*Nevertheless she takes it, and wipes her eyes and then blows her nose.*)

Fidel: Don Nimfo said I could carve the church doors for him. But he said I would have to move to Topo Grande to work on them. He said I had to leave right away.

Berta (*perking up her interest*): You mean—move away from here?

Fidel: And I was wondering if we could get married tomorrow. I know this is very sudden, Berta, but after all, think how long I have waited to carve a church door.

Berta: Tomorrow. (*She looks toward Salome's house.*) They would both be too sore to do anything by tomorrow.

Fidel (*too concerned with his own plans to hear what she is saying*): Of course I know that you may not be able to forgive me—

Berta: Fidel, I want you to understand that if I do marry you tomorrow— that means we will leave here tomorrow, eh?

Fidel: Ay, yes. I have to be in Topo Grande on Tuesday.

Berta: I hope you will always understand what a great thing I have done for you. It is not every girl who would forgive so easily as I.

Fidel (*humbly*): Indeed, I know that, Berta.

Berta: Are you quite sure that we will leave here tomorrow?

Fidel: Quite sure.

Berta: Very well. I will marry you.

Fidel (*joyfully*): Berta! (*Bends forward to kiss her. She jumps up.*)

Berta: Just a moment. We are not married yet. Do you think that I am just any girl that you can kiss me—like that! (*She snaps her fingers.*)

Fidel (*humbly*): I thought—just this once—

Berta (*gravely thoughtful*): Well, perhaps—just this once—you may kiss my hand.

> (*As he kisses it*
> THE CURTAINS CLOSE.*)

Copies of this play, in individual paper-covered acting editions, are available from Samuel French, Inc., 25 W. 45th St., New York, N.Y. or 7623 Sunset Blvd., Hollywood, Calif., or in Canada from Samuel French (Canada) Ltd., 26 Grenville St., Toronto, Canada.

Talking it over

1. *a.* Describe Salome's plan to bring Fidel and Berta together again.

b. What are Berta's objections to the plan?

c. How does Salome finally convince Berta to coöperate?

d. What happens which ruins Salome's plans?

2. At the end of the play, when Berta learns that Fidel has to leave town right away and that he wants the wedding to be the next day, why is she suddenly willing to marry him?

3. *a.* Who is smarter: Fidel or Berta? Support your answer with evidence from the play.

b. Which of the characters act foolishly?

4. Is this play meant to be serious or humorous? Explain.

Words in action

Actors in a play must give a lot of thought to which words in their dialogue they will speak with special force or stress, because the emphasis can make a big difference in meaning. In this exercise you will practice using word stress in order to get across a particular idea. The quoted passages are from *Sunday Costs Five Pesos*.

A

It is early afternoon on a Sunday. All sensible people are sleeping, but through the arch comes Fidel Duran.

1. If you wanted to make the point that Fidel is a rather foolish young man, which word or words in these stage directions would you stress?

2. If you wanted to make the point that Fidel is the only person awake at this hour, which word would you stress?

3. Which of these two ideas did the author probably have in mind? Explain.

B

Berta: ... When you marry [Celestina] she will bring you a fine dowry, and there will be no more need of Fidel Duran trying to carve wooden doors.

Fidel (*his pride wounded*): Trying? But I have carved them. ...

4. If Fidel wants to say that *he* is the person who has carved the doors, which word should he stress?

5. If Fidel wants to say that he is not just *trying* to carve doors, but that he actually has carved such doors, which word or words should he stress?

6. Which of these two do you think Fidel wants to say?

Football

by Walt Mason

The Game was ended, and the noise at last had died away, and now they gathered up the boys where they in pieces lay. And one was hammered in the ground by many a jolt and jar; some fragments never have been found, they flew away so far. They found a stack of tawny hair, some fourteen cubits high; it was the halfback, lying there, where he had crawled to die. They placed the pieces on a door, and from the crimson field, that hero then they gently bore, like soldier on his shield. The surgeon toiled the livelong night above the gory wreck; he got the ribs adjusted right, the wishbone and the neck. He soldered on the ears and toes, and got the spine in place, and fixed a gutta-percha nose upon the mangled face. And then he washed his hands and said: "I'm glad that task is done!" The halfback raised his fractured head, and cried: "I call this fun!"

Talking it over

1. What is exaggerated in this poem?
2. Why does it seem strange that the halfback would say, "I call this fun!"?
3. If the author were to reply to the halfback's words, what might he say?
4. *a.* What is unusual about the way this poem is printed?

   b. What does this poem have in common with some other poems you have read?

From *Walt Mason His Book* by Walt Mason, ©1916 by Barse & Hopkins.

*As she slowly lowered her hand,
we heard the unearthly hiss
of a deadly snake.*

WOMAN
WITHOUT
FEAR

by Daniel P. Mannix

I FIRST heard of Grace Wiley when Dr. William Mann, former director of the National Zoological Park in Washington, D.C., handed me a picture of a tiny woman with a gigantic king cobra draped over her shoulders like a garden hose. The snake had partly spread his hood and was looking intently into the camera while his mistress stroked his head to quiet him. Dr. Mann told me: "Grace lives in a little house full of poisonous snakes, imported from all over the world. She lets them wander around like cats. There's been more nonsense written about 'snake charming' than nearly any other subject. Grace is probably the only non-Oriental who knows the real secrets of this curious business."

Looking at the picture of that deadly creature, I knew what a famous writer meant when he described a snake as a "running brook of horror." Still, I like snakes and when my wife, Jule, and I moved into our Malibu house, I made it a point to call on Grace Wiley.

She was living near Cypress, outside Los Angeles, in a small three-room cottage surrounded by open fields. Behind the cottage was a big, ramshackle barn where the snakes were kept. Grace was cleaning snake boxes with a hose when I arrived. She was a surprisingly little lady, scarcely over five feet tall, and probably weighed less than a hundred pounds. Although Grace was sixty-four years old, she was as active as a boy and worked with smooth dexterity.

Adapted from *All Creatures Great and Small* by Daniel P. Mannix. Copyright © 1963 by Daniel P. Mannix. McGraw-Hill Book Company. Used by permission.

When she saw me, she hurriedly picked up the four-foot rattlesnake who had been sunning himself while his box was being cleaned and poured him into his cage. The snake raised his head but made no attempt to strike or even to rattle. I was impressed but not astonished. In captivity, rattlers often grow sluggish and can be handled with comparative impunity.

Grace came forward, drying her hands on her apron. "Oh dear, I meant to get dressed up for you," she said, trying to smooth down her thatch of brown hair. "But I haven't anybody here to help me with the snakes except Mother—and she's eighty-four years old. Don't trip over an alligator," she added as I came forward. I noticed for the first time in the high grass a dozen or so alligators and crocodiles. They ranged from a three-foot Chinese croc to a big Florida 'gator more than twelve feet long. I threaded my way among them without mishap, although several opened their huge jaws to hiss at me.

"They don't mean anything by that, any more than a dog barking," Grace explained fondly. "They're very tame and most of them know their names. Now come in and meet my little family of snakes."

We entered the barn. The walls were lined with cages of all sizes and shapes containing snakes. Grace stopped at each cage, casually lifting the occupant and pointing out his fine points while she stroked and examined him. Grace unquestionably had one of the world's finest collections of reptiles. I watched her handle diamondback rattlesnakes from Texas, vipers from Italy, fer-de-lance from the West Indies, a little Egyptian cobra, and the deadly karait from India.

Then I saw Grace perform a feat I would have believed impossible.

We had stopped in front of a large, glass-fronted cage containing apparently nothing but newspaper. "These little fellows arrived only a short time ago, so they're very wild," explained Grace indulgently. She quietly lifted the paper. Instantly a forest of heads sprang up in the cage. Grace moved the paper slightly. At the movement, the heads seemed to spread and flatten. Then I saw that they were not heads but hoods. I was looking at the world's most deadly creature—the Indian cobra.

Man-eating tigers are said to kill 600 natives a year, but cobras kill 25,000 people a year in India alone. Hunters have been mauled by wounded elephants and lived to tell about it, but no one survives a body bite from a big cobra. I have caught rattlesnakes with a forked stick and my bare hands, but I'm not ashamed to say I jumped back from that cage as though the devil were inside—as indeed he was.

Grace advanced her hand toward the nearest cobra. The snake swayed like a reed in the wind, feinting for the strike. Grace raised her hand above the snake's head, the reptile twisting around to watch her. As the woman slowly lowered her hand, the snake gave that most terrible of all animal noises—the unearthly hiss of a deadly snake. I have seen children laugh with excitement at the roar of a lion, but I have never seen anyone who did not cringe at that cold, uncanny sound. Grace deliberately tried to touch the rigid, quivering hood. The cobra struck at her hand. He

missed. Quietly, Grace presented her open palm. The cobra hesitated a split second, his reared body quivering like a plucked banjo string. Then he struck.

I felt sick as I saw his head hit Grace's hand, but the cobra did not bite. He struck with his mouth closed. As rapidly as an expert boxer drumming on a punching bag, the snake struck three times against Grace's palm, always for some incredible reason with his mouth shut. Then Grace slid her open hand over his head and stroked his hood. The snake hissed again and struggled violently under her touch. Grace continued to caress him. Suddenly the snake went limp and his hood began to close. Grace slipped her other hand under the snake's body and lifted him out of the cage. She held the reptile in her arms as though he were a baby. The cobra raised his head to look Grace in the face; his dancing tongue was less than a foot from her mouth. Grace braced her hand against the curve of his body and talked calmly to him until he folded his hood. He curled up in her arms quietly until I made a slight movement; then he instantly reared up again, threatening me.

I had never seen anything to match this performance. Later, Grace opened the cobra's mouth to show me that the fangs were still intact. The yellow venom was slowly oozing over their tips.

If Grace Wiley had wished to make a mystery out of her amazing ability I am certain she could have made a fortune by posing as a woman with supernatural power. There isn't a zoologist alive who could have debunked her. But Grace was a perfectly honest person who was happy to explain in detail exactly how she could handle these terrible creatures. I spent several weeks with her studying her technique and now that I understand it I'm even more impressed than I was before.

When a cobra attacks, it rears straight upward. If you put your elbow on a table, cup your hand to represent the open hood, and sway your forearm back and forth, you have a good idea of the fighting stance of a cobra. Your index finger represents the tiny, mouse-like head that does the business. Your range is limited to the length of your forearm. Here is a large part of the secret in handling cobras. With a little practice you can tell a cobra's range to the inch. Also, the blow of a cobra is comparatively slow. A man with steady nerves can jerk away in time to avoid being bitten.

Another important thing to understand in handling a cobra is his method of striking. His fangs are short and do not fold back. Instead of stabbing, he must actually bite. He grabs his victims and then deliberately chews while the venom runs down into the wound he is making.

When Grace approached a wild cobra, she moved her hand back and forth just outside the snake's range. The cobra would then strike angrily until he became tired. Then he was reluctant to strike again. Grace's next move was to raise her hand over the snake's hood and bring it down slowly. Because of his method of rearing, a cobra cannot strike directly upward, and Grace could actually touch the top of the snake's head. The snake became puzzled and frustrated. He felt that he was fighting an invulnerable opponent who, after all, didn't seem to mean him any harm.

Then came the final touch. Grace would put her open palm toward the snake. At last the cobra was able to hit her. But he had to bite and he could not get a grip on the flat surface of the palm. If he could get a finger or a loose fold of skin he could fasten his teeth in it and start chewing. But his strike is sufficiently slow that Grace could meet each blow with the flat of her palm. At last Grace would be able to get her hand over the snake's head and stroke his hood. This seemed to relax the reptile and from then on Grace could handle him with some degree of confidence.

I don't mean to suggest that this is a cut-and-dried procedure. Grace knew snakes perfectly and could tell by tiny, subtle indications what the reptile would probably do next. She had been bitten many times—she would never tell me just how many—but never by a cobra. You're only bitten once by a cobra.

"Now I'll show you what I know you're waiting to see," said Grace as she put the snake away. "My mated pair of king cobras." Dropping her voice reverently, she added, "I call the big male 'The King of Kings.' " She led the way to a large enclosure and for the first time in my life I was looking into the eyes of that dread reptile, the king cobra or hamadryad.

The common cobra is rarely more than five feet long. Even so, he has enough venom in his poison glands to kill fifty men. Grace's king cobras were more than fifteen feet long. The two hamadryads contained enough venom, if injected drop by drop, to kill nearly a thousand human beings. That wasn't all. The hamadryad is the only snake known to attack without any provocation. These fearful creatures have been reported to trail a man through a jungle for the express purpose of biting him. They are so aggressive that they have closed roads in India by driving away all traffic. This is probably because the hamadryads, unlike other snakes, guard their eggs and young, and if a pair sets up housekeeping in a district, every other living thing must get out—including elephants. When a king cobra rears up, he stands higher than the head of a kneeling man. They are unquestionably the most dangerous animal in the world today.

When Grace first got these monsters, she was unable to handle them as she would ordinary cobras; so she had to devise an entirely new method of working with them. When the kings first arrived, they were completely unapproachable. They reared up more than four feet, snorting and hissing, their lower jaws open to expose the poison fangs. "A very threatening look, indeed," Grace called it. She put them in a large cage with a sliding partition. Unlike other snakes, hamadryads are knowing enough to notice that when their keeper opens the door in the side of the cage to put in fresh water, he must expose his hand for a fraction of a second. These cobras soon learned to lie against the side of the cage and wait for Grace to open the door. She outwitted them by waiting until both of the hamadryads were on one side of the cage and then sliding in the partition before changing water pans.

She did not dare to go near them with her bare hands; she used a padded stick to stroke them. Yet she was able to touch them four days after their arrival. "I petted the kings on their tails when their heads were far away," she told me. "Later in the day I had a little visit with them and told them how perfectly lovely they were—that I liked them and was sure we were going to be good friends."

A few weeks later, the King of Kings began shedding his skin. Snakes are irritable and nervous while shedding, and the hamadryad had trouble sloughing off the thin membrane covering his eyes. Grace wrote in her diary: "I stroked his head and then pulled off the eyelids with eyebrow forceps. He flinched a little but was unafraid. He put out his tongue in such a knowing manner! I mounted the eyelids and they looked just like pearls. What a pity that there have been nothing but unfriendly, aggressive accounts about this sweet snake. Really, the intelligence of these creatures is unbelievable."

The King of Kings was so heavy that Grace was unable to lift him by herself. Jule offered to help her carry the snake outside for a picture. While Jule and Grace were staggering out the door with the monster reptile between them, the king suddenly reared and rapped Jule several times on her forehead with his closed mouth. "He's trying to tell you something!" exclaimed Grace. He was indeed. I saw that the Chinese crocodile had rushed out from under a table and had grabbed the hamadryad by the tail. Jule relaxed her grip and the king dropped his head and gave a single hiss. The croc promptly let go and the ladies bore the cobra out into the sunlight. I was the only person who seemed upset by the incident.

Out of curiosity, I asked Grace if she ever used music in taming her snakes. She laughed and told me what I already knew: all snakes are deaf. Grace assured me that the Hindu fakir uses his flute only to attract a crowd and by swaying his own body back and forth the fakir keeps the snake swaying as the cobra is feinting to strike. The man times his music to correspond to

the snake's movements and it appears to dance to the tune. The fakir naturally keeps well outside the cobra's striking range. Years later when I was in India, I discovered that this is exactly what happens. I never saw any Oriental snake-charmer even approximate Grace's marvelous power over reptiles.

Grace's main source of income was to exhibit her snakes to tourists, although she was occasionally able to rent a snake to a movie studio (she always went along to make sure the reptile wasn't frightened or injured), and sometimes she bought ailing snakes from dealers, cured them, and resold them for a small profit to zoos. While I was with her, a dusty car stopped and discharged a plump couple with three noisy children who had seen her modest sign *Grace Wiley—Reptiles*. Grace explained that she would show them her collection, handle the poisonous snakes, call over the tame alligators, and let the children play with Rocky, an eighteen-foot Indian Rock python which she had raised from a baby. The charge was twenty-five cents. "That's too much," the woman said to her husband, and they went back to the car. Grace sighed. "No one seems interested in my snakes. No one really cares about them. And they're so wonderful."

One day Grace telephoned me to say that she had gotten a new shipment of snakes, including some Indian cobras from Siam. "One of them has markings that form a complete *G* on the back of his hood," she told me. "Isn't it curious that the snake and I have the same initial! I call him My Snake." We laughed about this, and then Jule and I went out to Cypress to take a last set of pictures of Grace and her snakes for an article I was doing about this remarkable woman.

We took several pictures and then I asked Grace to let me get a picture of the cobra with the *G* on the hood. "I didn't look very well in those other pictures," said Grace anxiously. "I'll comb my hair and put on another blouse." She was back in a few minutes. Jule and I had set up our cameras in the yard behind the barn. I wanted a shot of the cobra with spread hood, and Grace brought him out cradled in her arms. Before allowing me to take the picture, she removed her glasses as she felt that she looked better without them. The cobra refused to spread and Grace put him down on the ground and extended her flat palm toward him to make him rear—something I had often seen her do before, but never without her glasses.

I was watching through the finder of my camera. I saw the cobra spread and strike as I clicked the shutter. As the image disappeared from the ground glass of my Graflex, I looked up and saw that the snake had seized Grace by the middle finger. She said in her usual quiet voice, "Oh, he's bitten me."

I dropped the camera and ran toward her, feeling an almost paralyzing sense of shock, for I knew that Grace Wiley was a dead woman. At the same time I thought, "Good Lord, it's just like the book," for the cobra was behaving exactly as textbooks on cobras say they behave. He was deliberately chewing on the wound to make the venom run out of his glands. It was a terrible sight.

Quietly and expertly, Grace took hold of the snake and gently forced his mouth open. I knew that her only chance for life was to put a tourniquet around the finger instantly and slash open the wound to allow the venom to run out. Seconds counted. I reached out my hand to take the snake above the hood so she could immediately start squeezing out the venom, but Grace motioned me away. She stood up, still holding the cobra, and walked into the barn. Carefully, she put the snake into his cage and closed the door.

This must have taken a couple of minutes and I knew that the venom was spreading through her system each moment. "Jule," said Grace, "call Wesley Dickinson. He's a herpetologist and a friend of mine. He'll know what to do." Calmly and distinctly she gave Jule the telephone number and Jule ran to the phone. Then Grace turned to me. Suddenly she said, "He didn't really bite me, did he?" It was the only emotion I saw her show. I could only say, "Grace, where's your snake-bite kit?" We both knew that nothing except immediate amputation of her arm could save her, but anything was worth a chance.

She pointed to a cabinet. There was a tremendous collection of the surgical aids used for snake bite but I don't believe any of the stuff had been touched for twenty years. I pulled out a rubber tourniquet and tried to twist it around her finger. The old rubber snapped in my hands. Grace didn't seem to notice. I pulled out my handkerchief and tried that. It was too thick to go around her finger and I twisted it around her wrist. "I'll faint in a few minutes," said Grace. "I want to show you where everything is before I lose consciousness."

Cobra venom, unlike rattlesnake venom, affects the nervous system. In a few minutes the victim becomes paralyzed and the heart stops beating. I knew Grace was thinking of this. She said, "You must give me strychnine injections to keep my heart going when I begin to pass out. I'll show you where the strychnine is kept. You may have to give me caffeine also."

She walked to the other end of the room and I ran alongside trying to keep the tourniquet in place. She got out the tiny glass vials of strychnine and caffeine and also a hypodermic syringe with several needles. I saw some razor blades with the outfit and picked one up, intending to make a deep incision to let out as much of the venom as possible. Grace shook her head. "That won't do any good," she told me. Cobra venom travels along the nerves, so making the wound bleed wouldn't be very effective, but it was all I could think of to do.

Jule came back with a Mr. Tanner, Grace's cousin who lived next door. Tanner immediately got out his jackknife, intending to cut open the wound, but Grace stopped him. "Wait until Wesley comes," she said. Tanner told me afterward that he was convinced that if he had amputated the finger Grace might have lived. This is doubtful. Probably nothing except amputation of her arm would have saved her then, and we had nothing but a jackknife. She probably would have died of shock and loss of blood.

Grace lay on the floor to keep as quiet as possible and slow the absorption of the venom. "You'd better give me the strychnine now, dear," she told Jule. Jule snapped off the tip of one of the glass vials but the cylinder broke in her hands. She opened another tube and tried to fill the syringe; the needle was rusted shut. Jule selected another needle, tested it, and filled the syringe. "I'm afraid it will hurt," she told Grace.

"Now don't worry, dear," said Grace comfortingly. "I know you'll do it very well."

After the injection, Grace asked Jule to put a newspaper under her head to keep her hair from getting dirty. A few minutes later, the ambulance arrived, with Wesley Dickinson following in his own car. Wesley had telephoned the hospital and arranged for blood transfusions and an iron lung. As Grace was lifted into the ambulance, she called back to Tanner, "Remember to cut up the meat for my frogs very fine and take good care of my snakes." That was the last we ever saw of her.

Grace died in the hospital half an hour later. She lived about ninety minutes after being bitten. In the hospital, Wesley directed the doctors to drain the blood out of her arm and pump in fresh blood. When her heart began to fail she was put into the lung. She had become unconscious. Then her heart stopped. Stimulants were given. The slow beating began again but grew steadily weaker. Each time stimulants were given, the heart responded less strongly and finally stopped forever.

We waited with Mr. and Mrs. Tanner at the snake barn, calling the hospital at intervals. When we heard that Grace was dead, Mrs. Tanner burst into tears. "Grace was such a beautiful young girl—and so talented," she moaned. "There wasn't anything she couldn't do. Why did she ever want to mess around with those awful snakes?"

"I guess that's something none of us will ever understand," said her husband sadly.

Grace was born in Kansas in 1884. She studied entomology at the University of Kansas and during field trips to collect insects it was a great joke among Grace's fellow students that she was terrified of even harmless garter snakes. Later, however, after her marriage failed, Grace turned with a passionate interest to the creatures she had so long feared. In 1923 she became curator of the Museum of Natural History at the Minneapolis Public Library but quarreled with the directors, who felt that her reckless handling of poisonous snakes endangered not only her own life but that of others. She went to the Brookfield Zoo in Chicago; here the same difficulty arose. Finally Grace moved to California where she could work with reptiles as she wished.

An attempt was made by several of Grace's friends to keep her collection together for a Grace Wiley Memorial Reptile House, but this failed. The snakes were auctioned off and the snake that had killed Grace was purchased by a roadside zoo in Arizona. Huge signboards bearing an artist's conception of the incident were erected for miles along the highways.

So passed one of the most remarkable people I have ever known.

THE END

🔄 **Talking it over**

1. The author says, "If Grace Wiley had wished to make a mystery out of her amazing ability, I am certain she could have made a fortune by posing as a woman with supernatural power."

a. What "secrets" did Grace know about snakes that made it possible for her to handle them?

b. What tricks does a Hindu fakir use to fool his audience?

c. Why didn't Miss Wiley advertise herself as a "snake charmer"?

2. Although Miss Wiley needed immediate treatment after she was bitten, she remained calm.

a. Why did she put the cobra back in its cage before letting herself be helped?

b. What did she mean when she said, "He didn't really bite me, did he?"

c. Was Grace Wiley in any way responsible for the accident? Explain.

He likes the unusual

⇄ Words in action

Follow the author's directions on page 51 for imitating the fighting pose of a cobra. Now, using your imagination, imitate what the snake is doing in each of the following descriptions. If necessary, check a dictionary for meanings, especially of the words in bold type.

1. "The snake swayed like a **reed** in the wind, **feinting** for a strike."

2. (Use your other hand to "help.") "The cobra hesitated a split second, his rear body **quivering** like a **plucked** banjo string. Then he struck."

3. (Hold up the open palm of your other hand as a target for the snake.) "He struck with his mouth closed—as rapidly as an expert boxer **drumming** on a punching bag."

4. (Slide the same hand over the snake's "hood" and stroke its "head.") "The snake hissed and struggled **violently.**"

5. "Suddenly the snake went **limp** and his hood began to close."

"Ever since I was a kid, I've been interested in the strange and unusual," writes Dan Mannix. "I liked to dream about traveling to strange places and seeing strange people."

And that is exactly what he has done. After college, he worked as a magician and sword-swallower in carnivals. He and his wife Jule have hunted iguanas (giant lizards) in Mexico with their pet eagle, explored caves and tamed vampire bats, and hunted in the wilds with their pet cheetah. Mannix has reported his experiences in books and magazine articles, in films and lectures, and on television.

The Mannix children, Danny and Julie, grew up with a menagerie of animals in their Philadelphia home. For her coming-out party, Julie's idea of having a circus tent and animal acts was a huge success—the guests said it was the best party they had ever attended.

In 1967, Mannix received the Dutton Animal Book Award for his book *The Fox and the Hound.*

He knew it was murder, but how could he prove it?

WALLY, THE WATCHFUL EYE

by Paul W. Fairman

The Watchful Eye Detective School
Parker Building
New York, New York

Mr. Walter A. Watts
Lettyville, New York

Dear Mr. Watts:

As President of Watchful Eye, I wish to thank you
for your application; also, to congratulate you on
your decision to move into the highly lucrative field
of private investigation. I was greatly impressed
by the enthusiasm your letter revealed and for that
reason am rushing you Lesson Number One of the ten
lessons that make up the Watchful Eye course.

However, in your haste to become one of us, you
neglected to enclose the $25 tuition payment. An
oversight, of course, so please send it along by
return mail. In the meantime, allow me to assure
you that our expert instruction, coupled with your
obvious drive and ambition, will assure you
swift progress.

Sincerely,

John Hayden, President

Dear Johnny:

Your letter and the first lesson, <u>Shadowing the Suspect</u>, received. Thanks a million, and you were right about my enthusiasm. You were real top-drawer to send the lesson without the loot and I'll get it to you as soon as possible.

You see, I'm clerking in old Tom Barton's grocery store here in Lettyville and old Tom's not exactly loose with the lettuce. But there won't be much delay with the dough because I've got a bonus coming from old Tom for watching the store three weeks ago while he took a two-day trip to Boston.

Now you might wonder why old Tom hasn't kicked in with this cabbage being as it's due me for almost a month. Well, Johnny, there's a reason for that. You see old Tom never gives out any green unless he's prodded plenty and I haven't felt like hounding him because he's having a hard time just now. You see, his wife, old Martha, committed suicide while he was in Boston.

As you can imagine, a suicide in a little place like Lettyville—pop. 3,000—is a real big deal. So old Tom has been long-facing it all over town with everybody squirting out the sympathy like they were spraying him down for fleas. Everybody helping him moan it up with hardly a thought for Martha who did the dutch while old Tom was in Boston.

And she didn't wait long, either. He'd hardly pulled out for the railroad depot before she turned on the gas range in their kitchen and sat down for a farewell snooze right in front of it.

That's how it had to happen because the coroner said she'd been dead the whole two days when old Tom got back and found her there with the place full of gas. Nobody went to see her while he was gone because we all thought she was going with him. That was how it was supposed to be but old Tom said she changed her mind at the last minute. Probably, I guess, so she could do this one last thing without old Tom griping and heckling her.

And now the whole town's on his side because they know him better and besides, a lot of them owe him money, his claws being in real estate and mortgages and everything else along with the grocery store I work for him in. And they didn't know old Martha very well. She kept to herself in their house about a mile out of town and people said she was snooty.

But that wasn't true. I delivered groceries out there and met her several times and she was real nice. I think old Tom just kept her there by never giving her a dime for duds and she was ashamed to socialize in the sloppy sister smocks and socks he said were good enough for anybody.

And so, Johnny old man, that explains why I'm a little tardy with the tuition. But I know everything costs money these days and I'm going to lean a limb against old Tom tomorrow and bust out the bonus which I've got coming.

In the meantime I'm cramming like crazy, shadowing suspects all over the place until I've hardly got time to pitch and pash with Pearl. Pearl's my girl. She works at the local utility company and I'm planning to put the handcuffs on her as soon as I finish your course and get my license and come through on a couple of big cases. But I've got to really roll because I'm already 17 and I want to have an office by the time I'm 21 with a few ops on my payroll so I can sit back and mastermind their moves and have more time for Pearl.

Yours in a hurry,

Wally Watts

The Watchful Eye Detective School
Parker Building
New York, New York

Mr. Walter A. Watts
Lettyville, New York

Dear Walter:

Your letter received and I am sending along Lesson Number Two in the series—The Art of Obtaining Information Indirectly—even though the check you enclosed was to the amount of only $7.40. My better judgment tells me to withhold the lessons until the

total tuition is forthcoming as per contract. But
one seldom encounters a push and ambition such as
yours so I am forced to stretch a point, knowing
you will remit the entire amount as soon as Mr.
Barton gets around to paying you your bonus.

In the meantime, please allow me to suggest a little
restraint in your activities relative to the course.
"Shadowing suspects all over the place"—as you put
it—can lead to unhappy complications, what with
your lack of experience and the suspects being under
no suspicion whatever. Therefore I suggest that you
confine yourself to the academic aspects of detection
as set forth in the Watchful Eye course, avoiding
practical application for now.

Cordially,

John Hayden, President

Dear Johnny:

I'm afraid you got the wrong idea from my last
letter—about the bonus from old Tom covering all the
tuition. Old Tom paid up when I prodded him but the
bonus was only five bucks—I told you he was tight
with the tips—and I hadn't figured on that to finish
off the finances with you. As a matter of fact, I'm
peddling my pig to pay the balance. I live on a small
farm out of town with my parents and this pig was the
runt of the litter and got the short shake on everything. So Dad gave him to me and I bottle-babied him
up to a shoat. Now I'm selling him to Frank Gilmore,
a nearby farmer, to clean up our contract.

As to the other part, don't worry about a thing.
I've stopped shadowing all and sundry and am
concentrating all my skill on old Tom. Because here's
a hunch right out of the hat, Johnny, and I know
you'll keep it confidential—I'm dead sure old Martha
didn't commit suicide. Old Tom gave her the gas
himself. So it's murder and I don't know why I didn't
figure it before. If you were here and could take a
gander at the ghoul, you'd catalogue him for a killer
right away. Low, slanty forehead. Beady little eyes. A
scowl he puts on every morning like his pants.

Oh, he's the criminal type all right and I'm giving
him my undivided attention. Of course, I do need a

little more shadowing experience. Old Tom made me realize this when he turned around the other evening and said, "Wally, I'm getting tired of banging my heels against your shins every time I stop short. Can't you find your way around town any more without a guide?" Right away, I soaped him real soft and he isn't suspicious, but as I say, I guess I need a little more experience.

And cracking this case won't be easy. Old Tom's probably got the ticket stubs to show he was in Boston all the time. But don't worry. I'll amputate his alibi and keep you posted.

Meantime, I'm studying Lesson Number Two—learning how to obtain the info on old Tom.

The best,

Wally

The Watchful Eye Detective School
Parker Building
New York, New York

Dear Wally:

Even though you sent only $4.20 in lieu of the total balance due, I'm rushing you the next lessons—all of them up to and including Lesson Number Six which I beg you to read carefully. Even its title—<u>Logic: The Basis of Successful Detection</u>—should be enlightening. This lesson brings out basic truths—that there is no such thing as a criminal type from a physical stand-point. Some of the finest people alive have slanty foreheads; beady eyes may indicate an abnormal optical condition but nothing more. And if we arrested all the scowlers in this world there wouldn't be enough of us left to feed them.

So read Lesson Number Six carefully and stop annoy-ing poor old Mr. Barton. He no doubt has enough to contend with already.

Sincerely,

Johnny

Dear Johnny:

About the $4.20—I sold my pig all right and deliv-
ered him and made off with the moola. But that night
he stymied his new sty and then tunneled out under Mr.
Gilmore's fence and hiked home. That's how pampering
pigs pays off. Hand-feed one and he's yours forever.
So Mom made me give Mr. Gilmore back his dough.

But don't worry. I went right out and pressured Pete
Policheck, a real pal, into buying my old bike. He's
paying the price tomorrow.

Also, thanks for all those lessons in one big lump.
They help because I'll get to be a real clever op just
that much sooner. But I haven't got Lesson Number Two,
about obtaining information, down quite pat yet. I
know I'm a little rough in this department because Mr.
Ingalls, the insurance man hereabouts, almost saw
through my efforts. He said, "Wally, whether or not
Tom Barton had a life insurance policy on Martha is
none of your business. A man's insurance program is
confidential and an agent wouldn't get much business
if he talked about his client's coverage."

But that info wasn't really too important. I'm about
ready to close in. Old Tom is scowling harder and his
eyes are getting beadier every day.

The best,

Wally

The Watchful Eye Detective School
Parker Building
New York, New York

Dear Wally:

Look, old pal, I'll level with you. This isn't a big
operation I'm running. The address is just a mail drop
and I do it all from my furnished room on Sixth Avenue. So you can see I'm just a young fellow like yourself, trying to better myself and make an honest buck
—so please lay off Mr. Barton!

If you want to get sued for your shirt and maybe
thrown in the clink it's okay, but my lawyer says I
could get the works too. Old Tom might extend his

coverage to include me when he gets around to suing
for libel or maybe false arrest and heaven knows what.

Anyhow, my lawyer says I could be held legally
liable along with you, the way you're probably sounding off up there. So please—please!—do me a favor
and go back to your pigs and groceries. And forget the
balance you owe me—the last few lessons are on the
house.

Desperately,

Johnny

Dear Johnny:

I'm going to give your school a big boost, old pal.
You can use my name and picture in your advertising
and get a lot of business. An ad in the big magazines
that would say something like—"After Two Watchful Eye
Lessons I Nailed My Boss for Murder."

Because that's about how it happened. Old Tom confessed to everything. He did old Martha in with a few
whiffs of gas before he went to Boston to establish
his alibi. Then when he got back from Boston he turned
the gas on for a few minutes to smell up the place,
opened the windows, and ran out yelling for help.

Of course none of it could have been proved unless
old Tom confessed, even with the twenty-five grand
policy on old Martha, because everybody figured him to
be a solid citizen. But he did confess and that's
that. My first case is all wrapped up, signed, sealed,
and delivered! And you can go ahead and put that ad in
the magazines.

The best,

Wally

121 Sixth Avenue
New York City

Wally, Old Pal:

It's not fair to leave me hanging this way. I know
darned well old Tom didn't break down and confess just

because you asked him to. Things don't work out that
way in this business. You had more on him than you
told me. So let me in on it and then maybe I'll be
able to sleep nights again.

Johnny

Dear Johnny:

   It was that logic lesson you sent that steered me
right. Knowing old Tom as I did, it wasn't logical
that he'd waste two days' gas on a ten-minute job. And
I knew he wouldn't risk a fire by leaving a gas stove
going for two whole days.
   So Pearl, she's my girl, being employed at the utility company made it easy to check old Tom's gas bills.
They always ran around $3.00 a month, give or take a
dime. Forty-eight straight hours would have shoved it
up around 80¢ or $1.00 more than usual. But old Tom's
bill for last month read the usual—this time, $3.05.
   So old Tom could shill the sheriff and con the
coroner all right, but he couldn't make a monkey out
of the gas meter. Or maybe he forgot that everything
costs money these days, even murdering old Martha.
   I'm enclosing a snapshot for that ad you'll want to
run. The one on the left is Pearl, my girl. She
says hello.

All the best,

Walter A. Watts
(the A is for Alert)

1. *a.* What did Wally notice about Tom Barton which made him start investigating his boss?

b. Explain how Wally figured out how Martha Barton died.

2. *a.* How are Mr. Hayden's letters different from those Wally writes?

b. From their letters, what do you learn about the kinds of persons Wally and Mr. Hayden are? You will find clues both in the way each one writes and in what he says about himself.

c. Mr. Hayden's last two letters sound different from the others. What might explain this change?

Words in action

Part of the fun of reading Wally's letters is being able to understand the slang that he uses.

1. Find and write on your paper at least two expressions Wally uses in referring to each of these:
   a. Mrs. Barton's death
   b. Wally's attempts to get Mr. Barton to pay him the bonus
   c. Mrs. Barton's clothing
   d. Wally's feelings toward Pearl
   e. money

2. Find and write on your paper at least one slang word or phrase for each of these:
   a. jail
   b. detective
   c. how Wally stopped Tom Barton's suspicions of being tailed
   d. how Wally will prove Tom Barton is the murderer

3. For each of the slang expressions you wrote in 1 and 2, consider whether you and your friends would use the same expression or a different one. If you would use the same expression Wally does, write "same" after it. If you would use a different one, write the word or expression you would use.

4. Wally often puts words together in his own special way. If you noticed what this is, explain and give examples.

5. What does Wally's slang add to the enjoyment of the selection?

6. What happens to slang over a period of time?

Outsmarted by Wally

"Wally the Watchful Eye" is one of a series of stories about a clever boy who tells his experiences in the form of letters to the Watchful Eye Detective School. Usually the stories have a clever twist at the end.

Author Paul Fairman says he is sometimes outsmarted by his characters. He writes, "Wally might be called a symbol of all the kids I've known who did crazy things that came out all right.

"My sympathies are all with poor Johnny Hayden, an upstanding young man trying to make an honest dollar and furnish a needed service. I always try to help him out as much as possible, but so far Wally has been too smart for both of us. I promise myself that some day he will get his comeuppance. He is a hard lad to catch napping, though."

The other stories about Wally appeared in *Ellery Queen's Mystery Magazine* from 1959 to 1962.

I stumbled into the black night, sobbing,

my legs wobbly from fear.

THE Kitten

by Richard Wright

IN MEMPHIS we lived in a one-story brick tenement. The stone buildings and the concrete pavements looked bleak and hostile to me. The absence of green, growing things made the city seem dead. Living space for the four of us—my mother, my brother, my father, and me—was a kitchen and a bedroom. In the front and rear were paved areas in which my brother and I could play, but for days I was afraid to go into the strange city streets alone.

It was in this tenement that the personality of my father first came fully into the orbit of my concern. He worked as a night porter in a Beale Street drugstore and he became important and forbidding to me only when I learned that I could not make noise when he was asleep in the daytime. He

was the lawgiver in our family and I never laughed in his presence. I used to lurk timidly in the kitchen doorway and watch his huge body sitting slumped at the table. I stared at him with awe as he gulped his beer from a tin bucket, as he ate long and heavily, sighed, belched, closed his eyes to nod on a stuffed belly. He was quite fat and his bloated stomach always lapped over his belt. He was always a stranger to me, always somehow alien and remote.

One morning my brother and I, while playing in the rear of our flat, found a stray kitten that set up a loud, persistent meowing. We fed it some scraps of food and gave it water, but it still meowed. My father, clad in his underwear, stumbled sleepily to the back door and demanded that we keep quiet. We told him that it was the kitten that was making the noise and he ordered us to drive it away. We tried to make the kitten leave, but it would not budge. My father took a hand.

"Scat!" he shouted.

The scrawny kitten lingered, brushing itself against our legs, and meowing plaintively.

"Kill that damn thing!" my father exploded. "Do anything, but get it away from here!"

He went inside, grumbling. I resented his shouting and it irked me that I could never make him feel my resentment. How could I hit back at him? Oh, yes. . . . He had said to kill the kitten and I would kill it! I knew that he had not really meant for me to kill the kitten, but my deep hate of him urged me toward a literal acceptance of his word.

"He said for us to kill the kitten," I told my brother.

"He didn't mean it," my brother said.

"He did, and I'm going to kill 'im."

"Then he *will* howl," my brother said.

"He can't howl if he's dead," I said.

"He didn't really say kill 'im," my brother protested.

"He did!" I said. "And you heard him!"

My brother ran away in fright. I found a piece of rope, made a noose, slipped it about the kitten's neck, pulled it over a nail, then jerked the animal clear of the ground. It gasped, slobbered, spun, doubled, clawed the air frantically; finally its mouth gaped and its pink-white tongue shot out stiffly. I tied the rope to a nail and went to find my brother. He was crouching behind a corner of the building.

"I killed 'im," I whispered.

"You did bad," my brother said.

"Now Papa can sleep," I said, deeply satisfied.

"He didn't mean for you to kill 'im," my brother said.

"Then why did he *tell* me to do it?" I demanded.

My brother could not answer; he stared fearfully at the dangling kitten.

"That kitten's going to get you," he warned me.

"That kitten can't even breathe now," I said.

"I'm going to tell," my brother said, running into the house.

I waited, resolving to defend myself with my father's rash words, anticipating my enjoyment in repeating them to him even though I knew that he had spoken them in anger. My mother hurried toward me, drying her hands upon her apron. She stopped and paled when she saw the kitten suspended from the rope.

"What in God's name have you done?" she asked.

"The kitten was making noise and Papa said to kill it," I explained.

"You little fool!" she said. "Your father's going to beat you for this!"

"But he told me to kill it," I said.

"You shut your mouth!"

She grabbed my hand and dragged me to my father's bedside and told him what I had done.

"You know better than that!" my father stormed.

"You told me to kill 'im," I said.

"I told you to drive him away," he said.

"You told me to kill 'im," I countered positively.

"You get out of my eyes before I smack you down!" my father bellowed in disgust, then turned over in bed.

I had had my first triumph over my

father. I had made him believe that I had taken his words literally. He could not punish me now without risking his authority. I was happy because I had at last found a way to throw my criticism of him into his face. I had made him feel that, if he whipped me for killing the kitten, I would never give serious weight to his words again. I had made him know that I felt he was cruel and I had done it without his punishing me.

But my mother, being more imaginative, retaliated with an assault upon my sensibilities that crushed me with the moral horror involved in taking a life. All that afternoon she directed toward me calculated words that spawned in my mind a horde of invisible demons bent upon exacting vengeance for what I had done. As evening drew near, anxiety filled me and I was afraid to go into an empty room alone.

"You owe a debt you can never pay," my mother said.

"I'm sorry," I mumbled.

"Being sorry can't make that kitten live again," she said.

Then, just before I was to go to bed, she uttered a paralyzing injunction: she ordered me to go out into the dark, dig a grave, and bury the kitten.

"No!" I screamed, feeling that if I went out of doors some evil spirit would whisk me away.

"Get out there and bury that poor kitten," she ordered.

"I'm scared!"

"And wasn't that kitten scared when you put that rope around its neck?" she asked.

"But it was only a kitten," I explained.

"But it was alive," she said. "Can you make it live again?"

"But Papa said to kill it," I said, trying to shift the moral blame upon my father.

My mother whacked me across my mouth with the flat palm of her hand.

"You stop that lying! You knew what he meant!"

"I didn't!" I bawled.

She shoved a tiny spade into my hands.

"Go out there and dig a hole and bury that kitten!"

I stumbled out into the black night, sobbing, my legs wobbly from fear. Though I knew that I had killed the kitten, my mother's words had made it live again in my mind. What would that kitten do to me when I touched it? Would it claw at my eyes? As I groped toward the dead kitten, my mother lingered behind me, unseen in the dark, her disembodied voice egging me on.

"Mama, come and stand by me," I begged.

"You didn't stand by that kitten, so why should I stand by you?" she asked tauntingly from the menacing darkness.

"I can't touch it," I whimpered, feeling that the kitten was staring at me with reproachful eyes.

"Untie it!" she ordered.

Shuddering, I fumbled at the rope and the kitten dropped to the pavement with a thud that echoed in my mind for many days and nights. Then, obeying my mother's floating voice, I hunted for a spot of earth, dug a shallow hole, and buried the stiff kitten; as I handled its cold body my skin prickled. When I had completed the burial, I sighed and started back to the flat, but my mother caught hold of my hand and led me again to the kitten's grave.

"Shut your eyes and repeat after me," she said.

I closed my eyes tightly, my hand clinging to hers.

"Dear God, our Father, forgive me, for I knew not what I was doing. . . ."

"Dear God, our Father, forgive me, for I knew not what I was doing," I repeated.

"And spare my poor life, even though I did not spare the life of the kitten. . . ."

"And spare my poor life, even though I did not spare the life of the kitten," I repeated.

"And while I sleep tonight, do not snatch the breath of life from me. . . ."

I opened my mouth but no words came. My mind was frozen with horror. I pictured myself gasping for breath and dying in my sleep. I broke away from my mother and ran into the night, crying, shaking with dread.

"No," I sobbed.

My mother called to me many times, but I would not go to her.

"Well, I suppose you've learned your lesson," she said at last.

Contrite, I went to bed, hoping that I would never see another kitten.

THE END

His life in his books

"The Kitten," an excerpt from Richard Wright's autobiography *Black Boy*, describes only one of the many harsh experiences that marked the author's boyhood. When his father deserted the family and his mother's paralyzing illness seemed incurable, Richard and his brother stayed briefly in an orphanage and then with whatever relative would take them. Richard's unhappiness drove him to rebel against everybody and everything; his lying, fighting, and school-cutting led his grandmother to predict that he would die at the end of a hangman's noose.

In his later teen years, Richard was strongly attracted to books, and he resolved to become a writer. The books he wrote reflected what he had seen and felt as a Negro struggling for survival, for freedom, and for the freedom of all black people. *Native Son* contains characters based on boys he met in a Chicago reform school. Some of his other books are *Uncle Tom's Children, Twelve Million Black Voices,* and *Black Power.*

Richard Wright died in France in 1960 at the age of fifty-two.

GOOD BOOKS TO READ

RANGE

Big Nick
by George Laycock
Johnny Swope releases a bear cub from a trap and treats his injured foot, but cannot keep him as a pet. Johnny sees Nick occasionally, recognizing him by his injured foot. He saves the bear from troubles that beset him as he wanders in a national park, raiding camps for food. (Norton, 1967, 186 pages)

The Fledgling
by John Tomerlin
Because of a car accident in which Richard was injured and his brother killed, his mother worries that he, too, may be killed. Her fears threaten to cut Richard off from what he most wants to do: learn to fly a plane. No one knows that Rich also carries a secret load that hampers him as much as his mother's feelings. (Dutton, 1968, 188 pages)

Henry 3
by Joseph Krumgold
Because of his father's job, Henry has lived all over the U.S.A. His problem is that he can't make friends. Somehow the news of his high IQ always gets around, and the other kids are afraid of him. Now his family has moved once again and this time he is determined to keep his brains a secret. (Atheneum, 1967, 268 pages)

The Soul Brothers and Sister Lou
by Kristin Hunter
In the part of the city where Louretta lives there are usually too many people for the space. Lou and her brother Fess feel only hate when a white policeman kills an innocent member of their gang. But they start activities that lead the young people away from violence and despair. Sister Lou learns what "soul" is and finds it in her own singing. (Scribner's, 1968, 248 pages)

COURAGE

Cave of Danger
by Bryce Walton
Matt Wilde is interested in just one thing—finding a cave that he can show to tourists. That is the only way he knows to earn needed money for his family. But he and his friend Spot Jessup find more than they are looking for when they go exploring underground. (Crowell, 1967, 264 pages)

The Little Fishes
by Erik Haugaard
Guido, orphaned in World War II, takes on the responsibility of two younger children whose aunt has been killed in a bombing raid. As the three homeless children travel toward what they hope will be a safer part of the country, they meet with kindness as well as treachery. (Houghton, 1967, 214 pages)

The Pit
by Reginald Maddock
Almost everyone says that Butch Reece is no good. His father beats him and his schoolmates taunt him. He has little to enjoy except the wild moorland of England, where he lives. Blamed for a theft he did not commit, Butch decides

to make the real thief confess. (Little, Brown, 1968, 191 pages)

The Pool of Fire
by John Christopher
When human boys and girls are fourteen, the Tripods that are ruling the world fit a metal mesh over their skulls and make them slaves. A boy who has escaped the capping tells the story of an underground movement among humans struggling to overthrow the conquerors and win freedom back again. (Macmillan, 1968, 178 pages)

To the Wild Sky
by Ivan Southall
Bewilderment and terror follow when the pilot who is flying six Australian children to a weekend birthday celebration dies. After a crash landing, the children find themselves cut off from the world on an uninhabited island. This story tells of their struggle to survive. (St. Martin's, 1967, 184 pages)

SEARCH

Coyote in Manhattan
by Jean Craighead George
When Tenny Harkness meets her father at the boat dock, she discovers aboard the freighter a caged coyote and impulsively turns it loose. Soon New York City is taking sides: those who are bent on capturing the animal because it is a danger to the city, and those who would like to see it outwit its pursuers. (Crowell, 1968, 203 pages)

Overdrive
by Leslie Waller
John Francis Regan, a high-school senior, tells of his love for cars, his work as a mechanic, and of a mistake that could have spoiled his life. (Holt, 1967, 118 pages)

Sicilian Mystery
by Arthur Catherall
Sixteen-year-old Neville Brown, vacationing on the Italian island of Stromboli, near Sicily, is looking for good scenes to photograph. He is particularly interested in getting some good views of the volcano. But as he gets acquainted with a fisherman and his son, Neville finds himself in dark caverns under the volcano where even the turtles carry secrets, and he must search for a way to save his own life and that of a friend. (Lothrop, 1967, 160 pages)

Smugglers' Road
by Hal G. Evarts
Facing the probability of being sent to Juvenile Hall because of his offenses, Kern Dawson chooses an alternative suggested by one of his teachers—a summer of working in a clinic in a Mexican seaside village. The work is hard, and seasoned with the danger and excitement of tracking down some lawbreakers. (Scribner's, 1968, 192 pages)

Stranger in the Hills
by Madeleine Polland
Two British families vacationing in Scotland learn that a Russian sailor has fled from his ship and is hiding to avoid capture. The young people of the families find Sergei and do their best to keep him safe. Their experiences in this complicated adventure lead through fear and laughter to a conclusion quite unexpected. (Doubleday, 1968, 190 pages)

SECOND LOOK

The Big Wheels
by William E. Huntsberry

A Committee of Six, formed to organize the activities of the senior class, gains power that threatens to control a much wider area than the school. Can anything stop them? (Lothrop, 1967, 158 pages)

Bryan's Dog
by Edmund Scholefield

Bryan, son of a poor Alabama farmer, sees fire threatening a neighbor's pine forest. Although the neighbor had once had Bryan's father arrested for trespassing, the boy cuts through the fence and turns soil over to keep the trees from burning. This action brings many changes to his life, including the chance to buy a dog he has wanted. A later decision about the dog forces him to take a second look at his future. (World, 1967, 158 pages)

Haunted Summer
by Hope Dahle Jordan

Marilla Marston, about to graduate from high school, has made the golfing team. She has a job, too, and is interested in the boy next door. Then her life becomes haunted because of something she has done that no one knows about. (Lothrop, 1967, 158 pages)

The Nitty Gritty
by Frank Bonham

Charlie is smart, and his talent for writing arouses the enthusiasm of his high-school teacher. But Charlie's father says education doesn't do a Negro any good. Wanting to make something of his life, Charlie works to earn money for a share in his Uncle Baron's secret venture—and then has to take a second look at what his uncle can do for him. (Dutton, 1968, 156 pages)

Smoke
by William Corbin

Chris finds a lost German shepherd dog. Believing that the stepfather he resents so much won't let him keep the dog, Chris tries to take care of it secretly. But the dog needs a doctor, and Chris must find a way to help him. (Coward, 1967, 253 pages)

TURNING POINT

Edge of Two Worlds
by Weyman Jones

The wagon train in which he has been traveling from Texas to New England is halted by Comanches and everyone is killed except Calvin. The boy is dangerously near dying of starvation when he meets an old Indian. Calvin has to choose between probable death in traveling alone, and possible torture at the hands of the Indian, whose interest in him he doesn't understand. The old Indian is now famous in American history. (Dial, 1968, 143 pages)

The Pigeon Pair
by Elisabeth Ogilvie

Ingrid Snow looks back from her eighteenth year through all the hardships she and her twin brother experienced in a family that never had enough money. She tells how she and Greg dream toward a better life in a better house than their tar-paper shack until the hopelessness of it all makes Greg bitter. Then, with tragedy, comes change. (McGraw-Hill, 1967, 182 pages)

The Starveling
by Nina Warner Hooke
A trailer family in England heartlessly leaves a kitten behind. The villagers make half-hearted attempts to help the cat, but nobody carries through. An interesting character is an elderly woman who lost her family in a bombing raid during the war, while she was saved because she was away from home seeing about a cat. She has hated cats ever since. (Day, 1968, 128 pages)

The Troubled Summer
by Ben Haas
Clay Williams, who attends a segregated high school for Negroes, finds it hard to accept the second-rate books and equipment the white school board provides. Then a civil rights team comes into the community to change things. Clay resents the leader because he is white, and finds he has a personal problem to solve before he can wholeheartedly join the cause of his people. (Bobbs-Merrill, 1966, 192 pages)

THEN

Jed McLane and Storm Cloud
by Donald Honig
Jed, son of a sergeant, lives in a frontier Army Post in Montana Territory. He earns his reputation of being the leading mischief-maker at the Post as he tries to save a Blackfoot Indian accused of murder and an Army deserter hiding in the hills. (McGraw-Hill, 1968, 140 pages)

Me, California Perkins
by Patricia Beatty
The Perkins family is often uprooted because Papa has an itchy foot. This time they head for a California silver mining town where Papa hopes to get rich. Mama and the children settle into a house built of whiskey bottles, but because Mama is angry, Papa boards at the Lion's Den. A lively and amusing story. (Morrow, 1968, 255 pages)

A Peculiar Magic
by Annabel and Edgar Johnson
Cindy's mother is a dance-hall girl of the Old West. When the police raid the hall and send the girls away, Cindy manages to slip away before the Ladies' Reform Society can get her. By chance she meets a theatrical company. Believing they will play Denver, where she thinks her mother has gone, she joins the troupe. Their adventures and hers make exciting reading. (Houghton, 1965, 256 pages)

Riders of Enchanted Valley
by Lee McGiffin
Luke Morgan goes from Kentucky to California by ship. Once ashore, he sees a white man knock down a Chinese man for no reason. He strikes the white man. This gives him one friend and one enemy. Later he becomes involved in a fight to save land from unscrupulous men and finds that the man he struck on his first day in San Francisco is still to be reckoned with. (Dutton, 1966, 158 pages)

The Travels of Colin O'Dae
by Ruth Franchere
Colin runs away from the Chicago boarding house where he and his father live, in order to avoid having to work on the Illinois-Michigan canal. Colin joins a traveling show, going by showboat to New Orleans. His efforts to be helpful both on- and off-stage are entertaining. (Crowell, 1966, 261 pages)

2

Word Attack

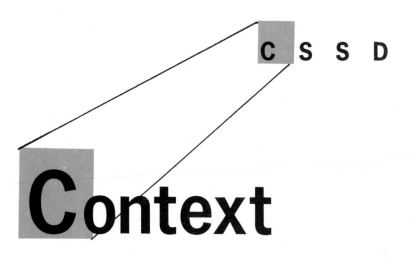

C S S D

Context

LESSON ONE: Recognizing context clues

> "...a ten-foot blue shark sighted the flash of bare, white feet, then eight dangling, waving human legs. The beast heard the splashings of the men—and planed upward to investigate.
>
> His dorsal fin broke the surface perhaps twenty feet from the little knot of men."
>
> From "The Tigers and the Sharks" (page 165)

If you don't know the word in the colored block, you should still be able to figure out what it means by thinking about what you know from experience and applying this to certain clues in the passage both before and after the word—the **context** of the word.

1. Where are the men?
2. What is the surface that is referred to?
3. To what does the fin belong?
4. Try to picture the fin "breaking the surface." Where would this fin be—on the belly, the back, the right or left side, or the tail of the beast? (Common sense and what you know about fish in general should tell you.)

If you have ever heard or said *dorsal* (dôr'səl), you probably can pronounce the word as soon as context gives you its meaning.

EXERCISE I. Using context clues to recognize words

See if you can figure out the meaning of the words in colored blocks. The questions will help you find the context clues.

1. Jackie Robinson's first year in major league baseball was crucial . If he wasn't good enough, it would be years before another black player would be given a chance.
   - a. Would Robinson's success or failure make much difference? Why or why not?
   - b. Which is the best definition of *crucial?* (1) very important   (2) just ordinary   (3) of no importance

2. I stood looking into the eyes of the most dangerous animal in the world today, that dread reptile, the king cobra or hamadryad .
   - a. Which word or words in the sentence mean the same thing as *hamadryad?*
   - b. How do you know?

3. To celebrate the joyful occasion, Joseph's mother invited everyone in the village to a feast of groundnut stew. Her own household could hardly supply enough food to feed all these people, but other women brought rice, peppers, or a bit of meat to augment the stew.
   - a. Did Joseph's mother have enough food on hand to feed all the people of the village?
   - b. Which is the best definition for *augment?*
     (1) eat along with   (2) add to   (3) replace

4. We were sure John didn't start the fight, but we were certain he could name the culprit .
   - a. What does *but* mean in this sentence?
   - b. Complete this statement with as many words as you need: "He didn't start the fight but he knew _____."
   - c. *Culprit* probably means: (1) a missing person (2) an innocent person   (3) a guilty person

5. The men closest to where the gold piece fell began to fight each other for it. Finally, Jim wrested it from the others and ran off.
   - a. What does *it* refer to in the second sentence?
   - b. Do you think Jim ran off with the gold or without it?
   - c. *Wrested* probably means: (1) took by force (2) accepted   (3) refused to accept

6. As Loretta approached the dark, silent house, she glanced up and was suddenly frightened. There was something sinister about the place.

   a. How is the house described in the first sentence?

   b. How did Loretta feel?

   c. Sinister probably means: (1) cheerful, welcoming (2) evil, threatening (3) dirty, disorderly

7. Before the captain would try to land with only one engine operating, he ordered the crew to jettison the cargo so that the plane would be lighter.

   a. What will be the effect on the plane once the cargo is jettisoned?

   b. In other stories you have read or movies you have seen about a plane or a ship in trouble, how does the crew usually lighten the load?

   c. Jettison here means: (1) pump up with air (2) tie together (3) throw overboard

8. Which words could you figure out from the general sense of the passage?

9. Which word is explained directly?

10. For which word were the context clues weakest or least helpful?

11. Were there any words you were able to pronounce only after you had figured out their meaning through context? Which ones?

LESSON TWO: When context clues don't help

"The house had just been painted and its pristine walls gleamed in the sunlight." Could *pristine* mean "pure white"? "yellow"? "lower"? "upper"? "wooden"? "rough-textured"? "newly plastered"? "shiny"? "fresh and clean"? Try each of these meanings in the sentence. Do all make sense?

Sometimes the context suggests several possible meanings for a word, any of which could be right. In other cases there are no clues at all, as in a sentence like "Mrs. Lunt brought each of her nieces a *huipil* from Guatemala." You must learn to recognize when you can probably rely on the context for the meaning of a word and when you will need to use a dictionary or other source of information.

EXERCISE II.   Recognizing whether context clues help

In the following paragraph from a story which appears later in *Focus,* nonsense words are substituted for actual words in the story. As you read each sentence, decide whether context tells you the exact meaning of the word. Then answer the questions.

> It was too bad about Joe's hog because it was his last one, all he and Tildy had to provide **grox** for the winter. Joe was the kind of man that seemed born for bad **culos.** If he planted a **nebb** patch, there would be rain all around the **rolser** but never a drop in his field. His neighbors' **nebb** would grow tall and green, and Joe's would burn up for lack of water. His **tickstroms** were always dying off with one thing or another, and it seemed he just couldn't get ahead.
>
> From "The Man Who Rode the Bear" (page 148)

1. Which of the following could *grox* mean?
   (a) shelter   (b) meat   (c) transportation
   Is that the only possible meaning?
2. Which of the following words could be substituted for *culos?*
   (a) luck   (b) habits   (c) hogs
   How much of the paragraph did you have to read in order to be sure?
3. Is there more than one possible meaning for *nebb?* Which of the following choices fit in the sentence beginning "If he planted a nebb patch"?
   (a) cabbage   (b) potato   (c) corn   (d) weed
4. Notice that *nebb* also appears in a later sentence beginning

"His neighbors' nebb . . . ." Which of the choices in 3 do you now think is the right one? Why?

5. Which of the following do you think *rolser* means?
   (a) neighborhood   (b) area   (c) state   (d) barn
   (e) house
   Can you tell the EXACT meaning from context?

6. Which of the following could *tickstroms* be?
   (a) animals   (b) crops   (c) children

7. Which nonsense words are least clear from context clues?

What you should know about using context clues

When you meet a word that looks unfamiliar, check first to see if there are any helpful clues in the context. Sometimes a writer explains unusual words he uses. More often, you must figure out the word by using information in the passage and applying common sense.

If you are reading an exciting story and don't want to lose the thread by stopping to look up words, you may get along well enough by guessing meanings in this way. When you need to understand exactly what is said, and in special kinds of reading (math or science or social studies, for instance), you may also need to use the other methods of word attack which are reviewed on the following pages. But always BEGIN by looking for context clues. When you have to figure out the meaning of a word by another method, check out the meaning in context to see if it fits.

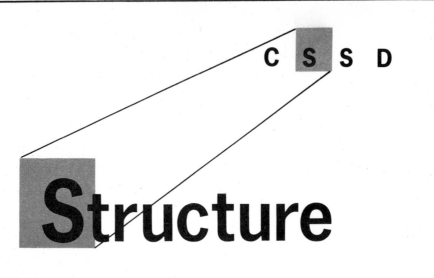

Structure

LESSON ONE: Derivatives

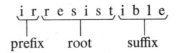

$$i \; r \;\; r \; e \; s \; i \; s \; t \;\; i \; b \; l \; e$$

prefix   root   suffix

If you had an *irresistible* craving for popcorn, would you say no if someone offered you some? Why or why not?

A word like *irresistible* may look hard, but if you recognize its structural parts (and think about the context in which it is used), you should be able to figure out what it means.

1. What is the root word in *irresistible?*
2. How does the prefix change the meaning of the root word?
3. What is the suffix?
4. Could either *resist* or *resistible* be used in "a _____ urge"? in "to _____ arrest"? How does a suffix change a word?

Words like *irresistible,* which are formed by adding a prefix or a suffix, or both, to another word are called **derivatives.**

What are the structural parts of the derivative in this sentence? "In those days, **combativeness** was the rule among Bridgeport boys. Fist fights were frequent, yet long-standing grudges were rare."

How many suffixes are in *combativeness*? What is the root word? What does it mean? What do you think *combativeness* means?

EXERCISE I. Recognizing prefixes and suffixes

1. What is the advantage of nonbreakable dishes?
2. What possible problems might be faced by someone with an unpaid debt?
3. Could solidifying fudge be poured quickly out of the pan?
4. If someone is active in an anticruelty society, is he likely to be in favor of treating animals kindly, or cruelly?
5. Why can't one nation legally keep the ships of other countries from using international waters?
6. If noise and disorder are customary in a particular home, is it usually a quiet, or a noisy, place?
7. Write the following words on your paper: **nonbreakable, unpaid, solidifying, anticruelty, international, customary.** Each of these words has one or more suffixes, and some have a prefix as well. Circle each prefix and each suffix. Underline the root word.
8. How many prefixes did you circle?
9. How many suffixes did you circle?

SOME COMMON PREFIXES

ab-.....from, away, off
ante-...before
anti-...against; not; preventing; curing
co-.....with; equally
com- (con-)..with, together
dis-....opposite of, reverse of
ex-.....former
extra-..outside, beyond; besides
in- (il-, im-, ir-)..not; the opposite of;
     the absence of
in-.....in, into
inter-..together, one with the other;
    between or among
intra-..within, inside

mis-....bad, badly; wrong, wrongly
non-....not; opposite of; lack of
post-...after
pre-....before
pro-....in favor of; forward; in place of
re-.....back; again
semi-..half, partly; twice
sub-....under, below; further; again;
    of less importance
super-.over, above; to excess, exceedingly
trans-..across, over; beyond; into a different
    place, condition, etc.
un-.....not, the opposite of

SOME COMMON SUFFIXES

FORMING NOUNS		FORMING VERBS	FORMING ADJECTIVES	
-age	-er	-ate	-able	-ish
-al	-ess	-en	-al (-ial)	-ive
-an (-ian)	-ion (-tion, -ation)	-fy (-ify)	-an (-ian)	-less
-ance	-ism	-ize	-ant	-ly
-ant	-ist		-ary	-ory
-dom	-ity		-ful	-ous
-eer	-ment		-ible	-y
-ence (-ency)	-ness		-ic (-ical)	
-ent	-or			

LESSON TWO: Compound words

$$\underbrace{\text{h i t c h}}_{\text{root}}\underbrace{\text{h i k e}}_{\text{root}}$$

Compound words are made up of two or more root words. Each part of a compound influences its meaning. Sometimes the meaning of a compound is exactly what you would expect from combining the meanings of its parts, as in *raincoat, logjam, poolside, eyesight, teen-ager, daytime, haircut.* In other compounds, you have to use your imagination (or even a dictionary) to figure out the meaning. Examples are *network, freeloader, skinflint, blackmail, stiff-necked.* But usually the context, plus the meaning of at least one of the parts of the compound, will suggest what it means.

Prefixes or suffixes, or both, may be added to a compound:

$$\underbrace{\text{p r e}}_{\text{prefix}}\underbrace{\text{t e e n}}_{\text{root}}\text{-}\underbrace{\text{a g e}}_{\text{root}}\underbrace{\text{r}}_{\text{suffix}}$$

EXERCISE II. Analyzing compounds

Part A

Write the words in the colored blocks in a column on your paper. Draw a slanting line between the root words that form the compound. If a compound has one or more prefixes or suffixes, circle these.

1. Caught in quicksand
2. Spellbound by the music
3. Exact time of splashdown
4. Work done by longshoremen
5. A plan that backfired
6. Get on the bandwagon
7. A cheapskate trick
8. Ungentlemanly behavior
9. Anti-aircraft missiles
10. The carefreeness of youth

Part B

11. In which of the compounds in Part A can you get the meaning by combining the usual meanings of the parts?
12. Which compounds have a special meaning that is different from what you would expect from the usual meanings of the parts?

EXERCISE III. Combining structure and context clues

Part A

Write the numbered words in a list on your paper. Circle the prefixes and suffixes. If a word is a compound, draw a slanting line between its parts. After each word, write the letter of the definition that you think fits.

1. stouthearted
2. baleful
3. repossess
4. accusation
5. impale
6. preoccupied
7. improper
8. restive

a. a statement that someone has done something wrong
b. occupied beforehand
c. take ownership of again
d. full of bundles of grain
e. having enlarged internal organs because of disease
f. restless
g. not suitable; not correct
h. pierce with something pointed; fasten
i. resting quietly
j. have color drain from one's face because of fear, anger, illness, etc.
k. harm, damage
l. brave
m. evil
n. having all one's attention on something

Part B

On the next page are sentences using the words from Part A. After you have read a word in context, take another look at the meaning you selected. Does it fit? If you still choose the same definition, write O.K. after the choice on your paper. If you think your first choice was wrong, cross it out and write the letter of your new choice after it.

1. There isn't a man in all these hills **stouthearted** enough to take the job of sheriff.
2. Exhausted from his work, the young steel worker sat on the crowded train ignoring the **baleful** looks of standing women.
3. If you can't make a payment of twenty-five dollars by Monday, the car will be **repossessed.**
4. A quarter was missing from Lorri's desk, and Sandra had an extra quarter at lunch time. The girls stood close to Lorri, daring her to make the **accusation.**
5. The walls were lined with huge chunks of beef **impaled** on giant hooks.
6. Daydreaming, **preoccupied** with thoughts of the coming vacation, Bill didn't realize the bus had passed his corner.
7. Every once in a while Mrs. Sheehan gets after the girls for wearing what she calls "**improper** clothing."
8. A **restive** herd, uneasy and hard to handle, is frightening to any cowhand who's seen a stampede.

If you chose a different definition in Part B than you did in Part A, check the word in a dictionary to see which meaning is correct.

> When you guess the meaning of an unfamiliar word from structure clues, always be sure the meaning makes sense in context. If it doesn't, your guess is probably wrong and you need to check the word in a dictionary.

LESSON THREE: Word parts from Greek and Latin

A biped has two feet .

A uniped has one foot .

A multiped has many feet .

Study these statements, especially the material in colored blocks. What is the meaning of the word part *ped*? What tells you?

What does *bi-* mean? *uni-*? *multi-*? How do the colored blocks help you understand the meaning of the word parts?

The word parts *uni-*, *bi-*, and *ped* come from ancient Greek and Latin words. They, and others like them, have been adopted into English, and form parts of many English words, especially words that have to do with science and technology. Learning what some of these word parts mean will help you figure out the meaning of many technical words as well as words in ordinary use.

On a piece of paper, write the list of word parts from column I. Then read the statements in column II, which will help you figure out the meaning of the parts in column I. When the class agrees on a short definition for each word part, write it on your paper.

I	II
1. -logy	A. Cosmology is a science that deals with the universe.
2. cosmo-	
3. bio-	B. Biology is a science that deals with life, especially the growth, reproduction, etc., of living things.
4. hydro-	
5. geo-	
6. psycho-	C. Hydrology is a science that deals with water.
	D. Geology is a science that deals with the earth.
	E. Psychology is a science that deals with the mind.
7. -naut	F. A cosmonaut is one who sails through the universe.
8. astro-	
	G. An astronaut is one who sails among the stars.
9. -meter	H. A photometer is an instrument for measuring light.
10. photo-	
11. thermo-	I. A thermometer is an instrument for measuring degrees of heat.
12. -scope	J. A telescope is an instrument for viewing distant objects.
13. tele-	
14. micro-	K. A microscope is an instrument for viewing extremely small objects.

EXERCISE IV.   Using structure and context clues

Part A

Read the following sentences. Copy on your paper the words in colored blocks. In each word, circle the part or parts listed in Lesson Three.

1. Multiengine aircraft carry a device that warns the pilot when one engine is putting out more power than the others. If this situation is not corrected, the pilot may lose control.

2. A thermograph , a special kind of camera, can help doctors discover health problems. The idea behind the device is that tissues in trouble are slightly warmer than healthy tissues. On a thermograph, "hot spots" show up white, while "cool spots" register black.

3. With a process called microprinting , a hundred pages of a book can be printed on a seven-by-nine card.

4. An adult who has been bilingual since childhood will probably learn still another language easily. On the other hand, a unilingual adult usually has a good deal more difficulty in learning another language.

5. Using hydrophones , scientists have listened to and recorded the sounds of hundreds of animals, from shrimps to porpoises.

6. A Telecopier will produce a copy of a page on a machine in New York when the original page is placed in a similar machine in Los Angeles.

7. Nature seems to have designed the human body to walk on all fours. The fact that we have become bipeds has resulted in a few medical problems that would not exist if men had remained quadrupeds .

8. Serious students of oceanology have taken up the popular sport of skin diving—flippers, aqualung, and all.

9. Certain types of psychopathic patients are being treated with photoshock . After being given a drug that makes them very aware of brightness, they are put in a room with flashing lights.

10. Does life exist anywhere besides on earth? It may not be long before we find out. Astrobiologists are working on devices which someday will be landed on Mars and perhaps on Venus to collect and analyze samples of planetary material to see if they contain any living organisms.

Part B

Now choose the correct definition for each word you copied from Part A. Write its letter after the word. There are two definitions you will not use. In deciding on a definition, think about the sentence context as well as the meaning of the word parts.

a. two-footed creatures
b. four-footed creatures
c. able to speak and understand two languages
d. able to speak and understand only one language
e. having many engines
f. scientists who are investigating life on other planets
g. having a disorder of the mind
h. a science that deals with the ocean
i. a device that picks up sound under water
j. a device that detects differences in the amount of heat being given off by different parts of a person's body
k. men who study the ocean
l. shock treatment using light rather than electricity
m. a device that automatically prints the temperature every hour
n. a device that makes copies appear a great distance from where the original is located
o. printing something in extremely small type

What you should know about word structure

Many longer words are either compounds or derivatives. A **compound** is formed by combining two or more root words, as in *south/paw* or *head/light*. A **derivative** is formed by adding a prefix or a suffix, or both, to a root word, as in *un/common/ly*. The meaning of such words is a combination of the meanings of their parts.

Word parts like *cosmo-, hydro-, bi-,* and *-logy* are often combined to form words. Knowing what these parts mean will help you figure out the meaning of many technical and scientific words. These parts are sometimes called "living," because they are still being put together to form new words.

By using what you know about word parts and what you can guess from the context, you can figure out the meanings of many words. Always check back to be sure that your meaning makes sense in the context.

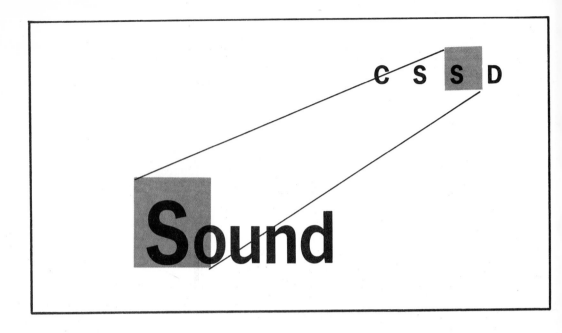

C S S D

Sound

LESSON ONE: Review of syllables and accent

In words of two or more syllables, one syllable is pronounced with greater force or stress. This greater force is called **accent**. The syllable that is pronounced with greater force is the **accented syllable**.

Choose the correct pronunciations for the words that will complete the following statements. If you do not understand the pronunciation symbols, turn to the key at the beginning of the Glossary.

1. In September the winners in the major leagues play each other in the World _____. (sir′ ēz) (sir ēz′)

2. Courage and loyalty are things to _____.
(ad′ mīr) (ad mīr′)

3. Blue and _____ combine to make green.
(yel′ ō) (yel ō′)

4. The opposite of destroy is _____. (krē′ āt) krē āt′)

5. Hens, mares, and lionesses are _____. (fē′ māl) (fē māl′)

The first syllable of *series, yellow,* and *female* is pronounced with greater force than the second syllable. Therefore the first pronunciation is correct for 1, 3, and 5. The second syllable of *admire* and *create* is pronounced with greater force than the first. The second pronunciation is correct for 2 and 4.

Pronounce the words in A and B below.

A	B
Carlos	Irene
Sally	supreme
Robert	attend
people	retire
damage	deny
temper	invent
total	remain

How many syllables are in each word in list A? in list B? Which syllable is accented in each group?

You may find it helpful to show accented and unaccented syllables with symbols: (′) for the accented syllable, (⌣) for the unaccented syllable. The accent pattern for the words in A will look like this: ′⌣ . How will you show the accent pattern for the words in B?

In which group—A or B—does each of the following words belong?

Thomas	problem	captain
Michael	bombard	remove
Edward	sincere	suggest
Louise	tunnel	capsule
Diane	heavy	adult

Pronounce the words in groups C–F. For each group, write the accent pattern, using the symbols (′) and (⌣).

C	D	E	F
Jennifer	Loretta	literature	Elizabeth
Winifred	emotion	candidacy	America
Africa	diploma	spiritual	emergency
multiply	addition	caricature	peninsula
cannibal	mechanic	eligible	analysis
incident	department	nationalize	bacteria
celebrate			arithmetic
melody			magnificent

Study what you have on your paper—the accent patterns of the words in groups C–F. Then complete the following statement:

> "Words of three or more syllables have an accent on
> either the _____ or the _____ syllable."

EXERCISE I. Listening for syllables and accent

Write words 1-12 in a column on your paper. Pronounce each word softly to yourself. Listen for the number of syllables and the position of the accented syllable. Then write the letter of the group in Lesson One (C, D, E, or F) in which the word belongs. If you need to, write the accent pattern for the word, using the symbols (′) and (˘). Number 1 should look like this on your paper: 1. carnation—(˘/˘)—D

1. carnation	7. aluminum
2. astronaut	8. Geraldine
3. charitable	9. destruction
4. fraternity	10. mercilessly
5. Veronica	11. catalog
6. confusion	12. courteously

LESSON TWO: Words accented on more than one syllable

Words that have three or more syllables are called **multisyllabic words**. Many multisyllabic words are accented on more than one syllable. For example, *territory* is accented on the first and third syllables. The first syllable of *territory* is pronounced with the heaviest force or stress. It receives the **primary accent**. In dictionary pronunciations, this kind of stress is marked with the symbol (′). The third syllable of *territory* also has stress, but it has a less heavy stress than the first syllable. It receives **secondary accent**, which is shown by the symbol (′).

The first word in each list below is divided into syllables and marked to indicate the primary and secondary accent. After pronouncing the first word, pronounce the rest of the words in the list, using the same accent pattern.

A	B
ag′ ri cul′ture	ed′ u ca′ tion
necessary	universal
semicircle	macaroni
fertilizer	adolescent
cemetery	celebration
matrimony	ornamental
alligator	satisfaction
supermarket	entertainment

What kind of syllable comes between the accented syllables in all the words in A and B?

> In multisyllabic words, there may be more than one accented syllable. Usually there is at least one unstressed syllable between the syllables that are accented.

EXERCISE II. Listening for accent patterns

Pronounce the phrases to yourself and listen to the accent patterns in the words in colored blocks. On your paper, after the number of the phrase, write either A or B to indicate which list in Lesson Two the word belongs in.

1. Microscopic in size
2. Living in the boys' dormitory
3. Singing patriotic songs
4. Military service
5. An armed desperado
6. A swift undercurrent
7. A good television program

LESSON THREE: Suffixes that are clues to primary accent

One of the biggest problems in pronouncing multisyllabic words is knowing where to place the accent or accents. The principles you have just learned are helpful:

A. There is always some kind of accent on either the first or second syllable.
B. A word may have both primary and secondary accent.
C. There is likely to be at least one unstressed syllable between the syllables that are accented.

It is also helpful to know that certain suffixes are clues to where the primary accent comes in a multisyllabic word. Once you know where the primary or strongest accent comes, you can usually pronounce the word—especially if you have heard it before. If there is a secondary accent, it seems to fall into place according to the natural rhythm of English.

What part of the word is the same in all the following words?

protection
discussion
destination
interruption
dimension

Pronounce the words, listening especially for the primary accent. Where does this accent fall in relation to the ending *-ion?*

When you see an unfamiliar word ending in *-ion,* which syllable should you accent most strongly?

The syllable just before certain other endings also receives stress. Other suffixes which tell you where to put the primary accent are *-ial, -ian, -ic,* and *-ity.*

Pronounce the words below. Listen for the primary accent.

presidential	comedian
secretarial	Norwegian
celestial	Italian
essential	musician
artificial	disciplinarian
automatic	electricity
Atlantic	similarity
Pacific	velocity
ballistic	activity
catastrophic	nationality

LESSON FOUR: Clues to the pronunciation of vowel letters

How to pronounce vowel letters can be a problem because the same letter may represent different sounds. For example, can you hear that *u* represents different sounds in *club, burn, use,* and *rule?* To make matters worse, a single vowel sound may be represented by many different spellings. For example, listen to the vowel sounds as you pronounce these words: *eve, seat, need, field, key.* Did you make the same *e* sound in each word? In how many different ways is the sound spelled in these words?

Often you can't tell what sound a vowel has until you try more than one. Certain spellings are clues that suggest which vowel sound to try first. These clues are most helpful with words of one syllable or with the vowel sound in an accented syllable.

The following chart summarizes two of the spelling patterns that are clues to the long* or the short sound of vowel letters. The letter V stands for any vowel letter. C stands for any consonant letter except *r*. (A vowel letter followed by *r* is often pronounced with a special sound, one that is different from either the long or the short sound of the vowel.)

CLUE	VOWEL SOUND	EXAMPLE WORDS
1. V C + silent *e*	long	rate, these, side
2. V C C + silent *e*	short	hinge, bronze

*In the case of *u*, both (yü) as in *use* and (ü) as in *rule* are considered to be long vowel sounds.

EXERCISE III.   Applying clues 1 and 2 to final accented syllables

Copy the words in column A on your paper. They are either one-syllable words or are accented on the last syllable. Study the spelling of each accented syllable, decide which clue gives you the vowel sound, and write the clue after the word. Finally, choose the word in column B which rhymes with the first word and write it in a third column on your paper. The first word should look like this on your paper:

1. incite—V C + silent *e*—light

A	B
1. incite	bit, light
2. cede	red, reed
3. statuette	met, meet
4. dote	boat, cot
5. serene	seen, hen
6. finesse	geese, bless
7. collapse	apes, snaps
8. mete	wheat, set
9. copse	hopes, hops
10. parole	bowl, doll

EXERCISE IV.   Applying clues 1 and 2 to other accented syllables

In compound words or in words to which a suffix has been added, the spelling V C + silent *e* or V C C + silent *e* may appear in an accented syllable within the word, rather than at the end. Examples: hedgehog, homesick, amusement, revengeful.

Do you hear a long or a short *e* sound in *hedgehog*? Is the *o* sound in *homesick* long or short? Which clue applies in each case?

Copy words 1-12 on your paper. Circle the vowel letters in the accented syllable. Write *long* after the word if the spelling pattern in the word suggests that this vowel is long. Write *short* if the spelling suggests a short vowel sound. Number 1 is done for you.

In deciding which syllable is accented, remember two things: (1) In a compound word, the first root word usually receives the primary accent. (2) In a derivative, the primary accent usually falls within the root word.

1. advancement—*short*	7. princedom
2. elsewhere	8. graceful
3. vengeful	9. trademark
4. engagement	10. safety
5. faceless	11. defenseless
6. namely	12. mincemeat

LESSON FIVE: More clues to vowel sound in accented syllables

What vowel sound—long or short—do you hear in the accented syllable of *capsule*? of *ambush*? of *republic*? How many consonant letters follow the accented vowel? This spelling pattern is indicated like this: V' C C.

Do you hear a long or short vowel sound in the accented syllable of *cubic*? of *study*? How many consonant letters follow the accented vowel in *cubic* and *study*? This spelling pattern is indicated by: V' C V. The pattern V' C V is a clue to EITHER the long or the short sound of the vowel. In words with this spelling pattern, you may need to try first one, then the other, sound of the vowel in the accented syllable.

CLUE	VOWEL SOUND	EXAMPLE WORDS
3. V'C C	short	capsule, ambush, republic
4. V'C V	either long or short	cubic, study, wagon, bacon

EXERCISE V. Applying clues 3 and 4

The following sentences either define the words in the colored blocks or supply very strong context clues. Using this information, together with spelling clues to vowel sound, see if you can recognize the words.

Write the answers to the questions below for each word in a colored block. If you can answer B, you can omit question C. The words you are to deal with in 1-5 are all accented on the first syllable.

    A. How many consonant letters follow the vowel letter in the accented syllable? Which clue applies?

    B. Is the vowel pronounced with a long or a short sound?

    C. If you still don't recognize the word, look it up in the Glossary. Is the vowel sound in the accented syllable long, or short?

1. A ring of light around the moon is called a halo .
2. If a job is risky and full of danger, like a miner's, it is said to have many hazards .
3. A person in a long, deep sleep caused by illness or injury is said to be in a coma .
4. A person who makes or sells women's hats is a milliner .
5. A trombone is a brass musical instrument with a sliding U-shaped tube.

In sentences 6-10, the words in colored blocks are accented on the second syllable. Continue to answer the same questions.

6. The four middle teeth in the top or bottom of your mouth are called incisors .
7. If one is fearless or very courageous, he is said to be intrepid .
8. Florida is nearly surrounded by water; it is a peninsula .
9. The word community is used to refer to neighborhoods, towns, cities, states, nations, and sometimes all the world.
10. A stenographer must be good at shorthand and typing.

LESSON SIX: Two vowel letters appearing together

When two vowel letters appear together in a word they often represent only one vowel sound—that is, they are pronounced as the vowel sound of one syllable. But they also may represent two vowel sounds—that is, they may belong in separate syllables.

Which word in each list is pronounced in two syllables?

A	B	C	D	E
friend	pie	weird	break	triumph
peace	bruise	neon	diet	hail
bias	trial	yield	juice	veil

Pronounce the words in list F, and then choose the correct word to complete Clue 5.

Then pronounce the lists G, H, I, and J and complete Clue 6.

F	G	H	I	J
liar	main	mean	fleet	oak
coed	raid	steal	teen	soap
riot	sail	peak	sleep	goal
dual	vain	teach	steel	coach

Clue 5

When two vowel letters appear together in a word and are pronounced as two separate syllables, the first vowel usually represents the (**long/short**) sound.

Clue 6

Two vowel letters appearing together in a word may represent only one vowel sound. The vowel pairs —, —, —, and — usually represent the long sound of the first vowel letter.

EXERCISE VI.   Applying clues 5 and 6

A. Write the words in column I on your paper.
B. Circle the two vowel letters that appear together.
C. Does either Clue 5 or Clue 6 suggest a familiar pronunciation? Write the number of the clue after the word.
D. If you recognize the word, write the letter of the correct definition from column II. There is one definition you will not use. Number 1 is done for you.

I	II
1. thr(oa)ty—Clue 6—*b*	*a.* a kind of medicine
2. dainty	*b.* low-pitched (said of a woman's voice)
3. upheaval	*c.* three-sided figure
4. coastal	*d.* tool for pulling out hairs
5. ruin	*e.* destroy, spoil
6. velveteen	*f.* bridge
7. iodine	*g.* a beautiful large house
8. tweezer	*h.* near the seashore
9. triangle	*i.* a forcing upwards
10. viaduct	*j.* fresh and pretty
	k. soft cotton material with a thick pile

What you should know about sounding out words

1. In words of two or more syllables, one syllable is pronounced with greater force, or accent. Multisyllabic words have some kind of accent on either the first or the second syllable. There may be more than one accent in such words. Usually there is at least one unstressed syllable between syllables that are accented.

2. Certain suffixes, including -ion, -ial, -ian, -ic, and -ity, are clues to where the primary accent falls.

3. Certain spelling patterns, or arrangements of consonants and vowels, suggest whether the vowel sound in an accented syllable is long or short. These clues do not always work, but they tell you which vowel sound to try first. Always check whether spelling clues give you a word that makes sense in context. If you don't recognize the word, look it up in a dictionary.

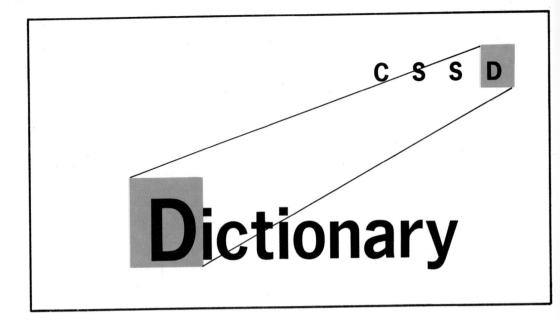

LESSON ONE: When do you use a dictionary?

CASE 1: Morris knows what the railing on a stairway is. He also knows what a derailed train is. But he doesn't know any other meanings for *rail*. Then he reads: "If the watchman had been younger, he would have fought them, broken their heads. But he was old, and they ignored his *railing*."

Will Morris have any problem pronouncing *railing*? No, but he will probably need a dictionary to find a meaning for *railing* that makes sense.

CASE 2: As far as you know, you have never seen or heard the word *egregious*. You read in a Hollywood gossip column: "X will never again be invited to introduce a candidate for an Academy Award. His appearance last night was shocking, and his manners were *egregious*."

From context, would you guess that X's manners were good, bad, or terrible? Context gives you strong clues to the meaning of *egregious*, but suppose this sentence were your line in a play and you had to say it aloud. You would need a dictionary to find out how to pronounce the word. You would probably need to check the exact meaning as well.

CASE 3: So far as you know, you have never seen or heard the word *cynosure*. You read: "Gregory was surprised to find that his height made him a *cynosure* in Japan."

In this case, the context gives you little help with the meaning of *cynosure*. Are you sure you can pronounce the word correctly? You would probably need to consult a dictionary for both the pronunciation and the meaning of *cynosure*.

LESSON TWO: Using a dictionary for word meanings

> **gin ger** (jin′jər), **1.** spice made from the root of a tropical plant, used for flavoring and in medicine. **2.** the root, often preserved in syrup or candied. **3.** the plant. **4.** *Informal.* liveliness; energy. **5.** light, reddish or brownish yellow. 1-5 *n.,* 5 *adj.*

"How about a combo to add a little ginger to the Veterans' Day assembly?"

"Charlie had a straggly ginger beard."

1. How many meanings are given for *ginger* in the dictionary entry?
2. How are the definitions clearly separated?
3. If you weren't told, how could you tell which definition fits in a particular sentence?
4. Use *ginger* in a sentence where its meaning is definition 1.

EXERCISE I.   Finding the correct meaning

Number from 1-12 on a piece of paper, for the twelve sentences in this exercise. After the number of the sentence, write the word in the colored block. Read the dictionary entry for the word and decide which definition tells what the word means in the sentence. Write the number of the correct definition after the word.

1. He called himself a "lull" pianist. He played during the lull while the pop combo was on its break.

2. The shaft into the cave was so narrow and tortuous that a man over 150 pounds could never get through it.

3. A great fault running north and south through California causes the many earthquakes in that region.

4. The farther the river flows the deeper it cuts; at one point the gorge is a mile deep.

5. After a steamy shower he gorged himself on eggs, bacon, oatmeal, toast, wheat cakes, and coffee.

6. All their dashing about in trench coats is vain. They've never caught a spy.

7. At 80, Grandmother is still vain about her beautiful hands.

8. A blunt teacher gave him honest advice: forget acting and take up carpentry.

9. You may as well try to divert teen-agers with Mother Goose as show some of those 1950 movies to today's moviegoer.

10. Dr. Fiedler considers it vital that Latin still be taught in high school.

11. The word in cars this year is "big"—big wheel base, big tread width, big interior space.

12. Each knob on the dashboard is in its separate padded recess.

---

blunt (blunt), **1.** without a sharp edge or point; dull. **2.** make less sharp; make less keen. **3.** plain-spoken; outspoken; frank: *He thinks that blunt speech proves he is honest.* 1,3 *adj.,* 2 *v.* —**blunt′ly,** *adv.* —**blunt′ness,** *n.*

di vert (də vért′), **1.** turn aside: *A ditch diverted water from the stream into the fields.* **2.** amuse; entertain: *Music diverted him after a hard day's work. v.*

fault (fôlt), **1.** something that is not as it should be: *Sloppiness is his greatest fault. Her dog has two faults: it eats too much and it howls at night.* **2.** mistake. **3.** cause for blame; responsibility: *Whose fault was it?* **4.** a break in a mass of rock with the segment on one side of the break pushed up or down. **5.** failure to serve the ball into the right place in tennis and similar games. *n.*

gorge (gôrj), **1.** a deep narrow valley, usually steep and rocky. **2.** eat greedily until full; stuff with food. **3.** fill full; stuff. **4.** a gorging; gluttonous meal. **5.** contents of a stomach. **6.** feeling of disgust, indignation, resentment, or the like. **7.** a narrow rear entrance from a fort into an outwork or outer part. **8.** mass stopping up a narrow passage: *An ice gorge blocked the river.* **9.** *Archaic.* throat. 1,4-9 *n.,* 2,3 *v.,* **gorged, gorg ing.** —**gorg′er,** *n.*

lull (lul), **1.** hush to sleep: *The mother lulled the crying baby.* **2.** quiet: *lull one's suspicions.* **3.** become calm or more nearly calm: *The wind lulled.* **4.** period of less noise or violence; brief calm: *a lull in a storm.* 1-3 *v.,* 4 *n.*

re cess (rē′ses or ri ses′ for 1,3,6; ri ses′ for 2,4,5), **1.** time during which work stops: *There will be a short recess before the next meeting.* **2.** take a recess: *The convention recessed until afternoon.* **3.** part in a wall set back from the rest; alcove; niche. **4.** put in a recess; set back. **5.** make a recess in. **6.** an inner place or part; quiet, secluded place: *the recesses of a cave, the recesses of one's secret thoughts.* 1,3,6 *n.,* 2,4,5 *v.*

tor tu ous (tôr′chu əs), **1.** full of twists, turns, or bends; twisting; winding; crooked: *a tortuous path.* **2.** mentally or morally crooked; not straightforward: *tortuous reasoning. adj.* —**tor′tu ous ly,** *adv.* —**tor′tu ous ness,** *n.*

tread (tred), **1.** walk; step; set the foot down: *Don't tread on the flower beds.* **2.** set the feet on; walk on or through; step on: *tread the streets.* **3.** press under the feet; trample; trample on; crush: *tread grapes.* **4.** make, form, or do by walking: *Cattle had trodden a path to the pond.* **5.** act or sound of treading: *We heard the tread of marching feet.* **6.** way of walking: *He walks with a heavy tread.* **7.** the part of stairs or a ladder that a person steps on: *The stair treads were covered with rubber to prevent slipping.* **8.** the part of a wheel or tire that touches the ground. **9.** part of a rail or rails that the wheels touch. **10.** sole of the foot or of a shoe. 1-4 *v.*, **trod** or (*Archaic*) **trode, trod den** or **trod, tread ing;** 5-10 *n.* —**tread′er,** *n.*

vain (vān), **1.** having too much pride in one's looks, ability, etc.: *She is vain of her beauty.* **2.** of no use; without effect or success; producing no good result: *I made vain attempts to reach her by telephone.* **3.** of no value or importance; worthless; empty: *a vain boast. adj.* —**vain′ness,** *n.*

vi tal (vī′təl), **1.** of life; having to do with life: *vital forces.* Vital statistics give facts about births, deaths, marriages, etc. **2.** necessary to life: *Eating is a vital function. The heart is a vital organ.* **3.** very necessary; very important; essential: *An adequate army is vital to the defense of a nation.* **4.** causing death, failure, or ruin: *a vital wound, a vital blow to an industry.* **5.** full of life and spirit; lively. *adj.* —**vi′tal ly,** *adv.*

LESSON THREE: Words not defined in the dictionary

You will remember that words made by adding a prefix or a suffix to another word are called **derivatives**. Some derivatives are not entered separately in the dictionary. If you know the meaning of the original word and the meaning of the prefix or suffix, you can figure out what the derivative means.

If you have trouble with this lesson, review pages 82-83, Word Attack/Structure.

Part A. Words with prefixes

1. Suppose you discover that the word *nonabsorbent* is not entered in your dictionary. What word will you have to look up?

2. What meaning must you add to that definition to get the full meaning of *nonabsorbent*?

3. Which of these things is nonabsorbent? (a) wax paper (b) a sponge (c) a woolen coat

4. Suppose you cannot find the word *overzealous* in your dictionary. What word will you have to look up?

5. What meaning must you add to that definition to get the full meaning of *overzealous*?   (*over*)

6. Which of these men is overzealous?

    a. A man who does his job faithfully and thoroughly

    b. A man who wastes time attending to all the unimportant details of his job

    c. A man who neglects his job

7. What words would you look up to get the meaning of each of the following? (a) nonofficial (b) unalloyed (c) overcritical

Part B. Words with suffixes

8. Look up the word *decipherable* in the Glossary. It is not a separate entry, but it is easy to find. At the end of what word entry is *decipherable* listed?

9. Is *decipherable* defined? What information is given?

10. Which of the choices below explains the sentence "Your letter was not decipherable"?

    a. The letter arrived too late.

    b. The letter could not be read.

    c. The letter did not contain any useful information.

11. Look up the word *manifestly.* Where is it listed?

12. After reading the whole entry, choose the correct meaning for this sentence: "The woman had manifestly been injured severely."

    a. It was impossible to tell whether or not the woman had been hurt badly.

    b. The woman's injuries actually were not very serious.

    c. It was easy to see that the woman had been badly hurt.

LESSON FOUR: Recognizing dictionary pronunciations

Pronounce the dictionary spellings, using the pronunciation key which follows them. If this short key doesn't offer enough help, turn to the complete pronunciation key at the beginning of the Glossary. After pronouncing each word, find a phrase or sentence in the right-hand column that is a clue to the meaning of the word.

a. (in′ə sənt)	1. Put it on buttered toast.
b. (dē′sən sē)	2. The bathroom sink is made of it.
c. (pôr′sə lin)	3. The best possible verdict.
d. (sin′ə mən)	4. It's what makes good people good.
e. (i nish′əl)	5. Old-fashioned dance.
f. (wôlts)	6. Mary's is M; Jack's is J.
g. (ung′kəl)	7. Your father's brother.
h. (plak)	8. It hangs on the wall.
i. (lēg)	9. For a girl's hair.
j. (sit′ə zən)	10. Organization of baseball teams.
k. (sėr′kəs)	11. A person born in the U.S.A.
l. (bə ret′)	12. Clowns, animals, acrobats.
m. (kü′kü)	13. Flowers.
n. (bō kā′)	14. It's shot into the arm.
o. (vak′sēn)	15. Summer is one.
p. (sē′zən)	16. A clock; or crazy, silly.
q. (ĭ′si kəl)	17. Frozen drips.
r. (tėr′kē)	18. Park the car.
s. (tish′ü)	19. Paper handkerchief.
t. (gə räzh′)	20. Rough and tumble.
u. (kôr′də roi)	21. Gobble-gobble.
v. (rou′dē)	22. Good for sports clothes.

---

hat, āge, fär; let, bē, tėrm; it, īce; hot, gō, ôrder; oil, out; cup, put, rüle; ch, child; ng, long; th, thin; ŦH, then; zh, measure; ə represents *a* in about, *e* in taken, *i* in April, *o* in lemon, *u* in circus.

EXERCISE II. Pronouncing words

Using your Glossary, prepare to read the following sentences orally. Pay special attention to the pronunciation of the words in colored blocks. A good way to check the accent in an unfamiliar word is to pronounce it after a familiar word that has the same accent pattern. (You may want to review the lessons on accent patterns, pages 90-94.)

What you learned in the lesson on suffix clues to accent (pages 93-94) should help you pronounce the words in 5, 6, 8, 13, and 14.

1. Men on furlough often hitchhike home on military planes.
2. Two men in the boat grabbed him and got his chest and shoulders over the gunwale .
3. The slope was broken by a huge crevasse not visible from the valley.
4. Jesse has about him a kind of roguery that makes him popular among boys.
5. In three lazy years Teddy has grown fat and lethargic .
6. Setting the fire was an atrocity beyond anything the principal had believed possible.
7. The nefarious scheme was discovered just in time.
8. Alice is an expert at prevarication .
9. Cars all look alike, but each one has its eccentricities .
10. He took a horse and worked reconnaissance, staying two or three miles ahead of the column.
11. Speaking in the manner of a ventriloquist, the medicine man keeps repeating "Who has broken the taboo?"
12. A paroxysm of fear gripped the town as the sound of planes grew louder.
13. The evidence is circumstantial .
14. You can imagine the consternation of the people in the valley when the volcano begins to rumble.
15. The principal asked for silence in the auditorium; what he got was a slight diminuendo .

LESSON FIVE: Words with two pronunciations, depending on use

> **ex ploit** (eks′ploit for 1; eks ploit′ for 2,3), **1.** a bold, unusual act; daring deed: *Old stories tell about the exploits of famous heroes.* **2.** make use of; turn to practical account: *A mine is exploited for its minerals.* **3.** make unfair use of; use selfishly for one's own advantage: *Nations sometimes exploit their colonies, taking as much wealth out of them as they can.* 1 *n.*, 2,3 *v.*, —**ex-ploit′a ble,** *adj.* —**ex ploit′er,** *n.*

Study the dictionary entry above. How many ways are there to pronounce *exploit*?

When is *exploit* pronounced with the first syllable accented? When is it pronounced with an accent on the second syllable?

Certain words, like *exploit*, are pronounced one way when they are used as a verb, and pronounced differently when they are used in some other way in a sentence—for example, as a noun. The dictionary entry always includes such information.

EXERCISE III.   Choosing the right pronunciation

Sentences A, B, and C below all use the word *exploit,* but in different ways. Copy the sentences on your paper, leaving at least a one-line space between sentences. Underline the word printed in bold type. Then follow the numbered directions.

A. When Mr. Richey checked on how much work the manager of the prison farm was making the boys do, he found that the manager was **exploiting** the boys.

B. By bringing in water from the mountains, the farmers were able to **exploit** part of the desert.

C. Killing a dragon is a famous **exploit** in the story of St. George.

1. Read the various meanings of *exploit* given in the dictionary entry in Lesson Five. After each of the three sentences you copied, write the number of the meaning that applies to it.

2. For each sentence, decide which pronunciation of *exploit* is correct. Copy the pronunciation after the sentence.

3. Practice reading the sentences aloud, being sure you pronounce *exploit* correctly.   (*over*)

Follow the same procedure with sentences D, E, and F.

> **con fed er ate** (kən fed′ər it for 1-3; kən fed′ər āt for 4), **1.** joined together for a special purpose; allied. **2.** country, person, etc., joined with another for a special purpose; ally; companion. **3.** accomplice; partner in crime: *The thief was arrested, but his confederate escaped.* **4.** join (countries, people, etc.) together for a special purpose; ally. 1 *adj.*, 2,3 *n.*, 4 *v.*

D. Several small countries, fearful that they could not separately fight off an enemy attack, decided to **confederate.**

E. Each little nation was a **confederate** of the others.

F. In robbing the bank, the criminal used three **confederates:** two stationed at key points in the building, and one in the car parked around the corner.

LESSON SIX: Words with two correct pronunciations

> **hos pi ta ble** (hos′pi tə bl or hos pit′ə bl), **1.** giving or liking to give a welcome, food and shelter, and friendly treatment to guests or strangers: *a hospitable family, reception, etc.* **2.** willing and ready to entertain; favorably receptive or open: *a person hospitable to new ideas.* *adj.* —**hos′pi ta bly,** *adv.*

> **con serve** (kən sėrv′ for 1,2; kon′sėrv or kən sėrv′ for 3), **1.** keep from harm or decay; protect from loss or from being used up: *Try to conserve your strength for the end of the race.* **2.** preserve (fruit) with sugar. **3.** fruit preserved in sugar; jam. 1,2 *v.*, **con served, con serving;** 3 *n.*

Compare the dictionary pronunciations of *hospitable* and *conserve*. How many pronunciations does each word have?

For which word are you told when to pronounce it one way and when another way? For which word is either pronunciation correct for all its meanings?

The pronunciation of words like *hospitable* does not depend on how the words are used. The fact is that some educated people say the word one way, while others say it the other way. Sometimes one correct pronunciation is used in one part of the country and another equally correct pronunciation is more common in another section.

When you find two such pronunciations given in the dictionary, try saying both of them. If one sounds more familiar to you, use that pronunciation. It is probably the way the word is said in the part of the country where you live. If neither pronunciation sounds familiar, use the first one.

EXERCISE IV.   Choosing between two correct pronunciations

Look up in the Glossary the words printed in bold type in the sentences below. Choose the pronunciation you think you ought to use and be ready to read the sentences aloud.

1. He feared that the strangers would be **hostile.**
2. The pain was followed by **nausea.**
3. The others continued to **harass** him.
4. Far away they heard the howling of a **coyote.**
5. The track star **patronized** the younger boys.

What you should know about using a dictionary

1. Most dictionary entries include more than one meaning. When you are looking for the meaning of a word, first read all the meanings. Then choose the one that makes the best sense in the context.

2. Some derivatives (like *nonabsorbent* and *decipherable*) are not entered separately. You can figure out their meaning by combining the meaning of the root word (*absorbent* or *decipher*) and the meaning of the prefix or suffix (*non-* or *-able*).

3. The pronunciation key tells what sound each pronunciation symbol stands for. You should not try to memorize the key but should use it for reference as needed.

3

Sensory Images

Photo courtesy of Chicago's *American.*

LESSON ONE: Using all your senses

What are your feelings as you look at this photograph? Can you
imagine yourself throwing the punch of the boxer on the right?
Can you almost feel the sting and impact of the punch bouncing
off the chin of the boxer on the left?

What would your senses tell you if you were one or the other
of the boxers? What would you feel? What would you hear?
What would you see around you? What might you smell? What
might you taste?

Suppose there were no pictures of the fight and a friend wanted
to make you imagine what it was like. How could he do it?

Pictures and words often serve as substitutes for real things,
and they can stimulate your five senses—make them react—

almost as strongly as the actual happenings. (Try thinking about a big juicy hamburger.) When you are remembering or imagining the sights, smells, and sounds of an event you are **forming sensory images.**

Some people form sensory images easily. That is, it is easy for them to call up in their minds tastes, smells, feelings, sights, and sounds. When they read about an experience that is filled with sights, sounds, and smells, they are able to put themselves in the scene and "sense" what they are reading about. For other people, image-making is not easy. But everyone has imagination, and everyone can improve his powers of image-making.

EXERCISE I. Image-making words

Part A

Certain words make your senses react more strongly than others. Here are fifteen sense-appealing words. Say each word to yourself and decide which of the five senses—sight, touch or feeling, hearing, smell, taste—it affects most directly. Next, think of an object which the word could describe. The first one is done as an example.

1. prickly . . . *touch* . . . *cactus*
2. gigantic
3. sticky
4. peppery
5. rumbling
6. fragrant
7. clanging
8. damp
9. pink
10. smoky
11. bitter
12. creaking
13. teeter-tottering
14. polka-dot
15. sour

When you form images in your mind, you are probably remembering sensations that your five senses experienced at some earlier time. Tell what experiences any one of the words reminded you of.

Part B

People who write advertising depend heavily on image-making words—words that appeal to your senses. They try to make products attractive so that you will want to buy them. Some of the advertising phrases on the next page may make you want to buy the product. Others may call up mental images that are not very appealing. Make a list of those phrases you think are unappealing or ineffective and be prepared to explain why you feel as you do. Then think up a phrase to replace ONE of those you don't like.

16. mud-pack make-up
17. crunchy, crackly breakfast flakes
18. wrinkled prunes
19. velvet-soft facial tissues
20. thick, oozy paint
21. juicy, sun-ripened tomatoes
22. flaky Danish pastry
23. a car with the strength of a tank
24. star-shaped grains of laundry detergent
25. gummy cheese spread

Part C

The things you can imagine are not limited to what you have actually experienced. Such things as TV, movies, reading, and what other people tell you can provide information which appeals to your senses almost as if you had had the experiences yourself.

Think of the words "cowboy country." Many students reading this book have not actually been on a western cattle ranch, but all readers have some ideas about the West. Test how good you are at forming mental images by listing under the five senses as many images about "cowboy country" as come to your mind in a few minutes. The image under *sight* is an example. (Your other headings should be *hearing, smell, touch or feeling,* and *taste.*)

SIGHT
Cowboys on galloping horses

LESSON TWO: Visualizing accurately

When you read an action-filled story, do you form mental pictures of what is happening? Unless you visualize accurately what the author is describing or suggesting, you will miss a great deal or get hopelessly confused.

EXERCISE II.   Visualizing what happens

Here is a short incident from a longer story. As you read, picture the setting and the actions of the characters. You will be asked to prove without looking back that you did visualize accurately.

(Henry Reed, who is telling the story, is visiting the Grand Canyon with Midge and her parents. They meet Terry, another young tourist, who is dressed in a very fancy cowboy outfit. They all want to do something exciting and dangerous. Finally they decide to shoot off firecrackers in the Canyon, hoping to create a big noise.)

WE STARTED down the trail. We hadn't gone far when we found a spot with a guardrail right on the edge of the Canyon and no one around. I lighted a firecracker and tossed it out into space. It was a big cracker, but Midge was right. The noise seemed to get lost and was dwarfed by the Canyon.

"I hope the fall-out kills that bug that is biting me," Midge said, trying to slap a spot between her shoulder blades.

I lighted a second firecracker and tossed it straight up in the air. It exploded before it got back down to our level. This one was much better, and I thought I heard an echo.

"Hey! I dropped the keys!" Midge shouted.

"What keys?" I asked. I knew but I hoped I was wrong.

"The car keys," she said. "I was carrying them in my hand. Now what will I do?"

"We could drop you after them," Terry said. "That's what my pop would probably do with me if I lost our car keys."

"Is it the only set?" I asked.

"I don't know. I'd rather not have to find out."

"If you were going to get scared and drop something, why did you stand so close to the edge?" Terry asked.

"I wasn't scared!" Midge said scornfully. "The keys were on a little loop of chain hooked over my finger. That bug was biting me, and I tried to brush it off. The keys came off my finger."

The rail looked solid, but no rail looks solid enough to me on the edge of something as deep as the Grand Canyon. I had Midge and Terry hold my belt, and I leaned between the top and middle rails and looked down. About ten feet below us was a ledge, and there on the edge of it were the keys.

"That does us a lot of good," Midge said bitterly. "No one is going down there after them."

"We need a fish line," Terry said.

"Maybe your rope will do."

We didn't have any fishhooks, so we tried a big wad of gum on the end of Terry's rope. The rope was a little too stiff, and we couldn't seem to maneuver it around to touch the gum against the keys.

"Hey, I've got a paper clip in my pocket," Midge said suddenly. "And that bug has crawled down inside my blouse, and it's driving me crazy," she said. "I'm going in back of those bushes and take off my blouse and get rid of it."

The bushes were about ten feet away. Midge disappeared behind them, and we began fishing for the keys. I was doing the fishing, and I didn't care for leaning out between those rails at all. I tied a loop of the rope around my stomach and then around the rail. That still left enough rope to let me reach the keys. I was maneuvering our wire hook around when suddenly I heard a woman's voice.

"What on earth are you doing?" she asked. "That's terribly dangerous."

"We lost some car keys over the edge," Terry explained. "They're on a ledge about ten feet down."

"What are you trying to do with the rope?"

"The girl who dropped the keys is on the other end," Terry said.

I wish I could have seen the expression on her face, but I had the keys almost hooked and didn't dare turn around. Terry told us later that he had one foot braced against the rail and was pretending to be pulling the rope with all his might. Of course he was pulling against the part tied to the rail. He can say almost anything with a straight face, and I suppose the woman thought anyone crazy enough to wear a cowboy costume like his would be crazy enough to lower a girl over the edge. She gave a surprised squeak followed by a dismal "Oh my!"

She turned and hurried back along the path, but I didn't know that, because just then I hooked the keys.

"Got 'em!" I said, pulling the rope up.

"Quick, Midge, she's coming back!" Terry said.

Midge came out from behind the bushes, and I handed her the keys. She was still tucking her blouse into her skirt when two women came hurrying around the curve. They were timid-looking women, probably in their sixties. The one in the lead, a tall woman with white hair, put her hand to her mouth, gave a weak gasp, and wilted. She leaned against the other, shorter woman.

"Thank heavens, you're safe," she said.

"She's been safe all along," Terry said. "We had the end of the rope tied to the rail."

"Please don't do anything like that again, children," the short woman said.

"We won't need to," Midge said. "I'm going to hold on to the keys this time."

As you read this story, did you "see" the setting and what the characters were doing? To find out how well you visualized what happened, look at the pictures and decide which ones are scenes from the story. Then figure out what is wrong with the pictures you did not choose. Do not look back at the story.

EXERCISE III.   Visualizing what probably happened

To solve this "minute mystery" you must visualize the setting and also a series of actions performed by the murderer. Read slowly and carefully, and think about the possible meaning or significance of every detail given. The information you will need is given in the story.

A Significant Fact
by Austin Ripley

"THE MURDERER climbed up to Lord Melford's open bedroom window, all right," insisted Detective Sergeant Boland, addressing Professor Fordney, the master detective. "We discovered, you know, that all the entrance doors were locked on the inside and all the windows but the one in question were fastened. See those footprints in the flower bed?"

Suddenly Detective Sergeant Boland grasped Fordney's arm in excitement and pointed to the ivy-covered wall of the old mansion. Starting ten feet from the ground, and all the way up to Melford's window on the third floor, the leaves were stripped and broken. "See, Professor, I was right! That's how the murderer did get in. Let's have another look inside."

Lord Melford lay on his bed, his throat cut, the pillow and spread covered with blood. One arm dangled over the edge of the bed. The night lamp was still burning. Walking to the open window, Boland discovered fresh scratches on the outside sill.

"That clinches it, Professor. Gosh, I'm glad to find you wrong just once! Your theory that it's an inside job and that the murderer did not make his entrance by the window is all shot now. The only one to gain by Melford's death is his nephew, and—I don't believe he'd have the courage for a job like this."

"Appearances are deceiving, old fellow—you've learned that. I'm really surprised that you've overlooked the most significant fact." Fordney leaned out of the window and looked down. "Do you see what I mean?"

Adapted from *Minute Mysteries* by Austin Ripley. Copyright, 1949, by Press Alliance, Inc. Reprinted by permission of Opera Mundi, Inc.

1. What is Detective Sergeant Boland's theory about the murder?
2. Suppose Boland is correct. Try to picture in your mind the actions of the murderer:
   a. How would he enter the bedroom from the outside?
   b. Would he leave footprints in the flower bed?
   c. What would he use to get up to the window?

(*over*)

3. Professor Fordney disagrees with the Detective Sergeant. What is the Professor's theory?
4. Suppose the Professor is correct. Picture in your mind a murderer who is already in the house.

   a. By what means would he probably enter Lord Melford's bedroom?

   b. Now try to form a mental picture of the murderer leaving the room quickly and in such a way that he would not be observed by someone inside the house. Does this way fit the physical evidence? Explain.
5. *a.* What would happen to the leaves on the vine if the murderer climbed up the vine and entered the bedroom from the outside?

   b. What would happen to the leaves on the vine if he left the room by the window and let himself down by means of the vine?
6. What, then, is the significant fact that Boland didn't notice?

LESSON THREE: Filling in details

A story in which the author tried to tell you everything about his characters, what is happening to them, and where it is happening, would probably seem long and dull. Instead, an author will usually give a few important details—enough so that the reader can form an image in his mind—and then he will expect the reader to supply the rest through imagination. If the author has given the right kind of details, and if you read the story accurately, your mental images will fit in with what the author had in mind.

Read the paragraph below and try to imagine what it would be like to be one of the boys riding through the desert.

> For a while Mike drove in silence while the city boys in the back seat looked curiously at the cactus-studded scenery. Finally Mike turned off the highway onto the desert. The rough wheel-tracks on which they bumped along indicated that other people must have traveled here too, but nothing except cactus and a few stunted bushes could be seen for miles in every direction. The midday sun beat down relentlessly, and the gritty sand flats seemed endless.

Which of the details below would fit into this scene?

1. A rushing stream
2. Dry, cracked lips
3. Smell of decaying leaves
4. Dairy cows grazing
5. Feeling of being jerked from side to side
6. Hot sand blowing into a traveler's eyes
7. Dry bones from a small animal
8. A cool breeze

In a sandy desert in the middle of the day you would not be likely to find a rushing stream or a cool breeze, or to smell wet, decaying leaves. Dairy cows would not be able to find enough food or water in this desert. However, a traveler in this desert might well have lips cracked by the hot, dry wind and feel hot sand blowing into his eyes. The dried bones of an animal which had died in the desert would be a likely sight. And a person riding in a car over a bumpy desert road would probably be thrown from side to side.

When you read, you must draw on what you already know—from your own experiences or from TV, movies, and reading—to fill in details the author has left out.

EXERCISE IV. Filling in details

Part A

Read the paragraph below and answer the questions. Then select from the list of details the ones that would fit into the situation described, details which the author might have included but didn't.

> As Meg jerked open the door, three books and a crumpled candy wrapper fell to the floor. Her home economics book skidded across the hall and landed with a thud. The hall was unusually quiet, except for the momentary noise Meg had made in her haste. She smiled to herself as she glanced at the picture of a long-haired, guitar-strumming young man on the inside of the door. What was she looking for—oh yes, a pen and a pad of notebook paper. She muttered in annoyance when she saw that in rummaging around, her hand had gotten smudged by her charcoal drawing pencil. Finally she found some paper, and then suddenly remembered that she had a pen in her pocket. (*over*)

1. Where is Meg?
2. To what does the door belong?
3. Why is it unusually quiet?

DETAILS:

Select the details that fit into the situation. There is room here for some differences of opinion, but be sure you can give a good reason for each detail you include.

4. A pad of drawing paper
5. *Popular Mechanics* magazine
6. A fancy ribbon
7. A potted plant
8. A red mitten
9. The loud voice of a girl at the next locker
10. File cards containing recipes
11. A portable radio
12. A smell of floor wax
13. A class bell ringing
14. An empty coke bottle
15. A long mink coat

Part B

Continue as you did in Part A.

The movie theater is brimming with people. From where I'm standing in the crowded lobby, I hear the high-pitched screams of women in the audience. I wonder why I ever came. My little brother begged me to take him to see "Igor of the Unknown Planet," and here I am. I feel a sudden jerk on my arm and I reel around, but it's only Billy telling me "Let's go in!"

Once we're in our seats I glance at the greenish-purple monster on the screen and quickly look away. I'd rather not watch. For diversion I count the seats in my row and then start to count the rows. But a gigantic crash forces me to look at the screen. Igor has smashed the rocket ship and is trying to get at the men trapped inside.

Choose from the list on the next page (numbers 16-35) the details you think would be included in this outer-space horror movie. Be prepared to tell how each of your details would work into the story.

16. enormous craters
17. shadowy scenes
18. surfers on the beach
19. a love scene
20. deadly rays
21. a gigantic balloon
22. stone-age people
23. lush green forests
24. a hammer and saw
25. vast deserts

26. comic song and dance routine
27. choking dust and fog
28. a hairy, multicolored monster
29. eerie music
30. a department store
31. huge, scaly beasts
32. motorcyclists
33. flowers as high as trees
34. rushing mountain streams
35. a rope ladder

Part C

Make a list of details you could include if you were describing things you experienced in the theater but that were not a part of the movie. List at least five items, but try for ten or more. Next to each detail write which sense or senses it would be acting on. Here is an example:

gum stuck on floor . . . touch or feeling

LESSON FOUR: Experiencing emotional effect

Do "empty streets and strange silence" suggest a cheerful state of mind, or a gloomy one? Do you have different feelings about the words "slithering snake" than you do about "playful puppy"?

Depending on the kind of images they call up, words can suggest various feelings. A writer can make you feel sad or happy. He can make you shudder with dread, hold your breath in suspense, or break up with laughter.

EXERCISE V.   Reacting through emotions

Part A

On the next page are several paragraphs which are intended to create certain feelings or emotions through the way they appeal to your senses. Read each one thoughtfully and then answer the questions that follow.

The signal was like a banshee[1] wail that rose higher and higher and louder and louder until it became a prolonged shriek; then it slid down the scale and back to its low, mournful note, only to rise again in a renewed scream of terror.

From "Adventure in the Blackout" from *Night Boat and Other Tod Moran Mysteries* by Howard Pease. Published by Doubleday & Company, Inc.

1. What is being described?
2. How would you feel if you heard this sound?
3. What words or phrases do the most to make you feel this way?

Suddenly, nose to the ground, I became aware of a rank, musky odor that brought my head up with a jerk. Something queerly crawling touched my cheek. I slapped my hand over it and, with a chill of premonition, looked at what I'd caught—a long tuft of coarse brown hair dangling from a twig above.

From "One Alaska Night" by Barrett Willoughby. Reprinted by permission of Paul R. Reynolds, Inc.

4. To what senses does this passage appeal?
5. How do you think the person who is speaking felt at this point?
6. How is the feeling you get from this passage similar to the feeling in the first one you read?

. . . The October night was warm, the slowly rising moon etching faint shadows on the ground and lying yellow on the corn shocks and pumpkins in the field. On the light south wind that blew from somewhere among the stars, the pungence of autumn lay; leaf-fire smoke, drying leaves, the fragrance of apples and nuts. Somewhere in the bottomland near Grell's Millpond a killdeer rode the wind, crying his loneliness down the quiet night.

From "The Blue Goose" by August Derleth. Copyright 1939, 1967 by August Derleth.

7. What kind of feeling do you get from this description?
8. What senses does the author appeal to?

---

[1]**banshee,** in Irish folklore, a spirit whose wails mean there will soon be a death in the family.

Part B

Continue as before. Read slowly enough so you can enter into the experience being described.

> The filtered sunlight warms her back as she wanders barefoot through the ferns. In the trees overhead the breeze playfully tosses the younger branches back and forth, creating spring-green shadows on the path ahead.

9. If this girl's mood matches her surroundings, how does she feel?
10. What senses does this passage appeal to?

RAIN[2]

by Jane Stembridge

It is raining
such
soft
warm
drips
with
wet
soft
splash

splish,
ping.

11. Is the author trying to make you think of rain as pleasant or as unpleasant? What words tell you?
12. What senses does the poet appeal to? What kind of images do you think are the strongest?
13. The author has used several words that sound like what they describe. *Splish* is one. What others do you find?
14. What besides the sound of the words makes you think of raindrops falling?

[2]From *I Play Flute* by Jane Stembridge. Copyright © 1966. Reprinted by permission of Flute Publications, Tougaloo, Mississippi, for the author.

EXERCISE VI.   Reacting to story characters

In each passage below, a father is seen through the eyes of his son. As you read, try to picture each father in your mind.

I

He was the lawgiver in our family and I never laughed in his presence. I used to lurk timidly in the kitchen doorway and watch his huge body sitting slumped at the table. I stared at him with awe as he gulped his beer from a tin bucket, as he ate long and heavily, sighed, belched, closed his eyes to nod on a stuffed belly. He was quite fat and his bloated stomach always lapped over his belt. He was always a stranger to me, always somehow alien and remote.

From *Black Boy* by Richard Wright. Copyright 1945 by Richard Wright. Reprinted by permission of Harper & Row, Publishers, and Paul R. Reynolds, Inc.

1. How did Richard Wright feel toward his father? What details in the passage tell you?
2. Is this father someone you yourself would like? Why or why not?
3. Think of something this father might say to his son. Then imitate the way he would say it.
4. Below are some of the image-making words the author used. To which sense does each phrase mainly appeal?

    a. sitting slumped   *e.* stuffed belly
    b. gulped his beer   *f.* bloated stomach
    c. ate long and heavily   *g.* lapped over his belt
    d. belched

II

His father, standing at the end of the bargain counter, was planted squarely on his two feet, turning a book over thoughtfully in his hands. Then he took out his glasses from an old, worn leather case and adjusted them on the end of his nose, looking down over them at the book. His coat was thrown open, two buttons on his vest were undone, his hair was too long, and in his rather shabby clothes he looked very much like a workingman, a carpenter perhaps. Such a resentment rose in young Harcourt that he wanted to cry out bitterly, "Why does he dress as if he never owned a decent suit in his life? He doesn't care what the whole world thinks of him. He never did. I've told him a hundred times he ought to wear his good clothes when he goes out.

Mother's told him the same thing. He just laughs. And now Grace may see him. Grace may meet him."

5. How does Harcourt feel toward his father? What things about his father make him feel that way? (Quote words in the paragraph that describe the father.)

6. Compare the two fathers described in this exercise. How does Harcourt's attitude toward his father differ from that of Richard Wright? Is there anything similar about their feelings?

7. Would you yourself like Harcourt's father? Why or why not?

LESSON FIVE: Imagining the unfamiliar

Your ability to form mental images can change a picture or a description of something unfamiliar into something real and believable. The thrill of exploring other planets, of living in another period of history, of being someone you admire, is possible through your imagination.

Here is an excerpt from a science fiction story which appears later in this book. Peter Claney is describing his experiences on the planet Mercury to James Baron, who is planning an expedition there. They are seated in a tavern.

> ". . . we had an inch of Fiberglas and a half-inch of dead air between us and a surface temperature where lead flowed like water and zinc was almost at melting point and the pools of sulfur in the shadows were boiling like oatmeal over a campfire."
>
> Baron licked his lips. His fingers stroked the cool, wet glass.
>
> From "Brightside Crossing" (page 249)

Instead of telling what the temperature is on Mercury, Peter Claney describes what he saw, leaving Baron to draw his own conclusions. Why do these details suggest how hot it is on Mercury? Could you have come to the same conclusion if the speaker had described "*ligil* flowing like water, *rampter* at the melting point, and *krint* boiling"? Explain.

Why is it important in this description that the speaker mentions metals that are familiar to most readers? What other familiar substance does he refer to in order to help you picture the scene? If you think it is an effective comparison, explain why.

The author adds one further touch to make certain that you get the picture. How do Baron's actions bring out the feeling the author wants to give? What do these actions tell you about Baron himself? Did you find the use of contrast effective?

EXERCISE VII.   Imagining the unfamiliar

A little later in "Brightside Crossing" you are given this picture of Mercury as seen through the eyes of the men who are traveling in little enclosed vehicles:

> We couldn't detect a wind, but we knew there was a hot, sulfurous breeze sweeping in great continental tides across the face of the planet. Not enough for erosion, though. The craters rose up out of jagged gorges, huge towering spears of rock and rubble. Below were the vast yellow flatlands, smoking and hissing from beneath the crust. Over everything was gray dust—silicates and salts, pumice and limestone and granite ash, filling crevices and declivities—offering a soft, treacherous surface for the Bug's pillow tires.

1. What sense or senses does the first sentence appeal to?
2. Do the men actually feel the sensation the speaker describes, or have they formed a mental image of the sensation? Explain.
3. From the second sentence on, the details appeal mainly to sight. Describe what shapes, sizes, colors, and movements the author has included to give you a sharp visual image.
4. What kind of tires are "pillow tires"?
5. What past experiences would help you picture this scene?

What you should know about forming sensory images

Pictures and words can make your five senses react almost as strongly as actual happenings. When you read, you should take time
  —to imagine you are characters you are reading about
  —to visualize, or picture in your mind, what is happening
  —to fill in suitable details that the author has not included
  —to respond through your emotions as well as through your mind.

4

Central Idea

These pictures all show different parts of one activity. What is that activity?

You might say simply that all the pictures are about putting on a play. But you can say more than that about them. You can also express one or more ideas which connect all the pictures together.

Before considering what these ideas might be, read the following paragraph:

There are the actors and actresses who actually appear on stage, of course, but in addition there are many other people connected with a play who are never seen by the audience. Their work is every bit as important to the play as what the actors do. Scenery must be designed, built, and painted, and the set must be furnished. For some productions the scenery must also be changed while the play is in progress. The scenery must be carefully lighted, and this lighting often must be changed during the play, as when an actor onstage turns on a lamp. Making or getting together costumes and "props"—things the actor must handle, such as letters or glasses or swords—requires the work of many people. Someone must put make-up on the actors. Other workers handle publicity, make posters, and sell tickets. Ushers are needed to show people to their seats. And of course, none of these efforts would have any effect without someone to open and close the curtains.

1. What does the paragraph suggest might happen to a play if the boys shown in picture 6 did not do their job? What might happen if the job shown in picture 5 were not done? Why is each job shown in pictures 1-4 necessary?

2. Which of the following sentences best sums up the answers you gave to question 1?
   a. In a play, actors and actresses appear on a stage.
   b. Sometimes people working on a play don't do the jobs they're supposed to do.
   c. It takes many people working together to put on a play.
   d. Scenery is designed, built, and painted, and the set is furnished.

3. a. Look at the pictures once again, and imagine that the sentence you chose is printed at the top of the page. What does it do for the pictures?
   b. Reread the paragraph, but imagine the sentence you chose as the first sentence in the paragraph. What does it do for the paragraph?

If your sentence fits both the pictures and the paragraph, you understand the idea that they both express. You see how the pictures are all connected and what point the paragraph is making. A summary statement of this kind is called the **central idea.**

The different kinds of work involved in putting on a play are the **details** the writer uses to help you understand the point he is making or to convince you that his idea is true.

LESSON TWO: Deciding what it's all about

Part A. When the central idea is stated

The person who wrote the following paragraph made it easy for you to get the idea, by stating it twice and giving six examples which all lead you to the same conclusion.

> I am convinced that my cat understands words. Of course he learned very early in our lives together the meaning of a sharp "No," but that, I am told, is a response to the tone of voice. However, I may stand quietly in my living room and ask Pasha if he wants something to eat. If interested, he will go toward the kitchen and take up a waiting position near the refrigerator. A suggestion that it is time for bed starts him ambling toward the bedroom and his sleeping basket there. Two questions send him to the door: "Would you like to go outside?" and "How about a ride in the car?" An encouraging "O.K." from me gives him faith to venture from the porch without checking first for the presence of dogs or starlings. If I call to him as he strolls through the yard, "Upstairs, Pasha," he usually obliges with a quick run to the rear entrance of our second floor apartment. To me it seems that the words have a definite meaning for him.

1. What six examples of Pasha's behavior are mentioned?
2. If someone were to give you these six examples without telling you what he thought they showed, what might the examples lead you to believe about Pasha?
3. *a.* What two sentences in the paragraph tell you what the writer thinks Pasha's behavior means? Do these two sentences say the same thing?

   b. Does your conclusion from question 2 agree with these statements of the writer?

Examples are one kind of **detail** a writer uses to convince you, or to make it easier for you to understand.

Part B. When the central idea isn't stated

Quite often a writer doesn't actually state the point he wants to make, but instead gives details from which you must draw your own conclusions. Here is a paragraph of this kind:

> Nobody goes swimming in Lake Erie any more. Commercial fishing has almost disappeared on the lake. In the center

of the lake there is a patch of water covering 2600 square miles which contains practically no oxygen in the summer. A similar pattern is beginning to develop in Lake Michigan. During a recent summer, thousands of dead and rotting fish washed up on Chicago beaches in the space of a few days. That same year, an oil slick spread for five miles over the lower part of the lake. Wispy green algae clogged the intake screens of Chicago's water filtration plant and stained Milwaukee's beaches for days. In the Green Bay area, fishing for sport has dropped way off.

Which of the sentences below (4-10) is a good summary of what the paragraph says? Why is that sentence better than the others? What is wrong with each of the others?

4. People no longer go swimming in Lake Erie.
5. The Great Lakes provide one of our country's greatest natural resources.
6. The study of algae and other water plants is fascinating.
7. Commercial fishing is disappearing on Lake Erie.
8. The government needs to pay much more attention to conserving our natural resources.
9. The water in at least two of the Great Lakes is becoming polluted.
10. Fewer and fewer people want to use Lake Michigan for recreational purposes.

When a statement is unsatisfactory as a summary, it is usually for one of these reasons:

   a. **It is too broad**—includes more than the material actually says.
   b. **It is too narrow**—only one detail out of many.
   c. **It isn't true, or it contains information not in the selection.**

A summary statement which expresses the basic—or main—idea the author wants to get across is called the **central idea**—the one idea "central" to the whole work. It is impossible, of course, for a summary to contain all the ideas and details of the original, for then it would be the same as the original. But it must contain the most important idea or ideas.

In some pieces of writing the central idea is clearly stated and easy to find, while in others it is not. But in either case you can find the central idea by considering together all the ideas and details. You then find what broad idea they all work together to describe or explain.

LESSON THREE: Finding the central idea of a group of paragraphs

Sometimes several paragraphs together develop a single idea. In the following short article, each paragraph gives an example which contributes to or illustrates one basic idea. This idea is not stated, but it should be fairly obvious what it is.

ALL HIS LIFE Roy had been interested in art. From the time he was old enough to hold a crayon or a pencil, he loved to draw and paint. In school he especially liked his course in commercial art. Finally Roy was old enough to get a job during summer vacation. He thought about the usual jobs available to teen-agers—working in a supermarket, mowing lawns, delivery boy—but none of these really interested him. Instead, he had the good idea of asking for work at a local printing shop. After a while, the printer was letting him do simple layout work and even the handlettering on some signs.

Jeff, who was very skillful with motors and knew how to take good care of his motorcycle, proved he could be quite useful working part time in his older brother's auto repair shop.

Ella didn't think she could earn enough money baby-sitting. When she considered what else she might do, she remembered that she had spent considerable time helping her mother in their backyard flower garden. The knowledge of plants she had picked up helped her get a vacation job in a florist's shop.

Susan loved animals and had had several pets. She and a friend formed their own "pet-sitting" service to take care of other people's pets while the owners were away on vacation.

1. What did all these young people have in common, besides wanting a job?
2. What enabled each one to get a job?
3. State in one sentence the point you think the writer of these paragraphs wanted to make. This will be the central idea of all four paragraphs.

LESSON FOUR: Finding the central idea of a short article

Each of the four paragraphs in Lesson Three gave an example that illustrated the same point. There are other kinds of articles which use a different method to develop a central idea. Each paragraph in such an article may talk about a different aspect of the subject, yet each paragraph contributes to the general understanding the writer wants you to get. Here is an example of this kind of article:

THE VIGILANCE committees came out of the mining camps of California during the Gold Rush. Even if there had been good law officers in the camps, enforcing the law would have been almost impossible because there were no jails. There was simply no safe way to hold a prisoner for trial, so the citizens tried a suspect on the spot and carried out the sentence immediately. With no jails, there were generally only three punishments to choose from—whipping, hanging, or forcing the prisoner to leave town.

Originally the punishment was decided by all the miners together, but as the camps grew larger the responsibility was given to a chosen group of men. This vigilance committee or miners' court was influenced by public opinion. It had to be, for no group of men could be found willing to cross a whole camp of angry miners.

In the city of San Francisco hordes of criminals mixed with honest adventurers—who were not always perfectly law-abiding themselves. It was here that the vigilance committees gained their greatest fame.

And it was in San Francisco that the dangers of citizens' taking the law into their own hands became apparent. The vigilantes had wide support during most of their active period and they threw terror into the large and active underworld of the city. Yet many citizens were shocked when the vigilantes broke into the jail, carried off two prisoners, and hanged them before a great crowd at the committee's headquarters. Another time the vigilantes seized two prisoners after setting up a cannon and threatening to blow up the jail.

The activities of the San Francisco vigilance committees became known throughout the West. Because of them, similar groups were formed in nearly every western state at one time or another. Most of these groups lasted but a short time. One of the most famous cases of vigilante action outside of San Francisco was in Montana where citizens banded together to overthrow the reign of terror of Sheriff Henry Plummer, who built up one of the most active outlaw gangs in the West.

Adapted from *Western Sheriffs and Marshals* by Thomas Penfield. Copyright © 1955 by Thomas Penfield. By permission of the publisher, Grosset & Dunlap, Inc.

(over)

Is either of the following statements a good summary of the main point this article makes?

1. Vigilantes used to break into jails and hang the prisoners.
2. The vigilantes were groups of private citizens who provided effective law and order in some parts of the West.

While both of these statements are true, neither of them does a very satisfactory job of telling what the article as a whole is about. They are only two out of many other ideas in the article.

Which of the following statements best expresses the central idea of the article—the main point the writer wanted to make? What is wrong with the others? (Remember the three faults to look for: **too broad, too narrow, not in the article.**)

3. Enforcing law and order in the Old West was a difficult job.
4. Vigilance committees gained their greatest fame in San Francisco, where there were a great many criminals.
5. In Montana, citizens banded together to overthrow the reign of terror of Sheriff Henry Plummer, who was more of an outlaw than an officer of the law.
6. Attempts at law enforcement by private citizens can lead to great injustice.
7. Vigilance committees in the Old West did a necessary job of keeping peace and dealing with criminals, but sometimes went too far.
8. The vigilance committees were the product of the mining camps of California during the Gold Rush.
9. Vigilance committees were necessary because of the lack of jails on the frontier.

LESSON FIVE: Finding the central idea of an article

To find the central idea of the article[1] which begins on the next page you will need to analyze each of its paragraphs. First look at the illustration at the top of the page and read the caption. Then go on to the opening paragraph of the article.

[1]From Boys' Life (February 1965). Reprinted by permission of the author and Boys' Life, published by the Boy Scouts of America.

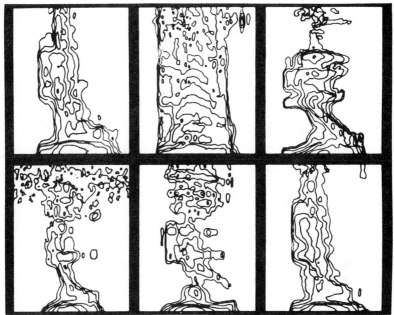

These six voiceprints were made from five different people saying the word "you."
One of the speakers said it twice. Which two voiceprints are from the same speaker?
Experts say the ones at upper left and lower right are from the same person.

Voiceprints

by Albert I. Mayer

Sometimes called visible speech, voiceprints are usually referred to by scientists as voice spectrograms and the machine
used is called a spectrograph. "A voiceprint," according to
Bell Laboratory acoustics scientist Lawrence G. Kersta, "is
a little picture of one spoken word. It reveals the pattern
of a person's voice energy in various levels of pitch. These
patterns can be identified."

No one sentence in this opening paragraph contains enough information to be the central idea of the whole paragraph. You
will have to construct a sentence of your own. Suppose you write,
"A voice spectrogram is a kind of picture showing patterns in a
person's voice which can be identified." How well does this sentence cover the information in the paragraph? Why were some
details left out?

The six paragraphs which follow complete the article on
voiceprints. For each paragraph, write a sentence which expresses its central idea. You may use words and phrases from
the paragraph, or, if you think one of the sentences in the paragraph does the job well, copy it, using quotation marks.

2 Naturally police chiefs and the FBI are interested in the voiceprint. Suppose a kidnaper calls his victim from a pay telephone booth, states his ransom demands, and says: "I'll call tomorrow to give you pay-off details"— then hangs up. Today it's still virtually impossible to catch him when he makes his second call. In the future, with a spectrograph making a print of his voice, he could be identified on his second call.

3 Surprisingly, when a trained person looks at a voiceprint he can see speech patterns which he missed when he listened. In 1962, before the Acoustical Society of America, Dr. Kersta played a record of President Kennedy's voice, then that of the mimic Elliot Reed. Those in the audience couldn't tell which was which. But voiceprints made it easy. The late President's print was "muddy"; Elliot Reed's was clear.

4 In another experiment Dr. Kersta had ventriloquist Shari Lewis say some words—first in her natural voice, then in the voices of her puppet characters Lamb Chop, Charley Horse, Hush-Puppy, and Minnie Owl. Identification was easy, for voiceprints showed that basic characteristics of Shari Lewis' voice existed in all of her characters.

5 Suppose you muffle your voice by talking through a handkerchief, lower or raise its pitch, speak in a whisper, affect an accent? You can't fool a voiceprint because the natural shape of your mouth, throat, and nasal cavities cause your voice energy to be concentrated into bands of frequencies that are impossible to disguise.

6 To identify a single person's voice out of millions will require the training of experts and the development of an efficient system of classification. Dr. Kersta suggests that voiceprints can be analyzed and coded by computer. The code of an unidentified voice can then be matched against those on file.

7 It will take more than one spoken word to positively identify a person by means of a voiceprint. Dr. Kersta proposes using the following ten of the most commonly used words in the English language: *it, me, you, the, on, I, is, and, a,* and *to.*

1. *a.* Reread the seven central idea statements you wrote. Choose the one sentence which best serves as a summary statement for the whole article. Remember to include the one for the first paragraph.

   b. How well does this sentence cover the main ideas from the entire article? Why must many ideas be left out?

2. A paragraph marks a division in a piece of writing. Whenever a new paragraph begins, there is a shift or change of some kind. The shift may be to a different idea or part of an idea; to a different speaker or a different character; to a different place or time; or to a different action. What is different in each of the paragraphs in the article on voiceprints to cause the article to be divided as it is?

EXERCISE I. Finding the central idea in several paragraphs

The following paragraphs are taken from the middle of an article. The beginning and the end, which state the author's central idea, are missing, but the questions which follow will help you decide what the missing parts are about.

1 For several weeks, I had been studying the habit pattern of a huge white-tail buck and trying to get a good, close-up picture of him. Finally, as autumn approached, I located his favorite daytime bedding place.

2 The deer had selected the spot with care, and it was practically foolproof. He bedded in a thinly wooded patch of underbrush at the head of a ravine, with old brambled fields on all sides. From his bed the buck had a good view on both right and left as well as downhill. Any approach from those directions was out of the question. His only blind spot was uphill to the rear, but there he was protected by the prevailing winds, which would carry any danger scents down through his woods. Thus, the old buck was safe and he knew it—while I watched helplessly with binoculars from across the valley.

3 Then, one afternoon, the wind changed. Blowing *uphill,* it left his back door unprotected, but he apparently liked his hidey-hole so well that he took the risk rather than seek another bed. The binocs showed me his exact spot—almost under a small overhang in the hillside.

4 Circling the valley, I found the leaves and ground cover damp and ideal for easy stalking. Approaching quietly, I finally was only about ten yards from the overhang. By stretching my neck I could just see the tips of his huge antlers, moving gently as he chewed his cud. A few more careful steps and I could get my picture.

5 How often plans are scattered like a house of cards! A little way from the deer, a gray squirrel suddenly came flip-tailing up through the sparse timber. He suddenly rose up on his hind legs and looked directly at me. The deer's antler tips hadn't changed movement. Then the bushy-tail sprang up against a sapling and began jerking his tail. In a couple of seconds the "squacking" would begin. I watched the antlers.

6 One squack . . . the antlers became rock-still. Two more squacks! On the

Adapted from "Calls of the Wild" by Howard T. Sigler from *The Elks Magazine* (January 1967). Reprinted by permission of the author.

TONY CHEN

last, the buck waited no longer. In one motion, he was up and into the brush, quickly disappearing around the hillside.

7 In this instance, it seems obvious that the squirrel told the buck exactly where I was. Had the buck *not* known my exact location, he could just as easily have escaped straight downhill or to my right, in either case being in full view. He would have had identical wind protection either way. Instead he took the left route, *putting two large trees between us.*

8 One time I had lured a fox into the vicinity by using a commercial call imitating an injured rabbit, but the fox apparently decided there was something wrong with my rabbit yells. He would come no closer than about eighty yards, where he sat down on a scraggly fallen tree near a deer trail along the ridge.

9 Things came to a standstill for a while. I settled myself to outwait the fox and he apparently figured to make me move first.

10 Within minutes, out beyond the fox and in the trail, a buck deer appeared. The fox certainly heard the deer behind him, but evidently identified the sound as familiar because he remained motionless. On came the deer, passing the fox and heading straight for me. Raising the camera, I waited.

11 But again I was defeated—for when the deer was almost within camera range, the fox barked. The buck never broke stride. Instead, he immediately changed direction slightly, left the path, angled around the side of the ridge away from me and vanished *downwind* —a direction deer seldom take except in emergency.

12 Why hadn't the fox "said something" before the deer appeared? Why did he choose that particular moment to bark? He simply told the deer I was there!

1. What changes are signaled by the beginning of each new paragraph? For paragraphs 2-12, explain what change, large or small, might have caused the writer to begin each new paragraph.

2. What examples of animal behavior are described in the article?

3. What is the writer trying to show by these examples?

4. Write a single sentence which contains the central idea of the entire selection.

The central idea of a piece of writing made up of several paragraphs is found in the same way as the central idea for one paragraph. You can summarize the central ideas of all the paragraphs to get the central idea of the whole work. Or you can consider the examples, details, and ideas throughout and form a central idea statement which all the individual parts together seem to "prove."

LESSON SIX: Central idea in a narrative

The author of this modern fable tells you his "meaning," but it's really a kind of joke.

The Unicorn in the Garden
by James Thurber

ONCE UPON a sunny morning a man who sat in a breakfast nook looked up from his scrambled eggs to see a white unicorn with a golden horn quietly cropping the roses in the garden. The man went up to the bedroom where his wife was still asleep and woke her. "There's a unicorn in the garden," he said. "Eating roses." She opened one unfriendly eye and looked at him. "The unicorn is a mythical[1] beast," she said, and turned her back on him. The man walked slowly downstairs and out into the garden. The unicorn was still there; he was now browsing among the tulips. "Here, unicorn," said the man, and he pulled up a lily and gave it to him. The unicorn ate it gravely. With a high

[1]**mythical,** not real; made-up; imaginary.

heart, because there was a unicorn in his garden, the man went upstairs and roused his wife again. "The unicorn," he said, "ate a lily." His wife sat up in bed and looked at him, coldly. "You are a booby," she said, "and I am going to have you put in the booby-hatch." The man, who had never liked the words "booby" and "booby-hatch," and who liked them even less on a shining morning when there was a unicorn in the garden, thought for a moment. "We'll see about that," he said. He walked over to the door. "He has a golden horn in the middle of his forehead," he told her. Then he went back to the garden to watch the unicorn; but the unicorn had gone away. The man sat down among the roses and went to sleep.

As soon as the husband had gone out of the house, the wife got up and dressed as fast as she could. She was very excited and there was a gloat in her eye. She telephoned the police and she telephoned a psychiatrist; she told them to hurry to her house and bring a strait-jacket. When the police and the psychiatrist arrived they sat down in chairs and looked at her, with great interest. "My husband," she said, "saw a unicorn this morning." The police looked at the psychiatrist and the psychiatrist looked at the police. "He told me it ate a lily," she said. The psychiatrist looked at the police and the police looked at the psychiatrist. "He told me it had a golden horn in the middle of its forehead," she said. At a solemn signal from the psychiatrist, the police leaped from their chairs and seized the wife. They had a hard time subduing her, for she put up a terrific struggle, but they finally subdued her. Just as they got her into the strait-jacket, the husband came back into the house.

"Did you tell your wife you saw a unicorn?" asked the police. "Of course not," said the husband. "The unicorn is a mythical beast." "That's all I wanted to know," said the psychiatrist. "Take her away. I'm sorry, sir, but your wife is as crazy as a jaybird." So they took her away, cursing and screaming, and shut her up in an institution. The husband lived happily ever after.

Moral: Don't count your boobies until they are hatched.

1. The author of this brief story has set aside one sentence which is supposed to contain the "meaning" of the story. What is it?

2. *a.* What old familiar saying has he based this sentence on? What does it mean?

   b. How does the old saying apply to this story?

3. *a.* Does the author intend this story to be funny or serious? Why do you think so?

   b. Do you think he intends his "meaning" to be taken seriously? Explain your answer.

Very often, when an author tells a story in a comic way, he has based his story on a serious idea. In this way, he can make a serious point without seeming to do so.

A **narrative** is a writing in story form. It can be serious or comic, imaginary (fiction) or based on fact. Most narratives, of course, do not contain sentences such as this in which the author sets forth the "meaning" of his story. For most, you have to figure out the central idea for yourself. To do this you should look carefully at two things:

(1) What happens in the narrative.

(2) The way the author tells it.

Then you can put these two things together and draw from them an understanding of the story, which is the central idea.

EXERCISE II.   Finding the central idea in a narrative

Read the short story which follows. The questions at the end will help you understand its central idea.

A Private Place

by Donald Abramson

I DON'T know how to tell you, all I was looking for was a *place,* see? Just some place of my own where I could keep stuff and where I could go and be alone for a while. For instance, one of my cousins has this tree house that's all his, and nobody bothers it and it's great. But then they've got a house with a yard. All we have is this three-room apartment and there aren't any trees to speak of. There's Mom's bedroom, and a kitchen and sort of living room together, and a bedroom for me and my little brother, who always wants to be where I am. I mean, if I go in the bedroom and shut the door he wants to come in too. Well, that was all right when I was growing up, but sometimes you like to be by yourself, and then you don't like to have a little brother poking his nose in. We were getting along all right until one day I was in my room with my best friend Watt, and Billy started to come in.

"Scram, kid," I told him. "This is private."

Of course he had to tell Mom and then she came and wanted to know what we were doing in there. Well, we weren't doing anything—just looking at some old magazines—but I got mad.

"For gosh sakes, can't a guy be alone for a while?"

"What have you got to be alone for?" Mom wanted to know. Well, of course I couldn't explain so I just kept quiet.

"You let Billy come in, now. He's got rights in this house, just like you have!"

So Watt and I scraped up our stuff and put it away in the old wooden tool box I keep under my bed, then we opened the door to let Billy in and we started to go. "Where you goin'?" he wanted to know.

"I don't know. Out, somewhere."

"Can I come?"

"No, you can't!" I said, mad. "You wanted in there. Now you go in and stay there."

"I don't want to stay there."

I gave him a shove into the room. "Well, you're not coming with us!" And Watt and I beat it quick before Billy could follow.

After a while we were sitting on the steps talking. "Listen, Watt," I said finally. "This is getting me down. I've just got to have a place of my own to keep stuff. What d'you think?"

Watt pulled at his ear for a while, the way he does when he's thinking hard. Then he said, "My mom goes to the bank."

"Huh!" I said. "So what?"

"I mean, she's got a place there, a box, that she keeps stuff in. She rents it from them and they let her go in anytime she wants to, and she says she's got the only key."

"No kidding?" I said.

"Yeah. I've been there with her a couple times."

"But that's just a box. My junk, I like to—you know, look at it, and stuff."

"Well, they've got rooms there you can go in and take your box and nobody bothers you."

"And they don't ask you what's in it?"

"Naw. They don't care."

Well, I thought about it for a while, and it seemed like a pretty good idea. Lots of times I'd find out that Billy had been into my stuff because my box didn't have a lock on it, and he'd gotten it all mixed up. But when I said anything to Mom she'd just say, "Can't you let him play with it? He's just a little kid, he's not going to hurt anything. He doesn't have much of anything else. What've you got in there that's so almighty precious, anyway?"

Now, I don't have a lot of stuff, and even I know it isn't worth much. I mean, there's some old car magazines and a few comic books, an ID bracelet that I found, a bottle opener, and a big league baseball that had been hit for a home run that I swapped with my cousin for. Oh, and some other things, a fountain pen and some sea shells and a model car—well, you know the kind of stuff. But the thing is, how could I explain it to Mom? I mean, I could tell her what it is, but how could I tell her how important all of it is to me? And I just don't like anybody messing around with it. So the more I thought about it, the better Watt's idea sounded to me. So the two of us went over to the bank.

Watt knew right where to go so we went downstairs where there was this lady behind a desk. She gave us a pretty good look-over, but she must have decided that we weren't going to pull a stick-up or anything, so she asked us what we wanted.

I told her I wanted a box to keep stuff in.

"You mean a safety deposit box?"

"Uh, yeah. I guess so."

"What size did you have in mind?" she asked.

I looked over at Watt, but he was

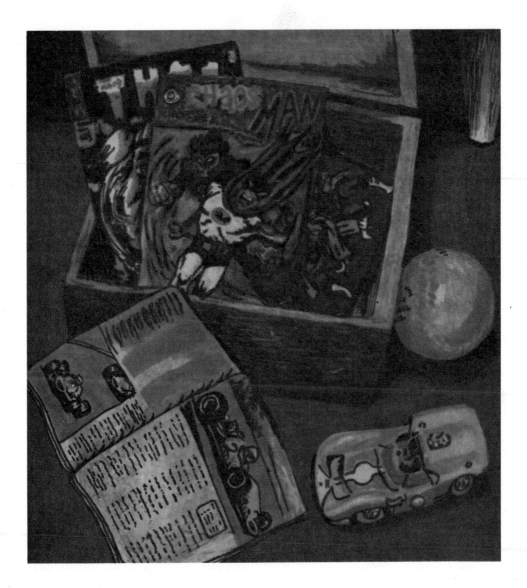

looking around, he wasn't looking at me. "I don't know," I said. "I'd have to see 'em."

So she took a key out of a drawer and came out from behind her desk and went and opened this big grilled gate and asked me to follow her inside. Well, I was disappointed. I mean, there were sure a lot of boxes, but they were all so small. But I thought, well, I'm here, so I might as well go through with it, and I told her I thought the biggest one would do. Then as she was leading the way out I asked her about the rooms.

"Oh yes," she said. "Right over here." And she pointed to a row of doors behind her desk. I went to look in one and that's what decided me. It was just right, with a couple of chairs and a desk and all, so I told her that'd be fine.

"All right," she said, and got out a card and started writing on it. "Did you want to rent it for one year or two years, or what?"

I had started to feel awfully uncomfortable, and now something nudged at my mind that there was something wrong. I said, "Ah—did you want the money now?"

A look came across her face but she smiled again right away. "Oh yes, it's all in advance." Then she looked at me again, close. "I'm sorry I didn't make that clear."

Right then I didn't want anything more than to be out of there. So I mumbled something about having to come back with the money and I thanked her very much and I said, "C'mon, Watt," and we left in a hurry.

"Hey, I'm sorry," Watt told me as we were leaving the bank. "I didn't know."

"Forget it," I told him.

So we went home again and I found Billy playing with my baseball that I've told him a hundred times not to touch, so I chased him out of the bedroom and I told him I'd kill him if I caught him messing around in there ever again, and I'd kill him anyway if he told Mom what I said.

Watt and I talked about it some more, and I guessed maybe I could fit a padlock on my box. That'd be a lot cheaper, anyway, but I still wouldn't have a place to go with it. Anyway, I'm planning to get a padlock just as soon as I have some extra money. That'd be better than nothing. After all, a guy's got to have something to himself.   THE END

1. Who is the main character in the story? Explain.
2. *a.* What does the main character want at the beginning of the story? What does he want at the end?
   b. Why is this thing important to him?
   c. What does he do to try to get what he wants?
3. Often, when a story ends happily for the main character, you feel glad for him. If a story ends unhappily, you may either feel sorry for him or feel that he got what he deserved. Does this story end either happily or unhappily for its main character?
4. Have you ever had feelings similar to those of the main character? Do you think other people also feel this way at times?
5. The questions you have just answered have helped you to think about some of the more important aspects of the story. Now you should be ready to consider the central idea. From the following sentences, choose the one you think best expresses the central idea of "A Private Place." Be prepared to explain why you chose the one you did, and also to explain why you did not choose each of the others.

a. The boy is selfish in wanting privacy in a home where there just isn't enough room.

b. A young boy tries unsuccessfully to rent a safety deposit box for his own "private place."

c. A safety deposit box is the best place for personal possessions, whether they are valuable or not.

d. Everyone needs a "private place" where he can be alone and also keep things important to him.

e. Not being able to keep other people away from his personal possessions will ruin this boy's life.

f. Something which is worthless to one person may be very important to someone else.

No two pieces of writing are exactly the same. The questions you ask yourself about a particular selection may have to be somewhat different from those in 1-4. But you will find that questions something like these will usually give you a good start.

What you should know about central idea

The **central idea** of a piece of writing, whether it is one paragraph or a whole book, is an understanding the reader gets from the whole piece with all its **details.** The central idea may be stated by the author, or it may be a general understanding the reader must piece together for himself.

In considering the central idea, it will be helpful to keep in mind the following points:

1. The *whole* piece must be considered, with all its details.

2. The central idea is an *idea,* not just a single fact, or detail, or action, or even a whole list of facts, details, or actions.

3. It must be *central* to the work; that is, the most important or most general idea expressed.

4. The central idea in a narrative will often be influenced by how the reader feels about the main character and about what happens to him.

5

COUR

Is it looking danger in the face

and not running away?

Is it wanting to live

but being willing to die?

Is it living with terror, hour after hour?

Is it killing?

Or maybe not killing?

Or shouldering heavy loads

without complaining?

Could it be closing your mouth

on a word you want to say?

Or saying the needed thing

that others don't want to hear?

What is courage?

*Riding a wild bear was only
the beginning!*

The Man Who Rode The Bear

by Ellis Credle

B ACK IN the times when the Indians were still a-raiding around in the Blue Ridge Mountains, there was an old bear that had the people more scarified than the Indians ever did. He was a terror—as big as a horse, people said, and ferocious, too. It seemed like a bullet didn't even tickle him. He raided pigpens, carried off sheep, and wasn't even afraid to hang around the cabins at night and take a grab at anybody that came out. It got so folks were afraid to be out after dark.

Well, the critter went over to Sowback Ridge one night and got into the pigpen of a fellow named Joe Dowdy. Joe and his wife Tildy didn't hear a sound. It was raining and they were moving the furniture here and there to keep the rain from wetting it. What with all the noise they made, dragging the bed and the chest and the table around, and with the rain beating down on the shingles overhead, they never heard their hog a-squealing.

The bear killed the pig and dragged him around behind the barn. There he made a meal of him, hair, hide, and hoof. Then, gorged with his meal, the bear lay down under the eaves of the barn, where he was protected from the rain, and went to sleep.

It was too bad about Joe's hog because it was his last one, all he and

Abridged from *Tall Tales from the High Hills* by Ellis Credle. ©1957 by Ellis Credle. Published by Thomas Nelson & Sons.

Tildy had to provide meat for the winter. Joe was the kind of man that seemed born for bad luck. If he planted a corn patch, there would be rain all around the country but never a drop in his field. His livestock were always dying off with one thing or another, and it seemed he just couldn't get ahead.

So it went until the night the bear paid them a visit. By that time Joe and Tildy had nothing in the world but the leaky cabin, the hog, and a poor decrepit old horse. And now, though they didn't know it, their hog was inside the bear.

Along about four o'clock in the morning, when the rain let up a little, Joe and Tildy sat down in front of the fireplace and began to talk about their situation.

"If I could only get the reward they're offering for that old bear, it would put us on Easy Street," Joe said. "It's a lot of money. I might just try it."

"Oh, talk sense," said Tildy impatiently. "Everybody in the mountains has tried it. Folks have gone in bands to get him. He's clawed Jake Sadler and raked open Solly Sneed. Everybody's scared for their lives of that critter. Do you think you can go out and bring him in all by your lonesome?"

"Well—" Joe hung his head.

"And what would you hunt him with?" Tildy went on. "Your gun has been sold these three months. Are you aiming to go out and get him with your bare hands?"

Joe sighed.

"You'd better think of looking for work," said Tildy. "I heard yesterday that the miller down the creek a piece is looking for a man to help with the grinding. Why don't you get down there and ask for the job?"

"Well," said Joe doubtfully, "I reckon it wouldn't hurt to try."

"Wouldn't hurt to try!" echoed Tildy. "Well, I reckon it wouldn't. Get out right now and saddle up the horse and get along."

"Why, it's dark now," said Joe, "I couldn't see to saddle the horse."

"Get along. You'll manage with the horse; do it by the feel."

Well, Joe got up, clamped some spurs on his boots—for his poor old horse needed plenty of urging—and put on his coat. Then he said good-bye and walked out to the barn. It had stopped raining but Joe couldn't make out a thing in the dark. He felt his way to the place in the barn where he kept his saddle and bridle, and took them off the peg. Then he made his way to the stall where the horse slept. He held out his hands and walked this way and that inside the stall, but he couldn't find the horse. He wasn't in his stall. The fact was that the horse had smelled the bear and had run clean away to the woods.

"Now where's that horse?" said Joe. He went outside and stumbled here and there, feeling along the fences and around the well. Then he went back to the barn and felt along the walls. At the back, he stumbled over the bear lying under the eaves sound asleep.

Joe put out his hand and felt the hair on the bear's neck. "Oh, so there you are, you crazy critter!" He grabbed the bear by the ear. "Haven't you got enough sense to stay in outen the rain?"

Well, the bear was so logy with a whole hog in his stomach that he didn't even wake up. While he snored away, Joe opened his mouth and put the bit in; he buckled the bridle on his head. He threw the saddle across the bear's back and then gave him a kick in the ribs.

"Get up, you no-count critter! Let me fasten this bellyband."

The bear roused himself groggily, and hoisted himself onto his feet. Joe quickly fastened the bellyband. Then he leaped into the saddle. He gave the critter a jab with his spurs.

That bear woke up for sure. He felt the thing tied around his middle and the load on his back. He gave himself a terrific shake. It almost threw poor old Joe from the saddle. "What's the matter with you?" he cried, and he beat the bear's head with the handle of his whip.

The bear had never had anything like this happen to him. He reached around to claw Joe off his back, but his arms wouldn't reach. He couldn't get his head back that far to bite. And all the time Joe was beating him about the ears with the handle of the whip and sticking him with his spurs.

That old bear was scarified outen his wits. He took off down the road as fast as he could gallop. Every now and then he'd hump himself and jump up in the air, trying to throw off whatever it was that had him around the middle. Never in his life had Joe had such a ride. Who would have thought the old horse had it in him? he wondered.

It was a good seven miles to the mill and that bear ran every step of the way. By the time he got there he was run near to death. When Joe pulled up on the reins to stop him, he just stood swaying, with his tongue hanging out and all the fight out of him.

In the dark, Joe threw the halter rope around the hitching post and tied it. Then he sat down on the steps of the mill to wait till the miller appeared.

It wasn't long before day came on. The miller entered the mill through the back door and unlocked the front one, ready to do business. He saw Joe leaning against the wall.

"Good morning, Joe Dowdy. Have you come for some meal? How'd you get here so early?"

"I rode," said Joe, pointing with his thumb over his shoulder. "There's my horse out there tied to the hitching post."

The miller looked. His eyes popped half out of his head. There stood the bear, saddled and bridled and tied to the hitching post.

"You—rode—that?" squalled the miller.

"Sure," said Joe without turning around. "Why not?"

The miller looked at Joe as though he'd never seen him before. He'd never thought Joe was much of a man—but there was the bear. The very bear that had been terrorizing the whole settlement. And here was Joe acting as though bear-taming was nothing at all.

"I came to see you about that j-job." Joe stuttered a little. "I'd admire to have it, if you ain't got a man no better."

"B-b-better!" stammered the miller. "Where would I find a better man than you? You can have the job, and welcome."

By that time folks had begun to arrive with their meal to be ground. When they saw the bear tied to the hitching post, they were struck dumb with astonishment. At first, they just stood; then they began carrying on— exclaiming and asking questions.

"Who—who rode him?" They stared at the bear and then at the miller.

"Joe, here, rode him up just before daybreak."

Joe turned around then, to see what all the commotion was about. When he saw the bear, his eyes flew open. His heart almost stopped.

"Well, Joe, you're the man that gets the reward!" the miller said. "You sure have earned it. Tell us—how did you manage it?"

Joe could only gasp. "I—I'd ruther not talk about it."

Well, the fame of old Joe Dowdy went all over the mountains. The money for capturing the bear came in mighty handy for Joe and Tildy. They put a new roof on their house, bought themselves a cow, several hogs, and some poultry. But if Joe thought he could settle down and enjoy his good fortune, he had another think a-coming.

When the time came to elect a sheriff, it was only natural that folks should think of Joe. All the mountain men met at the crossroads store and they agreed that he was the man for the job. There were some pretty rough horse thieves about; robbers appeared now and then, and sometimes rowdy fellows got to fighting with knives. Yes, Joe could handle them if anybody could.

The very thought of the sheriff's duties gave Joe the cold shivers. But he decided he'd better not refuse until he had talked it over with Tildy.

Tildy listened and looked thoughtful. "They pay the sheriff a mighty big salary," she said. "You'd better take the job. You know the sheriff has a man to help him out. A deputy, they call him. If anything dangerous turns up, you can send him to handle it, while you stay out of harm's way and direct things."

Well, that solved the problem. Joe accepted the job.

They gave Joe a big husky fellow for a deputy. If Joe didn't appear to take care of some ruffian, people said it was a job not worthy of a man like Joe. So everything went all right for a year or two. Then there was a serious problem for old Joe Dowdy.

Word got around that the Indians were going on the warpath, and all through the mountains people were worried. The men of the community got together at the store to see what could be done about it. They were all there but Joe, who had found an excuse to stay home.

"We'll have to get together and fight 'em," said Solly Sneed. "There's no other way."

"Within a week they'll be on us!" shouted Sam Cobble.

"Let's call on Joe Dowdy; he'll get us out of this!" someone cried.

Everybody gave a sigh of relief. Yes, Joe was the man to save the day.

So a messenger was sent to tell Joe they were all depending on him to save them from the Indians. It hardly needs saying that Joe was scared outen his wits.

"Why, Bud," he said to the messenger, "how can I do that?"

"Any way it suits you, Joe," Bud replied. "I'll go out and saddle your horse for you." And he set off for the barn.

Joe rushed into the house. "Tildy! Tildy!" he shouted.

Tildy came running. "What now?"

Joe poured out the story of what had happened. "What can I do? Bud's out there now, a-saddling my horse."

"Let me think," Tildy told him. She sat with her head in her hands. "Well," she said at last, "you might stall just a little and gain some time. Go over to the store and tell the men that you'll have to take a couple of days to scout out the situation.

"You wouldn't really have to go near the Indians. You could just ride over that-a-way. Then you can hide in the woods a day or so, and come on home with some tale to satisfy them. Meanwhile, I'll be thinking up some excuse to get us out of this fix."

Since there seemed nothing else to do, Joe decided to take his wife's advice. He went out and mounted his old nag and rode with the messenger down to the store. He said to the gathering just what Tildy had told him to. They all agreed it was a sensible plan.

"But you ought not to go on a horse like that," the miller said. "That old bag of bones can hardly get into a trot. We'll get you a good horse."

"He can have mine," spoke up Solly Sneed. "I reckon he can outrun anything! Of course, he's a mite hard to handle, but anybody that could saddle up a bear and ride it ought to be able to manage my horse."

Now everybody in the mountains knew Solly's horse. He was a half-wild brute that only Solly could ride. The thought of getting on his back scared Joe almost as much as facing the Indians. But there was nothing for it but to accept Solly's offer.

"Well, I'll just ride my old horse home," Joe said, "and get some grub. I'll lead Sol's horse on behind, and he'll be there ready to mount after I've fixed up something to eat."

The men all agreed that this was a good idea. "We'll stay here at the store to wish you good luck as you go by," they said.

Home went poor Joe, feeling that his last day had come for sure. He showed Tildy the horse. "I'll never stay on his back a minute," he said. "He'll hump me off like I was a rabbit. Then he'll trample me, just outen spite. And the men all waiting at the store to see me go by!"

"Oh my!" cried Tildy, "what shall we do?" And she put her head in her hands, to think. In a few minutes she came up with a plan.

"We'll feed him some corn," she said, "and while he's eating I can tie your feet under his stomach. That way he can't buck you off. You ride by the store, then circle around the woods and come back home. You can hide in the barn loft a few days until it's time to report to the men at the store."

So they fed the horse a big helping of corn and, while he was munching it, Joe mounted and Tildy tied his feet with a rope under the horse's belly.

Joe set off easily enough. The horse was full of corn and in no mood for acting up. But when they came to the store, Joe kicked him in the ribs. If he passed the store at a fast clip, he thought, the fellows wouldn't see that his feet were tied. Well, kicking that horse was a mighty rash act, and Joe soon found it out. The critter let out a whinny and hoisted himself up on his hind legs. Then he set off for other places. Joe whizzed by the store like he was shot out of a cannon. The men hardly saw him before he was out of sight.

Joe couldn't stop that horse to save his life. The worst of it was, he was headed right for the Indian camp.

Now the Indians had set guards along the road to warn them in case the whites should attack. As Joe came abreast of them, they leaped out in all their war paint. They tried to stop the horse. But lawsy! They didn't have a chance. That horse upped with his back feet and kicked one Indian half a mile down the road. He reached around with his teeth and took a bite out of the other one. The fellow squalled and jumped back. The horse humped himself and galloped on.

The guards were scared a sight. They bellowed on to the camp: "Here come the white men! Their horses are worse fighters than the men. They thrash with their hoofs and crack people's skulls; they bite off arms with their teeth!"

This news set the Indian camp in an uproar. Everybody was running around telling the news to everybody else, and with every telling the tale got bigger. How could they defend themselves against an army of such terrible critters?

Meanwhile, the horse thundered on. But with all the kicking he had done, the rope that tied Joe's feet began to work loose. Joe knew he'd have a terrible fall if it came untied. I'll grab a

tree limb over the road, he thought, and haul myself offen this hog-wild critter.

He reached out to grab the first tree he came near. It was small and had hardly any roots. It came out in his hand and there he went, galloping past a second set of guards brandishing a tree torn up by the roots.

"Here come the white men!" the guards shouted. "They pull up trees by the roots without getting outen their saddles. Here they come, a-shaking them over their heads for war clubs!"

This news struck terror into the whole Indian camp. Like a swarm of locusts, they fled to the woods. When Joe and the horse came charging in among the tents, not a red man was left.

Joe hadn't thought to drop the tree, and it was banging and beating against the horse's side. It set the critter wild for sure. He charged around, kicking and bucking. He knocked down tee-pees, kicked over cooking pots, and trampled the Indians' belongings.

From behind the trees the Indians saw all the rampaging. The chief yelled for his counselors. "We'd better send him a peace pipe," he cried, "before the rest of 'em get here!"

By the time Joe had thought to drop the tree and his horse had quieted a bit, an Indian brave was there.

"Peace, we have peace!" the red man cried, holding out the pipe.

Joe grabbed the thing—what it was he didn't know. He stuck it in his mouth. There was no other way of holding it, for he had all he could do to stay in the saddle. The horse was wheeling; he'd had his run and his mind was set for home.

By the time he got back to the store, where the men were still gathered, the horse had gentled down considerable.

Joe took the pipe from his mouth and held it out to see what it was the Indian fellow had offered him.

The men on the porch of the store let out a whoop. "They're routed!" they shouted and began to thump each other on the back. "The Indians have sent the peace pipe!"

"T-t-tore their camp all to pieces," stuttered Joe. He sank down on the steps, nearly finished off.

Old Joe had done it again. All by his lonesome he had met and routed the Indians—all two hundred of them.

Well, there never was a man like Joe, the settlers all decided then and there.

"He ought to be commander of the state militia," said the miller. "He ought to have the job of defending the whole state." The others heartily agreed.

When they got back to the store, they put it up to Joe. "No, boys." Joe shook his head. "I'm getting old. I've done enough. I hereby resign from public life. I don't even want to be sheriff any more. I want to settle down on my farm and live a quiet life."

That was his say and he stuck to it.

Well, in the end, the men had another meeting in the store. They decided that sure enough Joe had done his part for the settlement. Out of gratitude they voted him a pension, a nice tidy sum to be paid him every month for the rest of his life.

So, at last, Joe and Tildy were able to settle down and live peacefully on their little farm.   THE END

1. Something unexpected always happens when Joe Dowdy tries to follow Tildy's advice. Tell what Tildy intends and then what actually happens in each of these situations:

   a. Tildy tells Joe to saddle up his old horse immediately and ride to the mill.

   b. Tildy ties Joe's feet under Solly Sneed's horse and he sets off for the Indian camp.

2. *a.* At the end of the story, what reasons does Joe give for retiring from public life?

   b. What is his real reason for retiring?

3. From the following scale, choose a number which shows where you would rate Joe Dowdy for courage.

1	2	3
Very little courage	Average courage	More than average

Why do you rate him as you do?

4. Which of the following help make the story seem funny? Why?

   a. The bear kills Joe's pig.

   b. The people choose Joe to be sheriff.

   c. Joe pulls up a tree by the roots.

   d. Joe settles down to a quiet life.

Words in action

"The Indians were still **a-raiding around** in the mountains."

"An old bear had the people more **scarified** than the Indians did."

The words in bold type might be spoken in the Blue Ridge Mountain country. Words like these, which are used only in a particular part of the country or by certain groups of people, are called **dialect.** How would the same things be said where you live?

Here are some other mountain dialect words. What does each one mean?

1. The wild **critter** got into the pigpen.
2. The pig was **a-squealing.**
3. Stay in **outen** the rain.
4. Joe said he'd **admire** to have the job.
5. He rode over **that-a-way.**
6. The horse was a **mite** hard to handle.
7. Joe tried to get **offen** the animal.

Photo permission of Thomas Nelson & Sons

Hank's tall tales

When Ellis Credle moved to the Blue Ridge Mountains in North Carolina, she met Hank Huggins, an old mountaineer who lived in a little log house high on the mountainside.

Hank was full of stories—mostly tall tales handed down from the days, long before movies and TV, when people used to sit around the fire and tell tales and each man tried to outdo the rest. Miss Credle wrote down Hank's tales and put them into her book *Tall Tales from the High Hills.* "The Man Who Rode the Bear" is one of the stories Hank told.

It was time to find out: Was he a man or a coward?

ONE OF THE BRAVE

by Elliott Arnold

In the late 1770's a ten-year-old boy named John Tanner
was kidnaped from his Kentucky home. He grew up with
Indians of the Ottawa and Chippewa tribes. *White Falcon,*
the book from which "One of the Brave" is taken, tells the
true story of John's life with the Indians and his struggle to
be accepted by them.

The tests of courage, strength, and skill set before John
were difficult and sometimes cruel, thanks to the jealous
Begwais, son of the chief. The rivalry between the two was
known to the whole tribe. The war between the Chippewa
and the Sioux would test whether Begwais, John, and the
other young men of the tribe deserved the title of "warrior."

The selection begins in the midst of a battle at the edge
of Spirit Lake. John, determined to prove to Begwais and
the rest of the tribe that he is worthy of becoming one of
them, listens closely to the instructions of Little Clam, the
only Indian who has shown him friendliness and concern.

TRY TO think that you are hunting
game," the Little Clam said. "Remain calm. Make each musket ball
find its target."

"It is the biggest game," John said.
"And yet it is wrong, somehow—a man
killing other men he has never before
seen."

"The Sioux are enemies," the Little Clam said. "A man kills his enemies or they kill him."

John listened to the whistle of the musket balls and the deadly whine of the arrows. A branch, cut off by a ball, fell near him. An arrow passed so close to his face its sound screamed in his ear. A man lying a few feet from him grunted and then died with a ball in his head and another man fell unconscious with an arrow deep in his side.

What did he feel now, John asked himself. It was the time to ask. The time to know what was inside of him, whether it was manhood or something cowardly. He felt tight and tense, but he did not think he felt fear.

And yet he did not feel the true passion of battle, as he could see it in the faces of the men around him. The thing that was in him was cold. Men around him shook with excitement. They sang and shouted and made other strange noises as they reloaded and fired, as they whipped arrow after arrow out of their quivers.

Was this because he was a white man, he wondered. Was this part of the difference that Begwais and the others felt? The Sioux were enemies and they had done harmful things to the Chippewas. They must be fought, but he could feel no pleasure in the fighting.

Above the noise of musketry he heard a shout of defiance. He saw Begwais leap up. Begwais pounded his chest. He stood erect and in the open, his face proud, and he shouted scornful things to the Sioux.

"Squaws! Children who pretend to be men! I am Begwais, son of Peshawba, and I spit on you!"

The air around the chief's son black-ened with arrows, but as though by some miracle, none touched Begwais. He remained standing, a picture of arrogance, and then at last a Sioux shaft found a resting place in his arm.

Peshawba raised his head and opened his mouth to speak, to order his son to cover, but he closed his lips without uttering a word. This was the moment of his son's courage and he would say nothing.

Begwais made no effort to shield himself. Without haste he plucked the arrow from his arm, his face indifferent to the pain; then he fitted the arrow into his bow and fired it back.

"Begwais! Begwais!" Chippewa men shouted in compliment.

Begwais lay down again and picked up his musket and resumed firing. Peshawba looked at him proudly but still did not speak.

"That was a brave thing," John said.

"That was for you," the Little Clam said.

John looked over to where Begwais was lying. Begwais was gazing at him challengingly. When John continued to lie behind the protective stump Begwais laughed contemptuously.

"There are many kinds of courage," the Little Clam said. "There is noisy courage and there is silent courage. No man can say which is better."

John understood that the Little Clam was trying to make him feel secure. And that meant the Little Clam understood that Begwais had challenged him and that he had not accepted the challenge. There would be others who noticed that he had refused to match Begwais' feat of bravery.

A part of him called upon him to stand up and do what Begwais had done but he could not. Fear had nothing to do with it. It was that he could not make a spectacle of himself, not even a spectacle of courage. But who would see it that way?

He looked at his friend, the Lightning. The Lightning was not taking the fighting well. He had sweat on his face over the black ash-marks and there was nervousness in his eyes.

Then he saw a look of terror in the Lightning's eyes. He followed the Lightning's gaze. A Sioux warrior had crept forward and was aiming an arrow directly at the Lightning. The Lightning seemed paralyzed.

Swiftly John fired and the Sioux clutched his chest and fell.

The fighting went on through the hot day and men on both sides were wounded and died. Late in the afternoon the Sioux raised their war cry and streamed from the forest in a charge.

Now there was no time to reload muskets and pistols. Now the fighting was with bows and arrows and then there was no time for that either and the fighting was with lances and knives. The Chippewas could not retreat. Behind them was the lake. And yet as the Sioux continued to pour from the forest Peshawba's men saw they were outnumbered two to one.

A mounted Sioux bore down upon John, his lance out-thrust. John waited coolly until the Sioux was on him and then he leaped swiftly to one side. He seized the lance and with a powerful pull he jerked the Sioux from his horse. In a moment the two men were wrestling on the floor of the forest.

The Sioux raised his right arm, a knife gleaming in his hand. John caught the wrist and the Sioux pressed down, the knife coming closer. John smelled the sweat and paint on the Sioux and saw the light of murder in his eyes.

The powerful arm of the Sioux came closer. He was a man in the fullness of his strength, fully half again as heavy as John. John called upon all his power but he could not stop the slow movement of the knife toward his throat. He thought swiftly that perhaps that was how it was intended, that he die in his first battle, and then he saw the triumph fade from the eyes of the Sioux and the light in them glaze. The arm grew limp and the Sioux fell loosely upon him and then he saw that the Little Clam had driven his own blade into the back of the Sioux.

He pushed the dead body away and engaged another of the enemy. The shore of the lake shuddered as the men fought from horseback and on the ground and now to the sounds of the yelling and grunting was added the whinnying of horses as men stabbed them to bring down their riders.

Still John fought in silence. A knife thrust tore through his sleeve and opened his arm. A blow from a war club sent him reeling. A wounded Sioux jabbed at his leg with a lance. And still no word came from between his tightly compressed lips.

The Sioux slowly but relentlessly forced the Chippewas back toward the lake. Peshawba's men fought bravely but the weight of the enemy was too great and step by step the blue water came closer.

If it was to be the time of death John wanted to die at the side of the Little Clam. He craned his neck until he saw the Little Clam and then he fought his way to his side. The Little Clam was wounded in several places but he fought without weakening.

A Sioux rode down upon them and

leaped from his horse upon the Little Clam and at the same time thrust his lance into the chest of the Little Clam with such force the point emerged from the Little Clam's back. Blood bubbled from the lips of the Little Clam and he fell back upon the ground, the lance rising like a sapling from his chest.

Now a terrible shuddering came over John. He gave forth his first cry of rage. He fell upon the Sioux, hands closing on his throat. The Sioux struggled and tossed like an animal.

This is no otter, John shouted in his head. This is no polecat. This is the man who just killed the Little Clam.

Then the Sioux ceased his struggling. He became limp and he moved no more and still John could not take his hands from his throat. And from his own mouth came a wild babbling of rage.

He felt a blow upon his head but no pain. He was beyond pain. He shouted that he wished the Sioux had ten lives so he could strangle him ten times. It was not until he heard the Little Clam utter a weak warning that he remembered there were other Sioux.

He lifted the dead Sioux and hurled his body at another Sioux warrior who was rushing toward him, knife in hand. He picked up the Little Clam's war club and battered the man senseless.

Then John knelt over the Little Clam. He tugged gently at the lance.

The Little Clam shook his head. "It is useless," he said. "You will pull out my life with it."

John leaped to his feet, the Little Clam's war club in his hand. Again he heard himself shouting words of madness.

He threw himself into the battle, swinging the war club with blazing fury. The Lightning, whose feet were already in the water of Spirit Lake, caught the fury and joined him, and then another Chippewa warrior, and then another.

The fury passed from man to man and Peshawba raised the war cry. Men knee-deep in the water fought their way back to land, echoing the war cry with parched lips. Each man seemed now to find in himself the strength of many men. Arms that had grown tired and heavy were so no longer. Legs that had barely been able to remain upright now drove men in charge after charge.

Before this sudden and unexpected onslaught the Sioux fell back. Their leaders tried to rally them but they could not stop the retreat. They reached the edge of the forest and made one last attempt to stand, but first one man turned and fled and then another and in a few minutes the battle became a rout and every Sioux who could raced away on foot or horse.

The madness was still on John. He strode from place to place, swinging his war club at Sioux warriors who had been unable to flee, and when there was no man left for him to strike he jumped upon a horse to follow the others.

Peshawba seized the bridle of the horse and commanded him to stop. John kicked at the sides of the horse. Peshawba pulled the horse back. "It is enough," he said.

The madness went away. John slumped in his saddle. He slid to the ground and went to where the Little Clam lay.

The Little Clam's eyes were getting dim with the death that was creeping through his body. John fell to his knees and lifted the Little Clam's head and held it against his chest. His eyes burned with tears.

"Grieve not," the Little Clam said. "The path I am walking is one in which all men must follow."

The Little Clam closed his eyes and breathed no more.

The smoke of the fighting drifted away. The forest was silent again. Birds returned to the trees but they did not sing. In the air were the smell of death and the ghosts of dead warriors.

Peshawba's fighting men nursed their wounds and buried their dead. John dug a grave for the Little Clam, deep enough to lie in with the lance still in his chest.

"Take the lance out of him so he will feel no pain on his journey," the Lightning said.

"Let those who are where he is going know that he died a warrior, in battle," John said. He put the Little Clam's war club at his side in the grave. "He will want that with him. It sent many of his enemies ahead of him and he will want it to wave it at them there."

He filled the grave with earth and put stones on it and only then did he take himself to the lake to bathe his wounds.

After the setting of the sun Peshawba ordered that a great fire be built. He commanded the medicine men to make a Metai of thanks to Gitche-Manito for the victory he gave the Chippewas over their enemies.

"Not for a long time again will the Sioux come to put out our fires," Peshawba said to his men. "Not for a long time will they attack our hunting parties or steal our children. They will talk about this day in their villages and they will fear for the day when we may come to put out their fires."

An owl hooted in the night. A faint breeze from the lake touched the faces of the listening men.

"Men died," Peshawba said. "They died well, fighting their enemies, making life safer for their women and children. They will feel no shame when they meet old friends who died before them. We will not say their names again but we will never forget them and we will honor their families and see that they never hunger."

The listeners grunted softly.

"The Sioux will talk about this day," Peshawba said again. "And most of all they will talk about our warriors who fought for the first time. They will talk about my son who did not disgrace me. Begwais, come before me."

The son of the chief stepped before his father. Peshawba placed his hand upon his shoulder and looked at him with pride.

"This morning you were a novice and people wondered whether you were brave. No one wonders now. This day you have become a warrior. Henceforth you are a man among other men and the people will respect you and talk about the brave things you did. At the Sioux fires tonight they are talking about the son of Peshawba who stood before them and taunted them."

One by one Peshawba summoned the novices who had proven themselves in the battle. And nothing in his words or manner gave greater or lesser praise to any of them. To each he awarded the status of warrior. Then he said: "I have saved for the last the white youth called John. John, come before me."

When John faced the chief, Peshawba looked at him intently. "Men here are alive and can hear my voice because of what you did this day," Peshawba said. "It has long been known that your eye is keen and that you do not waste arrows. This day you showed the people that your heart is not less valiant than your eye."

Peshawba gripped John by both arms.

"You have been a stranger among us," the chief said. "You are stranger no longer. Henceforth no man will feel apart from you because your blood is that of a white man. Today you proved that no one among us has greater right to call himself a Chippewa warrior. Everyone will hold you in esteem and ask your counsel and women will be grateful because you returned their husbands and their sons to them. But for you the water of Spirit Lake would be filled with the bodies of the dead."

The listeners rumbled their approval.

"The name John is a name of your own people and without doubt it is a name of honor," Peshawba went on. "But I will give you an Indian name, a warrior's name, a name that will be carried by the winds to our enemies, the Sioux, to our friends, the Assiniboines, the Ojibwas, the Crees. By this name will you be known and friends will say it with pride and affection and enemies will whisper it with fear."

Peshawba's face grew stern. "I have said your eye is as keen as the eye of a hawk who can see the smallest things from great distances. Your heart too is that of the fighting hawk, which fears nothing. Therefore I give you his proud name to bear among us. From this time on every man will call you White Falcon."

The moon rose. The fire died to embers. Exhausted men slept. Spirit Lake was pale and ghostly.

The new warrior, the White Falcon, felt the weight of tiredness upon him but he could not sleep. He sat for a long time at the new grave of the Little Clam and he held tightly to the eagle's talon that the Little Clam had given him.

Spirit Lake was red with morning light before the White Falcon's eyes finally closed in sleep.   THE END

Talking it over

1. *a.* Why does John question his own courage early in the battle between the Chippewas and the Sioux?

b. What explanation does he have for being less eager to fight than his Indian companions are?

c. How does the Little Clam explain to John the necessity for killing?

2. *a.* How do Begwais' actions differ from John's when they are both under fire?

b. Why does Begwais show off his courage so obviously? Why doesn't John imitate Begwais' daring?

c. How does the Little Clam explain the difference in courage between the two boys?

3. How does John show that his quiet courage can accomplish something?

4. *a.* What changes John into a furious attacker who fights like a madman?

b. How does the change in him affect the battle?

c. Choose the number which shows how much courage you think

John's actions at this point required.

1	2	3	4
None	Little	Much	Very much

Explain your choice.

5. How do the Chippewas feel toward John after the battle? How do they show their feeling?

b. Tom was such a _____ at piling bricks that his shoulders ached for a week after the job was done.

c. Joe suggested a _____ idea for raising money to buy uniforms.

d. My old coat looked much better after my mother _____ it.

⇌ Words in action

"After their first battle, the Indian youths were no longer **novices,** but experienced warriors." From clues in the sentence, what do you think *novice* means? What words in the sentence mean the opposite of *novices?*

The words in bold type below come from the same Latin word as *novice* and are related to it in meaning. Knowing that the word part *nov-* means "new" should help you answer these questions:

1. Which one would probably be a **novelty** to an Eskimo? (*a*) snow (*b*) a merry-go-round (*c*) a polar bear

2. One meaning of the prefix *re-* is "again." Would a building be **renovated** (*a*) to make way for a highway, or (*b*) because it was badly in need of repair?

3. How many of these are **novel** ideas? (*a*) A car that can be flown like a plane. (*b*) A coat that keeps you warm in winter and cool in summer. (*c*) Moving sidewalks that make walking unnecessary.

4. Which word (novice, novelty, renovated, or novel) completes the meaning of each of the following sentences?

a. The _____ of traveling by plane for the first time helped Ellen forget her fear.

A friend of Indians

Elliott Arnold writes from first-hand knowledge about Indians. After working as a reporter and serving in the Army in World War II, he settled in Tucson, Arizona, where he became friendly with many of the Indians who live in the area. His interest in these people led him to study Indian life of the past and relations between Indians and whites. Much of what he has written about Indians is based on real events.

Blood Brother, a story of the Indian Wars of 1874, is his best-known novel. It was made into a movie called *Broken Arrow,* which then became the basis for a TV series by the same name.

For you to read

In Elliott Arnold's book *White Falcon,* from which "One of the Brave" is taken, you will find many other instances in which John faces danger.

In the empty night sky above the vacant sea,
the Flying Tiger crew began
a battle for their lives.

The Tigers and The Sharks

by Edward Peary Stafford

F̲ROM the surface of the empty sea, the single plane looked like a slowly moving star. Then, as it crossed the sky, an observer could have seen the shifting red-green flashes of its running lights and heard the high hum of its engines.

It was a Flying Tiger DC-4[1] airliner on a routine transpacific run with a crew of five and a cargo of jet engines for delivery in Tokyo. But man's incredible conquest of time and distance still hangs on the twin threads of mechanical reliability and human skill, and no flight across an ocean is ever really routine.

Yet aboard the DC-4 it certainly seemed that way. In the cockpit, Captain Tony Machado monitored the rows of red-lighted gauges from his accustomed left seat. To his right, First Officer Warren Gin made minor adjustments on the auto-pilot knobs to keep

---

Adapted from *Saga* Magazine, August 1964.
[1]**Flying Tiger DC-4,** a large, four-engine, propeller-driven transport plane.

the plane on course and at its assigned 8000-foot flight altitude.

Behind the two pilots, the navigators, Dominic Ventresca and Richard Olsen, kept the plane's position pinpointed, giving the pilots those changes necessary to keep the plane on the course planned before take-off from Honolulu. Machado knew exactly where he was —1000 miles west of Oahu, with Wake Island, their immediate destination, 1000 miles to the west. Midway Island was some 600 miles to the north, Johnston Island 500 miles southeast.

Machado had turned in an hour after take-off, when the flight was well started on its way and all going well. He had slept for five hours while Warren Gin took over command and young Bob Hightower rode the right seat. Machado had been back on the job just ten minutes, returning slowly to full consciousness with the help of black coffee, and Gin had moved to the right seat, replacing Hightower, when one of the threads on which man's mastery of the elements depends, began to fray.

Near the center of the instrument panel, on the left-hand gauge of a group of four, a needle wavered uncertainly and fell until it rested against a tiny peg labeled "zero." Number one engine had lost fuel pressure. The silent flicker and fall of that one slim needle was like the clang of an alarm bell in the minds of Machado and Gin. They saw it instantly and reacted instantly. All the crew felt the DC-4 swerve slightly to the left as the left outboard engine stopped and its windmilling prop dragged against the airstream. Almost imperceptibly the plane began to lose altitude as a quarter of its horsepower failed.

Captain Machado immediately rammed up the throttles on the other three engines while Gin snapped off the auto-pilot and got the yoke[2] in his hands and the rudders[2] under his feet. The plane leveled off again and Machado went to work to find and correct the trouble. In the cabin, Ventresca automatically rechecked the flight's position. Hightower and Olsen crowded anxiously into the cockpit.

In the empty night sky above the vacant sea, the Flying Tiger crew began a battle for their lives.

A minute after number one engine went out, the number three engine coughed and stopped, and on two of the four red gauges, the fuel pressure needles collapsed to zero. Olsen sat down at the radio position and began to click his key. His distress message crackled over the hemisphere of water.

Not far from where Tony Machado's men fought to stay out of the patient Pacific, the steamship *Steel Advocate* rolled and lifted gently in the swell, bound for Honolulu on the next-to-last leg of a round-the-world voyage. The men on the new watch had just settled down to their duties when the radio speaker guarding aircraft distress frequencies began a staccato chirping. The radioman clapped on his earphones, tuned his receiver, and began to tap the keys of his typewriter. He listened for a minute when the message was over, then pulled the paper from its roller and ran along the boat deck to the bridge. He handed the message to Dick Rausch, the ship's chief officer, who had the watch.

It was Olsen's "Mayday."[3] The message said that Flying Tiger Flight 433,

---

[2]**yoke, rudders,** the controls with which a pilot steers the plane.

[3]**Mayday,** radio signal calling for help, sent out by ships and airplanes in serious trouble.

now with three dead engines, was losing altitude rapidly and preparing to ditch. The position followed. Rausch plotted it quickly and found that it lay 280 miles to the south of the *Steel Advocate*'s location. He called the captain, and seconds later, the merchantman's high bow swung southward and her deck began to tremble as the engines worked up to full speed. Help was on its way.

And Tony Machado needed it. Aboard the faltering DC-4, all five men were desperately busy. Machado and Gin tried various positions of fuel selector valves, cross-feeds, and boost pumps, and attempted again and again to restart the dead engines. Only number four was still operating normally, and one engine cannot maintain an empty plane in level flight, to say nothing of one with a full load of cargo and half a load of fuel. Hightower, in the jump seat between the pilots, worked frantically with them to locate and remedy the trouble. Olsen clacked steadily away on his key, and back in the cargo compartment, Ventresca struggled to get the lashings off the heavy wooden boxes and shove them out the door to lighten the ship. And all the while the altimeter implacably unwound and the dark face of the sea loomed closer.

At 6000 feet, Machado punched the red feathering buttons[4] for number one, two, and three engines, and the big props twisted their blades into the airstream and stopped. The plunging descent leveled off slightly; the gauge now showed a loss of 500 feet a minute instead of nearly 800, but still the glide continued. While Gin held the plane straight and at the optimum speed,

Machado unfeathered each dead engine in turn, and attempted a restart. At 3000 feet, he ordered his crew into their life jackets, taking over the controls while Gin wiggled into his. Machado couldn't find his own jacket.

At 1000 feet, he ordered the crew to prepare for ditching. Olsen tapped out a final SOS, clamped down his key so that a single long dash began to be heard in all the listening receivers, then sat down on the deck behind Gin bracing himself for impact. Ventresca gave up his struggle with the cargo and wedged himself against a bulkhead as far aft as he could get. Bill Hightower left the jump seat and took the radio operator's position that Olsen had just left, swinging the seat around to face the tail.

The two pilots tightened their seat belts and braced their feet on the rudders. At 500 feet, they could make out the pattern of the swell on the dimly moonlit sea, and Machado took over the controls and banked left to parallel it. In a last-minute, nothing-to-lose effort, Gin unfeathered number three engine and was working throttle and mixture for a restart when the DC-4, nose high, its single good engine whining at absolute maximum power, ripped into the Pacific.

There was a banging jolt and a pause. Just as the first flicker of a thought which wanted to say, "That wasn't so bad and I'm still alive," began to enter the minds of the men, there came the final, sickening, sinking impact. Then after the strained howling of number four engine, the wind noise and the shouted commands—there was utter silence, and darkness, and water waistdeep in the cockpit.

It was the cold sea water around his

---

[4]**feathering button,** a device that turns the propeller blades to reduce wind resistance.

lower body that brought Machado to. His head ached and he could feel a welt across his forehead where he had slammed into the instrument panel. To his right, he could hear and dimly see Gin grunting and struggling, and he realized that the cargo, loosened by Ventresca in his attempt to jettison it, had slammed forward on impact, trapping Gin and Hightower under the heavy crates.

Reaching down into the rising water, Machado released his belt and bent down out of his seat to help Gin. By tugging alternately at the man and his crates, he got him loose and, working together, the two men then freed Hightower. The doorway to the cargo compartment where Ventresca was, was a broken, impassable jumble of wooden crates, but Olsen had already released the plastic astrodome in the plane's top, and one by one the four men who had been in the nose section crawled out. Gin and Hightower could feel the aluminum of the fuselage cool on their bare feet, having lost their shoes and socks in the struggle with the crates.

It was like riding the back of a dying whale. In the moonlight, the empty sea stretched all around them and the slow swell sloshed over the horizontal stabilizers and up onto the wings. Machado carefully made his way back until he was above the cargo door. He lay on his belly, and reached down but couldn't reach the handle. He banged on the top of the door with his fist and yelled.

"Ventresca! Hey, Dom! Dom! Open the door and get out fast! She's sinking!"

From beneath the shiny aluminum, they could all hear Ventresca's voice, calmer and steadier than any of them felt. "I can't see, Tony. Which way do I go?"

"Here, Dom, here!" Machado was still hammering with his clenched fist when the DC-4 lurched under them and was gone, and the four men were alone in the sea.

And yet they were not alone. A score of ship's bows had turned toward them. High in the air from where they had just fallen, the noses of a dozen planes homed in on their position. The air above them, although they could not hear it, buzzed and crackled with search and rescue orders. The long, electronic fingers of radars groped for them through the darkness.

The human beings closest to the Flying Tiger crew were the men aboard the *Steel Advocate,* and all that night, as she closed at the rate of a mile every three minutes, men on watch aboard the ship, or meeting as the watches changed, discussed the chances of rescue. The word quickly spread from a mate with a knowledge of aviation that the chances of a successful night ditching with only one engine turning out of four, were not good. There would probably be no time to launch life rafts, even if anyone survived the impact, so at the best they could only hope to have five tiny, dark heads in all that immensity of ocean as the objects of their search. Despite the pessimism, there was also determination. All sailors live with the thought of disaster at sea, and readily put themselves in the places of the shipwrecked and the lost.

At dawn, the *Steel Advocate*'s blunt bow was still a hundred miles away, but with daylight the air search could begin to have a chance. From Midway and Johnston, Oahu and Wake, Navy,

Air Force, and Coast Guard planes were converging on the crash position.

All things considered, it was not such a bad night for the men in the water. After the shock of the crash began to wear off, a kind of instinctive, blood-deep delight in their own survival dulled even their sorrow at the loss of Ventresca, and through the long night hours they bobbed and sloshed in a circle, facing each other at arm's length, laughing and joking at the ridiculousness of their situation. All were experienced airmen and all knew the magnitude of the effort that was being made to find and save them. The tropic sea, once they were used to it, was warm and not rough, and the air was clear and visibility good in the moonlight. Not one of the four doubted that rescue would come with daylight.

Tony Machado had reason to be more anxious than the others. He had no life jacket. All night he trod water, taking care to use just enough energy to keep his head out, and no more—but even working as easily as possible, there were times when he had to rest, wrapping arms and legs around one or another of the other men whose jacket would support them both for a while.

As the eastern sky began to lighten, and the four tiny human faces peered up hopefully out of that waste of water, it seemed that the faith in the Search and Rescue net which had kept up their spirits during the night would be justified. Over the rustle of the wavelets around them, they all heard the familiar and unmistakable hum of aircraft engines. The sound grew louder, faded, built again, and faded as the plane changed course and the wind broke and twisted the mutter of exhaust and spinning prop.

They didn't see the first plane—but the second, some thirty minutes later with the sun just breaking the horizon, they could make out clearly. At some 1500 feet it was obviously on a search mission. But it flew steadily on until it disappeared to the west, passing perhaps two miles north of the swimming men. The four survivors waved and splashed and could not help shouting— but then the sound of engines died out and there was only the slapping of the little waves and the breathy whisper of the sea breeze. Machado and Gin and Olsen and Hightower told each other there would be others, plenty of others, and one would be bound to sight them before long, they were sure of it.

Then, in a single, heart-sinking moment, it became desperately urgent that they be right.

Cruising only a hundred or so feet below the surface, looking upward hungrily for the dead or distressed creatures which were its prey, and which show up nicely against the sky, a ten-foot blue shark sighted the flash of bare, white feet, then eight dangling, waving human legs. The beast heard the splashings of the men—and planed upward to investigate.

His dorsal fin broke the surface perhaps twenty feet from the little knot of men. Warren Gin, who couldn't swim a stroke, saw it first and shouted a warning. The four airmen twisted to face the new danger, feeling their mouths go dry and their heartbeats increase as the shark circled. Frantically, they tried to remember all they had ever learned about sharks. Machado said that splashing and shouting would frighten them off, but Gin had heard

that they attacked anything wounded or in distress, and wouldn't splashing be a sign of distress?

The shark seemed to be in no hurry. Patiently, curiously, he circled, sometimes so closely they could almost touch him, sometimes farther out. Now the men's attention was divided between the circling beast and the sky which could hold deliverance.

In mid-morning, a dark-blue Neptune patrol plane swept overhead so low that they could read the Navy markings on its wings and tail—but it continued unswervingly on course, and a few minutes later two more fins joined the patient circler. That was when the crew began to pray.

The sharks edged in closer and began to snap at feet and legs. And as the planes flew by, unseeing, hope began to fade.

It was no fault of the men in the air that day that they came so close but never saw the Tiger crew. In all the vastness of the shifting, wind-ruffled, sun-flecked sea over which they were flying at some three miles every minute, the four dark heads, only inches across, were so tiny that a man could miss them if he blinked or sneezed or turned aside for one second for a gulp of coffee.

In mid-afternoon, with Gin and Olsen already bleeding in several places from shark bites and from the tearing sandpaper of the sharks' hides as they brushed by, the men saw the smudge

of a surface ship on the northern horizon. But after a few minutes she turned and they lost her. It was the *Steel Advocate*.

The big freighter, steering straight and navigating accurately, had arrived in the vicinity of the crash position at noon. Now, with every available man on look-out duty, she was executing a search pattern in the form of an expanding square, calculated so that with high-powered binoculars an observer should be able to sight a man in the water two and a half miles on either side. All afternoon she steamed slowly on her search plan, her men hoping and determined but half afraid they would find nothing. Dick Rausch rechecked his position with an observation of the sun at noon, and at twilight confirmed it with a five-star fix. As darkness fell, the vessel reduced speed to five knots and began to sweep the surface methodically with a 36-inch searchlight mounted on the bow.

As their second night began, the Tiger crew, hungry, thirsty, wounded, exhausted, chilled by now even in the 80-degree water, and still under sporadic attacks by half a dozen sharks, made up their minds to help themselves. They began the impossible 500-mile swim to Johnston Island. Feebly, they paddled to the southeast, resting and praying. Occasionally, a man would scream in pain as a shark clamped down on his foot or leg, and the others would come splashing and shouting to his aid. The shark would back off and the little foursome, trailing more blood now, and weaker, would resume its crippled crawling toward the land.

At some moment in that timeless nightmare of darkness, a shark killed Warren Gin. The others heard him groan and turned again to help, but his blood darkened all the moonlit sea around him, and in a few seconds he was dead. Tony Machado lifted his smarting eyes to the remote stars and offered a prayer for this man who only hours ago had been his partner in the near-miracle of flight. Then, sorrowfully, yet gratefully, Machado slipped the life jacket off his friend's body and shrugged into it himself. In the next second Gin was gone. Machado, Olsen, and Hightower resumed their hopeless marathon, while the *Steel Advocate,* somewhere over the horizon, swung her searchlight, and across the whole Pacific other ships and planes crisscrossed and groped, and the air pulsed with the waves of radio and radar as man fought for his own against the sea.

During the night the swells built up until the three survivors were now on a high peak in the full light of the moon, and now in a dark, watery valley from which they could see nothing. The *Steel Advocate* rolled and wallowed and her lookouts knew that if a swell shadowed the men as the light swept past, the ship would miss them.

By daylight of the second day, all three men knew that if rescue did not come before darkness, it would be too late. The sharks were still with them, and they were losing the strength to fight. A dozen planes flew past that morning, most of them commercial airliners diverted through the search area, but all were too high and none of them saw the three flyspecks on the horizon-to-horizon sea.

But a little after noon, a shout went up aboard the *Steel Advocate*—a lookout had sighted wreckage. The ship hove to, grappling hooks were lowered, and a 20" x 30" aluminum and plywood hatch cover was recovered. It was part of the DC-4. The ship's radio opened up and all the ships and planes within 500 miles turned and headed in. All sensed that they were in a race against the sun, that it was this afternoon or never.

But out in the narrow, lonely world a few inches above the sea's surface, where the little waves slap and choke and the sharks glide up to snap and tear, another man had already lost the race. Richard Olsen, starved, exhausted, and drained of half his blood, had quietly turned his face to the broiling sun and died. Machado and Hightower paddled feebly on with the sharks still circling, nipping, and worrying them.

In the early afternoon, the two men made out a ship in the distance and, with renewed strength, began swimming toward it. After a few minutes, it turned away. Four or five times it changed course, now toward, now away. Machado and Hightower were nearing the end of their endurance. Machado had one final prayer: "God," he said, "if it is Your will that I die or swim, let me know." When the next swell lifted him, he could see the ship clearly for the first time and she was backing down straight for them, "on as true a course," he said later, "as if God Himself were at the helm."

The *Steel Advocate* had seen them. A lifeboat was put over, with Dick Rausch in command. Its engine failed a few yards from the ship, but the men broke out the oars, and in a few minutes Machado looked out of salt-caked eyes to see human faces above him, felt himself hauled into the boat, and could only gasp, "My buddy, my buddy . . . over there."

Rausch maneuvered the boat alongside Hightower, and two men grabbed for him and got his chest and shoulders over the gunwale. There they froze in horror for a moment. A ten-foot shark had Hightower's left leg in his mouth and would not let go. Rausch jumped over the seats from his position at the tiller and, aiming carefully, emptied his .38 revolver into the fish's head. The shark's jaws opened and it slid downward in a cloud of blood. The men pulled Hightower into the boat.

Tony Machado, on the final edge of consciousness, looked straight up into the tropic sky and said very softly, "Thank you, God."   THE END

Talking it over

1. What "enemies" do the Flying Tiger crew have to fight?

2. What signs of courage do you see in the men as they face the prospect of ditching? Why don't they panic?

3. What do Machado's actions after the ditching tell you about him? Why is his situation more serious than that of the other survivors?

4. *a.* How did the sudden sinking of the plane make you feel? Why?

b. How would you rate Ventresca's courage? Explain your choice.
(1) little
(2) average
(3) much

5. *a.* Why were the men so sure they would be rescued? Why was rescue so long in coming?

b. What made their chances of survival less certain? What complicated the rescue at the last moment?

6. Which required more courage, preparing for ditching or awaiting rescue? Why?

7. Without modern science, how would the outcome have been different?

8. Select from the story a situation in which one of the men showed courage. How might his behavior have been different if he had not been courageous?

Words in action

1. "Near the center of the instrument panel on the left-hand gauge of a group of four, a needle wavered uncertainly and fell until it rested against a tiny peg labeled 'zero.' Number one engine had lost fuel pressure."

This quotation describes something the pilot sees. Can you see it, too? What words help make the picture clear?

2. "Over the rustle of the waves around them they all heard the familiar and unmistakable hum of aircraft engines."

What words help you hear the sounds the Tigers were hearing?

3. From the story, select passages that you feel are successful in making you aware of sights, sounds, or feelings. Be prepared to read the one you like best to the class and to explain why it seems real to you.

"Spare the rod and spoil the child," ma said.
I guess she licked me every day.

Spoil the Child

by Howard Fast

THE FIRST morning pa was gone, I tried to ride one of the mules. I didn't think that would hurt, because the mules were unharnessed anyway. But Maude told ma, and ma licked me. Ma was in the wagon, and she wouldn't have seen. I told Maude I'd remember.

Pa left about six in the morning

while ma still slept. "Goin' after meat?" I asked him. He had his rifle.

He nodded.

"Kin I go?"

"Stay with ma, sonny," he said. "She ain't well."

"You said I could hunt—"

"You stay with ma, sonny."

Maude got up a few minutes after that. I could see pa like a black dot out on the prairie. I pointed to him.

I said: "That's pa out there huntin'."
Maude was combing her hair, not paying a lot of attention to me. Then I tried to ride the mule. Pa would never let me ride his horse. It was only half-broken, cost four hundred dollars. Ma was always saying we could have lived a year on what that horse cost.

Maude woke ma. My mother was a tall, thin woman, tired looking. She wasn't well. I could see that she wasn't well.

"Dave, get off that mule," she said. "Where's pa?"

"Went out to hunt."

"Come here. Can't ever get it into your head to behave." I went over, and she slapped my face. "Don't bother them mules. When'll he be back? We can't stay here."

"He didn't say."

"Get some chips[1] for a fire," ma told me. "My land, I never seen such a lazy, shiftless boy." But she didn't say it the way she always did, as if she would want to bite my head off. She seemed too tired to really care.

I guess ma licked me every day. She said I was bad—a lot worse than you'd expect from a boy of twelve. You didn't expect them to be bad that young.

"You learn to leave the mules alone," Maude called.

"You shut up," I told her. Maude was fifteen, and pretty. She had light hair, and a thin, delicate face. Ma said that someday Maude would be a lady. She didn't expect much from me. She said I would be like pa.

I walked away from the wagon, looking for chips. By now, pa was out of sight, and where he had gone the prairie was just a roll of yellow and brown, a thread of cloud above it. It frightened me to be alone on the prairie. Pa laughed at it, and called it a big meadow. But it frightened me.

We had been on the prairie for a week now. Pa said in another few weeks we'd reach Fort Lee, due west. He said that if he had cattle stock, he'd settle down right on the prairie. This way, he'd cross the mountains, grow fruit,

[1] **chips,** pieces of dried buffalo dung, used for fuel by people on the prairie where there was no wood.

maybe, in California. Ma never believed much he said.

I went back to the wagon and started a fire. Ma had gone inside, and Maude sat on the driver's seat.

"You might gimme a hand," I told Maude.

"I don't see you overworking," Maude said.

"You'd better learn to shut up."

From inside the wagon, ma yelled: "You hold your tongue, Dave, or I'll wallop you!"

"You're a little beast," Maude said.

"You wait," I told her.

I went to the keg, drew some water, and set it up to boil. I could tell by the sound that there wasn't a lot of water left in the keg. Pa had said we'd reach water soon.

When I came back to the fire, I glanced up at the sky. It was an immense bowl of hot blue, bare except for a single buzzard that turned slowly, like a fish swimming. I guess I forgot. I kept looking up at the buzzard.

Ma climbed down from the wagon slowly. "You're the same as your pa," she said. "Lazy an' bad." Her face was tight-drawn. For the past few weeks she had hardly smiled, and now it seemed that she wouldn't smile again.

"And fresh," Maude said.

I put the water on the fire, not saying anything.

"Spare the rod and spoil the child," ma said.

Then her face twisted in pain, and she leaned against the wagon. "Well, don't stand there," she told me. "Water the mules."

I went to the keg. I knew there wasn't enough water for the mules. I hoped pa would come back soon; I had a funny, awful fear of what would hap-pen if he didn't come back soon. I kept glancing out at the prairie.

Pa had an itch in his feet. Ma said I would grow up the same way—having an itch in my feet. She was always sorry that she had married a man with an itch in his feet. Sometimes she said that the war had done it, that after the war between the North and the South, men were either broken or had to keep moving, like pa. Always west.

We lived in Columbus. Then we moved to St. Louis; then to Topeka. Pa couldn't stop, and ma got more and more worn out. She said that a wild land was no place to raise children. It was hard on ma, all right. Pa didn't do much, except when we were moving west, and then he would be like a different person. Ma never complained to him. She licked me instead.

I gave the mules enough water to cover the bottoms of their pails.

Ma came over, said: "That's not enough water."

"There ain't a damn sight more."

"Don't swear!" ma exclaimed. She clapped a hand across my head.

"He's always swearing," Maude said. "Thinks he's grown up."

Ma stared at me a moment, dully; then she went over and prepared breakfast. It was gruel and hardtack.

"Fresh meat would be good," ma said. She looked over the prairie, maybe looking for pa. I knew how much she cared for pa. She would talk a lot about itching feet, but that didn't matter.

After breakfast, I gave the mules some oats, and Maude cleaned up the dishes. I kept glancing at Maude, and she knew what I meant. She didn't care, until ma went back into the wagon. It hurt me to look at ma.

"He'll be back soon, I guess," ma said. Then she climbed into the wagon. It was a big sixteen-foot wagon, the kind they called freighters, with a hooped top, covered over with dirty brown canvas.

Maude said: "You leave me alone."

"I'll leave you alone now," I told Maude. "I gotta leave you alone now. Maybe you know what's the matter with ma?"

"That's none of your business," Maude said.

"It's my business, all right."

"You're just a kid."

I went to the back of the wagon and pulled out pa's carbine. It was the one he had used during the war, a short cavalry gun.

Ma saw me; she lay inside and I could hear her breathing hard. She said: "What're you up to now; pa back?"

"Not yet."

"Well, you tell me soon as he gets back. And don't get into any mischief."

"All right."

In front of the wagon, I sat down on a feed box, and cleaned the gun with an old rag. Maude watched me. Finally, she said: "I'm gonna tell ma you're fooling with pa's gun."

"You keep your mouth shut."

Ma groaned softly then, and we both turned around and looked at the wagon. I felt little shivers crawl up and down my spine. Where was pa? He should have been back already. I put down the gun and walked around the wagon. In a circle, the prairie rose and fell, like a sea of whispering yellow grass. There was nothing there, no living thing.

Maude was crying. "Why don't pa come back?" she said.

I didn't answer her. I guess it occurred to me for the first time that pa might not come back. I felt like crying. I felt like getting into a corner and crying. I hadn't felt so small for a long time. It would be a comfort to have ma lick me now. You get licked, and you know you're a kid, and you don't have to worry about anything else.

I said to Maude: "Go inside the wagon and stay with ma."

"Don't you order me around."

"All right," I said. I turned my back on her. I didn't hold much with girls when they're that age.

Then Maude went inside the wagon. I heard her crying, and I heard ma say: "You stop that crying right now."

I loaded the carbine. I untethered one of the mules, climbed onto it, and set out across the prairie in the direction pa had taken. I didn't know just what I'd do, but I knew it was time pa came back.

It wasn't easy, riding the mule just with harness straps. Mules have a funny gait. And we didn't go very fast. I was glad ma and Maude were in the wagon; otherwise ma would probably lick the pants off me.

In about a half hour, the wagon was just a tiny black dot. It might have been anything. I kept glancing at the sun to remember the direction I had taken. Then a swell hid the wagon. I kept going. I knew that if I stopped, even for a little while, I'd cry my head off.

I saw a coyote. He stood like a dog and watched me. An antelope hopped close, and I might have shot at him. But I couldn't bring myself to fire a rifle there. It would have done something to me.

I found pa. I guess I had been riding for about an hour when I saw him, over to one side. A buzzard flapped up, and

I felt my throat tighten until I thought it would choke me. I didn't want to go over to him. I got down from the mule, and I walked over slowly. But I didn't want to; something made me.

He was dead, all right. Maybe it was Indians and maybe it wasn't; I didn't know. He was shot four times, and his gun was gone.

The buzzard wouldn't go away; I shot the buzzard. I didn't cry. The carbine kicked back and made my shoulder ache. I was thinking about how pa always called me an undersized, freckled little runt. He said I wouldn't grow up. Maybe that's why I didn't cry.

I went away a little distance and sat down. I didn't look at pa. I tried to remember where we were, what pa had told me about going west. When I thought of ma, I had a sense of awful fear. Suppose it happened now.

The mule walked over and nuzzled my shoulder. I was glad the mule was there then. If he wasn't, I don't know what I would have done.

Pa had to be buried. I knew that men had to be buried, but I couldn't do it. The prairie was hard, baked mud. I went back to pa and stood over him; I guess that was the hardest thing I had ever done in my life. I straightened his clothes. I pulled off his boots. Men in the West were always talking about dying with their boots on. I didn't know how it meant anything, one way or another, but I thought pa would be pleased if he didn't have his boots on.

Then I climbed up on the mule and started back for the wagon. I tried not to think that I was twelve years old. If you get to thinking about that, then you're no good at all. When I got back, ma would lick me plenty.

The mule must have found its way back, because I didn't pay much attention to that. I let the reins loose, holding onto the harness straps, and I kept swallowing. Then I saw the wagon.

I thought: "I can't tell ma now—maybe later." Nobody had ever told me about a thing like that, but I knew it wouldn't do to tell ma now. I guess I only felt it instinctively, but I knew that the importance wasn't in pa any more. All that was important was life, and life was just a fleck of dust in the prairie. It was like a nightmare to think of the distance of the prairie, and how we were alone.

I rode up to the wagon, and Maude and ma were both standing next to it. I could tell from ma's face how worried she had been about me.

"There he is!" Maude screamed.

Ma said: "I guess there ain't nothing a body can do with you, Dave. Get off that mule."

I slipped off, tethered the mule. My whole body was twisted up with the strain of keeping what I had seen off my face. I came over to ma.

"Where you been?" she demanded.

"Hunting."

"I reckon there's nothing else for a little loafer like you. Spare the rod and spoil the child. Come here."

I went over and bent down, and she walloped me a bit, not too hard. She wasn't very strong then, I guess. I cried, but I wasn't crying because of the licking. I had had worse lickings than that and never opened my mouth. But it seemed to break the tension inside of me, and I had to cry. I went over and sat down with my back against one of the wagon wheels.

Maude walked past me and said: "I guess that learned you."

I just looked at her, without answering. I took out my jackknife and began to pare at one of the wagon boards. Then my eyes traveled to the water keg.

I got up and went around to ma. She was still standing there, staring off across the prairie in the direction pa had gone.

Without turning, she said to me: "Seen anything of your pa?"

"No."

The sun was westward now, a splotch of red that blazed the whole prairie into a fire. I could get a little of how ma felt; I could see the loneliness.

"Get a fire going," she said. "He ought to have enough sense to come back early. Stop that whimpering. God help a woman when a man has itching feet."

I gathered chips and started the fire. When I took the water from the keg for mush, the keg was just about empty. I didn't mention that to ma. She went about preparing supper slowly, awkwardly, and Maude watched her frightened.

Ma kept glancing at the west.

"Be dark soon," I said.

"Guess pa'll be here any minute," ma said dully. I could tell that she didn't believe that.

"I guess so," I nodded.

We ate without speaking much. Ma didn't eat a great deal. As soon as we had finished, she went into the wagon.

Maude was saying: "I don't see how I can clean dishes without water. You fetch some water, Dave."

"There ain't no water," I said.

Maude stared at me, her eyes wide and frightened. She had heard stories, just the same as I had, about pilgrims who ran out of water. She opened her mouth to say something.

"What about ma?" I asked her quietly, nodding at the wagon.

"Why don't pa come back?"

"Ain't no sense thinking about pa if he ain't here. What about ma? I guess it won't be long."

She shook her head.

"You don't need to be scared," I muttered. "It won't do no good to be scared. I reckon the worst part of this trip is over."

"Where's pa?" she whispered. "What happened?"

"How do I know what happened? You girls make me sick. I never seen anything to beat you girls."

I got up and went over to the water keg. I shook it, hoping, without having any reason to hope. I knew it was just about empty. We had plenty of food—dried meat and meal and dried beans—enough to last a month, I guess. But ma would need water.

Maude was crying.

"Why don't you go to bed?" I told her.

"Don't order me around."

"Well, you go to bed," I said. "Go in and sleep with ma. I'll stay out here."

"You're not big enough to stay out here alone," Maude said, but I knew she was afraid to stay inside the wagon with ma. I knew how she felt, and I didn't blame her for the way she felt, she was such a kid, with ma petting her all the time. We couldn't talk it over between ourselves, and that would have made it a lot better. But we couldn't.

"I'm plenty big enough," I said.

Inside the wagon ma groaned, and out on the prairie a coyote was barking. There's nothing like a coyote barking to make your insides crawl. I was all shivers, and I could see that Maude wanted to stay close to me. But that wouldn't have made it any better.

"Get in the wagon, damn you!" I cried. I was glad ma couldn't hear me swear. Ma would lick me good and plenty when I swore like that.

Surprised, Maude stared at me. Then, without a word, she went into the wagon.

I stood there, outside, for a while. It had grown quite dark. In the sky there was a faint, reflected light of the sun, but it was quite dark. I walked over to the wagon and picked up one of the mule blankets that hung on the shafts. It was a warm night, summertime; I decided to put the blanket under the wagon and lie down on it.

I heard Maude saying her prayers in the wagon, but no sound from ma. I couldn't say my prayers. Usually, ma saw to it that I did, but tonight I couldn't say a word aloud. I tried opening my mouth, but no words came out. I thought then, as much as I could. I tried not to think about pa. Spreading the blanket, I lay down on it, holding the carbine close to me. It seemed a part of pa and all that was left; I hugged it.

I couldn't sleep. I tried for a long time, but I couldn't sleep. It was quite dark now, with no moon in the sky. The mules were moving restlessly; probably because they wanted water.

I think I dozed a little. When I opened my eyes again, the moon was just coming up, yellow and bloated. I felt chilled thoroughly. Bit by bit, what had happened during the day came back, and now it was all more real than it had been in the daytime. While I lay there, thinking about it, I heard horses' hoofs; at first not noticing them, and only becoming aware of them when the

horses bulked out of the night, two men riding slowly.

They were in the moonlight, and I was hidden in the shadow of the wagon. They didn't see me. They stopped just about a dozen yards from the wagon, sitting on their horses and eyeing the mules. The mules moved restlessly.

When I realized they were Indians, I couldn't move, just lay there and watched them. They were naked to the waist, with their hair in two stiff braids to their shoulders. They both carried rifles.

I thought of pa. I thought of screaming to wake Maude and ma. I thought: "If they shot pa—"

They were cutting loose the mules.

I felt for the carbine, twisted around, so I lay on my belly. One of the men had dismounted and was coming toward the wagon. He held his gun in one hand and had drawn a knife with the other. I sighted the center of his breast and fired.

I remember how the sound blasted out the silence of the prairie. In the wagon someone screamed. The Indian stopped, seemed to stare at me, swayed a bit, and crumpled to the ground. I remembered the sharp pain in my shoulder from the blow of the recoil.

The mounted man's horse had wheeled about. He pulled it back, and fired at me. The shot threw sand in my face. I had a few cartridges and caps in my pocket, and I tried frantically to reload. The cartridges slipped through my fingers.

Then the Indian was gone. He had taken the other horse with him, and I heard their hoofs thundering across the prairie. I dropped the carbine. My shoulder ached terribly. Inside the

wagon, Maude was whimpering, my mother groaning.

I climbed from under the wagon. The Indian lay on his back, his face hard and twisted. I stood there, looking at him.

Maude climbed down out of the wagon. "What is it?" she cried. Then she saw the Indian and screamed.

"All right—I shot him."

She stood there, holding her hand to her mouth.

"You get back in the wagon. I guess he killed pa, all right. Don't tell that to ma."

She shook her head. Ma was groaning. "I can't go back," Maude said.

"Why?"

And then I knew. I should have known from the way ma was groaning. I went up to Maude and slapped her face. She didn't seem to feel it. I slapped her again.

"Get in there with ma."

"I can't—it's dark."

"Get in there!" I yelled.

We had lanterns on the outside of the wagon. I took one and lit it. I was trembling so much now. I gave the lantern to Maude, who was still standing the way she had been before.

"Go inside," I said.

Maude climbed into the wagon, taking the lantern with her. Then I cried. I crouched under the wagon, clutching the carbine and crying.

Finally, I went over to the Indian. I forced myself to do that. He lay half across the rifle he had carried. I pulled it out, and it was my father's rifle, all right.

I don't know how long I stood there holding the rifle. Then I put it under the seat, along with the carbine. I didn't want to look at the wagon.

I walked over to the mules, led them over to the shafts. It was hard to harness them. I had to balance myself on the shafts to get at their backs. When it was done, I ached all over, and my shoulder was swollen where the carbine had rested.

I climbed to the driver's seat. The curtains were down, and I couldn't see into the wagon, but the light still burned. Taking down pa's whip, I let it go onto the mules' backs. I had seen pa do that, and sometimes he let me try. The whip was fourteen feet long and I couldn't do much with it, but I got the mules moving. They had to keep moving. We had to find water.

At night, under the moon, the prairie was black and silver at the same time. Somehow, it didn't frighten me, the way it had during the day. I sat there thinking, I guess, of nothing at all, only awfully aware of the change inside me.

We drove on like that. I kept the mules at a slow pace, so the freighter wouldn't roll much. I was very tired, and after a while I didn't use the whip at all.

Then Maude came out of the wagon, sat down next to me. She looked at me and I looked at her, but she didn't say anything. She pressed close to me.

I whistled at the mules.

Inside the wagon something was whimpering. It made me tremble to hear that.

"Reckon we'll find water soon," I told Maude.

She nodded mechanically. Her head kept nodding and I dozed, myself. I guess I kept dozing through the night, fell asleep toward morning.

Maude woke me. The wagon had stopped, and the sun was an hour up. The mules had stopped on the bank of a slow, brown stream, lined with cottonwoods as far as I could see.

Maude was pointing at the water.

"Don't you start crying now," I said, rubbing my eyes.

"I won't," Maude nodded.

Ma called me, not very loud: "Dave, come here."

I climbed inside the wagon. Ma was lying on the bed, her arm curled around something. I peered at it.

"Do you know?" she said.

"I reckon I do. I reckon it's a boy. Girls ain't much use."

Ma was crying—not much; her eyes were just wetting themselves slowly.

"Where are we?" ma asked me.

"We been traveling through the night. There's a river out there. I guess we don't need to worry about water."

"All night—pa back?"

I said, slowly: "I killed an Indian last night, ma. He had pa's gun."

Then she just stared at me, and I stood there, shifting from one foot to another, wanting to run away. But I stood there. It must have been about five minutes, and she didn't say anything at all. The baby was whimpering.

Then she said: "You harnessed the mules?"

"Uh-huh. Maude didn't help me—"

Ma said: "You don't tease Maude. You don't tease Maude, or I'll take a stick to you. I never seen a boy like you for teasing."

"Uh-huh," I nodded.

"Just like your pa," ma whispered. "It don't pay to have a man whose heels are always itching—it don't pay."

"No use cryin'," I said.

Ma said: "What are we going to do?"

"Go on west. Ain't hard now to go a few hundred miles more. Reckon it won't be hard. Pa said—"

Ma was staring at me, her mouth trembling. I hadn't ever seen her look just like that before. I wanted to put my head down on her breast, hide it there.

I couldn't do that. I said: "Pa told me. We'll go west."

Then I went outside. I sat down on the wagon seat, looking at the river. I heard the baby making noises.

I said to Maude: "A man feels funny —with a kid."   THE END

Talking it over

1. *a.* What opinion does the mother have of her son? How does she treat him? For what things does she punish Dave?

b. What reason does the mother give for her actions? What does Dave think is the real reason for the lickings? Do you agree with Dave or with his mother?

2. *a.* How does Dave feel toward his mother? How do you explain his attitude?

b. What kind of person was his father? How can you tell?

c. What evidence is there of Dave's feeling toward his father?

3. *a.* Describe the feeling that seems to exist between the brother and sister. How do these two compare with brothers and sisters you know?   (*cont.*)

b. When in the story does the attitude of the girl change? What causes the change?

4. *a.* How does Dave feel about the prairie?

   b. What great fear haunts him through much of the story?

   c. Are his fears reasonable or do they indicate that he is a coward? Explain.

5. Describe several ways in which Dave shows courage. In which situations does he also experience fear?

6. Which statement best expresses the central idea of this story?

   a. It takes courage to accept responsibility before you are ready.

   b. Parents could help their children better if they themselves had more courage.

   c. Brave people were responsible for the settling of the West.

⇄ **Words in action**

(A) At one point in the story, the boy rides out on the prairie alone. As he looks back, he sees that a "swell" hides the wagon from his sight. What would a swell on the prairie be? How would this swell compare with the swell mentioned in "The Tigers and the Sharks"?

(B) Using clues from context and structure, try to figure out what the words in bold type mean in the sentences below. Be ready to explain what clues helped you.

1. Some people thought he was a **shiftless** boy, but really he worked hard.
2. He had never ridden a horse, but he could ride a **mule** bareback, and that was hard to do because of the peculiar **gait** of the animal.
3. When a person fires a gun, sometimes the **recoil** hurts his shoulder.
4. A person who sees he is about to step on a snake will usually **recoil instinctively.**
5. When hours of worry or fear have tightened a person's feelings, crying will often help break the **tension.**

He feels deeply about freedom

Howard Fast is best known for his stories and novels about periods of crisis in American history. He is a man who feels deeply the importance of human freedom, and he writes so powerfully about it that the reader often feels himself a part of the struggle. A book of his that can bring to life for you the struggle for freedom in the American Revolution (1776) is *Haym Salomon.*

Fast has often been honored for his skill in reviving the past. In 1962 he won the Secondary Education Board's annual book award.

RESCUE

One man buried alive for two weeks, and the

whole nation waiting for news . . .

A television play by David Shaw

RESCUE, a Television Play by David Shaw, based on Pulitzer Prize-winning news dispatches by William Burke Miller. Reprinted by permission of Ashley Famous Agency, Inc., from *Best T.V. Plays of the Year*, Volume III, edited by William I. Kaufman, published by Merlin Press, Inc., New York City. Copyright 1954 by William I. Kaufman. Originally produced by Philco Television Playhouse over the National Broadcasting Company Television.

CAUTION: Professionals and amateurs are hereby warned that *Rescue* being fully protected under the copyright laws of the United States of America, the British Empire, including the Dominion of Canada, and all other countries of the Copyright Union, is subject to royalty. All rights, including professional, amateur, motion picture, recitation, lecturing, reading in public, radio broadcasting, television, and the rights of translation into foreign languages are strictly reserved. All inquiries for rights should be addressed to the author's agent, Ashley Famous, 1301 Avenue of the Americas, New York City, N.Y., and William Burke Miller, c/o NBC, 30 Rockefeller Plaza, New York, N.Y.

CHARACTERS

Actual People:

William Burke (Skeets) Miller, *21-year-old reporter on the Louisville Courier-Journal*
Floyd Collins, *a Kentucky cave guide*
Homer Collins, *his brother*
Neil Dalton, *city editor of the Louisville Courier-Journal*
H. T. Carmichael, *superintendent of a mining company*
Everett Maddox, *a coal miner*

In addition, there are various fictitious characters who appear briefly.

ACT I

(FADE IN ON *a detailed automobile map of the "Cave Country" of Kentucky.* CAMERA GRADUALLY FOCUSES ON *the name "Cave City."*)

Announcer (*narrating over shot*): This is Kentucky. This is where it happened. This is "sink-hole" country, honeycombed with caves and fissures beneath the rocky ground. This is where a man named Floyd Collins lay buried alive for two weeks, while a nation held its breath. . . .

(CAMERA HAS MOVED IN ON *the black dot marking the exact location of the cave.* FADE TO *the black hole which is the mouth of the cave, about five feet in diameter.* CAMERA PULLS BACK SLOWLY *out of cave mouth which is at the bottom of a wedge-shaped ravine.*

Above the ravine is a cornfield, barren except for the scraggly cornstalks which stand brokenly against the white patches of snow.)

Announcer (*over the shot*): This is the story of Floyd Collins and the story of the man whose efforts to save him represented the hopes of an entire nation. . . . This is the true story!

(*A boy of fourteen is seen coming across the cornfield in the early morning. He scrambles down the sloping ravine, stands up and looks around curiously. As he looks at the cave mouth, a slightly frightened look comes into his eyes. He approaches the cave cautiously, stopping at the entrance. He listens.*)

Boy (*calling tentatively*): Floyd!

(*The voice reverberates hollowly down into the cave. The youngster starts into the cavern hesitantly.*)

Boy: Floyd!

(*He listens again. Then he goes deeper into the darkening cave, stepping into muddy puddles as he goes. He reaches a point where he is forced to get down on his knees to advance. He crawls a few feet and then stops, fright plain in his eyes, and whimpers.*)

Boy: I'm scared. . . . (*He waits, then shouts tremulously.*) Floyd . . . Floyd Collins!

(*The name echoes and re-echoes as it travels downward into the black void. After a few seconds, a voice is heard, as though from a distant grave.*)

Floyd: Help!

Boy (*more frightened than ever*): Is— is that you, Floyd?

Floyd: Get help! I'm trapped down

here! Can you hear me? I'm trapped. Go get help!

(DISSOLVE TO *a door marked "City Room."*[1] *Miller enters and opens door. He walks quickly to the desk of Neil Dalton, the city editor.*[2] *Dalton is speaking into the telephone.*)

Dalton: All right, Michaels, I'll switch you over to rewrite. Yeah. (*Jiggles phone.*) Switch this to Browning. (*Hangs up phone. Notices Miller.*) Well? Miller, how did you make out?

Miller: No dice. They refuse to send the rescue squad.

Dalton: Any reason?

Miller: Just that the taxpayers of Louisville aren't supporting a rescue squad to save lives in Cave City . . . a hundred miles away.

Dalton: Okay, Skeets. I got another assignment for you. There's been a shooting reported over on—

Miller (*incredulously*): Another assignment? But what about this guy in the cave?

Dalton: All right, what about him?

Miller: You can't drop the story just like that, Neil.

Dalton: Listen, Skeets, we're only trying to put out a newspaper, not to be the conscience of the world. If you had convinced the rescue squad to go down there it might've made a nice story. But this way—so a guy gets trapped in a cave. It's happened before; it'll happen again. Now about this shooting—

(*A copy boy*[3] *enters with a newspaper and lays it on Dalton's desk.*)

Copy boy: Bulldog edition[4] of the *Herald,* Mr. Dalton.

Dalton: Thanks. (*Boy exits. Dalton scans paper.*) Well—let's see if we've been scooped[5] on anything today. . . .

Miller: Listen, Neil, why don't you send me down to Cave City to—

Dalton (*frowning as he reads*): You're going to cover that shooting.

Miller: But—what about that guy in the cave?

Dalton: But nothing. There's no more story in Cave City. (*He slams newspaper down on desk disgustedly and picks up phone.*) Get me our "great" correspondent in Cave City. Right away. . . .

Miller: What happened?

Dalton (*to Miller*): These country correspondents give me a swift pain in the—Hello. Asleep? Well, wake him up . . . Yeah, I'll hold here. Read our competition to find out.

(*He shoves newspaper across the desk toward Miller. Miller takes paper and reads.*)

Miller: "Collins, freed, says never again." Well, that's good news.

Dalton (*irritatedly*): Great!

Miller: What's the matter with you?

Dalton: We've been scooped; that's all. (*into phone*) Hello, Jenkins? . . . Neil Dalton . . . I just saw the *Herald* story on Floyd Collins and I'd like to know where the devil you were when they freed him? I—What? . . . You sure? . . . I see. All right, you stay on the job there and let me know when something breaks . . . Yeah. (*He hangs up phone.*) He says

---

[1]**City Room,** department in a newspaper office where local news is gathered and written.

[2]**city editor,** responsible for a newspaper's coverage of local news. He makes assignments to reporters.

[3]**copy boy,** errand boy in a newspaper office.

[4]**Bulldog edition,** earliest edition of a morning paper.

[5]**see if we've been scooped,** see if a rival newspaper has published an important story ahead of us, or gotten information we didn't get. [Journalism slang]

he just came from there. He says Collins is still trapped.

Miller: Why don't you send me down there, Neil? At least you'll get the straight story.

Dalton (*musing*): At least to know what's going on . . . .

Miller (*eagerly*): Then I can go?

Dalton (*after a pause*): All right, Skeets. There's a train around seven tonight. But you have the assignment on one condition—no monkey business. I know you're just a twenty-one-year-old kid with a lot of fool notions, but remember: we're not paying you twenty-five bucks a week to risk your neck. Don't go in that cave!

Miller: Me? Go in a cave? Do I look crazy?

Dalton: Now get going. (*Sits down to get back to work.*) And give us the straight story.

(FADE OUT TO *shot of a small campfire with a coffee pot boiling above it. Three people are huddled around the fire. One is the young boy of the first scene. Another is his father, a typical farmer of the Kentucky hill country. The third is Homer Collins, aged thirty. His clothes are wet and sticky, his face mud-splattered. The three watch the coffee pot mutely.*)

Homer (*after a pause, lifts the coffee pot and pours the steaming liquid into three tin cans*): Guess we's about ready now.

Farmer (*gingerly sipping his*): Bet this coffee tastes better to you than to us even, Homer. You bein' wet an' all.

Homer: Floyd's a lot wetter an' colder than I am an' he ain't drinkin' coffee neither.

Farmer: Maybe you can take him some after you finish yourn.

Homer: Be ice cold by the time I got it down to him. Anyways, it's too narra in there to be carryin' coffee.

Boy (*looking toward top of ravine*): Looka!

Farmer: Who's that?

Boy: I dunno.

Farmer: Stranger. I never seen him before.

Miller (*calling down*): Morning!

Homer (*without turning*): What's he want?

Farmer: Looks like a city feller. Pretty little, too.

(*Miller scrambles down the ravine.*)

Miller: Is this the cave where Floyd Collins is trapped?

Boy: It sure is. I was the one who found him in the cave. I . . .

Homer: Pay him no mind, boy.

(*The three go silently back to their coffee.*)

Miller (*after an awkward silence*): Coffee smells good.

Homer: He'p yourself, if you c'n find a tin can.

Miller: I doubt if I'll find a can around here.

Homer: I'll be finished with mine in a minute. You c'n use it if you want.

Miller: Thanks. I haven't eaten since yesterday and after sitting up all night in a train a cup of coffee would sure hit the spot.

Homer: Floyd ain't had anythin' hot for two days.

Miller: How is he? I mean—he's still alive, isn't he?

Homer: He's still alive.

Miller: Are you sure about that?

(*Homer looks at him contemptuously and goes back to drinking.*)

Farmer (*to Miller*): He ought to be sure. He just seen Floyd a coupla minutes ago.

Miller (*to Homer*): You saw him?

Homer: Who are you, mister?

Miller: My name's Miller. I'm a reporter from the Louisville *Courier-Journal.*

Homer: Reporter, eh?

Farmer: I told you he looked to me like a city feller.

Homer: How come they make a young kid like you a reporter?

Miller: I'm twenty-one.

Boy: Maybe he'll put all our pictures in the papers, Homer.

Farmer (*to Miller*): This here's Homer Collins, Floyd's brother.

Miller: Glad to meet you. Would you answer a few questions, Mr. Collins?

Homer: Mebbe.

Miller: Why did your brother go into this cave in the first place?

Homer: Floyd makes his livin' goin' into caves. He's a tourist guide.

Miller: Guess you don't get many tourists around here. They all go to Mammoth Cave,[6] don't they?

Homer: Floyd thinks mebbe this here's another entrance to Mammoth. Y'know they found another entrance over there some years back and this here cave is on the same ridge.

Farmer: This is my property and Floyd and I are goin' to split fifty-fifty if this is another entrance. Make lots of money out of it if it is.

Miller: How did Floyd get stuck in there?

Homer: It's a pretty narrow passage an' a big rock fell on his leg. Got him trapped.

Farmer: Don't worry about Floyd. He'll work hisself loose.

Miller: But if he's pinned—

---

[6] **Mammoth Cave,** a huge limestone cavern in central Kentucky which attracts thousands of tourists each year; made a National Park in 1936.

Farmer: Floyd's been trapped before in caves. Twicet. He always wiggled out before. He'll do it again, I reckon.

Boy: He's the best cave guide in the state, Floyd is.

Miller: How can he possibly get out if he's pinned under a rock?

Homer: 'Stead of askin' so many questions, Mister, why don't you go down an' see Floyd fer yourself?

Miller (*uneasily*): Go down—there?

Homer: Sure. I expect you're little enough to squeeze through the narrow places.

Miller: I—I don't know very much about caves.

Homer: 'Tain't much you have to know. Jest feel your way down 'til you reach him. You ain't a-scared, are you?

Miller (*unconvincingly*): Of course not. But I—

Homer (*putting down his coffee and starting toward the cave*): Then, come on.

Miller: Are you going with me?

Homer: Jest part of the way. Ain't room enough for two of us after a piece. (*Miller hesitates and looks at the farmer and the boy almost pleadingly.*)

Homer (*turns at the cave mouth and calls to Miller*): You comin', Mister?

Miller (*after a soul-searching pause*): Sure . . . Sure, I'm coming. (*Miller walks to Homer and together they enter the cave mouth.*

Cut to cave interior. After a few steps Homer drops to his knees and Miller follows suit.)

Homer: Guess I should've warned you. It's pretty wet in here. You're goin' to spoil that suit of yours.

Miller: That's all right. (*They crawl a bit further and Homer stops.*) Are we close?

Homer: We hardly started, Mister. Floyd's about a hundred an' twenty feet down . . . . Want to keep goin'?

Miller: Yes.

Homer: I'm turning back here. Jest keep goin'. You'll find Floyd, all right.

Miller: It's—so dark down there.

Homer: There's only one way down. You won't get lost. Here, take my flashlight.

Miller (*takes flashlight*): Thanks.

(*Homer moves to crawl back. Stops.*)

Homer: Oh. I'm obliged to you for takin' all this interest in my brother. . . . I'll see you outside in a little while.

(*Homer crawls out. Miller watches him, then turns and faces the black tunnel ahead of him. He takes a deep breath, shudders with cold, and, falling on his stomach, starts to squirm down into the passage.*

CAMERA FOLLOWS HIM *while the narrator speaks over shot.*)

Narrator: And so started one of the strangest and most harrowing journeys of our time. A young reporter risks his life to reach a man he doesn't know and has never seen. A stranger trapped.

(SUPERIMPOSE OVER SHOT OF *Miller the front page of a newspaper containing Miller's first dispatch.*)

Narrator: Here is William Burke Miller's first report to the world on Floyd Collins: "Cave City, Kentucky, February 2, 1925—* * * From here on I had to squirm like a snake. Water covers almost every inch of the ground, and after the first few feet I was wet through and through. Every moment it got colder. It seemed that I would crawl forever."

(TAKE OUT NEWSPAPER SUPERIMPOSITION.)

Miller (*shouting, his voice re-echoing*): Collins! . . . Collins, can you hear me?

(*No response. The only sound is the dripping water and Miller's heavy breathing. Miller resumes his journey.*)

Narrator: "The dirty water splashed in my face and numbed my body, but I couldn't stop. . . ."

(*Miller squirms on in silence. He reaches a downward bend in the channel and his body slides, lubricated by the oozing mud until he bumps into something soft. A pained, muffled moan is heard. Miller gasps, frightened, and brings his light around to see.*)

Miller: Collins!

(*He focuses the light on Collins' face. It is covered by a small piece of burlap which Miller lifts in order to see the face.*)

Collins: Put it back. Put it back—the water!

(*Miller turns his flashlight upward, to a spot above Collins' head where he sees a place on the tunnel roof from which a drop of water falls every few seconds.*)

Narrator: "Then I noticed a small drip-drip-drip from above. Each drop struck Collins' face. The constant dripping almost drove him insane. His brother had taken the burlap to him earlier in the day."

Collins: The leg. It hurts—hurts awful.

(*Miller backs away and shines the flashlight on his face again.*)

Narrator: "I realized then that something must be done before long if this man is to live."

(FADE OUT ON *Collins' suffering face.*
DISSOLVE TO *shot of papers coming*

Floyd Collins trapped in cave.

off the presses. OVER SHOT SUPERIM-POSE *headline and byline:*

Reporter Contacts Floyd Collins in Cave
by Wm. Burke Miller

DISSOLVE TO *phone ringing in Miller's hotel room. It rings for a long time. Miller, still fully clothed, is lying on top of the blanket in deep sleep. Finally he hears the ringing and staggers over to the phone.*)

Miller (*on phone*): Yes?

(CUT TO *Dalton at his desk speaking into phone.*)

Dalton: What about this Floyd Collins? Do you think he'll be able to get out?

Miller (*after a pause*): I doubt it. He's stuck in that passage like a cork in the neck of a bottle. . . . Sure, keep trying to get the rescue squad. We've got to try everything.

(CUT TO *Dalton.*)

Dalton: Do you want to come back here? You sound pretty tired. I can send another man down there.

(CUT TO *Miller.*)

Miller: I'm staying here, Neil. I'm going to try to get Floyd Collins out of that cave. Okay?

(*He hangs up.* CUT TO *Dalton jiggling receiver hook.*)

Dalton: Right. Get me Burdon at the Fire Department. Fast!

(*Copy boy enters with some papers.*)

Boy: Here are the morning releases, Mr. Dalton.

Dalton: Never mind that. I want you to go in and tell the boss that I'm leaving. I don't know when I'll be back.

Boy: Leaving, Mr. Dalton?

Dalton: You heard me. Now go—(*on phone*) Hello, Burdon? Dalton. Did you see Miller's story on Floyd Col-lins this afternoon? . . . What? . . . No, don't leave right away. Wait'll I get over there. Right.

(*Hangs up and grabs his hat and starts for the door.*)

Boy: Don't you think you'd better tell the boss yourself, Mr. Dalton?

Dalton: If he wants to see me, tell him my new address is Sand Cave, Kentucky. So long.

(*He leaves and the copy boy looks after him open-mouthed.*

DISSOLVE TO *the map seen in Scene One.* CLOSE-UP *of the area surrounding Cave City. Now* CAMERA STARTS TO PULL BACK, *revealing larger and larger area. It begins to cross state lines and slowly covers the whole nation.* OVER THIS SHOT ARE SUPERIMPOSED *the following headlines:*

Floyd Collins Still in Cave

Young Reporter Will Make Second Descent into Sand Cave

DISSOLVE TO *Collins trapped in cave.* CLOSE-UP *of his face. We see that he has a rubber tube in his mouth on which he is sucking.* CAMERA FOLLOWS *the tube upward until it sees the other end in a bottle of milk. Miller is holding the bottle in one hand. His other hand is holding the tube so that he can pinch off the flow of milk. Suddenly Collins gets too much milk and starts to choke. Miller pinches the tube. Collins' coughing subsides.*)

Miller: Want some more?

Collins: That's enough, fellow.

Miller: Feel any better?

Collins: Yeah. Better. . . . How long have I been down here?

Miller: Three and a half days. It's Monday night now.

Collins: Three and a half days of prayin' to God to get me out of this.

Miller: We'll get you out, Floyd.

Collins: With both my feet. I want to get out with both my feet, fellow.

Miller: Sure. . . . Does the leg hurt much?

Collins: Let's—let's talk about somethin' else. When I start thinkin' about the pain . . . (*wincing in agony*) . . . I try not to think about the leg. Or about dyin'. I jest keep prayin' whenever I'm conscious. Keep thinkin' about Heaven, too.

Miller: There are a lot of people praying with you, Floyd—a lot of people.

Collins: Can't you do something to free my leg, fella? Can't somebody do something? I can't stand the pain much more, fellow. I've faced death before. It doesn't frighten me, but it's so long. Oh, God, be merciful.

Miller (*softly*): God be merciful. (FADE OUT.)

↻ **Talking it over**

1. *a.* Why does Floyd Collins go into the cave in the first place?

b. How serious is his accident? What details in the play make you feel how uncomfortable he must be?

2. What is the first reaction of the following people when they learn that Collins is trapped and needs help?

   a. the residents of Louisville in general

   b. Dalton

   c. Miller

3. *a.* Why does Miller go into the cave the first time?

b. Why does he continue going in later on?

c. What changes in attitude do you notice in Dalton and the people of Louisville? Why do these changes occur?

⇄ **Words in action**

Actors must learn lines and follow the directions given in the script of a play. If you were preparing to play the part of the young boy who discovers that Floyd is trapped in the cave, you would have to understand the following directions. Use the Glossary if you need help with the words in bold type.

1. (*He approaches the cave* **cautiously** . . . .)

2. (*calling* **tentatively**):

3. (. . . *starts into the cavern* **hesitantly**.)

4. (*He waits, then shouts* **tremulously**.)

If you follow these directions, will you:

—(*a*) hurry up to the cave, or (*b*) act as if you are a little afraid of the cave?

—call Floyd's name (*c*) as if you are sure he is in there, or (*d*) as if you aren't sure he is there?

—start into the cave (*e*) as if you aren't sure you want to go in, or (*f*) as if you are eager to go?

—shout (*g*) in a shaky voice, or (*h*) in a firm tone?

ACT II

(FADE IN ON *Collins, still trapped. A small chip hammer is banging away at the rock near him. Miller is using the hammer as best he can within the confines of the narrow tunnel.*)

Announcer: "Special to the Louisville *Courier-Journal*. By William Burke Miller. Sand Cave, Cave City, Kentucky. February 3—I have been in the cave three times since 5:30 o'clock this afternoon at the head of as many rescue parties. I am very small and able to get back to the prisoner with the least possible difficulty. I am confident we are working now on a plan that will save Collins' life, and Collins shares my views. Our plan is simple. Thirteen other men crawl in behind me and pass a small chip hammer along to me. With this I work as best I can enlarging the cave and, as soon as I have succeeded in getting loose a large piece, I pass it back to the men behind me and, in this way, it is relayed out to the entrance."

(SHOT OF *Miller chipping off a piece of rock and passing it back close to his body to the next man. Camera follows the small rock-chip as it passes from man to man. It is with the greatest difficulty that even this is accomplished in the small confines of the passage.*

CUT TO *cave mouth, exterior, with many men around it looking into cave.*)

Voice (*calling from inside cave*): Stand clear out there!

(*The small knot of men separates and we see the small rock-chip as it emerges from the cave after the last man has hurled it. It is a painfully small reward after all the effort that has gone into getting it.*

Immediately, and from all angles, many people dive for the little piece of rock, like baseball fans grabbing for a foul ball that has been hit into the stands. They fight each other for the rock furiously until one man wrests it from the others and dashes off with it, triumphantly waving it over his head. The others follow him off. Neil Dalton and Homer have been watching.)

Homer: What do they want with them?

Dalton: Souvenirs, Homer. You'll find people like that any time something unusual happens. They collect like flies around a garbage pail.

Homer: We ought to chase them away.

Dalton: They've just begun. There'll be more of them, by the thousands, they'll bring their kids and their sweethearts. They'll come on foot and in old jalopies. They'll pitch tents and open hot-dog stands. I hear the railroad is running special sightseeing trains from Louisville, loaded with the curious people who will come to gape and stare and collect souvenirs if they can.

(DISSOLVE TO *newspaper headlines:*

Thousands at Sand Cave

Collins Still in Tomb

Rescue Work Continues

DISSOLVE TO *interior of a tent at Sand Cave. An operator is sending out Morse code and a reporter named Maxwell is standing above him holding a few sheets of paper in his hand.*)

Maxwell (*impatiently*): Say, am I ever going to get this story filed?

Operator (*still working*): As soon as I get Skeets Miller's story out.

Maxwell: Listen, Buster, I'm as much of a reporter as Skeets Miller. How come he gets all this special attention? My story's as good as his. Maybe better.

Operator: Miller filed his an hour ago. You just came in.

Maxwell: He's making a real hero out of himself out of this story, isn't he? Big shot! Skeets Miller! That's all I've heard since I hit this burg.

Operator: Miller deserves all the credit he's getting.

Maxwell: Maybe he'll get more than he bargained for when this story of mine gets printed.

Operator: What do you mean?

Maxwell: Never mind, Buster. You just get Miller's story out of the way and—

(*Miller enters the tent with his story.*)

Miller (*to operator*): Got another dispatch for you, Ray.

Operator: Okay, Skeets, but it won't go out for at least a half hour.

Miller: Good enough.

Maxwell: I thought you were down the hole chipping rock away, Miller.

Miller: We had to stop. It's too slow that way.

Maxwell: That's funny. I thought the longer it took to pull Collins out of there, the better you'd like it.

Miller: What does that mean?

Maxwell: As long as Floyd Collins is trapped in that cave, you're the big hero around here. Once Collins is free you're just a nobody again!

(*Miller stares at Maxwell incredulously, then decides to ignore him.*)

Miller (*turns to operator*): Will you see that that story's filed, Ray?

Maxwell: You didn't tell me what you thought of my theory, Miller.

Miller: I think less of your theory than I do of you, mister, and that's mighty little.

Maxwell: All right, I have another theory which you might like better. How come that you're the only reporter around here who's actually seen Floyd Collins in that cave?

Miller: I'm the only reporter small enough to fit down there.

Maxwell: Then how do we know what you're telling us is the truth?

Miller: You don't. You just have to take my word. Unless—unless you'd like to come down in the cave with me.

Maxwell: You know you don't want me down there, Miller. I might see things you don't want known.

Miller: Things like what?

Maxwell: I'll give it to you straight, Miller. I don't think Floyd Collins is in that cave at all.

Miller: Of course not. I just keep risking my neck going down there because I love caves so much.

Maxwell: It's been worth it to you. You're getting all the glory. In my opinion this is all a big hoax you've cooked up about a guy stuck in a cave. I've got to give you credit, though, because it's a honey of an idea. But the picnic's just about over for you, Miller. This story—(*waving his papers*)—is going to expose you and your whole rotten scheme.

(*Homer enters tent.*)

Homer: Skeets, we got the small jack now. You ready to go down?

Miller (*looking straight at Maxwell*): Yes, Homer. I'm coming.

(*He turns and leaves. Maxwell watches him, then turns to the operator who has stopped his work.*)

Maxwell (*irritably to operator*): Well —get busy on that key, Buster. I want this story to hit the morning papers. . . .

(DISSOLVE TO *newspaper headlines:*

**Skeets Miller Accused of Hoax—
Doubt Floyd Collins Trapped**

**Call National Guard to Keep
Order at Sand Cave**

**H. T. Carmichael Named
to Direct Rescue Operations**

FADE TO *a medium close shot of Carmichael and Miller standing at the mouth of the cave. Carmichael is a big, hulking man with a calm, kind face.*)

Carmichael: My name's Carmichael and I'm superintendent of the Kentucky Asphalt Company. I've been reading your reports about this cave, but I want to get some more of the facts. I've brought seven of my own drillers along with me to dig a shaft down to Collins and maybe pull him out that way.

Miller: Sounds like a good idea, Mr. Carmichael.

Carmichael: Now you've been in that cave as much as anyone, Miller. Tell me, just as nearly as you can, exactly how this cave is laid out.

Miller: I'll try. I'll show you a sketch I made. (*Picks up a twig and starts to draw a diagram in the damp sand.* CAMERA GOES IN CLOSE *on diagram during next speech.*) There's an eighty foot drop just inside the mouth. After that there's a fairly level place. A few feet of that and then it gets very small and narrow. So narrow there you have to let your breath out to fit through. Collins is lying on his side. Down here. His left leg is caught by a big rock and his left arm is pinned under him.

Carmichael: What about the other arm? Can he use that?

Miller: Very slightly. You see, the tunnel is so narrow that the moment he tries to lift it, it hits the roof. He's just about helpless.

Carmichael: I see. . . . Seems to me the only thing to do is sink a new shaft down to him.

(*Carmichael and Miller have been squatting over the diagram.*)

Maddox (*off screen*): No, Mr. Carmichael, a shaft is out.

Carmichael: Oh, Maddox, this is Skeets Miller.

Miller (*shaking hands with Maddox*): Hello.

Carmichael: This is Everett Maddox. He's a coal miner fom Central City. (*to Maddox*) Why no shaft?

Maddox: I've just been surveying the ground. The whole area is full of sandstone. I'm afraid that the vibrations of the drills would collapse the passage completely.

Carmichael: That's a rotten break. All right, we'll have to try to get to him through the cave itself.

Miller: It's not big enough down there for your men to work, Mr. Carmichael.

Carmichael: We'll make it big enough. We'll start right from the mouth and work in. Make it bigger all the way down until we reach Collins. (*to Maddox*) Just be sure to shore it up every foot of the way so she doesn't cave in on you.

Miller: How long will that take?

Carmichael: I don't know. Maybe a week, maybe a month, who knows. It depends on what the ground's like down there.

Miller: I don't think Collins can hang on much longer. He's pretty weak now.

Carmichael: I'm still open to suggestions.

Miller: I'd like your permission to keep

Left to right: Floyd Collins' sister, father, and brothers Homer and Marshall.   UPI Photo

on going down to try to release Collins some other way. It won't interfere with your men.

Carmichael: Sure. Go in as much as you like, Miller. I'm not particular who does it or how. Let's get Collins out of there.

(DISSOLVE TO *a small generator just outside the cave mouth, a rope wound around its flywheel. A man's hand pulls the rope hard. The motor sputters a few times and then starts, chugging away noisily.*

CAMERA SLOWLY FOLLOWS *the wires leading from the generator into the mouth of the cave and down through the torturous route. At fifteen-foot intervals are light bulbs which glare harshly in the small, muddy tunnel.* CAMERA PANS ALONG *the strung lights until it reaches a bulb just above Collins' head.*

We get a good look, for the first time, at Collins' tortured face. He seems asleep at first. Slowly, because of the light, his eyelids start to flutter. Then he blinks a few times, the bright light hurting his eyes.)

Collins (*when his eyes can finally focus, looks up to see Miller crouching above him holding the bulb*): Hello, fellow.

Miller: How's it going, Floyd?

Collins: All right, I guess.

Miller: Is the light too bright for you?

Collins: No. It feels good. Could you leave it here when you go back up?

Miller: Sure. . . . Unless we're able to take you out with us this trip.

Collins: I'll never get out of this. I'm half dead already.

Miller: Take it easy, Floyd. (*Calls over his shoulder.*) Homer!

Homer's voice: Yeah?

Miller: We're ready for the jack down here. Pass the word on back.

Homer's voice: Send down the jack! Pass the word!

Voice (*far off*): Send down the jack!

Collins: What are you fixing to do now?

Miller: We're bringing an automobile jack down, Floyd. We're going to try to jack the rock off your foot.

Collins: You've tried just about everything else; you might as well try that, too.

Miller: I think it'll work, Floyd.

Collins: Did you bring the whiskey down like I asked you to? I'm freezing.

Miller: Yes, I've got it.

(*He struggles to pull flask out of his pocket. He raises Collins' head so that it rests on his knee, then puts flask to Collins' mouth. Collins takes a long gulp, then turns his head away.*)

Collins: That feels better. Maybe you'd better take a drink yourself. Your leg's shivering.

Miller: It's pretty cold down here.

Collins: Next time you're up top, tell 'em to cover the mouth of the cave with a piece of canvas. A trick I used. It'll make it a lot warmer for you when you're in here. Give me another drink, will you?

Miller: Sure. (*He does so.*) Tell me, Floyd, when you were exploring around here, were you able to find out if this connects with Mammoth Cave?

Collins: I don't know. I did find a cave. Beautiful! Big! I don't know where it led. Right below where the rock's got my foot, is an eighty-foot drop, straight down. (*He takes another drink.*) By the way, fellow, who are you anyway?

Miller: I'm a reporter from the *Courier-Journal.*

Collins: You mean you're writing all this up in the papers?

Miller: Not only me, Floyd. Every paper in the country is full of this story. Wait'll you get out of here and see what's doing up top in that old cornfield. You'll think the carnival's come to town. There are thousands of people up there just waiting for you to come out free, Floyd.

Collins: It's—it's nice to know that I'm not in this alone.

Miller: Every man, woman, and child old enough to think is thinking about you, Floyd. Hoping with you and praying with you.

Collins: Tell them to pray hard, will ya, fella?

Miller: Sure.

Homer's voice: Skeets. Here's the jack.

Miller: Okay.

(*He reaches back and pulls in a tiny jack.*)

Collins: You think maybe this will do the trick?

Miller: There's a good chance.

Collins: Somehow I think it will. I don't know why but I got a hunch it will.

Miller: You keep on thinking that and you'll get out, Floyd. . . .

(*Suddenly Miller seems faint. He stops what he's doing to rest.*)

Collins: You feeling all right, fellow?

Miller: It's so cold down here. . . . Hard to breathe. . . . I'll be all right in a minute.

Collins: Maybe you'd better go back up and rest. Come down again when you're feeling better.

Miller: If I feel this way I can imagine how you must feel.

Collins: I can't help myself. You can.

Miller: Now, you're going to have to try to place this jack under the rock. I can't reach it.

Collins: Give it here.

(*He takes the jack and with his right arm reaches down to put it in place.*)

Miller: Can you make it?

Collins: I think so. . . . There. . . . She's under the rock. Okay, fellow, start turning.

(DISSOLVE TO *Carmichael at cave mouth as Dalton enters.*)

Dalton: Anything new here?

Carmichael: Not that I know of. They're having a rough time trying to dig the passage wider. That wall keeps crumbling. It's like trying to dig a hole in quicksand.

Dalton: What about Skeets and that automobile jack?

Carmichael: He hasn't come up yet. Guess they're still working it down there.

(*A girl of about twenty-eight approaches them, gaudily but cheaply dressed in the 1925 fashion.*)

Girl: I beg your pardon, but could you gentlemen tell me where I could find this Mr. Skeets Miller?

Carmichael: I'm sorry, miss, but you'll have to get back behind the police lines. Only authorized people are—

Girl: But I've just got to speak to Mr. Miller. (*sweetly*) Won't y'all tell me where I can find him?

Dalton (*sarcastically*): Yes, ma'am. Just go in that cave and follow your nose for about 165 feet. You can't miss him.

Girl: Y'all wouldn't make fun of me if you knew who I was.

Dalton: And just who are you?

Girl: I'm Floyd Collins' sweetheart, that's who I am.

Dalton: Oh, are you? It took you quite some time to show up here, didn't it?

Girl: I don't have to speak to you. I want to speak to Mr. Miller.

Dalton: You can tell me everything, miss. I'm Mr. Miller's editor.

Girl: Oh, are you a newspaperman, too?

Dalton: Now what's your story?

Girl (*dabbing at her eyes with her handkerchief*): Floyd and me planned to elope next Saturday. I told him not to go down in that old cave, but he wouldn't listen to me—

Dalton (*calling a nearby soldier*): Hey, sergeant!

Soldier: Yes, sir?

Dalton: Take this lady back behind the ropes, will you?

Soldier (*taking girl's arm gently but firmly*): This way, miss.

Girl: Take your hands off me. (*to Dalton*) Don't you even want to know what my name is?

Dalton (*to soldier*): Get her out of here!

(*Soldier leads girl off.*)

Carmichael (*looks after girl, then to Dalton*): You newspapermen can be pretty hard at times.

Dalton: Don't waste your pity on her, Carmichael. She's no more Floyd Collins' sweetheart than I am. She thinks this is a good way to get her name in the papers, that's all.

Carmichael: How can you be so sure?

Dalton: Because she's the third girl that's come to me to say she was Collins' girl. . . . I wonder what's keeping Skeets so long.

(DISSOLVE TO *shot of screw jack in cave being turned.* CAMERA PULLS BACK *to reveal full scene. Miller is still turning jack handle. He is near exhaustion.*)

Miller: Can you move your foot at all?

Collins (*tries it, winces*): No.

Miller: I don't think we've budged it an inch.

Collins: The wall is too soft. The jack just sinks into it.

Miller (*wearily*): Well, we'll just keep trying it until it works.

(*He lays his head down on the ground to rest.*)

Collins: You're too cold and tired to do any good down here now, fellow. You get out of here and rest a bit and get warm—then come back down here and try it again. You'll make it next time.

Miller (*after a pause*): You're quite a guy, Floyd.

Collins: Before you go, would you put that bulb behind my neck?

Miller: It'll cut off all the light that way.

Collins: I don't care. It'll be warm against my neck and I'm so cold— so cold.

Miller: Sure. Hope she doesn't short circuit.

(*He places the bulb under Collins' head.*)

Collins: Ah—that feels good!

Miller (*placing the hip flask on a small ledge above Collins' head*): I'll leave the liquor down here in case you want some more when I come back.

Collins: Thanks, fellow. Thanks a lot.

Miller (*starting to slide out*): I'll be back.

(DISSOLVE TO *cave entrance, exterior.* CLOSE-UP *of Dalton.*)

Dalton: Amputate the leg?

Doctor: That would be one way of getting him out.

Dalton: But that's not the best place in the world to perform an operation, doctor.

Doctor: We could try.

(*There is a flurry of excitement at the cave mouth. Doctor, Carmichael, and Dalton cross to cave entrance. After a short pause, Miller comes out of cave mouth almost faint with fatigue. Dalton and Carmichael grab him to keep him from collapsing.*)

Carmichael: This boy better get some rest.

Dalton: This boy's going to get some rest, if I have to tie him down.

Miller: The jack wouldn't hold, Neil . . . wall too soft.

Dalton: Never mind that now, Skeets. I'm taking you back to the hotel in Cave City.

Miller (*nodding toward the cave*): What about him?

Dalton: You can't do him any good when you're half dead yourself.

Doctor: Mr. Dalton, what do you think of my idea? And you, Miller?

Dalton: This is a doctor, Skeets. He wants to amputate.

Miller (*looking doctor over*): He's too big. Wouldn't fit down there.

(*Voice comes from crowd of onlookers.*)

Voice: Maybe Skeets could do it.

(*All look to Miller.*)

Miller: I don't know much about amputating a man's leg. . . . Anyway, how would we ever get him out? It's hard enough to get out of there with two good legs. He'd bleed to death before we pulled him ten feet. . . . Couldn't get to the leg anyway. Too narrow down there. . . . Much too narrow. . . . We'll have to get him out of there, whole, in one piece— or not at all.

(*Suddenly there is pandemonium in the cave entrance as the men who have been digging in the cave start to scramble out. Immediately a large crowd gathers at the entrance.*)

Dalton: What's the matter now?

Carmichael: Something's wrong. The diggers are coming out.

(*He pushes his way through the crowd and reaches the entrance just as the last digger is being helped out.*)

Digger: Cave in. . . . She caved in about half way down. . . . Whole passage is blocked!

Carmichael: Any more men down there?

Digger: No. I'm the last one. All out—except Collins!

(FADE-OUT.)

Talking it over

1. *a.* What attempts does Miller make to free Floyd Collins? Why do they fail?

  b. Why isn't the doctor's suggestion taken?

  c. What does Mr. Carmichael first plan to do? Why is that plan discarded? What plan does he substitute? How does that one turn out?

2. *a.* Of what does Maxwell accuse Miller?

  b. What do you infer is his reason for doing this?

  c. How does Miller react to Maxwell's accusation?

3. *a.* When Dalton says "They collect like flies around a garbage pail," to whom is he referring? What does he mean?

  b. Miller tells Floyd that there are so many people outside, it's as if the carnival's come to town. What actions of the crowd is Miller probably thinking of?

  c. What impression of human beings do you get from the behavior of the crowd? Include the girl who claims to be Floyd's sweetheart.

4. What evidence of courage do you see in Act II?

Words in action

In each of the following sentences, the word in bold type describes a very specific kind of movement.

1. The frightened boy **scrambled** up the slopes of the ravine.

2. Rescuers had to **squirm** through the narrow tunnel.

3. Waking from a nap, the young reporter **staggered** over to the ringing phone.

4. The last man in line **hurled** a small rock-chip from the cave.

5. Souvenir-hunters **dived** for the pieces of rock.

Match each of the boldface words with one of the following general words which is closest in meaning to the specific word: **crawl, throw, run, walk, reach.** If you are not sure of the meaning of a word from the way it is used in the sentence, look it up in the Glossary.

Which word of each pair helps you see the action better?

ACT III

(FADE IN ON *the following headlines:*

Cave-in Seals Collins
in Sand Cave
Contact with Floyd Broken—
Fear Collins May Be Dead

FADE TO *cave interior where cave-in has occurred. Miller and Everett Maddox examine the slimy wall of mud and debris that blocks the passage to where Collins is trapped.*)

Miller: Here's the cave-in.

Maddox (*probing the wall*): Just what I was afraid of.

Miller: It's not very far down from here to where Collins is. Couldn't you dig through this?

Maddox: It's too soft and too wet. For every shovelful we took out two would seep down from above.

Miller: But we've got to get to him.

Maddox: Sure. But it'll have to be some other way. I've been mining most of my life, Skeets, and I tell you there ain't a chance to cut through this muck.

Miller: Do you think there's a chance he's still alive?

Maddox: There's a chance—if this cave-in didn't pile onto him. Why don't you try calling to him?

Miller (*uneasily*): All right. (*Pause while he steels himself for the worst possible news. Then he calls loudly.*) Floyd! . . . Floyd!

(*Silence. Miller and Maddox exchange glances.*)

Maddox: Hello, Collins!

Miller (*at the same time*): Floyd! Floyd, are you there?

(*Silence again as they listen. Then very faintly, they hear a reply.*)

Collins: Hello . . .

Miller (*excitedly*): He's alive! (*shouting*) Floyd! Floyd, can you hear me?

Collins (*his voice muffled through the mud wall*): I can hear you. . . . Come on down, I'm free!

Miller: He's free, Maddox! He says he's free!

Maddox: This cave-in caused the rock on his foot to move. The whole formation must've shifted. Talk about rotten breaks.

Miller: Maybe he isn't free.

Maddox: Why would he lie about it?

Miller: Maybe he knows about this cave-in. Maybe he thinks we'll stop trying to get to him.

Maddox: He'd know better than that.

Miller: What would you think if you'd been lying in this hole for five days with a six-ton rock on your leg? (*shouting*) Floyd!

Collins: Hello!

Miller: Are you sure you're free?

Collins (*after a pause*): Come on down.

Miller (*to Maddox*): You see? He's trying to urge us on.

Maddox: Maybe. But you can't be sure.

Miller: No, I can't be sure. Wait a minute—(*shouting*) Floyd, we can't make it right now. Are you hungry?

Collins: Yes. Why don't you bring me something to eat?

Miller: We can't get to you right away, but if you're hungry, I left that milk bottle above your head. Do you see it?

Collins: Yes.

Miller: Well, if you're free, reach up and get it. (*long silence*) Floyd, can you reach the bottle?

Collins (*long pause*): No, I can't.

Miller: Then you're not free, are you? (*silence*) Floyd, you're not free, are you?

Collins (*finally, almost sullenly*): No, I am not free.

(*Maddox and Miller look at each other grimly.*)

Miller: Don't worry, Floyd! We're doing all we can. We'll keep doing it until we get you out. Do you hear me, Floyd? We'll get you out!

Maddox (*after a slight pause*): We'd better go up and tell Carmichael he's still alive and that it's impossible to get to him from here. Come on!

(*Maddox starts to squirm out. Miller stays at the wall for a moment, almost reluctant to leave.*)

Miller (*shouting*): We'll get you out.

(*He starts to crawl out. He stops as he reaches Maddox, who has stopped in the larger compartment of the cave.*)

Maddox: I hear someone coming.

(*Miller squirms up alongside Maddox, and they both peer ahead.*)

Miller (*surprised*): Homer!

(*Homer appears; his eyes are glazed.*)

Homer: Let me by. I'm going to my brother.

Maddox: You can't get to him this way, Collins. The cave-in is—

Homer: I'm goin' to my brother.

Miller: You shouldn't be down here, Homer. How did you get past the guards?

Homer: Nobody's tellin' me the truth. You're all jest a bunch of outsiders who do more talkin' than anything else. I'm tired of listenin' to all the talkin'. I'm going to help Floyd out of here. Let me by.

Maddox: Get him to go back, Miller. If he tries to push by us he's liable to cause another cave-in. This whole place is ready to fall.

Homer: I'm going to Floyd.

Miller: You can't. You'll get us all killed. We'll all be trapped down here.

Homer: My brother's trapped down here.

Miller: That's why we've got to stay alive, Homer. We want to help him. We can't help him if we're trapped, too.

Homer: Jest some more of your talk. There's got to be less talkin' and more action around here. I ain't leavin' Floyd to die in this cave.

Miller: Nobody's leaving him. We'll get to him a better way. Back out, Homer!

Homer: How do I know you're telling me the truth? How do I know this ain't just a trick?

Miller: Homer, I've been trying to free Floyd for almost as long as you have. And I promise you I'm going to keep on trying.

Homer: I trust you, Skeets. You're a good fella, but I don't trust none of the rest of 'em.

Miller: Then trust me now, Homer. Go back. I give you my word that everything that can be done will be done for Floyd. Back up now.

Homer: I want to get Floyd out of here.

(*Homer seems undecided and Miller has to talk quickly and convincingly.*)

Miller: We all want to get Floyd out of here. Every man connected with the rescue work is just waiting for the good news that your brother is alive and free. The whole country is praying for him, Homer. Back out now. For Floyd's safety you've got to back out of here. Go ahead, Homer.

(*Homer looks at him a long time.*)

Homer: All right. But I'm warnin' you,

Skeets, if they don't start some real action pretty soon, I'm comin' back down here and gettin' Floyd myself. Understand?

Miller: Sure, Homer—sure.

Homer: All right.

(*Homer starts to back out as the others squirm forward.*

DISSOLVE TO *cave entrance, exterior.* SHOT OF *Carmichael speaking. There is a large blackboard behind him. As he speaks,* CAMERA PULLS BACK *to reveal a large group of men listening.*)

Carmichael: All right, here's the story. Miller and Maddox have just told me that Floyd Collins is still alive. (*The men cheer.*) There's nothing to cheer about yet. Collins is still trapped in that cave and we've still got to get him out of there. Now the only thing left for us to do is to dig a shaft from here, straight clean to Collins. That's sixty-seven feet. It won't be easy. We can't use dynamite, we can't use any machinery. Nothing but a core drill to keep a few feet ahead of us to let us know what kind of ground we're coming to. We're going to dig, with picks and with shovels and plain human muscle. We're going to dig steadily. We're going to dig all day, and we're going to dig all night. It's going to be hard work, and dirty work, but it's going to be done. And now that I've given you all the facts, I want volunteers!

(SUPERIMPOSE OVER A SHOT OF *revolving drill, the following headlines:*

Shaft Begun at Sand Cave

Collins Still Alive

Carmichael Calls for Volunteer Rescuers to Save Collins

DISSOLVE TO *series of portrait shots.*)

Saunders (*a heavy-set man of twenty-eight*): My name's Saunders. I drive a truck. I was deliverin' coal to Louisville when I passed by this place. That was two days ago. I've been waitin' here ever since, hopin' I could help that poor fella in the cave. I want to help dig that shaft, Mister. . . .

(DISSOLVE TO *a tall, lean farmer.*)

Farmer: I live 'round here. I knew Floyd. Used to see him come past the farm now and then. One of my boys went to school with him when they were kids. . . . No, I'm not too old to work. Please, mister, give me a shovel.

(DISSOLVE TO *a slight man of thirty-five.*)

Man: I brought my family here all the way from Tennessee after reading all about it in the papers. Guess I was just curious. Been living in our car for four days. . . . But I ain't just curious no more, mister. I can use a pick as good as the next one.

(DISSOLVE TO *a young man of twenty.*)

Young Man: I work in the feed store over to Cave City. Nine to five. My folks need the money I make, otherwise I'd quit the job to work in this shaft. But I only work in the store nine to five, mister. I can dig in the shaft nights—Sundays, too. What do you say, mister?

(DISSOLVE TO *men digging in the shaft.*)

NOTE: *The actual shaft at Sand Cave was eight feet square. It was braced with wooden beams and the sides were shored with boards to avoid cave-ins. Above ground, at the top of the shaft, was a crude structure very much like the mechanism above a well. The dirt from below was hauled up in buckets.*

Voice (*shouting*): Take her up!

(CAMERA FOLLOWS *bucket as it is pulled upward in the shaft.*

DISSOLVE TO *men digging in shaft.*

SUPERIMPOSE *masthead: "The Louisville Courier-Journal Friday, Feb. 7, 1925"*

FADE TO *farmer who is digging diligently. He suddenly stops, wearily, and leans against the shaft wall for support. The man working next to him grabs him to keep him from falling.)*

Young Man: You all right, Pop?

Farmer: Sure—sure, I'm doin' fine.

Young Man (*unconvinced, he shouts up*): Replacement down here!

Farmer (*angrily*): I'm all right, I told you. Don't need no replacement.

Young Man: Don't try to dig this shaft all by yourself, Pop.

Farmer: We got to get to Collins before he starves to death down there.

Young Man: Sure, but a fresh man can dig twice as fast as a guy after two hours in this hole.

Farmer: Maybe you're right. (*Starts to put shovel down.*) I'll go on up for a spell.

Young Man: Not yet, Pop. Keep digging until your replacement gets here. Every minute counts.

(*Farmer picks up shovel and starts to dig again.*

DISSOLVE TO *masthead: "The Louisville Courier-Journal Saturday, Feb. 8, 1925"*

DISSOLVE TO *press tent interior. Present are Miller and Carmichael, both looking dirty and exhausted.)*

Miller: Not a sign of life for three days. Maybe he's dead.

Carmichael: Maybe.

Miller: Then let me try going in through the passage again and see if I can call to him.

Carmichael: Forget it, Skeets. I don't want to have to start digging two of you out. We're having a tough enough time with one. The old cave's sealed itself up. You wouldn't get thirty feet. And if you did you'd never get out alive. We've just got to keep digging that shaft!

(DISSOLVE TO *masthead: "The Louisville Courier-Journal Sunday, Feb. 9, 1925"*

CAMERA PANS DOWN *front page of newspaper to headline in large type:*

Rain over Sand Cave

EFFECT OF *large raindrops hitting the newspaper until the paper is soaking wet, fluid, limp.*

DISSOLVE TO *men standing ankle-deep in soft mud, digging furiously in the water-soaked shaft.* AS CAMERA PANS *from man to man,* SUPERIMPOSE *the following series of dates:*

> *Monday, Feb. 10*
> *Tuesday, Feb. 11*
> *Wednesday, Feb. 12*
> *Thursday, Feb. 13*

FADE TO PRESS TENT. CLOSE SHOT OF *Dalton holding tent flap back and looking outside.)*

Miller: Any sign of its letting up?

Dalton: No, if anything, it's raining harder than ever.

Miller: Poor Collins. Everything seems to be against him—even the weather. Carmichael says we'd probably have the shaft deep enough by now if not for this deluge. You know, Neil— sometimes I get the feeling that we haven't got a chance. Every attempt we make to get at him seems doomed from the start. And now this rain. . . .

Dalton (*after a pause*): I don't like this rain any more than you do. But it's taught me something, too. Something I never knew before.

As part of rescue attempt, a miner is about to be lowered
into a shaft in the cave where Collins is trapped.

Miller: Like what?

Dalton: Even the rain can't stop the people out there. When I first got here and saw all these sightseers, here, I hated them, Skeets. I considered them parasites, getting some sort of vicarious thrill out of Floyd Collins' misfortune. There were times when I would have gladly blown up the special trains they were coming in. I would've volunteered to mine the roads to keep them away.

Miller: But not now.

Dalton: No, not now. They're out there now, digging like madmen in that rain. The same people; same souvenir hunters; same hot-dog eaters. They'll dig straight down to China if they think it will help Floyd Collins.

(*He stops, a little self-conscious after his long speech. He sits down wearily. Carmichael enters quickly and looks around.*)

Dalton: Hello, Carmichael.

Carmichael: Oh, there's a fellow over at the shaft wants to speak to you.

Miller: What about?

Carmichael: He's an electrical engineer. Claims he's got a gadget that can tell us whether Collins is still alive.

Dalton: Sounds like another one of these crackpots with a brainstorm.

Carmichael: I don't think so, Dalton. Anyway, we've got to listen to everybody. If Collins is dead there's no use in continuing that shaft. It's dangerous; could bury the men alive.

Miller: Well, what does he want of me?

Carmichael: He read about you leaving that electric light under Collins' neck the last time you saw him. It has something to do with that. He wants you to tell him exactly where you left the bulb in relation to Collins. That's important, he says.

Miller (*starting out*): All right. Let's go tell him.

(DISSOLVE TO *the cave entrance, near the generator.*)

Engineer: I'm going to break the circuit so that the light next to Collins will go off. If he's alive and conscious he'll see it go off. It'll get pitch dark down there. He'll wonder what's happened. The sudden darkness might cause him to move as much as he can and that action would jar the electric bulb under him.

Miller (*skeptically*): And even if all that happens—then what?

Engineer: The moment I break the circuit from this generator, I'll switch the wires to this circuit here.

Dalton: What's that?

Engineer: Just a battery and a radio amplifier. If Collins moves at all after the lights go out down there, he'll jar that bulb under him and we'll hear noises through the amplifier. And if we hear noises . . . he's alive!

(*Miller scratches his head uncertainly.*)

Miller: I don't know. What do you think, Mr. Carmichael?

Carmichael: It's worth a try. I say "go ahead."

Engineer: Good! But I'm going to have to have absolute quiet while I make this test. Any noise we hear isn't going to be very loud. (*to Carmichael*) And you'll have to order the men to stop digging in the shaft while the test is going on. This is a sensitive machine and it might pick up the noise of the shovels down there.

Carmichael: I don't like to stop the digging. We're going too slow as it is.

Engineer: This test won't take more than a few minutes, Mr. Carmichael.

Carmichael (*after a thoughtful pause, to one of the men standing behind him*): Order the digging in the shaft stopped! Tell the men to stand by.
(CUT TO *shaft interior where men are working furiously.*)

Voice (*unseen, shouting from above*): You men in the shaft! Stop all digging and stand by!
(*The men stop work and all look upward.*)

Voice: Just be as quiet as you can. I'll let you know as soon as it's over.
(*The men all stand quietly in the black, wet hole.* CAMERA MOVES *from face to face showing the dirt and fatigue on each one.*
CUT TO *Carmichael.*)

Carmichael (*calling loudly*): Let's have absolute quiet. Please.
(*All noise ceases except for the chugging of the generator motor.*)

Carmichael (*to engineer*): All ready now?

Engineer: All ready. . . . Turn off the generator.
(*A man presses "ground wire button" and the motor slowly comes to a stop. There is absolute silence now. The engineer takes the wires from the generator and hooks them into his radio amplifier. The bedraggled men watch intently, their ears straining for some noise from the loud speaker.*)

Carmichael (*after a long pause*): Well?

Engineer (*his ear up against the loudspeaker*): I don't hear anything. . . . He hasn't moved. He must be—Wait a minute! I think—I can't be sure, but I think I hear. It's a steady sound. Steady—steady like a heartbeat. Listen!
(SOUND: *faintly at first, but growing louder, a dull, thumping sound, like a slow heartbeat.*)

Carmichael (*shouting excitedly*): Grab those shovels down there and dig. He's alive! Collins is still alive!
(*With a roar combining relief and happiness, the men resume their digging with renewed fervor.*

CAMERA REMAINS ON *the digging shovels as the following dates are superimposed over the shot:*

> *Friday, Feb. 14*
> *Saturday, Feb. 15*
> *Sunday, Feb. 16*

CUT TO *shot of one man digging in a corner of the shaft. Suddenly the ground beneath him gives way, the whole shaft trembles, the man falls against the wall for support.*)

Man (*yelling*): She's caving in! She's caving in!
(DISSOLVE TO *shaft head. Carmichael is surrounded by a crowd of men. Behind him stands the blackboard showing the layout of the cave. He points to the diagram as he speaks.*)

Carmichael: Collins said that there was an eighty-foot drop right below him. That might've been what caused the floor of the shaft to give way. Whatever the reason, we know we can't dig down any further. However, we'll try to tunnel across to Collins from the shaft. We probably won't be able to pull Collins out that way, but we'll find out whether there's any reason for further rescue operations. Now —let's dig that tunnel!
(DISSOLVE TO *following headlines:*

Tunnel Started Toward Collins
Nation Awaits News
Collins' Fate
Will Be Known Today

DISSOLVE TO *shaft interior near the spot where the tunnel has been dug.*

Two men stand and stare at the jagged hole.)

1st Man: Why don't he come out and tell us?

2nd Man: It ain't easy slidin' through that muck in there. We'll know soon enough. Just take it easy.

(*Now* CAMERA PANS TO *other men in the shaft, all waiting anxiously, their eyes glued to the tunnel entrance.*

CUT TO *Dalton and Miller standing at the shaft head. Miller throws cup.*)

Dalton: Take it easy, Skeets.

Miller: Why can't they hurry?

Dalton: Just take it easy.

(*A commotion is heard in the bottom of the shaft. Dalton leans over and looks in.*)

Miller: Well?

Dalton: Brennan's coming out now. We'll know in a minute.

(CAMERA CLOSES IN ON *Miller's face during the next sequence. There is a deathly hush over the whole area. Then, from deep in the shaft, a man's voice is heard saying something which is too far away to be understood. But as his words are passed from one man to the next through the shaft they become more and more distinguishable until we can make out that the words are: "He's dead!"*

The words grow louder and louder over the shot of Miller sitting stunned, in stony silence.)

Miller (*almost to himself*): He's dead . . . Floyd Collins is dead . . . Why? Why couldn't he die right away? All that agony and torture, for what?

Dalton: We're just human beings, Skeets. We can't know "why" and "for what."

Miller: A man gets trapped in a rotten hole and the whole world couldn't save him.

WILLIAM FLOYD COLLINS
BORN
JULY 20, 1887.
BURIED
APRIL 26, 1925.

TRAPPED IN SAND CAVE, JAN. 30, 1925.
DISCOVERED CRYSTAL CAVE, JAN. 18, 1917.
GREATEST CAVE EXPLORER EVER KNOWN.

Wide World Photo

Dalton: No, the whole world couldn't save him. But what's more important is that the whole world tried. If you're looking to make any sense out of this tragedy, that's where to look. We fought a war, remember? We learn to live with casualty lists and killing on a grand scale. We think we're getting calloused, hard, unfeeling; but then one day a man— one single man—gets trapped in a hole and every decent person in the country wants to help him. They've come here by the thousands. They came here because a fellow human being was fighting to stay alive and they wanted only to be near him and to help dig him out if possible. That's an important thing, Skeets. More important than you or me or Floyd Collins . . . or anybody. . . .

(*Carmichael enters.*)

Carmichael: I'm sorry, Skeets.

Miller: Will you be able to get the body out now?

Carmichael: No, the family wants him left where he is. I've ordered the men to fill in the hole . . . and may God rest his soul.

Miller: God rest his soul.

(CUT TO *shaft where tunnel entrance is being filled.* THE PICTURE GROWS VERY SHARP, THEN FADES OUT.)

THE END

⟳ **Talking it over**

1. *a.* Why does Floyd call out that he is free?

b. How does Miller know that he is not?

2. *a.* What final method of rescue is tried? Who does the digging?

b. Explain the change in the mood of the crowd.

3. *a.* How does the electrical engineer prove that Floyd is still alive?

b. What happens that delays the rescue more?

4. *a.* When one rescuer reaches Floyd, what is the situation?

b. How does Miller feel about Floyd's long agony?

c. What does Dalton consider the most important point in this true story? Do you agree or disagree with him? Why?

The story is true

David Shaw, recalling interesting experiences he had while *Rescue* was being prepared for television, writes:

"At the time, the night program manager for NBC in New York was William Burke Miller—the same Miller who tried to rescue Collins and who earned a Pulitzer Prize for his newspaper articles on the Collins story. He supplied me with a great deal of personal information which I put into the script.

"It was a highly successful show, quite ambitious for its time. Television then was not used to carrying out the complicated techniques required for filming *Rescue*. The director said it was really too big a thing for television. That was in 1954. Now such a statement seems very funny."

JOURNEY INTO A TOMB

by William Burke Miller

CAVE CITY, KY., Feb. 2—Floyd Collins is suffering torture almost beyond description, but he is still hopeful he will be taken out alive, he told me at 6:20 o'clock tonight on my most recent visit to him.

Until I went inside myself I could not understand exactly what the situation was. I wondered why someone couldn't do something quick, but I found out why.

I was lowered by my heels into the entrance of Sand Cave. The passageway is about five feet in diameter. After reaching the end of an eighty-foot drop I reached fairly level ground for a moment.

From here on I had to squirm like a snake. Water covers almost every inch of the ground, and after the first few feet I was wet through and through. Every moment it got colder. It seemed that I would crawl forever, but after going about ninety feet I reached a very small compartment, slightly larger than the remainder of the channel.

This afforded a breathing spell before I started on again toward the prisoner. The dirty water splashed in my face and numbed my body, but I couldn't stop.

Finally I slid down an eight-foot drop and, a moment later, saw Collins and called to him. He mumbled an answer.

My flashlight revealed a face on which is written suffering of many long hours, because Collins has been in agony every conscious moment since he was trapped at 10 o'clock Friday morning.

I saw the purple of his lips, the pallor on the face, and realized that something must be done before long if this man is to live.

Before I could see his face, however, I was forced to raise a small piece of oil cloth covering it.

"Put it back," he said. "Put it back— the water!"

Then I noticed a small drip-drip-drip from above. Each drop struck Collins' face. The first few hours he didn't mind, but the constant dripping almost drove him insane. His brother had taken the oil cloth to him earlier in the day.

Reprinted by permission of Wyatt, Grafton & Sloss, attorneys for the Louisville *Courier-Journal*.

This reminded me of the old water torture used in ages past. I shuddered.

Here I was at the end of the journey, and I saw quickly why it was that workmen who had penetrated as far as I had accomplished but little. I was exhausted, as they had been. I was numb from head to foot. Chills raced through my body. I missed the fresh air. I came to know in this brief time what Collins had suffered, but I could not comprehend fully. I felt certain I would get out. Collins has hopes, nothing more. I was in no physical pain. Collins' foot, held by a six-ton rock in a natural crevice, is never without pain.

I tried to squirm over Collins' body to reach the rock, but his body takes up nearly all the space. I squeezed in, hunting for some way to help, until he begged me to get off.

"It hurts—hurts awful," he said.

Collins is lying on his back, resting more on the left side, so that his left cheek rests on the ground. His two arms are held fast in the crevice beside his body, so that he really is in a natural straightjacket.

I was behind Lieut. Robert Burdon of the Louisville Fire Department and followed by Homer Collins, brother of the victim, and Guy Turner. Homer Collins had brought with him some body harness to place around his brother and we finally succeeded in putting it on him.

The prisoner helped as best he could by squirming and turning as much as possible, and finally we were ready to haul away on the rope attached to Collins. We pulled as much as we could and it seemed as though we made headway. It was estimated we moved the prisoner five inches.

Perhaps we did, but I can hardly realize it. All of us were on the point of collapse and after a short time our strength failed. We couldn't do any more.

We saw that the blankets and covering which Collins' brother had brought to him were in place and that he was resting as comfortably as we could make him.

Then we left near his head a lantern well filled with oil. It isn't much, but the tiny light it throws means much in that relentless trap and it may bring some bit of consolation to a daring underground explorer whose chance for life is small.

We said farewell and the last man started backward. I found soon that the trip out is worse than the one in. I encountered difficulty in crawling backward for a time, but practice soon enabled me to make progress.

Every foot it seemed the dirty water would splash in my face. I didn't mind it on my body any more, because I was numb to it. Frequently I had to back up in an incline, and the water would flow down to my neck, but as I said, I already was as cold as I could get.

It was with the utmost relief that I came to the small compartment about midway from the entrance which affords to the rescuer his only resting place. I found that by working my head down to my feet and by easing my feet backward I could face about.

This aided a great deal and within twenty minutes I came in sight of lights at the entrance. But, before reaching it, I discovered that two members of our party were unable to proceed farther. I spent what little strength remained in me to get them out.

THE END

It took guts to be

The Man Who Wouldn't Fight Back

by Mickey Mantle

SOMETIMES courage is very quiet. People who saw Jackie Robinson play baseball remember him as a hard, aggressive, noisy ballplayer who was always in the middle of every argument —when he wasn't winning a game by

stealing home or driving in the go-ahead run[1] or making a game-saving play in the field. I thought he was one of the best ballplayers I ever saw, and when he played against teams that I was on—in the World Series of 1952 and 1953 and 1955 and 1956—he always showed a lot of guts.

But he had even more courage his

[1] **driving in the go-ahead run,** making a hit that permits a man on base to score and put his team one run ahead.

first year in the majors, 1947, when I was still a young high-school kid in Oklahoma. That year Robinson hardly ever opened his mouth, he never argued, he didn't get into any fights, he was the quietest, politest player anyone ever saw. When you think of Jackie's natural personality—he liked action, arguments, rough games, give and take, and he liked to be in the center of the stage, talking, yelling, taking charge— you wonder how he ever was able to control himself that first year. Especially in the face of the riding he took, the things he was called.

Jackie was the first Negro player in the major leagues. When he broke in, he was all alone, the only one. Any new player takes a certain amount of kidding, and if the older players don't like him for some reason the kidding can get pretty rough. When Robinson came up, a lot of the older players—and some of the younger ones, as well— resented him because he was a Negro. They didn't care how well he could play ball, or what kind of a man he was. Robinson was a college man, a Pacific Coast Conference[2] all-star in football, basketball, and track, a National Junior College record-holder in the broad jump, a well-educated man with a cultured way of speaking (when he wasn't sore!) and a fine vocabulary. He was a great athlete and a gentleman. But men who didn't have half his brains or education or ability got on his back and called him names that I cannot write down on paper, they were so bad. Terrible, insulting things. If anybody had called him one tenth of those things five or six years later, Jackie would have gone over the stadium roof after them.

But that first year Jackie took everything. He didn't say a word, hardly, against the ones who were jockeying[3] him. Branch Rickey, the president of the Brooklyn Dodgers, who had signed Robinson out of the Negro leagues and made him the first Negro player in organized baseball (when he sent him to Montreal in the International League[4] in 1946) and the first Negro player in major league ball (when he brought him up to the Dodgers in 1947) warned Jackie that he could not lose his temper that first year.

Rickey told Robinson that he had to take every insult, every nasty name, every dirty play, and do it without showing anger or temper or even resentment. He had to turn the other cheek and keep it turned all season long. When Rickey told him this, Robinson didn't like it. He said, "Mr. Rickey, do you want a ballplayer who's afraid to fight back?" And Rickey shouted at Robinson, "I want a ballplayer with guts enough *not* to fight back!"

That first year was a crucial one for the Negro ballplayer. Jackie broke the color line, but if he blew his assignment —if he lost his temper, got in a fight, struck back at the men who were riding him—the barrier would have gone right back up again. Jackie not only had to prove himself as a major league player, which is a pretty tough job all by itself, as you can find out by asking any ballplayer who ever had a shot at the big leagues, but he had to prove it fast.

---

[2]**Pacific Coast Conference,** Pacific Coast Intercollegiate Athletic Conference. A group of colleges whose athletic teams compete against one another is called a conference.

[3]**jockeying,** heckling; taunting.
[4]**International League,** a minor baseball league in the northeastern United States and southeastern Canada.

There wasn't time for a second or third chance. If he failed the first time and had to be sent back down to the minors, Rickey's experiment would have been called a failure, and no telling how many years it would have been before another Negro got a chance. So that was a strain. But on top of that strain, if Robinson lost his temper and exploded under the daily bench-jockeying he was hit with every day, there would have been news stories and editorials saying it was too soon to break the color line in baseball, and again the experiment would have been called a bust. What a spot Robinson was in.

Jackie's natural style of play was aggressive, slam-bang, hardrock baseball, but he had to break into the majors without using that style. He could run wild on the bases if he wanted to, but he couldn't bang into people. He had to play his best game, but he had to be gentle and quiet. So the bench-jockeys called him a coward. It seems sort of funny now in light of the Robinson everybody got to know later, but that's what they called him. Yellow. Scared. Chicken. All those things. It must have galled Robinson, but he remembered what Rickey had told him: "I want a ballplayer with guts enough *not* to fight back!"

I've been told that all the clubs around the National League rode Robinson pretty hard, but no club was as rough as the Philadelphia Phillies. The Phils were managed at that time by Ben Chapman, who had been a hot-tempered guy when he was an active player (he was as aggressive a player as Robinson, I suppose, when you stop to think of it), and as a manager he was still quick to anger.

Chapman and the Phils were so rough in their riding of Robinson that finally Baseball Commissioner Happy Chandler stepped in, and Chapman and the Phils had to quiet down. The next time the Phillies and the Dodgers met, Branch Rickey asked Robinson to pose for a picture shaking hands with Chapman. Rickey's idea was that it would be good for baseball and might help to ease things all around.

Robinson didn't want to. The things that Chapman had called him still burned in his memory, but he finally agreed to do what Rickey asked. And then Ben Chapman refused to shake hands. He said that he was willing to pose with Robinson holding a bat, but that he wouldn't shake hands with him.

When I heard this story years later, I sort of cringed because I knew Jackie's temper and I guess I was instinctively waiting even then for something to explode. I think things like this cause as many fights as anything—where one person or side controls its feelings and agrees to be friendly only to have the other person or side aggravate things all over again. It happens to kids, it happens to husbands and wives, it happens to countries.

But Branch Rickey talked to Robinson and asked him to pose anyway, and Robinson did. Jackie said he had to swallow more pride to pose for that photograph with Chapman than in any other thing he could remember. It must have taken tremendous effort to keep his mouth shut and his feelings under control, to suppress his natural personality for the future good not only of baseball but for the Negro in baseball.

But he did it. He did it all year. Ballplayers stepped on his feet at first base. They elbowed him. They said insulting things half under their breath but knowing he could hear. They came up with remarks that would have had peaceful Connie Mack red-necked and howling and ready to fight.

But old hot-tempered Jackie took it all year long. He made it. He made the big leagues and he didn't cause any trouble. He broke the ice. He broke the color line. He proved not only that a Negro could be good enough to play and star in the majors, he proved also that the presence of a Negro player on a ball field would not start fights and riots.

Other Negro players came in quickly after Robinson opened the door, and now some of the best players in the majors, some of the best players who ever appeared in the majors, are Negroes. And they got their chance because of Jackie Robinson's skill and courage. If it wasn't for Jackie Robinson you may never have heard of players like Elston Howard, Willie Mays, Henry Aaron, Tommy Davis. I think of kids like Al Downing, the fine young left-hander on the Yanks. I guess Al was only about six years old when Robinson broke into the majors. At that time, as I said before, I was in high

school and dreaming of playing in the big leagues some day. But up to that time a Negro kid couldn't even dream. After Jackie Robinson made it, it was different and an Al Downing grew up knowing that the door was open for him if he could pitch well enough. And it opened the door for a great catcher like Elston Howard. In other words, Robinson's courage in 1947 made it possible for Al Downing to be a major league pitcher in 1963 and for Elston Howard to be the Most Valuable Player in the American League the same year.

WIDE WORLD PHOTO

There's an odd thing about Jackie Robinson. I myself was never very friendly with him, and I have found that a lot of people who knew him in and out of baseball really dislike him. He's a hard man for some people to like because he isn't soft and smooth-talking and syrupy. He's tough and independent and he says what he thinks, and he rubs people the wrong way. But I have never heard of anyone who knew Jackie Robinson, whether they liked him or disliked him, who didn't respect and admire him. That might be more important than being liked.

THE END

Talking it over

1. *a.* In what two ways did Robinson have to prove himself?

b. What would happen if he failed?

c. Why was it hard for him to keep his promise not to fight back?

d. How was his calmness misunderstood by many people?

2. *a.* What did Robinson accomplish by refusing to fight during his first year?

b. In what way was his first year an example of outstanding courage?

3. How did Branch Rickey show courage? *(cont.)*

⟳ Words in action

1. What part of the words below is the same in all three? In what way are they alike in meaning? (Use the Glossary for help.)

judicial

judiciary

judicious

2. What part of the word below must have a meaning similar to that of the three words above?

prejudice

3. What do you do when you **precede** someone else in line? What is a movie **preview?** What does the word part *pre-* mean in these two words?

4. What do you guess is the meaning of the word *prejudice?* How does your guess compare with the meaning given in the Glossary?

5. In which of the situations below is a person prejudiced? Explain.

a. Martha has never eaten frog legs but is certain they must taste terrible.

b. Mr. Charles has driven both Chevrolets and Volkswagens many times. He feels the Chevrolet is better as a family car for his family of five.

c. Tom has never become well acquainted with a Mexican. He dislikes Mexicans because some of his friends have made remarks about them; and anyway, Mexicans have darker skins than his.

d. Connie's family has always lived on Ridge Avenue. She claims it is the only place in town where people are friendly.

e. Henry is a black American. Once some white boys beat him up for no good reason. He has never known a white person well. He hates them all.

He made the Baseball Hall of Fame

In 1962, Jack Roosevelt Robinson was elected to the Baseball Hall of Fame, both for his skill in playing baseball and for his courage in opening professional sports to blacks.

Once during Robinson's first year in the majors, his life was threatened. One teammate suggested that all the players wear Jackie's number so that the assassin wouldn't know which man to shoot. Robinson laughed. "It wouldn't work," he said, "unless we all painted our faces!"

In the years since he retired from the Brooklyn Dodgers, Robinson has held high executive positions with a bank, an insurance company, and a professional baseball team. He has served as a political aide to Governor Nelson Rockefeller of New York. In addition, he is a popular speaker.

Courage: Views and viewpoints

1. In which selections in this unit did people—or a person—act bravely under dangerous conditions they could not avoid?

2. In which selections did someone *choose* to face danger or hardship, for a good reason?

3. What word would describe a person who does something dangerous just for the thrill of taking a risk? Give an example of this kind of act. How much courage is involved here?

4. Estimate the courage involved in each of the situations below. Are they examples of cowardice, little courage, average courage, great courage, or recklessness?

   a. A house is burning. One child is still inside. Firemen say further rescue is impossible, but the father dashes back into the flames anyway. The house collapses and the father is killed, too.

   b. A platoon leader who is on a search mission with his men close to the battle line sees a grenade land close by. He throws himself over the grenade to protect his men. He himself is killed. The others are unharmed.

   c. A man goes alone and unarmed into a violent riot scene to try to quiet the rioters.

   d. Someone is being beaten up on the street. People who pass and people who look from their windows do not call the police or try to stop the beating. They say they don't want to become involved.

   e. A girl swims to a man who has been attacked by a shark. She drives the shark away and brings the man to shore and help.

   f. A man sets up a small business but goes bankrupt. He finds a job, but his wife becomes ill and almost all his salary goes for expensive care. She dies, and he is left with three young children to care for. He finds a woman to look after them while he works, but the store in which he clerks is closed and soon he doesn't have money to pay her while he looks for another job. He walks onto a high bridge and jumps to certain death.

   g. A young man dislikes his job, which is rather monotonous, but it pays well, so he stays with it.

5. Suggest other situations that you feel require courage. Have the class help you evaluate them.

6. Do you think it is easier or harder to define courage now that you have read the selections in this unit? Why? Write a paper in which you explain courage to someone who has not read the unit.

6

What do you want from life?

... plenty of money, and

free time to enjoy it?

... the admiration and

respect of others?

... a chance to make something

all by yourself?

... the satisfaction of doing

something no one else

has ever done?

People want different things—

but all are on

some kind of SEARCH.

THE BIG ROCK CANDY MOUNTAINS

Anonymous

INTRODUCTION:
On a summer's day in the month of May,
A burly little bum come a-hiking,
Traveling down that lonesome road
A-looking for his liking.
5 He was headed for a land that was far away,
Beside them crystal fountains—
"I'll see you all this coming fall
In the Big Rock Candy Mountains."

I

In the Big Rock Candy Mountains
10 You never change your socks,
And little streams of alcohol
Come a-trickling down the rocks.
The box cars are all empty
And the railroad bulls are blind,
15 There's a lake of stew and whiskey, too,
You can paddle all around 'em in a big canoe
In the Big Rock Candy Mountains.

CHORUS:
O—the buzzing of the bees in the cigarette trees
Round the soda-water fountain,
20 Where the lemonade springs and the bluebird sings
In the Big Rock Candy Mountains.

II

In the Big Rock Candy Mountains,
There's a land that's fair and bright,
Where the hand-outs grow on bushes
25 And you sleep out every night,
Where the box cars are all empty
And the sun shines every day,

O I'm bound to go where there ain't no snow,
Where the rain don't fall and the wind don't blow
30 In the Big Rock Candy Mountains.

CHORUS:
O—the buzzing of the bees in the cigarette trees
Round the soda-water fountain,
Where the lemonade springs and the bluebird sings
In the Big Rock Candy Mountains.

III

35 In the Big Rock Candy Mountains
The jails are made of tin,
And you can bust right out again
As soon as they put you in;
The farmer's trees are full of fruit,
40 The barns are full of hay,
I'm going to stay where you sleep all day,
Where they boiled in oil the inventor of toil
In the Big Rock Candy Mountains.

CHORUS:
O—the buzzing of the bees in the cigarette trees
45 Round the soda-water fountain,
Where the lemonade springs and the bluebird sings
In the Big Rock Candy Mountains.

Talking it over

1. What kind of man would enjoy living in the Big Rock Candy Mountains? Be specific.

2. If you could build your own Big Rock Candy Mountain, what would you put on it?

"I just couldn't stand there and watch them drink your blood," Jule told me.

VAMPIRES!

by Daniel P. Mannix

M Y wife Jule and I had a number of animals while we lived in Mexico, each of whom had his own personality and his own place in our lives. In fact, after two years in Mexico we thought we had kept virtually every sort of Mexican fauna but we were in for a surprise. That was the year we acquired several vampire bats.

I first heard about the vampires through a doctor who had proved that vampire bats were carriers of a sickness that had caused the death of thousands of cattle. The vampires were also known to carry rabies. In 1936, forty-seven people were attacked by vampires with rabies.

Most interesting to us was that possibly vampires had migrated north and crossed the Texas border. The skull of a vampire bat was reportedly found in a cave in the Big Bend area of Texas. Together with scientist Charles Mohr, we decided to explore caves in northern Mexico and find out how close the vampire colonies were to the border.

Charles Mohr's interest in the bats was purely scientific, but Jule and I determined to keep a few as pets and see if we could tame them. No one seemed to know much about the weird creatures. We couldn't understand why a sleeper attacked by a vampire never seemed to wake up, how the bats went about their nocturnal raids, or how an animal as small as a bat could apparently show considerable intelligence in plotting his forays. Perhaps by keeping pet vampires we could answer some of these questions.

Vampires are comparatively small bats. Their bodies are only about three inches long and they have a wingspread of little more than a foot. A single vampire can drink only about a tablespoon of blood, but a horde of them can cause a sleeper to lose enough blood to weaken him. They are found only in this hemisphere and were first reported by the conquistadors.[1] European scientists thought these men were simply repeating a native legend until Charles Darwin[2] proved the existence of the vampires by sleeping out in the jungle and letting himself be bitten. But not until it was discovered that the vampires could transmit disease was any real interest taken in them.

We discovered our first vampires in the cave of Los Sabinos,[3] about two hundred miles south of the border. At the time, this was the northernmost colony of vampires ever reported, although since then another colony has been found fifty miles closer to the United States. The village of Los Sabinos consisted of half a dozen thatched huts deep in the jungle, a few people, and several sheep, pigs, and goats. I spent some time talking to the Indians as I was curious to find out what sort of people would voluntarily live next to a community of vampire bats. The villagers discussed the bats as calmly as New Jerseyites would talk about mosquitoes. The bats came every night to feed on their stock—and on them. The villagers retired to their huts as soon as the sun went down and carefully filled in every chink. If anyone forgot a chink, when he awoke the next morning he was dripping blood from half a dozen little wounds. When the animals got bitten so badly they became weak, the villagers took them into the huts too.

I asked if they'd ever thought of moving. They had, but this was a good, high spot in the jungle with a spring of excellent water. There were no ticks, mosquitoes, or polluted wells. What were a few vampires?

Two Indians, a father and a son, offered to act as guides to the cave. I noticed them calmly testing a 150-foot fiber rope of a type usually used by climbers preparing to ascend the Matterhorn.

"How high is the roof of this cave?" Jule asked.

"How high is the sky, señora?"[4] the son replied carelessly.

The Indians insisted on taking along a double handful of the rough, home-

---

[1] **conquistadors** (kon kwis′ tə dôrz), leaders in the Spanish conquest of the Americas in the sixteenth century.

[2] **Charles Darwin**, 1809-1882, an English scientist, famous for his theory of evolution. He made many studies of animal behavior.

[3] **Los Sabinos** (lôs sä bē′nōs).

[4] **señora** (sā nyō′rä), Spanish for "Mrs." or "madam."

dipped candles that hung in bunches from the ceilings of the huts.

"The candles don't give as much light as our miners' headlamps," Charlie Mohr pointed out.

"The candles don't have batteries that go dead, either," said the old man stubbornly.

The Indians told us that no one knew how deep the cave might be. "Several people have tried to reach the end, señores," he explained. "Maybe some succeeded. Nobody knows because they never came out again."

It was several miles to the cave and part of the path led up the steep slope of a mountain. The entrance to the cave was shrouded by a forest of curiously twisted trees that looked like the papier-mâché creation of a Hollywood murder-mystery set. Our guides led the way down a steep slope into a natural amphitheater, hung with jungle creepers as big as cables. Across from us a black slit like a giant, toothless mouth showed in the white limestone. Vines overhung it like a straggly mustache. The older guide pointed. "This is the vampire grotto."

We climbed through the opening into the great entrance hall, seventy feet high. We lighted the lamps in our miners' helmets and started downward into the cave. The entrance hall was filled with boulders, piled together like children's marbles. We stepped from one to another, descending deeper and deeper into the earth. The vast mouth of the cave diminished behind us until it looked no bigger than a rathole. Then it vanished completely. We began feeling our way down a great slope in complete darkness except for the puddles of light from our headlamps. At intervals the guides lit candles and left them

sticking to the rocks to mark our path back. They showed in the intense darkness like tiny fireflies.

Then the slope ended in a steep drop, falling away into a vast black hole so deep that not even our powerful flashlights could reach the bottom of it. The guides started climbing down the sheer wall, working their way from handhold to handhold. As each of us climbed down the rock, the others held their flashlights so we could see the handholds. Bats began to pour out of the hole like clouds of black confetti but they were the little, insect-eating kind and although I could feel the wind of their leathery wings, none of them touched us.

Below us, the guides had stopped on a ledge. I could see them playing their lights back and forth along an overhang which projected over nothingness. One after another we landed on the ledge and looked over into the abyss. "This is where we use the rope, señor," the old man explained.

They doubled the rope so we could use one strand as a safety line and climb down the other length. I wrapped my feet around the climbing rope and, gripping the safety line, slowly inched backward over the edge. I began to let myself down seventy feet, and then the rope ended. I hung there, knowing I could never climb up hand over hand, especially with a knapsack on my back containing sixty pounds of scientific equipment.

"I've come to the end of the rope. What shall I do?" I yelled.

"Just let go," the guides shouted.

"What do you mean by that?"

"There's a ledge right under you. Let go and you'll drop onto it."

I turned my headlamp down and saw

the ledge. As soon as I was off the rope, the rest came down one after another. We climbed down to the floor of the cave and Charlie Mohr held up his hand. "Hear them?"

I listened and heard a noise that sounded like the chittering call of ordinary bats combined with the whistle of steam from a teakettle. "That's the cry of the vampires," said Charlie.

We moved forward slowly into a big room with passages branching off on all sides. They were separated from the main hall by fringes of stalactites hanging like draperies around the openings. Getting down on our hands and knees, we crawled under a strip of the stone teeth. Ahead of us was a series of great, billowing terraces like monster fountains turned to stone.

We began to climb up the terraces. The rock was as smooth and as slippery as ice, but there were occasional hollows full of water where we could sit and rest. Suddenly on the wall ahead we saw little shapes running and leaping among the formations. The long shadows thrown by our lamps added to their height and they looked exactly like little men rushing frantically about, trying to decide what to do. Every now and then one of them would crane himself up to peer down at us. They did not look in the least animal-like. They looked like goblins. An artist trying to illustrate a child's book of fairy stories could not have done better than to reproduce that scene.

These were the vampires. Running on their hind feet and the elbows of their wings, they could go as fast as a four-legged animal. They kept turning their enormous ears about as a rabbit would to pick up the noise we made. As we came closer, several ran to the edge of the ledges and sprang into the air. Others stood their ground, baring their teeth and chattering fiercely.

I grabbed one old warrior whose fur was a deep reddish-brown and as soft as moleskin. He fought savagely in my gloved hand, screaming with rage. As we put him into the collection box, he spit out two slivers of a brown substance we could not identify, but later we found that he had sliced out two small pieces of leather from my glove. They were not bitten out; they were slashed out with his scalpel-sharp incisors. A razor could not have dug out those gouges in my glove as neatly.

Charlie tried to catch some with a net. The vampires seemed to understand perfectly what he was doing. Several of them leaped straight up in the air to avoid his strokes. Others bounced along the ledges like rubber balls and vanished into holes. Some vampires ran up the walls, lifting themselves with two long fingers growing out of the elbows of their wings. These fingers are amazing instruments, each ending in a curved nail like a squirrel's claw. Turning up our lights, we could see dozens of vampires hanging head down on the walls above us. They looked like miniature bearskin rugs, hung upside down with the open mouths and grinning teeth pointing downward.

We found three young vampires in a pocket of the rock, all huddled together with their weird little bulldog faces peering out at us anxiously. Every time they saw the net coming near them, two of the little devils would grab the third and shove him forward while they hid behind him. The victim would stare at us for a moment and then dive under his friends, shoving them back over his shoulder. Jule pulled them apart and lined up all three on a stalagmite, but before I could get a picture one of them had kicked another and the fight started all over again.

When we got back to our hotel and opened our collecting box we found our vampires in a state of shock. We had three adults—including the tough old fellow who'd bitten my glove—and two little ones. The old warrior was the only one who showed any animation. He was still willing to fight, but the others seemed paralyzed. Charlie added to our troubles by telling us that vampires have to eat their own weight in blood every twenty-four hours or they'll die. The Los Sabinos Indians had told us that the bats, in addition to feeding on humans and cattle, will also drink blood from a chicken, biting the bird in the leg (they can't get through the feathers). We had invested in a couple of chickens but these bats were obviously in no condition to feed on anything and we didn't know when they had last eaten.

"You may as well let me make skins of them," Charlie suggested callously and I felt the same way, but Jule wouldn't listen to either of us. "There must be some way to save them," she insisted. "All they need to do is find out that we're their friends."

Jule went to work with a medicine dropper filled with fresh blood, contributed by the local butcher who frankly thought we were crazy. The only one she could work with was the old warrior who, we discovered, had only one eye. He had presumably lost the other in a fight with another vampire, possibly over a lady bat. The old fighter didn't take kindly to being force-fed. He bit, shrieked, whistled, and struggled in Jule's gloved hand. He positively refused to suck from the end of the dropper. The whole project seemed hopeless, but Jule refused to be discouraged. "Give him time; he'll have to quiet down a little first," she insisted. An hour later the old boy had quieted down enough so he'd sit crouched in Jule's palm, only snarling slightly when she scratched his head.

Then Jule tried the medicine dropper again. To make sure the blood was flowing easily, she pressed the bulb of the dropper slightly until a drop of blood appeared at the glass tip. An astonishing thing happened. The bat sat up, stretched out his neck, and with his curious pink, club-shaped tongue licked the drop off. Jule offered him another drop and he licked that away too. He was feeding.

The other bats were rigid from shock and Jule had to massage them gently until they came around. By two o'clock that morning, Jule had managed to feed them all. Her system was to put one of the bats next to the old warrior who was feeding readily. After a minute or so, the other bat would nudge over to get some and a fight would start. Then I'd decoy the old fellow away with another medicine dropper while Jule continued feeding the other bat.

Our main problem was keeping the blood from coagulating. Charlie Mohr solved that difficulty for us. By putting the fresh blood in a bottle with some marbles and shaking it up, the corpuscles of the blood were broken down and it would remain liquid for some time.

By the time we got back to our home in Taxco,[5] our bats were so used to us that we could feed them from a burro

---

[5]**Taxco** (tä ′skō).

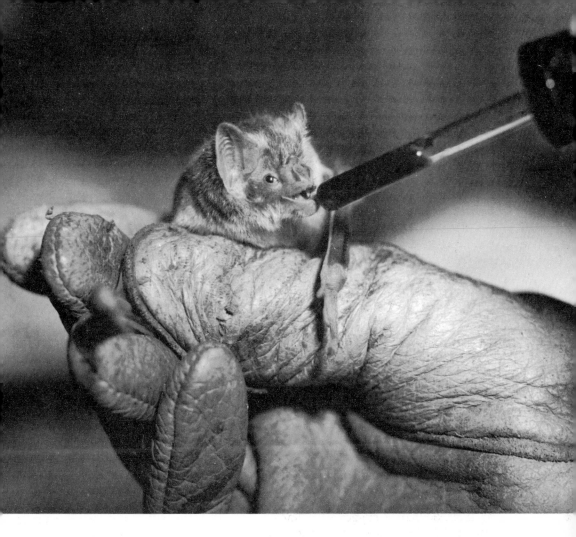

we rented for the purpose. The burro didn't mind the business—in fact, he was far more afraid of us than of the bats—and they took comparatively little blood. Most of the time, the burro didn't even know he was being bitten.

I wanted to see how vampires would attack a human being, but here Jule unreasonably rebelled. "Dan, I've been willing to do almost anything with you in the animal line, but I won't be eaten by vampire bats," she declared. So I had to act as the subject while Jule took notes.

But the bats positively refused to bite me. They would crawl up and down my bare arm or over my legs and never offer to bite. Finally Jule decided she would let the vampires bite her if they wanted to, but they wouldn't bite her either. It was very discouraging.

At last we decided that they were still nervous about us. I would have to pretend to be asleep while Jule hid in our bathroom and watched through the curtains.

In spite of all our precautions, the bats still stubbornly refused to coöperate. I finally did fall asleep and Jule reported what happened.

As usual, it was the old fellow who proved the boldest. He was hanging with the others from the cornice of our bedroom. He woke up, licked his lips, and then stretched his wings, one after the other. Then he began to turn his little bulldog head from side to side, his nose twitching as though he were scenting the air.

Instead of flying over to the bed, he climbed down the wall using his hooks, hopped across the floor like a toad, and then bounded onto the bed covers. He sat there some time watching me and listening to my breathing. Then he quietly reared up on the tips of his wings and crawled up the covers toward my face, every motion elaborately cautious.

When he reached my face, he moved back and forth around the pillow, looking for a good place to bite. We later found that a vampire tries to get a spot with few nerves and plenty of blood so he seldom chooses the throat—not as dramatic as sinking his fangs into the jugular vein but far more practical. When he finally decided on a good spot, he approached cautiously and nipped the side of my neck gently. I tossed and he scuttled back hurriedly and waited until I was quiet again. Then he tried the lobe of my ear.

Here Jule interfered. "I just couldn't stand there and watch him drink your blood," she told me later. I must say that I was just as happy.

We did, however, watch the bats drink from the burro. When a vampire bites, he stretches his mouth open to the fullest extent and makes a single quick slash with his two long incisors. He does not stab but slashes out two small gouges and then instantly jumps back to watch the quarry's reaction. If he has hit an insensitive spot, he then hurries in and begins to lap, not suck, the flowing blood. If the animal starts or shakes himself, the bat waits until he quiets down and then tries another spot. Once he has found a good spot, he will always return to that same place again. Each of our bats had a different spot where he fed on the burro. Indians told us that they can kill the bats by seeing where they've bitten an animal and then smearing poison on the scab. The bat will surely return to exactly the same spot.

A bite made by a vampire will continue to bleed long after the bat has left it, and more blood is lost this way than from the actual bite. Scientists have argued that the saliva of the bats must contain some chemical that prevents the blood from coagulating but apparently this is not so. The action of the tongue helps to keep the wound open while the bat is lapping but it seemed to us that the bats know enough to cut into a vein. The action of the victim's heart keeps pumping the blood out and this is why the wound continues to bleed. Our young vampires hadn't developed the approved technique and would bite the burro anywhere, but often they couldn't draw enough blood to satisfy them. Then they'd have to try somewhere else. But once they learned where a vein was, they never forgot the location.

I can't say the vampires made particularly good pets. They seemed to be highly specialized. Apart from their biting technique, they never showed any intelligence. They did learn to recognize Jule and would come to her for blood from the medicine dropper while they avoided me. Some even learned to lap from a saucer. Even when they became so tame that Jule could pick them up, stroke them, feed them, and then hang them up on the wall as though she were hanging up a scarf, they never responded to affection and never showed any interest in what was going on about them.

When it was time to leave Mexico, we let them go. As bats have an astonishing homing instinct, I've no doubt that they found their way back to their cave in Los Sabinos. They were interesting but hardly lovable.   THE END

Talking it over

1. How can you tell that the Mannixes had an unusually strong interest in finding out how vampire bats live?

2. It is certainly easier to check an encyclopedia for information than to gather it the way the Mannixes did. What advantages might there be, though, in getting information first-hand?

3. *a.* Why did the villagers stay in Los Sabinos in spite of the vampire bats?

   b. Discuss whether there is anything in your community which you are used to but which strangers might find unpleasant or even unbearable.

4. What description in this account about vampires seemed most vivid to you? To which of your senses did it appeal?

Words in action

Even if you have never been in a cave, you should be able to visualize what Dan Mannix saw because of the way he compares scenes in the cave to things with which you are probably more familiar.

Make a rough drawing of one or more of the following scenes. The idea is not to produce a work of art, but simply to show that you "see" what is described.

1. The entrance to the cave was shrouded by a forest of curiously twisted trees that looked like the papier mâché creation of a Hollywood murder-mystery set.

2. The entrance hall was filled with boulders, piled together like children's marbles.

3. The vast mouth of the cave diminished behind us until it looked no bigger than a rathole.

4. The candles left sticking in the rocks to mark our path back showed in the intense darkness like tiny fireflies.

5. Bats began to pour out of the hole like clouds of black confetti. . . .

6. Turning up our lights, we could see dozens of vampires hanging head down on the walls above us. They looked like miniature bearskin rugs, hung upside down with the open mouths and grinning teeth pointing downward.

7. Across from us a black slit like a giant, toothless mouth showed in the white limestone. Vines overhung it like a straggly mustache.

Counting Coup on a Wounded Buffalo

by Chief Plenty-coups

(as told to Frank B. Linderman)

To the plains Indians in the old days, war was a game
in which the score was kept by "counting coup."
A warrior who touched a living enemy with his hand
or with a feather-decorated willow stick called
a coup stick received the highest coup award.
Killing or scalping an enemy or stealing a horse
also called for an award, but one of less value.
Young boys were sometimes allowed to count coup for
brave deeds performed in connection with hunting.

ONE DAY when the chokecherries were black and the plums red on the trees, my grandfather rode through the village, calling twenty of us older boys by name. The buffalo-runners had been out since daybreak, and we guessed what was before us. "Get on your horses and follow me," said my grandfather, riding out on the plains.

We rode fast. Nothing was in sight until Grandfather led us over a hill. There we saw a circle of horsemen about one hundred yards across, and

in its center a huge buffalo bull. We knew he had been wounded and tormented until he was very dangerous, and when we saw him there defying the men on horseback we began to dread the ordeal that was at hand.

The circle parted as we rode through it, and the bull, angered by the stir we made, charged and sent us flying. The men were laughing at us when we returned, and this made me feel very small. They had again surrounded the bull, and I now saw an arrow sticking deep in his side. Only its feathers were sticking out of a wound that dripped blood on the ground.

"Get down from your horses, young men," said my grandfather. "A cool head, with quick feet, may strike this bull on the root of his tail with a bow. Be lively, and take care of yourselves. The young man who strikes, and is himself not hurt, may count coup."

I was first off my horse. Watching the bull, I slipped out of shirt and leggings, letting them fall where I stood. Naked, with only my bow in my right hand, I stepped away from my clothes, feeling that I might never see them again. I was not quite nine years old.

The bull saw me, a human being afoot! He seemed to know that now he might kill, and he began to paw the ground and bellow as I walked carefully toward him.

Suddenly he stopped pawing, and his voice was still. He came to meet me, his eyes green with anger and pain. I saw blood dropping from his side, not red blood now, but mixed with yellow.

I stopped walking and stood still. This seemed to puzzle the bull, and he too stopped in his tracks. We looked at each other, the sun hot on my naked back. Heat from the plains danced on the bull's horns and head; his sides were panting, and his mouth was bloody.

I knew that the men were watching me. I could feel their eyes on my back. I must go on. One step, two steps. The grass was soft and thick under my feet. Three steps. "I am a Crow. I have the heart of a grizzly bear,"[1] I said to myself. Three more steps. And then he charged!

A cheer went up out of a cloud of dust. I had struck the bull on the root of his tail! But I was in even greater danger than before.

Two other boys were after the bull now, but in spite of them he turned and came at me. To run was foolish. I stood still, waiting. The bull stopped very near me and bellowed, blowing bloody froth from his nose. The other boys, seeing my danger, did not move. The bull was not more than four bows' lengths from me, and I could feel my heart beating like a war-drum.

Two large gray wolves crossed the circle just behind him, but the bull did not notice them, did not move an eye. He saw only me, and I was growing tired from the strain of watching him. I must get relief, must tempt him to come on. I stepped to my right. Instantly he charged—but I had dodged back to my left, across his way, and I struck him when he passed. This time I ran among the horsemen, with a lump of bloody froth on my breast. I had had enough.   THE END

---

[1] Plenty-coups, like every young Crow boy, had recently been given a piece of the heart of a grizzly bear to eat, in order that he could truthfully say, "I have the heart of a grizzly." The Indians believed that this would make a person as brave and cool-headed as the grizzly, who supposedly is always ready to fight.

◯ **Talking it over**

1. Chief Plenty-coups described this incident without saying much about his deeper motives and feelings, but you can infer these things from his actions and the few comments he does make. What can you guess about the boy from each of the following statements?

    a. "I was first off my horse."

    b. "I stepped away from my

clothes, feeling that I might never see them again."

c. "I knew that men were watching me. I could feel their eyes on my back. I must go on."

d. "I am a Crow. I have the heart of a grizzly bear."

e. "This time I ran among the horsemen, with a lump of bloody froth on my breast. I had had enough."

2. *a.* What "sport" does this experience make you think of? What details are similar?

b. Why were the boys asked to perform this feat of striking a dangerous bull?

c. Why did the Indians place so much emphasis on self-control and daring?

Man of many achievements

When Chief Plenty-coups was born, in 1848, the Crows were still living the strenuous life of buffalo-hunters, following the big herds that provided them with food and clothing. His grandfather named him Aleek-chea-ahoosh, meaning "many achievements," because in a dream he saw the boy counting many coups. The boy felt he had to live up to his name by excelling his companions and becoming their leader. He became a war chief while still a young man.

Then suddenly life changed for the plains Indians. Within a few years, white fur-hunters had slaughtered all the buffalo. Other whites settled the land, fenced off the water holes, and forced the Crows onto reservations. It was at this time that Plenty-coups became the real leader of his people.

He saw that the Crows would have to readjust their way of life and get along with the whites. He himself began to cultivate the land, and later opened a general merchandise store. An impressive speaker and a man of great dignity, he several times went to Washington in the interests of his people. Later he was chosen to represent all Indian tribes in placing the red man's wreath of flowers on the grave of the Unknown Soldier in Arlington National Cemetery.

Sign-talker

Frank B. Linderman, who wrote down the old chief's life story as he told it, was called "Sign-talker" by his Indian friends. He lived for more than forty years in a cabin on the shores of Flathead Lake in Montana, where he became well acquainted with the Crows and other Indians in that part of the country.

Linderman felt that it was very difficult for a white man to understand the Indian's way of life. He wrote, "I have studied the Indian for more than forty years, not coldly, but with sympathy; yet even now I do not feel that I know much about him. He has told me many times that I *do* know him— that I have 'felt his heart,' but whether this is so I am not certain. And yet a stranger, after spending a week's vacation in our national parks, alternately fishing and talking to an English-speaking tribesman, will go home and glibly write all there is to learn about the habits, beliefs, and traditions of the Indian tribes of the Northwest."

It was hard work, lugging paper sacks and boxes of dirt
all the way up the stairs of our own building,
keeping out of the way of the grown-ups. . . .

ANTAEUS[1]

by Borden Deal

THIS WAS during the wartime, when lots of people were coming North for jobs in factories and war industries, when people moved around a lot more than they do now and sometimes kids were thrown into new groups and new lives that were completely different from anything they had ever known before. I remember this one kid, T.J. his name was, from somewhere down South, whose family moved into our building during that time. They'd come North with everything they owned piled into the back seat of an old-model sedan that you wouldn't expect could make the trip, with T.J. and his three younger sisters riding shakily on top of the load of junk.

Our building was just like all the others there, with families crowded into a few rooms, and I guess there were twenty-five or thirty kids about my age in that one building. Of course, there were a few of us who formed a gang and ran together all the time after school, and I was the one who brought T.J. in and started the whole thing.

The building right next door to us was a factory where they made walking dolls. It was a low building with a flat, tarred roof that had a parapet all around it about head high and we'd found out a long time before that no one, not even the watchman, paid any attention to the roof because it was higher than any of the other buildings around. So my gang used the roof as a headquarters. We could get up there by crossing over to the fire escape from

[1]**Antaeus** (an tē′əs), a giant in Greek mythology who became stronger each time he touched the earth.

our own roof on a plank and then going on up. It was a secret place for us, where nobody else could go without our permission.

I remember the day I first took T.J. up there to meet the gang. He was a stocky, robust kid with a shock of white hair, nothing sissy about him except his voice—he talked in this slow, gentle voice like you never heard before. He talked different from any of us and you noticed it right away. But I liked him anyway, so I told him to come on up.

We climbed up over the parapet and dropped down on the roof. The rest of the gang were already there.

"Hi," I said. I jerked my thumb at T.J. "He just moved into the building yesterday."

He just stood there, not scared or anything, just looking, like the first time you see somebody you're not sure you're going to like.

"Hi," Blackie said. "Where are you from?"

"Marion County," T.J. said.

We laughed. "Marion County?" I said. "Where's that?"

He looked at me for a moment like I was a stranger, too. "It's in Alabama," he said, like I ought to know where it was.

"What's your name?" Charley said.

"T.J.," he said, looking back at him. He had pale blue eyes that looked washed-out but he looked directly at Charley, waiting for his reaction. He'll be all right, I thought. No sissy in him . . . except that voice. Who ever talked like that?

"T.J.," Blackie said. "That's just initials. What's your real name? Nobody in the world has just initials."

"I do," he said. "And they're T.J. That's all the name I got."

His voice was resolute with the knowledge of his rightness and for a moment no one had anything to say. T.J. looked around at the rooftop and down at the black tar under his feet. "Down yonder where I come from," he said, "we played out in woods. Don't you-all have no woods around here?"

"Naw," Blackie said. "There's the park a few blocks over, but it's full of kids and cops and old women. You can't do a thing."

T.J. kept looking at the tar under his feet. "You mean you ain't got no fields to raise nothing in? . . . No watermelons or nothing?"

"Naw," I said scornfully. "What do you want to grow something for? The folks can buy everything they need at the store."

He looked at me again with that strange, unknowing look. "In Marion County," he said, "I had my own acre of cotton and my own acre of corn. It was mine to plant and make ever' year."

He sounded like it was something to be proud of, and in some obscure way it made the rest of us angry. "Who'd want to have their own acre of cotton and corn?" Blackie said. "That's just work. What can you do with an acre of cotton and corn?"

T.J. looked at him. "Well, you get part of the bale offen your acre," he said seriously. "And I fed my acre of corn to my calf."

We didn't really know what he was talking about, so we were more puzzled than angry; otherwise, I guess, we'd have chased him off the roof and wouldn't have let him be part of our gang. But he was strange and different and we were all attracted by his stolid sense of rightness and belonging, maybe by the strange softness of his voice contrasting our own tones of speech into harshness.

He moved his foot against the black tar. "We could make our own field right here," he said softly, thoughtfully. "Come spring we could raise us what we want to . . . watermelons and garden truck and no telling what all."

"You'd have to be a good farmer to make these tar roofs grow any watermelons," I said. We all laughed.

But T.J. looked serious. "We could haul us some dirt up here," he said. "And spread it out even and water it and before you know it we'd have us a crop in here." He looked at us intently. "Wouldn't that be fun?"

"They wouldn't let us," Blackie said quickly.

"I thought you said this was you-all's roof," T.J. said to me. "That you-all could do anything you wanted to up here."

"They've never bothered us," I said. I felt the idea beginning to catch fire in me. It was a big idea and it took a while for it to sink in but the more I thought about it the better I liked it. "Say," I said to the gang. "He might have something there. Just make us a regular roof garden, with flowers and grass and trees and everything. And all ours, too," I said. "We wouldn't let anybody up here except the ones we wanted to."

"It'd take a while to grow trees," T.J. said quickly, but we weren't paying any attention to him. They were all talking about it suddenly, all excited with the idea after I'd put it in a way they could catch hold of it. Only rich people had roof gardens, we knew, and the idea of our own private domain excited them.

"We could bring it up in sacks and boxes," Blackie said. "We'd have to do it while the folks weren't paying any attention to us, for we'd have to come up to the roof of our building and then cross over with it."

"Where could we get the dirt?" somebody said worriedly.

"Out of those vacant lots over close to school," Blackie said. "Nobody'd notice if we scraped it up."

I slapped T.J. on the shoulder. "Man, you had a wonderful idea," I said, and everybody grinned at him, remembering that he had started it. "Our own private roof garden."

He grinned back. "It'll be ourn," he said. "All ourn." Then he looked thoughtful again. "Maybe I can lay my hands on some cotton seed, too. You think we could raise us some cotton?"

We'd started big projects before at one time or another, like any gang of kids, but they'd always petered out for lack of organization and direction. But this one didn't . . . somehow or other T.J. kept it going all through the winter months. He kept talking about the watermelons and the cotton we'd raise, come spring, and when even that wouldn't work he'd switch around to my idea of flowers and grass and trees, though he was always honest enough to add that it'd take a while to get any trees started. He always had it on his mind and he'd mention it in school, getting them lined up to carry dirt that afternoon, saying in a casual way that he reckoned a few more weeks ought to see the job through.

Our little area of private earth grew slowly. T.J. was smart enough to start in one corner of the building, heaping up the carried earth two or three feet thick, so that we had an immediate result to look at, to contemplate with awe. Some of the evenings T.J. alone was carrying earth up to the building, the rest of the gang distracted by other enterprises or interests, but T.J. kept plugging along on his own and eventually we'd all come back to him again and then our own little acre would grow more rapidly.

He was careful about the kind of dirt he'd let us carry up there and more than once he dumped a sandy load over the parapet into the areaway below because it wasn't good enough. He found out the kinds of earth in all the vacant lots for blocks around. He'd pick it up and feel it and smell it, frozen though it was sometimes, and then he'd say it was good growing soil or it wasn't worth anything and we'd have to go on somewhere else.

Thinking about it now, I don't see how he kept us at it. It was hard work, lugging paper sacks and boxes of dirt all the way up the stairs of our own building, keeping out of the way of the grownups so they wouldn't catch on to what we were doing. They probably wouldn't have cared, for they didn't pay much attention to us, but we wanted to keep it secret anyway. Then we had to go through the trap door to our roof, teeter over a plank to the fire escape, then climb two or three stories to the parapet and drop down onto the roof. All that for a small pile of earth that sometimes didn't seem worth the effort. But T.J. kept the vision bright within us, his words shrewd and calculated toward the fulfillment of his dream; and he worked harder than any of us. He seemed driven toward a goal that we couldn't see, a particular point in time that would be definitely marked by signs and wonders that only he could see.

The laborious earth just lay there

during the cold months, inert and lifeless, the clods lumpy and cold under our feet when we walked over it. But one day it rained and afterward there was a softness in the air and the earth was alive and giving again with moisture and warmth. That evening T.J. smelled the air, his nostrils dilating with the odor of the earth under his feet.

"It's spring," he said, and there was a gladness rising in his voice that filled us all with the same feeling. "It's mighty late for it, but it's spring. I'd just about decided it wasn't never gonna get here at all."

We were all sniffing at the air, too, trying to smell it the way that T.J. did, and I can still remember the sweet odor of the earth under our feet. It was the first time in my life that spring and spring earth had meant anything to me. I looked at T.J. then, knowing in a faint way the hunger within him through the toilsome winter months, knowing the dream that lay behind his plan. He was a new Antaeus, preparing his own bed of strength.

"Planting time," he said. "We'll have to find us some seed."

"What do we do?" Blackie said. "How do we do it?"

"First we'll have to break up the clods," T.J. said. "That won't be hard to do. Then we plant the seed and after a while they come up. Then you got you a crop." He frowned. "But you ain't got it raised yet. You got to tend it and hoe it and take care of it and all the time it's growing and growing, while you're awake and while you're asleep. Then you lay it by when it's growed and let it ripen and then you got you a crop."

"There's those wholesale seed houses over on Sixth," I said. "We could probably swipe some grass seed over there."

T.J. looked at the earth. "You-all seem mighty set on raising some grass," he said. "I ain't never put no effort into that. I spent all my life trying not to raise grass."

"But it's pretty," Blackie said. "We could play on it and take sunbaths on it. Like having our own lawn. Lots of people got lawns."

"Well," T.J. said. He looked at the rest of us, hesitant for the first time. He kept on looking at us for a moment. "I did have it in mind to raise some corn and vegetables. But we'll plant grass."

He was smart. He knew where to give in. And I don't suppose it made any difference to him, really. He just wanted to grow something, even if it was grass.

"Of course," he said, "I do think we ought to plant a row of watermelons. They'd be mighty nice to eat while we was a-laying on that grass."

We all laughed. "All right," I said. "We'll plant us a row of watermelons."

Things went very quickly then. Perhaps half the roof was covered with the earth, the half that wasn't broken by ventilators, and we swiped pocketfuls of grass seed from the open bins in the wholesale seed house, mingling among the buyers on Saturdays and during the school lunch hour. T.J. showed us how to prepare the earth, breaking up the clods and smoothing it and sowing the grass seed. It looked rich and black now with moisture, receiving of the seed, and it seemed that the grass sprang up overnight, pale green in the early spring.

We couldn't keep from looking at it, unable to believe that we had created this delicate growth. We looked at T.J. with understanding now, knowing the

fulfillment of the plan he had carried alone within his mind. We had worked without full understanding of the task but he had known all the time.

We found that we couldn't walk or play on the delicate blades, as we had expected to, but we didn't mind. It was enough just to look at it, to realize that it was the work of our own hands, and each evening the whole gang was there, trying to measure the growth that had been achieved that day.

One time a foot was placed on the plot of ground . . . one time only, Blackie stepping onto it with sudden bravado. Then he looked at the crushed blades and there was shame in his face. He did not do it again. This was his grass, too, and not to be desecrated. No one said anything, for it was not necessary.

T.J. had reserved a small section for watermelons and he was still trying to find some seed for it. The wholesale house didn't have any watermelon seed and we didn't know where we could lay our hands on them. T.J. shaped the earth into mounds, ready to receive them, three mounds lying in a straight line along the edge of the grass plot.

We had just about decided that we'd have to buy the seed if we were to get them. It was a violation of our principles, but we were anxious to get the watermelons started. Somewhere or other, T.J. got his hands on a seed catalogue and brought it one evening to our roof garden.

"We can order them now," he said, showing us the catalogue. "Look!"

We all crowded around, looking at the fat, green watermelons pictured in full color on the pages. Some of them were split open, showing the red, tempting meat, making our mouths water.

"Now we got to scrape up some seed money," T.J. said, looking at us. "I got a quarter. How much you-all got?"

We made up a couple of dollars between us and T.J. nodded his head. "That'll be more than enough. Now we got to decide what kind to get. I think them Kleckley Sweets. What do you-all think?"

He was going into esoteric matters beyond our reach. We hadn't even known there were different kinds of melons. So we just nodded our heads and agreed that Yes, we thought the Kleckley Sweets too.

"I'll order them tonight," T.J. said. "We ought to have them in a few days."

"What are you boys doing up here?" an adult voice said behind us.

It startled us, for no one had ever come up here before, in all the time we had been using the roof of the factory. We jerked around and saw three men standing near the trap door at the other end of the roof. They weren't policemen, or night watchmen, but three men in plump business suits, looking at us. They walked toward us.

"What are you boys doing up here?" the one in the middle said again.

We stood still, guilt heavy among us, levied by the tone of voice, and looked at the three strangers.

The men stared at the grass flourishing behind us. "What's this?" the man said. "How did this get up here?"

"Sure is growing good, ain't it?" T.J. said conversationally. "We planted it."

The men kept looking at the grass as if they didn't believe it. It was a thick carpet over the earth now, a patch of deep greenness startling in the sterile industrial surroundings.

"Yes sir," T.J. said proudly. "We toted that earth up here and planted that grass." He fluttered the seed catalogue. "And we're just fixing to plant us some watermelon."

The man looked at him then, his eyes strange and faraway. "What do you mean, putting this on the roof of my building?" he said. "Do you want to go to jail?"

T.J. looked shaken. The rest of us were silent, frightened by the authority of his voice. We had grown up aware of adult authority, of policemen and night watchmen and teachers, and this man sounded like all the others. But it was a new thing to T.J.

"Well, you wan't using the roof," T.J. said. He paused a moment and added shrewdly, "So we just thought to pretty it up a little bit."

"And sag it so I'd have to rebuild it," the man said sharply. He started turning away, saying to another man beside him, "See that all that junk is shoveled off by tomorrow."

"Yes sir," the man said.

T.J. started forward. "You can't do that," he said. "We toted it up here and it's our earth. We planted it and raised it and toted it up here."

The man stared at him coldly. "But it's my building," he said. "It's to be shoveled off tomorrow."

"It's our earth," T.J. said desperately. "You ain't got no right!"

The men walked on without listening and descended clumsily through the trap door. T.J. stood looking after them, his body tense with anger, until they had disappeared. They wouldn't even argue with him, wouldn't let him defend his earth-rights.

He turned to us. "We won't let 'em do it," he said fiercely. "We'll stay up here all day tomorrow and the day after that and we won't let 'em do it."

We just looked at him. We knew that there was no stopping it. He saw it in our faces and his face wavered for a moment before he gripped it into determination.

"They ain't got no right," he said. "It's our earth. It's our land. Can't nobody touch a man's own land."

We kept on looking at him, listening to the words but knowing that it was no use. The adult world had descended on us even in our richest dream and we knew there was no calculating the adult world, no fighting it, no winning against it.

We started moving slowly toward the parapet and the fire escape, avoiding a last look at the green beauty of the earth that T.J. had planted for us . . . had planted deeply in our minds as well as in our experience. We filed slowly over the edge and down the steps to the plank, T.J. coming last, and all of us could feel the weight of his grief behind us.

"Wait a minute," he said suddenly, his voice harsh with the effort of calling. We stopped and turned, held by the tone of his voice, and looked up at him standing above us on the fire escape.

"We can't stop them?" he said, looking down at us, his face strange in the dusky light. "There ain't no way to stop 'em?"

"No," Blackie said with finality. "They own the building."

We stood still for a moment, looking up at T.J., caught into inaction by the decision working in his face. He stared back at us and his face was pale and mean in the poor light, with a bald nakedness in his skin like sick people have sometimes.

"They ain't gonna touch my earth,"

he said fiercely. "They ain't gonna lay a hand on it! Come on."

He turned around and started up the fire escape again, almost running against the effort of climbing. We followed more slowly, not knowing what he intended. By the time we reached him, he had seized a board and thrust it into the soil, scooping it up and flinging it over the parapet into the areaway below. He straightened and looked at us.

"They can't touch it," he said. "I won't let 'em lay a dirty hand on it!"

We saw it then. He stooped to his labor again and we followed, the gusts of his anger moving in frenzied labor among us as we scattered along the edge of earth, scooping it and throwing it over the parapet, destroying with anger the growth we had nurtured with such tender care. The soil carried so laboriously upward to the light and the sun cascaded swiftly into the dark areaway, the green blades of grass crumpled and twisted in the falling.

It took less time than you would think . . . the task of destruction is infinitely easier than that of creation. We stopped at the end, leaving only a scattering of loose soil, and when it was finally over, a stillness stood among the group and over the factory building. We looked down at the bare sterility of black tar, felt the harsh texture of it under the soles of our shoes, and the anger had gone out of us, leaving only a sore aching in our minds like overstretched muscles.

T.J. stood for a moment, his breathing slowing from anger and effort, caught into the same contemplation of destruction as all of us. He stooped slowly, finally, and picked up a lonely blade of grass left trampled under our feet and put it between his teeth, tasting it, sucking the greenness out of it into his mouth. Then he started walking toward the fire escape, moving before any of us were ready to move, and disappeared over the edge.

We followed him but he was already halfway down to the ground, going on past the board where we crossed over, climbing down into the areaway. We saw the last section swing down with his weight and then he stood on the concrete below us, looking at the small pile of anonymous earth scattered by our throwing. Then he walked across the place where we could see him and disappeared toward the street without glancing back, without looking up to see us watching him.

They did not find him for two weeks. Then the Nashville police caught him just outside the Nashville freight yards. He was walking along the railroad track; still heading south, still heading home.

As for us, who had no remembered home to call us . . . none of us ever again climbed the escape-way to the roof.

THE END

Talking it over

1. In the part of the city where the boys live, how is life different from life where T.J. came from?

2. *a.* What is T.J.'s dream? How does he keep it alive through the winter?

   b. Why does T.J. go along with the other boys' wish to plant grass?

3. Describe the feelings of the boys when their grass begins to grow.

4. What happens that keeps the

boys from buying the watermelon seeds?

5. *a.* Why does it take T.J. longer than the other boys to accept the fact that they cannot stop the destruction of their garden?

b. How do you think the boys will be affected by the experience of growing the grass?

6. *It is generally easier to destroy something than to make or create it.* How does this statement apply to the story?

7. *a.* What do you think is the reason why T.J. leaves the city and heads for Alabama?

b. Why do you suppose the other boys never again visit the roof?

3. ". . . none of us ever again climbed the **escape-way** to the roof."

a. How did the boys get from their building to the factory roof?

b. What is an escape-way on a building?

c. In what other sense is it an escape-way for the boys?

Words in action

1. "He stared back at us and his face was pale and **mean** in the poor light." (end, 241B). Which of the following sentences uses *mean* in much the same way as it is used above?

a. Today is my first day back at school after the flu, and I still feel *mean.*

b. John's unfair treatment of his little brother is *mean.*

c. A *mean* number is something like an average.

2. Choose the two definitions below that come closest to explaining *mean* as used in sentence 1.

a. of little importance
b. humiliated; ashamed
c. stingy
d. in poor physical condition
e. halfway between two extremes

It came in a dream

Have you ever had an idea in a dream? Borden Deal's "Antaeus" came to him in a dream, "practically complete word for word."

"Dreaming a story is not unusual for me," Deal writes. "What was unusual was the fact that it took ten years for 'Antaeus' to be published. It was turned down by virtually every popular and literary magazine in the country, not once but several times. When it was finally published, it was chosen for a collection of the best American short stories of the year. It has been reprinted more times than any of my other hundred or so short stories."

Mr. Deal was born in Mississippi. He lives in Florida in a house that "stands with its feet in the Gulf of Mexico."

OUR HOUSE

by Jane Stembridge

Our house is filled
with emptiness

which acts upon
the flesh

and crowds me out
to wandering

again.

 Talking it over

1. How can a house be "filled" with emptiness?

2. Which house would seem more empty—a house where there has never been happiness or one where former happiness is gone?

3. How does the emptiness affect the person who is speaking?

4. When the speaker is wandering, what might he be looking for?

THE FOOLISH MAN

Armenian Folk Tale

O NCE there was and was not in ancient Armenia a poor man who
worked and toiled hard from morn till
night, but nevertheless remained poor.

Finally one day he became so discouraged that he decided to go in
search of God in order to ask Him how
long he must endure such poverty—
and to beg of Him a favor.

On his way, the man met a wolf.

"Good day, brother man," asked the
wolf. "Where are you bound in such a
hurry?"

"I go in search of God," replied the
man. "I have a complaint to lodge
with Him."

"Well," said the wolf, "would you do
me a kindness? When you find God,
will you complain to Him for me, too?
Tell Him you met a half-starved wolf
who searches the woods and fields for
food from morning till night—and
though he works hard and long, still
finds nothing to eat. Ask God why He
does not provide for wolves since He
created them?"

"I will tell Him of your complaint,"
agreed the poor man, and continued
on his way.

As he hurried over the hills and through the valleys, he chanced to meet a beautiful maid.

"Where do you go in such a hurry, my brother?" asked the maid.

"I go in search of God," replied the man.

"Oh, kind friend, when you find God, would you ask Him something for me? Tell Him you met a maid on your way. Tell Him she is young and fair and very rich—but very unhappy. Ask God why she cannot know happiness. What will become of her? Ask God why He will not help her to be happy."

"I will tell Him of your trouble," promised the poor man, and continued on his way.

Soon he met a tree which seemed all dried up and dying even though it grew by the side of a river.

"Where do you go in such a hurry, O traveler?" called the dry tree.

"I go in search of God," answered the man. "I have a complaint to lodge with Him."

"Wait a moment, O traveler," begged the tree. "I, too, have a question for God.

"Please ask Him why I am dry both in summer and winter. Though I live by this wet river, my leaves do not turn green. Ask God how long I must suffer. Ask Him that for me, good friend," said the tree.

The man listened to the tree's complaint, promised to tell God, and continued once again upon his way.

Finally, the poor man reached the end of his journey. He found God seated beneath the ledge of a cliff.

"Good day," said the man as he approached God.

"Welcome, traveler," God returned his greeting. "Why have you journeyed so far? What is your trouble?"

"Well, I want to know why there is injustice in the world. Is it fair that I toil and labor from morn till night— and yet never seem to earn enough for a full stomach, while many who do not work half as hard as I live and eat as rich men do?"

"Go then," replied God. "I present the Gift of Luck. Go find it and enjoy it to the end of your days."

"I have yet another complaint, my Lord," continued the man—and he proceeded to list the complaints and requests of the starved wolf, the beautiful maid, and the parched tree.

God gave appropriate answers to each of the three complaints, whereupon the poor man thanked Him and started on his way homeward.

Soon he came upon the dry, parched tree.

"What message did God have for me?" asked the tree.

"He said that beneath your trunk there lies a pot of gold which prevents the water from seeping up your trunk to your leaves. God said your branches will never turn green until the pot of gold is removed."

"Well, what are you waiting for, foolish man!" exclaimed the tree. "Dig up that pot of gold. It will make you rich—and permit me to turn green and live again!"

"Oh, no," protested the man. "I have no time to dig up a pot of gold. God has given me the Gift of Luck. I must hurry and search for it." And he hurried on his way.

Presently, he met the beautiful maid who was waiting for him. "Oh, kind friend, what message did God have for me?"

"God said that you will soon meet a kind man who will prove to be a good life's companion to you. No longer will you be lonely. Happiness and contentment will come to you," reported the poor man.

"In that case, what are you waiting for, foolish man?" exclaimed the maid. "Why don't you stay here and be my life's companion?"

"Oh, no! I have no time to stay with you. God has given me the Gift of Luck. I must hurry and search for it." And the man hurried on his way.

Some distance away, the starving wolf impatiently awaited the man's coming, and hailed him with a shout.

"Well, what did God say? What message did He send to me?"

"Brother wolf, so many things have happened since I saw you last," said the man. "I hardly know where to begin. On my way to seek God, I met a beautiful maid who begged me to ask God the reason for her unhappiness. And I met a parched tree who wanted God to explain the dryness of its branches even though it stood by a wet river.

"I told God about these matters. He bade me tell the maid to seek a life's companion in order to find happiness. He bade me warn the tree about a pot of gold buried near its trunk which must be removed before the branches can receive nourishment from the earth.

"On my return, I brought God's answers to the maid and to the tree. The maid asked me to stay and be her life's companion, while the tree asked me to dig up the pot of gold.

"Of course, I had to refuse both since God gave me the Gift of Luck— and I must hurry along to search for it!"

"Ah-h-h, brother man, and what was God's reply to me?" asked the starving wolf.

"As for you," replied the man, "God said that you would remain hungry until you met a silly and foolish man whom you could eat up. Only then, said God, would your hunger be satisfied."

"Hmmmmmm," mused the wolf, "where in the world will I find a man more silly and stupid than you?"

And he ate up the foolish man.

THE END

Talking it over

1. At what point in the story did you realize the man is foolish?

2. If you were to ask several people what they want from life, they might mention happiness, success, popularity, power, or wealth.

   a. Which of these would the man get by taking the pot of gold?

   b. Which would he get by marrying the maid?

3. Why doesn't the man recognize good fortune when he could have had it?

4. Which of the following is the best statement of the central idea of this story? Justify your choice.

   a. Wolves are not to be trusted.

   b. People sometimes don't recognize their opportunities.

   c. Greed can easily destroy a man.

   d. A fool and his luck are soon parted.

   e. Love is more important than wealth.

Brightside Crossing

by Alan E. Nourse

Painting by Chesley Bonestell

No one had crossed this land
before and lived
to tell about it.

JAMES Baron was not pleased to hear that he had had a visitor when he reached the Red Lion that evening. He had no stomach for mysteries, vast or trifling, and there were pressing things to think about at this time. Yet the doorman had flagged him as he came in from the street: "A thousand pardons, Mr. Baron. The gentleman—he would leave no name. He said you'd want to see him. He will be back by eight."

Baron drummed his fingers on the tabletop, staring about the quiet lounge. Street trade was discouraged at the Red Lion, gently but persuasively; the patrons were few in number. Across to the right was a group that Baron knew vaguely—Andean climbers, or at least two of them were. Over near the door he recognized old Balmer, who had mapped the first passage to the core of Vulcan Crater on Venus. Baron returned his smile with a nod. Then he settled back and waited impatiently for the intruder who demanded his time without justifying it.

Presently a small, grizzled man crossed the room and sat down at Baron's table. He was short and wiry. His face held no key to his age—he might have been thirty or a thousand—but he looked weary and immensely ugly. His cheeks and forehead were twisted and brown, with scars that were still healing.

The stranger said, "I'm glad you waited. I've heard you're planning to attempt the Brightside."[1]

Baron stared at the man for a moment. "I see you can read telecasts," he said coldly. "The news was correct. We are going to make a Brightside Crossing."

"At perihelion?"[2]

"Of course. When else?"

The grizzled man searched Baron's face for a moment without expression. Then he said slowly, "No, I'm afraid you're not going to make the Crossing."

"Say, who are you, if you don't mind?" Baron demanded.

"The name is Claney," said the stranger.

There was a silence. Then: "Claney? *Peter* Claney?"

"That's right."

Baron's eyes were wide with excitement, all trace of anger gone. "My God, man—*where have you been hiding?* We've been trying to contact you for months!"

"I know. I was hoping you'd quit looking and chuck the whole idea."

"Quit looking!" Baron bent forward over the table. "My friend, we'd given up hope, but we've never quit looking. Here, have a drink. There's so much you can tell us." His fingers were trembling.

Peter Claney shook his head. "I can't tell you anything you want to hear."

"But you've *got* to. You're the only man on Earth who's attempted a Brightside Crossing and lived through it! And the story you cleared for the news—it was nothing. We need *details*. Where did your equipment fall down? Where did you miscalculate? What were the trouble spots?" Baron jabbed a finger at Claney's face. "That, for instance—epithelioma?[3] Why? What was wrong with your glass? Your filters? We've got to know those things. If you can tell us, we can make it across where your attempt failed—"

---

[1] **Brightside,** the side of the planet Mercury which always faces the sun.

[2] **perihelion** (per′ ə hē′ lē ən), the point in the planet's orbit closest to the sun.

[3] **epithelioma** (ep′ə thē li ō′mə), skin cancer.

"You want to know why we failed?" asked Claney.

"Of course we want to know. We *have* to know."

"It's simple. We failed because it can't be done. We couldn't do it and neither can you. No human beings will ever cross the Brightside alive, not if they try for centuries."

"Nonsense," Baron declared. "We will."

Claney shrugged. "I was there. I know what I'm saying. You can blame the equipment or the men—there were flaws in both quarters—but we just didn't know what we were fighting. It was the *planet* that whipped us, that and the *Sun*. They'll whip you, too, if you try it."

"Never," said Baron.

"Let me tell you," Peter Claney said.

I'd been interested in the Brightside for almost as long as I can remember (Claney said). I guess I was about ten when Wyatt and Carpenter made the last attempt—that was in 2082, I think. I followed the news stories like a tri-V serial, and then I was heartbroken when they just disappeared.

I know now that they were a pair of idiots, starting off without proper equipment, with practically no knowledge of surface conditions, without any charts—but I didn't know that then and it was a terrible tragedy. After that, I followed Sanderson's work in the Twilight Lab up there and began to get Brightside into my blood.

But it was Mikuta's idea to attempt a Crossing. Did you ever know Tom Mikuta? I don't suppose you did. No, not Japanese—Polish-American. He was a major in the Interplanetary Service for some years and hung onto the title after he gave up his commission.

He was with Armstrong on Mars during his Service days, with a good deal of the original mapping and surveying for the colony to his credit. I first met him on Venus; we spent five years together up there doing some of the nastiest exploring since the Mato Grosso.[4] Then he made the attempt on Vulcan Crater that paved the way for Balmer a few years later.

I'd always liked the Major—he was big and quiet and cool, the sort of guy who always had things figured a little further ahead than anyone else and always knew what to do in a tight place. Too many men in this game are all nerve and luck, with no judgment. The Major had all three. He also had the kind of personality that could take a crew of wild men and make them work like a well-oiled machine across a thousand miles of Venus jungle. I liked him and I trusted him.

He contacted me in New York, and he was very casual at first. We spent an evening here at the Red Lion, talking about old times; he told me about the Vulcan business, and how he'd been out to see Sanderson and the Twilight Lab on Mercury, and how he preferred a hot trek to a cold one any day of the year—and then he wanted to know what I'd been doing since Venus and what my plans were.

"No particular plans," I told him. "Why?"

He looked me over. "How much do you weigh, Peter?"

I told him one thirty-five.

"That much!" he said. "Be damned. Well, there can't be much fat on you, at any rate. How do you take heat?"

---

[4] **Mato Grosso** (mä′tō grō′sō), an isolated section of Brazil in South America.

"You should know," I said. "Venus was no icebox."

"No, I mean *real* heat."

Then I began to get it. "You're planning a trip."

"That's right. A hot trip." He grinned at me. "Might be dangerous, too."

"What trip?"

"Brightside of Mercury," the Major said.

I whistled cautiously. "Aphelion?[5]"

He threw his head back. "Why try a Crossing at aphelion?[5] What have you done then? Four thousand miles of butcherous heat, just to have some joker come along, use your data, and drum you out of the glory by crossing at perihelion forty-four days later? No, thanks. I want the Brightside without any nonsense about it." He leaned toward me eagerly. "I want to make a Crossing at perihelion and I want to cross on the surface. If a man can do that, he's got Mercury. Until then, *nobody's* got Mercury. I want Mercury—but I'll need help getting it."

I'd thought of it a thousand times and never dared consider it. Nobody had, since Wyatt and Carpenter disappeared. Mercury turns on its axis in the same time that it wheels around the Sun, which means that the Brightside is always facing in. That makes the Brightside of Mercury at perihelion the hottest place in the Solar System, with one single exception: the surface of the Sun itself.

It would be a hellish trek. Only a few men had ever learned just *how* hellish and they never came back to tell about it. It was a real Hell's Crossing, but someday somebody would cross it.

I wanted to be along.

The Twilight Lab, near the northern pole of Mercury, was the obvious jumping-off place. The setup there wasn't very extensive—a rocket landing, the labs and quarters for Sanderson's crew sunk deep into the crust, and the tower that housed the Solar 'scope that Sanderson had built up there ten years before.

Twilight Lab wasn't particularly interested in the Brightside, of course—the Sun was Sanderson's baby and he'd picked Mercury as the closest chunk of rock to the Sun that could hold his observatory. He'd chosen a good location, too. On Mercury, the Brightside temperature hits 770° F. at perihelion and the Darkside runs pretty constant at −410° F. No permanent installation with a human crew could survive at either extreme. But with Mercury's wobble, the twilight zone between Brightside and Darkside offers something closer to survival temperatures.

Sanderson built the Lab up near the pole, where the zone is about five miles wide, so the temperature only varies fifty to sixty degrees with the libration.[6] The Solar 'scope could take that much change, and they'd get a good clear observation of the Sun for about seventy out of the eighty-eight days it takes the planet to wheel around.

The Major was counting on Sanderson knowing something about Mercury as well as the Sun when we camped at the Lab to make final preparations.

Sanderson did. He thought we'd lost our minds and he said so, but he gave us all the help he could. He spent a week briefing Jack Stone, the third member of our party, who had arrived with the supplies and equipment a few

---

[5]**aphelion** (ə fē′lē ən), the point in a planet's orbit farthest from the sun.

[6]**libration,** movement from side to side.

days earlier. Poor Jack met us at the rocket landing almost bawling, Sanderson had given him such a gloomy picture of what Brightside was like.

Stone was a youngster—hardly twenty-five, I'd say—but he'd been with the Major at Vulcan and had begged to join this trek. I had a funny feeling that Jack really didn't care for exploring too much, but he thought Mikuta was God, and followed him around like a puppy.

It didn't matter to me as long as he knew what he was getting in for. You don't go asking people in this game why they do it—they're liable to get awfully uneasy, and none of them can ever give you an answer that makes sense. Anyway, Stone had borrowed three men from the Lab and had the supplies and equipment all lined up when we got there, ready to check and test.

We dug right in. With plenty of funds—tri-V money and some government cash the Major had talked his way around—our equipment was new and good. Mikuta had done the designing and testing himself, with a big assist from Sanderson. We had four Bugs, three of them the light pillow-tire models, with special lead-cooled cut-in engines when the heat set in, and one heavy-duty tractor model for pulling the sledges.

The Major went over them like a kid at the circus. Then he said, "Have you heard anything from McIvers?"

"Who's he?" Stone wanted to know.

"He'll be joining us. He's a good man—got quite a name for climbing, back home." The Major turned to me. "You've probably heard of him."

I'd heard plenty of stories about Ted McIvers and I wasn't too happy to hear that he was joining us. "Kind of a daredevil, isn't he?"

"Maybe. He's lucky and skillful. Where do you draw the line? We'll need plenty of both."

"Have you ever worked with him?" I asked.

"No. Are you worried?"

"Not exactly. But Brightside is no place to count on luck."

The Major laughed. "I don't think we need to worry about McIvers. We understood each other when I talked up the trip to him, and we're going to need each other too much to do any fooling around." He turned back to the supply list. "Meanwhile, let's get this stuff listed and packed. We'll need to cut weight sharply and our time is short. Sanderson says we should leave in three days."

Two days later, McIvers hadn't arrived. The Major didn't say much about it: Stone was getting edgy and so was I. We spent the second day studying charts of the Brightside, such as they were. The best available were pretty poor, taken from so far out that the detail dissolved into blurs on blowup.[7] They showed the biggest ranges of peaks and craters and faults, and that was all. Still, we could use them to plan a broad outline of our course.

"This range here," the Major said as we crowded around the board, "is largely inactive, according to Sanderson. But these to the south and west *could* be active. Seismograph tracings suggest a lot of activity in that region, getting worse down toward the equator —not only volcanic, but sub-surface shifting."

Stone nodded. "Sanderson told me

[7] **on blowup,** when enlarged.

there was probably constant surface activity."

The Major shrugged. "Well, it's treacherous, there's no doubt of it. But the only way to avoid it is to travel over the Pole, which would lose us days and offer us no guarantee of less activity to the west. Now we might avoid some if we could find a pass through this range and cut sharp east—"

It seemed that the more we considered the problem, the further we got from a solution. We knew there were active volcanoes on the Brightside— even on the Darkside, though surface activity there was pretty much slowed down and localized.

But there were problems of atmosphere on Brightside, as well. There *was* an atmosphere and a constant atmospheric flow from Brightside to Darkside. Not much—the lighter gases had reached escape velocity and disappeared from Brightside millennia ago— but there was CO_2, and nitrogen, and traces of other heavier gases. There was also an abundance of sulfur vapor, as well as carbon disulfide and sulfur dioxide.[8]

The atmospheric tide moved toward the Darkside, where it condensed, carrying enough volcanic ash with it for Sanderson to estimate the depth and nature of the surface upheavals on Brightside from his samplings. The trick was to find a passage that avoided those upheavals as far as possible. But in the final analysis, we were barely scraping the surface. The only way we would find out what was happening there was to be there.

Finally, on the third day, McIvers

blew in on a freight rocket from Venus. He'd missed by a few hours the ship that the Major and I had taken and conned his way to Venus in hopes of getting a hop from there. He didn't seem too upset about it, as though this were his usual way of doing things, and he couldn't see why everyone should get so excited.

He was a tall, rangy man with long, wavy hair prematurely gray, and the sort of eyes that looked like a climber's —half closed, sleepy, almost indolent, but capable of abrupt alertness. And he never stood still; he was always moving, always doing something with his hands, or talking, or pacing about.

Evidently the Major decided not to press the issue of his arrival. There was still work to do, and an hour later we were running the final tests on the pressure suits. That evening, Stone and McIvers were thick as thieves, and everything was set for an early departure.

"And that," said Baron, finishing his drink and signaling the waiter for another pair, "was your first big mistake."

Peter Claney raised his eyebrows. "McIvers?"

"Of course."

Claney shrugged, glanced at the small quiet tables around them. "There are lots of bizarre personalities around a place like this, and some of the best wouldn't seem to be the most reliable at first glance. Anyway, personality problems weren't our big problem right then. *Equipment* worried us first and *route* next."

Baron nodded in agreement. "What kind of suits did you have?"

"The best insulating suits ever made," said Claney. "Each one had an inner lining of Fiberglas modification, to

[8] CO_2 . . . sulfur dioxide, various kinds of gases. Carbon dioxide (CO_2) and nitrogen are found in the earth's atmosphere, but the others are harmful to man.

avoid the clumsiness of asbestos, and carried the refrigerating unit and oxygen storage which we recharged from sledges every eight hours. Outer layer carried a monomolecular chrome reflecting surface that made us glitter like Christmas trees. And we had a half-inch dead-air space under positive pressure between the two layers. Warning thermocouples, of course—at 770 degrees, it wouldn't take long to fry us to cinders if the suits failed somewhere."

"How about the Bugs?"

"They were insulated, too, but we weren't counting on them too much for protection."

"You weren't!" Baron exclaimed. "Why not?"

"We'd be in and out of them too much. They gave us mobility and storage, but we knew we'd have to do a lot of forward work on foot." Claney smiled bitterly. "Which meant that we had an inch of Fiberglas and a half-inch of dead air between us and a surface temperature where lead flowed like water and zinc was almost at melting point and the pools of sulfur in the shadows were boiling like oatmeal over a campfire."

Baron licked his lips. His fingers stroked the cool, wet glass.

"Go on," he said tautly. "You started on schedule?"

"Oh, yes," said Claney, "we started on schedule, all right. We just didn't quite end on schedule, that was all. But I'm getting to that."

He settled back in his chair and continued.

We jumped off from Twilight on a course due southeast, with thirty days to make it to the Center of Brightside. If we could cross an average of seventy miles a day, we could hit Center exactly at perihelion, the point of Mercury's closest approach to the Sun—which made Center the hottest part of the planet at the hottest it ever gets.

The Sun was already huge and yellow over the horizon when we started, twice the size it appears on Earth. Every day that sun would grow bigger and whiter, and every day the surface would get hotter. But once we reached Center, the job was only half done—we would still have to travel another 2000 miles to the opposite twilight zone. Sanderson was to meet us on the other side in the Laboratory's scout ship approximately sixty days from the time we jumped off.

That was the plan, in outline. It was up to us to cross those seventy miles a day, no matter how hot it became, no matter what terrain we had to cross. Detours would be dangerous and time-consuming. Delays would cost us our lives. We all knew that.

The Major briefed us on details an hour before we left. "Peter, you'll take the lead Bug, the small one we stripped down for you. Stone and I will flank you on either side, giving you a hundred-yard lead. McIvers, you'll have the job of dragging the sledges, so we'll have to direct your course pretty closely. Peter's job is to pick the passage at any given point. If there's any doubt of safe passage, we'll all explore ahead on foot before we risk the Bugs. Got that?"

McIvers and Stone exchanged glances. McIvers said: "Jack and I were planning to change around. We figured he could take the sledges. That would give me a little more mobility."

The Major looked up sharply at Stone. "Do you buy that, Jack?"

Stone shrugged. "I don't mind. Mac wanted—"

McIvers made an impatient gesture with his hands. "It doesn't matter. I just feel better when I'm on the move. Does it make any difference?"

"I guess it doesn't," said the Major. "Then you'll flank Peter along with me. Right?"

"Sure, sure." McIvers pulled at his lower lip. "Who's going to do the advance scouting?"

"It sounds like I am," I cut in. "We want to keep the lead Bug as light as possible."

Mikuta nodded. "That's right. Peter's Bug is stripped down to the frame and wheels."

McIvers shook his head. "No, I mean the *advance* work. You need somebody out ahead—four or five miles, at least—to pick up the big flaws and active surface changes, don't you?" He stared at the Major. "I mean, how can we tell what sort of a hole we may be moving into, unless we have a scout up ahead?"

"That's what we have the charts for," the Major said sharply.

"Charts! I'm talking about *detail* work. We don't need to worry about the major topography. It's the little faults you can't see on the pictures that can kill us." He tossed the charts down excitedly. "Look, let me take a Bug out ahead and work reconnaissance, keep five, maybe ten miles ahead of the column. I can stay on good solid ground, of course, but scan the area closely and radio back to Peter where to avoid the flaws. Then—"

"No dice," the Major broke in.

"But why not? We could save ourselves days!"

"I don't care what we could save. We stay together. When we get to the Cen-

ter, I want live men along with me. That means we stay within easy sight of each other at all times. Any climber knows that everybody is safer in a party than one man alone—any time, any place."

McIvers stared at him, his cheeks an angry red. Finally he gave a sullen nod. "Okay. If you say so."

"Well, I say so and I mean it. I don't want any fancy stuff. We're going to hit Center together, and finish the Crossing together. Got that?"

McIvers nodded. Mikuta then looked at Stone and me and we nodded, too.

"All right," he said slowly. "Now that we've got it straight, let's go."

It was hot. If I forget everything else about that trek, I'll never forget that huge yellow Sun glaring down, without a break, hotter and hotter with every mile. We knew that the first few days would be the easiest, and we were rested and fresh when we started down the long ragged gorge southeast of the Twilight Lab.

I moved out first; back over my shoulder, I could see the Major and McIvers crawling out behind me, their pillow tires taking the rugged floor of the gorge smoothly. Behind them, Stone dragged the sledges.

Even at only thirty per cent Earth gravity they were a strain on the big tractor, until the ski-blades bit into the fluffy volcanic ash blanketing the valley. We even had a path to follow for the first twenty miles.

I kept my eyes pasted to the big polaroid binocs, picking out the track the early research teams had made out into the edge of Brightside. But in a couple of hours we rumbled past Sanderson's little outpost observatory and the tracks stopped. We were in virgin territory and already the Sun was beginning to bite.

We didn't *feel* that heat so much those first days out. We *saw* it. The refrig units kept our skins at a nice comfortable 75° F. inside our suits, but our eyes watched that glaring Sun and the baked yellow rocks going past, and some nerve pathways got twisted up, somehow. We poured out sweat as if we were in a superheated furnace.

We drove eight hours and slept five. When a sleep period came due, we pulled the Bugs together into a square, threw up a light aluminum sun-shield, and lay out in the dust and rocks. The sun-shield cut the temperature down sixty or seventy degrees, for whatever help that was. And then we ate from the forward sledge—sucking through tubes—protein, carbohydrates, bulk gelatin, vitamins.

The Major measured water out with an iron hand, because we'd have drunk ourselves into nephritis in a week otherwise. We were constantly, unceasingly thirsty.

We didn't sleep the first few stops, as a consequence. Our eyes burned in spite of the filters and we had roaring headaches, but we couldn't sleep them off. We sat around looking at each other. Then McIvers would say how good a beer would taste, and off we'd go. We'd have butchered our grandmothers for one ice-cold bottle of beer.

After a few driving periods, I began to get my bearings at the wheel. We were moving down into desolation that made Earth's old Death Valley[9] look like a Japanese rose garden. Huge sun-baked cracks opened up the floor of the gorge, with black cliffs jutting up on

[9] **Death Valley,** in eastern California. It is below sea level and one of the hottest regions on Earth.

either side; the air was filled with a barely visible yellowish mist of sulfur and sulfurous gases.

It was a hot, barren hell-hole, no place for any man to go, but the challenge was so powerful you could almost feel it. No one had ever crossed this land before and escaped. Those who had tried it had been cruelly punished, but the land was still there, so it had to be crossed. Not the easy way. It had to be crossed the hardest way possible: overland, through anything the land could throw up to us, at the most difficult time possible.

Yet we knew that even the land might have been conquered before, except for that Sun. We'd fought absolute cold before and won. We'd never fought heat like this and won. The only worse heat in the Solar System was the surface of the Sun itself.

Brightside was worth trying for. We would get it or it would get us. That was the bargain.

I learned a lot about Mercury those few driving periods. The gorge petered out after a hundred miles and we moved onto the slope of a range of ragged craters that ran south and east. This range had shown no activity since the first landing on Mercury forty years before, but beyond it there were active cones. Yellow fumes rose from the craters constantly; their sides were shrouded with heavy ash.

We couldn't detect a wind, but we knew there was a hot, sulfurous breeze sweeping in great continental tides across the face of the planet. Not enough for erosion, though. The craters rose up out of jagged gorges, huge towering spears of rock and rubble. Below were the vast yellow flatlands, smoking and hissing from the gases beneath the

Painting by Chesley Bonestell

crust. Over everything was gray dust—offering a soft, treacherous surface for the Bug's pillow tires.

I learned to read the ground, to tell a covered fault by the sag of the dust; I learned to spot a passable crack, and tell it from an impassable cut. Time after time the Bugs ground to a halt while we explored a passage on foot, tied together with light copper cable, digging, advancing, digging some more until we were sure the surface would carry the machines. It was cruel work; we slept in exhaustion. But it went smoothly, at first.

Too smoothly, it seemed to me, and the others seemed to think so, too.

McIvers' restlessness was beginning to grate on our nerves. He talked too much, while we were resting or while we were driving: wisecracks, witticisms, unfunny jokes that wore thin with repetition. He took to making side trips from the route now and then, never far, but a little farther each time.

Jack Stone reacted quite the opposite; he grew quieter with each stop, more reserved and apprehensive. I didn't like it, but I figured that it would pass off after a while. I was apprehensive enough myself; I just managed to hide it better.

And every mile the Sun got bigger and whiter and higher in the sky and hotter. Without our ultraviolet screens and glare filters we would have been blinded; as it was our eyes ached constantly, and the skin on our faces itched and tingled at the end of an eight-hour trek.

But it took one of those side trips of McIvers' to deliver the penultimate blow to our already fraying nerves. He had driven down a side branch of a long canyon running off west of our route and was almost out of sight in a cloud of ash when we heard a sharp cry through our earphones.

I wheeled my Bug around with my heart in my throat and spotted him through the binocs, waving frantically from the top of his machine. The Major and I took off, lumbering down the gulch after him as fast as the Bugs could go, with a thousand horrible pictures racing through our minds. . . .

We found him standing stock-still, pointing down the gorge and, for once, he didn't have anything to say. It was the wreck of a Bug, an old-fashioned half-track model of the sort that hadn't been in use for years. It was wedged tight in a cut in the rock, an axle broken, its casing split wide open up the middle, half buried in a rock slide. A dozen feet away were two insulated suits with white bones gleaming through the Fiberglas helmets.

This was as far as Wyatt and Carpenter had gotten on *their* Brightside Crossing.

II

On the fifth driving period out, the terrain began to change. It looked the same, but every now and then it *felt* different. On two occasions I felt my wheels spin, with a howl of protest from my engine. Then, quite suddenly, the Bug gave a lurch; I gunned my motor and nothing happened.

I could see the dull-gray stuff seeping up around the hubs, thick and tenacious, splattering around in steaming gobs as the wheels spun. I knew what had happened the moment the wheels gave and, a few minutes later, they chained me to the tractor and dragged me back out of the mire. It looked for all the world like thick gray mud, but it was a pit of molten lead, steaming under a soft layer of concealing ash.

I picked my way more cautiously then. We were getting into an area of recent surface activity; the surface was really treacherous. I caught myself wishing that the Major had okayed McIvers' scheme for an advance scout; more dangerous for the individual, maybe, but I was driving blind now and I didn't like it.

One error in judgment could sink us all, but I wasn't thinking much about the others. I was worried about *me,* plenty worried. I kept thinking, better McIvers should go than me. It wasn't healthy thinking and I knew it, but I couldn't get the thought out of my mind.

It was a grueling eight hours, and we slept poorly. Back in the Bugs again, we moved still more slowly—edging out on a broad flat plateau, dodging a network of gaping surface cracks—winding back and forth in an effort to keep the machines on solid rock. I couldn't see far ahead, because of the yellow haze rising from the cracks, so I was almost on top of it when I saw a sharp cut ahead where the surface dropped six feet beyond a deep crack.

I let out a shout to halt the others; then I edged my Bug forward, peering at the cleft. It was deep and wide. I moved fifty yards to the left, then back to the right.

There was only one place that looked like a possible crossing: a long, narrow ledge of gray stuff that lay down across a section of the fault like a ramp. Even as I watched it, I could feel the surface crust under the Bug trembling and saw the ledge shift over a few feet.

The Major's voice sounded in my ears. "How about it, Peter?"

"I don't know. This crust is on roller skates," I called back.

"How about that ledge?"

I hesitated. "I'm scared of it, Major. Let's backtrack and try to find a way around."

There was a roar of disgust in my earphones and McIvers' Bug suddenly lurched forward. It rolled down past me, picked up speed, with McIvers hunched behind the wheel like a race driver. He was heading past me straight for the gray ledge.

My shout caught in my throat; I heard the Major take a huge breath and roar: *"Stop that thing,* you fool!" and then McIvers' Bug was out on the ledge, lumbering across like a juggernaut.

The ledge jolted as the tires struck it; for a horrible moment, it seemed to be sliding out from under the machine. And then the Bug was across in a cloud of dust, and I heard McIvers' voice in my ears, shouting in glee, "Come on, you slowpokes. It'll hold you!"

Something unprintable came through the earphones as the Major drew up alongside me and moved his Bug out on the ledge slowly and over to the other side. Then he said, "Take it slow, Peter. Then give Jack a hand with the sledges." His voice sounded tight as a wire.

Ten minutes later, we were on the other side of the cleft. The Major checked the whole column; then he turned on McIvers angrily. "One more trick like that," he said, "and I'll strap you to a rock and leave you. Do you understand me? *One more time—*"

McIvers' voice was heavy with protest. "Look, Major, if we leave it up to Claney, he'll have us out here forever! Any blind fool could see that that ledge would hold."

"I saw it moving," I shot back.

"All right, all right, so you've got good eyes. Why all the fuss? We got across, didn't we? But I say we've got to have a little nerve and use it once in a while if we're ever going to get across this lousy hotbox."

"We need to use a little judgment, too," the Major snapped. "All right, let's roll. But if you think I was joking, you just try me out once." He let it soak in for a minute. Then he geared his Bug on around to my flank again.

At the stopover, the incident wasn't mentioned again, but the Major drew me aside just as I was settling down for sleep. "Peter, I'm worried," he said slowly.

"McIvers? Don't worry. He's not as reckless as he seems—just impatient. We are over a hundred miles behind schedule, and we're moving awfully slow. We only made forty miles this last drive."

The Major shook his head. "I don't mean McIvers. I mean the kid."

"Jack? What about him?"

"Take a look."

Stone was shaking. He was over near the tractor—away from the rest of us —and he was lying on his back, but he wasn't asleep. His whole body was shaking, convulsively. I saw him grip an outcropping of rock hard.

I walked over and sat down beside him. "Get your drink of water all right?" I said.

He didn't answer. He just kept on shaking.

"Hey, boy," I said. "What's the trouble?"

"It's hot," he said, choking out the words.

"Sure it's hot, but don't let it throw you. We're in really good shape."

"*We're not,*" he snapped. "We're in rotten shape, if you ask me. *We're not going to make it,* do you know that? That crazy fool's going to kill us for sure—" All of a sudden, he was bawling like a baby. "I'm scared—I shouldn't be here—I'm *scared.* What am I trying to prove by coming out here, for God's sake? I'm some kind of hero or something? I tell you I'm scared—"

"Look," I said. "Mikuta's scared, *I'm* scared. So what? We'll make it, don't worry. And nobody's trying to be a hero."

"Nobody but Hero Stone," he said bitterly. He shook himself and gave a tight little laugh. "Some hero, eh?"

"We'll make it," I said.

"Sure," he said finally. "Sorry. I'll be okay."

I rolled over, but waited until he was good and quiet. Then I tried to sleep, but I didn't sleep too well. I kept thinking about that ledge. I'd known from the look of it what it was; a zinc slough of the sort Sanderson had warned us about, a wide sheet of almost pure zinc that had been thrown up white-hot from below, quite recently, just waiting for oxygen or sulfur to rot it through.

I knew enough about zinc to know that at these temperatures it gets brittle as glass. Take a chance like McIvers had taken and the whole sheet could snap like a dry pine board. It wasn't McIvers' fault that it hadn't.

Five hours later, we were back at the wheel. We were hardly moving at all. The ragged surface was almost impassable—great jutting rocks peppered the plateau; ledges crumbled the moment my tires touched them; long, open canyons turned into lead-mires or sulfur pits.

A dozen times I climbed out of the

Bug to prod out an uncertain area with my boots and pikestaff. Whenever I did McIvers piled out behind me, running ahead like a schoolboy at the fair, then climbing back again, red-faced and panting, while we moved the machines ahead another mile or two.

Time was pressing us now, and McIvers wouldn't let me forget it. We had made only about 320 miles in six driving periods, so we were about a hundred miles or even more behind schedule.

"We're not going to make it," McIvers would complain angrily. "That Sun's going to be out to aphelion by the time we hit the Center—"

"Sorry, but I can't take it any faster," I told him. I was getting good and mad. I knew what he wanted but didn't dare let him have it. I was scared enough pushing the Bug out on those ledges, even knowing that at least *I* was making the decisions. Put him in the lead and we wouldn't last for eight hours. Our nerves wouldn't take it, at any rate, even if the machines did.

Jack Stone looked up from the aluminum chart sheets. "Another hundred miles and we should hit a good stretch," he said. "Maybe we can make up distance there for a couple of days."

The Major agreed, but McIvers couldn't hold his impatience. He kept staring up at the Sun as if he had a personal grudge against it, and stamped back and forth under the sun-shield. "That'll be just fine," he said. "*If* we ever get that far, that is."

We dropped it there, but the Major stopped me as we climbed aboard for the next run. "That guy's going to blow wide open if we don't move faster, Peter. I don't want him in the lead, no matter what happens. He's right, though, about the need to make better time. Keep your head, but crowd your luck a little, okay?"

"I'll try," I said. It was asking the impossible and Mikuta knew it. We were on a long downward slope that shifted and buckled all around us, as though there was a molten underlay beneath the crust; the slope was broken by huge crevasses, partly covered with dust and zinc sheeting, like a vast glacier of stone and metal. The outside temperature registered 547° F. and getting hotter. It was no place to start rushing ahead.

I tried it anyway. I took half a dozen shaky passages, edging slowly out on flat zinc ledges, then toppling over and across. It seemed easy for a while and we made progress. We hit an even stretch and raced ahead. And then I quickly jumped on my brakes and jerked the Bug to a halt in a cloud of dust.

I'd gone too far. We were out on a wide, flat sheet of gray stuff, apparently solid—until I'd suddenly caught sight of the crevasse beneath in the corner of my eye. It was an overhanging shelf that trembled under me as I stopped. McIvers' voice was in my ear. "What's the trouble now, Claney?"

"Move back!" I shouted. "It can't hold us!"

"Looks solid from here."

"You want to argue about it? It's too thin, it'll snap. Move back!"

I started edging back down the ledge. I heard McIvers swear; then I saw his Bug start to creep *outward* on the shelf. Not fast or reckless, this time, but slowly, churning up dust in a gentle cloud behind him.

I just stared and felt the blood rush to my head. It seemed so hot I could hardly breathe as he edged out beyond me, farther and farther—

I think I felt it snap before I saw it. My own machine gave a sickening lurch and a long black crack appeared across the shelf—and widened. Then the ledge began to upend. I heard a scream as McIvers' Bug rose up and up and then crashed down into the crevasse in a thundering slide of rock and shattered metal.

I just stared for a full minute, I think. I couldn't move until I heard Jack Stone groan and the Major shouting, "Claney! I couldn't see—*what happened?*"

"It snapped on him, that's what happened," I roared. I gunned my motor, edged forward toward the fresh-broken edge of the shelf. The crevasse gaped; I couldn't see any sign of the machine. Dust was still billowing up blindingly from below.

We stood staring down, the three of us. I caught a glimpse of Jack Stone's face through his helmet. It wasn't pretty.

"Well," said the Major heavily, "that's that."

"I guess so," I felt the way Stone looked.

"Wait," said Stone. "I heard something."

He had. It was a cry in the earphones —faint, but unmistakable.

"Mac!" the Major called. "Mac, can you hear me?"

"Yeah, yeah. I can hear you." The voice was very weak.

"Are you all right?"

"I don't know. Broken leg, I think. It's—hot." There was a long pause. Then: "I think my cooler's gone out."

The Major shot me a glance, then turned to Stone. "Get a cable from the second sledge fast. He'll fry alive if we don't get him out of there. Peter, I need you to lower me. Use the tractor winch."

I lowered him; he stayed down only a few moments. When I hauled him up, his face was drawn. "Still alive," he panted. "He won't be very long, though." He hesitated for just an instant. "We've got to make a try."

"I don't like this ledge," I said. "It's moved twice since I got out. Why not back off and lower him a cable?"

"No good. The Bug is smashed and he's inside it. We'll need torches and I'll need one of you to help." He looked at me and then gave Stone a long look. "Peter, you'd better come."

"Wait," said Stone. His face was very white. "Let me go down with you."

"Peter is lighter."

"I'm not so heavy. Let me go down."

"Okay, if that's the way you want it." The Major tossed him a torch. "Peter, check these hitches and lower us slowly. If you see any kind of trouble, *anything,* cast yourself free and back off this thing, do you understand? This whole ledge may go."

I nodded. "Good luck."

They went over the ledge. I let the cable down bit by bit until it hit two hundred and slacked off.

"How does it look?" I shouted.

"Bad," said the Major. "We'll have to work fast. This whole side of the crevasse is ready to crumble. Down a little more."

Minutes passed without a sound. I tried to relax, but I couldn't. Then I felt the ground shift, and the tractor lurched to the side.

The Major shouted, *"It's going, Peter —pull back!"* and I threw the tractor into reverse, jerked the controls as the tractor rumbled off the shelf. The cable snapped, coiled up in front like a broken clock-spring. The whole surface under me was shaking wildly now; ash rose in huge gray clouds. Then, with a roar, the whole shelf lurched sideways. It teetered on the edge for seconds before it crashed into the crevasse, tearing the side wall down with it in a mammoth slide. I jerked the tractor to a halt as the dust and flame billowed up.

They were gone—all three of them, McIvers and the Major and Jack Stone —buried under thousands of tons of rock and zinc and molten lead. There wasn't any danger of anybody ever finding their bones.

Peter Claney leaned back, finishing his drink, rubbing his scarred face as he looked across at Baron.

Slowly, Baron's grip relaxed on the chair arm. "*You* got back."

Claney nodded. "I got back, sure. I had the tractor and the sledges. I had seven days to drive back under that yellow Sun. I had plenty of time to think."

"You took the wrong man along," Baron said. "That was your mistake. Without him you would have made it."

"Never." Claney shook his head. "That's what I was thinking the first day or so—that it was *McIvers'* fault, that he was to blame. But that isn't true. He was wild, reckless, and had lots of nerve."

"But his judgment was bad!"

"It couldn't have been sounder. We had to keep to our schedule even if it killed us, because it would positively kill us if we didn't."

"But a man like that—"

"A man like McIvers was necessary.

Can't you see that? It was the Sun that beat us, that surface. Perhaps we were licked the very day we started." Claney leaned across the table, his eyes pleading. "We didn't realize that, but it was *true*. There are places that men can't go, conditions men can't tolerate. The others had to die to learn that. I was lucky, I came back. But I'm trying to tell you what I found out—that *nobody* will ever make a Brightside Crossing."

"We will," said Baron. "It won't be a picnic, but we'll make it."

"But suppose you do," said Claney, suddenly. "Suppose I'm all wrong, suppose you *do* make it. Then what? *What comes next?*"

"The Sun," said Baron.

Claney nodded slowly. "Yes. That would be it, wouldn't it!" He laughed. "Good-by, Baron. Jolly talk and all that. Thanks for listening."

Baron caught his wrist as he started to rise. "Just one question more, Claney. Why did you come here?"

"To try to talk you out of killing yourself," said Claney.

"You're a liar," said Baron.

Claney stared down at him for a long moment. Then he crumpled in the chair. There was defeat in his pale blue eyes and something else.

"Well?"

Peter Claney spread his hands, a helpless gesture. "When do you leave, Baron? I want you to take me along."

THE END

(over)

1. *a.* To which of your senses does the author appeal in describing the Brightside of Mercury? Give examples.

b. Why did Mikuta insist on crossing at perihelion instead of aphelion?

c. How did the expedition plan to meet the hostile conditions on Mercury?

2. *a.* What personal qualities made the Major a good leader?

b. What qualifications did each of the other three crew members have that led the Major to choose him?

3. *a.* According to Claney, why did the attempted crossing fail?

b. What reason does Claney give to back up his opinion that McIvers was NOT the cause of their failure?

c. Who or what do YOU think was responsible for the disastrous end to the expedition?

4. Claney says, "You don't go asking people in this game why they do it. . . ." What made Claney and the others want to undertake the Brightside Crossing? Find passages in the story that deal with this matter.

⇄ **Words in action**

In Word Attack/Structure, Lesson Three, you saw how knowing part of a word (together with clues in the context) often helps you figure out the meaning of an unfamiliar word.

In describing the space suits used for the crossing, Peter Claney mentions that they were equipped with warning thermocouples, for "at 770 degrees, it wouldn't take long to fry us to cinders

if the suits failed somewhere." *Thermocouples* is a technical word you wouldn't be expected to know, but context clues, plus knowing that *thermo-* means "heat," should give you a general idea of what a thermocouple does.

Look at these words:

monochromatic	**monotone**
monosyllabic	**monocle**
monogamy	**monorail**
monopoly	

Notice that each one begins with *mono-,* which means "one" or "single."

Now answer the questions below. You may need to consult a dictionary for some of the words in bold type, but knowing that each of them has something to do with the idea of "one" should help.

1. If a woman wears a **monochromatic** striped dress to a party, should she be worried about clashing colors in the stripes?

2. If a man accidentally breaks the **monocle** he wears to help him see better, how many new lenses will he have to buy?

3. Being married to more than one person at a time is against the law in the U.S., but would your next-door neighbor be arrested because he practices **monogamy**?

4. If one member of the family has been **monopolizing** the family car, what has he been doing?

5. Why would less track be needed for a ten-mile **monorail** than for a conventional railway the same length?

6. Which one would be likely to use a greater percentage of **monosyllabic** words—a young child or a college professor?

7. Why aren't **monotones** needed in choirs?

The weather was responsible

Alan E. Nourse explains that "Brightside Crossing" was written in Philadelphia during a very hot summer between his second and third years of medical school. "This not only accounts for the medical detail and terminology in the story but also may account for my choice of setting—in the midst of extreme heat."

Mr. Nourse didn't expect any editor to be interested in his story, because it was a type of science fiction not very popular at the time. To his surprise, it was accepted by the first editor he sent it to and has since become one of his most popular stories.

Search: Views and viewpoints

1. The following people in this unit are searching for something: **the bum . . . Daniel Mannix . . . young Plenty-coups . . . T.J. . . . the foolish man . . . the speaker in "Our House" . . . Peter Claney.**

    a. What is each one searching for?

    b. Is his goal realistic—one he should be able to reach—or would you call it foolish or impossible?

2. A person's search may be made difficult, or even defeated entirely, by physical obstacles, by weaknesses within himself, or by what other people do. Which of these kinds of obstacles were present in "Vampires!"? in "Antaeus"? in "The Foolish Man"? in "Brightside Crossing"? Which people succeeded in spite of the obstacles?

3. A few years ago there was a popular song called "The Impossible Dream." Do you think it is foolish to follow an impossible dream? What good might come of trying for something that seems unattainable?

4. What besides personal benefits might a person have as the goal of his life's search? What are some of the specific things in today's world that mankind is searching for?

7

Judgments

If you had seen these people behaving the way they do in the pictures, what would you expect to happen next? On the next page are four possibilities:

1. Which of these pictures, in your opinion, would best continue the story?
2. Why do you think so?
3. What clues in the original picture sequence led you to make your choice?
4. Have you had any personal experiences which might have led you to feel for or against one of the characters, or to guess a certain way about his actions?

Actually, there is no "right answer." Any of the choices *might* complete the story, but the first three pictures really do not give you enough information about the characters or the situation for you to be certain about what happens next.

In choosing any of the possible endings to the story, you had to **jump to a conclusion.** You had to jump to a conclusion about which character was the "bad guy." In fact, you jumped to a conclusion if you even decided there *was* a bad guy.

You also had to jump to a conclusion about how the characters were likely to behave. Perhaps you had some reason to understand one of the characters and to feel strongly in favor of him or strongly against him. In any case, your choice and the choices of your classmates probably were quite varied because you did not all see the pictures the same way.

You have probably heard both of the expressions, **draw a conclusion** and **jump to a conclusion.** Can you tell what the difference is?

To draw a conclusion suggests considering all the evidence in order to come to a reasonable and likely conclusion. Jumping to a conclusion suggests just what the word means: "jumping" ahead, either by ignoring evidence which may be there or by not getting enough evidence.

Every day we all make many judgments—about small things as well as large matters:

"Should I spend my last half-dollar on this magazine, or should I buy a milkshake?"

"Do I have enough time to stop by the hobby shop before I have to be home for supper?"

"Was Sheila really trying to hurt my feelings, or did I just misunderstand her?"

"Should I vote for Jim Reed or Earl Cohen for class president?"

There may be times when making a fast judgment is good— even absolutely necessary. For example, suppose you are crossing the street and you see a car coming much too fast to stop for a stoplight. A quick decision here may save your life. Can you think of other examples?

Often, however, when you make a hasty judgment or jump to a conclusion you have not taken the time to get a complete and true picture of the situation before making up your mind.

EXERCISE I. Recognizing too-hasty conclusions

Explain how each speaker below has jumped to a conclusion. Then use your imagination to construct a possible explanation for each situation—the "facts" which the speaker doesn't know but which would explain what happened.

1. "Stan is half an hour late already. I'll bet he's not coming."
2. "That boy is too sloppy and careless for a job in this store. He came for an interview wearing a shirt with a patched sleeve."
3. "Listen to that thumping noise! It must be a burglar!"
4. "Joan's such a liar! She told me that dress sale at Young-in-Heart was going to last until the end of the week."
5. "Bill Freeman stole your bicycle! I saw him ride off on it just a few minutes ago."

EXERCISE II. Recognizing too-hasty conclusions

Read the following article; then decide whether each of the statements made about it is based on enough information from the article for you to accept it as true, or whether the person making it is jumping to a conclusion.

How Intelligent Is the Dolphin?

FROM THE time of the ancient Greeks, man has known that the dolphin is an intelligent, friendly, often playful creature. In recent years, scientists have begun to wonder just how intelligent this seagoing mammal really is, and they have tried a great many experiments to find out. They have found that the dolphin has a very large brain—about a pound heavier than man's, in fact—and that the "thinking part" of the brain, the cerebrum (ser′ə brəm), is well developed.

Scientists have also found that the dolphin is very quick to learn tricks and games and apparently enjoys performing for an audience. Dolphins have learned to do such things as "shake hands," blow a horn, leap through hoops held out of water, ring bells, and play forms of water basketball and baseball. Dolphins also invent games for themselves and can learn games from each other. They can concentrate on the same game for a long period of time. They can even make changes in the way a game is played. All these things are signs of high intelligence.

One trainer commented that sometimes his dolphins respond to their training as though they were expected to train him.

Scientists have also noticed that dolphins have a sense of humor and are great teasers. One dolphin enjoyed teasing a large fish that was hiding in a rocky cave. The dolphin took a piece of food and laid it outside the mouth of the cave. Then he backed off to wait. As soon as the fish came out to eat the food, the dolphin snatched it away. Such teasing is a sign of thinking ahead. Only the more intelligent animals think ahead.

Dolphins are also very good at solving problems. Two dolphins were trying to tease an eel out from under a rock. After a while one dolphin swam off while the first one waited by the rock. The first dolphin came back with a newly killed scorpion fish—which has very sharp spines—and pricked the eel with it. When they succeeded in driving the eel out of its hiding place, the dolphins caught it, took it to the middle of the pool, and let it go.

Dolphins often coöperate with one another in this way. Some dolphins become close friends and stay close friends. When a friend dies, dolphins show signs of sorrow and may even refuse to eat.

Dolphins also help man. They have been trained to locate things lost at sea. Many people have reported that they had been in trouble in the water and had been helped ashore by a dolphin. Dolphins love to be with people; they love to play with them and to be stroked and petted. Some dolphins have given children rides upon their backs.

Some scientists think dolphins are so intelligent that the dolphin "language," which consists of squeaks, squawks, whistles, clicks, and similar noises, has a meaning similar to human language, and these scientists are trying to learn it. Still other scientists think dolphins could be taught to understand and even to speak English because the animals often try to mimic the human voice. These men have been working with dolphins for years to find out how much the animals can learn.

It may be that the first nonhuman species we communicate with will not be some intelligent form of life on another planet, but will turn out to be the dolphin.

Determine whether each of the following statements is true because it is backed up by information from the article, or whether it jumps to a conclusion. On your paper, write either "true" or "jump" after the number of the statement.

Be prepared to explain what is wrong with each of the statements you labeled "jump"—that is, the statements you cannot accept because they are not backed up by information in the article. What "jump" did the speaker make in each case?

1. Man has known about the dolphin for hundreds of years. If he hasn't succeeded in communicating with dolphins by now, he never will.

(over)

2. We know that dolphins are more intelligent than man because the dolphin's brain is larger than man's.
3. Dolphins can learn other tricks besides those invented for them by their trainers.
4. At the same time we are trying to train the dolphin, it is trying to train us.
5. Dolphins coöperate with man because they know that we want to be their friends.
6. Scientists feel that the ability to solve problems indicates a high type of intelligence.
7. Dolphins and eels are natural enemies.
8. Results of experiments so far make many scientists feel that it would be worth while to continue experiments with dolphins.
9. When scientists learn the meaning of the squeaks, squawks, whistles, and clicks made by the dolphins, we will be able to teach them English.
10. When we make contact with the dolphin we will stop trying to communicate with other nonhuman forms of life.

LESSON TWO: Stereotypes

Which of the characters on page 272 would probably be the hero of a western adventure story? Which character would be the villain, or "bad guy"? What details in the two pictures led you to make your choices?

Which character would probably be the hero's best friend, or "sidekick"? What details in this picture made you think so?

Which character would probably be the friendly, wise doctor in the town? What details in this picture influenced your choice?

Can you remember where you originally got your ideas about these various characters?

There is no reason why a western hero cannot wear glasses or have a black mustache. But most people would probably choose character C for the hero. They have been greatly influenced by the fact that, for many years, the heroes of almost all western movies have been young, strong, and brave—and they usually wear white hats.

Have almost all the western heroes you have seen in the movies or on television behaved pretty much the same way? Describe their behavior.

How does a "sidekick" usually behave?

The kind of standardized mental picture so many people have of a "western hero" or other popular character is called a **stereotype** (ster′ ē ə tīp′). When someone has the idea that all the people in a certain group are alike and will always act alike, he is thinking in terms of stereotypes. In a way, a stereotype represents a jump to a conclusion about a group of people.

You will find many stereotyped characters in books, in movies, and on television. You know just how they are going to talk and act. In fact, they could all be the same character, but with different names. Sometimes it is helpful to be able to recognize a stereotype and thus to know immediately what kind of person a certain character is. Some writers use stereotypes for just that reason. On the other hand, a writer will sometimes deliberately make a character *not* fit a stereotype in order to create humor or for some other reason.

In everyday life, is it more desirable to think of people as individuals or as types? Why?

EXERCISE III. Recognizing stereotypes

Part A

Here are four character descriptions as they might appear in a story. Decide which of the characters are stereotypes and which are not. Be prepared to explain your choices.

(A) Sloane had a nervous habit of hunching his shoulders high and lowering his head so that his chin, weak to begin with, seemed to disappear entirely into the too-loose collar of his shabby, ill-fitting suit. When he did this, and when he pulled his hat down low, almost all that could be seen of him was his sharp nose and his small, dark eyes, darting rapidly from one side to the other. These things, and the peculiar way he had of walking almost sideways, as if he wanted to keep his back against a wall, had well earned him the name by which he was known throughout the underworld—"Shifty" Sloane.

(B) Joe Speery barely glanced up when the young man escorted the young woman across the street to his taxicab, then opened the door and helped her inside. Instead, Joe continued reading until he had finished the poem. He carefully marked his place with a leather bookmark and put the book on the seat beside him. Straightening his tie, he flashed an apologetic grin at the young man's reflection in the rearview mirror. He leaned forward to switch off the symphony concert that had been playing on the cab's FM radio. Only then did he twist around in his seat to face the young couple and say pleasantly, "Yes, sir?"

(C) Even the dark glasses which she wore almost constantly, indoors and out, couldn't disguise Sheree Starr. No one could fail to recognize her famous heart-shaped face, or the way she opened her mouth wide when she laughed to show her gleaming white teeth—or the way she tossed her head so that a mass of honey-blond curls tumbled over her forehead to cover one eye. These things, which had made her the image of glamor for movie-goers all over the country, would surely have given her away.

(D) Miss Singer perched small and birdlike on the park bench in the afternoon sunshine and fumbled with her over-large handbag. The camera dangling by its cord around her neck seemed to get in her way, and she removed it and put it down beside her. Then she began rummaging around in her handbag, pulling out an amazing number of rolls of film, tourist maps, handkerchiefs, sunglasses, and other such equipment. So absorbed was she in this process that she apparently didn't notice the dark gentleman who sat down at the other end of the bench. When he spoke to her, however —using the curious sentence she recognized as the sign of her contact—she immediately gave the correct countersign. Then she added, "Now I'll give you that microfilm in just a moment, X-13. I know I put it in here somewhere . . ."

1. What type of character or occupation is represented in each of the character descriptions?
2. Which of the characters are stereotypes? Point out some of the qualities that make them stereotypes.

Part B

3. List some qualities which you think belong to a commonly held stereotype of a teen-ager.
4. Do you know someone who has some of these qualities? Which qualities?
5. Do you know someone who has *all* these qualities? someone who doesn't have any of them? Do you know more teen-agers who have these qualities than teen-agers who do not?
6. Do you know any teen-agers who *try* to show certain qualities which may make them seem like stereotypes? Why might they do this?

EXERCISE IV. Recognizing stereotyped characters

Consider the following list of characters from selections in earlier units of this book. Are any of them stereotypes? If so, explain why you feel that character is stereotyped.

1. David, **a cabin boy** in "The Long, Cold Night"
2. Berta, **a young Mexican girl** in "Sunday Costs Five Pesos"
3. Grace Wiley, **a snake charmer** in "Woman Without Fear"
4. Wally Watts, **a private eye** in "Wally the Watchful Eye"
5. Maude, **a young frontier girl** in "Spoil the Child"
6. Dalton, **city editor of a newspaper** in "Rescue"
7. T. J., **a young southern boy** in "Antaeus"
8. McIvers, **an explorer** in "Brightside Crossing"

LESSON THREE: Facts and opinions

Imagine yourself in a discussion with a friend. He is defending his favorite baseball team, and you are standing up for yours.

You say, "The Admirals are the best in the league." You go on to explain, "They won the league championship last year by two games and swept the World Series in four straight games."

Your friend isn't going to give up easily, however. "Oh, yeah?" he says. "Prove it!"

How can you prove what you have said?

Which of your statements is about something that actually happened? Where might you look to find a record of those events?

How does your remaining statement differ from the one about an actual happening? Can it be proved in the same way?

Imagine that you next say to your friend, "First baseman Jackson Lawler led the league in hitting last year with a .343 average."

Then you add, "Jackson is one of the most popular players on the team. Everybody likes him and respects him."

Suppose your friend then says, "'Dick Welling of the Trojans had a higher batting average than that last year, and he's more popular than Jackson Lawler!"

Can you prove whether Jackson Lawler or Dick Welling has the highest batting average? How would you do this?

Can you prove whether Jackson Lawler or Dick Welling is the more popular player? Why or why not?

The statements above which can be proved to be either true or false are called **statements of fact.** Fact statements are usually based on actual things that have happened or are happening, or on things in the world around us that can be observed or measured in some way. Even your friend would probably agree with your statements if you could show him a newspaper or magazine article which says that Jackson Lawler did lead the league in hitting.

The statements which cannot be proved true or false are called **statements of opinion.** Opinion statements are often based on personal feelings. Even if you found a third person to agree with you that the Admirals are the "best in the league," your friend might not change his opinion because his personal feelings have not been changed.

EXERCISE V. Recognizing fact statements and opinion statements

Decide whether each of the following statements is a fact statement or an opinion statement. On your paper, after the number of the sentence, write "fact" or "opinion." Be prepared to explain your decisions and to tell how you would go about proving whether the statements you have labeled "fact" are true or whether they are false.

1. Aside from having been painted once, our school building hasn't been remodeled in the last seventeen years.
2. My stamp collection has over 1400 stamps from forty-five countries.
3. Taking music lessons will be a waste of time unless you spend two hours a day practicing.
4. The boys' club drive to raise money for a playground went over its goal of $6500.
5. Football should be called our national sport instead of baseball.
6. Last year's dry spell was the longest one in this area for thirty years.
7. The Caesar XII is the best-looking car on the road.
8. A girl should be younger than the boy she goes with.
9. This year our neighborhood street fair had more rides and more booths than ever before.
10. Money is the most sensible gift to give.
11. Our science teacher, Mr. Hartman, worked on a government conservation project three summers in a row.
12. Dave Fischer is a cinch to win the school award for best all-around athlete.

LESSON FOUR: Evaluating opinions

Suppose you want to buy a transistor radio but you know very little about radios. After looking over the transistors in a store, you realize there are many different kinds to choose from, and so you decide to get the opinions of several other people. Here is what they say:

The salesman: "Brand A is our most expensive model, but it's a good buy because it has a special, newly developed tuner that will pull in more stations than any other."

Your mother: "Brand B is very attractive looking, and it's on sale."

Your little brother: "Brand C comes with earphones and a neat case that makes it easier to carry."

Your uncle, who is a radio-TV repairman: "Brand D will work just fine and will probably give you the least trouble."

A magazine ad: "Brand E is the radio of the future."

1. Which of these opinions come from people who probably don't know any more about radios than you do?
2. Which opinions are influenced by a desire to sell a certain brand?
3. Which speaker probably knows the most about radios, and is least likely to want to sell a certain brand?
4. Which opinion should you accept? How did you decide?

Someone who has been interested enough in a subject to devote time and effort to studying it, or to getting the facts about it, would probably have a more solid basis for his opinion than someone who knows little about the subject. A person who knows a great deal about a subject is called an **authority** on the subject.

When might you want to consult an authority before making a decision or forming an opinion? When would it be unnecessary? Consider these two statements:

> A. My room would look a lot better painted a light shade of blue.
>
> B. There's a lot more to being a really good airplane pilot than just having a pilot's license.

Which of these opinions is probably based on personal feelings and nothing more? Which is probably based on special knowledge or experience?

There are times when your personal feelings on a subject are all the basis you need to form an opinion or make a decision. Would you expect to ask anyone else before deciding what your favorite color or favorite ice-cream flavor is? However, there are other times when your opinion will not be worth much—that is, will not be valid—unless it is based on as much information as you can obtain.

EXERCISE VI. Supporting your opinions

Number from 1-10 on your paper. If a topic listed below is one on which you could make a sound decision merely by consulting your personal feelings, write "feeling" after its number. If your decision or opinion ought to be based on special knowledge that you could get only from an expert in that field, write "authority." Be prepared to explain your choices.

1. The prettiest girl in a beauty contest.
2. The best way to care for your complexion.
3. An enjoyable book for reading outside of school.
4. The most informative book on building an electric motor.
5. What courses to take if you want to be a TV repair man.
6. Whether your tonsils should be removed.
7. Your favorite recording by a certain singing group.
8. How to play a good game of golf.
9. Whether Indians ought to live on reservations.
10. The best restaurant in town.

What you should know about making judgments

A **judgment** is a conclusion you arrive at. If you try to get as much information as you can that applies to the situation, and if you think carefully about this information and the conclusions that can be made from it, you are said to **draw a conclusion.** If you do not get any information, or if you use only the information that appeals to you, you are said to **jump to a conclusion.**

A **stereotype** is a mental picture of an entire group of people, based upon wrong or incomplete information. A stereotype is based on a jump to the conclusion that all people belonging to a certain group are alike and will act alike.

A **fact** is information based upon things which can be proved or measured. Some subjects have much factual information associated with them. Expressing an **opinion** about one of these subjects without considering the facts associated with it is like jumping to a conclusion. A more **valid opinion** results when you draw a conclusion from facts or when you consult one or more **authorities.** There are other subjects, however, on which an opinion based just on personal feelings is perfectly valid.

8

Relationships

LESSON ONE: Ways ideas may be connected

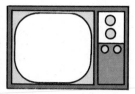

Suppose you were asked to make a brief statement that would include all three objects. Here are some things you might say:

1. The earliest books date back to almost 4500 years ago. It was not until the 1920's that people began to own radios. A little later came TV.

2. Reading a book takes more time and effort than listening to radio or watching TV, but when you read you can go at your own speed and also go back over what you didn't understand.

3. Almost everybody is curious enough about what other people do that he wants to read books and turn on radio and TV.

4. In the room there were a TV, a radio, and some books.

In each of the four statements the objects are connected in a different way. See if you can figure out what these ways are.

—In which statement are books, radio, and TV connected according to when things happened, or in order of time?

—In which statement is one thing compared to something else, and the differences between them mentioned?

—In which statement is a condition mentioned that causes or leads to the use of the three objects?

—In which statement are the three objects simply listed? Could you change the order in which the objects are mentioned without changing the meaning of the sentence?

If you were able to see how the ideas in each statement are connected, you have recognized, in a very simple form, four kinds of **relationships.** A relationship is a connection, and four of the most important ones are those you have just identified:

> **the time-order relationship**
> **the comparison-contrast relationship**
> **the cause-effect relationship**
> **the simple listing relationship**

Most writers frequently use all four of these methods of connecting ideas.

EXERCISE I.   Using relationships to connect ideas

Suppose you are planning a talk on each of the subjects listed. To illustrate the talks, you can use the pictures shown.

On your paper, after the number of the subject, write the letters of the pictures in the order in which you would show them. Then write the name of the kind of relationship (time order, comparison-contrast, cause-effect, or simple listing) you would use in your talk. For some subjects you may wish to use only two of the three pictures. The first one is done for you.

Part A

    a   *b*   *c*

1. SUBJECT: What happened last Saturday to our best player
    Order: c, b, a   *Relationship: time order*
2. SUBJECT: The exciting moments in last Saturday's game

Part B

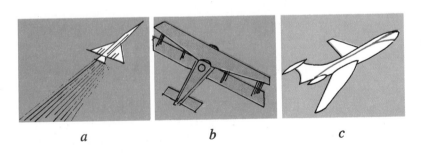

    a   *b*   *c*

3. SUBJECT: The development of passenger planes
4. SUBJECT: How a pilot of the twenties would feel in a plane of the future

Part C

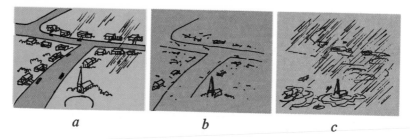

a   b   c

5. SUBJECT: How the rains destroyed Southbrook
6. SUBJECT: Southbrook as it was and Southbrook today

LESSON TWO: Clue words and phrases

In discovering the ways authors have connected their ideas, you usually get help from words and phrases which act as clues. Here are some typical passages in which ideas are related in specific ways.

TIME ORDER

Material written in time order is usually easy to recognize because the writer mentions dates or uses other words which have to do with time—words like *first, next, later, finally.* Here is a typical example:

> The whole cattle business suffered a great shock **in 1886. It began in the summer,** which was one of the hottest and dustiest on record. All through Dakota, Montana, and Wyoming cattle suffered as water holes dried up and grass turned brown. **By the end of July,** many streams had run low or stopped. Fires started up and roared through the dry grass of the plains. **By the end of summer** the best of the winter pastures had been destroyed.
>
> **Then came the worst winter** ever to strike the northern ranges. Temperatures dropped to zero **in November** and even lower **in December. By January,** when sixteen inches of snow fell in a few days and Montana temperatures went down to forty-five degrees below zero, some animals froze to death standing. . . . From *The Adventures of the Negro Cowboys* by Philip Durham and Everett L. Jones. Copyright © 1965, 1966 by Philip C. Durham and Everett L. Jones. Reprinted by permission of Dodd, Mead & Company.

COMPARISON-CONTRAST

When you **compare** two things you tell how they are alike and how they are different. The term **contrast** refers to differences, not to likenesses. Comparing and contrasting are good ways to explain or describe things. For example, you might explain how tall Bruce is by saying he's not as tall as Sam but taller than Billy.

What is being contrasted in the following?

> We in the United States have inherited a land of unrivaled beauty—spectacular mountain ranges, colorful tropical jungles, lovely lake-studded forests, rolling hills and rich farmlands, miles of sandy beaches. The only trouble is that we are turning it into the biggest slum on the face of the earth. Our towns and cities have many individual buildings that are attractive, even beautiful, but very few beautiful streets and neighborhoods. Our suburbs are endless wastelands dotted with millions of monotonous little houses. Highways running through the countryside are lined with billboards, jazzed-up diners, used-car lots, junkyards, drive-in movies, and gaudy motels.

Notice the contrast between "a land of unrivaled beauty" and "biggest slum." What are some of the specific things that are contrasted?

In other selections, words like *better, worse, bigger, smaller,* or expressions like *however, on the other hand, nevertheless* are clues that the writer is using a comparison-contrast relationship.

CAUSE-EFFECT

When a writer explains why something happened—what caused it—or what is the effect or result of something, he is using cause-effect relationship. Here is an example:

> The mess along the fringes of our communities has been created by hundreds of thousands of average citizens who toss trash out of their cars and tolerate the construction of ugly little buildings and glaring signs. Perhaps **because** Americans are so used to screaming colors and "spectaculars" of all sorts they are blinded to all this ugliness. Or perhaps it is **the result of** the throw-away civilization in which they live.

Expressions like "because," "as a result," "for this reason," "consequently" should alert you to cause-effect.

SIMPLE LISTING

The following is a common type of listing paragraph. Expressions like "many," "several," and "some of these" tell you that a listing will follow.

> An archaeologist is a scientist who studies the things that prehistoric men made and did. **Many other** scientists help the archaeologist find out about prehistoric men. **Some of these** are geologists who help him tell the age of the rocks or caves or gravel beds in which human bones or objects made by ancient men are found, and scientists with names which begin with "paleo" (the Greek word for "old") who contribute their special skills when needed. The paleontologists study fossil animals. Paleobotanists and paleoclimatologists study ancient plants and climates. . . .

> Adapted from *Prehistoric Men*, Seventh Edition, by Robert J. Braidwood. Copyright © 1964, 1967 by Scott, Foresman and Company.

EXERCISE II. Recognizing clue words and phrases

Read the sentences and answer the questions.

A. Joe's father was pleased with him because he'd been ambitious enough to mow some lawns.
   1. How did Joe's father feel?
   2. Why did he feel this way?
   3. What connection is there between the way Joe's father felt and what Joe had done?
   4. What word gives you a clue to this relationship?
   5. What kind of relationship is expressed in this sentence?

B. The bandmaster's encouragement was important to Jim, but even more important was Hank's invitation to join his rock group, the Polka Dot Wireless.
   6. What two things were important to Jim?
   7. Were these two things equally important?
   8. What kind of relationship is there between the two things?
   9. What is the clue phrase?   (*over*)

C. Justin's mother made him clean his room and throw out a lot of stuff—old comic books, candy and gum wrappers, empty coke bottles, and those worn-out blue sneakers.

  10. How many things are mentioned that Justin had to throw out?
  11. Could the writer have mentioned these things in a different order without changing the meaning of the sentence?
  12. What kind of relationship is used in this sentence?
  13. What phrase provides a clue?

D. A strange black cloud covered the sun in the southwest. Then a quietness settled over everything, followed by a burst of wind that drove sheets of rain across the road.

  14. Describe exactly what happened.
  15. Would you have described the event accurately if you had mentioned the rain as coming before the period of quiet?
  16. What kind of relationship did the author use here?
  17. What are the clue words?

EXERCISE III. More practice in recognizing clue words

On your paper, after the number of each passage, write at least one word or phrase which gives you a clue to the relationship used. Then write the name of the relationship (time order, cause-effect, comparison-contrast, or simple listing). The first one is done for you.

1. The sea is fascinating to most people, but Sarah hates and fears it. (*1. but—comparison-contrast*)
2. The ocean waves hide many valuable things: huge amounts of minerals, oil, and natural gas; diamonds and other jewels washed down by rivers; the hulks of sunken treasure ships; as well as millions of fish and other marine creatures.
3. Over a period of several thousand years, many men tried to develop a device that would enable a person to stay under water longer than he can hold his breath. Finally, in 1715, John Lethbridge, an Englishman, invented the first successful diving suit.
4. When a diver goes down into deep water, the pressure of the water forces nitrogen into his bloodstream. Therefore he has

to be "decompressed," or gradually freed of the extra nitrogen in his blood, when he comes to the surface.

5. If the deep diver were exposed to normal air pressure suddenly, the nitrogen would form bubbles in his blood which would result in great pain, perhaps death.

6. In deep dives, a mixture of helium and oxygen, called heliox, is better for men to use in their breathing apparatus than normal air.

EXERCISE IV.   Using relationships to understand paragraphs

Recognizing relationships helps you understand and remember what an author has said.

In the following paragraphs the clue words are printed in bold type, to help you recognize the relationship. As you read, think about the relationship as well as about the ideas. Then answer the questions.

(A)   **For a long time,** all exploring of the ocean depths had to be done from the surface with nets and bottom-grabs to bring things up to the top. **Then** various kinds of diving suits were invented. **One of the first** was a watertight leather suit with a large, barrel-like wooden helmet containing enough air for the diver to breathe for a few minutes. A diving helmet with a hose leading to an air supply on the surface came **next** and was probably invented **about 1820. In the early 1940's** came the aqualung which permits a diver to carry his own air supply. This has **since** been improved into the skin-diving equipment **of today.**

1. What kind of equipment did men use in their first attempts to find out what is hidden under the waves?

2. What three steps in the development of the diving suit are described?

3. What relationship is emphasized in paragraph A?

(B)   When men go down under the sea, they are in a world very **different from** the one they are used to. Things look out of focus and appear to be about a fourth **larger** and **nearer** than they really are. Also, it is **harder** to move about and one's body feels very strange. Sea water is much **heavier** than air. All the miles and miles of air in the earth's atmosphere press on a person standing at sea level with the weight of only 14.7 pounds per square inch of his body. In the deepest valleys of the ocean, **however,** the pressure has to be figured in tons per square inch, **rather than** pounds.

4. What two "worlds" are being compared?
5. In what two ways is man's condition under water different from his condition in the world of air?
6. What relationship is emphasized in paragraph B?

(C)   Some day there may be "cities" under the sea. They could have **many important uses. For example,** they could act as protected work sites from which to drill deep ocean oil wells and mines. They might **also** support docks for underwater vessels. They would be useful as centers of communication (sound travels in water more than four times faster than in air) **as well as** "homes" from which scientists could carry on studies of fish and plant life, the action of underwater volcanoes, and the effects upon the human body of living under the sea.

7. What uses would undersea cities have?
8. Would the meaning of the paragraph be changed in any important way if the uses were named in a different order?
9. What is the main relationship in paragraph C?

(D)   Study of the sea and its life may soon be a matter of life or death. The world's increasing population must have more and more food. Scientists believe we must learn how to "farm" the fish and plant life of the sea. Oil deposits on land are rapidly being used up. Fortunately, the United States alone has, it is estimated, over three trillion barrels of oil underwater just off its shores. This supply will have to be drawn on more and more to meet our increasing needs for oil. **Furthermore,** protection from nuclear submarines requires knowledge of the deep sea where these subs travel. **For all these reasons** we can no longer afford to be so ignorant about the ocean.

10. What is the central idea of paragraph D?
11. What facts does the author mention to prove that this central idea is true?
12. What relationship is emphasized?

(E)   **Although** the ocean floor is only a short distance away **as compared with** the moon, we know very little, if any, **more** about it. The moon is 240,000 miles away; the deepest part of the ocean, so far as we know, is only about seven miles down. **But** the back side of the moon has been successfully photographed and mapped, **whereas** only about 5 per cent of the ocean floor has been explored.

13. Which is the main point made in paragraph E?
    a. The moon is much farther away than the sea bottom.
    b. Since the moon is so far away, we have very little information about it.
    c. It is strange that we know quite a lot about the surface of the moon, which is far away, and very little about the sea bottom, which is close by.
14. What is the relationship used in paragraph E?

LESSON THREE: How relationships are combined

Authors often use more than one kind of relationship, even in a single sentence or a single paragraph. Think about the relationships in these two sentences:

    A. Jim worked hard on his homework and then decided to watch TV.
    B. Jim worked hard on his homework and then received permission from his father to take the car for the evening.

What relationship is there in both sentences? In which sentence is there probably also another kind of relationship between the events mentioned? What is it?

   Look again at paragraph D in Exercise IV. This paragraph actually consists of a list, but since the writer's main purpose is to explain why we need to learn more about the ocean, it seems more reasonable to call it a cause-effect paragraph.

   In each of the following paragraphs you will find more than one kind of relationship. Read each paragraph carefully and answer the questions.

    (A)   When the West was opened, explorers blazed the trails. Men like Daniel Boone crossed the Appalachians. Fremont and others pushed through to the Pacific, exploring and mapping as they went. Then came trappers, hunters, and gold miners, men who wanted to take as much as they could and get away. Following these came the men of the soil—the cattlemen and homesteaders—who brought their families and came to stay. "We want our women and children here," they said. "We want homes." Finally came the businessmen, the founders of cities who made money by using the labor of others in their factories. Some people think we are just at the beginning—the exploration stage—of a similar story on earth's last frontier beneath the sea.

1. What relationship do you find FIRST in this paragraph?
2. What second kind of relationship is suggested in the last sentence? What word in the sentence gives you a clue?
3. What four stages in the development of the West are described?
4. From the fact that he shifts to a different relationship at the *end* of his paragraph, what main point do you suspect the writer really wanted to make? Which relationship is probably the more important one?

(B) Black storm waves towering over a ship at sea are frightening things. Even more fearful are the great tidal waves caused by undersea earthquakes, which have destroyed thousands of people in a few moments. On the other hand, the blue-green waves or breakers rolling up onto the beach are pure delight to surfers riding on their crests, as well as to people merely watching them from the shore. A wave expert sitting on the beach, just by watching waves and by knowing something about seasonal winds, storm patterns, and coastlines, can make a pretty good guess as to where these breakers are coming from. If, while they are still far from shore, they have a steep, choppy look, they are probably young waves formed by a storm nearby. But if they seem slow and quiet as they roll in, and then, near the shore, crest and break with a roar, they are old waves which have traveled far, perhaps thousands of miles. Since time began, men have both loved and feared the everlasting movement of the sea.

5. How many major kinds of waves does the writer describe?
6. Which of these kinds does he describe most fully? How has he done this?
7. Has he merely described the kinds of waves, or is he making a special point about waves and the way people feel about them? If so, what relationship has he created?

8. What kind of relationship do you find in the second sentence?

9. In which other sentence has the writer used this kind of relationship?

10. What do you think is the main relationship in paragraph B?

(C) Tides seem at first to be small and unimportant compared with the huge waves which sometimes drown big ships and destroy seacoast towns. But this is a false impression. Tides actually move the whole ocean. They move the earth and the air, too. The continents rise about six inches every time there is a ten-foot tide, and the atmosphere around the earth bulges out toward the sun and the moon many miles. Even people are affected by the tides. Each of us gains or loses a fraction of an ounce of weight with each rise and fall of the tides.

11. What does the writer say that the tides do?

12. What does he point out about the relative effects of waves and tides?

13. Which of these two points do you think is more important in paragraph C?

14. Which kind of relationship receives the main emphasis?

EXERCISE V.   Using combined relationships in a longer article

Read the questions on page 293 before you read this article. They will help you find the relationships in it.

Seacamping

by Olive S. Niles

DANGER AND hardship were the hourly companions of America's earliest campers, the wilderness explorers. They camped because they had no other choice but to make a bed of some sort in whatever shelter they could find, start a fire with flint and steel to cook their game and scare wild animals away, and fall asleep from the fatigue of a daylong journey, usually on foot through an unmapped forest. They carried only a blanket, a gun and ammunition, a knife, and perhaps a small amount of food for the days when they couldn't find any game. Their purpose was altogether serious and practical.

America's modern campers, on the other hand, camp because they want to and because they expect to enjoy it. Perhaps their goal is to "get away from it all" or to seek the adventure which their daily life doesn't offer. They may carry as little equipment as the wilderness men did. In this case, they will rough it, though with less danger. They know that if they don't return when expected, some Forest Ranger or police officer will be out looking for them.

If today's camper is not the rough-it type, he can travel with a deluxe cabin on wheels which includes a kitchen sink, innerspring mattress, refrigerator, a closet with full-length mirror, wall-to-wall carpet, and a TV set. There are now thousands of campsites where these vehicles can be plugged into a source of electricity and a sewage system. However, many camp vehicles have completely independent electrical systems. The driver can pull up under the trees beside a lake deep in the wilderness and spend a night as comfortably as he would in his own home.

There are those who think the next quarter-century may bring even more dramatic developments in camping.

Soon people may be spending their vacations on earth's last frontier, under the sea, living in special vehicles and moving around with the fish. Though nobody has yet done this just for fun, it has already been proved that people can live for weeks at a time undersea.

Experiments have been going on to develop the needed equipment. Most nearly like the old-fashioned tent in which Boy Scouts and some of the more rugged family groups still camp on land is the inflatable, watertight tent for use in 35 to 50 feet of water. It is an open-ended bag which can be inflated from a diver's air bottle and anchored, open end down, to the sea floor. Pressure inside the bag equals pressure outside, so water does not come in. If the idea proves practical, it will provide a kind of home from which a diver can explore the water around him. Its furniture will probably consist of nothing more than a floating mattress. The tent can be used until the supply of air inside becomes polluted. Such camping would be as primitive in its way as that of the first explorer-campers.

More complicated is the SPID (Submersible Portable Inflatable Dwelling) which has been used experimentally. It carries its air supply in bottles, has a floor, and is equipped with an apparatus for purifying air. It is small and cramped, with no luxuries aboard, but it can be moved about under water.

Steel undersea houses permanently attached to the ocean bottom are also being planned. These will be roomier and more comfortable. A series of such houses may some day be built at points of special interest so that campers may move via a small sub from one to another, much as hikers move from shelter to shelter along the Appalachian Trail in the eastern United States.

Vehicles like the Navy's SeaLabs offer another possibility for undersea camping. These steel shells are weighted to make them sink to the bottom. When it is time to come to the surface, the weights are dropped off and the SeaLab floats on the surface, ready to be towed to a new site. This kind of vehicle is similar to a land trailer. It can be equipped with many of the comforts and even luxuries of these land vehicles.

Undersea camping may always be limited to the continental shelf along the shore, not only because this area is much safer than the deep ocean, but because its warm, shallow waters swarm with interesting marine life. The deep ocean is uninviting—black, cold, and dangerous.

For a while, at least, camping in inner space (as the ocean is now being called) will involve far greater dangers than ever an explorer-camper faced in the Western wilderness. One other big difference will be in terms of cost. Even the cheapest equipment for undersea camping will be expensive. The Daniel Boones of the ocean floor will have to be well-to-do.

1. To what does the author of this article compare seacamping?
2. In what two ways does *all* modern camping on land differ from the experiences of the early explorers?
3. What two kinds of modern camping are mentioned? Which is described more fully?
4. What are some of the things that make the deluxe trailer camp like home?
5. What kinds of equipment might be used for seacamping? How do they differ from each other?
6. In which type of equipment will seacampers come closest to the experience of the Western explorers?
7. Since camping under water is such a strange new idea, the author compares the various possible types of seacamping equipment to more familiar facilities for camping on land.
   a) To what kind of land camping is the inflatable tent compared?
   b) Houses permanently attached to the sea floor are compared to what kind of land camping?
   c) What is the SeaLab similar to?
8. How long does the author feel it may be before seacamping will be a common part of American recreation? Before the average American family can go seacamping, what will manufacturers have to do to the equipment besides make it safer to use?
9. Why will people probably camp on the continental shelf instead of in the deep ocean?

Writers of fiction also use the relationships you have been studying. In the following story, written by a high-school student, the relationships are not always expressed directly. However, you will understand the story only if you understand the relationships the author suggests.

In the Beginning

by Judi Lundberg

HE STOOD and stared at the window, pockets empty. "So easy," they said, "all it takes is guts." Guts, that was what you needed to be "in" around this stinkin' town. Guts, something he'd never had to prove before. Guts, that one thing everyone was so dependent on.

Well, he wanted to be "in," didn't he? Sure, it's no fun to be stuck in a town without any guys to goof off with. "The only way to get 'in,' " they said. Why, why, why did his family have to move here?

It was so clear, what he had to do.

He'd gone over and over it in his mind. Now, just to put the plan into action. The store was busy; good, they said it would be easier that way. He walked over to the Directory. His eyes found what he wanted and transplanted the "fourth floor—clothing" deep in his mind. He rode the elevator up and went over to the men's section. Nonchalantly, he walked around, acting interested, but not too interested so as not to draw attention. When he reached the jacket rack the familiar blue jacket with the black lettering seemed to stand out from all the rest. No, he couldn't chicken out now, he had to belong and there was only one way to get that jacket. Money didn't count. What did he care, he didn't have money anyhow. He had to do it right, he had to get "in." Okay, now do it just as you planned. That's right, try it on, admire it in the mirror, and while no one is looking, take off the tags. Muss it a little and act like you were born in the thing, walk around a little more, careful. Now clear out, fast.

He ran down the escalator and once he reached the outside he did run, fast, faster than he thought he could. The

From *Harp in the Willows* (Spring 1964). Reprinted by permission of Walter R. Johnson, Superintendent, Libertyville High School, Libertyville, Illinois.

sooner he got out of this neighborhood and out of range of that store, the better.

* * * * *

As HE STOOD in front of the window, pockets empty except for the gun he fingered carefully, he thought how easy it was now. All this was old stuff. He looked back and remembered the first time. Punk kid he was then, but he'd made it; he was "in."

THE END

After your answer to each of the following questions, write the name of the relationship you used in deciding on your answer.

1. Why did the boy in this story steal the jacket?
2. Describe exactly what he did.
3. Why did he run fast when he got out of the store?
4. What has happened between the last two paragraphs?
5. What evidence is there that he is no better off at the end of the story than he was at the beginning?
6. Why do you think the author has the setting for the last paragraph exactly the same as that for the first?

What you should know about the relationship of ideas

In all written material that makes sense, there are connections or **relationships** among the ideas. Four important kinds of relationships are:

       time order
       cause-effect
       comparison-contrast
       simple listing

Most writing contains more than one kind of relationship. The same kinds of relationships are used in fiction and in factual writing. Recognizing the way ideas are connected or related helps you understand and remember.

9

A savage dog . . .

a schoolgirl rival . . .

a motherless boy . . .

a murderer's ghost . . .

an old frontiersman . . .

each one surprises you

when you take a

SECOND LOOK.

Second Look

An open window,
muddy tracks,
a dog with a bloody mouth—
What could a frantic father think?

The Soul of Caliban

by Emma-Lindsay Squier

FROM French Louis I had this story, which you will accept as true or scout as impossible, according to your liking and knowledge of dogs. For myself, I think it is true, for Louis was not blessed—or cursed—with imagination.

French Louis is a curious mixture of savagery and simplicity. For many years he lived by trapping in the northern woods. And yet, despite his cruel occupation, he has always loved animals. One day when he heard a visitor remark that it was a pity that animals had no souls, he flew into a rage, fairly booted the visitor out of the place, and was still sputtering French and English when I dropped in upon him.

"No souls, they say!" he snorted, spreading his hands and puckering his lips in contemptuous mimicry. "Faugh! Listen, I tell you somet'ing I bet you nobody believe! Or they say, 'Oh, that dog he obey his instinct.' All I say is, who know what is instinct and what is soul?"

It was in the sheep country of Alberta[1] that Louis knew the dog, Caliban. Leon Suprenon[2] was his owner, and Louis used to visit the sheep man at his ranch, far removed from civilization.

"Leon he was one fine educated

Adapted from "The Soul of Caliban" by Emma-Lindsay Squier. Reprinted by permission of John Bransby.

[1]**Alberta** (al bėr′tə), a province in the western part of Canada.

[2]**Leon Suprenon** (lā ōN′ sü prä nōN′)

man," he told me. "That dog, Caliban, Leon name' him from a play by Shakespeare. You know a play with a dog name' Caliban in it?"

"Not a dog," I answered, "but a poor imprisoned monster, ugly, deformed, and very wicked, yet somehow very pitiful."

French Louis nodded vigorously.

"What kind of dog was Caliban?" I asked.

Louis shrugged his shoulders, spread out his hands, and shook his head. No kind, and every kind, was what I gathered from his description—a big, shaggy dog, as large as a sheep dog, and much more stockily built. His hair had no silky smoothness to it. Rather it was like the rough, matted fur of a wolf— and Louis maintained that Caliban had wolf blood in him. There was a strain of bulldog, too, that made his legs short and bowed a bit. His under jaw came out pugnaciously—always with that lifted lip which was no fault of his, but which gave his face a perpetually savage expression.

Ugly he must have been; yet useful, too. As a guard against tramps and the lawless characters who are to be found in any part of the country where civilization is at a distance, he was invaluable. As a sheep dog, too, he had not his equal in Alberta. Perhaps it is too much to say that he could count the sheep his master owned. But it is true that he would watch them passing into the big corrals, his sharp, shaggy ears pointed, his small, close-set eyes never wavering in their intense regard, his whole body taut with concentration. And if any lingered or did not come, Caliban would need no word of command to stir him to action. Like an arrow he would dart out, snapping at

the lagging heels, turning in a scatter-brained ewe, or dashing off across the fields to find a sheep which he knew had strayed or had fallen into the river.

A dog of stormy jealousies, and incomprehensible tenderness. So rough was he, when herding the sheep, that Leon Suprenon was always shouting: "Caliban, you devil! Stop biting that sheep or I'll beat your ugly brains out!"

Caliban would stop short, regard his master with a long, disdainful stare, and then look back at the sheep, as if to say: "Those silly things! What difference does it make whether I bite their heels or not?"

And yet—that was the dog that, after seeing the sheep into the corral one winter afternoon when a blizzard was threatening to blow down from the north, did not come into the house to dream and twitch under the kitchen stove as was his custom. When darkness fell Leon noticed the dog's absence at first with unconcern, and then with growing uneasiness. The rising wind flung itself viciously upon doors and windows, the white snow whirled up against the panes with hissing flurries. Leon went to the door and called. The blizzard drove his voice back in his throat.

Leon Suprenon was not the man to be daunted by a storm. He remembered that after the gates were shut, Caliban had stood steadily gazing away toward the dim fields, where the menacing curtain of oncoming wind and snow was blotting out the contours of stream and distant forest.

So he took a lantern and fought his way out into the terrible night. A mile he went—perhaps more—fighting his way against the fury of the storm. It was out by the cluster of pine trees that marks the east line of the ranch that he met Caliban, coming home.

The dim light of the lantern threw a weak golden circle against the driving white mistiness of the snow. And into the ring of light came Caliban, a grotesque monster looming out of the white darkness, his mouth strangely misshapen by something he was carrying—*a lamb,* newly born. Beside him, struggling weakly yet valiantly against the driving snow, came the mother sheep, which had given birth to her baby in the midst of the dreadful blizzard. Caliban was coming slowly, adapting his pace to hers, stopping when she would stop, yet with unmistakable signs that he expected her to struggle forward with him. And the lamb—the weak, bleating little thing swung from his teeth as lightly as if it had been a puff of thistledown.

Now the dog Caliban never begged for caresses. He was not the sort of dog to leap and bark and wag his tail when the master came home. Between him and Leon Suprenon there was an understanding—a man's understanding of mutual respect and restraint. A word of praise was enough for him, or sometimes a pat on the head.

Nevertheless, Caliban had his jealousies, fierce, deep, and primitive. He killed a dog that Leon petted casually; he took it by the throat and crushed it with his great teeth, then flung the quivering body down and stared at it with those baleful, close-set eyes. There was blood on the perpetual snarl of his lifted lip.

Then fearlessly he awaited his punishment. Leon beat him cruelly. But Caliban never flinched or whimpered, just stood there hunching himself up and shutting his eyes, licking his lips a bit as the blows hurt him more and more. When it was over, he shook himself, stretched, then pricked up his ears and looked Leon in the face, as if to say: "Well, that's over. Now have you any orders?" If he had whimpered once —but he did not. Leon swore furiously, and had the dead dog buried in the meadow. He did not caress the other dogs after that. They were valuable to him, but Caliban was priceless. And Leon knew that the only way of breaking his stubborn spirit would be to kill him.

Caliban had one abiding hatred: cats. Whereas the other dogs chased them joyously, or ignored them as inferior creatures, Caliban loathed them, chased them savagely, killed them mercilessly. He had a short, brutal way of doing it; if he caught a luckless cat— and he would run like a yearling buck, that dog Caliban—he would give it one shake, like the crack of a whip, and then toss the cat into the air. It usually died with a broken neck, and a broken back. And by the law of the survival of the fittest, the cats that escaped from Caliban were the wise ones which kept out of his way.

But there was one small cat, not yet out of kittenhood, that had either come recently to the ranch, or else by an accident had not crossed Caliban's path —a gentle little cat, all gray, with a white paw which she was always licking as if proud of it.

One day she sat sunning herself on the porch before the house. Caliban came by that way, and saw her.

With the savage, deep-throated growl that all the other cats had learned to fear as the most deadly thing of life, he leaped at her, caught her, flung her up into the air.

Perhaps it was supreme ignorance of danger that saved her from death. For the gentle little cat had not tried to run from the oncoming whirlwind of teeth and gleaming eyes. She lay where Caliban had flung her, dazed, motionless, staring at the terrible dog with round, uncomprehending eyes. He saw that he had not killed her. He came nearer, ready to shake her with the peculiarly deadly twist that he knew so well. Still she did not move. She could not. She only mewed, a very small, pitiful mew, and her stunned body twitched a little.

Caliban hesitated, sniffed at her, turned away. After all, he seemed to tell himself, you could not kill a weak, helpless thing like that—a thing that could not run.

Leon Suprenon came out and found the little cat. He took her up very gently, and she tried to purr as he stroked her quivering, hurt body.

"Caliban," Leon said sternly, "that was not a sportsmanlike thing to do. I am ashamed of you!"

And to his great surprise, Caliban put his tail between his legs and slunk down the porch steps. He too was ashamed.

But Caliban could make amends. And to the best of his ability he did. The gentle little cat did not die, but never did she fully recover the use of her legs. She had a slow, halting way of walking, and running was an impossibility. She would have been an easy prey for the joyous, roistering dogs that chased cats, not from enmity, but because it was the proper thing to do. But Caliban stood between her and eager, sniffing dogs like a savage warrior. Too well did the other ranch dogs know the menace of those close-set eyes, the ugly, undershot jaw, and the snarl that showed the glitter of deadly, clamping teeth. They learned—through experience—that the little gray cat was not to be molested.

Not only did Caliban become the little cat's protector; he became her friend. She would sit on the fence and watch for the sheep dogs to come up to the house after the day's work was done. When the other dogs filed past her, she paid no attention, realizing perfectly that they dared not harm her. And when Caliban came, close at the heels of Leon Suprenon, she would yawn and stretch, purr loudly, and drop squarely and lightly on the big dog's back. He would carry her gravely into the kitchen, lie down while she got slowly off his back, and would lie under the stove, with the little cat purring and rubbing about his face. It was not in him to show affection. But he permitted her carefully to wash his face and ears, tug at burrs that matted his heavy coat, and to sleep between his forefeet.

Once another cat, emboldened by the gray cat's immunity from danger, went to sleep between Caliban's great paws. When Caliban awoke and found the intruder peacefully purring against his chest, he gave one terrific growl, sprang to his feet, seized the strange cat and shook it. Savagely he flung it across the room. It was dead before it struck the floor.

Now it was at this time that Leon Suprenon married Amelie Morin[3] and brought her to the ranch. She felt the loneliness of the place, and shivered when at night the wolves howled far back on the distant slopes. But she loved Leon Suprenon, and in time became used to the loneliness of the ranch

---

[3]Amelie Morin (ä mä lē′ mô raN′)

—still more so when a baby was born to her, and was strong and healthy and beautiful.

Caliban had accepted the girl, Amelie, without apparent resentment. It was as if he knew that sooner or later his master would bring home a woman to share the lonely ranch house. But the baby—that was a different thing. He had not bargained on the small intruder who became at once the lord and tyrant of the household. When Leon took up the tiny baby in his arms, Caliban growled, and his eyes became a baleful red.

When Leon put the baby in its crib, and spoke to it foolishly, fondly, as all fathers do, Caliban came and stood beside him, looking down at the red-faced crinkly-eyed baby; and again the dog growled, deep in his throat.

One day when Leon caressed the child, Caliban sprang, trying to tear the infant out of his arms. Leon kicked the dog furiously aside, and beat him with a leather whip.

"Caliban, you devil!" he panted between the blows. "If you ever touch that baby, I'll kill you!"

And, as if he understood, the dog hunched himself and shut his eyes, licking his lips as the heavy lash fell again and again. Then he shook himself, stared at his master with somber, unwavering eyes, and went out of the house without once looking back.

For a whole week he did not return. One of the ranchmen reported that he had seen Caliban in the forest.

Leon Suprenon said that Caliban would come back. But Amelie cried out:

"No, no! That dog, he is a monster! Never again would I feel that my baby was safe!"

"You misjudge him," Leon said soothingly. "He is a little jealous of the baby, it is true, but he will overcome that in time. An ugly-looking dog, I grant you, but he is very gentle, nevertheless."

"*Gentle*—that beast!" The girl shut her eyes and shuddered.

Caliban did come back. He appeared at the kitchen door one day when Leon was out looking after the sheep—sullen, defiant, his glittering, close-set eyes seeming to question whether or not he would be welcomed. Amelie snatched up her baby from where he was playing on the floor, ran with him to the bedroom, and closed and bolted the door. But a royal welcome he received from the little gray cat, that dragged herself toward him with purring sounds of joy. She mewed delightedly, rubbed against his bowed legs, and tried to lick his face. Caliban, for the first and last time, bent his ugly head, and licked the little gray cat, briefly and furtively.

The dog had learned his lesson as to the status of the baby. And whether or not his heart was seared with that savage, primitive jealousy which he had shown at first so plainly, no hint of it now appeared. At first he ignored the child, even when it crawled toward him as he lay under the kitchen stove. Later he would watch the round-faced baby with rigid, attentive eyes—eyes in which there were blue-green wolf gleams behind the honest brown.

Little by little Amelie's distrust lessened, and she was willing that the baby should lie in his crib on the sunny porch, when Caliban was stretched out on the steps with the little gray cat sleeping between his paws.

Then one day, after a morning of housework within doors, she came out to take the baby—and he was gone. The crib was empty, the little blankets were rumpled into confusion. The dog Caliban still lay sleeping upon the porch, and the little gray cat purred drowsily against his furry chest.

Amelie screamed, and the men came running up from the sheep pens and barns, snatching up sticks of wood, or fumbling with guns. Leon came running with a face the color of chalk, and Amelie clung to him, screaming, sobbing, wild with hysterical fear. She was certain that some wild animal had snatched her baby out of his crib and devoured him.

"Nonsense!" said Leon Suprenon positively. "No wild animal could have come near the house with Caliban on guard."

After an hour of frantic searching they found the child. Back of the ranch house where the garbage was dumped and burned, there they found the baby, playing happily with an old tin can, dirty and bedraggled, yet quite unharmed.

In the first moment of acute relief, no one thought to question how the child had come so far. But afterward—

Leon stood in deep thought, staring down at Caliban, who returned his look steadily, unflinchingly. For the first time a doubt of the dog's integrity came into his mind. He knew Caliban's great strength, knew that the dog could have carried the baby as easily as he had carried the newborn lamb. And the garbage pile—there was a grim humor in that which pointed to Caliban's line of reasoning. . . .

"Caliban, you devil!" said Leon Suprenon between clenched teeth. Yet he could not beat the dog. The evidence was only circumstantial.

Had the thing happened to anyone else's child, he would have laughed heartily at the story. But to him it was not so funny. Anything might have happened to the child. The dog might have dropped it; or stray wolves might have come down out of the woods. The baby might have cut its hands terribly on broken glass or rusty tin cans.

"Caliban," said Leon Suprenon sternly, "you have spoiled my belief in you. I will never be able to trust you again."

The great ugly dog stared at him with those glittering, close-set eyes, then turned away abruptly and lay down. It was almost as if he had shrugged his shoulders.

Now there came the winter time—a lean, terrible winter, when the wolves howled about the ranch, sometimes becoming so bold as to come close to the house.

The spring was late, and even when the snow began to melt, and the first warm breezes began to come up from the south, still the howling of the wolf pack was heard on distant hills, and still tracks were found in the crusted snow about the barn and the sheep corrals.

One day in the spring an urgent message came to Amelie Suprenon, begging her to come to a neighboring ranch where a woman lay in childbirth.

She saddled her horse herself, for the men were out on the ranges. Then she hesitated as to leaving or taking the baby. But Leon had said he would return at noon. She scribbled a note for him, put the baby in the bedroom in the little pen which Leon had made for it, and shut the door. Then she mounted her horse and rode hard and fast to the woman who was in need of her.

Leon Suprenon did not get the note. A hint of spring sickness had come upon some of the sheep, and he worked through the morning and late into the afternoon with sheep dip and sprays. When he was about to return to the ranch house, one of the men told him that he had seen Amelie riding by, at noon, in the direction of the Pourers' ranch. Leon frowned a bit. He did not like to have Amelie ride alone, especially on the forest roads. He flung himself upon his horse, shouted to his men to go on with their work, and took a short cut across the fields to ride home with Amelie.

He met her just as she came out of the door, tired but smiling.

"Such a sweet little baby boy!" she called to Leon as he rode nearer. Then her face suddenly clouded.

"The baby—our baby—" she said uncertainly. "You did not leave him alone?"

Leon stared back at her, his forehead wrinkled.

"The baby?" he repeated. "Why surely, Amelie, he is with you?"

For an instant she did not reply. A slow fear was dawning in her heart that stretched her eyes wide and made them hard and glassy.

"No—no," she almost whispered. "I left a note—I thought you would come at noon. The baby then—he is there alone—perhaps with—*Caliban*—" Her voice died away, as if she were afraid of the name she had spoken.

Leon tried to laugh, to make light of her fears. But his lips were a bit stiff, and he breathed hard as he helped her into the saddle.

"Come, come, Amelie, you worry too much. The little one will be quite well—you shall see—only very hungry perhaps and exercising his small lungs terrifically. As for Caliban—"

Amelie slashed at her horse's flank with the whip. Her face was dead-white.

"Where was that dog—that terrible beast, when you came away?" she gasped as they galloped down the snowy road.

"I don't know," Leon jerked out grimly, as if thinking aloud. "I can't remember seeing him—yes, yes, he stood looking away toward the ranch house; I remember that he barked once —then trotted away. I thought he was rounding up a sheep. I did not call him back."

"*O grand Dieu,*[4] guard my baby!" cried Amelie. "He is in danger, I tell you, Leon. I feel it, I know it! That beast—that horrible beast—Oh, my baby, my little baby!"

She lashed her horse with frenzied, hysterical hands, and the startled animal reared and plunged forward. Fast, faster, the slender hoofs pounded through the snowy slush of the road, and Leon's horse followed, breathing hard and straining at the bit.

They did not speak again, but rode, rode as if for the saving of a life.

It was Amelie who dismounted first, when at the end of that wild ride her horse came to a stop, panting and trembling. She dashed the unlocked door wide open, and an instant later a wild scream sent the blood ebbing from Leon's face and made his hands numb clods of flesh as they fumbled for the gun in his belt.

The scene he saw as he stumbled through the hallway turned him sick with a deadly nausea of horror and despair.

---

[4] **O grand Dieu** (ō gräN dyoe), Oh great God. *French.*

Amelie lay fainting in the open doorway of the bedroom. Beyond, an empty pen, an open window, with muddy tracks on the window sill, told a dreadful story. But the thing that made him cry out, savagely, hoarsely, was the dog —Caliban. The snarling misshapen beast stood in the doorway, staring at him with red, malevolent eyes—*and there was blood on the heavy jowls and the thick, matted hair of the chest.*

"You—you devil!" Leon screamed like a madman—and fired.

The dog still stood there, just an instant. The small, close-set eyes blinking slightly, the ugly head jerked back once —and he fell in a silent, twitching heap.

"Oh God! Oh God!" Leon was sobbing, hardly knowing what he said or did. And then—he heard a baby crying.

Stunned, incredulous, almost believing himself in a tortured dream, the man went slowly forward. The baby lay behind the door, lay where it had been dragged to safety. It was crying with fright and hunger, beating the air vaguely with its pink little hands. And over by the dresser, in a pool of blood —lay a dead wolf.

"There is a grave on the ranch of Leon Suprenon," said French Louis solemnly, in the language of his people, "where the dog, Caliban, lies buried. And above it is a tombstone of marble —yes, the whitest of marble—with this inscription:

" 'Here lies Caliban, a dog. He died as he lived, misjudged, maligned, yet unafraid. In life he never failed in duty, and in death he was faithful to his trust.'

"And that is why," said Louis, "that I get so mad inside of me when people say animals they have no souls. Did not the dog, Caliban, have a soul? I know this: when he died that day, and his spirit went out of his big, ugly body and rose up to the skies, the good Saint who guards the gates up there he look out and say: 'Why, Caliban, is that you? Come in, *mon brave.*[5] I did not know you. How beautiful you have grown!' "

THE END

Talking it over

1. *a.* Why was Caliban so "priceless" to Leon Suprenon that he kept the dog in spite of all the trouble he caused?

   b. How does Caliban reveal early in the story that there is some kindness in his savage nature?

2. What two things does Caliban do which show he might harm the baby?

3. What judgment does Amelie make about Caliban?

4. *a.* What judgment has Leon Suprenon made when he shoots Caliban?

   b. What evidence leads him to make this judgment?

   c. When Leon takes a "second look," what does he find has actually happened?

5. *a.* French Louis insists that the good Saint who guards the gates of Heaven must have said, "Why Caliban, is that you? . . . I did not know you. How beautiful you have grown!" Why does French Louis feel that Caliban must have a beautiful soul?

   b. Explain whether you agree or disagree with French Louis that Caliban could be called "very pitiful."

---

[5]**mon brave** (mōN bräv), my good fellow. *French.*

Talking it over

1. *a.* Why does the speaker rescue the loon?

b. When he picks up the loon, he thinks "of the warmth within." What does he mean by this phrase?

c. How does the speaker feel toward the loon?

2. *a.* How do you know that the bird bit him very hard?

b. Why did the bird hurt someone who was trying to help him?

3. *a.* How does the description of the man's cry relate to the title of the poem?

b. Who takes a "second look"? What is it?

4. Explain whether "Chain" is a good or a poor title for the poem.

A real experience

Paul Petrie says, "I wrote the first draft of 'Chain' over seventeen years ago. The original impulse came from seeing an injured loon in a rabbit pen in the backyard of an old man at whose place my father and I used to go fishing. The old man had set a trap for some foxes who were harassing his chickens and had caught the bird by mistake. As he was removing it from the trap the loon had given him a vicious bite on the wrist. In writing the poem I turned the old man's experience into my own and added many imagined details."

Something really terrible
would happen now. . . .
But Enie wasn't sorry.

THE SLAP

by Mildred Lee

THE NEW English teacher was also Enie's home room teacher. Her name was Cecily Pritchard and she was small and very young-looking, but a quiet authority emanated from her in the first words she spoke.

At recess some of the girls glibly gave out information about the new teacher—most of which, Enie suspected, was without foundation. Her age, dress, shoes, and hair style were of major interest to the adolescent girls clustered under the big oak. But it was Mary Lee Williams' statement that fired Enie with excitement almost too great to be contained. Mary Lee's father, Green Pine's leading druggist, was on the school board—a fact Mary Lee did not let the others forget. With a toss of her curly brown head she said, knowingly, "Miss Pritchard lives in North

Carolina in some little town like this, but she went to college in New York City. I heard Daddy tell Mother so. That's why she's so stylish."

Enie, who always felt on the fringe of the town girls' gatherings anyway, withdrew to think this over. She had never known anyone who had been to New York City! She was still tingling with thrills when the bell rang and the home room noisily settled for the first day's work.

Right from the start Miss Pritchard took an interest in Enie as no teacher had before. It began with the first assignment she gave the class. She told them to write a composition, but gave them no subject or choice of suggested ones. It was an unheard-of procedure and promptly threw the students into a sea of consternation. Mary Lee Williams looked as blank as the rest, though she was smart and had always reigned like a little queen with teachers and

Reprinted (slightly abridged) by permission of Lothrop, Lee & Shepard Co., Inc., from *The Rock and the Willow* by Mildred Lee. © 1963, by Lothrop, Lee & Shepard Co., Inc.

students alike. Enie had always outstripped Mary Lee scholastically—sometimes by the narrowest margin—but the better grades were cold comfort when she had to endure the town girl's condescending manner year after year with never a real triumph of her own to alleviate the discomfort.

At recess that day Mary Lee left her town friends in their usual tight circle and approached Enie with an ingratiating smile. "Look, Earline, what are you going to write about for tomorrow's English?" Enie could feel Lou Addie's and Carol's eyes switch from the boys' side of the playground to her.

"I don't know. I hadn't thought about it." It was true; aside from the little quiver of interest when Miss Pritchard made the assignment, she had not given it a thought. Her composition book at home was full of scribbling that might easily furnish an idea if she had need of it. But she could not tell this to Mary Lee Williams; her composition book was as private and personal as a diary.

The dimple in Mary Lee's round cheek disappeared. "I don't see why she couldn't at least give us a title," she said, crossly. Enie moved uneasily, scuffing gravel with her ugly, heavy shoes. "Look, Earline," Mary Lee wheedled, "you could write something —just the beginning—for me. I can finish it, easy, if you will. It's just getting started that's so hard." The dimple flashed back. "I'll do something nice for you sometime, if you will."

Enie knew it had not been easy for Mary Lee Williams to ask a favor of her; at the same time she had a lightning vision of the advantages that might be hers if she chose to grant it. It was such a little thing to do and would cost her so little that she was half surprised to hear her own voice answering, "No. No, I can't. I've got my own to write. You'll have to do yours, Mary Lee— like everybody else."

Mary Lee's face turned crimson. She opened her mouth to say something, closed it without saying anything, and stalked angrily back to her friends.

The day after the compositions were turned in, Miss Pritchard devoted most of the period to poetry: its meaning and spirit. She explained smilingly that poetry did not have to rhyme—and that a rhyme was not necessarily a poem. "Prose frequently contains the beauty, the spirit of poetry," she said, glancing at the tiny gold watch on her wrist. "We have a minute or two before the bell. I'd like to give you an example that may illustrate better than what I've said—better, I think, than an essay written by someone you will never see and can think of only as someone dead and belonging to a faraway past."

She picked the sheaf of papers from her desk, slipped one from the elastic band that held them together. "This was written by a member of our own class—Earline Singleton. She has called it 'Imagination.'"

Before the light gasps of surprise had fluttered to silence, Miss Pritchard began to read: "My little brother told me of a pool he found in our woods. It was very, very deep, he said, and covered with ice. He said that when he looked at the frozen pool a long time he could see silver fishes swimming in silver rings beneath the ice. He said he heard music beneath the ice—distant and of an unearthly sweetness. When I searched for the pool, it was not there. I think I had known it would not be, yet I do not believe my brother lied to me."

Enie sat staring at her desk, not seeing its scars and ink stains, only hearing with burning ears Miss Pritchard reading the words she had written in her old composition book in her secret place behind the willows sometime last summer. Miss Pritchard's voice stopped and there was a peculiar hush. Enie could feel the eyes of every student upon her, making her hotter and hotter. The bell shattered the silence; there was the clatter of feet, the rustle of papers, the thwack of a dropped book. As Enie passed the teacher's desk, Miss Pritchard touched her shoulder. "You didn't mind, did you, Earline?" she asked, and Enie said on a caught breath, "No, ma'am."

Mary Lee Williams was waiting in the hall with her bosom friend, Hilda Reese. Her face was white with rage; her dark eyes raked Enie with hate. "Teacher's pet," she hissed. "You think you're something now, don't you? A big shot. Well, that doesn't stop you being a little old country tack!" Her eyes swept contemptuously over Enie's faded cotton dress with the hem that had been let out, showing a different shade of blue, the cotton stockings and ugly, sensible shoes. She thrust her arm through Hilda's so violently that both girls' friendship bracelets jingled, and turned a furious back on Enie.

Enie's pride staggered beneath the blow. All the way home on the bus she tried to salve it with Miss Pritchard's public praise. Mary Lee's wounding words were nothing, she told herself, against Miss Pritchard's. Always, before, her good marks had been their own reward; never had a teacher in the town school praised her before the class, making her achievement a shining example. Hadn't she said in front of them all that it was a better illustration than the writing of a dead and famous author? But the wound ached in spite of the praise; it left a deep and ugly scar, and what had been friction before settled into a cold and heavy enmity. It was not till late November that things came to a head between Enie and Mary Lee Williams.

Fifty cents mysteriously disappeared from Mary Lee's desk; Miss Pritchard allowed time for everyone in the room to take part in the search for it, but the money could not be found. Enie, secretly rather pleased at Mary Lee's misfortune, busied herself studiously while the search was going on.

"Perhaps you dropped it on your way to school," Miss Pritchard suggested, but Mary Lee was positive she had laid the two quarters on her desk. "Right by the inkwell," she said, and sent a flashing glance round the room. "Right where anybody could see it if they. . . ."

"That will do, Mary Lee," Miss Pritchard stopped her. "I'm sure that if anyone finds the money, it will be returned to you."

At recess a group of girls were standing round the washbowl in the girls' basement, taking turns at the mirror, when Enie hurried in with just time to wash her hands before the bell. In her haste she did not notice the silence that fell upon the town girls as she pushed past them to the washbowl. As she laid two coins on the ledge of the bowl and turned the spigot, a gasp went up, and something clicked in Enie's brain. It was then she knew it was going to happen. She could feel a gathering together of herself in readiness, yet she did not turn and look at the girls behind her— Hilda, Juanita, Paula, and Mary Lee.

A cold, unflustered fury took possession of her, making her actions precise and careful and unhurried: the drawing out of a paper towel, the wiping of her hands. Mary Lee's voice, asking the question, had the silkiness of a cat's purr.

"Would you mind telling me where you got that money?"

Enie gave a last rub with the damp piece of paper, then turned her eyes upon Mary Lee. "I got it from Louise Johnson and Carrie Knowles. They owed it for sugar cane I let them have over a month ago. Just about ten minutes ago they paid me—twenty-five cents apiece for five stalks of cane apiece." It occurred to Enie that she had not heard this particular voice of hers since the last time she and Henry Jim had a roll-and-tumble fight for which they had both been soundly whipped by Mamma. "If you don't believe me you can ask them. Right now. Go ahead, why don't you?" She took a step toward Mary Lee. Through the humming in her ears, she heard Mary Lee's voice, sounding thin and queer.

"I don't need to, thank you. I know some folks in this school are always mighty hard up for change."

Enie's hand cracked resoundingly across Mary Lee's cheek. Mary Lee's shriek echoed back from the concrete walls of the basement, and Enie slapped again—again—again. She struck Mary Lee for accusing her of stealing, for the hurts and humiliations of this year and those before it. She knew she had an overwhelming advantage over the sheltered, pampered only child who had never had to defend herself against tough-fisted brothers and who had no heritage of red hair and the temper that went with it.

The bell jangled across the bedlam about the washbowl. The other girls' squeals mingled with Mary Lee's cries that sank to moans and hysterical sobs as Enie wound up the battle with a vicious yank of the permanently waved hair falling about Mary Lee's shoulders, picked up her two quarters, and walked out, leaving the babel of horror and indignation behind her.

Her ears still hummed and there was a sick spot spreading through the middle of her. But she wasn't sorry for what she'd done; she was glad. Something really terrible would happen now; maybe she would be expelled from the school—Mary Lee's father was a member of the board—and the disgrace would include Mamma and break her heart with disappointment and shame. But Enie was even with Mary Lee Williams; she had paid her back for all the meanness—right down to the briefest glance which had emphasized Enie's shabby clothes, each ringing blow ramming the hated words "country tack" down Mary Lee's howling throat.

The last stragglers scuffed through the door of Miss Pritchard's room, and Enie crept along behind them and slid into her seat. The shuffling and whispering gradually died into comparative silence. Miss Pritchard was writing on the blackboard and had not seen the four empty seats.

The door flew open and agitated steps crossed the room to the blackboard. Every ear strained to catch the whispered words Juanita was pouring at Miss Pritchard. Enie saw bewilderment swallow the teacher's face. She laid the chalk on the ledge of the board. "Study quietly, please," she told the class. "Come with me, Earline."

Not a word was spoken as the two

girls and Miss Pritchard walked the length of the hall and descended the stairs into the carbolic aroma of the basement. Enie couldn't think and she had no feeling other than the faint sickness in her stomach. She had never been in trouble at school. She knew, in a detached sort of way, that each leaden step was bringing her closer to her doom, but she felt neither regret nor fear.

Paula, Hilda, and Mary Lee were sitting on the wooden bench that ran alongside the wall next to the basins. Mary Lee sobbed softly, her brown curls falling untidily over the hands that covered her face.

"You'd better go upstairs, girls," Miss Pritchard said. "All but Mary Lee and Earline. You're late, as it is." The three girls trailed disappointedly out. Their steps on the stairs, their subdued twitterings drifted back, grew fainter, and died. "Sit down, Earline," Miss Pritchard directed, not looking at Enie. "Stop crying, Mary Lee." Miss Pritchard took a handkerchief from the pocket of her blouse, pressed it into Mary Lee's hand. "I want you to tell me exactly what happened."

Mary Lee gave a hiccup and raised her face. She shook her hair back and fingered the scarlet weal on her cheek. "Go on, tell me," Miss Pritchard prompted. Enie stared at the gray wall opposite. Her legs had begun to tremble and she braced her feet to hide the telltale quivering of her skirt.

"*This* is what happened," Mary Lee cried, her voice shaking with outrage. "She slapped me in the face! *Earline Singleton*. She hit me and hit me till I know my jaw's broke," and she wailed in renewed anguish.

Miss Pritchard put a hand on either side of Mary Lee's face. She pressed gently, her attention all on Mary Lee; Enie might have been out at Tired Creek for all the notice Miss Pritchard took of her. "Your jaw isn't broken, but there is an ugly mark on your cheek. It's a pity—such a pretty face, too." Mollified, Mary Lee blinked through her tears. She dabbed at her eyes with Miss Pritchard's handkerchief, gave a gratified sniff at the violet scent of it. "Why did Earline slap your face, Mary Lee? What could have caused her to do such a thing?"

Mary Lee began to twist the handkerchief. Her lips parted, closed. "Ask her," she muttered at last.

"No," Miss Pritchard said. "I asked you."

"She—I—my two quarters. . . ." Mary Lee began, her face reddening evenly, so the print of the blows was lost. "Well, I had this fifty cents and it disappeared off my desk and. . . ." She bogged down, pulling nervously at the handkerchief.

"You believed Earline had taken your money? You accused her of—*stealing* it?"

Mary Lee's lip trembled. "I—I never said—I just. . . ."

Miss Pritchard frowned, musingly. "It's odd—I was under the impression you were such a well-bred girl. I've thought of you as—a lady. Your home, and your parents, your advantages. . . . How could the loss of fifty cents make you forget yourself and all that's expected of you?"

Mary Lee looked sullenly at the wall. Miss Pritchard sighed, and Enie saw genuine sadness settle over her face. A feeling of guilt crept over Enie, guilt and a tightness like grief in her throat. She jumped when Miss Pritchard's voice penetrated her welling misery. "Wasn't it really more than losing the money?"

She turned her look upon Enie, and under it Enie felt tears sting her lids. "And more for you, Earline, than the accusation? That's reason for anger, I grant you. But to strike out and do bodily hurt to anyone—I would never have believed you could behave so badly, either of you."

Silence drew out, heavy and painful, and Enie's trembling increased; the tears that had burned her lids crept out and down her pale cheeks. Miss Pritchard laid one hand on Enie's knee, the other on Mary Lee's. "I think the real problem is one you have in common. Jealousy isn't a pretty word and it isn't a pretty characteristic. It's unworthy of you both. I'd like to be proud of the two brightest students this year has given me."

She stood up and smoothed her skirt. "Now, wash your faces and report to class." And she walked out of the basement and up the stairs.

Enie was the first to speak, her prime feeling one of surprise that the whole episode had suddenly become childish and unimportant. "I'm sorry I slapped you, Mary Lee."

"Well, I'm—I'm sorry I—made you mad," Mary Lee returned after a brief hesitation. She gave a last sad little sniff. Awkwardly they stood up, moved toward the washbowl. Mary Lee touched her cheek tenderly, and began to comb her hair.

"I love Miss Pritchard!" Enie burst out.

Mary Lee carefully applied her lipstick. "Golly," she murmured when she had finished, "she didn't even *offer* to punish us."

"I reckon she thought we punished ourselves enough," Enie replied thoughtfully.

Mary Lee screwed the cap onto her lipstick. She drew a deep breath and said in a rush, not looking at Enie, "I'm sorry I've been mean to you before this."

Above, a bell rang, the echo of feet scraped along the halls, sounding far away. The two girls went sedately up the stairs, side by side.   THE END

↺ **Talking it over**

1. In what ways are Enie and Mary Lee alike? In what ways are they different?

2. *a.* What kind of judgment is Mary Lee expressing when she calls Enie a "country tack"? Explain whether she is justified.

b. What kind of judgment does Mary Lee make when she assumes Enie has stolen her money? Is she justified?

3. Why does Enie slap Mary Lee?

4. *a.* Explain whether Miss Pritchard is correct in saying that the girls have a problem in common.

b. What do you think of the way Miss Pritchard handles the situation? If you think there might have been a better way, explain.

5. *a.* When Enie takes a "second look" after the talk with Miss Pritchard, how does she see the situation?

b. At the end of the story, the girls go up the stairs side by side. What do you think about the possibility of their becoming close friends? Explain.

c. If this incident had occurred in your school, could it have ended the same way? If you think it would have ended differently, account for the difference.

Town girl

and

country girl

Words in action

Often there is a story connected with the way a word came into our language.

Bedlam (bed′ləm) is a nickname for The Hospital of Saint Mary in Bethlehem, which existed in London, England, in the 1600's. It was not so much a hospital as it was a madhouse; people who were mentally ill or insane were imprisoned there amidst noise, confusion, and filth.

Babel (bāb′l or bab′l) is a reference to the story in the Bible of the Tower of Babel. When some men tried to build a tower to reach Heaven, God punished them by changing their language into several new and different languages. When the men could no longer understand each other, they began to shout and fight among themselves, and in the confusion they left the tower unfinished.

Explain what **bedlam** and **babel** might mean when used today. How does each word fit into the excerpt below?

"The bell jangled across the **bedlam** about the washbowl. The other girls' squeals mingled with Mary Lee's cries that sank to moans and hysterical sobs as Enie wound up the battle with a vicious yank of the permanently waved hair falling about Mary Lee's shoulders and walked out, leaving the **babel** of horror and indignation behind her."

Mildred Lee has written numerous short stories for magazines in addition to books, including *The Invisible Sun* and *Honor Sands*. About *The Rock and the Willow,* the novel from which "The Slap" was taken, she writes:

"Enie was not I nor anyone I knew, actually, though, like her, I did creative writing in my teens—and at an earlier age. My father was a minister and we lived in a succession of small towns in Alabama. On his travels and visits about the countryside he used to take me with him along with my sisters and brother. In that way I must have got most of the book's background, though all the characters were, of course, entirely imaginary.

"The episode dealing with Enie and Mary Lee Williams grew out of an incident which made a deep impression on me in my preschool days. A town girl in my older sister's classroom called one of the girls from the country a country tack. The story, told at home, incensed my parents as well as my sister who had witnessed it. So far as I know the true incident resulted only in the country child's bursting into tears before the class. My Enie chose to deal differently with her situation once it had built up to sufficient crisis."

*I wondered why any woman would go away
and leave her son—
especially a boy like Jerry.*

A MOTHER IN MANNVILLE

by Marjorie Kinnan Rawlings

THE orphanage is high in the Carolina mountains. Sometimes in winter the snowdrifts are so deep that the institution is cut off from the village below, from all the world. Fog hides the mountain peaks, the snow swirls down the valleys, and a wind blows so bitterly that the orphanage boys who take the milk twice daily to the baby cottage reach the door with fingers stiff in an agony of numbness.

"Or when we carry trays from the cookhouse for the ones that are sick," Jerry said, "we get our faces frostbit, because we can't put our hands over them. I have gloves," he added. "Some of the boys don't have any."

He liked the late spring, he said. The rhododendron was in bloom, a carpet of color, across the mountainsides, soft as the May winds that stirred the hemlocks. He called it laurel.

"It's pretty when the laurel blooms," he said. "Some of it's pink and some of it's white."

I was there in autumn. I wanted quiet, isolation, to do some troublesome writing. I wanted mountain air to blow out the malaria from too long a time in the subtropics. I was homesick, too, for the flaming of maples in October, and for corn shocks and pumpkins and black-walnut trees and the lift of hills. I found them all, living in a cabin that belonged to the orphanage, half a mile beyond the orphanage farm. When I took the cabin, I asked for a boy or man to come and chop wood for the fireplace. The first few days were warm, I found what wood I needed about the cabin, no one came, and I forgot the order.

I looked up from my typewriter one late afternoon, a little startled. A boy stood at the door, and my pointer dog, my companion, was at his side and had not barked to warn me. The boy was probably twelve years old, but undersized. He wore overalls and a torn shirt, and was barefooted.

He said, "I can chop some wood today."

I said, "But I have a boy coming from the orphanage."

"I'm the boy."

"You? But you're small."

"Size don't matter, chopping wood," he said. "Some of the big boys don't chop good. I've been chopping wood at the orphanage a long time."

I visualized mangled and inadequate branches for my fires. I was well into my work and not inclined to conversation. I was a little blunt.

"Very well. There's the ax. Go ahead and see what you can do."

I went back to work, closing the door. At first the sound of the boy dragging brush annoyed me. Then he began to chop. The blows were rhythmic and steady, and shortly I had forgotten him, the sound no more of an interruption than a consistent rain. I suppose an hour and a half passed, for when I stopped and stretched, and heard the boy's steps on the cabin stoop, the sun was dropping behind the farthest mountain, and the valleys were purple with something deeper than the asters.

The boy said, "I have to go to supper now. I can come again tomorrow evening."

I said, "I'll pay you now for what you've done," thinking I should probably have to insist on an older boy. "Ten cents an hour?"

"Anything is all right."

We went together back of the cabin. An astonishing amount of solid wood had been cut. There were cherry logs and heavy roots of rhododendron, and blocks from the waste pine and oak left from the building of the cabin.

"But you've done as much as a man," I said. "This is a splendid pile."

I looked at him, actually, for the first time. His hair was the color of the corn shocks, and his eyes, very direct, were like the mountain sky when rain is pending—gray, with a showing of that miraculous blue. As I spoke a light came over him, as though the setting sun had touched him with the same suffused glory with which it touched the mountains. I gave him a quarter.

"You may come tomorrow," I said, "and thank you very much."

He looked at me, and at the coin, and seemed to want to speak, but could not, and turned away.

"I'll split the kindling tomorrow," he said over his thin ragged shoulder. "You'll need kindling and medium wood and logs and backlogs."

At daylight I was half awakened by the sound of chopping. Again it was so even in texture that I went back to sleep. When I left my bed in the cool morning, the boy had come and gone, and a stack of kindling was neat against the cabin wall. He came again after school in the afternoon and worked until time to return to the orphanage. His name was Jerry; he was twelve years old, and he had been at the orphanage since he was four. I could picture him at four, with the same gray-blue eyes and the same—independence? No, the word that comes to me is "integrity."

The word means something very spe-cial to me, and the quality for which I use it is a rare one. My father had it—there is another of whom I am almost sure—but almost no man of my acquaintance possesses it with the clarity, the purity, the simplicity of a mountain stream. But the boy Jerry had it. It is bedded on courage, but it is more than brave. It is honest, but it is more than honesty. The ax handle broke one day. Jerry said the woodshop at the orphanage would repair it. I brought money to pay for the job and he refused it.

"I'll pay for it," he said. "I broke it. I brought the ax down careless."

"But no one hits accurately every time," I told him. "The fault was in the wood of the handle. I'll see the man from whom I bought it."

It was only then that he would take the money. He was standing back of his own carelessness. He was a free-will agent and he chose to do careful work, and if he failed, he took the responsibility without subterfuge.

And he did for me the unnecessary thing, the gracious thing, that we find done only by the great of heart. Things no training can teach, for they are done on the instant, with no predicated experience. He found a cubbyhole beside the fireplace that I had not noticed. There, of his own accord, he put kindling and "medium" wood, so that I might always have dry fire material ready in case of sudden wet weather. A stone was loose in the rough walk to the cabin. He dug a deeper hole and steadied it, although he came, himself, by a short cut over the bank. I found that when I tried to return his thoughtfulness with such things as candy and apples, he was wordless. "Thank you" was, perhaps, an expression for which he had had no use, for his courtesy was instinctive. He only looked at the gift and at me, and a curtain lifted, so that I saw deep into the clear well of his eyes, and gratitude was there, and affection, soft over the firm granite of his character.

He made simple excuses to come and sit with me. I could no more have turned him away than if he had been physically hungry. I suggested once that the best time for us to visit was just before supper, when I left off my writing. After that, he waited always until my typewriter had been some time quiet. One day I worked until nearly dark. I went outside the cabin, having forgotten him. I saw him going up over the hill in the twilight toward the orphanage. When I sat down on my stoop, a place was warm from his body where he had been sitting.

He became intimate, of course, with my pointer, Pat. There is a strange communion between a boy and a dog. Perhaps they possess the same singleness of spirit, the same kind of wisdom. It is difficult to explain, but it exists. When I went across the state for a weekend I left the dog in Jerry's charge. I gave him the dog whistle and the key to the cabin, and left sufficient food. He was to come two or three times a day and let out the dog, and feed and exercise him. I should return Sunday night, and Jerry would take out the dog for the last time Sunday afternoon and then leave the key under an agreed hiding place.

My return was belated and fog filled the mountain passes so treacherously that I dared not drive at night. The fog held the next morning, and it was Monday noon before I reached the cabin. The dog had been fed and cared for that morning. Jerry came early in the afternoon, anxious.

"The superintendent said nobody would drive in the fog," he said. "I came just before bedtime last night and you hadn't come. So I brought Pat some of my breakfast this morning. I wouldn't have let anything happen to him."

"I was sure of that. I didn't worry."

"When I heard about the fog, I thought you'd know."

He was needed for work at the orphanage and he had to return at once. I gave him a dollar in payment, and he looked at it and went away. But that night he came in the darkness and knocked at the door.

"Come in, Jerry," I said, "if you're allowed to be away this late."

"I told maybe a story," he said. "I told them I thought you would want to see me."

"That's true," I assured him, and I saw his relief. "I want to hear about how you managed with the dog."

He sat by the fire with me, with no other light, and told me of their two days together. The dog lay close to him, and found a comfort there that I did not have for him. And it seemed to me that being with my dog, and caring for him, had brought the boy and me, too, together, so that he felt that he belonged to me as well as to the animal.

"He stayed right with me," he told me, "except when he ran in the laurel. He likes the laurel. I took him up over the hill and we both ran fast. There was a place where the grass was high and I lay down in it and hid. I could hear Pat hunting for me. He found my trail and he barked. When he found me, he acted crazy, and he ran around and around me, in circles."

We watched the flames.

"That's an apple log," he said. "It burns the prettiest of any wood."

We were very close.

He was suddenly impelled to speak of things he had not spoken of before, nor had I cared to ask him.

"You look a little bit like my mother," he said. "Especially in the dark, by the fire."

"But you were only four, Jerry, when you came here. You have remembered how she looked, all these years?"

"My mother lives in Mannville," he said.

For a moment, finding that he had a mother shocked me as greatly as anything in my life has ever done, and I did not know why it disturbed me. Then I understood my distress. I was filled with a passionate resentment that any woman should go away and leave her son. A fresh anger added itself. A son like this one— The orphanage was a wholesome place, the executives were kind, good people, the food was more than adequate, the boys were healthy, a ragged shirt was no hardship, nor the doing of clean labor. Granted, perhaps, that the boy felt no lack, what about the mother? At four he would have looked the same as now. Nothing, I thought, nothing in life could change those eyes. His quality must be apparent to an idiot, a fool. I burned with questions I could not ask. In any, I was afraid, there would be pain.

"Have you seen her, Jerry—lately?"

"I see her every summer. She sends for me."

I wanted to cry out. "Why are you not with her? How can she let you go away again?"

He said, "She comes up here from Mannville whenever she can. She doesn't have a job now."

His face shone in the firelight.

"She wanted to give me a puppy, but they can't let any one boy keep a puppy. You remember the suit I had on last Sunday?" He was plainly proud. "She sent me that for Christmas. The Christmas before that"—he drew a long breath, savoring the memory—"she sent me a pair of skates."

"Roller skates?"

My mind was busy, making pictures of her, trying to understand her. She had not, then, entirely deserted or forgotten him. But why, then— I thought, "But I must not condemn her without knowing."

"Roller skates. I let the other boys use them. They're always borrowing them. But they're careful of them."

What circumstance other than poverty—

"I'm going to take the dollar you gave me for taking care of Pat," he said, "and buy her a pair of gloves."

I could only say, "That will be nice. Do you know her size?"

"I think it's eight and a half," he said.

He looked at my hands.

"Do you wear eight and a half?" he asked.

"No. I wear a smaller size, a six."

"Oh! Then I guess her hands are bigger than yours."

I hated her. Poverty or no, there was other food than bread, and the soul could starve as quickly as the body. He was taking his dollar to buy gloves for her big stupid hands, and she lived away from him, in Mannville, and contented herself with sending him skates.

"She likes white gloves," he said. "Do you think I can get them for a dollar?"

"I think so," I said.

I decided that I should not leave the mountains without seeing her and knowing for myself why she had done this thing.

The human mind scatters its interests as though made of thistledown, and every wind stirs and moves it. I finished my work. It did not please me, and I gave my thoughts to another field. I should need some Mexican material.

I made arrangements to close my Florida place. Mexico immediately, and doing the writing there, if conditions were favorable. Then, Alaska with my brother. After that, heaven knew what or where.

I did not take time to go to Mannville to see Jerry's mother, nor even to talk with the orphanage officials about her. I was a trifle abstracted about the boy, because of my work and plans. And after my first fury at her—we did not speak of her again—his having a mother, any sort at all, not far away, in Mannville, relieved me of the ache I had had about him. He did not question the anomalous relation. He was not lonely. It was none of my concern.

He came every day and cut my wood and did small helpful favors and stayed to talk. The days had become cold, and often I let him come inside the cabin. He would lie on the floor in front of the fire, with one arm across the pointer, and they would both doze and wait quietly for me. Other days they ran with a common ecstasy through the laurel, and since the asters were now gone, he brought me back vermilion maple leaves, and chestnut boughs dripping with imperial yellow. I was ready to go.

I said to him, "You have been my good friend, Jerry. I shall often think of you and miss you. Pat will miss you too. I am leaving tomorrow."

He did not answer. When he went away, I remember that a new moon hung over the mountains, and I watched him go in silence up the hill. I expected him the next day, but he did not come. The details of packing my personal belongings, loading my car, arranging the bed over the seat, where the dog would ride, occupied me until late in the day. I closed the cabin and started the car, noticing that the sun was in the west and I should do well to be out of the mountains by nightfall. I stopped by the orphanage and left the cabin key and money for my light bill with Miss Clark.

"And will you call Jerry for me to say good-by to him?"

"I don't know where he is," she said. "I'm afraid he's not well. He didn't eat his dinner this noon. One of the boys saw him going over the hill into the laurel. He was supposed to fire the boiler this afternoon. It's not like him; he's unusually reliable."

I was almost relieved, for I knew I should never see him again, and it would be easier not to say good-by to him.

I said, "I wanted to talk with you about his mother—why he's here—but I'm in more of a hurry than I expected to be. It's out of the question for me to see her now. But here's some money I'd like to leave with you to buy things for him at Christmas and on his birthday. It will be better than for me to try to send him things. I could so easily duplicate—skates, for instance."

She blinked her honest spinster's eyes.

"There's not much use for skates here," she said.

Her stupidity annoyed me.

"What I mean," I said, "is that I

don't want to duplicate things his mother sends him. I might have chosen skates if I didn't know she had already given them to him."

"I don't understand," she said. "He has no mother. He has no skates."

THE END

She loved the South

Marjorie Kinnan Rawlings was raised in Washington, D.C., lived for a while on a farm in Maryland, and graduated from the University of Wisconsin. She decided to make a career in writing, for she had been writing—and selling—her stories since the age of eleven. After college she moved about a great deal, writing publicity and advertising and newspaper stories. She fell in love with the South when she went to visit there. Soon afterwards she bought an orange grove at Cross Creek, in northern Florida, where she lived most of the rest of her life. The beauty of the backwoods region and the interesting tales told by the people there gave her much material for her writing. Her Pulitzer Prize novel, *The Yearling,* is about a boy growing up in the depths of the Florida forest. Other books with the same setting are *South Moon Under, Cross Creek,* and *When the Whippoorwill.*

Talking it over

1. *a.* Describe the feelings between Jerry and the narrator.

b. Describe Jerry's feelings toward her dog.

2. *a.* The narrator describes Jerry by saying he has *integrity.* What special meaning does this word have for her?

b. Which of Jerry's actions throughout the story show his integrity?

3. *a.* Why doesn't the narrator do more to help Jerry?

b. How does she feel when Jerry tells her his mother is living in Mannville?

c. How do you think she must feel about Jerry at the end when she learns the truth from Miss Clark?

4. *a.* Why might Jerry have said what he did about having a mother and receiving presents from her?

b. Do you think the story Jerry tells makes him all the more a person of integrity, or less so? Explain.

When is a cat not a cat. . . ?

The Tale of the Skunk and Poor Jez

by John Becker

Jezebel Jones smelled really punk
From having tried to catch a skunk.
Her sister Sue, the little brat,
Had told the child it was a cat—
5 And so it was.

Some cats are white and some are blue
And quite a few are tiger too;
Some cats are Toms and some are not,
Some are neuter, some are pewter;
10 Some howl at night, all prowl at night,
Some are Persian, some Angora,
China, Cheshire, Glanamora;
Some are manx and some are lynx,
And one's a sphinx.

15 The lion lords it o'er them all,
Over the short and over the tall.
But he's no pet. To catch a cat
You catch him small. But sister Sue
Did not tell Jez what I tell you:
20 Only the pole-cat is a skunk,
And that's why Jezebel smelled so punk.

From *New Feathers for the Old Goose* by John Becker. Copyright © 1956 by John Becker. Reprinted by permission of Pantheon Books, a Division of Random House, Inc.

He writes plays for puppets

John Becker and his wife live in Rome, Italy, where they have a widely known private marionette theater. Mr. Becker writes the plays for the theater, his wife does the costumes and sets, and she and their children work the marionettes. Someday they hope to publish the plays, with illustrations of their productions.

Mr. Becker's writings include short stories, puppet plays, and books for young people, including *Melindy's Medal, Near-Tragedy at the Waterfall,* and *New Feathers for the Old Goose,* the book of poems from which "The Tale of the Skunk and Poor Jez" was taken. His wife is a painter, and has illustrated several of his works.

Talking it over

1. *a.* Why does the poet devote more lines to varieties of "cats" than he does to what actually happened to Jezebel?

   b. What *did* actually happen to Jezebel? Use your imagination to describe the scene.

2. Had her sister Sue lied to Jezebel? Explain.

The light fell on the thing which lay
half-concealed under the moonlit leaves.
It was a fleshless, skeleton hand
cut off at the wrist.

One Alaska Night

by Barrett Willoughby

A ROOT tripped me and threw me flat in the trail that led through the blueberry thicket. For a moment I was too tired to stir. I lay there, face on my arms, feeling that I'd been foolhardy to start out alone on a ten-mile hike across an unfamiliar peninsula. Yet I comforted myself with the thought that it could not be much farther to the coast fox ranch which was my destination. There Lonnie, a schoolmate of mine, was spending the summer with her father, who owned the place.

Suddenly, nose to the ground, I became aware of a rank, musky odor that brought my head up with a jerk. Something queerly crawling touched my cheek. I slapped my hand over it and, with a chill of premonition, looked at what I'd caught—a long tuft of coarse brown hair dangling from a twig above.

One startled glance told me it had been raked from the side of an Alaskan brown bear—the largest carnivorous animal that walks the world today. With the tuft of hair clutched in my hand and sudden alarm sharpening my senses, I looked closely at the path leading forward under the leafy tunnel in which I lay.

All along it, evenly spaced in the damp, brown mold, were deep depressions, round and large as dinner plates.

The truth came with a shock—I had been following a bear trail! It was already getting dark, and I was unarmed.

I'm not a hunter. I'm not even a brave woman. And I'd never before been alone in a bear-infested forest with night coming on. I recalled that bears do most of their traveling after dark—and I was lying flat in the middle of one of their thoroughfares.

I leaped to my feet, turned off the trail, and began plowing through the brush, intent only on putting all possible distance between me and that place before dark.

Almost at once the bushes thinned out and I was able to make good time through stretches of short ferns; but the

light was fading fast. Oddly, it was only now, when I was safely away from the bear trail, that it dawned on me that I had no idea which way to go.

I was lost.

In that instant of realization all my strength seemed to ooze out of me. Then panic came upon me. I had a senseless, almost uncontrollable impulse to dash madly through the trees, regardless of direction, bears, or anything else. But I got hold of myself, decided on a course, and with forced calmness went forward, watching tensely for that breaking away of the timber which foretells an approach to the sea.

Every step took me deeper into the darkening wilderness. There was no wind. Not a thing moved except myself —not a leaf, not a twig.

The very silence began to frighten me. I found myself stepping furtively, trying not to make any noise, and straining to hear the slightest sound. I kept glancing back over my shoulder. Every few feet I'd stop suddenly, holding my breath while I studied a moss-grown log or the long arm of a thorny shrub which I was sure had stirred a second before.

I was groping with my feet, my gaze fixed ahead, when out of the tail of my eye I saw a blurred stirring in the shadows under the hemlocks. I jerked my head around to look.

Nothing moved.

I wondered if the "woods-madness" that seizes lost persons was coming upon me so soon.

And then I paused to stare at a murky clump which I hoped was only bushes. The clump, big as a truck horse, started toward me. It kept coming, slowly, heavily, swinging a great, low head. Brush rattled under its sham-bling tread. I smelled the rank, musky odor of bear.

The next instant I had turned from the monster and was running madly through the semidarkness of the forest.

I was nearly exhausted when I burst through the timber and saw the log cabin. I was running toward this refuge with all the speed left in me when something in the look of the place caused me to slow up. I came to a stop and peered fearfully through the dusk.

There was something distinctly sinister in the very quality of the silence that hung over the cabin—a feeling as if death brooded there. The boarded windows on each side of the closed door stared back at me like eye sockets in a brown and weathered skull.

My recoil from the place was so strong that I turned to go back, but after one glance back into the black forest I changed my mind. I slipped my belt ax from its sheath, grasped it firmly, and moved forward.

At the edge of the dooryard I came upon a stump and again hesitated. My fingers, absently exploring the stump's broad top, felt a crosshatch of ax marks. A block for chopping firewood, I thought, glancing at the nearby stack of dead hemlock boughs.

For some reason, this evidence of human workaday activity heartened me. I moved on and paused before the closed door. It was a home-made door of heavy, rough planks, silvered by the beating of many storms. In place of a knob, it had a rawhide latch thong hanging outside. The thong had curled up into a hard, dry knot.

Obviously, no one had drawn this latchstring for many months. Yet when I gave it a pull, I leaped back, expecting—I don't know what.

The creaking door swung in of its own weight, revealing an interior so dark I could make out no details. I listened. All was silent. I sniffed. The place gave off the faint rancid odor that clings to a cabin in which raw furs have been dried.

Suddenly impatient at my senseless hesitancy, I plunged inside and bumped against a crude table in the middle of the floor. My outflung hand touched a bottle with dribbles of wax on the side. I struck a match, lighted the candle stub, and turned to inspect my shelter. Clearly, this was the very ordinary dwelling of some trapper who had abandoned it for other fields. There was nothing here to alarm even the most fearful woman, yet I continued to feel uneasy.

The sensible thing to do now was build a fire and then eat a sandwich. Luckily I had a couple remaining from lunch. I would go on to the fox ranch in the morning. A trail must lead out from here; and I knew I could find it when the sun came up. As I raked the ashes from the stove, I began searching my memory for all I had heard of this region.

The first thing that popped into my mind was the story of five prospectors who, a few years before, had vanished on this peninsula without leaving a trace. Rumor had it that they had met foul play at the hands of a crazy trapper—"Cub Bear" Butler. I didn't even know whether the mystery had ever been solved. But—a crazy trapper. . . . I glanced back over my shoulder, wishing I hadn't thought about that.

A moment later, ax in hand, I reluctantly went out of doors to the chopping block to cut some wood for the stove. In nervous haste I chopped an armload of wood, then began piling the sticks on my arm. As I was reaching for the last stick which had fallen in the bear weed, my groping fingers touched something which made me recoil so violently that all my wood fell to the ground. Hurriedly I struck a match and, leaning forward, lowered it until the tiny light fell on the thing which lay half-concealed under the moonlit leaves.

It was a fleshless, skeleton hand, cut off at the wrist.

The match burned my fingers. I dropped it. I was backing away when my eyes, now adjusted to the darkness, fell on another set of bony fingers thrust out from under a round leaf of bear weed. Then, just beyond that, a third skeleton hand took shape in the gloom.

My brain went into a sickening tailspin. I tried to scream, but could make no sound. I tried to run, but my legs seemed turned to water. Then the hope that my eyes had tricked me in the dim light brought back a measure of calmness. I struck another match and, sweeping aside the weeds with my foot, bent to look.

They were there—all three of them.

I don't know how I nerved myself to make a thorough search of the ground around that ax-marked stump, but I did. And in the dense bear weed I saw twelve skeleton hands, all cut off at the wrist. There wasn't a skull or bone of any other kind.

Somehow I got back inside the candlelit cabin with an armload of wood, and, shoving the door shut, latched it. The fastening was an unusually sturdy bar of wood. The only way to lift and lower the bar from the outside was by means of the latch thong. I pulled this through its small hole, grateful that the door was strong and that no one could enter unless I lifted the bar.

But I was hollow with dread. My mind kept swirling about Cub Bear Butler, the crazy trapper, and the five prospectors who had vanished. The men were last seen on this peninsula when Butler was living in the vicinity running his trap lines. Was it possible that I had stumbled on to Cub Bear's cabin? Could those skeleton hands belong to—

"But there were only *five* prospectors." I was startled to find I had spoken aloud. There were six pairs of fleshless hands out there. To whom did the sixth pair belong?

I was so unstrung by these thoughts that even after the fire was going I couldn't eat a sandwich. Instead, after making sure that the door was still barred, I snuffed the candle, knowing it would soon burn out anyway. With my wadded jacket for a pillow, I lay down in the bare bunk, my little ax handy by my side.

I didn't intend to go to sleep, but gradually fatigue began to triumph over nerves.

I don't know what awakened me; but suddenly I found myself sitting bolt upright, heart pounding, ears straining. In the sooty darkness I could see nothing except a streak of moonlight lancing in through a knothole in one of the slats over the window. The stillness was intense. Yet, I knew that some sound had penetrated my sleep.

I was about to get up to light the candle when it came again: *Thump! . . . Thump-thump-thump!* Someone was knocking to get in!

I chilled to the pit of my stomach, for the summons was curiously muffled

as if the visitor were rapping not with firm knuckles, but with— I shoved the horrible thought from me.

"Who—who's there?" I called unsteadily.

Silence.

Ax in hand, I eased out of the bunk, lighted the candle, and turned to inspect the door. It was barred. Everything in the dim room was just as it had been when I fell asleep.

"Who is it?" I demanded in a firmer voice.

I knew that anyone knocking at this hour of the night would identify himself —unless he were a—

Again I put from me the thought of a dead man with no hands. I do not believe in ghosts.

I was trying to convince myself that the knocking had been born of my overwrought nerves when—*Thump! . . . Thump-thump-thump! Thump! . . . Thump-thump-thump!* It was like the fleshy stub of an arm hammering on wood.

Leaden with fright, I managed to reach the door and press my ear against it. "Who—what do you want? Answer me!"

I heard a faint rustling, as of a loose garment brushing against the rough log wall outside. After a dozen seconds, I had a sudden, desperate impulse to end the suspense. I lifted the bar, flung open the door, and looked out.

Nothing.

The high moon lighted the clearing with a brilliance almost like that of day, but there was neither movement nor sound in the breathless Northern night.

Puzzled as well as frightened, I went back inside.

No sooner had I dropped the bar in place than it came again—*Thump! . . .*

Thump-thump-thump! Instantly I jerked open the door.

No one was there. But the slithering sound, plainer than before, seemed to come from the corner to the right, as if someone had knocked and then run, to play a joke on me.

A flash of anger banished my fear. I darted out and ran all the way around the cabin.

There was no one.

The nearest cover—a tall hemlock— was fully fifty feet away. Nothing human, no matter how fleet, could possibly have covered that distance in the second between the last knock and my abrupt opening of the door. No creature larger than a rabbit could have concealed itself in the meadow surrounding the cabin.

Then gooseflesh broke out all over me. With a rush of terror came the thought that I was gazing on no ordinary wild meadow. Under the bear weed were skeleton hands—so many of them that this was literally a meadow of the dead.

I was trembling, and though it was not from cold, I wanted the comfort of a fire—a great, flaming fire. I dragged the pile of dead limbs over to the hut and kindled a roaring blaze just outside the door. The crackling and the warmth of it put new courage into me. I sat in the doorway and watched the clearing.

Nothing further disturbed me. After a while I began to nod.

I woke with a start, thinking I heard laughter and someone calling my name. Late morning sun flooded the clearing. Then I saw a slim, blonde young woman in breeches and a windbreaker, running across the meadow toward me. Lonnie, my friend of the fox ranch! Behind her strode her father, a lean, sourdough Alaskan who had, as I well knew, no very high opinion of a woman's ability to take care of herself in the woods.

I was so overjoyed to see them that I could have rushed upon them and fallen to embrace their knees. But pride kept me from betraying myself to the quizzical eyes of Lonnie's father, whom I always called "Dad." I assumed a nonchalant manner and strolled out to greet them.

"There, Dad!" said Lonnie, laughing. "I told you she'd be cool as a cucumber!" She gave me a hug. "I knew you'd be all right, but Dad had a fit when you failed to show up last night."

"A woman," declared Dad, "should never go into the woods alone. Women are always getting lost." He readjusted the heavy holster on his hip. "I was afraid you'd run into a bear—there are a lot of brownies around this summer. You can thank your lucky star you stumbled onto Butler's cabin."

Butler's cabin! But even as a shivering thrill ran through me, Dad's I-told-you-so manner nettled me.

"It's not only women who get lost," I retorted. "How about those five prospectors who disappeared in these woods a few years ago?"

"Oh, those chaps! It's likely they were drowned in the tide-rips off the Cape."

"No, they weren't, Dad," I said quietly. "They were killed—murdered—right here at Butler's cabin."

He and Lonnie stared at me as if they thought I had gone insane. Then Dad began to laugh. "Now, Sis, don't try to put over any of your writer's imaginings on an old fellow like me."

"It's not imagination. Come. I'll show you."

I led the way to the chopping block, and, brushing aside the bear weed with my foot, one by one revealed the skeleton hands, stark white in the sunlight.

Dad looked grave. "By George," he muttered. "This looks bad. I remember there was some talk about Cub Bear Butler, but—" He stooped and picked up one of the bony things.

After a moment's inspection he tossed it back into the weeds, and brushed his hands together. "Just like a woman!" he drawled, grinning at me. "Those are not human hands, Sister. They're the skeleton paws of cub bears."

I must have looked uncommonly foolish for he patted my shoulder consolingly. "Nine men out of ten would have made the same mistake. You see, the skeleton of a bear's paw, particularly a cub's, is almost identical with that of the human hand."

"But—why are there no other bones here?"

"Cub Bear Butler, like all other trappers, skinned his catch at the traps in the woods—all except the feet, which need a good deal of care. He brought the pelts back here to his cabin to skin the paws. He trapped only cubs, yearlings. That's how he got his nickname."

Feeling very much deflated, I followed him into the cabin.

"Poor old Cub Bear," he said. "They finally got him."

"Who got him?" I asked, remembering that Butler had been called "the crazy trapper."

"Bears. The Indians round here swear it was the Great She-Bear, the Spirit Bear, who took revenge on him for killing so many cubs. At any rate he was found crumpled down right there"—Dad pointed to a spot just outside the door—"killed as a bear kills a man. He'd been dead only a couple of days and the tracks of a big brownie were still visible in the dooryard."

"But why didn't he shoot the beast if it jumped him in his own yard?"

"Couldn't reach his gun. When they found him, his rifle, his ax, and a fresh cub pelt were all here in the cabin, and the door was barred and the latch thong broken off."

"What a strange thing!"

"Nothing strange about it. What happened was plain enough. Cub Bear must have come in from his trap line with the pelt. He dropped it when he put his rifle on the table, and then went out—for water, likely—shutting the door behind him. Possibly the mother of the cub he'd just killed did follow him home, and—well, an angry she-brownie is just about the most terrifying creature a man can run up against.

When she went for him, he ran for his cabin to get his rifle. In his haste, he jerked the latch thong so hard he broke it off. Then he couldn't open the door. And it is so heavy he couldn't break it in. So—the beast got him."

"How terrible—and ironic!" I shuddered as I pictured what had happened.

"Tough luck, all right. Bert Slocum, one of my ranch hands now, spent a couple of months here afterward, trapping mink. He came out with a fine, large tale about Cub Bear's ghost hanging around here, and—"

"Ghost," I started, and turned to stare at the spot where Butler must have stood frantically beating on the heavy plank door trying to get in.

"Yes, so Bert claims." Dad chuckled. "But Bert's the biggest liar in Alaska. The way he tells it, Cub Bear—"

Thump! . . . Thump-thump-thump! With the door wide open it came, and before I knew it I had leaped to my feet.

"What in heck's the matter with you, Sis?" inquired Dad.

I looked from the empty door to the faces of my companions. "Didn't you hear it?" I demanded.

"Hear what?"

"That knocking."

"Oh, those pesky flying squirrels," drawled Dad. "The country's getting overrun with 'em. On a moonlight night a man can't get a wink of sleep, the way they play humpty-dumpty on the roof. They—"

"Flying squirrels," I interrupted, doubtingly. "I'd like to see one—playing."

"No trouble. Just stand there inside the door, sort of hidden, and keep your eye on that lone hemlock out in front."

I took up the position he indicated. After a moment, sure enough, a small, furry form soared out from the top of the tree and, with little legs outspread, came gliding down to land with that soft, solid *thump!* on the roof. Then, quickly, *thump-thump-thump!* it bounded down to the eaves, and off, racing back toward the tree.

"What a cunning little creature," I observed, turning around with what must have been a sickly smile.

As I did so, my attention was caught by the door, swung in so that the outside of it was very close to me. Years of Alaska weather—beating rain and wind and snow, alternating with hot summer sun—had worked the rough grain of the unfinished planks into a coarse, light-gray nap. Visible now on the sunstruck surface, and about even with the top of my head, were curious marks—depressions in the weathernap of the wood, such as might have been made by the edge of heavily pounding fists.

"What are you staring at now, Sis?" Dad broke in on my thoughts.

"Those marks on the door."

He laughed. "You must have been pretty excited when you got here last night—knocking that hard. But that's just like a woman—never able to tell whether a cabin's deserted or not." He picked up my jacket from the bunk and held it for me. "Come, now. Slip into this. It's time we were moving. I'm hungry enough to eat boiled owl, and it's eight miles to the ranch."

A few minutes later, as we were walking away across the sunny clearing, I fell a step behind the other two and turned to look back at the cabin in which I had spent the most terrifying night of my life.

I was remembering that two days ago there had been a heavy southeast gale which must have beat directly on that closed door. Yesterday's sun drying out the planks would have raised the wood-nap, obliterating any depressions that might have been there before I reached the cabin. Yet marks were there, as if two fists had pounded on the door. Dad thought I had made them.

I looked down at my hands, and though I don't believe in ghosts, I had a queer feeling in the pit of my stomach. The marks were there, plainly visible when the sun struck the door just right. But I knew that my two small fists had never made them.

For I had never knocked, or even thought of knocking, on the door of that grim, deserted cabin in the clearing.

THE END

○ **Talking it over**

1. There are three things which most frighten the narrator:
   (1) the skeleton hands
   (2) the knocking noises
   (3) the depressions in the
       wood of the door.

   a. Why is she frightened about each of these things?

   b. What explanation does Dad give for each one?

   c. What mystery remains in her mind in spite of Dad's explanations?

2. Dad makes several statements about the character of the narrator and

the character of women in general. (See 334a, 6; 334b, 5 & 9; 336a, 5.)

a. What stereotyped picture of women does Dad have?

b. Explain whether he is right in his comments about the character of the narrator.

3. How does the narrator feel about her nighttime experiences, after they are over? What does she think about there being a ghost?

⇄ Words in action

In "One Alaska Night" the author has used many colorful expressions that don't mean exactly what the words say. Many of these expressions you were probably familiar with already. Those you didn't know you could probably guess from context.

Try your hand at creating colorful expressions of your own. First decide what the speaker actually means by each of the italicized expressions in the following sentences taken from the story. Then make up a new and original expression that means the same thing.

1. "In that instant of realization *all my strength seemed to ooze out of me.*" (330a, 2)

2. "I told you she'd be *cool as a cucumber.*" (334a, 5)

3. "You can *thank your lucky star* you stumbled onto Butler's cabin." (334a, 6)

4. "On a moonlight night a man *can't get a wink of sleep.* . . ." (335b, 10)

5. ". . . the way they play *humpty-dumpty* on the roof." (335b, 10)

6. "I'm *hungry enough to eat boiled owl.*" (336a, 5)

Her school was a trading post

Barrett Willoughby's first home was her father's trading schooner which cruised up and down the coast of Alaska. She got much of her education from listening to the traders, trappers, Indians, explorers, scientists, and seafaring men who gathered at her father's Alaskan trading post.

She went to San Francisco to write her first novel, *Where the Sun Swings North,* but ran out of money before it was completed. Then she became a secretary to a famous writer and gradually finished her novel.

Barrett Willoughby wrote novels, travel books, and biographies of Alaskans, as well as magazine articles. She was the first native Alaskan to write of her own country.

Jerry Linton was living two lives. One was neat, orderly, and unvarying; the other pushed haphazardly into the exciting past of an old man who had never stuck to roads.

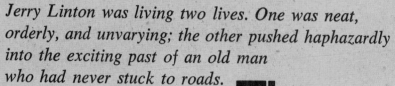

The Old Man and the Last Ambush

by Jack Schaefer

JERRY LINTON was ten the year the old man came to live with them in the still-new house his parents had built the year before. He knew the old man was coming, knew it the day the letter came and his mother read it with her lips folding into a tight line and put it up on the mantelpiece and in the evening he sat cross-legged in his flannel nightshirt on the floor of the dark upstairs hall and heard his parents discussing it in the parlor.

"Frozen his feet," said his father dry-voiced and precise, nailing down the essential fact in invariable precise manner. "Well, something was bound to happen to the old fool sometime. I suppose this means we'll have to take him in."

"Trapped," said his mother. "That's how it makes me feel. Just plain trapped. If we don't, you know what they'll all say. We have the room. We're about the only ones can afford it right now. But if we do—well, you know what he is."

"Yes," his father said. "I know. But he's your kin and that's that."

So that was that as it always was when his father spoke and Jerry Linton knew the old man was coming, the not even imaginable old man who lived alone off up somewhere in the far mountains, whom he had never dared ask questions about because his parents and all the relatives, the few times the old man was ever mentioned, looked at each other as if even thinking about him was a mistake and hurried on to talk of almost anything else. But Jerry Linton did not know what to expect and the excitement in him that he kept

From *The Plainsmen* by Jack Schaefer. Copyright© 1963 by Houghton Mifflin Company. Reprinted (slightly abridged) by permission of the publisher, Houghton Mifflin Company.

hidden because his mother did not believe in noise and disturbance about the house reached a high pitch that Saturday morning as he and his mother stood on the front porch and watched his father, coming back from the station, drive their new Ford with its gleaming brass oil lamps into their alleyway and stop it and get out of it all alone and come toward them and shrug his shoulders in an exasperated way and say: "He wouldn't come in the machine. I've got him coming in a carriage from the livery stable."

Then the carriage came and stopped out front and the driver swung down and opened the door and Jerry Linton was disappointed at first because what climbed out, slow and awkward, backing out and down and leaning against the side of the carriage to turn around, was just an ordinary old man, thin and stooped in wrinkled and dirty clothes. He held a battered old carpetbag with one hand and leaned away from it to balance the weight and hobbled up the walk, taking slow short steps and easing down carefully on each foot in turn as if it hurt him to step on it. He was a very old man with skin drawn tight over high cheekbones and a scraggly gray tobacco-stained mustache hanging down over his mouth and bright old eyes sunk below heavy brows. He stopped by the porch steps and set the old carpetbag down. Strapped along its side was an old heavy-barreled rifle. He straightened and peered up at the three of them on the porch.

"Made it," he said. "Bet ye thought I wouldn't. Mebbe hoped so. Ain't nothin' wrong with me 'cept these gol-danged feet." He poked his head forward a bit at Jerry's mother. "Mary, ain't ye? Young Tom's girl."

"That's right, Grandpa Jonas," said Jerry's mother in her careful company-manners voice. "It's so nice seeing you again. It'll be so nice having you with us."

"Will it now?" said the old man and he peered straight up at her and there was a short embarrassing silence and Jerry's mother broke it by turning to him. "Gerald. This is Jonas Brandt, your great-grandfather."

The old man turned his head a little and his bright old eyes peered at Jerry. "Looks like his father," the old man said and leaned and picked up the carpetbag and hobbled up the steps. "Where'll ye be puttin' me?"

But Jerry's mother had noticed the rifle. Her voice was normal again, with an extra little thin cutting edge. "Grandpa Jonas. We might as well get some things straight. One is I won't have any firearms in my house."

The old man looked at Jerry's mother and she looked right back at him and he lowered his head and looked down at the porch floor. "Ain't no hurt in it," he said. "It's broke. Won't work no more." He turned his head sideways towards Jerry Linton and put up his free hand as if to rub his cheek but the hand was there just to hide his face from the other side and far back in Jerry Linton's consciousness a slight tremor of shock and a kind of savage joy shook him because the old man was winking at him. And then his father was making it that's that again by saying: "Well, then, Mary, there's no real harm in it. Just so he keeps it where the boy can't get at it."

So the old man was living with them and at first it was difficult because Jerry's parents didn't know what to do with him, what he could or would do to pass the long hours of just being alive. But the old man solved that problem himself. At the suppertable, after only a few days, he suddenly put down his knife, which he always held in his right hand all through the meal while he used his fork with his left hand, and poked his old head forward a bit diagonally across the table corner at Jerry's father and said: "Ye payin' that coalman much a anythin'?" He meant the man who stopped by three times a day to tend the big round furnace in the basement.

Jerry's father stared a little in surprise. He pressed his lips together in a small frown because he disapproved of discussing financial matters at the table. "I'm paying him enough," he said. "Probably more than the job is worth."

"Get rid a him," said the old man.

"Now, Grandpa Jonas—" began Jerry's mother.

"These goldanged feet ain't that bad," said the old man. He picked up his knife in his right hand and let the fork drop from his left hand and reached with it and took a slice of bread from the dish in the center of the table and began mopping at the gravy on his plate. Jerry's mother watched him shove the dripping bread through his drooping old mustache into his mouth and take half of the slice in one bite and chew it briefly and shove the rest of the slice in. She turned her head and saw Jerry staring in fascination as the old man pushed out his tongue and pulled it back in through the mustache hairs with a tiny sucking noise to get the traces of gravy there. She looked straight across the table at Jerry's father and raised her eyebrows and sighed.

"Bein' fancy ain't never made food

taste better," said the old man and reached for another slice of bread and bent his head over his plate to concentrate on the last of the gravy and an almost imperceptible little shivery tingle ran down Jerry Linton's spine because he saw, just as the old head bent down, the glint, the unholy fleeting sparkle in the old eyes under the heavy brows.

So tending the furnace kept the old man busy much of the time. He was always up at the first light of dawn and this filled the early morning for him. After breakfast there was the job of taking the ashes and clinkers out to the growing pile behind the garage. Then there was only an hour or two to sit smoking one of his stubby old pipes, in good weather when the sun was bright on the front porch steps, in bad weather in the parlor by the front window looking on the street, before it was lunchtime and the furnace to be tended again and only a few hours more of sitting and smoking before it was suppertime and the furnace to be tended yet again. And when the warm weather really arrived there would be the other chores the coalman had done, cutting the grass, trimming the hedge, cleaning out the basement and getting rid of accumulated trash. For an old man with frozen feet these things could consume many hours.

That left the evenings and at first these were particularly difficult because Jerry's parents tried to be polite and include the old man in at least some of whatever talk there was and he just couldn't or wouldn't fit into their kind of talk and almost always said things that seemed to irritate or embarrass them. But the old man solved that problem too. There was the evening they were all in the parlor, and Jerry's mother looked up from her sewing and said in her half-joking voice that meant she was trying to make a point without any fuss about it: "Grandpa Jonas, don't you think it would be nice if you trimmed your mustache more often?"

The old man looked at her what seemed a long time. He looked at Jerry's father who was being very quiet behind the paper. He turned his head to look out the window. "Mebbe so," he said and Jerry's mother took up her sewing again with a triumphant little half-smile curving her lips. And suddenly the old man turned his head back again and said right out into the middle of the room, his old voice cracking some: "Don't ye folks ever do anythin' diff'rent? Allus the same doin's the same time. Like a bunch of goldanged clocks."

Jerry's mother stopped sewing. She stared at the old man and two spots of color began to show on her cheeks. Jerry's father lowered the paper and looked over it at first one of them then the other. "Regularity," he said. "That's the secret of success." But for once Jerry's mother paid no attention to his father. She had her hands folded in her lap over the sewing and she stared at the old man. Her voice was prim and sharp. "Grandpa Jonas. We are decent, respectable people. The least you can do is try to understand that. You, of all people, trying to tell us how to live."

The old man pushed up from his chair and balanced himself on his sore old feet. "Wasn't tryin' to tell ye a goldanged thing," he said. "Was just wonderin' why." He hobbled across the room and into the front hall and they could hear him making his slow way upstairs.

And the very next day his deafness began to develop. It came on fast and within a few days he couldn't hear a thing that was said to him unless a person was close and shouted. That was peculiar because the way his eyes moved and the look in them changed off and on when there was talking going on around him made it seem as if he knew who was speaking and maybe even what was being said. But he kept quiet and when anyone spoke directly to him he poked his old head forward and cupped one hand by an ear and the remark or question had to be repeated in a loud voice before he would understand it.

So his being deaf made the evenings easier because there wasn't much sense in trying to talk to a person who couldn't hear. It wasn't long before none of them ever said much of anything at all except to shout things absolutely necessary.

All the first weeks he was something new and strange to Jerry Linton and the boy couldn't help staring at him and watching him. Jerry's mother worried about that and had one of her talks with him about it. "Gerald," she said, "you're still a child and children are very impressionable. I don't want you ever to forget that you are a Linton and I intend you to grow up to be a gentleman like your father. Jonas Brandt," she said—she usually spoke of him not as if he were her grandfather, Jerry's great-grandfather, but someone removed who had no real connection with them—"well, Jonas Brandt is, well, he is just not a very nice person. That may not be altogether his fault because he didn't have a very good upbringing and, well, he just couldn't be after what he did. I don't want you watching him all the time and maybe learning habits that—"

"But, Mother, what was it that was so bad that he did?"

"Gerald. It's not nice to interrupt. Jonas Brandt just wouldn't ever settle down and take care of his family the way a decent man would. Expecting a woman with children to go off into wild country and not live decent when there was nice work he could do at home. He was always going off by himself and doing what he wanted and not even thinking of them and getting just cruder and coarser all the time. And then he—well, I'm sorry, Gerald, but you're not old enough yet to know about that. You just have to take my word about him. After all, I'm your mother. He has to stay with us because there's no place for him to go and after all he is related. The least you can do for my sake is just not pay much attention to him at all."

And after the first weeks that was not hard to do. The newness of the old man was gone. He was there, but he was less and less there in actual seeing and noticing, somehow quietly slipping or being pushed ever further into the background of household affairs. He took to using the back stairs all the time. He was no longer sleeping in the back bedroom across the hall from Jerry's room. When Aunt Ella came to stay a few days he moved up into the little finished room in the attic so she could have his room and after she left he stayed on up there where he didn't have to bother so much about Jerry's mother wanting things neat and tidy.

He was no longer on the front porch steps when Jerry came home from school, just before lunch and again in midafternoon. Jerry's mother worried about him sitting there, what people would think, seeing him dirty and disreputable sitting there, drawing on his bubbly old pipe and spitting sideways into the shrubbery. She must have said something then because he shifted around to the back steps and, later, to a bench he built behind the garage.

He was no longer even in the parlor, even in bad weather, except for a brief silent time each evening when he waited for the paper. He stayed down in the basement, sitting and smoking on an old kitchen chair with an old cushion pad on it in the recess between the coalbin and the basement stairs where a window up behind him just above the ground level gave some light.

Jerry Linton hardly ever even thought or wondered about him any more. Every morning, for some reason, lying in his bed in the second-story back room, the boy would suddenly be awake and the first light of dawn would be creeping in his window and he would hear, overhead, slow hobbling footsteps, quiet and muffled, that would fade away then be heard again coming down the narrow attic stairway and going past his door and fading out again down the back stairway to the kitchen. But even then he would not think of the old man. The hobbling steps were simply another sound out of the familiar round that measured existence and they simply meant there would be time for more sleep.

II

Jerry Linton was two weeks past his fourteenth birthday when the man from the historical society came to call. Jerry answered the door because he was in the stage of being taught how a gentleman greeted strangers and he did very well, inviting the man in and showing him into the parlor before running to get his mother.

The man sat in the platform rocker facing Jerry and his mother on the high-backed sofa. He introduced himself as a Mr. Finley, as the secretary of the state historical society, and said he was assembling information for an article he was writing for the society's quarterly publication. Jerry's mother sat up straighter with a proud little smile on her face and then suddenly she looked as astonished as Jerry felt because Mr. Finley was saying that he wanted to talk to a Jonas Brandt.

Jonas Brandt?

Why certainly. Of course, what was happening nowadays in the state, the tremendous strides forward of economic and social progress, was what was really important. But still it was interesting to get down facts about the past and the time to do that was now while some of the old-time settlers and pioneers were still alive. Of course, their memories were not always to be trusted but the scholarly approach, checking this against that, sifting out the probable truth, often yielded excellent results.

Mr. Finley was somewhat self-important as he explained his work. Jerry's mother listened and seemed a bit worried as she listened and she gave a little sigh of relief when Mr. Finley said his article was about the Sioux outbreak of 1862, about one aspect of it, one incident, that had been generally overlooked in the wealth of material available. He had his article well in hand. In fact, he was quite satisfied with it. But his scholar's conscience told him he should check his facts with every source and, after all, he liked traveling about so where was Jonas Brandt?

He was out on his bench behind the garage but Jerry's mother did not tell that. She simply excused herself and went out to get him and in a few minutes he had hobbled in after her. He sat on the edge of his chair hunched forward in his wrinkled and dirty clothes, his old hands on his knees, peering at Mr. Finley from under his heavy old brows.

"Mr. Brandt—" began Mr. Finley.

"You'll have to speak up," said Jerry's mother. "He doesn't hear very well."

"Mr. Brandt—" began Mr. Finley again in almost a shout.

"What ye shoutin' fer?" said the old man.

"Well," said Jerry's mother quickly. "This must be one of his good days."

"Mr. Brandt," began Mr. Finley again. He spoke slowly, separating the words, almost as if he were speaking to a child. "In August of 1862 you were living in a little crossroads settlement about ten miles from the town of New Ulm."

"Nope," said the old man. "Just passin' through. Freightin'."

Mr. Finley cleared his throat. "In any event, you were there when the Santee Sioux under Little Crow went on the warpath and began massacring defenseless women and children."

"Men too," said the old man. "Fightin' men." His old eyes were beginning to brighten.

"Well, yes," said Mr. Finley. "In any event, you were one of the party, all the people there, who set out to slip through those massacring Indians and get to Fort Ridgely."

"Yep," said the old man.

"Thirteen of you, including the children."

"Sixteen," said the old man.

"Very good, Mr. Brandt. I was just testing your memory. And who was in charge?"

"Feller named Schultz. Marty Schultz."

"Splendid, Mr. Brandt. And this Martin Schultz was an excellent leader, was he not? Took charge and—"

"Nope. Seven kinds a fool. Didn't know much. About Injuns anyway."

"Now, Mr. Brandt." Mr. Finley seemed somewhat irritated. "Let's not permit personal feelings or perhaps even jealousy to creep in here. The facts prove otherwise. There were only five of you men and the rest were women and children and Martin Schultz was in charge and you were three days getting to the fort with just about no food at all and unable to make a fire with murdering Indians all about—and yet you all got through safely. Now, didn't you?"

"Yep."

"And on the last day you wouldn't have. You were hiding in a ravine and an Indian way off on a hilltop sighted you and if he had got word to the rest of his band or been able to signal them you would all have been slaughtered. But he didn't because—"

"Ye're goldanged right he didn't!"

Mr. Finley was excited now. He jumped from the platform rocker and began pacing back and forth in front of it. "There you are, Mrs. Linton. That is my article. With full details added of course. I got it first from Martin Schultz himself. And two of the women are still living. They check it on most points. Can you see it? Of course you can. What a climax. That murdering Indian off on the hilltop and sixteen innocent white people hiding in that ravine. And Martin Schultz takes his rifle and steadies it on a rock and takes

his aim. It was all of nine hundred yards, Schultz claims, but of course that's exaggerated. Those old guns you know. But it was quite a distance anyway. And sixteen lives dependent on that one shot. And Martin Schultz knows that and maybe offers up a little prayer and—"

"Quit yappin'," said the old man. "Marty allus was one to hog it. Never made that shot." The old man raised his old hands and slapped them down on his old knees. "I did."

Mr. Finley stopped pacing. He raised one hand and looked down at it and turned and studied his neat fingernails. He cleared his throat. "Yes, yes, of course, Mr. Brandt. After all these years and thinking about it so much, perhaps it seems—"

"It was better'n a thousand yards too!"

Mr. Finley looked at Jerry's mother and raised his eyebrows and shrugged his shoulders. He cleared his throat again and followed this with a little cough and turned toward the old man. "Well, thank you, Mr. Brandt. You have been most helpful. At least I'm sure you meant to be. Perhaps sometime I will want to consult you about some of your other—"

The old man was not even trying to hear him. The old man was pushing up from the easy chair and hobbling toward the hall. "Thought ye wanted facts," he said and disappeared toward the back of the house.

So Jerry's mother was out in the front hall with Mr. Finley by the front door and she was saying apologetic things to him and Mr. Finley was saying polite things to reassure her and alone in the parlor, tense upright on the high-backed sofa, was Jerry Linton, shaking, shaking far down inside with a kind of savage joy and a desire for knowing, knowing, knowing—

"Mother. What was that other thing he did?"

"Oh, Gerald. I don't want you thinking about such things. We're civilized now. I don't see why, even if it is history, people have to go raking up all those horrible old things and making people remember them. People ought to just try to forget things ever weren't as decent and quiet as they are now. I wish that Mr. Finley, even if he is a gentleman—"

"Mother. What did he do?"

"Well . . . I suppose you do have to know sometime, Gerald. He, well, after his wife died—worried her into her grave, I'm sure that's what happened—he took up with, well, with an Indian woman. And he, well, he never even married her. There. I've told you. Now I want you to just put it out of your mind and not go around thinking about it. . . ."

Out of mind?

So Jerry Linton had to wait until his mother was busy again picking up and tidying about upstairs, then go find the old man. He was not out behind the garage. He was in the basement, on his old chair in the recess by the coalbin. Jerry Linton, stretching and gangling into his fifteenth year, almost as tall already as his father, stood on the basement steps near the bottom and saw the old man sitting there sucking on a bubbly old pipe and was afraid, afraid of this suddenly strange-again old man, thinner and more stooped than when he first came, with old eyes dulled now.

Jerry Linton could barely get the word out. "Grandpa."

It was really one of the old man's good days. He did not turn his head but he heard. "Eh, boy?"

"Did you—did you really shoot that Indian?"

Long seconds of waiting, then the old man's head turned slowly toward Jerry and nodded. "With that rifle a mine. That's a Sharps, boy."

"They—they don't believe you."

"That don't mean nothin'. How'd they know? Thing is, I know."

It was peculiar. Grown folks couldn't talk to the old man. But a boy could. Jerry Linton sat down on the second step from the bottom.

"That Indian woman—why didn't you ever marry her?"

"Yer mother's been talkin'." The old man chuckled. "Fact is, I did. Injun style. Good enough fer her so good enough fer me. Stuck with me till she finished."

And after that Saturdays were special because in the mornings when Jerry's mother was uptown doing her household shopping he was with the old man, in the basement or out behind the garage, and there was no end to the questions that kept coming.

"Grandpa. Did you ever shoot a buffalo?"

"Buffler, boy? That's fer sure. Partner'n me worked hides two-three years. Toted in more'n 'leven hundred once. Worked out a Bismarck up in North Dakoty. . . ."

That was the way it was, simply the plain unslicked statements somehow more real and exciting because of their very matter-of-fact plainness, to be expanded in imagination and given meaning in the thinking over afterwards.

"But why won't you ever ride in the car?"

"Goldanged machine. Leg or a hoss's

the way to get around. What good'd that thing be fer rough goin'? Up in the mount'ns? Ain't worth a buffler chip off a road. Me, I ain't never stuck to roads. . . ."

"Did you ever see Jesse James?"

"Nope. Didn't miss much nuther. Saw Boone Helm once. Knife man, he was. Killed a lot a people. Folks got together an' used a rope up in Montanny. Used to see the place freightin' into Virginny City. . . ."

"But, Grandpa, weren't you ever scared? Indians and wild animals and things like that?"

"Why, fer sure, boy. Lots of times. Bein' scared's all right. Backin' away ain't. I'd start shivering and I'd say, Jonas, ye goldanged mule, ye got yerself into this here fix an' so what comes ye can just take—an' after that it wouldn't be so goldanged bad. . . ."

So Jerry Linton, in a sense, was living two lives, one neat and orderly, bounded by school and family meals and the rules and almost unvarying routine of his parents' household, the other unruly and exciting, pushing haphazard into the long echoing past of an old man who had never stuck to roads. After a while the two lives began to merge in almost unnoticed small ways, unnoticed even by Jerry Linton himself. But one day in history class a picture of Andrew Jackson came alive on the page and he suddenly knew that the names in the book were not just names but people and not people apart and different but ordinary everyday-seeming people who ate meals and dressed and undressed and sometimes were tired and sick and just went ahead and did things and lived and in time grew thin and stooped and old.

Walking to school he saw the other houses in their neat rectangles of yards, and the squared corners of the streets laid out in regular blocks, and he knew that almost everywhere out beyond the town were the neat sectioned farms with their neat cultivated fields and pastures. It was not always like that. Indians once roamed even this tamed land at will. And buffalo. Men had made it the way it was, men like his father, steady and dependable, careful with figures, planning ahead. And suddenly he knew, knew in real knowing not just as an idea taught in class, that other men had come first, men who didn't stick to roads and who knew Indians and fought them and sometimes even lived with them and could bring in eleven hundred buffalo hides in a single season.

When he was in grammar school he never played much with the older boys who stayed around after school and played on the grounds and on the athletic field beside the big building. His mother wanted him to come straight home. She couldn't see why boys always liked to play such rough games anyway. There were so many ways they could be hurt, like the boy in the next block who broke an arm playing football.

Now Jerry was in high school, even just the first year, it was different. His mother had one of her talks with him and told him he could stay around after school two or three days a week if he really wanted to because she was sure she could trust him not to be wild and rough like some of the boys. He stayed around and it was early fall and they were playing football and at first, for quite a few days, he just stood and watched. He wanted to play too but he couldn't help thinking about getting hurt. And one day he pushed in with the others and he was let be on one side just to fill in and then he was out on the field more frightened than he had ever been before and ready to run away. And suddenly he was telling himself without thinking how or why that he'd gotten himself into this fix so he'd just have to take what came and in a kind of savage joy almost as if he hoped to be hurt so he could show he could take it he plunged into the game and it wasn't so bad after all. In a little while it was even fun, to be running and yelling and bumping into other boys trying to block them and gasping for breath with the blood in him pounding strong.

III

It was spring and Jerry Linton was past the halfway mark of his fifteenth year when his mother came home one Saturday morning from her household shopping and called and called to him and at last he answered from behind the garage and then he forgot and she had to call him again.

"Gerald," she said. "I do wish you would come when I call. Now carry these parcels upstairs. The least you can do is help with all the running up and down stairs that has to be done in this house." And when he had put the parcels in the upstairs hall and was back down and starting out the kitchen door she stopped him. "Gerald. It seems to me you're spending entirely too much time with Jonas Brandt. It's beginning to show in your talk. And you're becoming entirely too loud and noisy lately."

Jerry Linton stood in the doorway shifting from one foot to the other and his mother said: "Sit down, Gerald. I want to have a talk with you. I don't see how it can do you any good to have

a man like Jonas Brandt filling your head with wild notions and horrible old stories that very likely aren't the least bit true anyway. I'm sure most of the time he's just trying to justify himself and make you think that after all he really was something. You know how old people are, getting things mixed up and getting to think maybe things are true that really weren't true at all. I'm sure you remember what happened when that Mr. Finley—"

"Oh-h-h, Mother. He really did shoot that Indian!"

So Jerry Linton had spoken back to his mother and spoken sharply too and his father had to have a talk with him. "Jerry. I know you didn't mean to upset your mother but you did and that's that. I know when we're through here you will go and tell her you are sorry. What you have to realize is that she is right. No doubt there is some truth in the things your great-grandfather has been telling you. But he is nearly ninety years old and they happened a long time ago. Most people's memories, especially old people's, are very faulty as we keep finding out at the bank. Trying to straighten out wills and property deeds and things like that. Your great-grandfather has not given much evidence in his life that he has much sense of responsibility. And, after all, what happened so long ago is not nearly as important to a growing boy as what is happening right now. This is a practical world we live in these days and it is run on business principles. What you should be doing is tending to your lessons and learning how best to get along in it."

So Jerry Linton told his mother he was sorry. But his parents saw the stubborn look on his face and worried about it and only a few days later his father brought home a copy of the historical society's quarterly and showed him Mr. Finley's article.

There it was, in the cold clear neat not-to-be-questioned authority of printed words, the whole story, very well told and with impressive footnotes, of sixteen people fleeing for their lives under the leadership of a Martin Schultz and evading the bloody-handed Sioux for three days and on the third day sighted by an Indian scout who never got word back to his band because of the cool courage and unerring marksmanship of Martin Schultz. The only mention of Jonas Brandt was in a footnote: *The fifth man was a freighter named Jonas Brandt, who joined the group for added safety in reaching the fort.*

So his parents were right. There were no more Saturday mornings behind the garage for Jerry Linton. He was too busy playing with the other boys. It wouldn't be exciting listening to the old man anyway. Jerry Linton saw him in sensible perspective now and realized that for quite a while his memory had been getting bad after all. He contradicted himself sometimes and when he tried to pin down a date he kept getting mixed up. He was an old relic out of another time who didn't fit in the modern practical world.

IV

Jerry Linton was fifteen, in his sophomore year at high school, when he woke one spring morning in his second-floor bedroom soon after the first light of dawn with a strange feeling that something was wrong. He found himself listening and not sure for what. Then he knew. There were no slow hobbling footsteps overhead. He lay quiet wondering about that and after a while slipped back into sleep and when his mother called him and he dressed and went downstairs there was a slight chill in the house and his father was in the basement rattling and banging at the furnace. While they were eating breakfast the doctor came and Jerry's father went off with him upstairs. In a few moments they were back down, the doctor bustling and good-natured, rubbing his hands together and saying: "Nothing to get too much upset about, Mrs. Linton. He's a bit feverish but that's to be expected. He's had some kind of a light stroke. A remarkably tough old constitution, I'd say. Wouldn't surprise me to see him up and about again in a few days."

But it was not a few days. It was the very next day, early in the morning with the first light of dawn. Jerry Linton woke and heard slow hobbling steps overhead, quiet and muffled, that faded away and then were heard again coming down the narrow attic stairway and going past his door and fading out again down the back stairway to the kitchen. A kind of warm feeling drifted through him and he slipped back into sleep and suddenly he was awake again. Wide awake. The footsteps were returning past his door and on up the attic steps, not slow and hobbling but quicker, lighter, hurrying. Jerry Linton lay still and listened and they came down the attic stairs again and were going past his door again. He eased quietly out of bed and tiptoed to the door and opened it a crack. The old man was just disappearing into the back stairway and he was carrying his old rifle.

Jerry Linton couldn't move at first.

He was still, motionless, with his face pressed close against the door crack. Then he opened the door and went, soft and quick, along the hall toward the front of the house and stopped by the closed door of his parents' bedroom. He stared at the door almost a full minute. And suddenly he turned and hurried back to his own room and dressed as fast as he could and pulled on a sweater and went out and down the back stairs.

The old man wasn't in the basement. He wasn't on the back porch or anywhere in sight in the yard. He was behind the garage and he was standing straight, hardly stooped at all, with the heavy old rifle firm in one hand, and his old eyes were brighter, brighter than they had ever been, when he looked at Jerry coming around the corner of the garage.

"Time ye were out a blankets," he said. "There's things doin'." He looked at Jerry in a strange way, almost as if Jerry were somone else who should have been out of blankets before this. "What's got into ye, Jed?" he said. "Can't ye sniff it? Injun smell." He pointed with his free hand off across the vacant lot behind theirs and the fields beyond to the slight rise that hid the town dump. In the growing light of dawn Jerry saw it, a last thin wisp of smoke floating upward and dissolving away. "That's just a fire over in—" he started to say but the old man was poking his old head at him and saying in a fierce whisper: "Tell me I don't know Injun sign! Someun's got to do scoutin' or they'll be on us afore we know it!"

The old man started off, striding fast, across the vacant lot, and Jerry Linton wavered and turned to hurry back to the house and stopped. Slowly he turned around again and saw the old man striding away, head forward and intent, striding fast on old feet that must hurt him but he didn't seem to notice that, striding ahead with his heavy old rifle in his right hand, and far down in Jerry Linton a tingling started and shook him and would not stop and he was running to catch up.

The old man flicked one sideways glance at him as he came alongside. "Right, Jed," the old man said. "Two's got more chance'n one."

They were across the vacant lot and they struck straight across the fields beyond, climbing fences as they came to them. They went over the rise that hid the dump and on past the dump itself where some fire still smoldered which the old man didn't even notice and he stopped and raised his left hand to shield his eyes against the sun just beginning to show over the horizon and peered all around studying the countryside. "They'll come snakin' down that draw," he said and struck off again toward the only rough land, the only untamed-to-farming land, anywhere around, toward the far base of the huge wide slow-sloping hill that rose west of town with its near slope torn and eroded by an ancient dry boulder-strewn stream bed. They reached the base of the hill and Jerry Linton's legs were tiring from the pace but he couldn't have stopped if he had wanted to. It was impossible how the old man kept going on his old frozen feet, striding forward, head swinging from side to side, old eyes bright and intent under their heavy brows. He struck straight up along the upper left side of the dry stream bed that widened upward like a vast shallow funnel and Jerry Linton followed and followed and his legs were aching

and the old man stopped. "Can't figger it," he said. "Sioux ain't been liftin' hair lately." He started on and they were near the top of the hill and Jerry Linton's legs were aching and suddenly the old man clapped him on the shoulder so hard he went forward on his knees. "Down," said the old man in a fierce whisper, dropping to the ground and scrambling over behind a boulder. "Over here."

So there they were, Jerry Linton and the old man, behind a boulder on the edge of a wide gully, really just a wide stretch of rough eroded hillside. And the old man raised and peered over the boulder, intent old eyes studying the wide gully. "Take a peek, Jed," he said. "See 'im? Ahind that rock looks like a keg. Straight across an' down some."

Jerry Linton, aching and scratched but with a tingling inside that wouldn't stop, peered over the boulder too and at last he saw the rock that looked like a keg, way off across and up the other side of the wide gully, but it was only a rock and that was all.

"Got it," said the old man. "Pawnee. Sneakin' devils they are. Paint up like that." And then Jerry Linton, squeezing his eyes to sharp focus, saw showing above the rock in a small patch an outcropping of red sandstone in the ground beyond, bright and shimmering a little in the early morning sun.

"Likely a passel a bucks over the ridge," said the old man. He turned toward Jerry. His old voice was an urgent whisper. "Git amovin' Jed, an' rouse the folks. I'll slow' 'm here while ye get help."

It was the tingling in Jerry Linton that pushed him up and started him a few steps away. Then he felt foolish and he stopped and looked around. The old man was beside the boulder, flat on his stomach, and he was shoving the old rifle forward and muttering to himself. He put a finger in his mouth and licked it and stuck it up to test the air. "Wind about ten mile," he muttered. "Figger the drop across there maybe thirty feet." His left arm was out, resting on its elbow, and his left hand held and steadied the heavy old rifle barrel and the stock was snuggled up against his right shoulder and he squinted through the strange old double sights and suddenly the old Sharps roared like a Fourth of July cannon and the recoil smacked shaking through the old man's body. He rolled over and behind the boulder again and sat up with the rifle still in his hands and yanked down on the trigger guard and the breech opened and he clawed in a pocket and took out a funny old linen cartridge and started reloading and his fingers fumbled and dropped it and the old gun fell too, down and across his legs, and his whole body seemed to stiffen into a kind of rigidness. Slowly his old head came up and his eyes, dulling rapidly, looked around and stopped on Jerry Linton.

"What ye doin' up here, boy?" he said and his whole body sagged out of the rigidness into a kind of limpness and relaxed back against the boulder and slipped down sidewise to the ground.

Jerry Linton knew. He had never seen this before but he knew. He looked down at the crumpled still body a long time. He looked up and across the wide gully where a patch of red sandstone showed above a keg-shaped rock. Slowly he started down the rough eroded near side of the gully and then he was walking faster and then he was running, down and across the center dip and up the other side and then slowing, almost afraid to look.

There was the rock. There behind it, farther behind than it seemed from the other side, was the patch of red sandstone. And there, near the top of the patch where it would show over the rock, close to the edge but there, was the fresh, chipped, the shining gouge in the stone.

Jerry Linton stood with his back to the patch of sandstone. He started again across the gully, taking long steps, stretching them to what he judged the right length. Down and across and up. One thousand and twenty-seven. Taking into account the slope down and up that was still close enough.

Jerry Linton picked up the old rifle and looked at it. There was not a spot of rust on the metal. The old stock was sound. "Yes," he said. "Yes. I'm a Linton. But I'm Brandt too." He said it to the body of an old man who had given him what no one else could, what no one could ever take away from him because always, simply by closing his eyes, he would be able to see, acoss a thousand yards of untamed land, a patch of red chipped sandstone.

He turned and went down the slope toward the town to get his father, who, in his own precise way, steady and dependable, would make arangements to take care of what was left of the old man.   THE END

↻ **Talking it over**

Part I

1. *a.* How do Mr. and Mrs. Linton feel about having the old man come to live with them?

b. How do they treat him when he is there?

c. Name some specific things Mrs. Linton objects to in the old man.

d. How does his deafness seem to make it easier to have him around?

2. Jonas Brandt says to Jerry's parents, "Don't ye folks ever do anythin' diff'rent? Allus the same doin's the same time. Like a bunch a goldanged clocks." Jerry's father replies, "Regularity. That's the secret of success." Show the ways in which the lives of the two men reflect these statements.

3. *a.* How do Mr. and Mrs. Linton want Jerry to behave toward the old man?

b. How does Jerry actually treat him?

Part II

4. *a.* What kind of person is Mr. Finley?

b. Why does Mr. Finley ignore the information the old man gives him about the shot?

c. What judgments do Mr. Finley and Mr. and Mrs. Linton make about Jonas Brandt? What basis do they have for their judgments?

5. *a.* Jonas Brandt says, "Me, I ain't never stuck to roads. . . ." Apply this statement to his entire life.

b. How does he react to the fact that none of the adults believe him?

6. *a.* "It was peculiar. Grown folks couldn't talk to the old man. But a boy

could." Suggest reasons why this might have been true.

b. How do Jerry's feelings toward Jonas Brandt change in Part II?

7. *a.* How do the old man's stories affect Jerry's understanding of history?

b. Why does Jerry, who never had played much with the other boys, start playing football against his mother's wish?

Part III

8. In what way does the article in the historical society's publication change Jerry's feelings toward his great-grandfather?

Part IV

9. What probably causes Jonas Brandt's death after his rifle shot? Does it seem "right" that the last action he performs is firing this shot?

10. Why is the rifle shot so important that Jerry leaves the body of his great-grandfather to inspect the red sandstone and to measure the distance?

11. *a.* What "second look" does Jerry take toward Jonas Brandt in Part IV? What causes him to take this second look?

b. What had the old man given him that no one else could, that "no one could ever take away from him"?

c. Reread the next-to-last paragraph in the story. What does Jerry mean by saying to his dead great-grandfather, "Yes, I'm a Linton. But I'm a Brandt too"?

12. How many years of Jerry Linton's life are covered in the story? Why do you suppose each part begins with a statement of how old he is?

His characters were real people

Jack Schaefer is the author of many stories and novels about the old West. His best-known novel is *Shane,* which was made into a popular motion picture. Some of his short stories are collected in *The Big Range, The Kean Land, The Plainsmen,* and *The Collected Stories of Jack Schaefer.*

The characters in "The Old Man and the Last Ambush" were based largely upon real people. Jack Schaefer says, "In a sense, I knew personally every character in that story. . . . With the old man I was paying a sort of belated tribute to my own grandfather, who lived in our house almost precisely as did the old man in Jerry Linton's— and who was, to us kids, just as much a mere fixture with no real existence as a separate human being with a real and interesting past. No historical society dimwit ever came along and we kids never ever really focused on him. It was only later that I learned some things about him. He was not, of course, an old Indian fighter or frontiersman. But in his earlier days, he had had quite a past, about as interesting as one could be in the Middle West of his time. He, too, was pretty much incapacitated by trouble with his feet, which was why he was living with my parents . . . ."

Second Look: Views and viewpoints

1. What does it mean to take a "second look"? Explain in your own words the theme developed in this unit.

2. The people listed below appear in the stories you have just read in this unit.

    (1) Leon Suprenon in "The Soul of Caliban"

    (2) The speaker in "Chain"

    (3) Enie in "The Slap"

    (4) Mary Lee in "The Slap"

    (5) The narrator in "A Mother in Mannville"

    (6) Jezebel Jones

    (7) The narrator in "One Alaska Night"

    (8) Jerry Linton in "The Old Man"

    (9) Mr. Finley in "The Old Man"

    a. Which ones profited from a second look? How?

    b. Which ones took a second look too late or not at all? How might the results have been different if they had taken a second look, or if they had taken one earlier?

3. Have you ever taken a second look at someone or something and found that the person or the situation was quite different from what you first expected? Have you ever jumped to a conclusion that you later found to be false? Describe your experience.

10

What should you do

. . . when you've done something terribly wrong?

. . . when you know you're going to die?

. . . when you are faced with a dangerous challenge?

. . . when what you believe may land you in jail?

. . . when the decision you make <u>right</u> <u>now</u>

will affect your whole life?

Any decision, large or small, may be a

TURNING POINT

TURNING POINT·TURNING POINT·TURNING POINT·TURNING POINT·TURNING POINT·TURNING POINT·TURNING POINT·TURNING POINT·TURNING POINT·TURNING POINT·TURNING POINT·TURNING POINT·TURNING

BLOODSTAIN

*"Coward, coward, coward!" he cried
over and over. "You're afraid to tell!"*

by Christopher W. Rowan

THE BOY with the gun was fourteen, and he was consciously walking pigeon-toed, like an Indian, as he picked his way along a corridor-like path through the willows. Carrying the shotgun at trail, he fixed his whole attention on the underbrush ahead.

Back in the deep brush, away from the river and the footbridge, he began to walk more boldly. No one would know he had taken the gun. His parents were away for the afternoon, and he had met no one as he slipped out.

Fred chuckled as a nesting jay flew before his face, then clattered angrily in a cottonwood. With elaborate care the boy cocked both barrels, raised the gun, aimed, and pretended to snap the triggers.

"If I was as mad as you," he said, "you'd be a dead jay."

His whole body was vibrant, drunken with the smells and sounds and sights his senses brought him. Wild roses and dogwood were in bloom, and every sunny spot was heavy with their scent. Beyond the willows the spring hills, striped with the brighter green of aspen coulees, rolled up to a china sky. His ears were filled with the vanishing diminuendo of woodmice, and he raised his head to sniff as a puff of wind brought him the spicy tang of chokecherry blossoms.

Around a bend in the path ahead stepped a white-haired man with a book under his arm. The boy stopped

This selection first appeared in *American Prefaces* published by the State University of Iowa. Reprinted by permission.

short, pressing the gun close to his body.

"Well!" the man said. "Big game hunter, eh?"

"I . . . uh . . . uh-huh. . . . Huntin' rabbits."

Under his eyebrows Fred studied the man. Mr. Haskell knew all about the gun, he could tell. No use to play that he didn't steal it for the afternoon. But Mr. Haskell was a swell guy. Maybe he wouldn't tell on him. His eyes were twinkling now, and Fred started to grin, but the twinkle changed abruptly to something hard and severe, and the gun was picked out of the boy's hands.

Dumbly, red with shame, Fred saw the old man uncock both hammers.

"You ought to know better than that."

"I do," the boy mumbled. "Forgot, I guess."

"I tanned Jerry for that just once," said Mr. Haskell. "Maybe I ought to tan you, for a lesson."

The twinkle had returned, and he handed the gun back with a playful cuff on the ear. Fred grinned openly now. It was all right. Mr. Haskell was a swell fellow.

"Folks know you got that blunderbuss out?"

"No sir."

Mr. Haskell cuffed him again, tucked his book under his arm, and started on. "Just be careful. If I hear of you shooting anybody's cow I *will* give you that tanning."

"Yes sir," Fred said. "Thanks, Mr. Haskell."

Gratefully he watched the old man disappear behind the screen of willows, and then he was back at his stalking, pigeon-toeing carefully in the half crouch he had been told frontiersmen used. This time his gun was uncocked, and the safety on.

For an hour he slipped quietly through the willow breaks, up into the fringe of heavier timber at the edge of the bench hills, and back in a wide circle along the inside of the horseshoe bend. In all that time he had not started a single rabbit, and his vigilance had flagged, so that when a snowshoe broke and vanished under his very nose he didn't even get the gun to his shoulder.

With cautious haste he followed until he found himself facing a tangled thicket. On his left the willows thinned, and Fred was circling through the clearing when something moved behind a clump of dogwood.

By careful creeping he flanked the clump so that something white showed. Raising the gun with trembling hands, he aimed a long time and pressed the right-hand trigger. The recoil hit his shoulder like a club, and the white object disappeared. Breathless with excitement, he circled the flowering bush.

His shout of triumph died to a sound, half-scream, half-whimper, that trailed out of his lips and left his mouth open. Behind the bush lay Mr. Haskell, one hand still clinging to the book, his white head spattered with red. A trickle of blood, shining like oil, started from the wound and dripped in a quickening patter on the ground.

Stupidly the boy stared. A drop of blood glistening on a leaf, a ladybug crawling on the dead man's wrist . . . . Every particular was seared into his brain, yet none of these things penetrated his consciousness. For minutes he stood still, until the erratic wind rustled the pages of the book and released him from paralysis.

A shrill scream split his throat as he whirled and ran back the way he had come, still grasping the gun by the barrels. The sun slipped under a cloud, and a wave of shadow crossed the quiet glade behind him, moving with incredible swiftness. Gasping, the boy fled blindly through the brush, and shrieked aloud when the shadow, swooping on swift wings, caught and engulfed him.

On and on he ran, tearing through matted clumps, lunging frantically when grasping branches held him back, mouth open, heart pounding, brain one black convulsion. At last he gave out, and after a hard fall could not rise, but lay completely spent. A nerve in his cheek twitched violently, pulling his mouth into a one-sided grin. With gritted teeth he buried his face in his hands and dug flesh with fingers, but still, under the tense hands, he felt the spasmodic jerk of the nerves.

The twitching was actually a relief, for he could concentrate on controlling it, and shut out the picture in the woods behind. After a half hour the nerve quieted. Now the first blank horror was gone, and in its place came fear, and guilt, and the thought of escape.

Rising stiffly, still sobbing a little, he saw the gun, and snatched it from the ground in a frenzy of fear. Getting his bearings from the sun and hills, he picked up the east-west trail. At the river bank he looked carefully up and down stream before crossing on the line of wet stones below the rapids. On the opposite bank he covered the gun with leaves and brush, then walked swiftly homeward.

His parents were not yet home, and the big house was unnaturally still. The stairs creaked under his feet, and he walked on tiptoe. In his room, after he had carefully locked the door, he stood miserably wondering why he had come home. Looking around, he saw the glass-topped box that contained his prized collection of rocks and minerals, the stuffed pike on its board between the windows, the bookcase with its battered books: *Treasure Island, Huckleberry Finn, Tom Sawyer, A History of the World War, The Autobiography of Davy Crockett of Tennessee.* Dully his eyes saw the titles, saw the comfortable cluttered boy's room, but the charm was gone. The air was like the air of a prison.

Reaching out, he pulled the *Davy Crockett* from its shelf, opened it to the thumb-printed page where Davy grinned the coons out of the tree, but his mind, veering back to the tragedy, swung to the book in Mr. Haskell's dead hand, the red blotted stains, and the dry dead look of it, as if it had died with its owner.

He put *Davy Crockett* back again, and for the first time saw the mark on his index finger, an irregular spatter of blood half covering the nail. How it had come there he could not even guess.

Feverishly he poured a basin of water and scrubbed his hands until they hurt, but in the one finger was a feeling as of a deep burn that throbbed with every pound of his pulse. Even then, still stunned with the pain of what he had done, he realized that the stain of blood goes deeper than the skin.

Before the mirror he stared into his own eyes, wild and dark and swollen with crying. With the same keen, impersonal regard he noticed that the hair of the boy in the glass was ruffled and untidy, with twigs and bits of leaves in it, and that the eyes were red and inflamed. Automatically he combed his hair, washed his face in cool water, and went to the window. Through the half-drawn curtains he saw a group of boys playing baseball in the vacant lot next door.

Jerry Haskell was at bat.

Fred slipped down on his knees beside the window, hands clenched in the curtain's starched folds. Out of his misery he fashioned an incoherent, fumbling prayer.

"Oh, God, don't let Jerry find out! Don't make my best friend hate me! Help me, God, I pray. . . . Our Father which art in Heaven, Hallowed be Thy name. . . ."

He loosed his hold on the curtain and bent his head to the hard sill. From the lot next door came the shouts of boys playing.

All afternoon the boy lay face downward on the bed, the suffering growing keener as the numb shock wore off. Thoughts raced in agitated circles . . . confession, flight, denial, silence . . . and back again to bitter sorrow. For one shattered instant suicide hung over him like a black bird, but he chased the thing away.

What could he do? If he ran away, they would catch him and bring him back. He could see them . . . parents, friends . . . a ring of faces staring, shuddering, turning away. And if he stayed, said nothing, went about as usual? There might be a chance that he would not be suspected. He centered on the hope, seized it, let it go again as he thought of Jerry, how he would have to face him, act as if he knew nothing, sympathize. . . .

Fred got up and took a long drink, avoiding the mirror. His mind still whirled in a chaos of doubt and fear. His head dropped on the pillow, and his clenched teeth met through the edge of the slip.

"Coward, coward, coward!" he cried over and over. "You're afraid to tell!"

Late in the afternoon, when his parents returned, he sat up on the bed in sudden fright. The shotgun! Obsessed with grief, he had forgotten all about it.

A splash of cool water to hide the tear stains, and he slipped downstairs. His mother was in the kitchen. Stealthily he crossed the hall. The front door closed behind him. He was just going out the gate when Jerry came around the corner of the house.

With no strength in his legs, his throat and tongue frozen rigid, Fred held tightly to the gate post and waited.

"Seen anything of Dad?"

Fred's head swung sideways.

"He ain't come back from his walk, and Mom's getting worried."

Somehow, in ten seconds, Fred fought his mind calm.

"Think he might've got lost?"

Jerry snorted. "He knows the woods like a book. Let's go up by the dam and look for him. He probably got reading and forgot what time it was."

The terror was upon Fred again. Not go with Jerry, hunting! He hung on the gate.

"Got to . . . go get the cows."

"Oh, come on! The cows'll come home alone."

Fred hesitated, thinking of the pile of brush and leaves under which the gun was hidden, of the empty pegs in the cellarway where it should hang.

"Well . . . ."

He started, stopped.

"Wait a minute."

Running up the front steps, he opened the door and shouted to his mother.

"Ma!"

"Yes?"

"I won't be home for supper. I'm going out with Jerry to look for Mr. Haskell. They think he's lost. Be back quick as I can."

He slammed the door and rejoined Jerry. He saw Jerry looking at him queerly.

"What's the matter with you? You look like you've been bawling."

"I know. Something's the matter with my eyes. Been sore all day. Maybe I'm getting pinkeye."

The lie had come smoothly. All paroxysms of grief had disappeared magically there at the gate, where his problem had been taken out of his hands. The death of Mr. Haskell now was a furtive secret, something to hide, not something to agonize about. His concern now was all for himself.

Up along the river cliffs Jerry raised echoes with his shrill call. Fred tried to shout too, but his throat was tight, and he gave up after a few halloos.

In an hour they had turned back through the flattening shadows. At the Haskell gate Fred waited while Jerry went in to see if his father had returned; waited miserably, fearful of the gathering dark, haunted by the thought of the missing shotgun. In a few minutes Jerry came back and without a word started off toward town. Fred followed.

At the frame building that served as City Hall and jail, Jerry told his story to the constable, who asked a few questions, put on his hat, and led the way to the hotel.

Six men were having an after-dinner poker game in the lobby, while the proprietor and two loungers looked on.

The constable nodded to the proprietor, casually important. " 'Lo, Frank. Say, Pop Haskell's lost. Want to get up a searching party."

The proprietor was all alacrity. "Why sure! I'll get some lanterns. Come on, you guys. Pop Haskell's lost."

He dove into a back room and emerged with four lanterns.

"Where d'you suppose he's likely to be?"

"Out along the river somewhere. We'll split. You take three men and go up along the cliffs, and I'll take the other bunch into the timber. If you find him, send somebody with a lantern to let us know. We'll do the same."

Crowded out by the importance of the searchers, Fred inched away through the veranda door. Once free, he ran toward the spot where he had hidden the gun. Fear gathered behind him; with the fiend at his back he cleared the irrigation ditch in a single leap, and he was in a gibbering panic when he found the spot, pulled away the brush, and groped around in the dark.

With the weapon in his hands his terror passed. He ejected the empty shell and threw it far into the river. The thin splash was instantly swallowed in the dark, but long after the sound had died the boy found himself poised with strained ears, listening.

Throwing the unused shell after the first, he cleaned the barrels with a willow stick and his handkerchief, wrapped the handkerchief around a stone and dropped it in the water. Then he crept out into the open. The bobbing lanterns of one search party were just crossing the footbridge.

Behind a tree near his house he stopped. There was no light in the kitchen, but a lamp was lighted in the front room, and shadows moved between it and the window. He hurried to the door and tiptoed in. There were voices in the other room, discussing the disappearance of Mr. Haskell.

"Perhaps some accident," his father was saying. "Maybe hurt. If that's it, they'll find him before morning."

Soundlessly Fred stole across the room, hung the gun on its pegs in the cellarway, and sneaked out, too wretched to feel relieved.

The spectre of discovery was off his mind for the moment, but in its place came other phantoms, the picture of death in the bright woods, the blood-spattered book, the ghastly wound in the white head. And other pictures of Mr. Haskell: on hands and knees showing him and Jerry how to build a bridge with the Erector set; floating comfortably on his back in the river with a tiny child perched on his chest clutching his bathing suit; playing ball with them only the other day, bare-headed as usual, showing them how to throw a drop. . . .

There would be dew on the old hair, now, and on the pages of the book, and the dead man's face would be pale and cold. And there had been a ladybug crawling on the dead wrist, a bug the color of blood, and the streams of blood that ran on the ground had been quick and bright. They would be clotted now, and dark, and cold. . . .

He wandered over by Jerry's house, lurking behind the hedge, peering into the windows, gnawed by conscience, fear-ridden, miserable. Shadows frightened him; every tree was an accuser, every pool of blackness a menace.

Toward morning they brought the body in. From where he crouched by the hedge Fred saw dark figures carrying the shadow that had been Jerry's father, and Jerry walking beside the body. The men were silent, except for the tramp of their feet on the board sidewalk.

They turned in at the gate, and the porch sounded hollowly under their steps. The door opened; a woman cried out, a single, sharp cry, and the men went inside. The door shut with a dull note of finality, like a clod thudding on a coffin. The big house remained lighted, glaring into the night with yellow eyes, until someone inside pulled down the blinds, one by one.

It was hard to face Jerry the next day, but he had to go, had to go outside with him and stand while Jerry talked. He had to watch the tears rise suddenly, out of Jerry's control, and his own tears blinded him so that he fled.

Away from Jerry, back in his room, he felt curiously relieved. If he could only avoid his friend from now on, never have to speak to him. . . . If they could move to another town and never write. . . . Without realizing why, he felt their friendship as something vanished and impossible and repugnant.

Fred did not go to the funeral. He would have to walk past the coffin, look at the body. Everyone would be there, would be crying, and Jerry would try to get him to sit with the mourners. . . . He would be sure to give himself away.

In poignant contrast he saw the boy who had sneaked along the willow trail, playing Indian, and the furtive hunted animal who had crouched by the hedge to watch the searchers bring in the body

of the man he had killed. All the torturing doubts came back. Once more he was whirled through a maelstrom of indecision and fear. He prayed, and remembered the prayer he had made in his room that day, before anybody knew. It occurred to him as strange that he had not prayed since.

But the second prayer was bitter, too. It gave him no relief, only a hard, mean feeling of loneliness. He didn't want even God to know. All he wanted was to be left alone in his furtive waiting for what would happen.

That night the subject of Mr. Haskell came up again.

"Funny," said Fred's father. "They haven't found a trace of the murderer, except for the kicked-up leaves and the mark where he fell down as he was running away."

"The whole town was at his funeral," his wife said. "Mrs. Haskell was terribly broken up, poor thing. What she'll do now, Heaven knows. Alone with those two poor boys, and not a cent of insurance, I hear."

Fred ate stolidly without looking up, his food like rubber in his mouth.

"Where were you this afternoon?" his mother asked. "I didn't see you at the funeral."

"No . . . I didn't go, Mom. It's. . . . Oh, I don't know! It's too sad!"

"Yes," said his father, "and the saddest thing is that the man who shot him will probably never be caught and get what he deserves."

The boy sat caged and sullen, waiting to be excused from table, unconsciously feeling the end of his right index finger, testing it against his thumb and the table edge. The burning sensation was there still. Whenever he had thought about it since that first day he had felt it begin to swell and throb. Inside him a voice kept saying, "You'll have to tell! You'll have to tell! It'll burn forever if you don't tell."

He jerked his hand down to his lap as he saw his mother's eyes on him.

"What's the matter with your finger? You've been doing that for two or three days."

"Nothing. It ain't sore. Just a habit, I guess."

"I'll never tell," he told himself. "They'll never even suspect me."

And after dinner, when he went in to help his mother with the dishes, he found that the fear and agony had left him. His mind was full of a strange and sorrowful peace, and the finger no longer throbbed.

He was safe, he assured himself secretly, intensely. He would never tell.

THE END

↻ **Talking it over**

1. *a.* How does Fred feel about the Haskells? How do his feelings toward them make the accident seem even more horrible to him?

b. What kind of person is Fred? Give evidence from the story. What effect would these qualities have on the way he feels?

2. *a.* Why does Fred's home seem like a prison to him after the accident?

b. As Fred agonizes about what to do next, what possible solutions occur to him? Why does he reject each of them except one?

c. Why does the author keep our

attention focused on Fred, rather than taking us along with the search party when it discovers the body?

3. At a certain point, Fred stops worrying about what he should do. He feels that "his problem had been taken out of his hands" (363b, 10) and that from now on he can act only in a certain way. In what way have Fred's feelings changed?

4. *a.* Why does Fred feel a burning in his index finger? What does it mean to him?

b. What is meant by the statement, ". . . he realized that the stain of blood goes deeper than the skin" (361a, 4)?

c. Discuss whether "Bloodstain" is a good title for this story. If you think it is not, suggest a better one.

5. The author of "Bloodstain" again and again uses comparison and contrast to emphasize certain ideas. For example, when he says, "[Fred's] shout of triumph died to a sound half-scream, half-whimper, that trailed out of his lips and left his mouth open" he is contrasting SOUNDS to make you feel Fred's shock and horror.

Reread the passages indicated below. In each one, what is being compared or contrasted? What point is the author making?

a. The description beginning "His whole body was vibrant . . . ." (359a, 5) and the description in the paragraph beginning "A shrill scream split his throat . . . ." (360b, 1)

b. The section beginning with the sentence "Through the half-drawn curtains he saw a group of boys playing baseball in the vacant lot next door" (end of paragraph at top of 361b) and continuing through the next four paragraphs.

c. The descriptions of Mr. Haskell in the paragraph beginning "The spectre of discovery . . . ." (364b, 4) and the paragraph following.

6. *a.* At the end of the story, Fred no longer feels fear and agony and his finger no longer throbs. Does this mean that he no longer feels guilty? Explain your answer.

b. Reread the last sentence in the story. Do you think he really will be able to go through life without ever confessing? Explain.

Words in action

People who take up certain sports, hobbies, and occupations often find that words they already know have taken on new and special meanings. Hunting is one sport that has its own special vocabulary.

The following sentences are from "Bloodstain." In each one, the word or words in bold type have a special meaning when used by a hunter. Try to figure out this special meaning from the context, then explain it in your own words. Use a dictionary if you need help.

1. Carrying the shotgun **at trail,** he fixed his whole attention on the underbrush ahead.

2. In all that time he had not **started** a single rabbit, and his vigilance had flagged, so that when a snowshoe **broke** and vanished under his very nose he didn't even get the gun to his shoulder.

3. With elaborate care the boy **cocked** both **barrels,** raised the gun, aimed, and pretended to snap the triggers.

4. This time his gun was **uncocked,** and the **safety on.**

I began to think how sad my mother would feel, losing her son and all.

When you run away

by George H. Freitag

THERE was a time when my brother David was a small boy and I was twelve or so that my mother seemed to favor him more than she did me. It seemed that she was always being nicer to him. He was a good-looking boy with large brown eyes and deep dimples and pudgy soft hands, and I did not have brown eyes or deep dimples or pudgy soft hands; not that I wanted them. I was tall and skinny and my face was starting to come out with pimples.

One time when I was out in the back yard I thought about my brother. I hid behind a bush and watched my mother spread a piece of jelly bread for him and noticed how tender she was and the way she not only handed him the jelly bread but kissed him on the forehead. It wasn't that I wanted to be kissed on the forehead; it was just the fact that

she didn't have to do it to David. While I sat under the bush in the back yard I began to think how sad it would be if I ran off. I don't mean how sad I would feel but how sad my mother would feel, losing her twelve-year-old son and all. I guess when you came right down to it I wasn't much to have or not have; it was just that I was the older child and had been around a long time. I knew my mother would fret and be sorry. I don't think she ever realized that she wasn't spreading jelly bread for me any more. Maybe she thought I was old enough to do it myself. Just the same she never did it any more, but all David had to do when he wanted a slice of jelly bread was look hungry and undernourished and he got it.

In a way it made me a little sad myself at the thought of my mother's feeling sad that I might leave. I spent some time drawing maps of ways to run away. I showed the icehouse and the

This selection first appeared in *Atlantic Monthly* (December 1959). Reprinted by permission of the author.

train tracks and the large maple tree; things that would serve as specific places. The weather was nice; it was summer and the lilacs were in bloom and the nights were filled with lovely sounds and scents. There wouldn't be any problem about it. I thought for a while that I might go around and say farewell to my friends. But I liked them too well to have them feel sad at my going away. I was at an age when one is apt to make a very important decision quite by accident. And I did not want to let anyone know I was going. When you are old you make planned decisions, everything carefully worked out, but when you are a boy of twelve there is still time to make a few accidental decisions that change the course of your life.

I used to pity my father, who was tied so to my mother's apron strings. He went about his life in such a calculated way, doing all the proper things like going to work and coming home and wiping his mouth with a napkin during meals, coming and going with punctual regularity. I guess the town clock was even set by his routine. He did not have a thought of his own. He went to work and worked. He came home and was home. On the lines that were woven across my father's forehead was written the word "obligation." Poor, poor man.

A fellow knows pretty much what he is about at twelve. So just to try out my brother, I asked him to fetch me things. I wanted him to refuse so that I would have more reason to run away. "Go fetch me my lousy shoes, David," I yelled at him. He was four years old. He went to where I had hidden my shoes and brought them back.

"Here's your shoes," he said.

"Go fetch me a pencil and paper and an eraser and a box of crayons and don't come back until you have everything."

My little brother went out of the room and in about an hour he came back with everything; he even found the lost crayons. Then he made more trips and brought back things I never knew we had.

"See what a nice brother you have?" my mother said, giving him a smack-kiss on the cheek, but I only glowered at my mother. Then I spent more time drawing maps and getting my clothes together, a shirt, a pair of sandals to keep from getting stone bruises, my spyglass that I got with breakfast cereal, the one where the magnifying glass came in one box and another part in a different box until after forty-three boxes of breakfast cereal I had the spyglass. You don't know how many parts a spyglass has until you commence to eat breakfast cereal. I put my slingshot in the pack, too, and a calendar to know what day it was and how long I was gone, and a picture of my mother and father taken coming out of the Ritz-Balou picture show carrying a potted fern that my mother had won. I had other things in the pack, too, things like rope and a candle and a piece of moving-picture film of Rin Tin Tin[1] moving his head from one side of the picture to the other, and a harmonica. Everybody who runs away carries a harmonica and sometimes it is just on the strength of one that a fellow gets a free meal somewhere.

The night I went away was very quiet and peaceful. My mother and my brother had gone to bed early. My father had been marched off to work,

---

[1] Rin Tin Tin, a German shepherd dog who appeared in many movies in the 1920's.

carrying his dinner bucket, and was already doing his job because the whole sky was ablaze. My father worked in a steel mill and you could see the reflection of fire in the sky. That was my father opening the furnace doors of the mill. I looked into the sky and my father seemed to be all over it, skipping around in the fleecy clouds like a spirit. He was working hard just so he could come back home in the morning and walk down the street and nod good morning to all the neighbors who were getting up and having their breakfast and start the dogs to barking and the cats to scurrying over the back-yard fences.

Men coming home in the evening can be just as tired as men coming home in the morning, but in the evening the sun is going down and one does not see the tiredness on a worker's face. In the morning the sun is fresh and new and it seeks out all kinds of things about a man's face and you can see fatigue on it then.

My father came home under the gaze of the new clean sun. Then he fitted himself back in the mold of being a husband and a father, of sprinkling the lawn and mowing it, of picking things up if my mother dropped them.

I was going to let myself down from the second-story window of my bedroom, but even though my mother had forgotten to bring in the mattress that she had put out to air, the drop was too much for a fellow my age, and I tiptoed down the stairs with my sack of things thrown over my shoulder. When I got outside I turned around and looked the neighborhood over. I had never seen it that late except once when my father and I had to find a doctor for my mother. All of my father's garden lay under

a film of dew and was so still that you could hear the things grow. When a leaf died you could hear it drop from the stalk and fall to the ground.

I remembered watching my grandfather die a year or so before. He had been a shoemaker. He lay in the long white bed and his long tapered fingers spread out across his chest and he said to me in German: "It is like being a petal on a flower. First you are a part of the flower, then you are growing into a grandfather, and after you are a grandfather you commence to shrivel up and I am shriveling up now." In the way the silence of the night spread itself across the expanse of yard, I remembered my grandfather's voice as it died. I remembered the cold room and the fragrance of sickness in the room. I remembered the light that flickered by my grandfather's bed. I never smell a pair of good shoes that I do not think of my grandfather's hands.

I said good-bye to the yard where my father's garden lay. I said good-bye to the alley and even the rotten clothesline post at the corner of the lot. I turned and grew sadder still at the darkness of the whole house and at the windows that looked empty and evil, like a toothless woman. As I walked in the direction of the railroad tracks, the light my father made in the sky, now pink, now a deep vermilion, followed me. It pranced about and cavorted with the clouds and rolled and billowed like a wave of fire. I wanted to wake everyone up and say to them: "That is my father doing the fire," like you would say of someone on the stage: "The sound you hear is my brother making the wind blow."

Finally I heard the train. I swung the pack over my shoulder and went

through the back yards of houses until I saw the whirling, searching headlights of the train. Then the whistle blew, two long utterances of sound the way I always heard them while I lay in my bed in my own room and made up stories in my head about where the train would take me. And now I was there close to it, so close, in fact, that I could feel the suction of air and the pressure of steam and the vibration of its energy upon the ground. Then I got on and lifted myself into an open boxcar that didn't really seem to want to belong to the rest, for it swayed and pulled al-

ways in opposite ways from the others, and I said to myself, that it, too, was a part of a plan of things just like my father.

The buildings of my own town went by, the back yards of houses went by, and the fences and street lights and churches. Then we went into a strange kind of place and I looked out again to find that the train was coming to a stop and all the boxcars were being sidetracked. We were in the freightyards and a man said, his face against the flickering lantern: "I guess that winds it up for tonight." Then the engine itself went somewhere and the engineer climbed down and soon the whole place, like my own back yard, was still. I crawled down out of the car and I knew the night was growing old. I looked into the sky; there was just a flicker of my father glowing there, just a flash now and then of him opening the furnace doors. I walked over to the engine. "How do I get back to the place you found me?" I cried, but the engine was still. It gasped once or twice, as if from indigestion, but it was cooling down and resting. The thirty-one cars that had comprised the full train stood scattered at every conceivable angle, yellow cars, white and red cars, blue and black.

I began to follow the tracks; there were so many. Some did nothing more than circle; others went out and stopped. It was difficult to find the one I wanted. In the distance I heard a dog. The dog seemed to be calling for its master. Where could the master be? I walked in every direction for a short while, then doubled back. Then I sat down and rested. I opened the pack to get out my red sweater, the one I used to wear selling garden seeds house to house. My harmonica fell out, so I played a few tunes on it just to hear how a harmonica sounded in the freight-yard. It sounded weak. When I put the harmonica back was when a sandwich that my mother must have fixed for me fell out, and an orange. I ripped off the wax paper and commenced to eat. It was my mother's way, I guess, of fitting me to the mold; you never know what a woman has in her head. I ate the whole sandwich and the orange, too, and played my harmonica again. Then I stood up and commenced to run, wiping my mouth with the back of my hand. I don't know why I was in such a hurry, unless I was afraid the sun would soon come out and show the homesickness written across my face.

THE END

↻ **Talking it over**

1. *a.* What reasons does the boy give for wanting to run away? Are his judgments sound, or is he jumping to conclusions? Explain.

   b. Why does he ask his brother to do certain things for him?

2. *a.* What things does he plan to take with him when he runs away? Do you think his selections show careful thought? Explain.

   b. What repeatedly reminds the boy of his father? How does this affect him as he is running away?

3. *a.* What finally prevents him from running away?

   b. At the end of the story, how do you know he is running toward home?

   c. In the time that the boy has been gone, would the things that caused him to run away have changed? Why then does he decide to go back?

4. What do you think the mother had in mind when she put the sandwich and the orange in the boy's sack?

5. Reread the following: the opening sentence of the story; the last sentence in paragraph 3; the first sentence in paragraph 5; paragraph 11. Which of the following seems to you to best describe the author of this selection? Why?

   a. A boy of twelve years, writing about his own experiences

b. A boy of twelve, making up a story

c. An older man, writing about his boyhood experiences

d. An older man, making up a story about a boy

3. Before Grace joined the chorus she had never sung in _____ with anyone before.

4. I think a lighter blue would _____ better with the colors you already have in your room.

5. All the neighborhood children played together in a _____ group.

6. It's fun at a party to _____ while someone plays the guitar.

⇄ **Words in action**

The boy who runs away takes with him a **harmonica**. "Everybody who runs away carries a harmonica," he claims, "and sometimes it is just on the strength of one that a fellow gets a free meal somewhere."

What kind of musical instrument is a harmonica? How might the boy get a free meal with it?

Harmonious, harmonize, and **harmony** are three other words which begin with *harmon-*. They all have something to do with music, but they have other meanings as well. Look up these words in a dictionary. What do these other meanings have in common? In the sentences which follow, these three *harmon-* words are used in both their musical sense and their other sense.

Decide which word—*harmonious, harmonize,* or *harmony*—belongs in each of the following sentences and write that word on your paper after the number of the sentence. Each word is used twice.

1. We were surprised when we visited the farm to find three cats, a couple of dogs, and a tame skunk living together in perfect _____.

2. The wind chimes tinkling gently in the doorway made a _____ sound

Photo by Curt Armstrong

He had a love for expressing himself

George H. Freitag gained an international reputation for his short stories, most of which, like "When You Run Away," are based on events remembered from his childhood. His stories have been translated into many languages and have been broadcast by Radio Free Europe and Radio Free Asia. He was most proud, however, of those stories which were published in Braille for the blind.

Mr. Freitag also wrote a novel and taught creative writing, yet he always earned his living as a sign painter. "I have a love for expressing myself," he said. When he was unable to type after suffering a stroke, he continued to write stories in longhand, standing up at a work table in his shop.

The Day the TV Broke

by Gerald Jonas

It was awful. First,
the silence. I thought I'd die.
This is the worst,
I said to myself, but I
5 was wrong. Soon, the house began to speak.
(There are boards in the halls
that creak
when no foot falls.
The wind strains
10 at the door, as if in pursuit
of someone inside, and when it rains,
the drainpipe croaks. Nothing is mute.)
That night, there came a noise from the shelves
like mice creeping.
15 It was the books, reading themselves
out loud to keep me from sleeping.
I can tell you I was glad to see
the repairman arrive.
Say what you will about a TV—
20 at least it isn't alive.

From *Saturday Review*, February 25, 1967. Reprinted
by permission of the author and *Saturday Review*.

1. *a.* With what words does the poem suggest that *things* in the house sometimes seem alive?

b. Why does each of the things mentioned seem threatening?

2. Why does the speaker prefer the "dead" TV set to the other more "alive" objects in the house? How does he express this feeling? ("Who's afraid of TV?" below will help you answer this question.)

3. *a.* What central idea does the poem suggest about the effect of TV on people's lives?

b. Do you think the poem is meant to be serious or funny? Explain your answer.

Who's afraid of TV?

Gerald Jonas did not own a television set at the time he wrote this poem. A friend had loaned him his set, and when Mr. Jonas returned it after several months, he became aware of strange noises in the house—noises that he had not noticed before.

He feels that one thing wrong with television is that it does not cause you to be involved in what is going on. Being really involved—as in a close relationship between people—can mean danger, and risk, and a kind of fear, fear of not measuring up. "Television has a great impact in many ways, but who ever heard of someone being *afraid* of a television set? I can think of a number of books that frightened me—and I don't mean horror tales. Rather, books that challenge me, books that make me feel inadequate because I sense their importance but have trouble understanding them, books that leave me with the truly terrifying thought: Maybe I've been wrong about a lot of things (or even, Maybe I've been wrong about everything)."

Mr. Jonas is a staff writer for the *New Yorker* magazine. He has written short stories, poems, and articles on sports, drama, and many other subjects. Some of his stories and poems are science fiction; he considers "The Day the TV Broke" to be one of these.

WANTED:
Nice people to adopt a little girl.
References required.

by Zona Gale

BILL WAS thirty when his wife died, and little Minna was four. Bill's carpenter shop was in the yard of his house, so he thought that he could keep up his home for Minna and himself. All day while he worked at his bench, she played in the yard, and when he was obliged to be absent for a few hours, the woman next door looked after her.

Bill could cook a little, coffee and bacon and fried potatoes and flapjacks, and he found bananas and sardines and crackers useful. When the woman next door said this was not the diet for four-year-olds, he asked her to teach him to cook oatmeal and vegetables, and though he always burned the dishes in which he cooked these things, he cooked them every day.

He swept, all but the corners, and he dusted, dabbing at every object; and he complained that after he had cleaned the windows he could not see out as well as he could before. He washed and patched Minna's little garments and mended her doll. He found a kitten for her so that she wouldn't be lonely.

At night he heard her say her prayer, kneeling in the middle of the floor with her hands folded and speaking like lightning. If he forgot the prayer, he either woke her up, or else he made her say it the first thing next morning. He himself used to try to pray: "Lord, make me do right by her if you see me doing wrong." On Sundays he took her to church and sat listening with his head on one side, trying to understand, and giving Minna peppermints when she rustled. He stopped work for a day and took her to the Sunday school picnic. "Her mother would of," he explained.

When Minna was old enough to go to kindergarten, Bill used to take her morning or afternoon, and he would call for her. Once he dressed himself in his best clothes and went to visit the school. "I think her mother would of," he told the teacher, diffidently. But he could make little of the colored paper and the designs and the games, and he did not go again. "There's some things I can't be any help to her with," he thought.

Minna was six when Bill fell ill. On a May afternoon he went to a doctor. When he came home he sat in his shop for a long time and did nothing. The sun was beaming through the window in bright squares. He was not going to get well. It might be that he had six months. . . . He could hear Minna singing to her doll.

When she came to kiss him that night, he made an excuse, for he must never kiss her now. He held her at arm's length, looked in her eyes, said, "Minna's a big girl now. She doesn't want papa to kiss her." But her lip curled and she turned away sorrowful, so the next day Bill went to another doctor to make sure. The other doctor made him sure.

He tried to think what to do. He had a sister in Nebraska, but she was a tired woman. His wife had a brother in the city, but he was a man of many words. And little Minna—there were things known to her which he himself did not know—matters of fairies and the words of songs. He wished that he could hear of somebody who would understand her. And he had only six months. . . .

Then the woman next door told him bluntly that he ought not to have the child there, and him coughing as he was; and he knew that his decision was already upon him.

One whole night he thought. Then he advertised in a city paper:

A man with a few months to live would like nice people to adopt his little girl, six, blue eyes, curls. References required.

They came in a limousine, as he had hoped that they would come. Their clothes were as he had hoped. They had with them a little girl who cried, "Is this my little sister?" On which the woman in the smart frock said sharply:

"Now then, you do as Mama tells you and keep out of this, or we'll leave you here and take this darling little girl away with us."

So Bill looked at this woman and said steadily that he had now other plans for his little girl. He watched the great blue car roll away. "For the land sake!" said the woman next door when she heard. "You done her out of a fortune. You hadn't the right—a man in your health." And when other cars came, and he let them go, this woman told her husband that Bill ought most certainly to be reported to the authorities.

The man and woman who walked into Bill's shop one morning were still mourning their own little girl. The woman was not sad—only sorrowful —and the man, who was tender of her, was a carpenter. In a blooming of his hope and his dread, Bill said to them, "You're the ones." When they asked, "How long before we can have her?" Bill said, "One day more."

That day he spent in the shop. It was summer and Minna was playing in the yard. He could hear the words of her songs. He cooked their supper and while she ate, he watched. When he had tucked her in her bed, he stood in the dark, hearing her breathing. "I'm a little girl tonight—kiss me," she said, but he shook his head. "A big girl, a big girl," he told her.

When they came for her the next morning, he had her ready, and her little garments were ready, washed and mended, and he had mended her doll. "Minna's never been for a visit!" he told her buoyantly. And when she ran toward him, "A big girl, a big girl," he reminded her.

He stood and watched the man and woman walking down the street with Minna between them. They had brought her a little blue parasol in case the parting should be hard. This parasol Minna held bobbing above her head, and she was so absorbed in looking up at the blue silk that she did not remember to turn and wave her hand. THE END

⟳ **Talking it over**

1. Each of the following character descriptions gives a clear impression of the person. Explain what you infer about each of these people.

a. ". . . a sister in Nebraska, but she was a tired woman."

b. ". . . a brother in the city, but he was a man of many words."

c. ". . . there were things known to [Minna] which he himself did not know—matters of fairies and the words of songs."

2. The author also makes it possible for you to infer a great deal about people from what they do and say. Check through the story to find what the fol-lowing people do and say, and then de-scribe each person in your own words.

a. The woman next door
b. The woman in the blue car
c. Bill

3. What leads Bill to select the family he does?

4. Why do you think the author didn't call the story "Minna"? What title would you have given it?

Small-town life made her famous

Zona Gale was born in Portage, Wisconsin, and lived there most of her life. She became well known as a writer of realistic stories filled with "local color"—details of life which are asso-ciated with one particular part of the country. Her home town became fa-mous as "Friendship Village," the name she gave it in her stories.

In addition to short stories, Miss Gale wrote poetry, novels, plays, and articles for newspapers. Her novelette *Miss Lulu Bett* became a best seller. She rewrote it into a play, which won the Pulitzer Prize.

How Zona Gale came to write "Bill" is interesting. She explained, "The city editor of the New York *Evening World* once handed me a cutting from the want ads of that day's *Morning World*. 'Go and find what lies back of that,' he said.

"The advertisement was that one which I have included in the story of Bill. His story is rather like that of the man who had advertised.

"I do not recall this man's name. I never saw him again. But I still have his photograph, with that of the little girl."

THE GOLDEN AXE

*With the spirit of George Washington
in him, coming into his arms,
he raised the axe, and . . .*

by Ralph Scholl

CHARACTERS: **Jeb Wiliker**
Sheriff Henry Thompson
Young Widow Evans

TIME: **The present.**
PLACE: **An old-fashioned farmhouse
in the Missouri Ozarks.**

SCENE ONE:

It is late on a summer afternoon, in an old-fashioned farmhouse kitchen in the Missouri Ozarks. It has that "bachelor lives here" quality. There is a cookstove and an old-fashioned sink upon which sits a bucket of drinking water and a dipper. Above the sink hangs a cracked mirror. A door at the right of the stage leads to the outside; near this door is a large window. Left of center is a large old-fashioned table with three

chairs. A fourth chair is near the outside door. To the left of the room is another door which is closed.

When the curtain opens, we see Jeb sitting in the chair near the outside door. He is Lincolnesque, and moves his long gangly body rather lazily. He wears bib overalls, a blue shirt, and clodhopper shoes. Right now, his face serious, he is bending over a double-bitted axe while he sharpens it to a fine edge with a whetstone.

The Sheriff is striding back and forth in front of Jeb. He is one of those short, fat men who are constantly moving about, never at rest, and consequently always puffing. Ordinarily, his jowled face is good-humored, jovial, and friendly; but right now he is upset and wears a worried expression. Like Jeb, the Sheriff wears bib overalls, but owing to the dignity of his position in life (that of Sheriff of Saline Creek County) he wears a white shirt, a large red tie, and a double-breasted suit coat. Pinned proudly and conspicuously to the front of this coat is a large silver star which says simply "Sheriff." On his hip he wears an old Colt revolver. Suddenly the Sheriff stops striding back and forth in front of Jeb and brings his fist down on the table.

Sheriff (*desperately*): Don't do it, Jeb, don't do it!

Jeb (*with quiet determination, still sharpening the axe*): Got to, Henry.

Sheriff (*after a thoughtful pause, regretfully*): If you go ahead and use that axe, you know what that means, Jeb.

Jeb: Yep, I know.

Sheriff (*exasperated*): Then why do it?

Jeb: Got to.

Sheriff: But why?

Jeb: Cain't stop meself.

Sheriff: Well, why don't you *try?*

Jeb (*rubbing whetstone on the axe*): Wouldn't like meself.

Sheriff: But the *law,* Jeb?

Jeb (*disgustedly*): Humph!

Sheriff (*suddenly brisk and efficient, taking command of the situation*): Jeb, as Sheriff of this here county, I got to take action. God knows what they'll do to you! So I just ain't agonna let you do it!

Jeb: No?

Sheriff: No! I'll put you in jail first— for your own good.

Jeb (*calmly, still whetting the axe*): Cain't.

Sheriff: Cain't what?

Jeb: Cain't put me in jail. Ain't done nothin'. You got to wait 'til I done somethin' 'fore you kin put me in jail. (*looking up from the axe to the Sheriff*) And I ain't done nothin', so you cain't put me in jail yet.

Sheriff (*moving away, reflectively rubbing his hand on his chin*): Yeah, I guess that's so, Jeb. (*shrewdly*) Well, I guess I cain't stop you, all

right. . . . (*in a casual, offhand manner*) When you figure on doin' it, Jeb?

Jeb (*testing the edge of the axe with his thumb*): Soon's this here axe is sharp 'nough—and you ain't around.

Sheriff (*triumphantly, sitting down*): Then, by Grabees, I'm goin' to just set here and watch you! And just as you go to do it, I'm goin' to stop you and put you in jail for disturbin' the peace!

Jeb: Cain't do that, Henry.

Sheriff: And why cain't I?

Jeb: 'Cause I kin outset you. I been settin' here a year and not doin' it, so I guess I kin set a little longer. (*continuing to whet the axe*) 'Sides, you got to go vote gettin' tonight. You know well as I do that sooner or later I'm goin' to do it. So you might jist as well traipse off 'fore it gits dark and git your votes, and let me do what I got to do now and git it over with.

(*The Sheriff puts his hand on Jeb's shoulder.*)

Sheriff (*sentimentally*): Jeb, me and you has always been friends, ain't we?

Jeb: Yep. We always been friends. We're still friends.

Sheriff: That's right. (*speaking warmly and affectionately*) Now look here, Jeb. . . . (*The Sheriff takes off his badge.*) I'm a-layin' down my badge on the table here. . . . (*He lays down the badge, takes his gun out and lays it on the table.*) And I'm a-layin' down my gun, too. . . . Now don't think of me as Sheriff no more. Think of me as a friend. We've had good times as friends, ain't we?

Jeb: Sure have.

Sheriff: How long've we knowed each other? How long've we been friends, Jeb?

Jeb: Ever since we been born.

Sheriff: Right! We been friends ever since both of us was born. Why, we growed up together. We played together as kids. We chased the gals together. We even both courted Sally. And when she chose me, who was the best man at my weddin' ten year ago?

Jeb: Me.

Sheriff: You sure was! That's the kind of friends we was! And it's the kind of friends we still are now.

Jeb: Sure are.

Sheriff: Why, even now when you're a-sparkin' the young Widder Evans, and I come right out and say what I think of her, and she comes right out and tells you what she thinks of me —it don't make no difference. 'Cause me and you are still the same old friends, ain't we?

Jeb: Yep, and we'll still be friends even if'n I get the young Widder to marry me—which ain't likely.

Sheriff (*getting emotional and oratorical*): Friends! Why, we been friends through good times and bad times, no matter what! Ain't that so?

Jeb: Yep.

Sheriff: Then as a friend, Jeb, I'm askin' you from the bottom of my heart: will you put that axe down before somethin' terrible happens? (*gently, softly*) Will you, Jeb, for a friend?

(*While the Sheriff leans toward him, tensed and waiting for an answer to his question, Jeb puts down the axe, slowly and thoughtfully uncrosses his legs, takes out of his pocket a plug of tobacco, then a pocketknife, and carves a piece off the plug into his mouth. He returns the knife to his pocket, absently puts the tobacco on the table, and very slowly recrosses his legs. Then he speaks to the waiting Sheriff.*)

Jeb: Nope.

Sheriff (*sighing*): I guess it jist ain't no use.

Jeb: I told you it weren't.

Sheriff: But why, Jeb? *Why?*

Jeb: Come here, Henry. (*Jeb goes to the open door that leads to the yard outside the house. The Sheriff follows him. They stand there, looking out.*) Look out there, Henry. Acrost that new highway in front of my door is the hills. And behind the hills is the settin' sun. You know, some folks like sunup, but me, I like my sundown best.

Sheriff: Never could figure out why some folks like one better'n t'other. Why do you like sunset best, Jeb?

Jeb: I'm awake more.

Sheriff (*thoughtfully*): Hmmm. . . . I ain't never thought of it that-a-way.

Jeb: You know, Henry, I ain't never seen nothin' prettier happen in God's whole world than what I seen right here, standin' at my own door or settin' out there on the porch.

Sheriff: I know just what you mean.

Jeb: Why, I seen them hills out there look like God had all of a sudden busted a great big gold egg plop smack dab on top of 'em—and I've watched while the gold all run down, catchin' on the tops of the trees and stumps and rocks, makin' the tree tops look all stickery with gold, like the hairs on the leg of a bee in the sun.

Sheriff: Purty, all right.

Jeb: Yep, I've set and watched while the evenin' run in like blue water, fillin' up all the hollers and then floodin' over the tops of the trees.

Sheriff (*sadness in his voice*): Yeah, Jeb, I seen it before like that myself.

Jeb: But do you see it now, Henry?

Sheriff: No.

Jeb (*angrily*): You gol-durned right you don't! And neither do I! And why? Because they put that infernal signboard up on the edge of the highway, and that signboard's as big as a barn. A body cain't stand here nor set out there on the porch and see the sunset on them hills no more. Everthin's all hid behind that sign! All you kin see is that great skinny woman on that signboard.

Sheriff (*sadly, but trying to calm Jeb down*): Well, I admit you cain't see the sunset no more, Jeb, and that gal is purty skinny—bet she's near a hundred foot tall—and she ain't actin' ladylike neither, come to think of it. But still, you oughtn't to go out there and chop that signboard down, Jeb.

(*Jeb goes back to his chair, still carrying his axe, and sits down. His shoulders sag, but he speaks with determination.*)

Jeb: Henry, that sign's been up there almost a year, now. I cain't fight it no more. I got to cut 'er down.

Sheriff: You do that and you'll have to go to jail, Jeb. And you cain't scrape up enough money to hire a lawyer, or even bail yourself out. I don't know what'll happen to you. Why, they'll prob'ly take you out of my jail and put you in some dirty old big city prison. And then you'll *never* git to see the sunset!

Jeb: Some things a man has got to do, Henry.

Sheriff: But Jeb, you ain't got no legal right to chop down that sign.

Jeb: I got a right to see the sunset, Henry. That's my right.

Sheriff: Maybe so, but that won't stand up in court.

(*Jeb gets up and goes to the cracked mirror over the sink. He carefully selects a hair, pulls it out of his head, and, holding it between the thumb and forefinger of his left hand, cuts it with the axe.*)

Jeb: Well, she's sharp 'nough.

Sheriff: Say, Jeb, how come you look in the mirror to pull out a hair?

Jeb: So's I git the gray ones while I'm at it. A young Widder don't like no gray-headed bachelor.

Sheriff: You know, sometimes when I think about you and the Widder I git to worryin' a little. I'm afeerd you'll marry her and then she'll boss you to death. You'll do nothin' but *work* from sunup to sundown.

Jeb: Well, Henry, I used to worry a little 'bout that, too. But I don't worry much no more.

Sheriff: How come?

Jeb: Well, I been sparkin' the Widder for two year now. And she still holds off. Somehow she don't seem eager to git married.

Sheriff: Heck, she'll marry you, Jeb. The Widder's young, and the Widder's good lookin', but you don't have too much competition. 'Cause she's got one little thing against her that scares off all the rest of the single bucks in the county.

Jeb: Maybe so, but she still don't seem eager.

Sheriff: You're a brave man, Jeb. All the other bachelors 'round here would spark the Widder, but they're 'fraid to, seein' as how she buried two husbands in ten year.

Jeb: Aw—her husbands jist got sick like everybody else does once't in awhile. Only they died, 'stead of gittin' well.

Sheriff: They died 'cause they was all wore out from workin' too hard. The Widder just managed them to death. Only you don't want to admit it, even to yourself. *(after a pause)* Maybe she's been holdin' off 'cause you ain't rich enough. . . .

Jeb: 'Tain't that. Why, I paid seven hundred dollar for this here farm. 'Course it ain't nothin' but red dirt, and rocks and scrub oak—but that seven hundred dollar was my life's work. And the farm's all mine, so I ain't so poor.

Sheriff: Jeb, the Widder's jist playin' hard to git.

Jeb: Think so?

Sheriff: Sure. Why, I seen her sell an old wore-out horse collar to John Hanks once't. And the way she acted you'd've thought it was the best horse collar in the county—even if the stuffin' was all comin' out of it. She acted like it plumb broke her heart to have to part with it. Why, poor old John was a-beggin' her to sell it to him for four dollar 'fore it was all over. And it weren't worth two-bits. But you know how it is, when a thing is hard to git, people wants it more. And the Widder knows that. . . . Excuse me for comparin' the woman you love to a wore-out horse collar, Jeb. Didn't mean it the way it sounded.

Jeb: That's all right, Henry. Lots of folks in this county think the Widder is a little greedy when it comes to money.

Sheriff: You know, Jeb, the Widder is a law abidin' woman. If you go ahead with that there axe, I kin tell you somethin' for sure: she ain't never goin' to have nothin' to do with you agin.

Jeb *(sadly)*: That so? *(with a touch of rancor)* Well, to tell the truth, I'm kind of mad at her now, anyways.

Sheriff: How come?

Jeb: Well, she come over here to borry some 'taters this mornin'.

Sheriff: Now Jeb, jist 'cause a body borries 'taters once't in awhile ain't no call to git mad at 'em—unless they don't pay 'em back.

Jeb: But her borryin' them 'taters was jist an excuse so's she could torment me to tell her what I was goin' to do 'bout that sign—and then to run to town and git you to stop me.

Sheriff: Jist doin' my duty, Jeb.

Jeb: I know, Henry, and I forgive you for it.

(The men are silent for a moment. The Sheriff is thinking. Then he speaks.)

Sheriff: Look here, Jeb: be reasonable.

Why, the Widder told me the sign company pays the county ninety dollar a year for that land. County got it for back taxes from John Hanks five year ago, you know. Now ain't they got a right to that money?

Jeb: Henry, I ain't sayin' it's wrong for the county to own a piece of ground. But does any man own the air?

Sheriff: No, I guess no man owns the air, Jeb.

Jeb: They sure don't. If they did, they'd charge you for breathin'. Ain't that so?

Sheriff (*thoughtfully*): Well—bein' a legal man—(*stopping and pondering for a moment*) my opinion is this: Yes. If somebody owned the air, they would charge you for usin' it. Besides, if somebody owned the air the government would tax 'em for it. . . . So I guess nobody owns the air. (*The Sheriff and Jeb are silent and thoughtful for a moment. Then the Sheriff speaks.*) Sure I cain't change your mind, Jeb?

Jeb: Yep, I'm sure.

Sheriff: Well, I done said my piece, and it's time to be off politickin' if I don't want to lose no votes. (*The Sheriff goes toward the door. Jeb gets up and follows him. The Sheriff, looking out the door, sees something that catches his interest. He cranes his neck, looking to his right.*) Hey, Jeb, here comes the Widder! She's runnin' lickety split down the highway toward us. Bet she's comin' here.

Jeb (*a little exasperated*): A man cain't seem to get a thing done 'round here with all this visitin' goin' on!

(*The Sheriff, at the door, turns around.*)

Sheriff: But I think you're makin' a mountain out of a molehill, Jeb. And that s'prises me—never knowed anythin' to rile *you* up afore. You was always so calm.

Jeb: Henry, did you ever look out of your winder and see a woman taller'n a barn? No matter if you look forty times a day, there she is, grinnin' down at you.

Sheriff: Yeah, I guess it's been purty bad for you, Jeb. But you know, what they'll do to you after you chop 'er down is goin' to be a whole lot worse than what you got now.

Jeb: (*paying no attention to the Sheriff*): Maybe I wouldn't mind so much if the signboard woman was sellin' somethin' I could use. Like if she was holdin' a big new shiny tractor in one hand and a manure spreader in th' other, maybe it wouldn't be so bad. (*talking like an obsessed man*) And she's skinny, too. She's so tall and she's all hollow cheeked, and one lip is all crooked where the paper was put on wrong, and . . . (*trying to get himself under control*) I tell you, Henry, that havin' a ninety-foot tall woman standin' over him all day *does* somethin' to a man! (*The Sheriff goes part way out the door.*)

Sheriff: Well, I sure hope there ain't no hard feelin's on your part when I have to put you in jail for choppin' 'er down, Jeb.

Jeb: There won't be, Henry.

Sheriff: Fine. And say, be sure and fell 'er off the highway, won't you, Jeb?

Jeb: Henry, did you ever know me to have a tree jump out of line?

Sheriff: No, but this ain't quite like no tree! (*after a slight pause*) Well, 'night, Jeb. See you in jail.

Jeb: 'Night, Henry.

(*The Sheriff exits. Jeb goes to the table. We hear the Sheriff speaking to someone outside.*)

Sheriff (*from off stage*): Evenin', Widder. Nice summer evenin', ain't it?

Widow (*from off stage, breathless from running*): Evenin', Sheriff. . . . I s'pose.

(*Jeb picks up a plug of tobacco and turns toward the door. The Widow Evans is standing in the open doorway. She is plump, and there is a shrewd, calculating look about her eyes and mouth, not in keeping with her flirtatious walk, or, at times, her glances. She is dressed in a neat print dress and in the pocket of her blouse she carries an account book and a pencil. Her chest heaves from the effort of running. She knocks on the door jamb. Jeb sighs, goes to the door with the axe still in his hand.*)

Jeb (*sighing*): Might's well come on in, Widder.

Widow (*out of breath*): Jeb, I run all the way over here.

Jeb (*calmly*): Runnin's bad for the heart, Widder. (*Jeb and the Widow cross to the table. Jeb gives the Widow a chair.*) Here, set down.

(*The Widow sits down. Jeb remains standing.*)

Widow: Ever since this mornin' when you told me what you was goin' to do, I been thinkin' about it. And a little while ago I made up my mind. I got to stop you. (*looking up at him meaningfully*) And that means I got to tell you somethin'. . . .

Jeb: Now you jist set there a minute, Widder, and rest a mite. I'll be right back.

(*Jeb moves toward the door with his axe in hand.*)

Widow (*standing up*): I run and I run and I run and I kept sayin', "I hope he ain't done it yet. I got to tell him afore it's too late."

(*Jeb turns around at the door, and faces her.*)

Jeb: 'Scuse me a minute, Widder. . . . Be back afore you kin ketch your breath.

(*The Widow runs toward him.*)

Widow: Jeb, wait!

Jeb: Cain't wait.

Widow: But will you do me one last little favor 'fore you do it, Jeb?

Jeb: What is it?

Widow: Set and talk with me for just a minute. I won't argue none. I jist want to talk. For jist one minute, Jeb.

(*The Widow grabs Jeb's free hand. Jeb allows himself to be led back to the table.*)

Jeb: Might's well, I guess. Already been waitin' a year. But I got to do it 'fore it gits dark outside. . . . So I kin only listen for a minute.

(*Jeb and the Widow go to the table and sit down.*)

Widow: Sure, Jeb. (*after a pause*) You know, Jeb, if I don't want to see somethin', I just close my eyes.

Jeb: *Why* do you think God made sunsets, Widder?

Widow: Don't know. Never thought about it.

Jeb: Well, I have—'specially for the last year. (*continuing, after a pause to gather his ideas together*) Now you take a man—any man. Day in, day out, he's a-workin' and a-fightin' and a-pushin' and a-shovin' like a hog in a trough, jist to git by. And when the day's over, and comes time to quit, he's bone tired. So he comes out on his porch and watches the sunset. . . . Pretty soon he ain't tired no more.

Widow: 'Course he ain't. He's rested up some.

Jeb: Nope, that ain't it, though I guess it helps out. It's 'cause he gits to thinkin' that sunsets and all the pretty things in the world are signs.

Widow (*eagerly*): Once't I seen a real purty sign. Showed a real good picture of a fur coat that was . . .

Jeb (*interrupting*): I mean Nature's signs: God's way of lookin' down and talkin' to us.

Widow (*suddenly deflated*): Oh.

Jeb: Yep, it's like He's sayin', "Hello, man, I ain't forgot you. Jist been a little busy, that's all. I know you're down there, and someday maybe me and you kin make this old world a purty good place to live in. But 'til I kin git to it, I just thought I'd put a few purty things like sunsets and rainbows and stuff like that in the sky for you to look up at—to sort of help you want to git your head out of the trough." (*slightest of pauses, then looking directly at the Widow*) And you know, Widder, that's jist what them things does.

Widow (*after a pause*): Well, maybe so, Jeb. . . . But I say that if you destroy other men's *property*, that ain't Christian.

Jeb: Widder, God made things like sunsets for everybody. And a few men ain't got no right to go around uglifying 'em up, even if they does make money by doin' it. (*Stands up.*) Well, I guess I better be gittin' along. Goin' to be dark purty soon.

(*The Widow stands, comes up close to Jeb, who, a little frightened, keeps the axe between them.*)

Widow: Jeb, I know you're a-goin' to

do it. But afore you do it, I got to tell you somethin'.

Jeb: Ma'am?

Widow (*kittenishly*): Jeb, if I was to tell you somethin'—somethin' a lady never tells a gentleman—you wouldn't think bad of me, would you?

Jeb: Guess not. (*curious*) What don't ladies tell gentlemen?

Widow (*pretending shyness*): Well— you know what I come over here for, don't you, Jeb?

Jeb: Heck, yes! Like ever'body else in the county you're tryin' to talk me out of choppin' down that signboard. (*Jeb turns toward the door.*) And that's just a waste of time. I got to go now.

Widow (*her hand on his arm, detaining him*): But Jeb, don't you know there's another reason why I come over? 'Course I come over to stop you. I admit that. You're too smart for me to try and fool you by lyin' about it, so I ain't even tried. But there's another reason why I come over, Jeb. (*insinuatingly*) Don't you know the other reason?

Jeb: Well, no. This mornin' you come over to borry some 'taters. (*straight-faced, kidding the Widow without her knowing it*) Need any more 'taters?

Widow: No, Jeb. That ain't why I come over. I got 'taters now. But why would a lady come over to visit a gentleman, Jeb?

Jeb: Same reason a gentleman comes over to visit a lady, I guess.

Widow (*suggestively*): And why is that, Jeb?

Jeb: You mean why does ladies and gentlemen visit each other?

Widow: Yes.

Jeb: To see each other, I guess. (*Jeb moves abruptly to go. The Widow tries desperately to detain him.*) 'Scuse me, Widder, I got to go now.

Widow (*frantically trying to detain him*): But Jeb, why should I run clear over here to stop you from goin' to prison if I didn't . . . (*pretending embarrassment*) if I didn't care for you?

Jeb (*unbelievingly*): Widder!

Widow (*coyly*): Now what would you say, Jeb, if a lady told you . . . Now mind you, I'm only sayin' "If"; I'm a self-respectable woman—but what would you say if a lady told you that she'd like to spend out the rest of her years with you in holy wedlock?

Jeb: Oh, Widder! (*Jeb puts down the axe and draws her toward him, though not quite hugging her.*) Oh, Widder, I sure do thank you for askin' me to marry you!

(*The Widow stands away from him suddenly and haughtily.*)

Widow: I never asked you to marry me, Jeb!

Jeb (*at a loss, not understanding*): You didn't?

Widow: I only said what "if" . . . I didn't say I would. A woman cain't.

Jeb (*relieved*): Oh, well, how ever you want to git around it . . . (*continuing as though making a formal speech*) Widder Evans, will you marry me?

Widow (*shyly*): 'Course. If you'll have me.

Jeb: Oh, Widder, I'll have you! Don't worry none about *that!*

Widow (*hesitatingly*): Would you marry me, Jeb, even if you found out somethin' about me that you never knowed afore?

Jeb: S'pose. People's all the time find-in' out things they didn't know—after the knot's tied.

Widow: Well, there's somethin' you don't know. Somethin' about me. . . . You see, Jeb, there's somethin' I been keepin' from you, and from the other people in Saline Crik County, too.

Jeb: You ain't done nothin' illegal?

Widow: Oh, no! Ain't that! It's just that I, I . . . (*decisively*) Well, I jist got to tell you. I own that there land the signboard's on. Bought it from the county over a year ago.

Jeb: Oh, Widder, why do you have to go and tell me that?

Widow: 'Cause someday you'd find out my secret. 'Sides, that signboard company pays me ninety dollar a year for that patch of ground. I won't git it, you know, if you cut their sign down, Jeb. (*coming close to him*) Jeb, for the love of me—for our future happiness in holy wedlock, will you *not* cut down that sign? Please?

Jeb (*suddenly a broken man*): Why do you ask that, Widder? The one thing I cain't do. (*Jeb, his shoulders drooping, stoops and picks up his axe, as he speaks brokenly.*) 'Bye, Widder!

(*Jeb runs out the door with his axe. The Widow stands shocked and still for a moment, then runs to the door, calling out.*)

Widow: Jeb! Wait! Stop! *Please* stop, Jeb! (*The Widow stands looking out the door, horrified and unable to move.*) Oh, no. Oh, no. Jeb, oh, no! Don't chop! Don't!

(*As the Widow stands there, we hear the furious chopping of wood. The Widow's body jerks as if in pain, with each stroke of the axe. The stage lights begin to dim. Just before the stage is in total darkness, we hear Jeb's voice.*)

Jeb (*calling out*): There she goes!

(*There is a tremendous crash. The stage is now totally dark.*)

SCENE TWO:

(*The stage remains dark for a short period, to indicate the passing of time. Then a faint light shows on Jeb's axe, which is leaning against the table. The light makes the axe appear to be gold, and it is for a moment the only thing to be seen on the completely dark stage. Then the stage becomes visible, and then, fully lit. We see the Widow sitting in Jeb's kitchen, in a chair facing the open doorway. The Sheriff is standing looking out the window, craning his neck to the right. On the table are a stack of opened letters, neat stacks of bills and rolls of silver, the Widow's account book, her purse—a scalloped leather affair in keeping with her taste—and a large cardboard box. The Widow is slowly and painstakingly writing something on a large tablet, her lips moving slowly as she wets her pencil and writes.*)

Sheriff: Sure wish't he'd git here.

Widow (*looking up from the tablet*): Think he'll bring the mail out from town with him? Noon train prob'ly brought lots to the postoffice.

Sheriff: Don't know. (*with a gesture of impatience*) I just wish't he'd *git* here! You know, I ought to've gone into town special to git him.

Widow: Body cain't be in two places at once't, Sheriff. (*gesturing toward the money*) You sure cain't leave here with all *this* around!

Sheriff: I know, but jist the same, it don't seem right. When your best friend gits bailed out of jail, you ought to at least be there to greet him.

Widow: Maybe he got helt up with his fancy new lawyer. You know how them people talk.

Sheriff: No, t'aint that. I'll bet a dollar that John Hankses' old car broke down on the way out of town and he's havin' to walk home.

Widow: How's Jeb lookin', Sheriff— poorly?

Sheriff: Naw! Why, Jeb looks better'n he ever did. Ought to. Ate 'nough of Sally's good cookin'. Never seen a man eat so much and stay so skinny. (*continuing, after a pause*) He ate all his meals over home, you know. Easier to take him to the house than bring all that food over to the jail. (*another pause*) In all that time, how come you didn't visit him? (*sarcastically*) Visitin's allowed, y'know.

Widow: You don't think he'll hold it agin me, do you?

Sheriff: Don't know. (*looking out the window*) Sun'll be down in a little while. Hope he don't miss his very first sunset at home. You know how he is about sunsets.

(*The Sheriff turns away from the window, goes to the table, and starts to lift up the top flap of the box just as the Widow looks up from her writing tablet. Like a flash, her arm goes out and she slaps the top of the box down. The Sheriff looks a little hurt, a little guilty.*)

Widow: For the last time, Sheriff, I'm tellin' you not to peek into that box! It's a s'prise for Jeb. And if I kin stand not lookin', so kin you.

Sheriff: But *you* know what's in it, and I don't.

Widow: Don't make no difference.

Sheriff (*very inquisitive*): Is it somethin' you bought out of the catalogue?

Widow: No, I had it made up and sent here to Headquarters. Now you go on and watch out the winder for Jeb! Maybe he'll bring us some letters from places we ain't even heard of yit. (*The Widow selects an envelope from the stack on the table in front of her.*) Did you see this one? Come in jist yestiday. (*reading, by syllables*) It's from Henry Hamson, Esq., from Barnstaples, Somersetshire, England, to Jeb Wiliker, Esq. (*looking up at the Sheriff*) And he sent ten dollar, too! Seems like the whole world knows about Jeb now. And everybody's tryin' to help him out.

Sheriff: Funny how people is that way.

Widow: Yeah, ever'body tryin' to help him fight it out in court—and emergency citizens' committees formin' themselves. Why, I tell you, Sheriff, it's really somethin'!

Sheriff: Yep, I ain't never seen nothin' like it in Saline Crik County before.

Widow: Did you hear the latest the newspapers was sayin' about me and you?

Sheriff: No, don't read what they say. They don't seem to like Jeb none, and I git mad when they say mean things about him.

Widow: They say you're his best friend. They say I'm his manager—(*with a simper*)—and his love life.

Sheriff: Are you Jeb's manager, Widder?

Widow: Sure. Now he's been bailed out of jail and has got a fancy lawyer and people has sent in all that money, we're goin' to make us a national campaign.

Sheriff: A what what?

Widow (*very excited*): Tell you all about it later. But it's really goin' to be somethin'! Oh, I tell you, Sheriff, I'm so excited about it all, I cain't hardly set still.

Sheriff (*calmly*): Uh huh. . . . How much money've people sent in so far?

Widow (*reaching across the table for her account book, and reading it*): Well, let me see. Just three week ago this afternoon Jeb chopped 'er down. (*looking up at the Sheriff*) We didn't git nothin' the first week hardly, 'til the people heard about it in the papers. (*looking down at the account book*) And we got seventy-two dollar and twenty cents today. That makes . . . .

(*The Sheriff, who has just glanced out the window again, sees something slightly to his left. He interrupts the Widow before she can finish her sentence.*)

Sheriff (*joyfully*): Here he comes! And he's walkin'! He's comin' right acrost the new highway to'ards us!

Widow: Oh, Sheriff, my heart's jist a-goin' pitter-patter.

Sheriff: By Grabees, I bet John Hankses' old car broke down, and Jeb's taken the short cut over the ridge. And all the time I was lookin' for him to come down the highway.

Widow: Has he got any mail?

Sheriff: Don't see any. (*abstracted*) Dang it, a man oughtn't to cross a highway lookin' back over his shoulder at the sunset, like that! (*moving quickly to the door*) 'Scuse me, Widder.

(*The Sheriff goes out the door. The Widow primps furiously. From her purse, she whips out a mirror, checks her make-up, adds some lipstick, then pats at her hair. She stands up, facing the door, and twists, turns, pulls and straightens her girdle. We hear steps on the porch outside, the Sheriff's laugh, Jeb's chuckle, and then the Sheriff and Jeb enter. Jeb carries an ancient and battered suitcase. He walks toward the sink as the Widow speaks.*)

Widow (*her words coming out in a rush*): Oh, Jeb, I'm *so* glad to see you! I missed you so. And I wanted real bad to visit you in jail, but . . . (*a little embarrassed*) you know how people talks about a woman what hangs around jails.

(*Jeb puts the suitcase down on the sink.*)

Sheriff (*to Jeb*): I was tellin' the Widder that John Hankses' old car broke down on the way out from town, and you had to walk, so you took a short cut over the ridge. Bet I was right, wasn't I, Jeb?

Jeb (*turning around, to the Sheriff*): Sure was.

Widow (*with a rush of words*): Oh, Jeb, I got so much to tell you and show you. Oh, I got so many wonderful plans, I jist don't know where to begin!

Jeb: I got somethin' to tell you too, Widder. . . .

Widow (*interrupting*): Say, Jeb, did you git things all fixed up with your fancy new lawyer? (*Jeb nods, and opens his mouth to speak. The Widow again cuts him off. She speaks softly, affectionately.*) Bet he near talked your arm off, didn't he?

Jeb (*sighing, shaking head like a man who has suffered*): Sure did. But Widder, I . . .

Widow (*interrupting*): Oh, Jeb, I know how you must have suffered in jail and all. No, you don't need to say you ain't. I know how it must've been. Jeb, I want you to know I forgive you for everthin'. Everthin'! I forgive you and make up with you. (*Jeb tries to speak; the Widow holds up her hand.*) No, don't say anythin', Jeb! We'll jist forgit it all. You don't need to say a thing, 'cause it's all forgot. (*moving quickly, picking up the account book*) Now, Jeb, first off I want to show you this! Nine hundred and eighty-six dollar and seventy-four cents! That's how much people sent in since you chopped 'er down. Just three weeks ago this afternoon, and we already got near a thousand dollar! (*Jeb whistles a long, low whistle.*)

Sheriff: Makes you feel real good when people are so nice they send money to bail you out of jail, don't it, Jeb?

Jeb (*to the Sheriff*): Sure does. (*to the Widow*) But I . . .

Widow (*interrupting*): Oh, we're jist beginnin', Jeb! Now you're out of jail, we kin really git our national campaign started. I tell you it's really goin' to be somethin', too.

Sheriff: What's a national campaign?

Widow: You know—what you have when you have a national organization. When you have a national organization, you have a national campaign. Ain't you never heerd of them?

Sheriff: No.

Widow: Well, this is the way it works. (*to Jeb*) You go around different places, Jeb. You go all over the country. And everywhere you go you make speeches. . . . (*Jeb opens his mouth to say something, but before*

he can speak the Widow cuts him off, pointing to the tablet on the table.) Like the one I'm writin' now. And after you make your speech, people gives money so's they can join up in the organization.

Sheriff: What organization?

Widow (*proudly*): We call it the organization of the Golden Axe! (*The Sheriff and Jeb look blank.*) People has always hated signboards, but 'til Jeb here done it, they was always afeered to cut 'em down. So now we form committees—organizations always does that—and the people goes out at night in secret and chops 'em down. (*The Widow reaches into the cardboard box.*) And whenever they chops down a signboard, they gits a little golden axe (*taking out a tiny gold pin and holding it up*) like this! (*The Sheriff takes the pin from the Widow and inspects it closely. He is impressed. While the Sheriff and Widow talk, Jeb drifts inconspicuously toward the door, where he leans against the door-jamb, looking out at the sunset. The Widow continues talking to the Sheriff.*) They jist come in this mornin'. Ain't they somethin'? (*pretending modesty*) 'Course they ain't *real* gold. But they *look* like it.

Sheriff: But what happens when people gits caught choppin' down the signboards?

Widow: We use some of our money we collected to git 'em out of jail and hire a fancy lawyer. Oh, I tell you, Sheriff, it's really goin' to be somethin'! And Jeb will make a real good president for the organization.

Sheriff: I see. And what did you say you'd be, Widder?

Widow: Jeb's manager. That's all I

want. . . . No, sir, no limelight for me! If I kin help out a little, that's all *I* want. (*seeing Jeb start out the door*) Where you goin', Jeb?

Jeb: Out on the porch.

Widow: But you won't be able to hear me out there, Jeb.

Jeb: I kin hear you real good, Widder. (*Jeb goes out the door.*)

Widow (*to the Sheriff*): Wish't he'd stay and set in the house, stid of out there on the porch watchin' the sun go down. Ain't civilized to set out there like that.

Sheriff: You know, I ain't never seen a man about sunsets the way Jeb is. He waits for sunsets like a cat waits for milkin' time.

(*The Widow reaches for the writing tablet.*)

Widow: 'Scuse me for jist a minute, Sheriff. Got to finish my speech— jist a couple a words and then you kin hear me read it. (*The Widow begins to read what she has written on the pad, her lips moving slightly. Once she wets her pencil and makes a slight change. The Sheriff gets up, takes a bag from his pocket, and puts the money from the table into it.*) You goin', Sheriff?

Sheriff: Yep, cain't stay, Widder, though I'd like to. But I got to take keer of this, seein' as how it's my official responsibility. Then I'd best be gittin' on home, I guess. (*The Sheriff goes to the door, looks out, and speaks to Jeb.*) Say, Jeb, that's a real purty one this evenin'. And you can really see it, too, now that the sign's down.

Widow (*looking up*): Ain't you goin' to stay and listen to the speech I writ for Jeb, Sheriff?

Sheriff: No, thank you jist the same.

But I got to take this to town and put it in the safe—then I'd best be gittin' on.

Widow: Why don't you stay for jist a minute, Sheriff? (*gesturing toward the tablet*) It's a real good speech. I'd like to have you hear it.

Sheriff: No, don't guess I'd better stay, Widder. One time I stayed too long where they was havin' a fire and I got all my hair burnt off. So I guess I'd better be goin'.

Widow (*miffed*): Oh, all right. Evenin' to you, then.

Sheriff: 'Bye, Widder. (*The Sheriff exits, then speaks from off stage.*) See you later, Jeb.

Jeb (*off stage*): You bet, Henry. And thanks again to you and Sally for makin' everthin' so nice for me while I was in your jail.

Widow (*puzzled, speaking to herself*): Now I wonder what he meant by that business about a fire? (*She shrugs her shoulders, turns toward the door, and yells out to Jeb, commandingly.*) Jeb, you git in here and hear my speech! Right now, 'fore I git mad agin and decide to change my mind about makin' up with you! (*Jeb enters lazily. He leans against the door-jamb and looks outside.*) Jeb, I got you a real good speech writ. It's the kind that gits people all worked up so they start puttin' out the money. With you president, and me manager, we ought to do real well. But I'll tell you all about that later. Right now I want to read you my speech. (*The Widow does not notice Jeb's posture at the door, his back to her. She continues oratorically, with flourishes.*) Dear Friends! (*to Jeb, who still has his back turned*) They always start out speeches that way. . . . Dear Friends! Makes a nice friendly touch, don't it? Dear Friends, what do you think of when you think of an axe? Why, you think of George Washington, that's what you think of! 'Course he didn't use an axe, properly speakin'; he used a hatchet, but that was only 'cause he was a boy. If he'd've been a man he'd've used an axe. And Dear Friends, what do you think of when you think of George Washington? Why, you think of honesty, and presidents, and great national heroes. Don't you, Friends? Oh, I know, lots of you right now are sayin', "Humph! George Washington, he was a great national hero, all right, but that was a long time ago. And he's dead now." (*waving her arms and pounding the table*) But I'll tell you all somethin' you didn't know! GEORGE WASHINGTON AIN'T DEAD! No, he's alive, right here in this very room—in this very auditorium—in this big city, that seats thousands. . . . (*interpolating to Jeb, who still has his back to her*) I say that, you see, 'cause that's where you'll be givin' the speech, Jeb. (*continuing in speech-making tone*) No, sir, Friends! GEORGE WASHINGTON AIN'T DEAD; HE'S RIGHT HERE IN THIS AUDITORIUM! No, don't turn your heads! You cain't see him. 'Cause he ain't here in the flesh, Friends. IT'S HIS SPIRIT THAT'S HERE! George Washington's spirit's right here in this room! And his spirit is carryin' an axe! And his spirit's in the heart of us all! How do I know this? I FEEL IT! I FEEL THE SPIRIT OF GEORGE WASHINGTON IN ME! I FEEL HIS STRENGTH NOW! POURIN' INTO MY ARMS, MAKIN'

THEM WANT TO CHOP DOWN MORE SIGNS, AND MORE SIGNS AND MORE AND MORE AND MORE SIGNS. . . . (*interpolating again, Jeb still with his back to her*) Now how's *that* for a beginnin'? Oh, but that's just a beginnin'! (*Suddenly aware of Jeb's back being turned, she interrupts herself.*) Why Jeb, you ain't listenin'! Don't you like my speech?

Jeb: *Nice* speech.

Widow: Do you think you kin make a speech like this, Jeb?

Jeb: Nope.

Widow: Why not? (*offhandedly, trying to build his confidence*) Oh, jist 'cause you're a little afeerd is okay. Everbody's a little afeerd to make a speech in front of a lot of strangers, the first couple times.

Jeb: Sorry, Widder, cain't make no speech.

Widow (*regretfully*): Well, I guess we *could* git around it somehow. Maybe I could make it, and tell them you was too modest. But you'll have to *be* there, seein' as how you're goin' to be president.

Jeb: Cain't be no president, neither.

Widow (*surprised*): Cain't be president? (*her confidence a little shaken*) Oh, I'll bet you'll change your mind after awhile—when you see there ain't nothin' to it. Why, I'll do all the work, if that's what's botherin' you. You kin kind of lean on me at first. (*shyly*) 'Course, that'll be easy, 'cause we'll be married pretty soon now. Have to be. People talks about single ladies what travels around with single gentlemen, you know.

Jeb: Sorry, Widder, cain't marry you, neither.

Widow (*astonished*): What? You cain't *marry* me?

(Jeb turns away from the door and faces her.)

Jeb: Widder, I spent three weeks in jail, and that gives a man time to think. For the last two year I been sparkin' you, and all that time I been tryin' not to see some things. But now I cain't help seein' 'em. Not no more! You're the greediest, skin-flintinest, crabbiest, jabberinest, lie-inest, managinest, bossyinest, ugly-fyinest woman in the whole county!

Widow *(with outraged dignity)*: Why, I never . . .

Jeb: So now git on out of here.

Widow: Well!

Jeb: Widder, all of a sudden after I chopped down that there sign, you found out you was in business. So you tell me you forgive me, and you're goin' to make me president of a national organization, and sich stuff as that. And all the time you figure on gittin' rich!

Widow: I'm jist a poor helpless Widder, Jeb. Try to understand!

Jeb: Git out of here, woman!

Widow *(turning to tears)*: Oh, Jeb, please give me a chance't!

Jeb: I said *git!*

(Jeb picks up the axe from where it leans against the table and slowly advances on the Widow. She retreats before him, backing to the door leading outside.)

Widow *(desperately pleading)*: Oh, Jeb, I'm all alone! I ain't got nobody to lean on. I'm jist a lonely widder, Jeb. That's what I am, a poor, weak, lonely widder.

(Jeb continues advancing.)

Jeb: No, you ain't! You're an uglyfyer! That's what you are!

Widow *(frantic)*: Please, Jeb! Think of the national organization! All them people needs strength to use their axes! They needs leadership!

Jeb *(still advancing)*: Ever' man has got to chop down his own sign soon-er or later. And he's got to do it all by himself. Now *git!*

Widow *(threatening)*: I'll tell ever'-body you're a bad man, Jeb!

(Jeb raises the axe menacingly.)

Jeb: Woman, I feel the spirit of George Washington in me—COMIN' INTO MY ARMS! *(The Widow breaks, turns, and runs out the door. Jeb chuckles and puts the axe down against the door-jamb. For a moment, he stands there looking out the open door, watching the sunset sift slowly through the trees. He speaks quietly to himself.)* Sure is a purty sunset.

CURTAIN

 Talking it over

Scene One

1. In the opening scene, Jeb is calm-ly sharpening his axe while the Sheriff desperately tries to persuade him not to do "it," without mentioning what "it" actually is.

   a. What did you think "it" was? How did you feel about "it"?

   b. What were your feelings when you found out what Jeb was really go-ing to do?

2. *a.* What arguments do the Sher-iff and the Widow use to persuade Jeb not to do as he plans?

b. How does Jeb answer their arguments?

3. What does the Sheriff think of Widow Evans? What incidents does he mention to explain his attitude toward her?

Scene Two

1. When the news of Jeb's act becomes widely known, how do many people react? How would you explain their reaction?

2. *a.* How does the Widow plan to take advantage of the interest shown in Jeb? What does she plan to do with the money she has collected?

b. Does the Widow share Jeb's interest in sunsets? Find the line or lines which prove your answer.

c. How sincere is she when she says, "No limelight for me"? What does she want?

3. Why does the Sheriff feel he had better leave so soon after Jeb comes home from jail?

4. *a.* In the speech Widow Evans writes for Jeb, she refers to a legend about George Washington. What legend is this?

b. How is this legend connected with what Jeb has done?

5. Jeb calls the Widow the "greediest, skin-flintinest, crabbiest, jabberinest, lieinest, managinest, bossyinest, uglyfyinest woman in the whole county!" From what you have seen of the Widow, how fair is Jeb's description?

6. When Jeb chases Widow Evans out, he uses the words, "Woman, I feel the spirit of George Washington in me —COMIN' INTO MY ARMS!" Why is this speech funny?

7. *a.* What *two* important decisions does Jeb make? How is his life changed by each one?

b. What does Jeb mean when he says, "Ever' man has got to chop down his own sign sooner or later. And he's got to do it all by himself"?

8. If you were casting the play, what would you look for in the appearance of the actress who would play the Widow? Mention details from the play which helped you decide.

9. *a.* Are Jeb, the Sheriff, and Widow Evans stereotypes, or are they realistic characters? Support your viewpoint with evidence.

b. Is the play basically funny, or serious? Explain your answer.

⇄ **Words in action**

Do you know that you speak a dialect? A **dialect** is nothing more than a form of speech which seems natural in a certain part of the country or to a certain group of people. The teen-age slang which you probably use and understand without giving it a second thought is a dialect, and it is no doubt a puzzle to most adults.

"The Golden Axe" is written in the dialect of the Missouri Ozarks. This accounts for many of the expressions the characters use—expressions which may seem "quaint" and amusing to someone from another part of the country.

Some of these expressions are in the speeches on the next page. Be sure you know what each expression means. Then try to put it into *your* dialect.

1. "So you might jist as well traipse off 'fore it gits dark. . . ."

2. "Why, even now when you're a-sparkin' the young Widder Evans . . . it don't make no difference."

3. "She acted like it plumb broke her heart to have to part with it."

4. "She's runnin' lickety split down the highway toward us."

5. "But I think you're makin' a mountain out of a molehill, Jeb. And that s'prises me—never knowed anythin' to rile *you* up afore."

6. "Day in, day out, he's a-workin' and a-fightin' and a-pushin' and a-shovin' like a hog in a trough, jist to get by. And when the day's over, and comes time to quit, he's bone tired."

Photo by Doug Kilgour, Manhattan Beach, Calif.

He'd rather see the view

"A writer writes out of love, joy, and anger," comments Ralph Scholl. "I believe 'The Golden Axe' came out of all three."

He tells of the time he was driving through the California countryside, hoping to refresh himself for some work which lay ahead. But every time he turned a corner to what should have opened up into a great view of pines running down to a valley full of the play of sunlight and shadows—there was a signboard. It seemed to him that these signboards were cluttering up and covering the beauty of the land.

"I came home that evening not very refreshed after a day in the country," he continues. "I came home very angry. Beauty belongs to everyone. No man has a right to destroy it. How fine and brave a thing it would be, I thought, to go out that evening with axes and saws and crowbars and torches and cut down these hideous billboards.

"But the advantage of being a writer —and a reader—is that one can do all the things he wishes to and not suffer real consequences for them. The writer, or reader, can be the most heroic of men, yet never suffer the pain that inevitably comes to all real heroes (and the jail sentence that would surely come to anyone who dared to destroy a signboard).

"So I decided my best course would be to write a play."

Mr. Scholl chose for the setting the most beautiful view he had ever known: a hillside overlooking the creek on the farm in Missouri where he lived for several years. He based the characters on farmers and neighbors living nearby.

"I had thought—even hoped—that with the coming of the new legislation on highways and billboards, the play would no longer have any meaning, for there would be no billboards. But one should never misjudge the power and tenacity of the uglyfyers . . . . Billboards still sprout like great ugly weeds in the most scenic areas of our country."

Would he get the thumbs-up sign, meaning life,
or the thumbs-down, meaning he must die?

The Gloucester Gladiator

by Stephen Langley

IT WAS spring in Korea. May, 1951. The sun shone on the bare countryside, still frozen from the hardness of winter.

On a bleak hillside, a small group of Korean soldiers stood on a terrace of paddy fields. Rice straw crackled in the wind, and frozen dust stirred under the padded winter boots of the troops.

Nearby, two British soldiers knelt, hands tied behind their backs, waiting for the bullets from a firing squad which would carry out the death sentence that had been passed on them.

Yet those two men lived to tell the tale, because of a feud between two Communist officers, a curious sense of oriental humor and fair play.

It is a true story. It remained untold until recently because the soldiers, both shy and unassuming men, looking back on the experience, realized that it was almost unbelievable.

Desmond Fox and Herbert Graham were private soldiers in the "Glorious" Gloucestershire[1] Regiment, one of the first British units sent to fight in Korea shortly after the North Korean Communists attacked and overran South Korea.

They were captured at the end of the battle of the Imjin, when most of the regiment were imprisoned after a gallant stand on "Gloster" Hill. Taken northwards by the Chinese, they escaped and were recaptured three times. Finally the Chinese handed them over to a battalion of North Koreans. For a

This selection by Stephen Langley slightly adapted from *Young Elizabethan* (Vol. 11, No. 5). © 1958 by Periodical Publications Ltd.

[1]**Gloucestershire** (glos 'tər shir), a county in southwest England.

few days they were marched along. The Koreans showed them off to villagers as "long noses" they, themselves, had captured in battle.

Then on this bright, sunny morning —May 12, 1951—their guards escorted them from a mud-walled hut, across the frozen rice fields to where the group of Korean soldiers stood with their officers.

The enemy colonel spoke to them through an interpreter.

"Can you say why we should keep on feeding you, foreigners and enemies? No, we have been good to you long enough. You must be killed."

A firing squad of unkempt soldiers in ragged, padded uniforms stood ready with carbines.

The guards forced the Englishmen's hands behind them and tied their wrists tightly with signal cable. Then they pushed them to their knees.

Desmond Fox told me recently that he cannot remember what he thought about. "My brain was numbed. We just knelt there waiting for the end," he said.

Suddenly the interpreter stepped up to them and said, "The colonel says he will give you one chance."

What could it mean?

They were pulled to their feet. The colonel pointed to a powerfully built Korean lieutenant—the bully of the regiment. He said, "This officer thinks he is the strongest man in Korea. I say he is not. If you"—and he pointed to Fox—"can beat him in a fight, I will let you both go free."

Communist troops formed a tight ring around the contestants, and a guard undid the bonds which held the Englishman's wrists.

Fox rubbed at his wrists and hands, trying to force the blood back into his fingers. He is today a blond, blue-eyed six-footer of nearly two hundred pounds, but then, on a starvation diet, he was down to one hundred forty, gaunt faced, with a straggly ginger beard.

He looked across the ring at his giant opponent who was at least six inches taller than he, and very powerful.

There were to be no rules in this fight. It was fists and feet, elbows and knees, teeth and nails.

The two of them stood and fought. They fell and struggled on the ground. For twenty minutes the Korean soldiers watched with cruel eyes and expressionless faces.

Fox was fighting for his life and for a comrade's life. The Korean was fighting for his pride and for what the Oriental calls "face."

Herbert Graham, a stolid Yorkshireman,[2] stood surrounded by his captors, watching and silently praying.

Then the Korean made his fatal mistake. For a joke he grabbed with both hands at the Englishman's beard. Desmond Fox saw his chance and got a grip on the Korean's throat. With a heave he had him on the frozen mud. The lieutenant kicked and struggled, but Fox got on top. With two mighty punches, one on each side of the face, he knocked him out.

Recalling that moment, Desmond says, "It was so quiet, I could hear my heart beating. I was almost out myself, and trembling from fatigue. I could hardly think."

Slowly he got to his feet. Sweat was pouring down his face into his eyes and salting his lips. He must have felt like a gladiator in a Roman arena. Would

---

[2]**Yorkshireman** (yôrk'shir mən), a citizen of Yorkshire, a county in northern England.

he get the thumbs-up sign, meaning life, or the thumbs-down, indicating death? Looking into the black slit eyes of his enemies he was soon to know.

Suddenly one Korean face broke into a broad grin. Another man whooped with delight. And then the two lone Englishmen were surrounded by a horde of soldiers slapping them on their backs and showering them with cigarettes, matches, and apples.

It was thumbs up. The Korean colonel was to keep his promise.

At dawn an escort took them to just behind the front line and handed them over with safe conduct passes to a Chinese battalion.

A Chinese captain led them through the dugouts and gun positions. Pointing down a dusty lane he said, "Three miles along this road you will find the Americans. Don't delay."

Into No Man's Land they stepped. Once only did they stop. That was when an amazed Korean villager, stepping from a battered, shell-torn hut, offered them some hot rice. It was tasteless, but it was warm and filling and the first hot food they had tasted for days.

At a forward American post they were challenged by a soldier who could hardly believe his ears when they replied to him in English.

The next thing that Desmond Fox remembers was the feast of twelve eggs, twelve bacon rashers, and a whole box of Scottish shortbread which he ate.

What does he think about it now?

He has married and works with a road gang on the Isle of Man.[3] He enjoys his open-air life and the company of his friends.

That May day seems a lifetime away. He prefers to forget the past, and lives for the present and the future. But he has never completely forgotten that little Korean colonel who held his life in his hands.   THE END

---

[3]**Isle of Man,** a small island west of northern England, in the Irish Sea.

Talking it over

1. *a.* Why were the Englishmen to be executed?

   b. Why was the execution delayed?

2. *a.* How evenly matched physically were the men who fought?

   b. How do you account for Fox's winning even though his condition was poor?

3. *a.* Why were the Korean soldiers pleased with the outcome?

   b. What did they do to the prisoners after the fight?

4. What evidence of stereotyping do you find in the descriptions of the enemy soldiers? What evidences do you find in the descriptions of the British soldiers? How do you account for the difference in the author's attitude in each case?

DESERTION

*If he went back, he would be
among human beings again.
But if he didn't . . .*

by Clifford D. Simak

FOUR men, two by two, had gone into the howling maelstrom that was Jupiter and had not returned. They had walked into the keening gale—or rather, they had loped, bellies low against the ground, wet sides gleaming in the rain.

For they did not go in the shape of men.

Now the fifth man stood before the desk of Kent Fowler, head of Dome No. 3, Jovian Survey Commission.

Under Fowler's desk, old Towser scratched a flea, then settled down to sleep again.

Harold Allen, Fowler saw with a sudden pang, was young—too young. He had the easy confidence of youth, the face of one who never had known fear. And that was strange. For men in the domes of Jupiter did know fear—fear and humility. It was hard for Man

to reconcile his puny self with the mighty forces of the monstrous planet.

"You understand," said Fowler, "that you need not do this. You understand that you need not go."

It was formula, of course. The other four had been told the same thing, but they had gone. This fifth one, Fowler knew, would go as well. But suddenly he felt a dull hope stir within him that Allen wouldn't go.

"When do I start?" asked Allen.

There had been a time when Fowler might have taken quiet pride in that answer, but not now. He frowned briefly.

"Within the hour," he said.

Allen stood waiting, quietly.

"Four other men have gone out and have not returned," said Fowler. "You know that, of course. We want you to return. We don't want you going off on any heroic rescue expedition. The main thing, the only thing, is that you come back, that you prove man can live in a Jovian form. Go to the first survey stake, no farther, then come back. Don't take any chances. Don't investigate anything. Just come back."

Allen nodded. "I understand all that."

"Miss Stanley will operate the converter," Fowler went on. "You need have no fear on that particular score. The other men were converted without mishap. They left the converter in apparently perfect condition. You will be in thoroughly competent hands. Miss Stanley is the best qualified conversion operator in the solar system. She has had experience on most of the other planets. That is why she's here."

Allen grinned at the woman and Fowler saw something flicker across Miss Stanley's face—something that might have been pity, or rage—or just plain fear. But it was gone again and she was smiling back at the youth who stood before the desk. Smiling in that prim, schoolteacherish way she had of smiling, almost as if she hated herself for doing it.

"I shall be looking forward," said Allen, "to my conversion."

And the way he said it, he made it all a joke, a vast, ironic joke.

But it was no joke.

It was serious business, deadly serious. Upon these tests, Fowler knew, depended the fate of men on Jupiter. If the tests succeeded, the resources of the giant planet would be thrown open. Man would take over Jupiter as he already had taken over the other smaller planets. And if they failed—

If they failed, Man would continue to be chained and hampered by the terrific pressure, the greater force of gravity, the weird chemistry of the planet. He would continue to be shut within the domes, unable to set actual foot upon the planet, unable to see it with direct, unaided vision, forced to rely upon the awkward tractors and the televisor, forced to work with clumsy tools and mechanisms or through the medium of robots that themselves were clumsy.

For Man, unprotected and in his natural form, would be blotted out by Jupiter's terrific pressure of fifteen thousand pounds per square inch, pressure that made terrestrial sea bottoms seem a vacuum by comparison.

Even the strongest metal Earthmen could devise couldn't exist under pressure such as that, under the pressure and the alkaline rains that forever swept the planet. It grew brittle and flaky, crumbling like clay, or it ran away in little streams and puddles of ammonia salts. Only by stepping up the toughness and strength of that metal could it be made to withstand the weight of thousands of miles of swirling, choking gases that made up the atmosphere. And even when that was done, everything had to be coated with tough quartz to keep away the rain—liquid ammonia that fell as bitter rain.

Fowler sat listening to the engines in the sub-floor of the dome—engines that ran on endlessly, the dome never quiet of them. They had to run and keep on running, for if they stopped, the power flowing into the metal walls of the dome would stop, the electronic tension would ease up, and that would be the end of everything.

Towser roused himself under Fowler's desk and scratched another flea, his leg thumping hard against the floor.

"Is there anything else?" asked Allen.

Fowler shook his head. "Perhaps there's something you want to do," he said. "Perhaps you—"

He had meant to say write a letter and he was glad he caught himself quick enough so he didn't say it.

Allen looked at his watch. "I'll be there on time," he said. He swung around and headed for the door.

Fowler knew Miss Stanley was watching him and he didn't want to turn and meet her eyes. He fumbled with a sheaf of papers on the desk before him.

"How long are you going to keep this up?" asked Miss Stanley, and she bit off each word with a vicious snap.

He swung around in his chair and faced her then. Her lips were drawn into a straight, thin line, her hair seemed skinned back from her forehead tighter than ever, giving her face that queer, almost startling deathmask quality.

He tried to make his voice cool and level. "As long as there's any need of it," he said. "As long as there's any hope."

"You're going to keep on sentencing them to death," she said. "You're going to keep marching them out face to face with Jupiter. You're going to sit here safe and comfortable and send them out to die."

"There is no room for sentimentality, Miss Stanley," Fowler said, trying to keep the note of anger from his voice. "You know as well as I do why we're doing this. You realize that Man in his own form simply cannot cope with Jupiter. The only answer is to turn men into the sort of things that can cope with it. We've done it on the other planets.

"If a few men die, but we finally succeed, the price is small. Through the ages men have thrown away their lives on foolish things, for foolish reasons. Why should we hesitate, then, at a little death in a thing as great as this?"

Miss Stanley sat stiff and straight, hands folded in her lap, the lights shining on her graying hair. Fowler, watching her, tried to imagine what she might feel, what she might be thinking. He wasn't exactly afraid of her, but he didn't feel comfortable when she was around. Those sharp blue eyes saw too much, her hands looked far too competent. She should be somebody's aunt sitting in a rocking chair with her knitting needles. But she wasn't. She was the top-notch conversion unit operator in the solar system and she didn't like the way he was doing things.

"There is something wrong, **Mr.** Fowler," she declared.

"Precisely," agreed Fowler. "That's why I'm sending young Allen out alone. He may find out what it is."

"And if he doesn't?"

"I'll send someone else."

She rose slowly from her chair, started toward the door, then stopped before his desk.

"Some day," she said, "you will be a great man. You never let a chance go by. This is your chance. You knew it was when this dome was picked for the tests. If you put it through, you'll go up a notch or two. No matter how many men may die, you'll go up a notch or two."

"Miss Stanley," he said and his voice was curt, "young Allen is going out soon. Please be sure that your machine—"

"My machine," she told him icily, "is not to blame. It operates along the coördinates the biologists set up."

He sat hunched at his desk, listening to her footsteps go down the corridor.

What she said was true, of course. The biologists had set up the coördinates. But the biologists could be wrong. Just a hairbreadth of difference, and the converter would be sending out something that wasn't the thing they meant to send.

For Man didn't know much about what was going on outside. Only what his instruments told him was going on. And the samplings of those happenings furnished by those instruments and mechanisms had been no more than samplings, for Jupiter was unbelievably large and the domes were very few.

Even the work of the biologists in getting the data on the Lopers, apparently the highest form of Jovian life, had involved more than three years of intensive study, and after that, two years of checking to make sure.

Yet it was work that had to be done if Man ever hoped to go about Jupiter in the life form of the Lopers. For before the converter could change a man to another life form, every detailed physical characteristic of that life form must be known—surely and positively, with no chance of mistake.

Allen did not come back.

The tractors, combing the nearby terrain, found no trace of him, unless the skulking thing reported by one of the drivers had been the missing Earthman in Loper form.

The biologists sneered when Fowler suggested the coördinates might be wrong. Carefully they pointed out, the coördinates worked. When a man was put into the converter and the switch was thrown, the man became a Loper. He left the machine and moved away, out of sight, into the soupy atmosphere.

Some quirk, Fowler had suggested; some tiny deviation from the thing a Loper should be, some minor defect.

If there were, the biologists said, it would take years to find it. And Fowler knew they were right.

So there were five men now instead of four, and Harold Allen had walked out into Jupiter for nothing at all.

Fowler reached across his desk and picked up the personnel file, a thin sheaf of papers neatly clipped together. It was a thing he dreaded but a thing he had to do. Somehow the reason for these strange disappearances must be found. And there was no other way than to send out more men.

He sat for a moment listening to the howling of the wind above the dome, the everlasting thundering gale that swept across the planet in boiling, twisting wrath.

Was there some threat out there, he asked himself? Some danger they did not know about? Something that lay in wait and gobbled up the Lopers?

Or had there been a basic fault in selecting the Lopers as the type of life best fitted for existence on this planet? The evident intelligence of the Lopers, he knew, had been one factor in that determination. For if the thing Man became did not have capacity for intelligence, Man could not for long retain his own intelligence in such a guise.

Had the biologists let that one factor weigh too heavily, using it to offset some other factor that might be unsatisfactory, even disastrous? It didn't seem likely. Stiffnecked as they might be, the biologists knew their business.

Or was the whole thing impossible, doomed from the very start? Conversion to other life forms had worked on other planets, but that did not necessarily mean it would work on Jupiter. Perhaps Man's intelligence could not function correctly through the sensory apparatus provided to Jovian life forms. Perhaps the Lopers were so alien there was no common ground for human knowledge and the Jovian conception of existence to meet and work together.

Or the fault might lie with Man. Perhaps just one ordinary human trait, accepted as commonplace on Earth, would be so violently at odds with Jovian existence that it would blast human sanity.

Claws rattled and clicked down the corridor. Listening to them, Fowler smiled wanly. It was Towser coming back from the kitchen, where he had gone to see his friend, the cook.

Towser came into the room, carrying a bone. He wagged his tail at Fowler and flopped down beside the desk. For a long moment his rheumy old eyes regarded his master, and Fowler reached down a hand to ruffle a ragged ear.

"You still like me, Towser?" Fowler asked, and Towser thumped his tail.

"You're the only one," said Fowler.

He straightened and swung back to the desk. His hand reached out and picked up the file.

Bennett? Bennett had a girl waiting for him back on Earth.

Andrews? Andrews was planning on going back to Mars Tech just as soon as he earned enough to see him through a year.

Olson? Olson was nearing pension age. All the time telling the boys how he was going to settle down and grow roses.

Carefully, Fowler laid the file back on the desk.

Sentencing men to death. Miss Stanley had said that, her pale lips scarcely moving in her parchment face. Marching men out to die while he, Fowler, sat here safe and comfortable.

They were saying it all through the dome, no doubt, especially since Allen had failed to return. They wouldn't say it to his face, of course. Even the man or men he called before this desk and told they were the next to go wouldn't say it to him.

But he would see it in their eyes.

He picked up the file again. Bennett, Andrews, Olson. There were others, but there was no use in going on.

Kent Fowler knew that he couldn't do it, couldn't face them, couldn't send more men out to die.

He leaned forward and flipped up the toggle on the intercommunicator.

"Yes, Mr. Fowler."

"Miss Stanley, please."

He waited for Miss Stanley, listening to Towser chewing half-heartedly on the bone. Towser's teeth were getting bad.

"Miss Stanley," said Miss Stanley's voice.

"Just wanted to tell you, Miss Stanley, to get ready for two more."

"Aren't you afraid," asked Miss Stanley, "that you'll run out of them? Sending them out one at a time, they'd last longer, give you twice the satisfaction."

"One of them," said Fowler, "will be a dog."

"A dog!"

"Yes, Towser."

He heard the quick, cold rage that iced her voice. "Your own dog! He's been with you all these years——"

"That's the point," said Fowler. "Towser would be unhappy if I left him behind."

It was not the Jupiter he had known through the televisor. He had expected it to be different, but not like this. He had expected a hell of ammonia rain and stinking fumes and the deafening, thundering tumult of the storm. He had expected swirling clouds and fog and the snarling flicker of monstrous thunderbolts.

He had not expected that the lashing downpour would be reduced to drifting purple mist that moved like fleeing shadows over a red and purple sward. He had not even guessed the snaking bolts of lightning would be flares of pure ecstasy across a painted sky.

Waiting for Towser, Fowler flexed the muscles of his body, amazed at the smooth, sleek strength he found. Not a bad body, he decided, and grimaced at remembering how he had pitied the Lopers when he glimpsed them through a television screen.

For it had been hard to imagine a living organism based upon ammonia and hydrogen rather than upon water and oxygen, hard to believe that such a form of life could know the same quick thrill of life that humankind could know. Hard to conceive of life out in the soupy maelstrom that was Jupiter, not knowing, of course, that through Jovian eyes it was no soupy maelstrom at all.

The wind brushed against him with what seemed gentle fingers and he remembered with a start that by Earth standards the wind was a roaring gale, a two-hundred-mile-an-hour howler laden with deadly gases.

Pleasant scents seeped into his body. And yet scarcely scents, for it was not the sense of smell as he remembered it. It was as if his whole being was soaking up the sensation of lavender—and yet not lavender. It was something, he knew, for which he had no word. For the words he knew, the thought symbols that served him as an Earthman, would not serve him as a Jovian.

The lock in the side of the dome opened and Towser came tumbling out —at least he thought it must be Towser.

He started to call to the dog, his mind shaping the words he meant to say. But he couldn't say them. There was no way to say them. He had nothing to say them with.

For a moment his mind swirled in muddy terror, a blind fear that eddied in little puffs of panic through his brain.

How did Jovians talk? How—

Suddenly he was aware of Towser, intensely aware of the bumbling, eager friendliness of the shaggy animal that had followed him from Earth to many planets. As if the thing that was Towser had reached out and for a moment sat within his brain.

And out of the bubbling welcome that he sensed, came words.

"Hiya, pal."

Not words really, better than words. Thought symbols in his brain, communicated thought symbols that had shades of meaning words could never have.

"Hiya, Towser," he said.

"I feel good," said Towser. "Like I was a pup. Lately I've been feeling pretty punk. Legs stiffening up on me and teeth wearing down to almost nothing. Hard to mumble a bone with teeth like that. Besides, the fleas bother me a lot. Used to be I never paid much attention to them. A couple of fleas more or less never meant much in my early days."

"But . . . but—" Fowler's thoughts tumbled awkwardly. "You're talking to me!"

"Sure thing," said Towser. "I always talked to you, but you couldn't hear me. I tried to say things to you, but I couldn't make the grade."

"I understood you sometimes," Fowler said.

"Not very well," said Towser. "You knew when I wanted food and when I wanted a drink, and when I wanted out, but that's about all you ever managed."

"I'm sorry," Fowler said.

"Forget it," Towser told him. "I'll race you to the cliff."

For the first time, Fowler saw the cliff, apparently many miles away, but with a strange crystalline beauty that sparkled in the shadow of the many-colored clouds.

Fowler hesitated. "It's a long way—"

"Ah, come on," said Towser, and even as he said it he started for the cliff.

Fowler followed, testing his legs, testing the strength in that new body of his, a bit doubtful at first, amazed a moment later, then running with a sheer joyousness that was one with the red and purple sward, with the drifting smoke of the rain across the land.

As he ran the consciousness of music came to him, a music that beat into his body, that surged throughout his being, that lifted him on wings of silver speed. Music like bells might make from some steeple on a sunny springtime hill.

As the cliff drew nearer the music deepened and filled the universe with a spray of magic sound. And he knew the music came from the tumbling waterfall that feathered down the face of the shining cliff.

Only, he knew, it was no waterfall, but an ammonia-fall, and the cliff was white because it was oxygen, solidified.

He skidded to a stop beside Towser where the waterfall broke into a glittering rainbow of many hundred colors.

"The music," said Towser.

"Yes, what about it?"

"The music," said Towser, "is vibrations. Vibrations of water falling."

"But, Towser, you don't know about vibrations."

"Yes, I do," contended Towser. "It just popped into my head."

Fowler gulped mentally. "Just popped!"

And suddenly, within his own head, he held a formula—the formula for a process that would make metal to withstand the pressure of Jupiter.

He stared, astounded, at the waterfall and swiftly his mind took the many colors and placed them in their exact sequence in the spectrum. Just like that. Just out of blue sky. Out of nothing, for he knew nothing either of metals or of colors.

"Towser," he cried. "Towser, something's happening to us!"

"Yeah, I know," said Towser.

"It's our brains," said Fowler. "We're using them, all of them, down to the last hidden corner. Using them to figure out things we should have known all the time. Maybe the brains of Earth-things naturally are slow and foggy. Maybe we are the morons of the universe. Maybe we are fixed so we have to do things the hard way."

And, in the new sharp clarity of thought that seemed to grip him, he knew that it would not only be the matter of colors in a waterfall, or metals that would resist the pressure of Jupiter. He sensed other things, things not yet quite clear. A vague whispering that hinted of greater things, of mysteries beyond the pale of human thought, beyond even the pale of human imagination.

"We're still mostly Earth," he said.

"We're just beginning to learn a few things we are to know—a few of the things that were kept from us as human beings, perhaps because we *were* human beings. Because our human bodies were poor bodies. Poorly equipped for thinking, poorly equipped in certain senses that one has to have to know. Perhaps even lacking in certain senses that are necessary to true knowledge."

He stared back at the dome, a tiny black thing dwarfed by the distance.

Back there were men who couldn't see the beauty that was Jupiter. Men who thought that swirling clouds and lashing rain obscured the planet's face. Unseeing human eyes. Poor eyes. Eyes that could not see the beauty in the clouds, that could not see through the storm. Bodies that could not feel the thrill of trilling music stemming from the rush of broken water.

Men who walked alone, in terrible loneliness, talking with their tongues like Boy Scouts wigwagging out their messages, unable to reach out and touch one another's mind as he could reach out and touch Towser's mind. Shut off forever from that personal, intimate contact with other living things.

He, Fowler, had expected terror inspired by alien things out here on the surface, had steeled himself against disgust of a situation that was not of Earth.

But instead he had found something greater than Man had ever known. A swifter, surer body. A sense of exhileration, a deeper sense of life. A sharper mind. A world of beauty that even the dreamers of the Earth had not yet imagined.

"Let's get going," Towser urged.

"Where do you want to go?"

"Anywhere," said Towser. "Just start

going and see where we end up. I have a feeling . . . well, a feeling—"

"Yes, I know," said Fowler.

For he had the feeling, too. The feeling of high destiny. A certain sense of greatness. A knowledge that somewhere off beyond the horizons lay adventure and things greater than adventure.

Those other five had felt it, too.

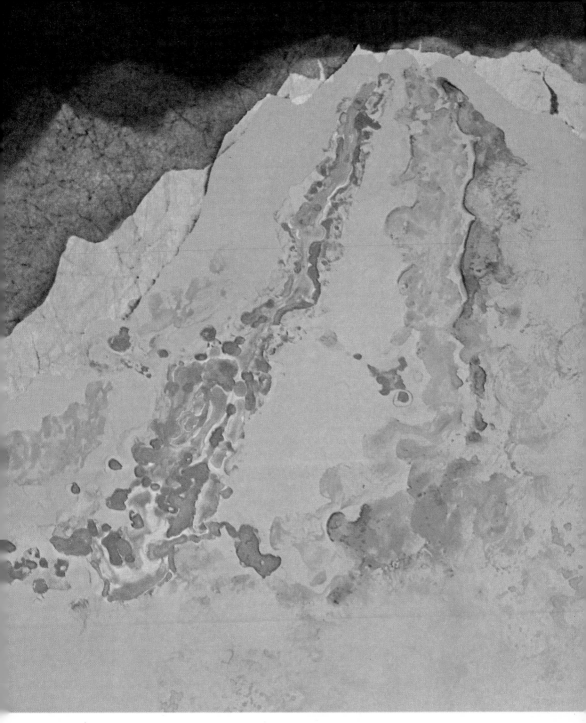

Had felt the urge to go and see, the compelling sense that here lay a life of fullness and of knowledge.

That, he knew, was why they had not returned.

"I won't go back," said Towser.

"We can't let them down," said Fowler.

Fowler took a step or two, back toward the dome, then stopped.

Back to the dome. Back to that aching, poison-laden body he had left. It hadn't seemed aching before, but now he knew it was.

Back to the fuzzy brain. Back to muddled thinking. Back to the flapping mouths that formed signals others misunderstood. Back to eyes that now would be worse than no sight at all. Back to squalor, back to crawling, back to ignorance.

"Perhaps some day," he said, muttering to himself.

"We got a lot to do and a lot to see," said Towser. "We got a lot to learn. We'll find things—"

Yes, they could find things. Civilizations, perhaps. Civilizations that would make the civilization of Man seem puny by comparison. Beauty and, more important, an understanding of that beauty. And comradeship no one had ever known before—that no man, no dog had ever known before.

And life. The quickness of life after what seemed a drugged existence.

"I can't go back," said Towser.

"Nor I," said Fowler.

"They would turn me back into a dog," said Towser.

"And me," said Fowler, "back into a man."   THE END

↻ **Talking it over**

1. *a*. Why does Man want to take over Jupiter?

b. What problems does Man in his own form face on Jupiter?

2. *a*. Why does Fowler continue to send men out, even though none have come back?

b. Why does Miss Stanley disapprove of what Fowler is doing?

3. *a*. What possible explanations does Fowler think of for the men's failure to return?

b. Why does Fowler decide to go himself?

c. Why does he take Towser along?

4. *a*. How is Jupiter different from what Fowler expects it to be?

b. What happens to the bodies of Fowler and Towser when they are converted to Lopers? What happens to their minds?

5. What differences did you find between the way you on earth and Fowler on Jupiter experience each of the following?

  a. rain

  b. wind

  c. a waterfall

  d. clouds

6. *a*. What is the "turning point" in Fowler's life? Why does he make the decision he does?

b. Do you think Fowler's decision involves an act of "desertion"? Explain.

c. Why is Towser important to the story?

7. Read "Science fiction and science fact" on the next page. Keeping Clifford Simak's comments in mind, express in a sentence what you think is the central idea of this story. (The section on "Central Idea," pages 127-145, may help you.)

⇄ **Words in action**

In science fiction stories, you often find the word *Terra* used as another name for the planet earth. Then you may see the word *terrestrial* used to refer to things about the earth, as in the following sentence from "Desertion": "For Man, unprotected and in his natural form, would be blotted out by Jupiter's terrific pressure . . . that made *terrestrial* sea bottoms seem a vacuum by comparison." Can you guess the meaning of *terra*, the Latin word from which this word comes?

When you know the meaning of *terra* you may recognize it in other words. Guess at the meaning of each of the boldface words in the following sentences, then look up the words in a dictionary to see if you are right.

1. He shaded his eyes with his hand and slowly scanned the **terrain** from north to south.

2. I like to ride in a plane, but I always breathe a sigh of relief when I set my feet once again on good old **terra firma.**

3. He threw himself down on the **terrace** and panted, out of breath from the exertion of climbing the hill.

4. The Indian jar my uncle brought me from his vacation in the Southwest is a beautiful **terra cotta** color.

5. For her science project my sister set up a small **terrarium** in the science lab and kept the plants and reptiles in it carefully tended.

Science fiction and science fact

As an author, Clifford Simak has won several awards—including one international award—for his stories and novels of science fiction and fantasy. As a newspaperman, Mr. Simak originated and continues to manage an educational program called the Science Reading Series for the Minneapolis, Minnesota, *Tribune*.

Some of his stories, he says, are based on an event, others on an idea, still others on a remark he happened to overhear. "Desertion" came from Mr. Simak's disgust at the pride some people feel in just being human. Too many people, he says, are convinced that mankind must be the highest and best form of life.

"We are too inclined to feel sorry for other forms of life because they aren't humans or to disregard their welfare or 'rights' as life forms simply because they aren't like us. A little humility at times would make us better life forms ourselves. So in this story the old dog, scratching fleas underneath the desk, becomes the equal of the man and both of them find a better life in yet another form and on another world which is blurred when viewed by dog or human eyes."

Turning Point: Views and viewpoints

1. *a.* Both Fred in "Bloodstain" and Jeb in "The Golden Axe" do something which might send them to jail; yet, one accepts his punishment and the other does not. How are their crimes different? Compare the way Fred and Jeb feel about what they have done.

    b. Both the boy in "When You Run Away" and Fowler in "Desertion" make up their minds to leave what they have for something else. What difference is there between their reasons for wanting to go? Why does one of them want to return and the other prefer not to?

    c. Both Desmond Fox, "The Gloucester Gladiator," and Bill face death. Contrast the kinds of courage they show and the kinds of situations they face.

2. Several of the characters in this unit make decisions which change their lives. Which character do you think makes the best decision? Which character makes the worst? Defend your choices.

3. *a.* What is a "turning point"? Use specific characters from the stories in this unit to help explain the understanding you have gotten from this unit.

    b. Have you experienced a turning point in your own life? How was your life changed because of it? If not, do you know someone else who has experienced one?

11

Flexibility

LESSON ONE: Why you read in different ways

(A) "Did you watch 'Saturday Night at the Movies'?" Tony asked his friend Butch as the boys waited for the bus.

"No. My dad was watching the Chicago Bears. What was on?"

"It was John Wayne—a real old picture. But it was real cool. John Wayne was this marshal out West, and there were some guys who wanted to get him, but he knew what they were up to and . . ."

"Yeah?"

(B) The nature of the acting beast makes him complex. The fact that he desires to constantly put on other "skins," become other characters, is not in itself unusual —we all do it daily, often subconsciously—but to go on stage for a livelihood, making a career of make-believe, lifts him forever from the mundane world of butcher, baker, candlestick-maker—all parts he will gladly assume in front of an audience.

There are all types in any profession, or art, and there are all types of actors and actresses. Some, like the enduring John Wayne, essentially play themselves. Wayne *is* the Wayne character, picture to picture, and this does not lessen his stature or ability. . . .

From *People Who Make Movies* by Theodore Taylor. Copyright © 1967 by Theodore Taylor. Reprinted by permission of Doubleday & Company, Inc. and A. Watkins, Inc.

Which passage did you read faster—A or B? Most people would be able to read the familiar conversation in A faster than a passage like B. Involved sentence patterns and unfamiliar words are likely to slow you up. It's like speeding on a bicycle down a smooth new blacktop when no cars are in sight, as compared with riding on a street where the pavement is torn up and there are barricades every few feet.

There are other things, too, that make a difference in the way you ride a bike or walk down the street. Can you imagine, for example, how different it would be to run to get to school on time —and then to walk slowly home with a report card you weren't proud of? The route is the same either way, but your purpose is quite different.

Reading is like that, too. For example, in which situation

would you carefully read all of a sports article describing a baseball game?

1. You only want to know the score.
2. You want to know what happened in the game, play by play.

Material can be skimmed quickly when you are looking for only one particular name or fact. When you are looking for fuller information, you will read straight through, more slowly and carefully. Your reading rate varies not only with the difficulty of the material, but also with your purpose.

LESSON TWO: Reading for different purposes

Situation 1

You are giving a report on leopards. The first thing you need to do is to collect as much information about leopards as possible.

Read the following so you will remember in detail what it says. Then try to answer the questions without looking back.

> The leopard is the shrewdest, the loneliest, the most patient, and the most vicious of the great cats. He stares with cold amber eyes across the body of his prey, measuring the intruder, ready to defend his kill—or to run. Small compared to a lion, only 140 pounds or so, he is so heavily muscled that no animal near his size can stand up against him and no other animal means anything to him —not his mate, with whom he stays only briefly, nor his young, whom he never sees. The leopard's fierce efficiency is disguised by spotted beauty or, in the uncommon black leopard, by rich sable fur. Almost anywhere in Africa is home to him—bush, forest, mountain, desert. Watchful and cautious, he naps by day amid rocks, high grass, or lying in leaf-dappled shadows on the limb of a tree. But if the prey comes near, he rouses himself to hunt, gliding from cover to cover as secretly as a snake.

> From "The Great Cats of Africa," *Life* Magazine, January 6, 1967. Copyright © 1967 Time, Inc.

1. How much does a full-grown leopard weigh?
2. What makes him dangerous?
3. Where does he live?
4. What are three of his traits?

Situation 2

Sometimes you don't need to concern yourself with small details; you just want to know in general what a selection is about, or what happens in a story. Read the next paragraph for a general idea of what it says.

> I was surrounded by wild jungle animals—lions, cheetahs, elephants, and rhinos. But I wasn't in any danger. Most of them were in comfortable cages or large pens. And just to make this photographer's paradise complete, the sun was shining brightly. I began to take pictures, not conscious of anything but what I saw in my viewfinder. Suddenly I heard someone yell "Freeze!" I stopped dead in my tracks and looked up. Coming straight at me was a giant tiger. Behind him, a muscular handler was straining with all his might against the chain leash that stretched taut from the collar of the beast.

5. Is this paragraph probably from an encyclopedia article about African animals, or is it from a personal-experience narrative?
6. What is the most startling incident in the paragraph?

Situation 3

Your class has been discussing wildcats and there is some dispute about their size. You are delegated to find out the facts. You begin by looking through some articles on wildcats in a nature magazine.

Read the following paragraph quickly to see if it tells how big a wildcat is.

> Suddenly I was stopped by a pair of blazing eyes. Then I saw his mouth open in a soundless snarl. I saw four white fangs, long and terribly sharp. Brown and white streaks gave his face a look of savagery as he laid his ears back against his head. The yellow eyes narrowed until the pupils were just slits. And there we stood in the swamp—a boy and a wildcat, ten feet from each other.

7. Does the paragraph tell the size of a wildcat?

In which of the three situations did you read at the fastest rate? What were you looking for?

In which situation did you read at the slowest rate? What were you trying to accomplish?

Which paragraph did you read at a medium rate? What were you trying to find out?

Before you start to read any material, you should know what your purpose is, and use it to help you decide on a general reading speed. If the rate you choose is too slow, you will spend more time reading than is necessary. If the rate is too fast, you will waste time by having to go back and reread. A good reader is **flexible**—that is, he varies his speed and method according to his purpose.

LESSON THREE: Skimming

What does "skimming" mean to you? It is a kind of very fast reading, but it is different from other kinds of reading. When you skim you do not actually take in every word. You simply let your eyes run very quickly over the print until you spot the particular thing you are looking for. Skimming is a useful reading "tool." Like all tools, it should be used only for the purpose for which it is designed—to find specific information quickly.

Suppose you are reading a book about how movies are made. You come across the unfamiliar term *arc light*. The book has a Glossary at the back, so you look there for the meaning.

In what kind of order are terms in a Glossary usually listed? Would you expect to find *arc light* near the beginning, the middle, or the end of the Glossary?

Of course you won't read all the entries until you find the one you want. You simply let your eyes run quickly down the left-hand side of the page. See how quickly you can find *arc light* in the Glossary section on the next page.

GLOSSARY

"A" property: a film with a large budget, usually of a million dollars or more. A "B" property is a more cheaply made film, usually with a budget of about $500,000.

Animation: a photographic process used in making films of drawings and cartoons that move.

Arc light: the large and powerful carbon lamp, also called "brute," used to light the set for filming.

Arrange: the technical job of adapting a composer's music for the various orchestral instruments, and voices, if any.

Bit player: an actor with a small part in the movie.

Book: to make a date for the running of a completed movie in a theatre.

Budget: the sheet issued daily to the cast and crew advising them which scenes will be filmed the next day and which people will be involved.

Camera angle: simply the standpoint of the camera—high, low, close-up, long-range, etc.—in terms of the scene being filmed.

Camera boom: a mechanized crane extending high into the air that serves as a camera platform for high shots.

Cast: the actors. Sometimes an important prop is listed as part of the "cast."

Commissary: the studio restaurant.

Composite print: the edited, completed strip of film, including all sound tracks.

Cover set: a stand-by set that is used if rain or other inclement weather prevents filming as scheduled.

Crab dolly: a small, hand-pushed camera platform mounted on wheels to move in any direction.

From *People Who Make Movies*

Does an arc light light the dressing rooms, the set, or the movie theater?

Now suppose you want to know what a *cover set* is. Skim to find the term. When is a cover set used?

You should have read only the definitions for *arc light* and *cover set*. If this is what you did, you **skimmed.** By learning how to skim, you can save yourself a lot of time and trouble.

EXERCISE I. Practice in skimming a table

Suppose you are traveling from Glenwood to Brownsville. You must arrive before noon. Below is a timetable for the train. Skim to answer questions 1-3.

1. Where on the timetable is Brownsville listed?
2. What is the best arrival time?
3. What time will that train leave Glenwood?

From Glenwood	AM	AM	AM	PM	PM
Leaves . . . .Glenwood	8:35	9:14	9:50	12:35	2:00
Park Heights	8:58	9:37	10:13	12:58	2:23
Wayne	9:10	9:49	10:25	1:10	2:35
Sheridan	9:24	10:03	10:39	1:24	2:49
Georgetown	9:29	10:08	10:44	1:29	2:54
Arrives . . . .Brownsville	9:53	10:32	11:08	1:53	3:18

4. Using the same timetable, and the tool of skimming, find which train you should take from Park Heights in order to arrive in Sheridan by 3:00 P.M.
5. What time will you need to leave Wayne in order to arrive in Georgetown before 10:00 in the morning?

EXERCISE II. Practice in skimming connected material

Skimming is fairly easy with tabular material. But often you need to locate information that appears in the middle of a paragraph or a long article. You must be able to let your eyes glance quickly over the paragraph or page, looking for what you want without reading everything on the page. Numbers, capital letters, and italic or boldface type all stand out from ordinary print and can help you locate an answer.

Part A

Skim each paragraph below to find the answer to the question which comes just before it.

1. Where is the saluqi found?

> The saluqi is a beautiful dog, gentle, affectionate, and loyal in personality, and is found on the Arabian peninsula. To an American, the smooth-haired saluqi looks like a greyhound. He has a long, narrow snout, deep chest, fine waist, and hocks that are well down. . . .

2. How large is the meteor crater in Arizona?

> Meteors of frightening bulk have invaded the earth's atmosphere and have been big enough to make good-sized dents in the earth's crust. One of these, weighing millions of tons, fell long ago in what is now Arizona. It gouged out a crater 600 feet deep and 4000 feet across. The meteorite itself has never been found, but drilling samples indicate that it may have burrowed down some 1200 feet under the crater.

Part B

When the information you need is not made conspicuous by capital letters, numbers, or special type, it often helps if you concentrate on the word or words you want to find. Let your eyes move rapidly over the material. Stop only when you come to the words you want. You should find that the words almost leap out at you.

Suppose you are looking for information on buildings made of *adobe brick*. Skim the following three paragraphs to see if adobe brick is mentioned.

> (A) From the Treasury a road leads to the right. There are temples, tombs, and caves everywhere. Farther on, to the left, is a fine Roman amphitheater with seats for 3000. It is cut out of the rocks, and many cave dwellings had to be sacrificed to make its building possible.

> (B) Rows of buildings, many twelve stories high, seem to soar much higher than their actual height. For centuries the people of the area have built their skyscraper homes of adobe brick. The first floor is used for storage, the second for servants, the third for guests, and the upper floors for the family.

> (C) It is made by wetting clay, adding something such as grass roots or straw, and then mixing these together. Later it is shaped into bricks of various sizes which are

called adobe bricks. In the southwestern United States, especially California, these bricks are used for building, and walls made of them are surprisingly durable in dry climates.

3. Did you find *adobe brick* in any of the three paragraphs? If so, in which?

LESSON FOUR: Reading to get a general idea

You see a newspaper review of a movie you are interested in. For which of the following reasons would you read the whole article?

> A. You want to find out if your favorite actor has a part in the movie.
>
> B. You want to know something about the plot of the movie. Is it the kind of story you enjoy?

In situation A, you want just one specific piece of information. There is no need to read all the article. Instead, you can skim. In situation B, however, you will probably need to read all or most of the review. But since your purpose is merely to get a general idea of what the movie is about, you should read fairly rapidly—more rapidly than you would if you needed to remember details. This is reading at a medium rate of speed.

Read the following paragraph at a medium rate, to determine what it is generally about.

> Thrilling sequences in motion pictures—a spectacular car crash, a sprawling, bloody battle, a fist-fight in a Western saloon, a leap from the tall mast of a ship—are performed by Hollywood *stuntmen,* and sometimes by *stuntwomen.* Without them, no action picture could be made.
>
> From *People Who Make Movies*

1. What is this paragraph about?

Now read the next paragraph, again at a medium rate.

> Teen-age fads often provide ideas for movies. A new dance, a new sport, a new beat in music, are all prime subjects for the low-budget B-type film. Surfing alone has provided at least a dozen movies. The Frug, Swim, and Watusi were all incorporated quickly into films. A teen-age singing idol, or a group, will inevitably be offered a contract if the popularity ratings show up around the world. Before the ink is dry on the contract, a writer will be working to build a story around the "Slick Chicks," a hot new group, and before he can collect his pay, the film might be in front of the cameras.
>
> Adapted from *People Who Make Movies*

2. What kinds of things often provide ideas for B-type movies?
3. Is a B-type film made slowly or quickly?

You could probably answer questions like these fairly easily after a medium-speed reading of the paragraph. However, unless you have an unusual memory, you would probably not be able to repeat all the details, like all the teen-age fads mentioned, the names of the dances, and the name of the singing group. When you need to remember details like this, you would use the slow, careful method of reading described in the section on Inventory, beginning on page 427.

EXERCISE III. Suiting rate to purpose

Below are three reasons for reading the following article on snow-mobiles. What rate of reading (slow rate, medium rate, or skimming) would you use for purpose A? for purpose B? for purpose C?

A. You want to know how much a snowmobile costs.
B. You are giving a talk on snowmobiles and want to learn as much as you can about them.
C. You have heard that snowmobiles are becoming popular and want to find out what they are and what they are used for.

Read the article for purpose C, using the appropriate rate. Then answer the questions that follow the article.

One of the fastest growing sports in the United States today is snowmobiling or snowcatting. In 1964 there were 15,000 snowmobiles, but by 1967 the number had grown to almost 200,000. A snowmobile is a machine with a tractor-like belt tread on the bottom for traction, a seat, and handlebars that steer a pair of skis in front. It is easy to operate and costs from $700 to $2000. Speeds of up to 50 or 60 m.p.h. are possible over flat country. Drivers usually kneel because it helps their vision and makes it easier to shift weight to control the machine. Experienced drivers will stand to soften the bumps over difficult land.

Snowmobiles are used most often for recreational purposes, but telephone linemen, doctors, and others who need to travel in remote areas with heavy snowfalls are now finding them a practical means of getting around—better than snowshoes.

1. What is a snowmobile?
2. What is the main use of snowmobiles at present?

What you should know about flexibility

The rate at which you read depends upon the difficulty of the content and the purpose for which you are reading.

1. Skim quickly when you are looking for a specific detail only. Do not read every word in the material.

2. Read at a medium rate of speed when you want to know in general what something says but don't need to remember all the details.

3. Read most slowly when you need to remember completely or when the material is really difficult.

12

Inventory

LESSON ONE: Remembering what you read

Read this newspaper article at your normal rate.

Thus the Ice-Cream Cone Was Born—as a Waffle!

The year 1969 marks the 65th anniversary of that summertime favorite, the ice-cream cone.

This fact may not be world-shaking headline news, but who can deny the good-to-the-last-lick enjoyment that the ice-cream cone has brought throughout these years.

Strangely enough, the first ice-cream cone was thought up on the spur of the moment by a waffle seller at the St. Louis World's Fair, in 1904. It was an extremely hot afternoon—perfect ice-cream weather—when Ernest Hamwi looked up from his waffle-making and noticed that his neighbor, an ice-cream vendor, had run out of ice-cream cups. The lack of cups was raising complaints from would-be customers seeking refreshment in some cooling ice cream.

Struck with an idea, Mr. Hamwi took a hot waffle from the griddle and quickly shaped it into a cone. He let it cool and harden, and then presented it to the troubled ice-cream vendor. The waiting customers were puzzled, then delighted, as they watched the vendor fill the cone with scoops of ice cream.

Thus the ice-cream cone was born—according to a legend which the ice-cream industry accepts as gospel truth.

Try to complete the following statements without looking back.

1. The article tells how the first _____ was made.
2. It was made in _____(year) at the _____ World's Fair.
3. A (n)_____ vendor teamed up with a (n)_____ vendor to produce the first dessert of this kind.

You were probably able to fill in the correct information, since the article is short, contains few facts, and is easy to understand.

Remembering what you read would be easy if every reading assignment were as short and simple as that one. However, many of the things you read in school (assignments in science and social studies, for example) may be fairly long, and packed with many facts you need to remember. When you need to understand and remember harder material, **taking inventory** of the material can be helpful.

To take inventory in reading, you do the following:

1. Get a general idea of what the material is about by reading the title, looking at illustrations if there are any, and reading the first few paragraphs (sometimes also the last). If the material is short, you may wish to read it all the way through very quickly.

2. Go back and read a small part of the selection (one or two paragraphs) slowly and carefully. Stop frequently to fix important details in your memory. (One way to do this is to ask yourself questions about what you have just read.) Look up the meaning of unfamiliar words and try to figure out the meaning of difficult sentences.

3. When you have read a paragraph or two, stop and think over what you have read. Then try to predict what the author will say next.

   Repeat steps 2 and 3 as many times as necessary to complete your study of the material.

4. Summarize the entire selection by telling briefly in your own words what it says.

LESSON TWO: Taking inventory of an article[1]

STEP I—Get a general idea of what the selection is about.

You don't have to read an article carefully to get a general idea of what it is about. Normally, all you need to do is read the title, look at the illustrations and any information printed under them, and then read the first paragraph or two.

---

[1]The article used in this lesson is abridged from pp. 16-17, 20-21 of *Kilauea: Case History of a Volcano* by Don Herber and Fulvio Bardossi. Copyright © 1968 by Prism Productions, Inc. Reprinted by permission of Harper & Row, Publishers.

Try the following example:

One of the Deadliest Volcanic Eruptions in History

One of the best-known islands in the West Indies is Martinique. In 1902, St. Pierre, Martinique, population 28,000, was a beautiful city. On May 8, in just a few minutes, it was completely devastated. The destruction came from Mount Pelée, a volcano about 4000 feet high, several miles north of the city.

Courtesy of the American Museum of Natural History

QUESTION: What will this article be about?

If you have a general idea of what an article is about before you read it carefully, you are better prepared to decide which information is important enough to remember.

STEP II—Read the selection slowly and carefully, a few paragraphs at a time.

Your purpose in reading carefully is to understand what is written and to remember all the important things the writer says. You will succeed if you

—figure out the meaning of unfamiliar words, using the CSSD approach.

—reread difficult sentences and think about what they mean.

—decide which information is most important and fix it in your mind.

If you have trouble deciding whether or not a detail is important, see if it answers one of these questions:

WHO or WHAT did WHAT?
WHEN?
WHERE?
WHY?
HOW?

Once you have decided that a fact is important, try to fix it in your memory. You might repeat the information over and over until you think you know it, you might relate it to something you know, or you might ask yourself questions about what you have read. Use the method that works best for you.

Following is some material on which to practice the second step of inventory, reading slowly and carefully. In the margins are questions the article answers, questions you might ask yourself to make sure you understand and remember these points. When you see this sign ☐, stop reading and answer the question. Questions at the right have to do with the most important points in the article. Those at the left refer to word meanings and less important details.

One of the Deadliest Volcanic Eruptions in History

DETAILS

MAIN POINTS

One of the best-known islands in the West Indies is Martinique. In 1902, St. Pierre, Martinique ☐, population 28,000 Ⓐ, was a beautiful city. On May 8, in just a few minutes, it was completely devastated Ⓑ. ☐ The destruction came from Mount Pelée, a

Ⓐ How large is St. Pierre?

Ⓑ What does "devastated" mean?

① What city is mentioned? Where is it?

② What happened to the city? When?

C — What is the name of the volcano?

D — About how long was this before the city was destroyed?

volcano about 4000 feet high C , several miles north of the city. ③

Only twice in a hundred years had Mount Pelée shown any signs of activity. The people of St. Pierre had no fear of the grand old mountain. Some looked on it as a protector against storms from land or sea. ④

So there was no alarm when, on April 23 D , a column of smoke rose from Mount Pelée and a light shower of ash fell in the streets. ⑤ But Mount Pelée continued to show signs of unrest.

③ — What caused the destruction?

④ — Why didn't people fear Mount Pelée?

⑤ — How did people first react to the smoke and ashes?

STEP III—Think back over what you have read and predict what will come next.

As you are reading carefully, stop occasionally to review what you have read and to try to predict what the author will say next. This step helps you become more alert to the remaining material.

In Step I, you looked at the picture, read the title, and read the first paragraph. Then you were asked to guess what the article would be about. This wasn't hard, since the clues were obvious: a picture of a volcano erupting, a title mentioning a deadly volcanic eruption, etc.

In Step III, you are again asked to predict on the basis of clues. Look again at the last paragraph you read in the article, paying special attention to the last sentence.

What will the next part of the article tell about—(1) additional danger warnings, or (2) past eruptions of Mount Pelée?

Continue reading to see if you predicted correctly.

E — What is a crater?

Observers sent to the rim to investigate reported that the crater's E normally dry bed now held a lake 200 yards wide, and that a small cone had formed at one side. But they saw no cause for undue concern. ⑥

The falling ash became heavier, masking the sun and muffling the street

⑥ — How had the crater changed? How did people react?

F Picture the
scene in your
mind.

G About how long
has all this been
going on?

H What is an
avalanche?

noises of bustling St. Pierre. Puffs of wind blew the ash in swirls of black snow from roofs and awnings. F Tension grew as earthquakes and the thunder of the volcano increased. 7 On May 5 G, water heated by the volcano flowed down a steep valley, forming a deluge of mud and huge boulders. Gathering speed as it rushed down the mountain, the flood swept over a sugar mill and killed more than 20 workmen. 8 In only three minutes, the boiling avalanche H, nearly a half mile wide, traveled three miles and poured into the sea at a point on the coast beyond St. Pierre. The water receded almost 100 yards from the west coast of the island and then piled shoreward again in a wave that flooded the St. Pierre waterfront and capsized several boats at anchor. 9

7 What first
caused people
to worry?

8 What was the
first serious
happening?

9 What other
damage was
done? What
caused it?

Review what has happened so far in St. Pierre. Then try to predict what will come next.

Will the next section tell (1) how the people calmly repaired the damage caused by the wave, refusing to get upset over the disturbance caused by Mount Pelée, or (2) how the people became worried that their lives and property were in real danger?

Continue reading to see if your prediction is correct. From here on there will be a few questions in the margin, and some additional stopping places indicated. When you come to a stopping point, ask yourself questions about what you have just read. You must decide for yourself what details are important to remember.

As you read the rest of the article about Mount Pelée, take time to form images of what is happening. What do you see in your mind? If you were there, what would you hear? What might you smell? When you have read a paragraph, stop to think back over what you have read.

The entire city was aroused. Confusion and fear were intensified ⑨ by the people flocking in from outlying areas near the volcano. Businesses closed and many of the citizens prepared to flee. ⑩ But panic was prevented by a report that a group of experts appointed by the governor of Martinique had decided that there was no need to evacuate Ⓙ the city. People were also reassured when the governor and his wife, in a show of confidence, settled down for a visit in St. Pierre. ⑪

⑪ How were the people assured there was no danger?

Most of the citizens stayed and endured several more frightening days and nights. May 8 Ⓚ dawned bright and sunny. Except for the vapor rising from the summit, Mount Pelée appeared normal. ⑫ At 7:50 A.M. a huge crack appeared in the side of the volcano, and with an explosive roar a glowing black "cloud" shot upward and outward from the summit. The cloud was so dense that only part of it spread out into the upper air. The rest swept down the mountainside with the speed of an avalanche—an avalanche of super-heated steam, dust, and ashes. In two minutes it swept through the entire city and fanned out over the sea, scorching vessels riding in the harbor and turning the water so hot that large numbers of fish died. ⑬

Ⓛ How many people died?

More than 30,000 people perished Ⓛ —practically the entire population of St. Pierre and many persons aboard the anchored ships. The roofs of all buildings were swept away. Cement and stone walls three feet thick were torn apart. A three-ton statue of the Virgin Mary was tossed 50 feet off its base. ⑭

⑭ What happened to the city?

Flames shot up in the wake Ⓜ of the "glowing cloud." The ground was so hot that rescuers could not approach the shore for hours. When they did, they found only three survivors. ⑮ The first, a woman, died within an hour. The second, a shoemaker, was severely burned, but had miraculously escaped from his seared Ⓝ house and run to a suburb. The third, a prisoner, was found three days after the eruption in a windowless dungeon of the city jail. ⑯ The only opening to the cell was a grating in the door. Even so, he suffered horrible burns. When he recovered, he was pardoned and joined a circus side show. Ⓞ

⑯ Who were the survivors?

During the summer there were several more eruptions from Mount Pelée. One of them partially destroyed five villages and claimed another 2000 victims. ⑰ Five months after the first eruption a stiff mass of lava rose like a gigantic tower from the throat of the crater to a height of 1000 feet. Then it slowly disintegrated Ⓟ into a stump standing in its own ruins. ⑱

STEP IV—Summarize the selection.

The last step in taking inventory is summarizing what you have read. In summarizing, you condense the selection into a few sentences which give the most important facts and sometimes the central idea. You should emphasize information that tells you WHO, WHAT, WHEN, WHERE, WHY, and HOW.

Here is a summary of the article you have just read.

On May 8, 1902, Mount Pelée, a volcano on the island of Martinique in the West Indies, erupted and destroyed practically the entire city of St. Pierre. For two weeks, the volcano had been showing signs of erupting. A lake had formed in the crater, black ash, boiling water, and mud came out, and the earth trembled. People were worried, but government officials assured them there was no danger. However, on the morning of May 8, a big crack opened in the mountain and a huge black "cloud" of hot steam, dust, and ashes shot out and swept down on the city, destroying it in two minutes. Only two people survived.

LESSON THREE: Applying the inventory method to poetry

The inventory method may help you read fiction and poetry, too. Whenever you are reading material (*a*) that is difficult, or (*b*) that contains many details which you need to remember, you should use this careful, intensive reading method.

Poetry often packs a great deal of meaning into a few words. This lesson shows how a poem should be read if you want to understand it thoroughly.

STEP I

Read the title and look at the illustrations, if there are any. Then read the entire poem straight through. You *may* find that the poem is easy to understand and therefore won't require the complete inventory process. More likely, though, there will be lines you don't understand completely on a first reading. Notice where these hard spots are. They will require special attention when you go through the poem again.

Read through the following poem to get an idea of what it is generally about.

The Domestic
by Thomas H. McNeal

At two in the cold winter morning
    I heard the geese fly over;
And I thought how good is a man-made bed,
    And the weight of the soft warm cover.

I thought how cold it was out there—
    How long it would be till day;
And then, like a knife, came the leader's call:
    To wing!—To wing and away!

And the poor goose inside me that I had tamed
    To a fowl most certain and stable
Got out of bed and turned on a light
    And studied an old timetable.

"The Domestic" from *Three Lyric Poets* by Thomas H. McNeal. Reprinted by permission of Swallow Press, Chicago, Illinois.

This isn't a really difficult poem, but there may be more in it than you would think from a first reading. The next step will show you.

STEP II

As you reread the poem, try to form mental images. Think about all the different things the words suggest. When you see this sign ③, stop and answer the question in the margin.

The Domestic [A]
by Thomas H. McNeal

DETAILS

[A] What does "domestic" mean?

[B] What kind of birds are usually called fowls?

[C] What do "certain" and "stable" mean?

At two in the cold winter morning [1]

I heard the geese fly over;

And I thought how good is a man-made bed,

And the weight of the soft warm cover. [2]

I thought how cold it was out there—

How long it would be till day; [3]

And then, like a knife, came the leader's [4] call:

To wing!—To wing and away! [5]

And the poor goose inside me [6] that I had tamed

To a fowl [B] most certain and stable [7] [C]

Got out of bed and turned on a light

And studied an old timetable. [8]

MAIN POINTS

[1] When does this happen?

[2] Where is the person who is speaking? How does he feel?

[3] What two things does the speaker think about?

[4] Who is the "leader"

[5] What does the speaker really hear?

[6] What does the speaker mean by "the poor goose inside me"?

[7] What is the speaker like now? What do you think he was like earlier in his life?

[8] Why does a person usually study a timetable? What is suggested by the fact that the timetable is old?

After you have gone through the poem slowly and carefully and answered the questions, go back and read it straight through again, to understand it as a whole. Think about these questions:

—What beyond geese is this poem about?

—What kind of people are like wild geese?

—What kind of people are "domestic"?

STEP III

Now you are ready for the final step. In just a few sentences, try to state the important facts that are given and the meaning or central idea of the poem.

You may have noticed that no mention was made of predicting. This step is unnecessary when the material is short.

LESSON FOUR: More practice with poetry

STEP I

Read the title and then read straight through the poem to get a general idea of what it says. How is the form of this poem different from "The Domestic"?

This Morning
by Jay Wright

This morning I threw the windows
of my room open, the light burst
in like crystal gauze and I hung
it on my wall to frame.
5 And here I am watching it take possession
of my room, watching the obscure love
match of light and shadow—of cold and warmth.
It is a matter of acceptance, I guess.
It is a matter of finding some room
10 with shadows to embrace, open. Now
the light has settled in, I don't think
I shall ever close my windows again.

This poem will probably require more careful reading than "The Domestic." The easiest lines are at the beginning and end; the middle lines may seem confusing. Taking inventory will help you understand what it is all about.

"This Morning" from *New Negro Poets: USA*, edited by Langston Hughes. Copyright © 1964 by Langston Hughes. Reprinted by permission of the publisher, Indiana University Press.

As you read through the poem again, try to find the meaning of difficult passages by answering the questions in the margin. Places where you should stop are marked with the sign ⬜.

This Morning
by Jay Wright

1 This morning I threw the windows

2 of my room open, the light burst

3 in like crystal gauze ⬜ and I hung

⬜ What would gauze made of crystal look like?

4 it on my wall to frame. ⬜

⬜ Did the speaker put a frame around the light, or did the light shine on a dark section of the wall, making the light part look as if it had a frame?

5 And here I am watching it take possession

6 of my room, ⬜ watching the obscure love

⬜ What takes possession of the room? What does the speaker see happening?

7 match of light and shadow—of cold

and warmth. ⬜

⬜ Are light and shadow alike, or different? What about cold and warmth?

Notice that the speaker sees the mingling or mixing of darkness and sunlight as a "love match," something only humans can experience. As you read the rest of the poem, see if what the speaker says could apply to love between humans.

8 It is a matter of acceptance, I guess.

9 It is a matter of finding some room

⬜ In what way does love depend on finding someone willing to accept you?

10 with shadows to embrace, open. ⬜ Now

⬜ Which of the following words could best be substituted for "light" in line 11? warmth, sun, happiness, love, person

11 the light has settled in, ⬜ I don't think

12 I shall ever close my windows again. ⬜

⬜ Why doesn't the speaker want to close his windows? Which of the following could best be substituted for "windows" in line 12? heart, shutters, eyes, life

Now go back and reread the entire poem again.

Which of these paragraphs best summarizes the central idea of the poem?

(A) When the speaker opened the windows of his room, the light came in, changing the cold and darkness to light and warmth. The light looked so pretty—just like crystal gauze—that he decided never to close his windows again.

(B) Just as a darkened room cannot be brightened unless its windows are opened to the sunlight, a person cannot experience love unless he opens his heart.

What you should know about taking inventory

When your purpose in reading is complete understanding and recall, you should use the inventory method. This is how you do it:

1. Read enough of the selection to get a general idea of what it is about. Usually this means looking at illustrations, reading the title, and reading the first few paragraphs.

2. Go back and read a small part of the selection slowly and carefully. Stop often to fix important details in your memory and to make sure you understand difficult sentences and unfamiliar words.

3. Stop occasionally to review what you have read. Then try to predict what will come next. Look for hints the author gives. Repeat steps 2 and 3 until you have completed the material.

4. Summarize the entire selection by giving briefly its main points.

13

How far away is THEN?

It depends on where you stand—

and when.

With today in your eye,

look at yesterday.

Does it seem

a long way back?

Ford's Fabulous Flivver

by Lyman M. Nash

You could usually patch up engine troubles with a paper clip or a safety pin. If the radiator leaked, you threw in a handful of oatmeal.

EARLY one morning near the end of June, 1909, a farmer in western Washington was consternated to hear what at first he thought was the end of the world. Rushing from his barn, he saw an object resembling an abbreviated coffin followed by a park bench. The strange contraption was mounted on four wheels and hurtling toward Seattle at forty miles an hour.

"Now what in thunderation's that?" he asked himself. But before he could investigate, the thing had disappeared in a cloud of dust and smoke. Not until the next day, when he picked up the Seattle *Times*, was the mystery solved.

He had seen a Model T Ford, winner of the "Ocean to Ocean Automobile Endurance Contest for the M. Robert Guggenheim Trophy."

Everything that could possibly happen to a car happened to that Ford. It ran out of gas, got lost, survived a fire, and traveled most of the way through gooey, axle-deep mud. It sank into quicksand in Colorado and into four feet of snow in Snoqualmie Pass, where it had to be rescued by a railroad section gang. Yet, 22 days and 55 minutes after leaving New York, it crossed the finish line in Seattle, 17 hours ahead of its closest rival, a much more powerful Shawmut.

"By golly," the farmer said, after reading an account of the trip, "the

Reprinted (slightly abridged) by permission of the author and *Boys' Life,* published by the Boy Scouts of America.

Model T is quite a car." Then he went out and bought one. So did a lot of other people, making Henry Ford a billionaire and his Model T the hottest selling vehicle since someone invented the wheel.

In less than ten years half the cars on the road were Model T's, in one form or another. They were converted into trucks, tractors, fire engines, ambulances, buses, taxicabs, and paddy wagons. Railroads added flanged wheels and used them as inspection cars. Hollywood made them collapsible and featured them in many a Keystone Cops comedy chase.

A Model T could plow fields in the spring, pull a harvester in the fall, and churn butter in between. By jacking up its rear end and attaching a drive belt, you could use it to pump water, grind feed, press cider, generate electricity, or run a buzz saw. About the only thing a Model T couldn't do was talk.

Not that Ford's flivver was perfect. It had more faults than a dollar watch, though none of the faults was fatal. There was, for instance, the matter of hills. Because of the gearing, you frequently had to attack steep grades backward, a maneuver which also helped preserve the front bearing. And even in the best of humor it was noisier than a canning factory with St. Vitus' Dance.

Getting a Model T started was a test of strength, endurance, and will power. First, you set the spark and throttle levers on the steering column at quarter to four. Going around to the front, you pulled out the choke wire emerging from the radiator. Then you took a firm grip on the crank and gave it a mighty spin. If the crank didn't snap back and break your arm, you grumbled a bit and spun a second time.

When the engine caught, you leaped back to the throttle and eased off on the gas; otherwise, the car was liable to shake itself into its component parts. Leaping was a necessity, as Model T's had a habit of advancing and nuzzling you like a friendly, oversized Great Dane.

Once the engine was going, however, the rest was simple. At your feet were three pedals: clutch on the left, reverse in the middle, brake on the right. Depressing the clutch pedal engaged the planetary transmission, starting you in low. When you reached what you judged to be twenty miles an hour, you lifted your foot and catapulted into high. That is all there was to it. In an emergency you could step on any of the pedals, and the car would at least slow down.

Until the advent of the Model T, automobiles were considered a needless extravagance. They cost as much as a house, were forever breaking down, and had an affinity for mud from which they refused to depart under their own power. Good old Dobbin still ruled the road, or what usually passed as a road. Any scalawag foolish enough to chug by in a newfangled gas buggy was rewarded with scowls of dark suspicion, if not outright violence.

Henry Ford changed all that in 1908. The Model T was cheap to buy, cheap to run, and hardly anything ever went wrong with it that could not be fixed with a monkey wrench and a jackknife. Tough and reliable, it proved so popular that Henry hung a permanent OUT TO LUNCH sign on his designing-room door and for nineteen years made nothing else.

Ford was born on a farm near Dearborn, Michigan, in 1863, and as soon as he was old enough, he hied himself to Detroit. He became an expert with steam engines, got married, and took a job as engineer with the Edison Illuminating Company.

He began tinkering with gas engines in his spare time, building them in a shed behind his home and testing them in the kitchen sink. Convinced that a mechanized bicycle was practical, he purchased two wheels and set to work.

One thing led to another, and the bicycle wound up as a quadricycle. He finished it at four o'clock on the morning of June 4, 1896. At 4:01 he discovered it was too wide to get out of the door. He made the necessary adjustments to the shed with an ax, spun the flywheel, and hopped into the driver's seat. A light rain was falling as he crept into the dawn, preceded by a friend on a bike to warn off any hayburners that might be afoot at that hour.

The first Ford automobile created a sensation on the streets of Detroit. It stopped traffic, scared horses, and had to be chained to a lamppost or, sure as shooting, some fool would hop in and try to drive away. Authorities considered it such a nuisance that Ford had to get a special permit from the mayor in order to drive it, making him for a time the only licensed driver in America.

His second car, two years later, was a nifty little runabout, notable mainly because only the front wheels turned, not the entire front axle. "That Henry," people began saying. "What won't he think of next?"

Henry thought next of racing cars, building a number of them. The most famous, 999, is now a legend. A real brute of a vehicle, it developed 80 horsepower in four seven-inch cylinders and spouted flame like an angry dragon. Ford drove it to a new speed record of 91.4 miles an hour on the ice of Lake St. Clair, but was afraid to open it up on a closed track. A young bicycle racer, Barney Oldfield, was recruited as a pilot, and under his lead foot Old 999 thundered to glory, beating everything in sight.

In 1903 Henry got down to real business. With twelve stockholders and $28,000 cash, he founded the Ford Motor Company. During the next five years he built a variety of cars. They had two, four, and six cylinders, and one had the engine behind the driver's seat. Starting with Model A, he skipped around the alphabet and in 1908 had finished with the letter "S."

He was now ready to challenge Dobbin.

As Henry saw it, automobiles were too blamed expensive. Why were they expensive? Because of all the ornate hardware. Eliminate the doodads, that was the answer, cut out the frills. Who needs a temperature gauge, anyway?

The result of this logic was the Model T. It had no bumpers, windshield wipers, water pump, speedometer, gas gauge, or battery, and merely the stamped outline of a left front door. The fuel tank was under the front seat, feeding the engine by gravity.

To find out how much gas you had, you removed the seat and everything on it, unscrewed the cap, and stuck in a sounding stick. To check your oil, you had to crawl underneath and fiddle with two petcocks on the rear of the crankcase. The one concession to styling was the fenders, and they looked as if they had been tacked on by mistake and were ready to fall off.

The Model T was ugly as sin to begin with, and throughout its long life Henry never got around to giving it a beauty treatment. But it sold. It sold like hotcakes. For years Ford's biggest headache was trying to keep up with the demand.

At a time when the average price of a car was over $2000, you could take home a Model T for $850, and the price kept dropping, down to a low of $260. Early Model T's came in red, gray, or Brewster green. Then Ford said, "Any customer can have a car painted any color he wants so long as it is black," and black the flivver remained forevermore.

Parts were available almost everywhere: the dime store, the blacksmith shop, the corner grocery; and they were cheap, too. A peck of potatoes and a muffler cost less than $2. A new fender set you back $6, the same as a carburetor. You could, if you wished, buy a Model T piece by piece and put it together yourself.

Whether you started from scratch or drove it off the showroom floor, you had a car weighing 1200 pounds with a wheelbase of 100 inches. It would turn inside a 12-foot circle and do 45 miles an hour, assisted by a tail wind. With its top up it stood 7 feet and was high enough off the ground to clear all bumps and most tree stumps.

The four-cylinder engine banged out 20 horsepower, giving the Model T a fantastic power-to-weight ratio compared to other cars on the road. You were fairly certain if it got you there it would bring you home, be it through mud, loose sand, or a foot of snow.

Most engine troubles could usually be patched up with a paper clip, a safety pin, or a piece of wire. Should a Model T conk out completely, a short rest was often enough to get it going again, good as new. Radiator leaks were easily stopped by throwing in a handful of oatmeal.

The Model T's myriad eccentricities endowed it with a certain curious personality. No two sounded alike, and no two ran alike. Yours might list to the right, your neighbor's to the left, and down the block was one that sagged in the middle. Nearly everybody took to calling his Model T "Lizzie," after the Queen of Spades in the game of Hearts.

A new Model T began rattling immediately. By the end of a year, you only had to look at it and it began to chatter. For 98 cents you could buy a set of antirattlers for the engine, but all they did was give the rattle a sort of muffled sound. You also bought antirattlers for the doors and fenders.

And that was only the beginning. Many other gadgets were on the market to dress up, diminish, or camouflage Lizzie's remarkable deficiencies. A set of bumpers sold for $2.95, a foot accelerator for 50 cents, and a steering-column brace for 75 cents. If you didn't like the shape of the radiator and had $11.75, you purchased a streamlined hood and radiator shell.

However, most Model T's went their way, unadorned and undisguised, doing things no car had done before and few have done since.

In 1911, Henry Alexander drove a Model T to the rugged, rocky summit of Ben Nevis, highest peak in the British Isles. Model T's uncomplainingly climbed the steps of the YMCA in Columbus, Nebraska, the courthouse in Duluth, Minnesota, and the state capitol of Tennessee.

The first car sold in Turkey was a Model T. Two Russian grand dukes and nineteen lesser princes bought flivvers. Arabian sheikhs and Indian maharajas took delivery by the dozen. By the 1920's, it was impossible to travel anywhere in the world without running into a Model T, or what had once been a Model T. They hauled mail in Alaska, tourists in Egypt, and explorers in the Philippines, while pieces of them kept cropping up in the most unlikely places.

Shortly after World War I, an American driving his Lizzie through a remote part of Palestine broke the drive-shaft pinion on the differential gear. Hiking to a village of mud huts, he noticed an Arab measuring dried beans on a primitive scale. Balancing the beans was, of all things, a Model T drive-shaft pinion. The Arab had picked it up at a British army repair depot during the war.

In the wake of the Model T came Model T jokes. No vaudeville program was complete without them.

Salesman: Can I sell you a speedometer?

Customer: I don't need one. At ten miles an hour my teeth rattle, at fifteen my fenders rattle, and when I'm going twenty the transmission falls out.

Or take this salty exchange, dated 1917: "I hear the new Ford isn't very noisy."

"Why is that?"

"They've taken the brass bands off the radiator."

Then there was the farmer who stripped the tin roof from his barn and sent it to the Ford factory. A few days later he received a letter saying, "While your car was one of the worst wrecks we've ever seen, we will be able to make repairs and return it to you by the end of the week."

Henry Ford didn't mind those jokes at all, even the bad ones. Every wisecrack was free publicity and kept him laughing all the way to the bank, for the Model T was a phenomenal moneymaker. A lady who invested $100 in the firm collected $95,000 in dividends and was paid $260,000 for her stock. A lawyer who put $5000 into the company got back $12,500,000.

Through nearly two decades the Model T remained unchanged, except for minor improvements. In 1915, the acetylene headlights were replaced with electric ones, but Ford still hadn't gotten around to providing a battery, so they worked off a magneto on the flywheel. They dimmed or brightened, depending on your speed. You had to travel at a good clip to see what lay ahead, and if you stopped to read a road sign, you raced the engine.

A self-starter was offered in 1919, as an extra, and you could also get demountable rims instead of clincher tires, also an extra. Those clincher tires were really something. To fix a puncture you had to pry the tire from the rim, take out the tube, patch it, return it to the tire, and somehow get the tire back in place. An amateur could finish the task in half an hour, an expert in thirty minutes. Then it took an hour to pump up the tire, which was good for any number of punctures but lasted only 3000 miles.

But as the years passed, the Model T began more and more to show her age. By the middle 1920's other makes of cars in snappy colors, with smoothly functioning gearshifts and annual beauty treatments, were catching on. Why buy a flivver and get only the bare essentials when, for a little more, you could get a flashier, more comfortable Chevrolet? The handwriting was on the wall. Ford saw it in 1927. On May 26, after nineteen unrivaled and untroubled years, Model T No. 15,007,-033 rolled off the assembly line.

Henry closed the plant, removed the OUT TO LUNCH sign from the designing room, and went inside. Six months later he came out with a new design: the Model A.

While it had lasted, America went from the horse-and-buggy to the gasoline age. The year Model T was born there were about 200,000 cars in the United States, moving haltingly on muddy, rutted roads. When the flivver went out of production, there were 30,000,000 cars sweeping effortlessly along smooth concrete highways, and half of them were Fords.

But Lizzie's day was far from over. Because of its simple durability the Model T became the perfect schoolboy's car. Decorated with catchy legends such as THE TIN YOU LOVE TO TOUCH and CAPACITY: 5 GALS, they blossomed around every high school in the land.

In time the Model T passed from the student to the antique car buff. Small fortunes were spent restoring them to mint condition, searching for the proper tires, locating an authentic acetylene headlamp. Model T clubs sprang up and sponsored meets, rallies, and tours, fostering renewed interest in the fabulous flivver that Henry made.

How good was the Model T? Well, some 300,000 are still alive today. True, many are cherished treasures, babied, pampered, and reserved for parades. But many more are in daily service after more than fifty years. With reasonable luck they will continue to shimmy, shake, wheeze, and rattle fifty more. And that marvel of machinery that made it go, the planetary transmission, is the basis of our modern automatic drives.

Perhaps, if you are lucky, you may discover a Model T standing quietly in a shed someplace, waiting for a new lease on life. Then, with time and patience and hard work, you can restore it to the way it used to be.

Or you might just possibly come upon a new one, coated only with a layer of dust. When a New Jersey woman heard that her favorite transportation was going out of production, she ordered several, ". . . so I'll never be without a Model T." A lot of other people did likewise. Those that didn't, have been kicking themselves ever since. THE END

Talking it over

1. *a.* Why did the Model T become so popular? How widely did its popularity spread?

b. What were the main disadvantages of the car?

c. What truly unusual things could the Model T do?

2. *a.* What is meant by the statement that Henry Ford "hung a permanent OUT TO LUNCH sign on his designing-room door"?

b. How long did the "sign" stay? What finally caused Ford to design a new model?

3. Model T's were around for a long time, even after Ford stopped producing them. Who continued to use these cars? What people are especially interested in them today?

4. Imagine you are a car manufacturer and find you can produce a simple, stripped-down car like the Model T to sell for $950 today. Would you go ahead with it? Give reasons.

Words in action

When you read that the Model T often had to attack steep *grades* backward, were you puzzled for a moment? *Grade* is one of the common words which has many meanings.

1. How many meanings are given in the dictionary entry for **grade?** Which meaning would fit best in "There were few **graded roads** at this time"?

2. How many meanings are given for **depress?** Which meaning would apply if you were to **depress the clutch pedal** on the Model T?

3. Which of the meanings given for **curious** would apply if you said that the Model T had a **curious personality?**

4. The five separate entries for **list** mean that there are five different words spelled this way. Which entry fits this sentence: "Yours might **list** to the right, your neighbor's to the left. . . ."?

5. If Ford's Old 999 "thundered to glory" under Barney Oldfield's **lead foot**, did Barney drive slowly, moderately fast, or fast, in terms of the car's possible speed? What does "lead foot" mean here? Which entry applies—**lead**[1] or **lead**[2]?

cu ri ous (kyür/ē əs), **1.** eager to know: *a curious student.* **2.** too eager to know; prying: *The old woman is too curious about other people's business.* **3.** strange; odd; unusual: *a curious old book.* **4.** very careful; exact: *a curious inquiry into the customs of the Pygmies.* **5.** *Informal.* very odd; eccentric: *curious notions.* *adj.* —**cu′ri ous ly,** *adv.* —**cu′ri ous ness,** *n.*

de press (di pres/), **1.** make sad or gloomy; cause to have low spirits: *She was depressed by the bad news from home.* **2.** press down; push down; lower: *When you play the piano, you depress the keys.* **3.** lower in amount or value: *The price of potatoes has been depressed by the tremendous size of the harvest this year.* **4.** reduce the activity of; weaken: *Some medicines depress the action of the heart.* *v.* **de press′ing ly,** *adv.*

grade (grād), **1.** any one division of a school arranged according to the pupils' progress: *the seventh grade.* **2.** step or stage in a course or process. **3.** degree in a scale of rank, quality, value, etc.: *Grade A milk is the best milk.* **4.** group of people or things having the same rank, quality, value, etc. **5.** place in classes; arrange in grades; sort: *These apples are graded by size.* **6.** be of a particular grade or quality. **7.** *U.S.* number or letter that shows how well one has done. **8.** *U.S.* give a grade to: *The teacher graded the papers.* **9.** slope of a road, railroad track, etc.: *a steep grade.* **10.** amount of slope. **11.** make more nearly level: *The road up the steep hill was graded.* **12.** change gradually; go through a series of steps, stages, or degrees: *Red and yellow grade into orange.* 1-4,7,9,10 *n.,* 5,6,8,11,12 *v.,* **grad ed, grad ing.**

lead¹ (lēd), **1.** show the way by going along with or in front of: *He leads the horses to water.* **2.** be first among: *She leads the class in spelling.* **3.** be a way or road: *Hard work leads to success.* **4.** pass or spend (time) in some special way: *He leads a quiet life in the country.* **5.** go first; begin a game: *You may lead this time.* **6.** place of leader; place in front: *He always takes the lead when we plan to do anything.* **7.** right to play first: *It is your lead this time.* **8.** amount that one is ahead: *He had a lead of 3 yards in the race.* 1-5 *v.,* **led, lead ing;** 6-8 *n.*
lead off, begin; start.
lead up to, prepare the way for.

lead² (led), **1.** a heavy, easily melted, bluish-gray metal, used to make pipe, etc. Lead is a chemical element. *Symbol:* Pb. **2.** something made of this metal or one of its alloys. **3.** made of lead. **4.** weight on a line used to find out the depth of water; plummet. **5.** bullets; shot: *a hail of lead.* **6.** a long, thin piece of graphite as used in pencils. **7.** a metal strip for widening the space between lines in printing. **8.** insert leads between the lines of (print). **9.** cover, frame, or weight with lead. 1,2,4-7 *n.,* 3 *adj.,* 8 *v.*

list¹ (list), **1.** series of names, numbers, words, etc.: *a shopping list.* **2.** make a list of; enter in a list: *I shall list my errands on a card.* **3.** enlist. 1 *n.,* 2,3 *v.*

list² (list), the woven edge of cloth, where the material is a little different; selvage. *n.*

list³ (list), **1.** a tipping to one side; tilt: *the list of a ship.* **2.** tip to one side; tilt. 1 *n.,* 2 *v.*

list⁴ (list), *Archaic.* **1.** be pleasing to; please: *Me lists not to speak.* **2.** like; wish: *The wind bloweth where it listeth.* *v.*

list⁵ (list), *Archaic and Poetic.* **1.** listen. **2.** listen to. *v.*

Inspired by a car buff

When asked how he happened to write "Ford's Fabulous Flivver," Mr. Nash wrote:

"The idea was in the back of my head for a long time. As a boy in Wisconsin I had several encounters with this rugged vehicle, and I remember one farmer who used his for everything from shelling corn to pulling a plow to sawing wood. It was an old car then, and I wouldn't be a bit surprised if it is still going strong. Later, I met many a Model T chugging along the back roads of Indiana, fenders crumpled, canvas rotted, but not yet ready for the junk heap. How many modern cars will be as vigorous after thirty years?

"But the thing that really got me going occurred in—of all places!—London, England. It was a chill, rainy night and the wife and I had spent the evening talking cars to an English motoring enthusiast. Fred offered to drive us to our hotel. But we didn't go straight there. Instead, he took us on an eery midnight tour of London, visit-all the ritzy car salons. . . .

"Eventually we did make it back to our hotel, and as we said goodnight, Fred gently patted a sagging fender of his decrepit Model T, saying, 'She's old and inclined to be cranky, but I wouldn't trade her for any of the fancy limousines we've seen tonight.' "

Everybody's father was out of work, and things you were lucky enough to own were things you might have to sell . . . .

Why the Iceman stopped coming to our flat

by Dick Perry

SUMMER was exactly six days away but at 4:33 P.M., Thursday, June 15, Raymond and I sat in my kitchen, sweating and waiting for Little Orphan Annie on the radio and hoping she wasn't as hot as we were. It promised to be a good summer: Roosevelt[1] was President, every father was out of work, and Raymond was my best friend.

Raymond was eleven and smarter than me. He had brown eyes, drank coffee, and was usually at the library, which was free. His family lived on the second floor rear in two rooms in the same tenement my family lived on the third floor front of. We lived in two rooms, too. My name is George and I was ten. Whenever we wanted each other we pounded on the water pipes with a special kind of code people could hear in every flat in the building.

But right now we were in my kitchen and Raymond was looking at the icebox.

"Let's chop some ice to eat," he said.

"All right," I said. "But we have to go to your place. My mother doesn't allow me to chop our ice."

"That's why I came here," he complained. "My mother doesn't, either."

My father walked in and said "Whew!"

He looked exhausted.

"Today is a scorcher," he said. "You could fry eggs on the sidewalk if you had eggs. That's how hot she is."

But he seemed more happy than hot. I could tell by the way he wiped sweat. I hoped it was about letting us chop ice. I hoped wrong. He was happy about a grown-up thing. He unfolded the Cincinnati *Post*. He held up its headline for us to read. The headline said:

NAVY TO BUILD 32 WARSHIPS
FOR TOTAL OF $238,000,000
TO CREATE JOBS FOR NEEDY

"Now there'll be work," said my father.

He believed in Roosevelt, standard time, the repeal of Prohibition,[2] heat

[1]**Roosevelt** (rō′zə velt), Franklin Delano Roosevelt, President of the U.S. from 1933 to 1945.

[2]**Prohibition** (prō′ə bish′ən). Between 1920 and 1933, the manufacture and sale of alcoholic beverages was forbidden, or prohibited, in the U.S.

waves, and the railroad. He was also a Mason and a member of the union, and once in a while he went to church.

My father moved around the kitchen searching for something. He looked in boxes, pulled out drawers, peered under cabinets. He went into the other room and did the same. He must have looked in every box and drawer we had before he said:

"Ah!"

He came back to the kitchen. He put the family revolver on the table, got rags and oil, and began cleaning the weapon.

Our stares bothered him. He stopped cleaning and said:

"Your mother's birthday is coming, George. *Now* we can get her something nice." He glanced at the headline. All those warships reassured him.

"Take her to the Strand," Raymond said. "They got vaudeville³ there. Five acts."

"We're not going to the Strand," my father said. "We're going to give her something special."

He looked around the kitchen.

"An *electric* refrigerator," he said.

Raymond and I were awed. *That* was a major purchase. The Strand cost only fifteen cents.

"We can afford a second-hand one," my father said. He looked at the revolver. "This will be the down payment. The way they're building warships, I'll be back to work before the next payment is due."

I was stunned. He was going to pawn the gun.

"But that's the gun that opened the West," I protested. It was. He had told

³**vaudeville** (vô′də vil), theater entertainment consisting of a series of acts—dancers, singers, acrobats, magicians, etc.—much like a TV variety show.

me so himself. That was the very gun that did it.

"Now," said my father with sudden melancholy, "it's the down payment on a second-hand electric refrigerator."

He sighed, wrapped the gun in newspaper, got up, and walked out the door.

I felt blue. The Singing Lady had gone; Orphan Annie was there, but I didn't listen. Orphan Annie didn't matter. Sandy would look out for her. But who would look out for our possessions that sat in pawnshop windows? My father's mandolin was there. The money we got for it got me a pair of shoes. My grandmother's spectacles—the ones with the frail gold frames—were there. That money had once paid the rent. Anyway, she was dead. She didn't wear them any more. And now the gun that opened the West would be there, too. It was sad. Soon we would run out of possessions the pawnshop wanted.

When "Orphan Annie" was over, Raymond said:

"You got a good icebox now. You don't need an electric one. My mother says they're dangerous. She says they can blow up."

I didn't argue. It *was* a good icebox —made of wood and wonderful. Its top compartment could hold a fifty-pound cake of ice. But because ice cost money we weren't allowed to chip off any to eat. My mother kept it from melting too fast by wrapping it with newspaper. But sooner or later it melted away. It melted twenty-four hours a day—drip, drip, drip—like a wet clock ticking. Its water pan underneath had to be emptied more often in hot weather. Sometimes when we forgot, it overflowed on the floor. But it was a good icebox. We'd had it for years. On hot nights when I couldn't sleep, its drip, drip, drip was comforting.

"If you get rid of it, you got trouble," Raymond said. "The iceman won't come here no more. And you know what happened to the Hasselbachs. The day they got their electric refrigerator, the iceman lowered the boom on Billy Hasselbach. No more climbing on his ice truck. No more eating free ice." Raymond looked thoughtfully at the icebox. "I'd think twice if I was your father."

That made me even bluer, but Raymond got up and went home anyway.

I didn't want to admit to him that I was already afraid of the iceman. The iceman walked around cold and damp. I guess this was from lugging cakes of ice to third-floor flats. He had great muscles, a resentful face, and wet shoulders. He never spoke with words; he spoke with grunts. His truck was old and he was old. Every day he drove it slowly along the street and searched with displeasure each third-floor window, searching the ice-card that told him his customers' wants: ten-, fifteen-, twenty-, or twenty-five-pound cakes of ice. He awed mothers. When my mother heard him coming up the stairs she ran in panic to remove the newspaper she had wrapped the ice in. She didn't want him to learn her treachery. Ice wrapped in newspapers lasted longer, as I said, and the longer it lasted, the less the iceman sold. A Cincinnati *Post* was a sound investment: it cost two cents and saved ten cents' worth of ice.

The iceman hated the Cincinnati *Post,* the Cincinnati *Times-Star,* the Cincinnati *Enquirer,* dogs, children, and third-floor flats. He never said hello. He never asked how things were. He barged into kitchens without knocking, dripped water, walked straight to the icebox, put in the ice, grunted, sweated, blew his nose, rattled his tongs, and left. He didn't say good-by, either.

In the winter he sold coal from his truck. He sold it by the ton, by the sack, and by the bushel basket.

Anyway, the next few days were mixed-up days. My father went about grinning wildly at nothing at all. This got on my mother's nerves as much as the heat wave did. He'd grin when she hurried to get the newspaper off the ice before the iceman came. She would look at him and ask what he was grinning at. He would say nothing, and grin some more—which made her frown harder. The harder she frowned, the harder he grinned. She would say he was making fun of her. He would say he wasn't. She would say prove it. And there they'd be, squared off and ready to punch each other in the nose. Well, right then, the kitchen door would bust open and in would come the iceman. He'd walk right between them as if they weren't there, shove the ice into the icebox, grunt, sweat, blow his nose, rattle his tongs, and go on. And my father would start grinning again. If you really want to know, it was awful. I considered running away from home three times.

Things weren't any better when I was down on the street.

One day Raymond and I were playing when the iceman's truck stopped. The iceman stared sullenly at third-floor windows where ice-cards were, muttered to himself, climbed up on the wooden step on the back of his truck, and, still muttering, chopped big ice cakes into small ice cakes. Then he lugged the cakes into the buildings. His truck was left unattended. This was our cue to climb on it and get as many slivers of ice to eat as we could before he returned. But that day was different.

"Better not," Raymond said.

"Why not?"

"Remember the Hasselbachs," Raymond said. "Suppose the iceman got wind of what your father's getting."

"We ordered ice today," I said. I pointed to the ice-card in our third-floor window. Fifteen pounds, it said. Fifteen pounds of ice was my passport to the iceman's truck.

"It's your funeral," Raymond said. He climbed on the truck and looked down at me.

"All I know is," he went on, "we're *not* getting an electric refrigerator. And," he added grandly, "we ordered twenty pounds of ice today."

"What's that got to do with anything?" I said.

"Everything," he said.

I got up on the truck anyway. I searched and found my slivers of ice. Only my heart wasn't in it. I was scared. The fun was gone. Suppose—just suppose—my father let slip what he was getting my mother. And suppose—just suppose—the iceman heard. That kind of supposing was too awful. I put the slivers of ice back and climbed off the truck. The ice was probably poisoned anyway.

The weekend was a scorcher. But Monday was no better. My father sat sweating and grinning. My mother sat frowning. The kitchen curtains stood stock still. Not a breath of air blew. At night the day's heat lingered in our rooms. The two rooms were filled with last week's fresh air warmed over by the sun. The walls were warm to touch. Even Kate Smith on the radio was no help. She talked about the heat wave, too.

But if the iceman was happy because the ice melted faster, he didn't show it. People who usually ordered twenty pounds of ice ordered twenty-five. People who usually ordered fifteen pounds ordered twenty. That was us.

"The ice goes so fast," my mother said, fanning herself. "Don't open the icebox so much."

My father didn't help the heat wave. When my mother said that, he grinned some more. Between the heat and his grins my mother got exasperated, but what could she do? All she could do was put more newspapers around the cake of ice and try to make it last.

Then Tuesday came and my father stopped grinning.

He got nervous. He spent the morning leaning out the front window, wiping sweat from his face, and watching for the delivery truck to come. He told Raymond and me to watch, too.

"They promised delivery today," he said. "Watch for a truck with an electric refrigerator on it."

Raymond and I sat all morning on the curb and watched. The day was important. Few families bought refrigerators—or anything else, for that matter. We knew when the truck stopped that people would watch from every window. Children would assemble. When a truck unloaded anything in our neighborhood it was an event. People didn't watch because they were nosy. They watched because they were surprised.

The iceman came, stopped, studied the ice-cards in the third-floor windows, muttered, climbed up in his truck, and chopped cakes of ice to fill the orders. I looked up at our two windows. My father was in one. Our ice-card was in the other. Twenty pounds, it said.

"Oh, no," Raymond said.

I looked quickly. Another truck had stopped behind the iceman's. Everybody, including the iceman, could see what it carried: our electric refrigerator.

Two men got out of the truck, checked papers, and asked the iceman if that was where we lived.

The iceman looked from them to what their truck brought.

"*Garf!*" he muttered.

"Thanks," said one of the men.

"*Garf!*" said the iceman, and turned back to chopping. But he chopped more angrily than ever. He created more slivers of ice than he meant to. He slammed his tongs into one cake, hurled the cake of ice to his wet shoulder, and stomped into the building where we lived.

From every window friends stared.

"I've never seen him *that* mad," Raymond said.

"But look at the electric refrigerator," I said. "Isn't it pretty?"

The white box gleamed. The two men moved it on a wheeled dolly into our building.

"It's the prettiest refrigerator I've ever seen," I said.

We followed everybody in: the two delivery men, the iceman, and the beautiful refrigerator.

Two minutes later on the third floor, our kitchen was crowded. The two men were there. The iceman was there. My mother and my father were there. Raymond and I were there.

Mother stood and looked. She was happy—and she was crying.

Well, she had earned the right to cry. The world owed her happy tears. She had the right to be stunned, to be awed, to be glad. She was my mother. She had lived for a long time in a bewildering place where possessions were just items to be pawned to get me shoes. The electric refrigerator was a kind of miracle. Its size staggered her. Its glory held her spellbound. Its being there at all flabbergasted her. It was a second-hand wonder in a second-hand world—and it made ice cubes. She couldn't believe it was real until she tasted the salt of her tears. The tears were real. The refrigerator was real.

She looked at my father and said:

"You shouldn't have, you shouldn't."

Which summed up the gladness in her heart.

My father leaned against the wall and grinned. The two delivery men manhandled the old icebox out into the hall and away. Raymond and I opened and closed the refrigerator door to see the light go on and off. The iceman— a twenty-pound cake still on his shoulder—watched the scene, his soul filled with resentment. The "National Farm and Home Hour" was on the radio and Everet Mitchell was saying what a beautiful day it was in Chicago.

"You shouldn't have," my mother said to my father. She said it soft like movie women say "I love you."

The iceman snorted, turned, and stomped out. He slammed the door hard. Where he had been, only puddles remained.

Alone at last—with Raymond, my father, and me—my mother dared approach the refrigerator. It was white, so white. It gleamed. It was beautiful.

On the other hand our stove was dinky and black. Our kitchen table— our only table—was covered with oilcloth, a cracked pattern. The pattern wasn't white. Nor was the couch where

I slept. Its comforters were patched and many colors, all faded, but not white. Nor was the kitchen cabinet. Nor was the sewing machine. Nor were the curtains at the window. Nor the wallpaper. Only the electric refrigerator was white —*pure white*—and it dominated the kitchen completely.

"Oh," my mother said. She spoke as a little girl does: small and breathless, full of wonder. "Oh."

She examined the refrigerator shelves, its doors, and the way its light went off and on.

"Oh," she said. "Oh."

Tomorrow or the day after, reality would return. There would be time then for her to worry what it cost.

My father leaned against the wall and grinned.

"*That's* why you grinned so much," my mother said.

She went to him and kissed him.

"Come on," said Raymond. "Let's scram."

When we reached the street both trucks had gone. We sat on the curb and watched three streetcars go by before we said a word. The headline on the Cincinnati *Post* said:

TEMPERATURE CLIMBING
TOWARD SUMMER HIGH;
LITTLE RELIEF IN SIGHT

Raymond and I laughed. For us the heat wave was over. Upstairs a machine was making ice cubes.

"Unless," Raymond said, "it blows up." THE END

Talking it over

1. *a.* Why are both adults and children so much interested in ice?

b. Why does the father plan to buy an electric refrigerator? How does he expect to pay for it?

2. *a.* Why is George saddened by what his father is going to do?

b. Why is Raymond against the idea of an electric refrigerator?

3. *a.* Describe the personality of the iceman as the boys see him. Why does the iceman feel the way he does about newspapers and electric refrigerators?

b. Why doesn't George take any ice from the truck? Why does he tell himself it is "probably poisoned"?

4. *a.* How does George's mother feel about the new refrigerator? How can you tell?

b. What might the refrigerator represent to her besides a way of making ice cubes? Find the passage which suggests this.

c. Do you think the father knew what the refrigerator might mean to his wife? Give reasons for your answer.

5. A writer may use contrast to create humor, to make a description more vivid, or to bring an idea or a situation into sharper focus.

a. What about the gun's background makes George feel especially sad when the gun has to be pawned as a down payment on the refrigerator? Why does this situation seem amusing to us?

b. What about the father's reaction to the mother's worry makes her worry even more?

c. What about the description of the kitchen makes the new refrigerator seem even more beautiful?

Sadness was so thick in our kitchen
I could slice it with a knife.

The reason my mother should win an Oscar

by Dick Perry

I KNEW something was wrong the minute I woke up. My mother sat at the kitchen table, stirring the coffee in her cup, but she didn't watch it stir. My father stared out the window, his back to me, his hands folded so tight behind him his knuckles were white. I usually woke up to their talk. That morning I woke up to their silence.

When my bed squeaked my mother snapped from her trance and my father turned around, sighed, walked to the stove, and poured himself a cup of coffee. He looked at me and said:

"Why don't you go for a hike today?"

"I'll fix you sandwiches," my mother said.

I got out of bed and padded about the kitchen in my BVD's.[1] I was sleepy. It takes me forever to wake up. Sometimes I walk around stumbling into

things till noon. I'm not a great conversationalist in the morning. I don't feel like talking or thinking or anything. That's why I didn't answer them. I didn't mean to be impolite. I was too sleepy to be impolite. Besides, it was only nine-thirty. The day, I could tell, was going to be another scorcher.

"This is a good day for a hike," my mother said.

A good day for a hike? In the broiling sun? Was that any way to treat their only child? Didn't they love me any more?

"I'd fall down dead from the heat," I said.

"Go take a hike!" my father said. He began to sound desperate.

"Are you trying to get rid of me?" I asked. I was confused. It's awful to wake up from a sound sleep to find nobody loves you.

"Please," he said. "Go."

When he said it that way my heart fell through the floor. There was a catch

[1] **BVD's,** one-piece suit of underwear.

in his voice. I knew he still loved me and my mother loved me, too. But I knew something else. The way they acted nailed it down. Something was wrong.

"What's wrong?" I said.

"I'll fix your breakfast," my mother said. "What would you like?"

They were avoiding me.

"What's wrong?" I repeated.

My father got up from the table and didn't answer. He walked to the door, turned, and looked at my mother. My mother looked back at him. Their eyes were sad.

"I'll be back," he said to her. "See if you can convince George to . . ." But he stopped, looked at me, winked at me, and said, "You worry too much. Nothing is wrong."

He didn't fool me. I had seen them sad before but never sad like that. Sadness was eating them up. I wasn't sleepy any more. I was wide awake and tormented by questions they wouldn't answer. They pretended I hadn't asked them. Whatever was wrong was a humdinger. Sadness was so thick in our kitchen I could slice it with a knife.

Raymond came in.

He was bubbling with a grand idea. He wanted to build a streetcar line through Mount Echo Park. When he saw the look on my face he stopped bubbling and frowned. He saw I wasn't interested.

"What's wrong?" he said.

I shrugged.

"I'm going to stick close to home today," I said.

"Why?"

But how could I tell him why? I didn't know.

He poured himself a cup of coffee and looked bewildered.

My mother had gone into our other room to make the bed. But she didn't hum as she usually hummed. She worked in silence. My father had gone out somewhere. The sadness, though, would not go away.

"I'll help you tomorrow," I said to Raymond. "Honest I will."

That didn't cheer him at all.

"I can't build an entire streetcar line by myself," he said. "I'll have to wait till tomorrow. But we'll be out millions. I was going to charge a penny a ride." He studied me carefully. "What's up, George?"

Before I could answer that I didn't know, my mother—preoccupied with gloom—came back into the kitchen. She went to the electric refrigerator, turned the dial, and made its humming stop.

"Going to defrost?" I said.

"Yes," she said. "That's it."

She opened the refrigerator door, the light went on, Raymond applauded, and she moved food from its shelves to the kitchen table. She carried the ice-cube trays to the sink. She seemed to move slower than usual.

"Dinky," she said.

"Huh?" I said.

"The cubes are dinky," she said. "You can't do a thing with them."

"You could eat them," I said.

She glared at me. "I'm *busy!*" she snapped and—instantly—was sorry. I could see regret in her eyes. "Go out and play, the both of you," she said. The gentleness in her voice surprised me. I knew more than ever something was wrong.

"Can I stay here?" I said.

"It doesn't matter," she said after a moment.

She took a cloth and wiped the ice-cube trays dry. She put them back empty into the silent refrigerator. She took another cloth and wiped the refrigerator clean, inside and out. She was forever doing that because she loved the refrigerator. She'd never let me touch it with my dirty hands. She'd never let me slam its door. She'd never let me get out an ice-cube tray. "You'll break something," she would say. "Let me do it." The refrigerator was her proudest possession. It was sacred.

Raymond and I watched in silence as she worked.

Then from the street came the cry: *"Here comes the Bean Wagon!"*

Children picked up the cry until the street was a Bean Wagon chorus. We heard grandfathers shout and the voices of two grandmothers, too. There was excitement and wonder on the streets but that morning I did not attend. I watched my mother wipe the refrigerator. The Bean Wagon would come again next week. I would see it then. I *had* to stay home. Something sad was happening.

"Go play," my mother said. Her back was to me. "Go play," she begged.

But she didn't turn around to see if I had gone.

My father entered. He looked at Raymond and me and finally at my mother's back.

"It *would* be the day the Bean Wagon came," he said. His voice was unhappy. "Of all the days," he said. "Of all the days. . . ."

He went to the stove, poured a cup of coffee, and walked to stand behind my mother.

"Can I help?" he asked.

She didn't turn around. Over and over again she wiped the same place on the refrigerator.

"There was never room enough in here," my mother said. She closed the refrigerator door. "It used so much electricity," she said. She turned and smiled at my father. It was a lonesome smile. "Drink your coffee before it gets cold," she said.

He stared out the window.

"Why didn't you let me do my watch?"

She stood beside him and they both looked at the river.

"No," she said.

"But you let me do your wedding band," he said.

"That was different."

"I wanted to give you something nice."

"It's all right," my mother said.

They stopped talking. They listened and so did Raymond and I. People were coming up the stairs. That was a nice thing about living on the third floor. It was easy to tell when company was coming. The stairs between the second- and third-floor landings creaked a special creak. Company was coming all right. I heard grunts, murmurs of "Easy does it," and commands of "Watch the banister, *watch the banister!*" The company was carrying something big. With a great "Whew" they stopped outside our door.

"I'll get it," I said, and ran to the door.

I liked surprises.

I swung the door wide and—*Oh!*

My heart sank.

Our old icebox stood there. The two men who had carried it up three flights leaned against it and panted with exhaustion. The climb had pooped them. But why had they brought it back? We didn't need it. We had the electric refrigerator.

"Is your old lady home, son?" the first man asked.

He looked over my shoulder as my mother stepped up.

"Morning, ma'am," he said. He sounded sad.

"Well," said my mother. "It's sure good to see the icebox again!"

She talked as if she were glad.

She invited the two men in.

"There," she said. She pointed to the electric refrigerator. "It's nice and clean. It's ready to go."

"Mother!" I cried, flabbergasted.

"Hush," she smiled. "Keep out of the way. These men have work to do."

"But they're going to take . . ."

"Quiet!" said my father. He sounded angry.

Distressed, I moved out of the way. The two men came into the kitchen. They looked reluctant. The first man—I suppose he was the boss—made a helpless motion.

"I only work for the store," he said to my mother. "This is not my doing." He sounded as if he hated himself. "If I had my way . . ." he started to say, but stopped. He looked at his partner. "Come on," he said, anger in his voice. "We haven't got all day. Come on." He stopped again, his anger fled. "Come on, Fred," he said to his partner. He almost whispered it. "Come on."

My mother didn't watch. She was busy at the stove. She poked the fire that didn't need poking. She moved pans around so much they ended where they began. Her hands fluttered, straightening this and moving that. All the time my father stared at the river.

Five minutes later the electric refrigerator was gone. The icebox stood where it had been. My mother and my father didn't have to explain. I knew.

The store had repossessed the refrigerator.

But why did my mother hum?

She actually hummed as she put the food back into the old icebox.

"This is better," she said. "Now there's *room* for food. That refrigerator was always cramped."

She took the coffee cup from my father's hand.

"You let it get cold," she said. "Shame on you. I'll pour you some fresh."

She started to say something to Raymond and me—some happy thing, I could tell by her eyes—but she stopped. The stairs between the second and third floors creaked again. It meant only one thing: more company.

The door burst open and without a word, not looking left or right, the iceman entered. Water dripping from the twenty-pound cake of ice on his wet shoulders, he padded straight across the kitchen. He opened the top of the icebox and put the ice in, grunted, sweated, blew his nose, rattled his tongs, and stomped to the door again.

He turned and glared—right at me!

"Boy!" he said.

I shook.

"You been avoiding me," he said. He glowered. "Your folks and me is friends. But ice slivers is rotting my truck bed. I count on you kids to keep the truck bed free of them ice slivers. How come you ain't been doing your job?"

And would you believe it, he smiled!

"Thanks," my mother said and grinned. She was the most beautiful grinner in the world. "I was afraid we'd have to do without till we saw you tomorrow . . ."

Her grin wavered.

"*Garf!*" he glowered and rattled his

tongs. "You're worse than your boy. I got eyes, ain't I? I knowed you'd be needing ice." He glared one final glare at all of us, started out the door but stopped again. "The ice is free for a week," he complained. "You're new customers on my route."

"But. . . ."

"Garf!" he said. "And a piece of advice. Wrap it in newspaper. It'll keep better that way."

He slammed the door and was gone. Raymond sighed.

"Now," he said, "I don't have to be afraid no more."

"About getting on the iceman's truck?" my mother said.

Raymond shook his head. "Not that. I mean about coming here. I never knew when your electric refrigerator was going to blow up and wipe out the entire neighborhood!"

He looked so relieved, we laughed at him. Then, he laughed, too. Suddenly, a morning that started out sad turned happy and silly. The four of us—my mother, my father, Raymond, and me—stood around the kitchen laughing our heads off. We laughed so hard my stomach hurt. We laughed so hard the neighbors turned off their radios to listen. It was a shining morning.

Then Raymond went home, my mother put newspaper around the ice, and my father drank another cup of coffee. We three smiled and kidded and had fun the rest of the day.

That night, as I tried to sleep, I heard my mother and my father talking softly in the next room.

"The ice cubes were dinky," my mother murmured. "They went so fast."

"Someday we'll get another," my father said.

My mother would have made a good actress; that night she was the greatest.

Much later, when an owl car[2] went by and woke me up, my father was sound asleep.

I stared at the ceiling and listened to my mother cry.   THE END

◯ **Talking it over**

1. *a.* Why do George's parents urge him to leave the house?

b. Why does George not want to go?

2. *a.* Contrast the mother's remarks about the refrigerator with those she made in "Why the Iceman Stopped Coming to Our Flat." Why does she criticize the refrigerator now?

b. Do her actions seem to prove or to disprove what she is saying?

3. *a.* Why do the men who come to take the refrigerator seem sad? What evidence of kindness do they show?

b. What error in judgment have George and Raymond made about the iceman? What proves they were wrong?

4. *a.* On the day the refrigerator was delivered, there was much laughter and happiness. What tells you that things are different now?

b. In spite of everything, the mood on this day is not completely gloomy. How do you account for the humor and laughter in this selection?

c. Why does George think his mother should win an Oscar?

5. Think back over your answers to questions 4*b* and 4*c* from "Why the Iceman . . . ," about what the refrigerator represented to George's father

---

[2]**owl car,** a streetcar that runs after midnight.

and mother. Which of the following statements do you feel is true? Explain.

a. The refrigerator has the same special meaning to the parents in both selections.

b. The refrigerator has come to mean something totally different in the second selection.

c. The refrigerator never really mattered to either parent.

⇌ **Words in action**

How did the golden statuette given as the Academy Award for the best performance in movies come to be called an "Oscar"? One story has it that a certain actress who received the award looked at it, at a loss for words. "I want to thank you for this—this—" Then something about the figure reminded her of her Uncle Oscar, and she blurted, "–this OSCAR!" The name stuck.

If this story is true, it is not the first time that someone made up a word which became popular. In this selection are several words whose origin no one knows.

Men who make a study of words have guessed that *flabbergast* (which has been around for about 200 years) might be a combination of "flabby" and "aghast." This explanation, which suggests being weak in the knees after seeing a ghost, does sound something like our modern meaning: "astonished or speechless." But no one knows for sure where *flabbergast* came from.

It is thought that *dinky,* meaning "small and inferior," may have come from an earlier word meaning "small

and dainty." If it did, it had changed in meaning by the time the small cap worn by college freshmen to show their lowly status was called a "dink."

But where *humdinger,* meaning "something special, rated very high," and *pooped,* as used in the phrase *pooped out,* meaning "exhausted, out of breath," came from—well, your guess might be as good as anyone's.

These words have been part of American slang for many years, and it is unlikely that anyone will be able to trace them now.

Slang comes and goes like other fads, however. What slang words do you use for the following?
1. Something very bad or inferior
2. Something unimportant
3. Being astonished
4. Something special, "the best"
5. Near collapse

How things were

The last two selections are from a book called *Raymond and Me That Summer.* The author, Dick Perry, says: "I wrote this book to tell my two boys —then the ages of Raymond and George in the book—how life was during the thirties when I was their age. I don't hold much with fathers who look stonily at their children and mutter, 'Listen, you've got it good. When *I* was your age . . .' For one thing, the children don't listen and I don't blame them. But all fathers are, nonetheless, human. They do want to pass along how things were. I happened to do it via this sketchy little novel."

MOONFLIGHT

WHEN Vilhjalmur Stefansson[1] explored the arctic regions of Alaska and Canada in the early part of the twentieth century, he became fascinated with the Eskimo people. Though their life was hard and bleak by our standards, most of them were cheerful and kind. They would share food with anyone who needed it.

Practically every part of the Eskimos' daily life was affected by their religion. There was religious meaning in every act and accident, and a religious formula to help in any situation.

Almost all natural things had spirits in them, they thought, and they had to be careful not to displease the spirits. When a child was born, the parents called to the spirit of some good and wise person who had died, asking it to enter their child and guide it until it

was old enough to make judgments of its own. Parents never punished a child, because they thought they would be punishing the spirit of a friend or relative—and this would bring extremely bad luck.

At the time of Stefansson's visits, Christianity was gradually spreading among the Eskimos, but many of the old ideas lingered and became mixed with the new religion. The Christian practice of not working on Sunday was accepted as a taboo and was followed so carefully that the Eskimos would not even save a life on Sunday!

In this selection Stefansson tells of the early Eskimos' belief in miracles, and describes a ceremony led by the shaman (shä′mən), a community leader whose connections with the spirit world gave him great influence among his people.

*"Now I am beginning to rise.
Now I am going to fly in circles slowly
just above the floor . . . fast . . . faster . . . ."*

by Vilhjalmur Stefansson

IT WOULD surprise most of us to see miracles happening all around us.

It is not so with the Eskimo. They expect them continually, and when anyone tells of having seen or heard of a miraculous thing, people accept the story without question.

To begin with, the Eskimo are very unclear in their religious thinking, a fact which does not, however, make them completely different from us. Questioning is unknown in religious matters. If they are familiar with my private character and they find me reliable about ordinary things—if I don't tell lies concerning the number of caribou I have killed, nor about the distance at which I shot them—they will believe anything I say about any subject. Once they have learned to rely on my statements regarding the thickness of the back-fat of the bull caribou I shot during the summer, they will accept anything I say about religion. On the other hand, if I told them there were ten caribou in a band I saw and they later discovered there were only five, they would not readily believe me if I told them there was but one God. The

Adapted from *My Life with the Eskimo* by Vilhjalmur Stefansson. Copyright 1913 by the Macmillan Company. Copyright renewed 1941 by Vilhjalmur Stefansson. Adapted by permission of McIntosh & Otis, Inc.

reasoning would simply be this: he did not tell us the truth about the number of caribou, therefore how can we rely on the truth of his statements about the number of gods?

Most miracles are supposed to be caused by the activities of a spirit controlled by some shaman or medicine man. There are many different kinds of miracles. Among the Mackenzie River Eskimo, the commonest of all miracles and the one best understood is the spirit flight in which the actual body of the shaman flies to some distant place. Sometimes his body flies to a neighboring village; often it goes to a faraway country. But most frequently, it goes to the sun, the moon, or the bottom of the sea. There is also another kind of spirit flight in which the body remains in its place and the soul alone goes abroad. These two sorts of spirit flights differ mainly in this way: while the first must be performed in darkness, the second can be managed in daylight.

The bodily flight of the shaman takes place usually at night in winter and in the dark of the moon. The event is announced beforehand and all those who wish to be present gather in the clubhouse or the largest available private home. In the Mackenzie River houses there is one window at the peak of the roof. Directly under this, near the center of the floor, sits the shaman. Two or three men who are skilled in the handling of ropes take a long thong and tie and truss the shaman until, humanly speaking, it is impossible for him to move. Usually a loop of the rope is passed under his knees and over the back of his neck and the rope is drawn tight until his chin rests between his knees. When the tying is done, there is always left over a loose rope-end about three inches long to which is attached a stone or other heavy object, such as a hammer or an ax-blade.

Before the beginning of the performance the window has been covered with a thick skin or blanket. All the people take their seats in a circle around the shaman as far away as possible from the center of the house, leaving him in an unoccupied circle perhaps ten feet in diameter. The lights are put out and the house is so dark that one can see absolutely nothing. Nevertheless everyone leans forward and closes his eyes tightly. If there are any children present, an older person sits behind each child and holds his hands over the child's eyes.

The moment after the light goes out the shaman begins to chant a magic song. Presently he says: "I do not feel so heavy now as I usually do. Somehow it seems as if I were not sitting very heavily on the floor. Now I am becoming as light as a feather. Now I am beginning to want to rise like a dry stick in water."

He says all these things in a low voice, speaking well in his throat so that it is difficult to judge how far away he is. But of course so far everyone knows exactly where he is, for he remains (as he himself says) in the center of the circle where he was when the lights were put out.

The next stage of the performance is that the shaman, still speaking in the manner of a ventriloquist, says: "Now I am beginning to rise; now I am going to fly in circles slowly just above the floor; now I am flying fast; now I am flying faster."

Presently the people begin to hear a whizzing noise. This is the stone or ax which was attached to the loose rope-end. The shaman is now flying in circles so fast that the centrifugal force makes the hammer on the rope-end produce a whizzing noise. If anyone were to open his eyes even a little to try to see what was going on, the hammer would strike him in the head, killing him instantly. Consequently, the louder the whizzing noise the more tightly is every eye squeezed shut, and the more firmly are the hands of the parents held over the eyes of their children.

While the hammer still continues the whizzing noise, the voice of the shaman is heard to say: "Now I am rising above your heads; now I am getting near the roof; now I am about to pass out through the window." Then the voice grows actually fainter and fainter as the shaman rises toward the roof and flies out through the window, and finally the whizzing noise dies away in the distance.

For half an hour or more the audience sits in absolute silence with eyes shut, and then the shaman's voice is heard again: "Now I am coming in through the window; now I am settling down; now I am down on the floor; now you may open your eyes and light the lamps." The lamps are lighted, and lo! there sits the shaman exactly where he was when the lights were put out three-quarters of an hour before.

Someone now unties the shaman and he relates to an attentive audience his adventures on the spirit flight. He went to the moon and approached the house of the man in the moon. He did not dare to enter, but waited outside until the wife of the man in the moon came out, saw him, and invited him in. Shortly afterward, the man in the moon himself came home from a caribou hunt, bringing with him a backload of meat and a number of marrow-bones. A meal was prepared of caribou meat, and after that the three of them cracked marrow-bones until the broken bones lay in a large heap on the floor.

The man in the moon said that last year the caribou hunt had not been very good in the moon, but this year it was much better. The caribou in the moon this year were fatter than usual, which was no doubt due to the fact that the summer had been cool and there had not been very many mosquitoes.

The wife of the man in the moon also joined in the conversation, saying that they had already obtained many skins for clothing for the coming winter, and that as for sinew with which to sew, they had enough already with which to sew, they had enough already for two years. She inquired about the shaman's wife, whether his little boy had begun yet to kill ptarmigan, whether the people in the shaman's village carefully kept all the taboos, and who it was that had broken some, for she knew from the vapor rising from the village that something was wrong.

The shaman had answered her questions to the best of his ability. He regretted that a certain young woman had been very careless in sewing caribou skin soon after the killing of white whales. The shaman was compelled to tell various other things of this sort, for he was a truthful man, but he was ashamed of his fellow countrymen and would gladly have been able to conceal the facts from the moon people.

Time is not measured the same way in the moon as upon earth, the shaman tells, and really he had been in the moon a long time, although on earth it seemed but a short while that he was away. He had lingered, feasted, and talked, but finally his visit was at an end, and he started off, promising the man in the moon to visit him again next year.

When the shaman's story is finished, a general discussion takes place, in which both men and women join, and finally when the crowd gets tired and sleepy they scatter to their own homes.

What we have described is not one of the most wonderful miracles, but merely the commonest one.

One day I was explaining to my Eskimo companions that there were mountains on the moon and was giving them other details about the moon's physical characteristics. The account I gave did not agree with the opinion held by my Eskimo listeners, and they asked me how I knew these things were so. I explained that we had telescopes as long as the masts of ships and that through them we could see the things on the moon's surface. "But has any white man ever been to the moon?" I was asked. When I replied that no one ever had, they said that while they did not have any telescopes as long as a ship's mast, yet they did have men, and truthful men, too, who had been to the moon. They had walked about there and seen everything, and they had come back and told them about it. With all respect to the cleverness of white men, they thought that under the circumstances the Eskimo ought to be better informed than the white men as to the facts regarding the moon. THE END

Talking it over

1. *a.* Stefansson visited the arctic lands in the early 1900's. How did the Eskimos feel about miracles at that time?

b. What was the most common miracle the Eskimos experienced? In what two ways could this take place?

2. What position did the shaman hold in the village? How much did the villagers rely on his judgment?

3. *a.* What preparations were made for the moonflight described here?

b. In what ways did the audience share in the moonflight? Which of their senses was most important during this experience?

4. *a.* Examine carefully the shaman's conversation with the moon people. What kinds of things did he discuss?

b. Why did he discuss these things?

5. *a.* What do you think was the purpose of the following?

   (1) The darkness
   (2) Tying the shaman with a rope
   (3) Keeping the eyes closed
   (4) The use of a heavy object on the end of the rope

b. Under what circumstances could the moonflight be made by daylight?

6. *a.* How did the Eskimos react to Stefansson's statements about the moon? Why did they react this way?

b. What two kinds of thinking are contrasted in the last paragraph of the selection?

Words in action

One word in each sentence below is printed in pronunciation symbols instead of being spelled out. Pronounce each word to yourself. (The pronunciation key in the Glossary will help if you're stuck.) Then follow the directions.

1. The Eskimos hunted **tar′mə ɣən** only when they couldn't find larger game such as caribou or seal.

2. The explorers had to be careful not to get **nü mōn′yə**.

3. Although the Eskimos often ate meat that we would consider spoiled, they did not get **tō′ mān** from it.

4. The chants of the shaman did not sound like the **sämz** the Christian missionaries taught the Eskimos.

5. Some of the Eskimos had made **nīvz** out of copper.

6. The Eskimos had no way to **nok** before entering a snow house, so they stopped outside and called that they were coming in.

Number on your paper from 1-6. From the lettered list below, select the correct spelling for each word printed in pronunciation symbols. Remember that a pronunciation symbol may represent more than one letter of the actual spelling of a word. Many words contain silent letters, too, and the silent letters do not appear among the pronunciation symbols.

Answers to choose from:

a. knives	*g.* psalms
b. knock	*h.* ptarmigan
c. neuralgia	*i.* ptomaine
d. niches	*j.* salves
e. notch	*k.* tarpaulin
f. pneumonia	*l.* tomahawk

What do the spellings of all the words you chose for sentences 1-6 have in common?

UPI photo

A modern Viking

Vilhjalmur Stefansson is thought to have discovered the last unknown islands of North America. People who trace the history of families say that Stefansson was a descendant of Leif Ericson, believed to be the Viking discoverer of the first new lands in North America 900 years before.

Stefansson was born in western Canada. His parents went there in 1876 from Iceland, where their ancestors had lived for almost a thousand years. From Canada the family moved to Dakota Territory in the United States, traveling across the prairies by ox wagon. There they homesteaded a farm.

Young Stefansson first learned to read in Icelandic, with the help of a traveling teacher who went from farm to farm teaching the children the alphabet and how to combine sounds into words. Since Icelandic is pronounced just the way it is written, the boy was able to sound out the words of the Bible by the time he was six. He did not learn English until somewhat later, when he began attending a regular school a few months in the year.

Two important experiences of his early years were getting acquainted with two college students who were Indians, and having a friend who was Irish. He had been brought up to believe that Indians and Irish should be scorned, but getting acquainted with these boys removed his prejudice.

Perhaps these experiences, plus his own unusual background, led him in college to take up anthropology, a science that studies the races of mankind —their beginnings, development, customs, and beliefs. Within a few years he began to be known for his arctic explorations and his studies of the Eskimo. His expeditions were sponsored by universities and museums.

Among the Eskimos, Stefansson lived and hunted and ate as they did. These primitive, friendly people soon thought of him as one of them and talked freely to him about their beliefs.

Stefansson's arctic studies became important to the Air Force and were valuable to the United States in World War II.

Stefansson died in 1962.

The Winning of the TV West

by John T. Alexander

When twilight comes to Prairie Street
On every TV channel,
The kids watch men with blazing guns
In jeans and checkered flannel.
5 Partner, the West is wild tonight—
There's going to be a battle
Between the sheriff's posse and
The gang that stole the cattle.
On every screen on Prairie Street
10 The sheriff roars his order:
"We've got to head those hombres off
Before they reach the border."
Clippoty-clop and bangity-bang
The lead flies left and right.
15 Paradise Valley is freed again
Until tomorrow night.
And all the kids on Prairie Street
Over and under ten
Can safely go to dinner now . . .
20 The West is won again.

Reprinted by permission of John T. Alexander and
The Kansas City Star.

Talking it over

1. *a.* Is Prairie Street a place in a TV show or a place where the TV watchers live?

b. Is Paradise Valley a place in a TV show or the place where the watchers live? How can you tell?

c. What does the name "Paradise Valley" suggest to you? Who lives there—the "good guys" or the "bad guys"?

d. Do you think either of these names refers just to one particular place, or does the speaker have something more general in mind?

2. *a.* Why can the kids on Prairie Street "safely go to dinner now"?

b. What does the last word, *again,* imply?

3. *a.* What lines from the poem best express how popular Westerns are?

b. Who are the "kids . . . over and under ten"?

Words in action

"Clippoty-clop and bangity-bang" make you realize what is going on in the poem without actually describing the actions. What action is suggested by *clippoty-clop?* Why? What action does *bang* suggest? Why?

Words like *bang* and *clip-clop* suggest the actual sounds made by the things they represent. Very often such "echoing" words represent the sounds made by animals: *buzz, oink, purr, quack,* or *baa.* Others represent the sounds made by objects. What words would you use to represent the following sounds?

1. Racing an automobile engine
2. Water running down a drain
3. An arrow flying past your ear
4. Pots and pans being dropped
5. Scissors cutting paper
6. Your heart beating
7. Someone falling into a pool of water
8. A telephone signaling a call

SCARS OF HONOR

by Dorothy Johnson

They had all done the best they could, the right thing, and they were ready to be warriors. They had endured in the old fashion.

CHARLEY Lockjaw died last summer on the reservation. He was very old—a hundred years, he had claimed. He still wore his hair in braids, as only the older men do in his tribe, and the braids were thin and white. His fierce old face was like a withered apple. He was bent and frail and trembling,

Slightly abridged from the story "Scars of Honor" published in the volume *Indian Country*, copyright 1949 by Dorothy M. Johnson, published by Ballantine Books.

and his voice was like a wailing of the wind across the prairie grass.

Old Charley died in his sleep in the canvas-covered tepee where he lived in warm weather. In the winter he was crowded with the younger ones among his descendants in a two-room log cabin, but in summer they pitched the tepee. Sometimes they left him alone there, and sometimes his great-grandchildren scrambled in with him like a bunch of puppies.

His death was no surprise to anyone. What startled the Indian agent[1] and some of Charley's own people, and the white ranchers when they heard about it, was the fact that some of the young men of the tribe sacrificed a horse on his grave. Charley wasn't buried on holy ground; he never went near the mission. He was buried in a grove of cottonwoods down by the creek that is named for a dead chief. His lame great-grandson, Joe Walking Wolf, and three other young Indians took his horse out there and shot it. It was a fine sorrel, only seven years old, broke fairly gentle and nothing wrong with it. Young Joe had been offered eighty dollars for that horse.

The mission priest was disturbed about the killing of the horse, justifiably suspecting some dark pagan significance, and he tried to find out the reason the young men killed it. He urged Joe's mother, Mary, to find out, but she never did—or if she did, she never told. Joe only said, with a shrug, "It was my horse."

The white ranchers chuckled indulgently, a little shocked about the horse but never too much upset about anything Indians did. The rancher who told the story oftenest and with most interest was the one who had made the eighty-dollar offer to Joe Walking Wolf. Joe had said to him, "Ain't my horse." But Joe was the one who shot it on old Charley's grave, and it didn't belong to anyone else.

But the Indian agent guessed what had been going on. He knew more

about Indians than the Federal Government required him to know. The horse was not government property nor the tribe's common property; everybody knew it belonged to Joe. The agent did not investigate, figuring it was none of his business.

That was last summer, when old Charley died and the young men took the horse out to where he was buried.

The story about the killing of the horse begins, though, in 1941, before that horse was even born. The young men were being drafted then, and the agent explained it all, over and over again, through an interpreter, so nobody would have an excuse for not understanding. In the agent's experience, even an Indian who had been clear through high school could fail completely to understand English if he didn't happen to want to.

Some of the white ranchers explained it, too. Some of them were expecting to go, or to have their sons or hired cowboys go, and the draft was a thing they mentioned casually to the Indians who worked for them at two or three dollars a day, digging irrigation ditches or hoeing in the kitchen garden or working in the hay fields. So the Indians understood the draft all right, with everybody talking about it.

The agent kept telling them, "In the World War you were not citizens, so you did not have to go in the Army." (He meant the First World War, of course. The United States hadn't got into the second one yet; there was only the draft.) "Many of your fathers enlisted in the Army anyway and they were good fighters. They did not have to go, but they wanted to. Now you are citizens, you can vote, and some of you will have to go in the Army. When the

---

[1]**Indian agent,** now called Agency Officer, an employee of the U.S. Department of the Interior Bureau of Indian Affairs, who counsels the Indians on or near a reservation and helps them with problems regarding education, employment, welfare, housing, etc.

letters come for you, we will talk about it again."

Well, some of the young men didn't want to wait until the letters came. Fighting was part of their tradition. It was in the old men's stories, and the names of their long-dead warriors were in history books, as well as in the stories the old men told around the cabin stoves when snow was deep outside and the cabins were crowded with many people and the air foul with much breathing and not much bathing. (Long ago, before any of these young men were born, their forefathers had bathed every morning in rivers or creeks, even if they had to break the ice, but that custom had passed with their glory.)

The middle-aged men of the tribe remembered the white man's war they had fought in, and some of them still had parts of their old uniforms put away. But the stories they told were of places too distant for understanding, foreign places with no meaning except for the men who had been there. The stories the grandfathers told were better. They were about the stealthy approach through the grass after the men had prayed and painted, the quick, sharp action on riverbanks that were familiar still or in tepee camps where white men now live in brick houses.

The grandfathers' stories were of warriors who never marched or drilled but walked softly in moccasins or rode naked on fleet war ponies. They had no uniforms; they wore mystic painted symbols on face and body. In those battles there was the proud waving of eagle-feathered war bonnets and the strong courage of warriors who dared to carry a sacred buffalo shield, although a man who carried one was pledged not to retreat. They were bat-tles without artillery, but with muzzle-loading rifles and iron-tipped lances and the long feathered arrows hissing out from a horn bow. Killing was not paramount in those old battles; more important was proof of a man's courage in the face of death, and the bravest were those few who dared to carry no weapon at all, but only a whip, for counting coup on a living, unhurt enemy. Nobody was drafted for those battles, and death was often the price of glory.

Only two or three of the old men remembered so far back. One of them was Charley Lockjaw. He was suddenly important. If he had not lived two generations too late, he would have been important simply because he was old. His people would have taken it for granted that he was wise, because his medicine had protected him for so long against death. They would have listened respectfully when he spoke. There was a time when it was a good thing to be an Indian, and old. But Charley was cheated—almost—of his honors, because he lived at the wrong time.

Suddenly he was needed. He was sitting in front of his summer tepee, nodding in the sun, with the good warmth seeping into his joints, when four young men came to him. They were modern Indians, with white men's haircuts. They wore torn blue jeans and faded shirts and white men's boots, because they were all cowboys, even the lame one, his great-grandson, Joe.

Charley looked up, ready to be angry, expecting some disrespectful, hurried greeting, like "Hey, grampa, look here."

They did not say anything for a while. Embarrassed, they shuffled their boots in the dust. Joe Walking Wolf took off his broad-brimmed hat, and the other three took their hats off, too, and laid them on the ground.

Joe cleared his throat and said in Cheyenne, "Greetings, my grandfather." It was the way a young man talked to a wise old one in the buffalo years that were gone.

Old Charley blinked and saw that Joe was carrying, with awkward care, an ancient ceremonial pipe of red stone.

Joe asked gravely, "Will you smoke with us, my grandfather?"

Charley was at first indignant, thinking they meant to tease him, because they were atheists who did not believe in the old religion or any of the new ones. He railed at them. But they did not go away; they stood there respectfully with their heads bent, accepting what he said and, in the old, courteous way, not interrupting.

He looked at their sober faces and their steady eyes, and he was ashamed for his own lack of courtesy. When he understood that they were sincere, he would have done anything for them, anything they asked. There was not much he could do any more, and nobody had asked him to do anything for a long time.

If he took the pipe and smoked, that said, "I will do whatever you ask." He did not know what they were going to ask, but he would have let them cut him into pieces if that was what they wanted, because his heart was full at being approached in the remembered, ceremonial way, clumsy as these modern Indians were about it. He answered in his reedy voice, "I will smoke with you."

They were going to do it all wrong. One of the young men brought out a sack of tobacco, and that was all right if there was none that had been raised with the right prayers said over it. But Joe pulled out a pocket lighter a white man had given him and another young man brought out some kitchen matches and old Charley could not endure such innovations.

He made them build a fire in the center of his summer tepee, under the fire hole in the peak, and he sat down with a groan of stiffness at the back, in the honor seat, the place of the lodge owner. The young men were patient. They sat where he told them to, on the old ragged carpet his granddaughter had put on the earth floor.

He filled the pipe with pinches of tobacco without touching the bowl and lighted it with a coal from the fire. With slow, remembered ceremony he offered the pipe to Heammawihio,[2] the Wise One Above, to Ahktunowihio,[3] the power of the earth below, and to the spirits of the four directions— where the sun comes up, where the cold wind goes to, where the sun comes over and where the cold wind comes from.

He spoke reverently to each of these. Then he himself took four puffs and passed the pipe, slowly, carefully, holding the stem upright, to young Yellowbird, who was on his left. Yellowbird smoked, though awkwardly, in the sacred manner and passed the pipe to Joe Walking Wolf. When Joe had finished, he stood up to take the pipe to the two young men on the other side of Charley, but the old man corrected him patiently. The pipe must not cross the doorway of the lodge; it must be passed back from hand to hand, first to Robert

---

[2]**Heammawihio** (hē′ä mä wī′hē ō)

[3]**Ahktunowihio** (ăk tun ō′wĭ hē ō)

Stands in Water and then on to Tom Little Hand.

The young men were humble when he corrected them. They thanked him when he told them how to do things right.

When he signified that the time had come for them to talk, young Joe, the lame one, said formally in Cheyenne, "My grandfather has told of the old times long ago, and we have listened. He has told how the warriors used to go on a hilltop with a wise old man and stay there and dream before they went on the warpath."

Old Charley said, "I told you those things and they were true. I dreamed on a hilltop when I was young."

Joe Walking Wolf said, "We want to dream that way, my grandfather, because we are going to war."

The old man did not have to promise to help them. He had promised when he took the pipe. He sat for a while with his eyes closed, his head bowed, trying to remember what his instructors had said to him the three times he had gone through the *wu-wun*,[4] the starving. How would anyone know the right way if the old men had forgotten? But he was able to remember, because he remembered his youth better than yesterday.

He remembered the chanted prayers and the hunger and thirst and the long waiting for mystery to be revealed. He remembered the grave warnings, the sympathetic teaching of the wise old men seventy years before.

"It is a hard thing to do," he told the young men. "Some men cannot do it. Alone on a high place for four days and four nights, without food or water.

Some men dream good medicine, and some dream bad medicine, and some have no dream. It is good to finish this hard thing, but it is no disgrace not to finish.

"A man lies on a bed of white sage," he told them, "and he is alone after his teacher, his grandfather, has taught him what to do. After four days, his grandfather goes up the hill and gets him—if he has not come back before that time."

Charley Lockjaw remembered something else that was important and added firmly, "The young men bring the grandfather a gift."

And so they went through the *wu-wun*, each of them alone on a high hill, hungering and thirsting for four days and nights. First they brought Charley gifts: four silver dollars from one, new moccasins from another, and two bottles of whiskey. (After the ordeals were over, he spent the four silver dollars for whiskey, too, getting it with difficulty through a man who was going off the reservation and who did not look like an Indian, so he could buy it, though it was against the law. An Indian could vote and be drafted, but he could not buy whiskey.)

The whole thing was secret, so that no one would complain to anybody who might want to interfere. Charley Lockjaw had been interfered with so much that he was suspicious. All his long life, white men had been interfering with him and, he thought, his own granddaughter might go to the priest if she knew what was going on, or the other young men's families might make trouble. No good would come of telling what went on.

Because of the secrecy, the old man had to ride horseback several times.

---

[4] **wu-wun** (wü ′wun)

Usually he had to be helped into a saddle because his joints were stiff and his legs hurt, so that if he did not stop himself and remember that now he could be proud again, he might groan.

He took each young man out separately to a hill chosen because of its height, its loneliness, and its location. It had to be south or west of a river; that had always been the rule. He had never known the reason, and neither did anyone else. It was one of the things that was right, that was all, and he was very anxious to do everything right.

At the foot of the hill, he and the young man left the horses hobbled. The young man helped Charley up the hill, respectfully and with great patience. He made a bed of white sage, and Charley sang his prayers to the Spirit above.

He added a humble plea that had not been in the ritual when he was young. "If I make a mistake," he cried to the blue sky, "it is because I am old. Do not blame the young man. He wants to do right. If he does wrong, it is my fault. Give him good medicine."

Then he stumbled down the hill and got on the borrowed horse by himself and rode home. If the young man should give up before his time had passed, he could catch up the horse that was left.

None of them gave up, and none of them cheated. Each of them lay alone on the sage bed on the hill, singing the songs Charley Lockjaw had taught him, sometimes watching the sky (and seeing airplanes more often than wheeling eagles) and three times a day smoking the sacred pipe.

The first was Joe Walking Wolf. Charley was proud of him when he toiled up the hill with a canteen of water and a chunk of dry bread. He was proud when the boy first splashed water on his face and then drank, unhurriedly, from the canteen.

When Joe's tongue was moistened enough so he could talk, he said briefly, "I dreamed a horse was kicking me."

"I do not know what that means," Charley told him. "Maybe you will know after you think about it."

He was afraid, though, that the dream was bad. The reason Joe limped was that a horse had kicked him when he was three years old.

The second man was Yellowbird. He was impatient. He was standing up, watching, when Charley Lockjaw came in sight on his old bag-of-bones, borrowed horse, and he came down the hill to gulp the water the old man had brought. But he had endured the whole four days.

He said in English, "I dreamed I was dead and gone to hell." Then he said it in Cheyenne, except "hell," and Charley knew what that word was. There was no hell for Cheyennes after they were dead, according to the old religion.

Charley said, "That may be good medicine. I do not know."

The third man was Robert Stands in Water. He was sick and he vomited the first water he drank, but he got better in a little while and they went home. He didn't say what his dream was.

The fourth and last was Tom Little Hand, a laughing young man except when there were white people around. He was a proud rider and a dandy; he wore green sunglasses when he went outdoors, and tight shirts like the white cowboys. When Charley brought the water, he was no dandy any more. Naked to the waist, he lay flat on the sage bed, and the old man had to help him sit up so he could drink and eat.

"There was a bright light," he said when he felt like talking. "It floated in the air and I tried to catch it."

Charley didn't know what kind of medicine that was, but he said Tom Little Hand would probably be able to understand it after a while.

Anyway, they had all done the best they could, the right thing, and they were ready to be warriors. They had endured in the old fashion.

When they got back to the cabin settlement beside the creek that is named for a dead chief, old Charley dug up his whiskey and went into his lodge and drank, and slept, and drank some more. A teacher is worthy of his hire, and Charley Lockjaw was tired out from all that riding and climbing of high hills. For all that time, four days for four men, sixteen days altogether, he had not slept very much. He had been singing in his lodge or in front of it, in his reedy voice like the wailing of the wind across the prairie. The little boys had not bothered him by crowding in to tumble around like puppies. They were afraid of him.

While Charley was having his drunk, the four young men went down to town to enlist in the Army. He did not know that. When he was sober again, two of them had come back—his grandson Joe and Tom Little Hand, the dandy.

Tom said, "They don't want me. I don't see so good."

Joe Walking Wolf didn't say anything. He went around with his bad limp and got a job for a few days on a white man's ranch, sawing branches off some trees in the yard. The cook gave him his meals separate from the white hired hands, but he heard them talking about the draft and joking with each other about being 4F. Some were 4F because cowboys get stove up by bad horses. Joe felt better, knowing he was not the only one.

In the winter the war clouds broke with lightning and thunder, and the Army decided Tom Little Hand could see plenty well enough to go to war. The Army began to take some married men, too, and almost all the single ones except lame Joe Walking Wolf, and a couple who had an eye disease, and six who had tuberculosis and one who was stone-deaf.

Then for a couple of years old Charley Lockjaw wasn't important any more. The people who were important were those who could read the letters that came to the cabin settlement, and those who could write the answers.

Some of the young men came back on furlough, hitchhiking eighty miles from the railroad. In wartime people would pick up a soldier, even if he was an Indian. They strolled around the settlement and rode over to the agency in their uniforms and went to the white men's store, and some of the white ranchers went out of their way to shake hands with them and say, "Well, boy, how goes it?" They were important, the fledgling warriors.

One of the letters that came to the reservation had bad news in it. It was in a yellow envelope, and the agent brought it over himself and explained it to the mother of Tom Little Hand.

Tom had been wounded, it said, and was in a hospital.

The next morning Joe Walking Wolf, the lame one, made a ceremonial visit to old Charley, carrying the old stone pipe. He was not embarrassed this time, because he knew how to smoke in the sacred way.

Charley drew in a breath sharply and was ashamed because he trembled.

"The gift for that, to the grandfather," he cautioned, "must be a big gift, because it is a hard ceremony."

"The gift is outside with the pole," Joe said humbly.

And outside was picketed Joe's good sorrel colt.

There was a time when the Cheyennes, the Cut Arm people, could be lordly in their generosity with gifts of captured horses, sometimes bought with their blood. They could be splendid in their charity, giving buffalo meat to the needy and fine robes to the poor. But that time was when Charley Lockjaw was young. He had not owned a horse of his own for thirty years. And this was the only horse his great-grandson had, for the old mare this colt belonged to had died.

Charley blinked at the horse, a beautiful colt without a blemish. He walked over to stroke its neck, and the colt threw its head back and tried to get away. Charley spoke to it sharply, with approval. The colt was no stable pet, but used to running across the prairie with its mane flying in the wind and the snow. It would throw a rider before it was broke, Charley thought.

He nodded and said, "The gift is enough."

When he was a young man, he had paid many fine horses to the old one who taught him the ceremony for swinging at the pole and whose hard, gentle hands had supported him when he fainted. But he had had many horses to give, and plenty of them left. This was a finer present than he had given, because it was all Joe had.

"We will have to wait," Charley said. "We cannot do this thing today. We will wait four days."

He chose four because it was the sacred number and because he needed time to remember. He had been a pupil for this sacrifice, but never a teacher.

"Come back in four days," he said.

In the time while he was remembering and praying for a return, in some

part, of his old strength and steadiness, he fasted for one whole day. His granddaughter fretted and murmured, coming out to the lodge to bring soup because he said he was sick and could not eat.

"I will send one of the children to tell the nurse at the agency," she decided, but he waved her away, promising, "I will be well tomorrow."

He was afraid, not only because he might forget something important or his hand might slip, but because someone might find out and try to stop him. Somebody was always interfering. For years the old religion had been outlawed by the government in Washington. For years no one dared even to make the Medicine Lodge when the grass was tall in summer, so those years passed without the old, careful ceremony of prayer and paint and reverence that brought new life to the tribe and honor to the Lodge Maker.

This was no longer true by the time of the Second World War, though. Every year now the Medicine Lodge was made by some man who could afford it and wanted to give thanks for something. Perhaps his child had been sick and was well again. A man who made the Lodge, who learned the ritual, could teach another man. So that was not lost, though some of it had changed and some was forgotten, and it was very hard to find a buffalo skull to use in the ceremony.

The white ranchers and their guests came to the reservation in July to watch the making of the Lodge and see the prayer cloths waving from the Thunderbird's nest, and Charley took part in those ceremonies. The white people vaguely approved of the Indians' keeping their quaint old customs.

But the Medicine Lodge, the Sun Dance, was a public ceremony. Swinging at the pole, as Joe Walking Wolf wanted to do it, was private suffering.

It was a long time since a young man had wished to swing at the pole. There was no one left in the tribe, except Charley Lockjaw, who could instruct a pupil in the ceremony. No one could teach it except a man who had himself endured it. And only Charley had on his withered breast the knotted scars of that ordeal.

Now that Joe was going to do it, Charley could not keep this great thing to himself. A man who suffered at the pole gained honor—but how could he be credited if no one knew what he had done?

At sunrise on the fourth day, Joe and Charley rode far out to a safe place among the sandstone cliffs.

Then Charley was shaken by terror. He denied his gods. He said, "Do not be too sure about this thing. Maybe the spirits will not hear my voice or yours. Maybe they are all dead and will never hear anything any more. Maybe they starved to death."

Joe Walking Wolf said, "I will do it anyway. Tom Little Hand has a bad wound, and he is my friend. I will make this sacrifice because maybe it will help him get well. Anyway, I will know what it is to be wounded. I did not go to war."

Charley dug a hole to set the pole in. He told Joe how to set up the pole and fasten a lariat to it, and all the time he was thinking about long ago. He could not remember the pain any more. He remembered his strong voice crying out prayers as he jerked against the thong. He had not flinched when the knife cut or when the thong jerked the skewers in the bloody flesh.

He said, "I did this to pay a pledge. My wife, Laughing Woman—my first wife—she was very sick, and I pledged this sacrifice. The baby died, because it was winter and the white soldiers chased our people through the snow in the bitter cold. Lots of people died. But Laughing Woman lived, and in the spring I paid what I had promised."

He had Joe make a bed of white sage. When everything was ready, Joe said, "Fasten it to my back. I don't want to see it."

Charley said, "Kneel on the sage bed."

He made his gnarled hands as steady as he could and pinched up the skin on Joe's right shoulder. He tunneled through the pinched part with a sharp knife, and the bright blood sprang to the dark skin. Through the tunnel he thrust a wooden skewer three inches long. Joe did not move or murmur. Kneeling on the sage bed, with his head bowed, he was silent as a stone.

Charley put another skewer under the skin on the left shoulder, and over each skewer he put a loop of rawhide, which he tied to the lariat that hung from the pole. The skewers would never be pulled out as they had been put in.

He lifted Joe to his feet and made him lean forward to see that the rope was tight and the pull even. Joe walked a quarter of a circle to the right four times, and back, sagging forward hard on the lariat's pull, trying to tear the skewers through. Then he walked four times to the left, with his blood running down his back.

Charley left the red stone pipe where he could reach it and said, "Three times before the sun goes down, stop and smoke for a little while."

His heart was full of Joe's pain. He ached with tenderness and pride.

"Break away if you can," he urged, "but if you cannot, there is no wrong thing done. If you cannot break away, I will cut you free when the sun goes down. Nobody can take away the honor."

Joe said, "I am not doing it to get honor. I am doing it to make Tom Little Hand get well again."

He kept walking with his bad limp and pulling mightily, but he could not break through the tough flesh that stretched like rubber.

"I will come back when the sun goes down," Charley Lockjaw said.

Back in the settlement he went around and told a few safe, religious men what was happening in the sandstone cliffs. They said their hearts were

with Joe, and Charley knew that Joe would have his honor among his people.

When he went back to the pole at sunset, Joe was still walking, still pulling.

Charley asked, "Did you have a dream?"

Joe said, "I saw Tom Little Hand riding a horse."

"What a man dreams when he swings at the pole," Charley told him, "is sure to come true. I saw myself with thin, white braids, and I have lived to be old instead of being killed in battle." He got out his knife and said, "Kneel down."

He cut out a small piece of skin from his right shoulder and the left, freeing the skewers, and laid the bits of bloody skin on the ground as an offering.

He touched Joe's arm and said gently, "It is ended."

Joe stood up, not even giving a deep breath to show he was glad the suffering was over.

Charley did something new then. He bandaged the wounds as well as he could, with clean gauze and tape from the white man's store. These were new things, not part of the ceremony, but he saw that some new things were good as long as there were young men strong enough to keep to the old ones.

"Tonight," he said, "you sleep in my lodge and nobody will bother you." In the sagging bed in the cabin where Joe slept, there were also two or three children who might hurt those wounds.

"Now," Charley said, "I am going to give you something."

He brought from a hiding place, behind a rock, a pint whiskey bottle, still half full, and said, "I am sorry there is not more here."

He told Joe, "Now you can teach the ritual of swinging at the pole. Two men can teach it, you and I, if anyone wants to learn. It will not be forgotten when my shadow walks the Hanging Road across the stars."

The spirits may be dead, he thought, but the strong hearts of the Cheyenne people still beat with courage like the steady sound of drums.

Charley never rode his sorrel horse, but when it was three years old, Joe broke it. The horse threw him two or three times, and the old man cackled, admiring its spirit, while Joe picked himself up from the dust, swearing. Joe used the horse, but he never put a saddle on that sorrel without first asking Charley's permission.

Some of the short-haired young men never did come back from the Army, but Joe's three friends came back, wearing their uniforms and their medals. Tom Little Hand walked on crutches the first time he came home, with a cane the second time, but when he came home to stay he needed only a brace on the leg that had been wounded, and a special shoe on that foot.

The three soldiers went to the agency to show off a little, and to the white man's store off the reservation, to buy tobacco and stand around. The white ranchers, coming in for the mail, shook hands with them and called each one by name and said, "Glad to see you back, boy! Sure glad to see you back!"

The Indian soldiers smiled a little and said "Yeah."

The ranchers never thought of shaking hands with Joe Walking Wolf. He had been around all the time, and the marks of his honor were not in any medals but in the angry scars under his faded shirt.

After all the girls had had a chance to admire the uniforms, the young men took off their medals, to be put away with the broken-feathered war bonnets and the ancient, unstrung bows. They wore parts of their uniforms to work in, as the white veterans did, and they went back to raising cattle or doing whatever work they could get.

Tom Little Hand, that proud rider, never wore his old cowboy boots again because of the brace on his leg. He could not even wear moccasins, but always the special shoe. But he walked and he rode, and pretty soon he married Joe's sister, Jennie, whose Cheyenne name was Laughing Woman, the same as her great-grandmother's.

That's all there is to the story, except that last summer Charley Lockjaw died. He had thought he was a hundred years old, but his granddaughter told the Indian agent that he had always said he was born the year a certain treaty was made with the white chiefs. The agent knew what year that treaty was, and he figured out that Charley must have been ninety when he died.

The agent was interested in history, and so he asked, "Was Charley in the fight with Yellow Hair at the Little Big Horn?" Charley's granddaughter said she didn't know.

Her son, Joe Walking Wolf, knew but did not say so. Charley Lockjaw had been there, a warrior seventeen years old, and had counted coup five times on blue-coated soldiers of the Seventh Cavalry that June day when General Custer and his men died in the great victory of the Cheyennes and the Sioux. But Joe did not tell everything Charley Lockjaw had told him.

When Charley died, he left his horse to Joe. So Joe wasn't lying when, after he shot the beautiful eighty-dollar sorrel on Charley's grave, he simply said, "It was my horse."

The three other young men were there when Joe killed it. That was the right thing to do, they agreed soberly, because in the old days when a warrior died, his best horse was sacrificed for him. Then he would have it to ride as he went along the Hanging Road to the place where the shadows of the Cheyenne people go. The place is neither heaven nor hell, but just like earth, with plenty of fighting and buffalo and horses, and tall peaked lodges to live in, and everybody there who has gone before. It is just like earth, as Charley Lockjaw remembered earth from his young days.

When Joe had shot the horse, the young men took the sharp knives they had brought along and peeled the hide off. They butchered the carcass and took the great hunks of horse meat home to their families.

Because the buffalo are gone from the earth now, and in the dirt-roofed cabins of the Cheyennes, the conquered people, there is not often enough food to get ready a feast.   THE END

⟳ Talking it over

1. *a.* What incident marks the real beginning of the story?

b. Why do the young men want to dream on a hilltop?

c. The young men had not shown much interest before in the traditions of their tribe. Why do they want to follow the old ways now?

2. *a.* Describe the ceremony of "dreaming on a hilltop." What is the dream supposed to tell each man?

b. Why does this ceremony have to be kept secret? Why were *some* of the old Indian ceremonies permitted?

3. *a.* Why does Joe Walking Wolf want to perform the old ceremony of "swinging at the pole"?

b. Describe the ceremony in detail.

4. *a.* Why do the young men sacrifice the horse on old Charley's grave?

b. How do you feel about the killing of the horse?

5. *a.* How is the title of the story connected with what happens in it?

b. What invisible scars has life left on all the Indians in this story?

6. *a.* How does the life of Indians in the twentieth century as seen in this story seem to compare with what Indians were like before the white man conquered them?

b. What is meant by the statement that Charley "lived at the wrong time"? (page 475b, 1)

c. What prejudices are shown by both whites and Indians in the story?

7. Select the statement you think best expresses the central idea of the story:

a. The world of the Indian is different from that of the white man.

b. All people need to feel pride in themselves.

c. Indians are just as brave as they used to be.

(over)

⇄ Words in action

This is a game of opposites. First read straight through the following paragraph. Then do what the directions after it tell you.

THE OLD Indian **distrusted** most people, even some of his own **descendants.** The white man had pushed his people into a corner. Bitterly he knew that, although the white man's treatment of the Indian was *unjustifiable,* the younger Indians had already accepted an *insignificant* position in the world. Many of the young men followed neither the **pagan** gods nor the *Christian* God, and that made them **atheists** in the old man's eyes. His suspicious attitude toward everyone was perhaps even more **justifiable** because many people both in and out of the tribe had treated him *disrespectfully.* He *trusted* only the very old members of the tribe who were *believers* in the old gods and who lived, as he did, according to the **traditions** of their *ancestors.* The old ways were of **paramount** importance to him. He scorned even small *innovations* such as cigarette lighters, preferring to light his **ceremonial** pipe with a hot coal. The *informal* way in which most of the young men spoke to him made him **indignant.** He was *proud,* though, and very *pleased* when four **humble** young men came to him to ask for instructions in some of the old ways. He spoke **reverently** to the old gods, asking help in doing the tasks right. Life was worth living again. There were others who cared about the past, too.

On your paper make two columns, as in the example. Starting at the same time as the rest of the group, write in the first column all the words from the paragraph which are printed in **boldface**. Write them in the order in which they appear.

For each boldface word there is a word in *italic* type that has the opposite meaning. The object of the game is to match each boldface word with its opposite, which you are to write beside it in the column headed "Opposites." You may use a dictionary for help if all players have one. The first word is done as a sample.

WORDS	OPPOSITES
1. **distrusted**	*trusted*

Her name is "Kills Both Places"

Dorothy Johnson is an honorary member of the Blackfeet Indian tribe. An old medicine man gave her his grandmother's name: Kills Both Places. She is also honorary police chief of Whitefish, Montana, where she grew up.

Most of her stories have to do with the frontier West. "Scars of Honor" resulted from a vacation trip to a ranch on the edge of the Northern Cheyenne Reservation in Montana. While there, Miss Johnson attended a Cheyenne rodeo, during which a bucking horse dropped dead. The Indians swarmed out and butchered it. This experience led her to read much about the tragic history of the Cheyennes. She developed a deep pity for the tribe, which has been called the Race of Sorrows.

Then: Views and viewpoints

1. *a.* Which selection or selections helped you most in understanding the past? Explain.

b. Which selection made best use of sensory images to help you experience life at that time? List several such passages.

c. In which selection did you most often have to adjust your speed to a slow, careful rate? Why?

2. Here are some judgments made by people in this unit:
   (1) In "Ford's Fabulous Flivver," the public makes a judgment about Henry Ford and his car.
   (2) In "Why the Iceman Stopped Coming . . . ," George and Raymond make a judgment about the iceman.
   (3) In "The Reason My Mother Should Win an Oscar," George makes a judgment about his mother.
   (4) In "Scars of Honor," Charley Lockjaw makes a judgment about the four young men when they first come to ask his help.
   (5) In "Moonflight," the Eskimos make judgments about their shaman and about Stefansson.

a. Which of these judgments and opinions were valid— that is, were based on sufficient evidence and careful thought?

b. Which judgments represented "jumping to conclusions"? On what were they based? Were any of these judgments changed for the better? If so, in what way?

3. Consider these questions:
   (1) What if the West still belonged to the Indians? Would it make any difference to you?
   (2) What if Stefansson and other explorers had never penetrated the far North?
   (3) What if someone like Henry Ford had not pioneered the mass production of cars?
   (4) What if mechanical refrigeration had never been invented?
   (5) What if the white man had accepted racial groups like the Indians on an equal basis from the start?

Answer one of these questions, showing relationships between now and the past. How do you think the present will relate to the future?

4. Write a paragraph based on the selection you like best, describing some of the changes that have taken place since that time. Have these changes been good for the people involved? Choose your examples and supporting details carefully, to help you prove your point.

A WIND OF CHANGE

A LETTER FROM THE AUTHOR

A WIND OF CHANGE is set in a West African country which was once a colony of Great Britain but has recently become independent. It is about a sixteen-year-old African boy, Joseph Konda, who is trying to continue his education. Before you begin reading, it will be helpful to know certain things about him and his country.

Many of the modern customs in Joseph's country have been adopted from Great Britain and are not so different from our own. But the people in this part of Africa had developed a culture of their own long before the British came. Some of their traditional ways of doing things may seem strange to you.

One thing you will notice is that Joseph's father has more than one wife. This is called polygamy, and it is an old and legal custom in West Africa. The family household, therefore, is quite different from the kind we know in America. There may be several wives and many children, all living together in one house or a group of houses called a compound. Because family ties are strong, you might find brothers or sisters of the various wives living there too, with their own children. Sometimes children are sent off alone to live with a relative for several months or even several years. In Joseph's case, he and his mother live in the village of Wainke near several relatives. His real father lives in another town, but his uncle, Vandi Tailo', acts as a father to him.

In Joseph's language there are no words for aunt, uncle, or cousin, and so he and his friends may call even a third cousin "brother." Gorba and Joseph, who are cousins, are often called brothers.

Names are much less permanent than in the United States. In some tribes, a boy may have only one name. If he travels away from his home, he can take the name of his village as his surname or last name; or, like Joseph's Uncle Vandi Tailo', he may use the name of his occupation. (Tailo' is a shortened form of *tailor*).

Schoolboys will also adopt the name of a person they admire; for example, Caesar. Joseph himself has taken new names. His family calls him Momo. His real father's surname is Karana, but Joseph prefers to use the name of his mother's family, Konda.

Before the British came to that part of Africa there was little education as we know it, and most of the people could not read or write. But there were secret societies, or sacred brotherhoods, which prepared young people to be good citizens of their villages and punished those whose behavior did not conform to their standards. Sometimes when a strong action had to be taken—such as making war on a neighboring village—the members would take an oath to follow through on the measure. They dared not break the oath. Even those who had not sworn to it themselves feared to oppose it, because they believed that terrible things would happen to them if they did. The boys who plan the fire in the story have taken such an oath.

Many of these customs have lingered on until the present, but Joseph's country has advanced rapidly in providing modern education for her people. The school system is modeled on the British system of education. Joseph, for example, attended primary school for six years, and then had to pass an examination to get into secondary school. At the end of his fifth year of secondary school, called Form V, he will take what he calls the "certificate examination" to determine whether or not he can go on to college. At present he is in Form III, which is about like ninth or tenth grade in the United States.

Like most secondary students in his country, Joseph attends a boarding school, and it is for boys only. To keep discipline in classrooms and dormitories, prefects (student officers) are elected, or are assigned by the headmaster (principal). The boy who is in charge of all the prefects, and who is mainly responsible for the good behavior of the students, is called the senior prefect.

Each of the masters (teachers) also is regularly on duty to supervise the school compound. Because Joseph's country does not have enough university graduates at present, many teachers without degrees are employed, called junior staff. Degree-holders are called the senior staff. Men and women from many foreign lands—Great Britain, Canada, the United States, India, Pakistan, Israel, and others—have also come to help in the schools. One of the teachers in the story, Mr. Jennings, is an American.

All subjects in Joseph's school are taught in English. Remember, however, that the boys come from many parts of their country and also speak their own various tribal languages. To communicate with one another they have developed a language known as West African Pidgin. It is something like English, but contains words from Spanish, Portuguese, and various African languages. You will see short examples of Pidgin in the story.

A Wind of Change is, of course, only a story, and the people and places in it are fictitious. Nevertheless, it will give you a good idea of the problems an ambitious teen-age boy from an African village must face as he tries to prepare himself for the modern world.

Sincerely yours,

Gregory Allen Barnes

Gregory Allen Barnes

He taught in Africa

Gregory Allen Barnes and his wife were members of the first group of Peace Corps Volunteers in a small West African country. Mr. Barnes taught for two years at a boys' school somewhat like the one described in his book. Later he was on the administrative staff of the Peace Corps program in Nigeria. Recently, while studying for his Ph.D. degree at the University of Wisconsin, he has been in charge of the office which advises foreign students.

PEOPLE IN THE STORY

Joseph Konda (kon′dä)............also called "Momo," a sixteen-year-old African schoolboy.

Gorba Konda ....Joseph's cousin, sometimes referred to as his brother.

Vandi Tailo' (vän′dē tā′lō)........Gorba's father, Joseph's uncle, who acts as Joseph's father and provides him with his school fees.

Mr. Karana (kä rä′ nä) ....Joseph's real father, who takes little interest in Joseph or his mother. He lives in another town.

Joseph's mother ....who is separated from Joseph's father and lives alone.

Meriema (mer ē ä′mä) ....a girl in Joseph's home village whom Joseph considers marrying.

Auntie ....Meriema's mother, not related to Joseph.

Peter Kaa (kä)...........................a student ringleader in the plan to burn the dormitories.

Mr. Jennings ....Joseph's English teacher, an American who has taken a personal interest in Joseph.

Mr. Koblo-Williams ....the Principal of Wayama School.

Michael Museh (mü′ze)............the prefect of Joseph's dormitory.

PLACES

Wayama (wä ē yä′mä) ....the boarding school attended by Joseph and Gorba.

Nkala (n kä′lä) ....the school dormitory in which Joseph and Gorba live.

Wainke (wä ēn′kä) ....the village where Joseph's family lives and where he grew up.

Ngolahun (n gō′lə hüN) ....larger town where Joseph's real father lives, eight miles from Wainke.

Michael Joseph Gorba Peter

Chapter 1

1

TEN OR twelve boys lay scattered around the long, low, hot dormitory, some talking in whispers, some resting. None of them was asleep. At one end Joseph Konda tossed and turned, unable to rest. He was nervous; so were the other boys, he could see.

The dormitory was unusually warm, even for three o'clock in the afternoon. The coolness of the West African rainy

CHANGE

by Gregory Allen Barnes

. Jennings   Mr. Koblo-Williams   Meriema   Auntie   Joseph's mother   Uncle Vandi

season had given way to the early "drys," when the clouds tended to linger on until blown away by the Harmattan, the cold desert wind of January. Other than the traditional Christmas rains, there would probably be no more rain until April. This day, December 12, was well chosen for the fire.

A friend made a comment on the heat, to which Joseph replied only with a nod. He was a slender boy, not overly dark, not overly large or handsome, but he was a good student and had his share of friends. Like many of the boys, he could best estimate his age by the changing locations of his family's farms, for because of the poor soil, a piece of land could be farmed only once every seven years. Joseph had been born while his father and Uncle Vandi were harvesting on what they called the "Bandu Road" farm; and because his uncle had sowed this farm twice since then, the last time two years ago, he calculated that he was just past sixteen. In recent months he had been gaining an awareness of his maturity. Already he found the confinement of a boarding school distasteful; and he was more than ever well dressed, for the girls' eyes, whenever he stepped off the compound.

After a time he found himself unwilling to remain on his bed. He stood, put on his shirt, for no particular reason, and walked along the aisle between the beds. A strip of raffia matting hung so low from the ceiling that he had to duck his head to pass beneath. The condition of the ceiling was a major grievance among the boys, but they had purposely pulled this strip down a few feet themselves, he knew.

"Joseph," said Samba Kpalu, a second-former. "How are you?"

"I'm all right," he said. "But this is foolishness."

"Yes." Samba, considered a jester by the other boys, was unusually sober.

"Is this your book?" Joseph picked up a library book from Samba's bed to examine it.

Samba told him in Pidgin to leave it alone: *"Lef' em, bo."*

"I wish to read it. May I keep it?"

"That is quite impossible."

"Well." Joseph handed the book back. He wasn't in the mood for teasing Samba. He wanted to read, but doubted if he could concentrate. With examinations scheduled for the day after next he should have been studying, but what was the use? He reseated himself on his bunk and let his chin sink into the heels of his palms.

2

About four o'clock his brother Gorba came in with Peter Kaa. Mr. Jennings, the English teacher from America, always insisted that Gorba was actually his cousin, because his mother and Gorba's father were sister and brother; but while Joseph understood this, it was the tradition to speak of any relative or even a close friend as a brother, and he could not break the habit. Gorba would always be his "brother," even though Joseph no longer thought highly of him. He was in fact greatly disappointed in him. He didn't want to tell Gorba's father that Gorba was considered unruly by the masters, or that he associated with boys like Peter Kaa, who was the leader in planning the fire. Kaa was a fifth-former, a tough, muscular boy who continually threatened and bullied the younger students. Gorba seemed to think that just by being in Kaa's company he could make the small boys fear him as well. He and Kaa swaggered in, talking loudly in Pidgin about their mischief and how angry it would make the teachers.

"Bo, we go humbug dey'ns," laughed Kaa.

"Ah say, bo, dey'ns no go like we," said Gorba.

"Look me, gentlemen," said Kaa. *"Ah want you for give dees man you*

coöperation. *You laugh me, bo?"* he said to Samba, challengingly.

"Eh! No, Ah no dey laugh you."

"You want fo' go army?"

A few months before, a list had been passed around by the National Army for those wanting to enlist. Unfortunately for Samba, he had been on sick call that day; someone had signed his name. "Gbooo!" he exclaimed. Joseph couldn't help smiling now at his dismay.

"Where are the sticks?" Kaa asked, still in Pidgin.

"Over there," said Gorba. He pointed to the hole caused by the sagging raffia matting, above which bundles of dry brush had been placed during the past few days. The boys had stolen the laborers' ladder to get them there.

"Do you have enough?" asked Kaa.

"Well, I need a little more."

"Kpalu, go bring sticks."

"Eh!" Samba clapped his hands together, then turned his palms out in a sign of dismay. "Why me?"

"Look, don't ask questions," said Kaa. "Just go. Greeners," he added to a pair of first-formers, all of whom were known as greeners, "the ladder is standing in Lambu one"—Kaa's dormitory. "Bring it here."

Joseph, on his bunk, turned his back to the other boys. He would have refused to go; not having taken the secret oath with Kaa, Gorba, and the others, he saw no reason why he should participate in their mischievous plans. He pretended to study. But when Samba and the greeners returned, he couldn't resist looking over his shoulder to watch. The ladder was placed against one of the sapling crossbeams, and Gorba climbed up to put in the brush. The boys were being careful to use plenty of dry sticks, for the walls were made of mud-bricks and the roof of zinc.

A little later, Kaa left. "I'll come back after dinner," he said, "and we'll get the kerosene."

Joseph closed the French book he'd been staring at, sprawled on his back, and fixed his gaze on the rotting, sagging raffia above. Gorba came over. "What's wrong?" he said.

"Nothing," said Joseph.

"You must help us."

"No."

"It's for the general good. That's why Brutus killed Caesar."[1]

"I know why Brutus killed Caesar. You think you are Brutus?"

"Anyway," said Gorba, "I am trying."

"Never mind." Joseph rolled onto his side.

Gorba laughed. "Oh, Momo."

"Yes?" Momo was the name by which he was known to his family.

"Let's go to the library. It's not pleasant here just now."

"All right." Joseph got up immediately and put on his sandals. "We will go." He tucked his shirttail in his shorts and the two of them stepped into the bright daylight. The twelve white dormitories stood atop a weedy hill. As they ambled down, they could see the two large classroom buildings to their left, part of the staff housing, the football field across the road, and behind that, the dense green rain forest.

3

How suddenly all this was happening, Joseph thought. He had never

---

[1]**Brutus, Caesar.** Julius Caesar, Roman ruler and general in ancient times, was killed in 44 B.C. by a group of conspirators led by his friend, Marcus Brutus.

really believed Kaa's scheme would be allowed to succeed, but now the awful day was at hand and it didn't seem that it could be stopped.

The fire had been planned for about six weeks. A year before, another school, the Kurampa[2] Government School, had suffered a fire which destroyed two classrooms and damaged two others. It was caused by faulty wiring; at least, this was the report published. The government immediately constructed four new classrooms, equipping them, it was said, with the finest school furnishings to be found in the country. A rumor was floating around, too, that the money spent on these classrooms had originally been budgeted for Wayama School; whether or not it was true, it stirred up the boys' feelings.

Then the soccer team, including Kaa and Gorba, played a game at Kurampa and saw the classrooms for themselves. They returned with their own plan for getting their school rebuilt. They and their supporters even went to the bush to take a secret society oath, which no one dared break.

As they walked past Mr. Jennings' house, Gorba waved jauntily to a few of his friends. He was wearing sunglasses and a small-brimmed straw hat tilted over his right ear. "In future," he was saying to Joseph, "the boys will be very thankful to Kaa, me, and all the rest. They will say we brought the school improvements."

He had acquired a boastfulness in the last year, and a superior pose which could often be overbearing. "I don't think so," Joseph replied.

"Well, we shall see."

_____
²**Kurampa** (kü räm′ pä)

"Do you think they will reward you for this? What if you are caught? Will the government give you a scholarship?"

"No one will learn who planned the fire. We have taken an oath of secrecy."

"Yes, but perhaps Mr. Jennings will see you."

"We have taken precautions," said Gorba.

Joseph was quiet for a moment. His brother was a tall, lithe, strong boy, and he was just a bit afraid of him. "You see," Joseph said then, "I want to stay in school. But they will stop classes, even now, before the exams."

"Perhaps."

"Yes. They will close school."

"But next year the government will give us new buildings. It will be the same thing that happened at Kurampa, you will see."

They entered the long portico that lay alongside the senior classroom building and fell silent, for other boys were strolling past them. In a few minutes they had entered the small, crowded library, found books, and taken seats. Like most of the other boys scattered around in the dozen or so chairs, however, they paid scant attention to their books; Joseph and the younger students gazed at their hands in passive fright, while Gorba and the older boys (at least, those in the conspiracy) exchanged nervous grins. But they all feigned interest in their books when Mr. Jennings' voice was heard outside. He was duty master this week.

"Good afternoon," he said, coming in. He was quite tall, and slender; Joseph suspected that despite his white hair, he was young.

"Good afternoon, sir," said all the boys.

He walked over to Joseph. "How are you, Joseph?" he said. "Hello, Gorba."

"Quite well, sir," Joseph replied.

"What are you reading?" He took Joseph's book to look at the title; Joseph himself couldn't remember what it was. " 'Black Beauty'?" he said. "Why are you reading this two days before exams?"

"The examinations will not be difficult," said Gorba.

"Oh?" said Mr. Jennings. Joseph, although he could never be sure what the man was thinking, sensed that he didn't care much for Gorba. "You always seem to have some difficulty."

Gorba laughed. But Mr. Jennings was right. Gorba had failed one year in primary school and had never received high marks.

"You'd better start studying," the teacher said.

"Yes, sir," said Joseph.

"No one seems to be studying. Why is that?"

"Well, I don't know."

"Very strange," said Mr. Jennings. "All right. I'll see you."

"Ha," said Gorba, when the American had left. "That man doesn't know what is going on in this school."

"He will be very disappointed."

"Well, perhaps. You like him too much, little Momo."

Joseph was annoyed at being called "little Momo," but he didn't let on. He did like Mr. Jennings. He was the top student in Mr. Jennings' class, whereas Gorba, who was in the slower stream of the third form, did poorly in English. The American was friendly, even more ready to help students than the other "Europeans," as all whites were called, on the staff. But such things didn't interest Gorba.

"Time to go eat," he said.

Joseph was only too ready to move on. Trying to read was useless; he couldn't even sit still. The two of them laid their books on the center table and walked out. The still-warm sun hardly suggested dinner-time, however. Normally at this hour they would still have been playing football, but games had been called off this week on the assumption that the boys would be studying. The staff was puzzled because none of them was.

"These people know something is wrong," said Joseph.

"The masters? Well, what business is it of theirs?"

"I'm telling you, they will be disappointed, and angry. And what of our father? He will be tired of paying our school fees."

"I can't help it," said Gorba, angrily. "This school is a disgrace to intellectuals. Do you know what the schools in Kurampa and Massaqui[3] look like? They are beautiful. Do not talk nonsense."

"Never mind."

"I hope you will not cause any trouble. This business must be settled."

"I cannot encourage it. I want to finish my schooling."

"But you will not interfere. And our father will never know."

"We are brothers," said Joseph. After all, Gorba was bigger than he.

Gorba laughed. "That's right, little Momo."

4

They had anticipated dinner by almost an hour. Without speaking again, they entered their dormitory and

---

[3]**Massaqui** (mä′ sä kē)

slumped onto their separate bunks. Joseph watched the descending sun, the last watchman over his school and schooling, preparing to go off duty. The gradual fading of the light brought home to him the imminence of the fire, instilling in him almost the sort of fear of the dark he had known in his very young years. He felt a sudden longing to be a child again, to be protected, to be free still to entertain those ambitions which seemed about to be shattered about him.

He thought of his mother, whose pride he was, quiet and perhaps lonely at their little home in Wainke; of his uncle, who had so often paid his school fees; of his brothers, sisters, and friends; of a girl called Meriema. His paternal home was Ngolahun, the chiefdom headquarters, but he had spent most of his childhood in (and had the fondest memories of) Wainke, eight miles east of Ngolahun and a little more than a hundred miles from Wayama. Little, remote place though it was, Wainke held a strong tie on him. It relaxed him slightly to recall his happy hours there.

Pictures came to his mind of his friends and relatives in the ways in which he best remembered them. In his mother's case it was perhaps not so simple. He saw the lonely, thin figure bent over a cooking pot; the healer of female sterility, for which she possessed special powers; and the teller of stories. She told two kinds of stories, those relating to the history of Wainke and the chiefdom, and those which were simply fables.

Of the fables he liked several, notwithstanding the fact that he had heard them over and over again. One was the story of the dog so greedy that upon seeing its reflection in the river with a bone in its mouth, it plunged in to get the "other" bone and drowned. Then there were all the "Mr. Spider" stories. Mr. Spider was also extremely greedy. Learning that feasts were to be given in three different towns, he tied three long ropes to his waist and sent his sons to these towns with the other ends of the ropes; they were to tug him the moment a feast began. But the villagers, tired of Mr. Spider's importuning, arranged to start all three feasts at the same moment. A tug-of-war ensued; and that was how Mr. Spider got his narrow waist.

Joseph's uncle could easily be pictured in his familiar seat behind his sewing machine, a slight smile on his lips. He was a tailor—more people knew him as "Vandi Tailo' " than Vandi Konda—and a good one, for he could make shorts and shirts as well as fine wrappers and robes of heavy-woven native cotton, called country-cloth. The smile, almost a permanent feature, gave a hint of his generosity. When he was making a good enough income (which was in December and sometimes still in April, when the farmers had money from the sale of their crops), he paid Joseph's school fees. During the rainy season, when he had little, he gave Joseph whatever he could. He had also to pay Gorba's fees, and to take care of several younger children, but he never forgot Joseph.

Joseph's most indelible memory of his uncle was far less happy, however. Vandi had two wives, the older of them Gorba's mother. The younger one, Jenniba, had after several years borne no child, a situation which saddened all who knew her. At last Joseph's mother cured her. She gave birth to a girl who became the joy of her life. But when the child was scarcely six months old, it fell ill with fever, which troubled Jenniba greatly. Finally Vandi decided he must take the child to Ngolahun for treatment, and he asked Joseph, who was only seven or eight, to accompany him. The mother insisted on going too. There was at that time no road through Wainke; the three of them had to walk the eight miles to Ngolahun with the sick infant which, they noticed, seemed to grow weaker during the trip. Jenniba was scarcely in control of herself. Vandi had to hold the baby and to keep her away from it. By the time they reached Ngolahun, the baby was suffering from shock (so the dispenser told them), and an injection came too late. Within an hour the child died. Jenniba became hysterical.

"Yela[4] has left me," she chanted. "Yela has died."

Joseph couldn't forget that day, for they had then to carry the small corpse back along their weary eight-mile path, while the woman chanted incessantly, "Yela has left me. Yela has died." His uncle asked him to take the baby's body while he held onto her, but being very young, he had become frightened. "Yela!" he screamed. "Why, Yela?" He began to cry. His uncle grabbed him.

"Momo! Do not be a woman!"

He stopped screaming.

"You are my son," said his uncle. "You shall not scream." But with the kindness that always characterized him, he took back the small body. Joseph wept quietly beside him but didn't wail. Nor had he ever again lost control of his emotions, for he had determined to be as good a man as his uncle. But the voice behind him would ever after

---

[4]**Yela** (yā′ lä)

haunt him: "Yela has left me. Yela has died. Yela has left me. Yela has died."

He had come to love his uncle far more than any other man. When he enrolled in secondary school, he used the surname "Konda" rather than his own father's name, which was "Karana." His father had been displeased, but Joseph didn't care; Mr. Karana had been cruel to Joseph's mother and finally left her. He considered Vandi Tailo' his father; and Gorba was as much his brother as Vailo,[5] his older brother by his own mother.

He looked at Gorba, now resting comfortably on his bed. Because he was angry with him at the moment he could see only his worst side: the thoughtless and often disrespectful son of the man Joseph loved. The mother, as Vandi Tailo' admitted, had been too lenient with the boy. He grew up thinking he should have privileges which others didn't, for the mother wouldn't make him carry water or do any of the other chores if he didn't want to, and Vandi was forever making him new robes for his mother to show him off in. This feeling was abetted by his becoming a school boy.

Joseph remembered particularly an incident two years before. The two boys had been asked to help brush Vandi's farm a day before returning to school. By this time Gorba had come to find farm labor intolerable, asserting as much to his parents. Joseph, in fact, also disliked manual labor, but he could deny his uncle nothing. Vandi was firm: they must help earn their school fees. But Gorba, the night before their day of work, came home with a terrible limp, which he claimed resulted from a

youngster's dropping a charcoal iron on his foot. Joseph went to the farm alone. He thought Gorba's story rather humorous, for he knew his brother had been with a girl that evening.

He had to admit that Gorba's pranks could be amusing. The year before, for example, when the upperclassmen were initiating the greeners, Gorba had made Samba Kpalu walk the length of the dormitory compound on all fours while he danced around the boy like a society devil, swatting him frequently on the rump with a stick. All the other boys shouted their approval. Gorba had about him a roguery that made him popular with them, and with girls as well. But the same roguery and lack of sincerity made him suspect with the teachers, and with Joseph, who had been hurt too often by it—by being called "little Momo," by having to work for both his mother and Vandi Tailo' while Gorba pretended to be sick; or by being accused of, and punished for, mischief which Gorba alone had committed. But he didn't quarrel with Gorba. This was due partly, he knew, to the fact that Gorba was bigger. But Gorba was also about two years older and Joseph would be respectful to his elders even if Gorba himself were not. As long as Gorba did not put his education in danger, Joseph would have to support him.

5

Gorba came over to Joseph's bunk. "Let's go bathe," he said.

"All right."

They still felt anger toward each other but tried to hide it. Talking familiarly, they bathed in the shower-stall behind the dorms, then went together to the dining hall at the southern end

[5]**Vailo** (vä′ ē lō)

of the compound, because dinner-time had come at last. The diet was the usual rice covered with a sauce of palm oil, dried fish, peppers, and potato greens. As a final gesture of amity, the two of them ate from the same bowl. Gorba had regained his good spirits.

"Eh, greener," he called to a very young and nervous first-former. "You want to sleep tonight?" A few boys laughed.

"Sh-h-h," said a fourth-former. "Mr. Jennings is here. You must be serious."

The clatter of more than two hundred spoons against tin bowls subsided as the American walked in. He had brought his own spoon with which to sample the food. "Well, Joseph," he said, "may I take a bite from your bowl?"

"Yes, sir. You are invited." He both liked and disliked the fact that Mr. Jennings seemed more attentive to him than to the other boys.

"You can take more," said Gorba.

"Thank you. This is enough. Are you boys going to study hard tonight?"

"Oh, yes," said Peter Kaa, who had walked up. "We shall be studying late into the night."

"You'd better," said Mr. Jennings. "Remember, Form III and Form V will be taking certificate examinations in a few months, too." He moved on; a moment later, he left the crowded dining hall.

Kaa and Gorba exchanged smirks which Joseph pretended not to see. "Do you want more rice?" he said.

"Uh-huh," said Gorba. *Ah done bell' full.*" He had eaten enough.

Joseph pushed the plate aside. Although not full himself, he had lost his appetite.

Talking it over

Parts 1-3

1. How do Gorba and Joseph differ in their feelings about (a) the plans for the fire? (b) Peter Kaa? (c) education?

2. How do Joseph and Gorba seem to feel toward each other? Why do they feel as they do?

3. *a.* How did the plans for the fire begin?

   b. How do Peter Kaa and Gorba figure in these plans? What do they hope to gain for the school? for themselves?

   c. What is the "secret society oath"? Why is it important?

Parts 4-5

4. Why does Joseph's mind dwell at this time upon scenes from his native village?

5. *a.* What does the story of Jenniba and Yela reveal about the character of Vandi Tailo'?

   b. How does Vandi Tailo' show his generosity toward Joseph?

6. How do Joseph and Gorba differ in their attitudes toward Vandi Tailo'? Give an example that illustrates it.

7. Why is Gorba so popular at school?

Chapter 2

1

BY THE time all the boys had wolfed down their rice, the sun was little more than a pink and orange edging on the miles of cotton clouds above. The beautiful sunset was watched but not appreciated; most of the boys now knew what the night would bring. The tension was heightened in Nkala, Joseph's dormitory, by the presence of Peter Kaa, who sat whispering with Gorba on the latter's bunk. As Joseph watched the white walls of the dormitory behind theirs change from a cheery yellow to furtive gray, he found himself hoping unreasonably that they were talking about a football game, or better, convincing themselves that the thing they had planned was too risky. But Kaa and Gorba too were absorbed in the fading daylight. The breezes started up, announcing the arrival of evening, and for this reason they were less welcome than usual. Above the opposite dormitory three cattle egrets cut the pale sky, followed by a vulture. The tall coconut palm in the bush behind became an uncertain shadow.

"Ah say," said Kaa in Pidgin, "this is the time to bring the kerosene."

Joseph began to perspire. He felt a tightening in his chest as his heart began to pound unnaturally.

"All right," said Gorba. "I'm going for it." He sounded nervous, Joseph thought.

The kerosene was in the charge of the Senior Prefect, who was a ringleader in the plot; he had authority to give it out only to the night watchman and to the dormitory prefects who marched the boys to study hall every night, and was expected to keep a strict record of his distribution. Kaa and the other dormitory prefects had skimped on the use of their lanterns in order to collect fuel in two four-gallon containers which lay hidden in the bush behind the compound. These were now to be brought to Nkala, where they would be stored until the kerosene could be spread around the four dormitories

selected for burning. So much Joseph knew, although he pretended complete ignorance.

"Take a small boy to help you," said Kaa. "Take a greener you can trust."

"I know the boy I want," said Gorba.

"Who's that?"

"My brother."

Gorba was grinning. This is his kind of joke, Joseph thought: to involve his own brother, who would have to share the guilt if they were caught; probably, being Gorba, he would try to shift all the guilt onto him.

"Do you hear me, little Momo?"

Kaa came up beside Gorba to look down at Joseph. "Do you trust him?"

"Oh, yes. I trust my own brother," said Gorba.

"I'm not going," said Joseph.

"Yes. You must."

"I can't."

"Why not?"

"I'm wearing my new shorts. I don't want to dirty them."

Gorba and Kaa laughed, but Kaa was angry. "You talk like that," he said, speaking in Pidgin so everyone would understand, "and we will flog you."

"Don't pick on me. I'm no greener. Look at Samba Kpalu." Joseph attempted a smile. "He wants to help."

"Eh! No!" Samba exclaimed with a jump.

"You see," said Joseph. "He is eager."

Apparently the idea appealed to Gorba. He laughed as Samba glared angrily at Joseph. *"Ah say,* Kpalu, you help me and you won't have to go to the army."

"I'm not a greener," Samba pleaded. "You can't take me."

Kaa said, "We're wasting time."

"Take a greener," Samba said. "I brought sticks."

Samba was careful not to affront the older boys, but he was so angry that there could be no doubt he would resist them physically. Because his thick torso gave promise of strength, they relented. Their faces reflected some concern, over either the delay or the fact that they were encountering unexpected opposition. In their next choice they were more careful: a small first-former who was afraid to go but afraid to resist, and altogether too frightened to speak.

"Come back quickly," Kaa instructed Gorba. "They're waiting for us to go down to study." He followed them out.

Joseph let out a long breath; it seemed he hadn't breathed since Gorba first spoke to him. When he glanced at Samba he found the other boy still glaring at him. He was glad Samba had stood up to Gorba and Kaa, showing them that some of the students, at least, were opposed to the fire. Like the other boys, he delighted in making Samba the butt of his jokes, but secretly he was very fond of him.

2

While they were resting and waiting for study period to begin, two boys became embroiled in a quarrel at the other end of the dormitory. Apparently one boy's shirt fell off the support of his cot onto the floor and the other stepped on it. Joseph heard a sharp "*Wetindu?*"[6] then a heated exchange in the tongue of an Eastern tribe, which he understood poorly. The owner of the shirt, whose name was John Ilbo,

demanded that the wrongdoer wash it; the latter refused. Without a word Ilbo hurried to the other boy's cot and overturned it. Other students jumped up to hold them until their tempers had cooled. Joseph was surprised; the boys seldom fought with their own tribesmen and moreover these two were close friends. Their quarrel irritated him. He had wanted to tell them to be still.

Quiet was restored as the dormitory dimmed into darkness. No one called for lights, least of all Joseph, who would have liked to fall asleep and wake up next day. He couldn't relax. What would his mother say? And Vandi Tailo'? He couldn't disappoint them. He was the only one of his mother's children to get so far in school. His brother Vailo had finished primary school but failed the common entrance exam—fortunately for Joseph, for there were no funds to send two sons to secondary school. Vailo now operated a filling station in Ngolahun. As for his sisters, they had received no schooling, since Joseph's father forbade it, but married immediately after entering the women's society, and now both had large families of their own.

He was the youngest, the favorite of the family, and its hope and pride. His mother liked to marvel at his learning.

"You know the white man's language well," she had said at Christmas time the year before. He had told her about receiving top marks in French. "And so you are learning another white man's language? Don't they all speak the same?"

"No," he said. "I think there are many tongues, as in our country."

"You have learned their secrets," she said. "That is good."

---

[6] **Wetindu?** What's the matter with you?

"Anyway, I am trying," he said uncertainly. He had come home just that afternoon and was a little disappointed with the report sheet that had preceded him in the mail. She had him translate the report sheet again. There was little that she could understand, but she showed great curiosity toward the idea of education and, vicariously, a strong belief in its intrinsic worth. Most pleasing to her were Joseph's consistent "Excellents" in rating of conduct.

"You are a good boy," she said, trying not to smile.

"And Mr. Jennings gave me the highest mark in English."

She was very pleased. With this in mind, she could afford to overlook his low grades in algebra and geometry. He never hid them from her, although it would have been easy to do so. If there was any one thing that angered him about Gorba, it was his falsehoods to his own father, Vandi Tailo'. His conduct rating was never better than "Fair," but he always translated it to Vandi as "Excellent," so that Joseph would not appear better-behaved. Similarly, he consistently finished at the bottom of his class, which was the slow stream, but reported his position as ninth or tenth of twenty-six, roughly equivalent to Joseph's. Their father suspected him at first, enough to ask Joseph once or twice to read him Gorba's report sheet, but Gorba was clever enough to get to Joseph first. Joseph felt impelled to support his elder brother, but he disliked it. He wouldn't do the same to his mother.

"I must do better if I want a scholarship," he told her that evening as they sat on the small veranda.

She asked again what that was, and he explained it to her. "It is so difficult to find the fees in September," he said.

"But perhaps you will be finished with school soon."

"No." He smiled, for he had explained to her several times that his schooling would require many years. But she didn't much understand the passage of years. All she knew was that he had been in school for a long, long time, surely long enough to be trained as a doctor, which he said he wanted to be. "A doctor must go to the university," he emphasized.

She shook her head. "They must be slow teachers."

He laughed. "You see, there is much to teach."

"Well, God will provide your fees."

There was nothing to worry about this time, he told her, because the rice harvest was in and his uncle, perhaps even she herself, could find the necessary eight pounds four shillings.[7] "But it is difficult in September," he said. "Did I tell you that the last time my father in Ngolahun gave me only three pounds? Vandi Tailo' gave me only two. I told my father I needed more but he said he could not help me. I had to ask Vailo and my brothers Mohammed and Robert to help me."

"Yes, your sisters told me. And Vailo gave you two pounds. He was never a serious boy, but he is kind."

"I will always be grateful to him."

"You see, there is always someone to provide for you."

Trying not to be disrespectful, he said, "But I had to pick a bushel of palm kernels to earn a pound. I am a schoolboy, but I had to climb a palm tree like any farmer and chop down the

---

[7] **eight pounds four shillings,** about $23 in U.S. money. A pound was equal to about $2.80.

clusters. You know how dangerous that is."

"Like any farmer." His mother laughed at him. "Oh, Momo."

"Besides," he said, "I was late. This caused my grades to be lower."

She smiled lovingly, but mockingly too.

"I am only in my second year," he said. He wished she could understand. "I must find fees for three more years, three times each year."

"God will provide."

Well, he thought, will He make me a doctor? Joseph had gone to a mission-run primary school, where he was baptized, given his Christian name, and taught to believe in God. Trusting his judgment, his mother had also placed her faith in God, perhaps more, in fact, than he; she felt certain that a kind deity would provide for a good boy. But he couldn't be sure the Lord would put him through six or eight or ten more years of schooling. If necessary, he would resign himself to being an engineer, or even a teacher, but he definitely would prefer being a doctor, so that he might cure his people's diseases. He wanted to treat them without charge, in fact; then they would say he was a good man. His mother thought the whole idea admirable, but she couldn't comprehend its magnitude.

"Momo?" she said. Noticing his reverie, she had reached over from her seat on a wooden box to touch his hand. "You shall sleep on the bed tonight." The small house had only one bed, which had been provided by Joseph's father for the increasingly rare occasions when he came to live with her.

"No, Mama. I will sleep on the mat."

"No. You are an educated man."

"Oh." He hesitated.

"You are still just a boy," she teased, "but you know book."

"Very well. You shall sleep on the bed."

"No. Am I not your mother? You must obey me."

"Well." After a moment's delay he gave in. Secretly—or not so secretly, since his mother knew it — he was pleased. Being a schoolboy was a wonderful thing; it made him one of the most important persons in Wainke. Not only did people seek his favor, and call on him to do such things as write letters for them, but his mother would let him have the use of her own bed.

3

Lying motionless on his cot, somewhat relaxed in the unnatural tranquility of the dorm, Joseph recalled something else that had happened that holiday. On one of his first evenings at home, Meriema's mother had visited them. She was a plump, light-skinned woman whom he called simply "Auntie," having explained to her the meaning of the word; formerly, because she had always been a close friend of his mother, he had called her "Mother" too. Auntie, like his mother, could not quite hide her happiness at seeing him. They talked, while other friends came and went, for an hour or so, often touching on Meriema and the fact that she had been initiated into the female society. His mother watched him closely the whole time. After the others had gone, she said,

"Let us say you become a doctor. Whom will you marry?"

So she had learned of it already. He was not surprised. Perhaps Meriema had let it be known that she liked him, but he rather suspected that someone,

probably Auntie, had discovered his interest in her (although it had begun only that day), and had passed the word along to his mother. It was hard to fool these wise old village women.

"I don't know," he replied.

"You should not marry a girl from the city, or another tribe. She might dislike me and be rude."

"Anyway, it is too early to discuss that."

She shook her head. "You can find the girl now and give her assurances. A good girl cannot live on hope while she waits."

Joseph might have been unsettled by his mother's untimely urging, had not Meriema been such a fresh and appealing new factor in his life. The idea of betrothing her was pleasant. That day he had visited Auntie, and Meriema was there, wearing only a wrapper and the special raffia necktie of the women's society, and when he smiled at her he noticed that she had become a woman. So new to him was his interest in girls that he was first startled, then embarrassed, to realize that he noticed it. He found his tongue quickly enough and greeted her, but undoubtedly Auntie had caught his reaction. It was a strange thing when one's erstwhile playmate and friend could no longer be thought of in the accustomed way. Several times his eyes slid toward her. He found himself inspecting her bit by bit, judging with pleasure that she was growing very pretty.

In evading his mother's prodding, then, he had made little effort to hide his pleasure; having his own woman was a tantalizing thought in that early stage of virility. Fortunately, he had

escaped from her, and from his own weaknesses, by excusing himself to go watch the society women dance. But it was hardly an escape, for Meriema would be dancing.

A crowd had already gathered around the court barrie, the open pavilion which was the town meeting place. What a joyful time of year was December, when all the rice was in, the nights were dry and cool, and the society women were training and initiating the young girls. It was most pleasant for the initiates, as they were transformed overnight from girls to women ready for marriage. Soon offers would be coming to their parents from men of the town and neighboring villages, and within a year they might have children of their own—the fondest dream of all girls.

The people of Wainke believed that their society dancers were the finest in the country, or at least, of their own tribe. The girls still danced the way their grandmothers, even their great-great-great-grandmothers, had, long before such things as machines and education were known. They were taught by a woman claiming to be 103 years old; certainly, Joseph thought, she looked 103, but she could still dance very well. Each year she chose twelve initiates, whom she arranged in order of ability for performance before the townspeople or visiting dignitaries. They wore a special costume: a feathered headband; a soft netting across their torsos; raffia skirts, which added a soft crackling to their movements; and leggings mounted with bells, so that they might accompany their own dancing.

Some of the girls were wearing their costumes that evening, although nothing formal had been planned. Soon they were prevailed upon to dance. The leader, called "Fireburst" (for she was an energetic and surprising dancer), began with a solo, accompanied by the skin drums, by the gourds wrapped in strings of beads, by the long hollow-bamboo drum. Then the others formed a bouncing sinuous line and whirled around the arena cleared for them in front of the barrie. The second girl was called "Flowing Water"; she was a smooth dancer. Meriema, who was the third, had been named "Leopard," for she was both graceful and strong. Joseph watched her to the exclusion of the others.

It was one of the happiest nights he had spent in Wainke. The moon shone in its fullness on the white barrie and the dust, and traced in soft lines the thatched roofs and the palm trees behind. After the girls had performed, small informal groups spread out across the town, so that in front of every veranda people were dancing, playing small native instruments, singing, or telling stories. Gorba and he stayed near Meriema and a group of society women singing initiation songs. Five women impersonated the initiates, seating themselves on the ground while the others danced; they tended to be older women, for Meriema and the other young girls no longer wished to be considered novices. But their song was a personal address to each girl in turn, and the young girls' names were used:

> Hawa, when you find your lover,
> How will you make him happy?
> Hawa, when you find your lover,
> How will you make him happy?
> Loom loom loom.

With each "Loom loom loom," three or four of the women, including Merie-

ma, would take three steps backwards, pushing their bottoms far out and wagging them saucily at the men behind. Then it was Meriema's name:

> Meriema, when you find your lover,
> How will you make him happy?
> Meriema, when you find your lover,
> How will you make him happy?
> Loom loom loom.

The men could not stay silent long. Soon they were dancing too. There were many dances that both men and women could do, usually in separate groups. The women, on one side, turned and twisted, while the men danced in place and chanted. Then the roles were reversed. Joseph lost himself in motion, oblivious to everything except his happiness, and perhaps its cause:

> Meriema, when you find your lover,
> How will you make him happy?

At last the men took over: the men's society dances were called for on the drums. Joseph had been initiated into the society two years before. He knew the dances well, and was a good dancer, although perhaps not so good as Gorba. The society recognized him as a man. He was ready to take a woman. Dancing, dancing, dancing, he came near delirium.

> Meriema, when you find your lover,
> How will you make him happy?

He saw her go home. For a moment, without missing a beat, he thought seriously of her. She was pretty. She liked him; he was sure of this, but no matter: Auntie did. Nothing else concerned him in that moment. He wanted a girl of his own, and Meriema was plump and strong. He lost himself again in the dance, recalling, despite the intricate rhythm making its demands on his feet, those words:

Meriema, when you find your lover,
How will you make him happy?

4

Not long afterwards he was to regret his weakness. He refused to relent to his mother's innuendoes, but in betraying his interest in Meriema he had allowed her to believe that time and her persistent urging would win him over. Once back in school, he had overcome his temptation. Not that he didn't daydream of Meriema occasionally; it was simply more important that he finish his education.

During Easter vacation, however, Auntie had decided to let Meriema see him alone, and they had talked together shyly until they had become quite fond of each other. One night, by chance or contrivance, she stood alone in front of her house, when he walked by—also alone. No one was watching; Auntie, feeling ill, had already gone to bed. He took her hand and they walked through the quiet darkness to the edge of the village, where he drew her close to him. It was wonderfully exciting; moreover, neither his mother nor Auntie, although they likely noticed, made any comment. So they walked together through the quiet darkness several nights more, also with impunity—or perhaps discreet blessings. If Joseph wondered the first time into what complications he might be falling, he saw fewer difficulties arising from each following meeting. He was enthralled with Meriema.

But when, shortly, he was again enrolled in the ascetic life of the boarding school, he fell in for a great deal of self-rebuke. In Meriema's eyes he had betrothed her; Auntie and his mother undoubtedly read the signs and felt the same. Well, she would make a good wife. But he was too young. And he wanted to be a doctor, or at least someone well educated and important, if not a doctor, and he had doubts about the propriety of a doctor marrying an illiterate. Once Mr. Jennings let the boys debate the question, "Should educated men marry educated women?" in English class. Joseph had argued against, but was impressed with Mr. Jennings' comments afterwards; although he wanted to remain neutral, the American said, he himself would want a wife who could advise him in his problems and appear with him socially. How could Meriema attend a party with cabinet ministers and the like? He had decided he would stall until she gave up on him.

But the fire put a different complexion on things. Surely the Principal would take severe action, and even if he himself were not punished, he would have no dorm in which to live. He would try by all means to get back into school, any school, but if he couldn't—well, he might have to yield to his mother's will. But he preferred to think the fire could still be averted.

5

"Be still!" Gorba ordered the greener, who was crying. "Be still, you," he said, angrily. Joseph could make them out bearing kerosene tins on their heads. They set the tins down with a clatter. Obviously frightened and ashamed, the greener fell on his bed and wrapped his country-cloth around his head to muffle his sobs.

"Why is there no light?" Gorba growled.

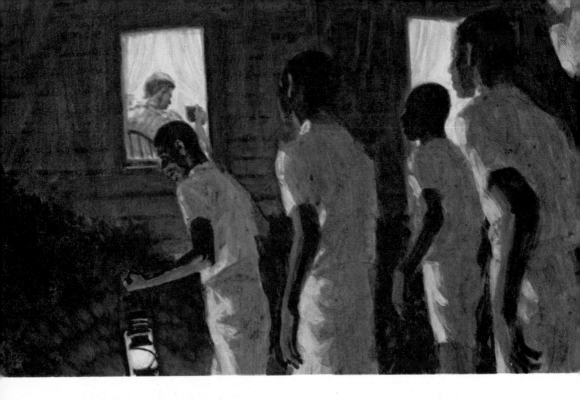

"Leave it off," said Michael Museh, the dormitory prefect. He was one of the few fifth-formers not actively engaged in the cabal, preferring to pretend ignorance. Joseph felt sorry for him, for he would certainly be accused in the burning of Nkala. Perhaps Michael was beginning to see this. "Leave the greener, too."

Gorba laughed shakily. He slumped onto his bed. "They'll think something is wrong if we don't have a light."

"Never mind."

So they lay in the dark. In a minute they were called to studies. Kaa, Gorba, and some of the other boys made sure that no one stayed behind. The night outside was black as ebony, though pierced below by Mr. Jennings' house lights. A fifth-former came along with a lantern. "March, gentlemen," he said. Quietly, with none of their usual banter, the students filed down the gravel path to their classrooms. Behind him, Joseph could hear the greener trying to con-

trol his sobs. That boy is too young, he thought.

They passed Mr. Jennings' house, where they could see the teacher drinking from a cup and smoking a cigarette. Strange food he eats, thought Joseph, who had once shared a meal there. Well, the Europeans were strange people. Sometimes they smiled until one would think their mouths were stuck. Other times they (Mr. Jennings excluded) would grow extremely angry, not for just a few minutes, but, seemingly, a week. The Canadian couple was very quiet, and the Englishmen very stiff, while Mr. Jennings, although he never flogged nor abused the boys, talked loudly and quickly so that it made one tired to listen to him. But all these people had degrees, and worked hard; Mr. Jennings, in fact, was his favorite teacher, for he helped the boys whenever asked. He seemed to take great pride in the school.

"We're going to make Wayama the

finest secondary school in the country," he would say. "Just wait until the results come out from this year's third- and fifth-form exams." Or he would discuss his hopes that the school would grow to sixth form. "All of you should go through fifth form at least. I hope most of you will go to sixth form and University. Hard work, that's the thing. That will do it."

Joseph wished Mr. Jennings would inspect the dormitories and find the kerosene. Or that one of the boys would tell him; but like himself, no one dared. The leaders claimed they would put a medicine on any who betrayed them, and whether or not they actually could or would, it was certain they would punish the guilty person. They had ways of revenging themselves, all right.

Between the classroom buildings the procession was halted and the boys dispersed to their individual rooms. Joseph, after seating himself at his desk, pulled out his French book, which he vainly attempted to read. Even if the fire failed to take place, he would be unprepared to do his final examinations. All he could do at the moment was glance idly at the pictures of France that filled the book: some chateaux, a big church in Paris, a train speeding across the countryside. He looked up at the sound of footsteps. There was Mr. Jennings again.

"Well, Joseph, you boys aren't taking your exams very seriously this year."

"Sir?"

"Why is everyone staring about tonight and not concentrating on his books?"

Joseph thought. "Well, I don't think whether they liked the food at dinner."

"Don't say 'think whether.' Say 'think that.' "

"Yes, sir."

"But no one has studied all day."

"I'm studying, sir."

"But most of the boys aren't."

Joseph nodded, jerking his head up and letting it fall.

"What are you studying? French?"

"Yes, sir."

"Are you going to be number one in your class this term?"

"Well, perhaps." Joseph returned the tall American's smile. Some of the boys said they couldn't respect Mr. Jennings, for he was too friendly. But Joseph, who was growing used to it, rather liked it.

"I want all the boys in your stream to pass the Form III exam in May. That means working hard, even now." He lifted his voice so that the other boys in the class could hear him. "All right, boys?"

"Yes, sir," they said in chorus. Usually there would have been an enthusiastic "That's right," and "Exactly," and "Indubitably," from a boy named Alfred Lahu, who spent his free hours learning big words.

"Well, I suppose you can't get any studying done while I stand here talking to you. Keep hard at it." He smiled and walked out.

Joseph found he was perspiring. He knew that Mr. Jennings disapproved of untruthfulness or evasiveness. Once he had arrived back from holiday in the evening, too late for dinner at the dining hall, and when he went to greet Mr. Jennings, the latter invited him to sit down and take dinner with him. While they were eating, Mr. Jennings talked about himself and his country, then about Africa, and his own reaction to living in Wayama. Much of what he said was too rapid for Joseph to comprehend accurately, but certain of his statements he remembered quite clearly.

"I find some trouble," Mr. Jennings had said toward the end of their meal, "in telling when someone from this country is truly pleased, or sad, for you tend to hide your emotions, don't you?"

Joseph was embarrassed by his inability to use a fork, aside from the fact that he didn't fully understand the question, and so he mumbled "Yes, sir."

"You see?" the teacher laughed loudly. "At this very moment I don't know whether you're pleased or displeased with me. Well, never mind. How do you like the green beans—there, the green stuff?"

"Oh, very sweet."

"Not sweet, delicious. Sugar is sweet. Excuse me for being a teacher all the time, but if people—in America, anyway—enjoy their jobs they devote all their time and energy to them." He talked in the same loud voice he used in front of the assembly. Sometimes he couldn't teach class because of hoarseness. "I hope you'll come to see that despite our peculiarities, we 'Europeans' are not such bad people. And we certainly enjoy living here."

Joseph had never had a teacher treat him in such a man-to-man fashion. To show respect for an elder, a boy should keep his eyes down and say very little, but Mr. Jennings apparently didn't understand that. Joseph wanted to express his respect, and his warm feelings toward the American, but wasn't quite sure how it should be put into words, and as a result, nothing came out.

"The one problem we face," said Mr. Jennings, with his wide smile, "is that we need someone to tell us what is expected of us. That's why we encourage you—at least, I do—to be frank. After all, I'm still fairly new here, and don't know many people, so I need friendship and advice. Have you ever heard of the English poet, Donne? A fine seventeenth century writer, who wrote a famous line: 'No man is an island.' Do you understand it? I think it's very accurate."

"Yes, sir," said Joseph, who understood little but was overwhelmed by the cascade of words.

"So please feel free to criticize. Well, enough of that. Don't care much for potatoes, eh? At least you got some meat, and we're having cookies for dessert, which you'll like, I think. Some day you may study in England or America, and you'll have to eat this kind of food."

"Please, sir. I am grateful, but I think I should go to the dormitory now." He was tired from his long trip, and ill at ease, too, although he sensed he didn't need to be.

Mr. Jennings seemed startled. "Well, certainly, if you've had enough," he said after a moment. "Feel free. I just didn't want you to go to bed hungry."

"Thank you very much, sir."

"No need to thank me. Thank *you* for being frank. Remember, you should always be truthful with me. I would appreciate it very much. Will you remember?"

"Yes, sir."

"That's the boy," he exclaimed, smiling broadly. "Well, good night."

"Good night, sir."

Joseph found Europeans utterly confusing for their alternating big smiles, seriousness, and angry scowls; it was hard to know how they felt about things. But he realized now that Mr. Jennings had been very kind to him, and he hoped he could find some way to show his appreciation. He also recognized that Mr. Jennings was a very good, if demanding, teacher. Whenever there was an argument about that, Joseph regularly took his part. He was subjected to a great deal of teasing for it, since the teacher's unusual attentiveness to him was widely noted, but he didn't let that bother him.

6

"That man asks too many questions," said a boy seated behind Joseph in the classroom, speaking in a southern tongue he understood reasonably well.

"He knows something is wrong," said another.

"We won't let him stop us," said yet another, who was in favor of the fire. "What business is it of his? He's a foreigner."

No one replied to that. Joseph suspected that a number of his classmates had never supported the idea of burning down the dormitories, while most of the rest were becoming uncertain as the time of the fire approached. But none of them, Joseph included, would reveal his feelings; to behave as had that greener, for example, would be disgraceful. So they thumbed through their books, twisted one hand in the other, stared into space, drew designs on scraps of paper.

Talking it over

1. *a.* How do the other students besides Joseph show their anxiety?

b. Why doesn't anyone reveal the plans for the fire to the school authorities?

2. *a.* How does Joseph's mother show her pride in the fact that he is a schoolboy?

b. How does she reveal ignorance of the practical problems he faces? What accounts for her lack of understanding?

3. *a.* What does Meriema's initiation into the female society mean?

b. How is she a problem for Joseph?

4. *a.* How does Joseph feel about Mr. Jennings as a teacher? as a friend?

b. How do the other boys judge Mr. Jennings? Why?

c. How does Mr. Jennings feel about Wayama School and his place in it?

Chapter 3

1

THE PREFECTS gathered all the boys together at twenty minutes past nine—ten minutes early. They retraced their steps along the tree-lined path running past Mr. Jennings' house to the darkened dormitories up the hill. Kaa had taken charge.

"Close all the shutters," he was telling his helpers in Pidgin, "so they can't see us. Bring in as many sticks as you need. We'll put the kerosene on soon, because time is short and we don't want to do everything in the dark." Joseph heard no more. When the ranks were dismissed, he went immediately to his bed and lay down. Gorba came in last.

"Close the shutters, gentlemen," he commanded.

"I am the prefect of this dormitory," said Michael Museh.

"Yes." Gorba grinned. "You tell them, sir."

"I choose not to."

"Eh! *Wetindu?*"

Michael preferred to register his indignation in English. "I have decided that this dormitory should not be burned."

"Good! Good!" said a fourth-former down the way. Joseph felt he should say nothing.

The two dissenters were of their tribe, so Gorba switched to their language. "Why are you talking that way?" he said, scrutinizing various faces carefully. "You know that's all been decided."

"I wasn't given a voice in the matter," Michael said in English. The fourth-former said nothing this time, for no one seemed willing to back him.

"You are standing against the wishes of the majority."

"Well," said Michael, looking vainly for support, "I don't think so."

Joseph started to speak but was interrupted by Gorba.

"You see how this boy refuses to yield to the will of the majority? It's treason to oppose us! This building is a disgrace to government scholars, and it should be burnt." Gorba's voice rose with his increasing confidence. "It *must* be burnt!"

"Education doesn't depend on the condition of the buildings," said Joseph.

"Ha! You heard that from your friend Mr. Jennings."

"You see," said Michael, "I'm not alone."

At that moment Kaa came in. Gorba's eyes read triumph. "Pooh!" he exclaimed. "That is little Momo. He is my brother. I know him, and I know he will not oppose us."

"What's wrong?" said Kaa.

Gorba pointed to Michael. "That boy is trying to delay us."

Michael turned away and sat down on his bunk.

"All right, gentlemen," said Gorba, "close the shutters. Mr. Museh, perhaps you will like to help."

Several boys, Joseph and Michael not included, jumped up to close the shutters.

"Where's the kerosene?" said Kaa.

"Here." Gorba pulled the two four-gallon containers from under his bed.

"Put some on the sticks above the matting now, in case you don't have time later," said Kaa. "We don't want to turn the lights on after ten, anyway."

"All right."

"You have enough sticks?" Kaa's voice sank as he became aware of the other boys' complete silence.

"Yes."

"Then you're ready. These boys can take their trunks to Akinbola"—a vacant dorm—"but leave some here in case a master should come around."

Another fifth-former stepped through the doorway.

"Have those boys been sent to the roads?" said Kaa.

"Yes."

"Where's the night watchman?"

"He is there, asleep."

Already, thought Joseph. The night watchman came on duty at seven every night and was usually asleep before the boys were. Sometimes he'd sleep ten or twelve hours there on the ground, with his lantern burning beside him. Soundly, too; Kaa and Gorba had been testing him. First they stole his lantern four or five times, then they threw bricks onto the zinc roofs, heavy bricks which made a terrible clatter when they rolled off. Mr. Jennings ran up from his house at the sound of them, but the watchman didn't wake.

Kaa walked out with the other fifth-former. "*Ah dey come here back,*"[8] he said. He took a tin of kerosene with him.

Gorba looked around at the other boys, all silent, none returning his look. Being unquestionably in control now, he took time to give a short speech. He told them they had been neglected and degraded by the government long enough. It was time to demonstrate their impatience and their pride. For this reason fifteen of the boys had taken

a society oath to the effect that they would at all costs carry out this plot. Those who hadn't taken the oath should give allegiance to those who had; let none think he could betray his brothers and escape revenge, said Gorba. Then he added, in a less threatening tone, that it was for the good of all concerned. He quoted Brutus—literature, especially Shakespeare, was one subject he enjoyed and worked at—

If it be aught toward the general good,
Set honor in one eye and death i' the
   other,
And I will look on both indifferently.[9]

He was fond of quotes and proverbs. He used "Nothing ventured, nothing gained," and made up a bromide of his own: "Shall he who is bitten by a snake thank the beast for its attention?" There was no doubting Gorba's speaking ability. Probably, Joseph thought, few listened to what he was saying, but they all admired his performance. From now on they would be docile.

"All right, gentlemen. Everybody pack his belongings in his trunk. You who are finished—*Ah say, take 'em na Akinbola.*"

They all did as he directed.

2

After Joseph had taken his trunk to the vacant dormitory, he wandered off in the cool dark to be alone. Below he could see Mr. Jennings' lights; farther, across the road, the Principal's. There was a night light burning by the classroom buildings, down the hill to his left, while thirty yards from him the

---

[8]**"Ah dey come here back,"** I'm going to come back here.

[9]**"If it be aught . . . indifferently,"** quoted from Shakespeare's play *Julius Caesar.* Gorba means that honor and death are of no importance as long as the goal of the general good is accomplished.

night watchman's lantern was humming softly in accompaniment to the old man's snoring. This might well have been the whole world but for the milky glow of lights from the town thrown against the nearby sky.

At such a moment he couldn't help wondering if he would have the opportunity again to look out over his school. He liked being a schoolboy, and he liked school, too, his French and English work, reading in the library, the afternoon soccer and cricket games. He was a good soccer player. Gorba, who had made the first eleven, was a little better, but next year they would both be "first-eleven." Next year! There might not be a next year at Wayama unless the fire was prevented.

Certain buildings on the compound were undeniably shabby. The older of the classroom buildings had been constructed with too much mud in proportion to concrete, so that the walls could be chipped with one's finger; moreover, the ceiling of one classroom had sagged so dangerously that the room had to be abandoned.

The dormitories, although more solidly constructed, were the boys' biggest complaint. They had inadequate electricity, and no electricity at all after 10 P.M. Many shutters would no longer close, or were mutilated, and the rain and the cold Harmattan in season came pouring in; some of the thief-proof screening in the windows had been torn out; and the raffia matting which formed the ceilings had in many places rotted through. Of all the school's buildings, his own dormitory, Nkala, was in the worst condition.

The staff knew the boys were dissatisfied. At more than one school assembly, Mr. Koblo-Williams, the Principal, had stated that he understood their problems and hoped the solutions were forthcoming. He would see to it, he said, that minor repairs of the dormitories would be effected at the first opportunity. "But money does not grow on trees," he never failed to add. Mr. Jennings made similar statements in English class. "Which is more important," he asked: "Getting a good education in plain buildings, or getting a bad education while living in comfort? Be happy that the school is progressing academically. As long as the facilities do not interfere with your studies, you have little right to complain."

The other boys, at least the rebellious among them, said that Mr. Jennings was a foreigner, that this was none of his business. Joseph was willing to accept his views, but Gorba said, "What does he know? As long as we are patient, no one will notice us or care. They must know that we cannot wait any longer for suitable buildings." Well, that was Gorba. He was a talker, and a persuasive one; whatever second thoughts the boys might be having, they were quite ready a few weeks ago to accept his point of view. Now, Joseph thought, they're probably recalling the statements of the Principal and Mr. Jennings and wondering who is right.

Below him, Mr. Jennings' house threw out lights as warm as fires on rainy nights. Although he could not see them, he knew that some of the fifth-formers were lurking under the trees near the house to keep boys from reporting the conspiracy to any of the masters. They would also be on the back path to the classroom block, and on the path leading to the compound's southeast gate and the town. He couldn't have imagined himself, even a week ago, risking their revenge to prevent the fire, but now it was different. The whole idea was wrong, if not for the students as a body, for him personally.

3

After these long weeks of planning, there was no easy way to oppose Kaa and his followers, because their confidence and determination grew as quickly as the more responsible boys' desperation. Kaa was not what the teachers called a "serious" boy. "Rascally" was the adjective usually applied to him, and it was a highly critical one. Once he had been suspended for being found in the town with a girl of ill repute, another time for cheating on a final examination. He had been flogged numerous times for smoking, breaking bounds, and other offenses. He was not permitted to hold any post higher than that of dormitory prefect, and the Principal often ridiculed him before the assembled students as an example of "unsavory characters" or what were sometimes called "cowboys." Kaa minded none of this as long as he retained his unspoken eminence among the boys. Where Gorba was jaunty and a tease, Kaa was a swaggerer and abusive. He was an outstanding fullback on the football team, a dormitory prefect, he was in the fifth form; and he had a certain popularity; these were more important to him than his grades or conduct rating. But for all his faults, he was courageous, a daredevil who would try anything. Joseph knew that he would start the fires in the dormitories with no hesitation.

When Joseph returned to his dorm, it was about ten minutes before ten, when the lights had to be turned out,

and Kaa was there giving final instructions. The boys were to wait fifteen minutes after lights-out, under their country-cloths but fully dressed, to make sure Mr. Jennings was not making a bed-check. At Gorba's word they were to carry the remaining trunks outside and lay them in haphazard order on the ground. They were to return to wait inside the dorms until the fires were lit and they heard Kaa yell "Fire!" Then they were to carry their bedding out over their shoulders, to create the illusion that they had been awakened by the blaze; it would be good, too, Kaa said, if their shirts were unbuttoned. The fires would not be started until Mr. Jennings went to bed.

Listening from the doorway, Joseph had an idea: he would wake the night watchman and send him to Mr. Jennings with a warning. He slipped back into the darkness. The dormitories lay in two rows, running northwest to southeast, between which lay a sort of commons which he wanted to avoid. The watchman slept at the northwest end of the dormitory rows, near a building the Moslem boys used as a mosque. He moved in that direction, along the outside of the next dormitory, past the spot where he had stood a few minutes earlier. As he approached, he could hear the night watchman snoring as steadily as before. He hoped he could wake him. It was quite natural for watchmen to go to sleep, but paying this old fellow to ward off thieves or troublemakers seemed like a waste of money, for he could scarcely be awakened unless someone kicked him; Gorba claimed he hadn't so much as rolled over while the bricks were bouncing off the roof.

He took a deep breath when he

reached the end of the dormitory wall, and the end of his cover. He wished the old man's lantern were not burning. For several seconds he looked around the little clearing, and fortunately, before he had stepped forward he caught a movement in the shadows by the mosque. A boy had just squatted on his haunches. Joseph couldn't recognize him, but it was obvious that the watchman was himself being watched, to make sure he didn't stir. With a sigh of disappointment, but also of relief, he made his way back to his dorm.

By the time he reached his bed he had conceived another, more hazardous plan. He would walk about the compound in hopes of meeting Mr. Jennings or another staff member, or even a small boy to carry a message. In preparation for the latter possibility, he would write a note. No one was looking. He pulled a piece of paper from his exercise book and wrote:

Dear Sir,
    The boys are going to burn the dormitories tonight. You must stop them from this nefarious action.

He started to sign his name, but caught himself. Folding the paper and placing it in his shirt pocket, he left the dorm hurriedly. There was little time before lights-out. He moved silently down the hill, aware that he might be stopped at any moment by the boys he knew were lurking in the shadows. He made up an excuse to give them; he was looking for his pen. If only he could get to the classrooms, he could cross the road and slip through the grass to the Principal's house. He feared the snakes that lurked in the weeds, but he was sure there would be boys patrolling

the road. He could only hope his mother's belief that snakes bit no one but witches and wizards was true.

As he expected, he was soon stopped. *"Who's man dey?"* came the muted but abrupt demand.

"It's all right," he answered in Pidgin. "I'm taking a walk."

"What is it?" another boy whispered.

"Come here," said the first boy. "What are you doing?"

"I'm going down to the school," said Joseph. "I lost my pen."

"What's your name?"

Joseph cleared his throat. "Momo Konda," he said.

"I know who it is," said one of the two boys who now stood close against him on either side. "It's Gorba's brother."

"Oh?" One of the boys was a member of his tribe, and the other spoke their language; they broke into it.

"He is friendly with Mr. Jennings."

"Won't you let me look for my pen?" said Joseph.

"No," said the larger boy, who had recognized him. "I think you are going to Mr. Jennings' house."

"I'm not!" Joseph exclaimed. "I'm going to the classroom block to look for my pen."

"Your pen? Why, at this time?"

"I just noticed it was gone."

"But it's lights-out."

"Then why don't you leave me, so I can find it quickly?"

"You're not going to need it," the smaller boy laughed.

"Look, Konda," said the bigger boy, "I know you want to talk to this European, but we're going to stop you. *You no can wash we eye.*" He would not be fooled.

"Eh!" said Joseph. "Let me go."

"No. You understand? Go to your dormitory."

"But the pen cost me a shilling. I don't have money for another."

The big boy stepped up menacingly. "Don't make trouble. Go."

Joseph turned around slowly. At that moment the lights-out signal was rung on the gong up the hill.

"Go quickly," the big boy whispered harshly. "They're waiting for you."

Thus foiled and with too little time to try another path, Joseph dragged himself up the hill. Fortunately, the boys hadn't laid hands on him and found the note. Still, they would inform Gorba and Kaa about his walk, and he could expect some suspicion, or anger, or even punishment directed at him. The thought of it made him resent all the troublemakers.

He had another idea. He rubbed his hands around the path until he found a large stone. Vaguely, against the light from the town, he could see Akinbola, the vacant dormitory; it was about sixty yards away. He hurled the stone as hard as he could. Nothing happened. He found another rock. This time he threw so hard he strained his shoulder, but he was rewarded by a *crack!* on the roof and two clattering bounces. He held his breath, watching Mr. Jennings' windows. Apparently the American had not heard.

Then, by the light falling out the front door, he saw the American step onto his veranda and look toward the dorms. Joseph scratched around for another stone and threw it. He missed. Breathless, he got hold of another but missed again. A third missed. Mr. Jennings walked back inside the house. But Joseph's arm, sore though it was, responded once more with a direct hit.

Mr. Jennings again came to his veranda, while from above came angry whispers. Joseph hurried on to his dormitory. Just before entering, he threw a rock high in the air. He was inside before it landed on the roof. He covered his head in mock alarm at its bang and noisy roll.

"Where have you been?" Gorba demanded angrily.

Joseph debated saying "At the lavatory," but decided against it. "Looking for my pen. Who's throwing rocks?"

"I don't know. Go to your bed. I want to turn out the light."

Joseph felt the gaze of every boy as he walked down the row of beds. When he reached his own cot he lay down and tried to muffle the long nervous breath that had to be released. Gorba turned off the lights.

A moment later Kaa burst in. "Gorba!" he called.

"Yes?"

"Who's throwing stones?"

"I don't know."

"Everyone present in this dorm?"

"Yes. Momo just came."

"Momo? Your brother?"

"Yes. He says he was looking for his pen."

"I want to talk to that boy."

"He's all right," Gorba said nervously. "He was inside when the stone hit our roof."

Kaa said nothing. Apparently he was satisfied. He started to leave but was prevented from doing so by the entrance of another student. From his voice, despite its unsteadiness, Joseph recognized the larger of the two boys who had intercepted him on the path below.

"Bed check! *Mr. Jennings dey come.*"

4

Kaa left quickly, and Gorba slipped under his country-cloth. They all listened for the teacher's footstep, ready to feign sleep. But he was a long time coming. There were apparently boys missing in the other dorms. If so, Mr. Jennings might be getting suspicious, Joseph thought; yet he knew that he could just as easily be investigating the stone-throwing, in which case he wouldn't learn or suspect anything.

At last they heard a scuffling of gravel outside, the door was pushed open, and the teacher's flashlight flicked about the long still room.

"All right," said Mr. Jennings, "who is prefect of this dormitory?"

"Sir?" said Michael Museh.

"What's your name?"

"Michael Museh."

"Michael, was any boy in here throwing stones, as far as you know?"

"No, sir."

"Was any boy out of the dorm when lights-out sounded?"

"Well—"

"I will hold you responsible for your answer." Mr. Jennings seemed irritated.

"Yes, sir, one boy was out, but he came back."

"Who is he?"

"Joseph Konda."

"Joseph? Where are you?"

"Here, sir."

Mr. Jennings threw the light on him and walked over. "Were you throwing rocks on the roofs?"

"No, sir. In fact, one hit this dorm after I had returned."

"Is that right, Michael?"

"Yes, sir."

"O.K. Now listen to me, all of you. I'm sorry to wake you; those who are asleep can stay asleep because I'm sure they're not guilty, anyway. But the rest of you can pass this word on to the whole school. I have been to every dorm, and I have found every boy in his bed. But ten minutes ago, after the bell had rung, somebody was throwing rocks on the dormitory roofs. And when I left my house to investigate, I heard boys running up the hill ahead of me. This means that several students were out doing mischief after lights-out. Now they're all in their beds, and not only will no one admit to being out, but the dormitory prefects refuse to report the guilty parties.

"I'm not sure just what I should do about this. Certainly I will report the matter to the Principal, and if my present mood continues, I will recommend the dismissal of every dormitory prefect."

His voice had risen, but he paused, and began again more quietly. "This may seem harsh, for it will affect innocent people, and I'm pretty sure, Michael, that you are one of them. But the prefects are the pivots of discipline here, so we must have boys we can rely on. There is no excuse for the displays of bad behavior that have taken place in recent days. Several times large rocks have been thrown on dormitory roofs. Besides this, no one is studying, with exams only two days off. Haven't we talked about making this the most outstanding school in the country?"

"Yes, sir," came several voices.

"We can't do this, can we, if the students don't study?"

"No, sir."

"All right. I'll expect you to adopt a better attitude, starting first thing in the morning. Is that understood?"

"Yes, sir."

"Good night," said Mr. Jennings, walking toward the door.

"Wait a minute." He stopped and sniffed. "I smell kerosene. Where is it coming from? Michael?"

"Sir?"

"Has someone had kerosene in here?"

"I don't think so, sir."

Mr. Jennings' light swung around the room, eventually to fall on Joseph's wide open eyes. "Joseph, do you know anything about kerosene being in here?"

"No, sir."

"You smell it, don't you?"

"Yes, sir. Well, maybe someone spilled it when he filled the lamps."

"Could be. Anyway, I guess it won't hurt anything." He again moved toward the door, but stopped. "Say, did you boys hear Michael's good grammar? He didn't say, 'I don't think,' as most of you do; he said 'I don't think so.' Did you hear him?"

"Yes, sir."

"Remember it. Not 'I don't think,' but 'I don't think so.' Understand?"

"Yes, sir."

"Good night." He sounded happier.

"Good night," the same voices repeated.

Joseph closed his eyes, setting his jaw to control himself. He had tried to tell the American that no kerosene should have been in the dorm, for the lamps were always filled at the kerosene shed; but he had on the contrary allayed the teacher's suspicions. Too late he thought of putting his note in Mr. Jennings' hand as the teacher walked by. It would have been dangerous, but it might have worked. Instead, after all, he had failed. He listened mournfully to Gorba's soft, mocking laughter.

Chapter 4

Talking it over

1. *a.* What justification do the boys have for their complaints?

b. How have Gorba and Kaa managed to persuade most of the boys to coöperate in the plans for the fire?

2. *a.* How does Michael Museh show his opposition? Who supports him?

b. When Peter Kaa enters the dormitory, what effect does he have on the disagreement between Gorba and Michael? Why?

3. *a.* Why does Joseph decide to risk the revenge of the conspirators by trying to warn Mr. Jennings?

b. Describe the four attempts Joseph makes to prevent the fire. Why does each attempt fail?

Words in action

The words in boldface all have prefixes which make their meanings negative. Guess at the answer to each question before checking in a dictionary to see if you are right.

1. The teachers at Wayama School consider Peter Kaa an **irresponsible** student. Does this mean that they approve of his behavior?

2. If Gorba is **unquestionably** in control, will many boys openly object to his decisions?

3. If the students, according to Gorba, are **degraded** by the government, does he mean that they are worse for it?

4. Are the **dissenters** to the plan to burn the dormitories more likely to go along with the plan, or object to it?

5. Would it be easy, or difficult, to study at night if your room had **inadequate** electricity? Why?

1

WHILE the others lay quietly, Gorba went to the door to watch Mr. Jennings. In a moment, he said, "He's gone to his house. Everyone wait quietly till I come back." He stepped outside. Joseph could hear him talking with the other ringleaders. Shortly he was back.

"Take the rest of the boxes to Akinbola," he ordered. "You hear me, everybody? Get up right now."

The boys slid from their beds without protest; even the greener who had cried earlier was quiet and resigned. Gorba ordered the shutters opened so that they might catch whatever light was coming from the outside, and then, in the still-blinding darkness, they struggled to find the remaining footlockers. Joseph did not help. He sat motionless on his bed for a time, sensing that others, including Michael, were doing the same. Later he stepped outside to see what was happening.

The central area between the dorms was now full of dark figures scurrying about like ants. They worked quietly; Kaa seemed to be in complete control. From four dormitories they came, setting box after box on the grass and paths. These four dormitories were the shabbiest of the twelve, but they were not all adjacent to each other, and so there could be no pretense of the fire catching in one and spreading to the others. No matter how the fire had started at Kurampa the year before, it

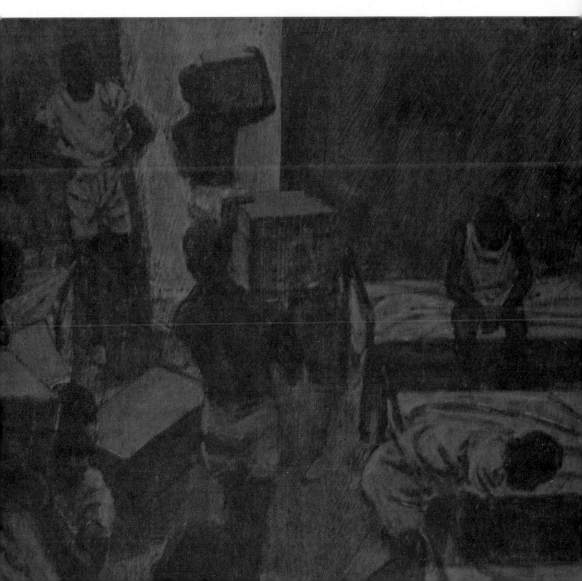

had looked like an accident. This one wouldn't. Apparently Kaa and the others intended to be defiant.

Joseph returned to his dorm and groped his way along to Michael Museh's bed. As he had thought, the older boy was still lying there.

"Michael."

"Joseph? What is it?"

"Those boys are crazy."

"Well."

"It won't work. It will only cause trouble."

"Yes."

Disappointed, he made his way back to his own bed. The bustle was subsiding; the trunks were all outside. The boys returned to their cots and lay down to await further instructions. A fifth-former came in to get kerosene for another dorm, bringing with him a small lantern which Gorba lit briefly, so that they could see to pour the fuel into the other boy's container. Afterwards he blew it out. Meanwhile the boy was giving Gorba the instructions from Kaa: as soon as the lights at the Principal's house and Mr. Jennings' house were out, he was to meet with Kaa and the others outside, where he would get a torch; he shouldn't spread any more kerosene until he was ready to start the fire, for it wouldn't work as well when it dried. He left then with his kerosene. Gorba told the boys they must wait quietly.

The shutters facing down the hill were left open, for every boy wanted to watch. Of all the senior-staff houses, only those of the Principal and Mr. Jennings were visible; the rest lay directly behind Mr. Jennings' house, cut off by it and by bougainvillaea shrubs and fruit trees, or were across the road opposite the classroom buildings. The junior-staff houses were actually visible to the right below, but had been discounted because, like the dorms, they had shutters instead of glass windows, which were always closed with the nightfall. Thus the boys' eyes were fastened on the only two houses whose occupants might be staring back at them.

The Principal's house, across the road, was soon dark. Mr. Koblo-Williams customarily retired at an early hour, for he rose before the boys —before 6:30 A.M.—to set the school laborers to work and to make his personal inspection of the grounds. This was his second year at Wayama. A native of "town"—as the boys called the capital city—and British educated, he was nearly as much a mystery to them as the Europeans. They knew him only as an aloof person, a strict disciplinarian and, according to the fifth-formers, to whom he taught literature, as a difficult but knowledgeable teacher. Joseph couldn't be sure how Mr. Koblo-Williams would react to the fire, but didn't want to think about it.

The Principal had a night watchman of his own, whose lantern still glowed in front of the large white bungalow. But the boys had watched him several nights, enough to predict that, like their own watchman, he would be in a deep sleep by this time.

They all looked at the windows of Mr. Jennings' house, three squares of light in the darkness. Some of the boys said they could see the teacher working at his desk. Joseph hurried to them, to peer over their shoulders. Although he couldn't see Mr. Jennings' face, he could make out his figure bent forward and his arm at work writing. There seemed never to be a waking hour when

Mr. Jennings wasn't at work. Of course, final examinations were approaching, but he worked like this most of the time. He was seldom seen with friends, not even other Europeans. Joseph marveled at this energy that kept him going until late in the evening. Maybe tonight he would keep working for hours.

They saw him once tilt and drain a cup, another time stretch and look up the hill towards them. Gorba laughed to see him yawn in their faces. Later, however, Gorba grew impatient because the American seemed still to want to work. One boy had a watch; he noted that it was eleven—then a quarter past.

At last Mr. Jennings turned off his parlor lights. They waited through the ten minutes that his bedroom light could be seen falling on the black night. Then the house was dark. The time had come.

2

Gorba left and was gone for about five minutes. When he came back, he ordered the shutters on the downhill side closed so that if anyone was walking in the compound he wouldn't notice the fire starting. Those facing the inside of the dormitory compound would remain open to catch the draft. The boys were to gather by the doors nearest them, their bedclothes wrapped around them. They were to wait there while the fires were being lit. No one was to open the doors or leave until he heard Kaa and the others call "Fire!"

"I'm not going to stay here while a fire's burning," Samba Kpalu blurted.

"You won't be hurt," Gorba argued nervously. "I'll start the fire in the roof, and on the beds in the center."

"Why should we burn the beds?"

Michael Museh countered softly. "We should make provision for sleeping."

"It's too late," said Gorba. "Besides, the mattresses are made of straw and they will burn well."

"They wouldn't have to close school if we didn't burn the beds," said Joseph.

"Shut up," Gorba told him. "I know you are unfaithful."

"This is foolishness," said Michael.

"What?"

Michael didn't want to repeat it. No one spoke. Gorba, taking a post by the door, said they should keep quiet until he was told to begin. In a few minutes he had his signal. He closed the door, slipped back to his bed, and lit the lantern. In the dim light Joseph saw the torch, a freshly-broken branch one end of which was wrapped in rags. Gorba got out the kerosene.

"Take up your bed-clothes," he told them.

Everyone moved speedily, wrapping himself in his country-cloth and, if he had such, his sheets.

"Stand by the door," was the next command. Joseph could see that Gorba, however much he tried to hide it, was frightened. Perhaps—but then a boy came in to help him. The two of them carried the kerosene tin to the center of the dorm and began to soak each of the mattresses. Samba seemed to resent his own being doused.

"Ah want fo' go out," he exclaimed.

"Be still," said Gorba angrily. "If you want to go outside, you want to be flogged, too."

"Eh! Well, you want to kill us, anyway."

"Be still, you!" Gorba noticed that other boys were restless. "Nobody leaves this place until I say so."

"Quick," said the boy helping him.

They hurriedly threw the rest of the kerosene around the center area, particularly dousing the raffia matting where it hung to head level. The last drops were used to soak the torch. They were ready now to start the fire, but Gorba fumbled the matches and dropped them. The other boy picked them up and lit the torch for him.

With obvious reluctance, Gorba approached one of the reeking mattresses. It burst into flames, striking fear through Joseph as though it were the visitation of an angry God. He jumped back, rubbing his eyes.

"Those others," said the older boy. Gorba too had flinched. When he hesitated, the fifth-former took the torch and fired two more beds. Abruptly the small greener again burst into tears.

"It's hot," exclaimed Samba. "We're going to die." He pushed toward the door.

"Open the door," cried others. But they pushed in so tightly that the door could not be moved. Joseph was first crushed against it, then assaulted by the others for his inability to pull it open. Ducking a second barrage of blows, he kicked and punched his way out of the throng. The fifth-former had given his torch back to Gorba in order that he might pull the boys away from the door. He mauled them as he pulled.

"Stop this!" he cried. "Imbeciles."

Joseph watched the frenzied boys fearfully. The greedy flames were becoming aggressive. Gorba was trying to set the raffia matting afire, but was being continually driven away by the heat of the flaming beds. At the other end of the dorm the door stood open; the other boys had escaped. When he turned around, he saw that the near door was being opened despite the fifth-former, enough so that boys could squeeze out one by one. At length the fifth-former stood alone, looking out after them. Recovering from his daze, he called to Gorba, "Be quick!"

Retreating slowly toward them, Gorba applied his torch to each mattress in turn. Joseph lingered on behind him, fascinated by his brother's new-found calm and daring. Outside he could hear Kaa and the others setting up their belated and ludicrous mock alarm: "Fire! . . . Fire! . . . Fire! Fire! Fire!"

3

Joseph waited no longer, but rushed past the lonely fifth-former to the outside. To his surprise, the night was no longer black but orange. He looked around the dormitory compound to find that the other three chosen dormitories were burning brightly; the flames of one were already reaching outside through the windows. Boys meanwhile were running frantically back and forth, uncertain what to do. Some of them were engaged in carrying their trunks farther from the blaze. Down the hill, Joseph saw, the lights at Mr. Jennings' house were already shining. While he watched, the Principal's lights were switched on. He was very much afraid, but like the other boys he tried to hide it by pacing up and down and shortly by removing his trunk from Akinbola to the bush a safe distance from the compound.

When he returned, he was surprised to see Gorba just emerging from their dorm, the torch still in his hand. He ran up to him. Gorba's face was sooty; he no longer had eyebrows.

"Throw the torch away," Joseph cried.

Gorba couldn't resist a victory cry

for the other boys' benefit. Raising the torch, he uttered a triumphant "yo-o-o-o-o," then ran to the bush and threw it away. But his theatrical display had attracted attention. Joseph saw the familiar white face approaching, and heard above the din, "Grab that boy! Get him!"

No one moved with any alacrity.

"Help me! Catch him!"

Gorba noticed then. Covering his face, he ran to the path leading towards the town, to the southeast. Mr. Jennings hesitated only briefly before dashing after him. Joseph didn't know who, but somebody yelled, "Don't let them catch him. We must help him." In the next moment he too was running down the path.

Had the fire been less bright, Gorba might have escaped in the dark. But the whole compound was now faintly glowing and there were no trees along this path to cast protective shadows. Besides, the long-legged American was very fast. With a tight heart, Joseph saw him overtake the fugitive and outdistance his pursuers. He seized Gorba by the neck and tried to wrest his hands from his face. Gorba ducked this way and that, making no reply to the shouted demands, "Who are you? What's your name?"

"We must pull him away," a boy said to Joseph in their own tongue. They came upon the two, still struggling, and took hold of Gorba. Mr. Jennings seemed surprised.

"Get away. What are you doing?"

Although careful not to assault the American—or even touch him—the boys dragged Gorba out of his grasp. He struggled with them, shouting angrily.

"You criminals! You arsonists! Let go of this boy, or I'll flog you all. Do you want to be expelled?"

They ran from him. He tripped one, threw another to the ground, but couldn't catch them all. Joseph ran as he had never run before, and felt himself safe when he stumbled into the midst of the other boys at the scene of the fire. To his dismay he heard the familiar voice behind him.

"Joseph! Joseph Konda!"

He ran on, gasping for breath.

"Stop, Joseph. Come back."

He didn't stop, although he knew Mr. Jennings would catch him. He had no wind left, but he was spurred on by the sight of the Principal, who was now hurrying up the hill.

"Joseph, I know it's you. Stop." Mr. Jennings' long arm had suddenly caught him. "You're in trouble, young man."

But Joseph didn't stop struggling. With a great effort he broke free and ran into the murk towards the classroom block.

"Come back here, you little fool!"

He didn't stop. He ran all the way to the darkened portico of the old classroom building. And—miraculously—no footsteps followed his.

4

From below, the dormitory compound looked like a giant, brightly lit stage containing a crowd of players. Joseph could compare it only with scenes from the American films he had seen on rare occasions. The four dormitories were now bursting with flames. The roofs of three were already burning, and the roof of the fourth (which was hidden from his view) seemed to be, from the glare in that direction. Figures scurried hither and about, but there was a general retreat from the immediate areas of the burning buildings. For a time individuals still ran at them with buckets of water, but not long, for this was dangerous as well as futile.

All the staff had appeared. Joseph picked them out one by one: the Principal, who had taken the time to put on a white shirt; Mr. Jennings, pushing, directing, pointing; Mr. Lawo, a junior staff member; Mr. Bainbridge, one of the young Englishmen, herding the boys from dangerous areas; Mr. Fowler, the Canadian, receiving instructions from the Principal; his wife; Mr. Hindell, the other Englishman; and so on. Even the night watchman got up and staggered toward the crowd, his lantern in his hand.

Joseph had been under his portico only a few minutes when he saw the boys being lined up in bucket brigades to save the remaining buildings. One line stretched from the washroom to the dorm between his and a second burning dorm; and another line of boys, behind, went from the well to the dorm he couldn't see. For a moment he hoped Nkala might be saved, but as soon knew there was no hope. The water bearers were not even interested in Nkala, but in the building next to it. They splashed water on the doors, the shutters, and the walls. A ladder was found and one boy, who looked like Michael Museh, went up on the roof and managed, though his footing was precarious, to dash water up the grooves of the corrugated zinc over the hump so that it could roll off the other side. Obviously he was being subjected to formidable heat when he approached either end of the roof, for he would reel back each time; once he almost fell.

A sudden roar startled Joseph. The roof of his dormitory had fallen in, sending balls of fire floating into the sky like giant balloons. So that was the end of Nkala. There he had studied, joked with his friends, and, secretly, danced twist, high-life, rock-'n-roll to phonograph records. He and his friends had often cooked on the dormitory floor, with a portable burner, animals they had caught in the bush. There they had ironed their shirts and shorts, engaged in "palabas,"[10] smoked their first cigarettes, talked about their girl friends. Joseph was not nostalgic, but wondering; how could a handful of boys change the lives of so many? His shock could have been no more profound had he suffered the death of a loved one—particularly since, also, he had himself fallen into trouble.

He never worried much about the past. He and the other boys had had their jolly moments, such as in March, when they went out collecting the huge flying ants that besieged every light, and later, after pulling off the wings and heads (which were bitter), fried them and ate them by handfuls; but these pleasures counted for little, once they were behind him. More than most of the boys, however, he looked forward to the future. He had dreamed, before, of becoming a doctor; in the past year he had been planning for it, or, at least, analyzing the difficulties involved. Now he saw dreams and plans in danger of burning with the fire, thanks, he thought bitterly, to his reckless brother.

The near wall of Nkala fell with a crash, revealing a blaze inside as bright as the sun. The gallery of onlookers quickly retreated before its hot breath.

---

[10]**palabas** (pä lä ′ bäz), discussions.

Another roof fell in. As the bucket brigades now stood in some danger, they were dismissed. Joseph could see Mr. Jennings and the biology master, Mr. Karima, rushing them out of the compound. The only thing left to do was to watch and wait. One by one the dormitories crumbled and fell apart. The flames were feeding on nothing but the cement foundations and steel cots, but they were slow to die. Fortunately their fingers had not reached out to grip the adjacent dorms.

For a long time he had stood, unaware that the night, like Nkala, was burning itself out. He scarcely realized his fatigue, despite the fact that he now sank automatically to the cement and shifted restlessly. But in any case he was not sleepy. He watched, as did the throngs of people up the hill, the gradual subsiding of the unreasonable flames. The vigil was long; the orange glow gave way only briefly to black and then to the lead-gray of approaching dawn. When the flames had disunited and concentrated in small numbers on odd bits of stone or steel, a new bucket brigade was formed and the fire was extinguished, or at least subdued. Joseph could make out his dormitory: a smoldering, meaningless, worthless ruin. He had never believed it would come to this. If only he could have realized beforehand what would be the result of Peter Kaa's mischief he would not have stood by so idly for such a long time.

The Principal's voice wafted to his ears: ". . . occupy the remaining dormitories . . . investigation begins now . . . crime against your school. . . ." He watched that vaguely seen person as though they faced each other across the latter's desk, fearing that such might

well be the case in a few hours. He heard the boys disassemble without a word and file into the dormitories that were still intact, but he himself did not move until he realized that sunrise was coming on in earnest. Mr. Koblo-Williams, Mr. Jennings, and the other staff members had not left, but seemed to be inspecting the compound. He would have to slip into a dormitory quickly to avoid notice. He moved up the hill by the back path, reaching the mosque first, then the dorm next to the remains of his own. The night watchman was sitting in his normal place, too groggy to pay him any attention.

It was extremely warm inside the dormitory. The other boys had moved their beds together against the end by which he had entered. There was scarcely a place to put one's foot, for students from the ruined dormitories were sprawled on the floor. Most were already asleep. Careful not to identify himself, he edged through the throng to a spot near the warm end of the dorm. The floor was hard and hot, but that didn't matter; in his fatigue he could lie on it comfortably. He wondered briefly if his school career might be finished, but cast the thought from his mind, for it was completely intolerable.

He closed his eyes. At last the long night was ended. Through all its cruel developments he had never let himself become emotional, had not even allowed his chin to tremble, and he didn't weaken now.

Talking it over

1. *a.* There is great tension at the moment of starting the fire. How does Gorba betray his feelings?

b. What near disaster occurs in Nkala? Why?

c. Why is Joseph one of the last to leave the dormitory?

2. *a.* How does Gorba attract Mr. Jennings' attention?

b. Why does Joseph go to Gorba's defense?

c. What special trouble does Joseph get into because he tries to help Gorba? In what way is his situation worse than that of any other boy?

3. How does Joseph feel as he watches the fire from the portico of the classroom building? Find passages that tell you.

⇄ **Words in action**

Each of the words in bold type has more than one meaning. Choose from the several definitions in the Glossary the one that seems most appropriate here. Explain your choice. Be sure you know how each word is pronounced.

1. "He looked around the dormitory **compound**. . . ."

2. ". . . even the greener who had cried earlier was quiet and **resigned**."

3. "The junior-staff houses were actually visible to the right below, but had been **discounted** because, . . . they had shutters . . . which were always closed with the nightfall."

4. " 'Why should we burn the beds?' Michael Museh **countered** softly."

5. "The two of them carried the kerosene tin to the center of the dorm and began to soak each of the mattresses. Samba seemed to resent his own being **doused**."

6. "Ducking a second **barrage** of blows, he kicked and punched. . . ."

Chapter 5

1

SLEEP at length overcame Joseph's anguish, but it was short relief; the boys were shouted and poked into wakefulness only, it seemed, a few minutes later. Joseph couldn't be sure what hour it was, except that the air still retained a morning freshness, and his eyes ached. However, he was quicker to rouse from his stupor than the other boys, for his heartbeat had already begun to accelerate.

The boys were told by Mr. Jennings, from whom Joseph kept his face averted, to take their tea in the dining hall; afterwards they would be called into assembly. Straggling up, they made a semblance of preparing for a school day. Some, like Joseph, first had to retrieve their trunks from the bush, or Akinbola, or wherever they had stored them during the fire. As they walked past the four still smoking heaps of rubble that twelve hours before had been, in fact, their homes, they stared in new surprise. The conspiracy had been completely successful. It frightened Joseph more at this moment than ever it had during the grotesque and spectacular events of the night before.

"Wetin? Wetin?" [11] exclaimed one boy. Others boys who had not questioned the plot the past evening now seemed to be wondering about the calamity they had permitted. But generally they said little.

In front of Akinbola, Joseph met Gorba carrying his trunk on his head. Gorba's normal jauntiness was miss-

---

[11] **"Wetin?"** Why?

ing, but a certain smugness was conveyed in the way he smiled without parting his lips.

"Little Momo," he said, "it is related that certain people tried to stop the boys last night, but they failed."

"Oh, well, I was not informed."

"I was told by people who should know."

"Never mind," said Joseph, angrily.

"There was some chance that a teacher might catch a certain boy."

"Yes. In fact friends and brothers saved him."

"Well, he will be grateful."

Joseph had thought of telling Gorba that Mr. Jennings had recognized him, but decided his brother would either threaten him or treat it as a joke. Receiving no answer, Gorba, who still bore the weight of his trunk on his head, was quick to move on.

Hurriedly Joseph retrieved his own trunk, which he carried atop his head to his adopted dormitory. Most of the boys had already washed and dressed for breakfast. He hurried to the washhouse and back, and was ready by the time the breakfast signal was rung on the gong. There was not the usual noise prevailing as the throng descended on the dining hall. They drank their tea and nibbled on their small loaves of bread in silence—although Gorba, Kaa, and the other ringleaders were subdued less because of any apprehension, it seemed, than because the silence suited their sense of drama. Joseph had purposely seated himself across the hall from them.

In a few minutes Mr. Jennings reappeared. The duty prefect, at his order, rang the bell and the boys assembled in ranks to march down the hill. They ordered themselves by class: IA, IB,

IC, then Form II, on through Form IV. Form V, by custom, enjoyed the privilege of sauntering down behind at their leisure, but this morning Mr. Jennings told them sharply that they were to fall in ranks behind the other boys. There was none of the grumbling that Kaa and his friends might normally have put up. No less than the small, frightened first-formers, the senior class moved down the hill with solemnity.

The school auditorium, which would seat five hundred people, was the largest room on the compound and the largest Joseph had ever seen. Here the Moslems' morning prayers were conducted, native plays and dances were given, and, on rare occasions, the boys were addressed by Mr. Koblo-Williams. This morning the staff was seated in its entirety on the platform to either side of the Principal, looking on gravely as the boys filed into their assigned rows. Mr. Koblo-Williams himself was composed, almost, it seemed, disinterested. Dressed in his usual dark suit and fresh white shirt, he gave no outward evidence of having lost sleep. When the fifth-formers had taken the front-row seats reserved for them, he moved somberly to the podium. Joseph anxiously chewed his thumb.

"Members of staff, students," began Mr. Koblo-Williams, "an act of mutiny unprecedented in its atrocity took place at this school yester evening. Four of our dormitories were consumed by fire. We know beyond all possible doubt that this deed was perpetrated by members of the student body, and it is to these young arsonists, and those who acquiesced in their villainy," he added, gazing around the entire assembly, "that I shall now address myself in particular. What I have to say, however, will be of great value to all for future reference.

"It would appear that in my short one and one-half years' tenure at this institution, my students have not come to understand me fully. Perhaps this is due to the fact that I do not belong to any of your tribes; I have indeed overheard one boy to remark that I am more peculiar than the Europeans. I am sorry for this misconception. Permit me to enlighten you.

"I finished my secondary schooling at St. Paul's, an institution certainly equal, and probably superior, to this one. During my last three years, I held various prefects' positions which, as you will admit, necessarily gave me insights into the tricks that boys can play. They say, 'You can't teach an old dog new tricks,' but you see, I was aware of this type of trick before most of you were even born. May I add that there were no fires in my days as prefect, nor did I stand by complacently when trouble arose.

"After my studies at our national university, and at Cambridge,[12] I embarked on my career of service to my native land. For three years I lectured to fifth- and sixth-formers at my old school, St. Paul's. From there I moved to the new Model Secondary School, which we all know to be the most progressive in the country, and then, in due time, I was asked to step into school administration. I spent several years building up the small rural school at Beima and now I have been promoted to this institution."

Joseph could not help glancing frequently at Mr. Jennings. The American sat slumped in his chair, arms folded across his chest, his long legs alternately stretched out before him or tucked under the seat. His face bore a scowl which Joseph couldn't translate.

"In all," the Principal continued, as the boys shifted restlessly, "I have been associated with schoolboys, many of them of your tribes, for twenty-one years, as friend, classmate, prefect, teacher, and principal. I know what to expect from them; I know their motives; and most importantly, I know how to react to their pranks. When I noticed your lack of application to your studies during the past week, I suspected trouble, and accordingly warned the staff to be on its guard. Then last night, a staff member smelled kerosene in one of the dormitories. Its presence was explained to his satisfaction, and he did not bother to inform me. Had I known, this disaster might have been averted. But we cannot bother with the 'ifs' of history. It would be as foolish for us to gaze backwards as it was for Lot's wife.[13] Arson was committed here last night. It was carefully planned by a number of boys; there is no doubt of this. It is the duty of the staff to redress the wrongs these students have perpetrated on their classmates, their school, and their country. We have therefore decided, based upon our collective experience, to take stringent measures, as follows:

"2521—Folana, Senior Prefect, stands expelled from this school. Petition will be made to the Ministry of Education to deny him entrance into any other government school.

---

[12]**Cambridge,** a leading university in England.

[13]**Lot's wife.** This refers to a story in the Old Testament of the Bible. Lot lived in the wicked city of Sodom which was destroyed by fire and brimstone, and from which Lot escaped with the help of an angel. Lot's wife, however, was turned into a pillar of salt when she disobeyed the angel's command not to look back at the city.

"2562—Gbowi, 2581—Museh, 2574—Lowai, 2509—Kakama, prefects of the destroyed dormitories, stand expelled from this school.

"2519—Boini, Duty Prefect, stands suspended for an indefinite period.

"All prefects are hereby deposed. Stronger action will be taken if any of them are found to be culpable.

"Pending approval of the government, this school shall be closed indefinitely for purposes of a thorough investigation of the fire. Terminal examinations are canceled. No boy shall receive credit for this term's work.

"Gentlemen, you can see that I consider your crime a personal affront to myself and the staff and that we shall pursue its rectification with all possible vigor. Any boy whose hands are stained shall receive his due reward. Finally, I wish to say that because you have betrayed yourselves and everyone connected with this school, I am sick at the sight of you. I expect you all to be out of this compound, and preferably out of town, immediately after lunch. Do not return until you receive notification authorizing you to do so. Good day." He walked off the platform and out of the building almost before the boys could rise to their feet.

Mr. Jennings stepped forward, his scowl more firmly implanted on his brow. "Go to your dormitories immediately," he said, in a tone they had never heard him use, "and get your belongings ready. If I find any boy still there at one o'clock, I will have him caned."

2

The expelled prefects were the object of every boy's attention. They all showed stony faces as they emerged from the assembly hall and made their way back to the dormitories, but Michael seemed unable to keep his head up; the other boys were saying, rather indignantly, that he had been the boy Joseph saw on the roof of the dorm adjacent to their own. Gorba and Kaa looked grim; obviously, harsh reprisals hadn't been expected. But they were still untarnished. How provident it had been of Kaa not to burn his own dormitory, Joseph thought.

But although the expelled boys might feel great dismay, it was a no more cruel sensation than the fright he felt. Why Mr. Koblo-Williams had said nothing of Gorba's being seen with a torch, and why Mr. Jennings had not sought him out, were questions he couldn't answer. Although there was no way to excuse his actions, he almost hoped to be summoned to Mr. Jennings' home. But nothing happened. The morning gave way to noon while he and most of the other boys slept.

They ate punctually at 12:00, after which they began to wend their way in clumps toward the southeast gate and the town, where they could find a lorry or wait for a train. Many of them had not received their fares from parents or guardians; no matter, they marched off with their trunks like the rest. Joseph and Gorba had shillings enough for only the first thirty-five miles of their journey, which they would cover by train, but at Yargbo, the town where they disembarked, they had an uncle who would see that they got home. Together, without speaking, they walked down the townward path, perspiring freely under the heavy loads on their heads.

Their train was due at 1:00 but as they had expected, it didn't arrive until almost 2:00. Some sixty or seventy boys, with their trunks, jammed into the five coaches. Usually the discomfort of the crowded quarters was offset by a holiday mood; this time it was merely discomfort, and the train's fifteen-mile-an-hour clip was wearing. The long halt at a market center along the way, normally a fine opportunity to explore and see new things, was also unwelcome. Joseph got off, however, for he saw Michael Museh outside talking with a friend. He ran over to him and took his hand. Michael seemed to appreciate it. For ten minutes they walked hand in hand, as good friends did, looking into Lebanese stores and listening to market women:

> "Fi' 'nanas, penny-penny."
> "Orange! You wa' orange?"
> "Ah got grou'nuts."

How seldom in recent years, Joseph realized, had Gorba or he made the friendly gesture of taking the other's hand, except around Wainke where it seemed proper. Disturbingly enough, he liked other boys, Michael certainly, better than his brother. But at that moment he couldn't worry about it. He was glad to show Michael his friendship. They had no need to talk and didn't. Usually they would have surveyed the crowd of women hawking on all sides and speculated on the younger ones' plumpness beneath their manifold brightly colored garments, but during this brief interlude they pretended to have nothing to say. The whistle blew. They returned hand in hand to the train. Because Joseph's stop was next, he said, "Michael, I will see you."

"We shall meet again, Joseph," said Michael, smiling. They dropped hands and mounted their separate coaches.

Michael was the only one of the expelled prefects who had not taken the secret society oath, but Joseph felt he wouldn't complain. All the members treated a society oath as irrevocable and would go to great lengths not to betray those who had taken it.

In another fifteen minutes he and Gorba descended from the train, unaccompanied by the usual cheers and cries of farewell. Joseph waved laconically, saw Michael wave back, and turned with Gorba to take up his trunk. A moment later the train was shuffling on.

The town into which they had dropped themselves was small, but lively, due to its location not merely on the railroad but on a broad navigable river which swept out of the bush to the tracks and away again. Six or eight boats a day plied up- and down-river, carrying passengers and mail. There was also a ferry connecting Yargbo with the southbound road on the other side. Inside the town there were always plenty of lorries waiting, as now, to pick up passengers discharged from the trains. The drivers and motor-boys called out their destinations:

"Kurampa, here! Express!"

"Wama! Wama! Wama!"

A driver Joseph knew called to them, *"Come, come, come, Ah dey take you na Yonima. Ngolahun tomarra."*

Gorba shook his head. *"Coppah no dey."*[14]

"Eh! You dey yeri?"[15] The man called to another driver. They were amused that Gorba should say he had no money, because schoolboys were considered a privileged class.

---

[14]**"Coppah no dey,"** I haven't any money.
[15]**"You dey yeri?"** Do you hear what he's saying?

"My sympathy!" the other driver laughed at them.

They ignored the taunts and walked on. They knew their way well, for they had spent part of several holidays in Yargbo with their uncle. Joseph had once thought he would like to be principal of the town's primary school, since life in Yargbo would be interesting and pleasant, despite the seventy miles it would put between himself and his mother. But now he wanted to be more than a primary school teacher.

Suddenly he had to tell Gorba. He controlled himself until they had passed, heading north, the few two-story shop-and-home buildings of the Syrians, and spoken to several acquaintances they encountered, then began.

"Michael Museh was punished unjustly."

"Yes." Gorba shrugged. "Well, I'm not sorry. 'The fault, dear Brutus, is not in our stars.'"[16]

"But you should be," Joseph said quietly. "He opposed you because he knew what was coming."

Gorba was impatient. "Oh, little Momo. You and your friend Museh would like to be slaves."

"But we don't deserve punishment."

"Museh will get in another school. As for you, the only thing that could happen is that Kaa and the others may decide to act against you for your misbehavior."

"No, that's not all," Joseph said. "I told Mr. Jennings the kerosene was spilled when the lamps were filled." He had forgotten this himself until a moment before. It was another reason why Mr. Jennings might be angry with him. He wondered again why the teacher hadn't contacted him.

"That is not important," Gorba was saying.

"Then there was this business of pulling you away."

Gorba clucked his tongue irritably. "I said, I will not forget that."

"But that man saw me."

His brother was sobered, more so with every step, as the implications of this unfolded themselves to him. "How do you know?"

"He called my name. I hid, but he knew it was me."

"You don't dare tell him."

"I shall remember," said Joseph, "that you are my brother. But I don't want to be expelled." For a moment this thought made him almost sick.

"Well," said Gorba, with a trace of his old jauntiness, "if he hasn't said anything yet, perhaps he will forget it. He treats you well."

"He will punish me. He will tell the Principal."

Their approach to their uncle's large yellow house was an excuse for Gorba to break off the conversation. But he admonished, as a final comment, "Of course, I shall stand by you like a brother if any trouble comes, and of course you shall stand by me like a brother."

Their uncle came out onto his veranda to greet them. He would have lorry fare for them, they knew, and heaping bowls of rice, for it was December and the harvest was in.

3

Being accustomed to visits from Gorba and Joseph, their uncle took them for granted and didn't trouble

---

[16]**"The fault . . . our stars,"** quoted from Shakespeare's play *Julius Caesar*. It means that the star a man is born under is not so important in determining what will happen to him as is his own character.

them with questions. He was a toothless, slight man, actually Vandi Tailo's uncle and not their own. One of his sons had been educated and now gave him money enough to live comfortably. Joseph had been considering approaching him the next time he needed fees; like Vandi Tailo', Pa Gulieu was generous.

He sent them off next morning with enough money for front-seat — first class—lorry fare to Wainke. Both boys said "Oh-h" upon receiving it, and nodded gravely, trying to hide their pleasure. Before long they had hailed a lorry, taken the soft seats in the cab, and were careening along the corrugated laterite roads. At Yonima, however, Joseph transferred to the benches in back. The ride was spine-shattering and dusty; he buttoned his shirt over his mouth to keep the filth out of his lungs, and sat on his hands to cushion the jolts. But it would save him three shillings on his trip.

They reached Ngolahun about noon. Joseph knew he had to greet his father, however much he dreaded the idea. While Gorba waited at the small roundabout serving as lorry park, with the trunks, he hurried along the back streets that led to his father's house. As usual, his father was there. He had four or five wives who tilled small farms while he carried out the slight duties of overseer of the Paramount Chief's[18] compound. After several years of idleness he had grown quite fat and lethargic. He didn't rise from his seat when Joseph entered.

"Have you kept well, Father?"

"God has kept my body well."

"May God keep it so." Joseph seated himself in the dark, bare parlor.

---

[17]**Paramount Chief,** the head chief of a district.

"Amen," said his father.

He shifted. "I have come to you, sir."

"Yes."

"I am returning from school."

"Oh." His father nodded. He hadn't much interest in school, a fact for which, on this occasion, Joseph was thankful.

"How are my mothers?"

"Well, they are there." His father yawned. "And we are hard on the work."

Joseph leaned forward in his hard wooden chair. "How is time?"

"Nothing to report."

They fell into silence for several minutes, Joseph surveying his dusty-red white shorts and shirt, his father lolling comfortably on a crude but padded settee across from him. Joseph had hoped his father might give him some food, but none of the women was there to prepare it for him.

"How is your mother?" his father said, at length.

"She was well when I left here three months ago."

"Give her my greetings."

Joseph nodded.

"Tell her I shall perhaps be coming to her very soon."

"I shall tell her," he said, although he doubted that his father meant it. They sat for another few minutes, at the end of which he said, "I want to leave now, sir."

"Yes. Thank you."

"Thank you. We shall see each other again."

"Yes. I shall see you."

They shook hands limply and Joseph stepped outside into the glare of the sunlight much relieved. His father would hear of the fire soon enough, but he himself wouldn't have to explain it.

Unless he got into trouble — but he didn't want to think of what his father might do. Stepping up his pace he returned to the small lorry park and Gorba.

The "Ngolahun Express," the only truck running to Wainke, was leaving Ngolahun about three, which was an hour or two away. Gorba wanted to greet some friends, so Joseph sat with the trunks. He was in no mood to visit anyone else; he didn't want to see his brothers or sisters, not even his mother or Vandi Tailo'. To divert himself he tried to think of Meriema, but found he didn't especially care to see her, either.

Three lorries sat around the small roundabout waiting for passengers. The driver of one walked over to him as he sat in the shade of an almond tree.

"Afternoon, Pa," said Joseph.

"Hello," said the driver. "Have you come from Wayama?"

Joseph debated quickly. "Yes," he said.

"They say there was a big fire there. The school was burned."

"Eh!" said Joseph, feigning surprise. "I don't think so."

"Oh, well, maybe they were wrong." He walked away.

So the news had reached Ngolahun. It had probably been broadcast over the national radio, but even if not, the communications network that the boys called "bush telegraph" would be operating. His father would hear of the fire before the day was out; the people in Wainke would know by tomorrow.

4

Wainke had one small shop, which carried soap, cigarettes, tomato paste, bottled drinks, cloth, razor blades, and a number of patent medicines. It was located along the road and served as community center as well as transport depot. Here, before the eyes of the dozen loiterers who always stood around gossiping, Joseph and Gorba stepped down from their lorry. After haggling over their fare a moment, eventually paying the amount demanded by the driver, they took up their trunks for the last portion of their journey. The idlers greeted them and dispersed to spread the news of their arrival to the town.

After mumbling a good-bye to Gorba, Joseph hurried to his mother's house. His greetings to the neighbors were briefer than usual.

"Have you slept?"

"Yes. Momo?"

"Yes?"

"Have you slept?"

"Yes, thank you. We shall meet later."

As he walked in the front door of his home he could see his mother cooking her evening meal in back. Setting his trunk on the dirt floor, he went to her. She paid no attention to the visitor, being busy in the preparation of her sauce.

"Mother, I have come," he said.

She looked up at him. "Oh, Momo," she said.

"Have you kept well?"

"The body is well." She stood and took his hand. She's always so happy to see me, Joseph thought. "Momo? How are you?"

"I am well."

"God keep it so." A slight smile drew her sunken mouth in further.

"Amen." He worried for a moment that she would notice he was home a week early. But she didn't think much of such things.

"Well, schoolboy," she said, "you look like a farmer."

"Eh!" He surveyed his filthy garments and laughed. "I think I must go to the stream," he said.

"But you cannot get clean without a shower, I think," she said, lifting the sauce from the three stones so that she might cook him some rice.

He laughed again. She liked to tease him about the modern conveniences at school. "Have you filtered my drinking water?" he retorted. Since she had forgotten what that meant, he had to explain again. "I can't drink plain river water," he said, from inside the house, where he was getting soap.

"Oh, Momo," she said, shaking her head. "They are teaching you many strange things at this school. But anyway, you still obey your mother and you still wash your face. Go now. I am not preparing food for any farmer."

He walked away greatly buoyed up. His mother always made him laugh, and besides this, he knew she trusted him. Somehow he felt secure now that he was in Wainke. He greeted acquaintances pleasantly, and at the stream chatted with another bather. Across the bridge he could hear young women's laughter, which made him wonder if Meriema was there. He couldn't look; when he joined the society, he had been given strict instructions that no matter how close men and women bathed together—in Wainke they were separated only nominally by a small wooden footbridge—they should not gaze upon one another. He was tempted sorely, and gave way, as he stepped up onto the bank, enough to cast his eyes quickly across the bridge. Meriema wasn't there. The young voice he had heard belonged to another girl about her age

who was already married. Since she too had finished bathing and had wrapped her hips in her cloth, she greeted him as he walked away. He turned to her and stared at her more directly than he should have. "Yes, Hawa. How are you?" he said. She was very attractive. As he redirected his steps onto the homeward path, he told himself that Meriema was even more attractive. He wanted to be with her.

His mother was bent over the pot of boiling rice when he returned. She was talking with other women in the cluster of small thatch huts as they all cooked their evening meals. Each of the women called to him. It was again the time of plenty, and he was infected with their good cheer. But then his mother said, "Where is your report card?"

He licked his lips. "It is sent through the mail," he said cautiously. "Don't you remember?"

She nodded. "But how was your behavior?"

"Well, I don't know yet."

Again she nodded. Fortunately some friends came around at that moment to greet him, and when they left, her mind was on something else.

"Did you visit your father?" She placed their rice in a big pan, added the sauce to it, and they fell to eating it in large handfuls.

"Yes," said Joseph. "He is well."

"That is good."

"He said he might be coming to you." He watched her face, but could catch no reaction. His father used to beat her severely. It made Joseph very angry, for sometimes she would have to stay in bed the next day, but she didn't complain. "I don't believe he will come," he added.

She changed the subject. "How is Gorba?"

"He came with me."

"Did you see your uncle in Yargbo?"

"Yes, we stayed with him last night. He sends greetings."

"Good," she said. "Well, the more book you get, the more you seem to eat."

He laughed. "I've had only bread today."

"Oh," she chuckled, "no tea? Didn't your father give you food?"

"No."

"Well, take more."

"No, you have not had enough."

"But I don't have to read books," she twitted him.

"And I don't either, tonight."

"But you are a schoolboy. Take that food as your mother tells you."

Usually he would have relented, but this time his conscience hurt. "My stomach is full," he said, rising to his feet. He wondered what Gorba was telling Vandi Tailo'.

She watched him wash his hands in a calabash. "How was Gorba's behavior?" she said. He couldn't fool her very easily.

"Well, I don't know."

"That boy is not serious," she said. He didn't reply.

"Are you going to greet Vandi Konda?"

"Oh, yes."

"And Auntie?"

"Yes, I must go there now."

"Meriema still has no husband. There are many offers, for she is very pretty, and everyone thinks it strange that her mother does not let her marry."

"Is Meriema well?"

"Yes, but she longs to have babies of her own."

He nodded. "I am coming back later."

"Very well. We shall see each other later."

He was as reluctant to see Auntie as to visit Vandi Tailo'. Things had not gone well during the last vacation. Several times in the first few days he had yielded to the temptation of seeing Meriema, but after his initial excitement he had questioned himself more and more as to whether he really wanted to marry her. Auntie kept hinting that Meriema should be betrothed, and when she looked at him expectantly, he grew frightened. He was sure she knew of their meetings; she would be angry if he didn't make their friendship formal, after the custom. He had spent most of the last month of the holiday with relatives in other towns. He couldn't do that again. As he walked along in the late dusk he told himself that he loved Meriema, and that he would marry her. He tried to imagine her living with him but saw incongruously Hawa, the girl at the stream, instead. Well, he just couldn't make the decision yet.

Auntie was standing out front talking to a passerby when he approached.

"Auntie, good evening to you."

"Thank you. Momo? How have you kept?"

"Well." He shook her hand and leaned against the veranda wall. "I have come to you."

They talked a moment about nothing in particular. Joseph saw that she was not as pleased to see him as usual. She didn't mention Meriema. Finally he asked about her.

"She is there," said Auntie, nodding toward the back.

"Is she well?"

"Yes, she is preparing our evening meal."

He waited for her to call Meriema, but she didn't. She didn't even suggest that he go around back to see her.

"I want to leave now," he said, after a respectful period.

"Very well," she said. "Good night."

Her "Good night" was so final that he couldn't restrain a little nervousness. It wasn't going to be a pleasant evening apparently; one unpleasant task had been performed unsuccessfully and another loomed ahead. Dutifully he walked on past the court barrie, where groups of people were dancing despite the darkness of the night, to Vandi Tailo's home on the west end of town. He didn't at all want to face his kind, trusting father. Already he had lost the happiness that had come to him at the stream.

Gorba was out front with his father, who lay in his hammock. "Good evening, my dear brother," he said.

"Good evening," Joseph replied, moodily.

"I have informed our father this of our accident," said Gorba.

Well, Joseph admitted to himself, that was very clever of Gorba. He went to Vandi Tailo' and took his hand. "Father, have you kept well?"

"Yes, Momo. I am happy to see you." Vandi Tailo' was wearing a stocking cap to protect his nearly bald head from the cool evening winds. He smiled at Joseph but seemed nevertheless to be in a serious frame of mind. "Gorba tells me there has been a fire at school."

"Yes, sir."

"Some boys did it by accident, perhaps," said Gorba. "Or maybe it was this electricity. You know, Father, it is a magic fire, and can do terrible things."

"Oh." Vandi Tailo' sat up in his hammock. "Will you be returning to school?"

"By the grace of God," said Joseph. "Of course the fees must be there."

Vandi smiled, his round flat face exuding warmth. "The rice harvest has been good."

"Oh, Father, I shall be grateful forever, for without you I would have been nothing. I will strive never to displease you."

Vandi nodded, still smiling. He was pleased. "But where can you stay?

Gorba says your dormitory has burned."

Joseph pondered that. "Well, anyway," he said, "we shall manage."

"This book business is very strange," said his father. "What is the good of electricity if it burns down buildings?"

"It does wonderful things," Joseph explained. "It makes wheels turn around, and it can keep things cold. Also, it makes very good light."

"But this lamp that works with kerosene gives enough light."

"Electricity is better, especially for reading."

"Oh." Vandi treated this as a joke. "For reading."

"We must read," said Gorba haughtily. In English, he said, "Our father is too old-fashioned and ignorant."

Vandi paid no attention, but Joseph, who didn't respond, was angry. The conversation took a turn for the better then, and he could forget the fire. But later, at home, he told his mother.

"I don't think we will be receiving report sheets this term," he said.

"Why not?" Her disappointment caused her to be direct.

"School closed early. There was a fire."

"Oh?" She waited.

"Yes, some dormitories"—he explained the word—"burned to the ground."

"You were not hurt?"

"No."

She nodded. It was late, and she was tired; besides, she didn't understand these things. He was glad she didn't try to find out the cause of the fire. What would she think if she heard that the whitewashed, zinc-roofed, concrete-floored dormitories were burned because the boys considered them dwellings unworthy of educated men?

Talking it over

1. *a.* The Principal, Mr. Koblo-Williams, includes in his speech an explanation of his career in education. Why does he do this? What impression do you get of him?

b. Why does he punish the prefects? What evidence against them does he have?

c. Does this punishment seem fair? Give reasons.

2. *a.* Describe the mood of the journey home. How does this contrast with the way the boys usually feel on such trips?

b. What makes Joseph and Michael Museh feel especially close?

c. Explain Gorba's reaction when he hears that Mr. Jennings recognized Joseph. For whose future is he most concerned?

3. Describe Joseph's father. Why does Joseph go to see him?

4. *a.* Why does Joseph dread visiting Auntie? How does she receive him? Why?

b. Why does Joseph also dread seeing Vandi Tailo'? How does Joseph show his feelings for his uncle?

5. *a.* How does Joseph respond to his mother's teasing? to her trust in him?

b. Try to answer the question that ends this chapter. What point does the author make by asking it?

Chapter 6

1

THE NEXT morning a rooster hopped up on the veranda wall and crowed. "Strangers will be here today," Joseph's mother announced immediately.

But the day went by without a visitor. Joseph spent his time talking with friends and swimming in the small stream. He talked about the fire with anyone who asked, and felt a little better about the whole affair. Of greater concern now was what to do about Meriema. Once, while with friends, he saw her walking from the stream with a bucket of water on her head. She looked away demurely. "Such a plump darling, and still not married," his friends remarked, knowing she liked him. But because he was a schoolboy, they didn't taunt him further.

Around noon the next day, however, he heard a vehicle come into town and was soon informed that a carload of important men, including one European, had arrived.

"You see," said his mother. "I told you there would be strangers." She readily forgot that her harbinger was a day off schedule.

Joseph was greatly fearful. He walked to the road, followed by his mother and the neighbors, to find the car parked by the court barrie. To his dismay he saw that the white man was Mr. Jennings. There were in addition three Africans, one of whom was Mr. Karima, the biology master, and another he knew to be the principal of Kurampa. Gorba came up and began to talk to them.

"What do you want here?" he demanded.

"This is one of our boys, isn't it?" Mr. Karima asked Mr. Jennings.

"Yes. This is the boy's brother, or cousin, I guess."

"What's your name?" said Mr. Karima.

"That is not your business. Why are you here?"

"His name is Gorba Konda," said Mr. Jennings. "Gorba, where is Joseph?"

"He is not here," said Gorba. Joseph winced. It was too late to hide.

"Yes, sir," he said, stepping up behind Mr. Jennings. "I am here."

Mr. Karima turned to the crowd of onlookers, among whom was Vandi Tailo'. "This boy is very rude," he said in the vernacular, pointing at Gorba.

"Joseph," said Mr. Jennings, "this is Mr. Johnson, principal of Kurampa School. And this is Mr. Telfa-Cole, Senior Master of Massaqui School. We would like to talk to you about the fire."

Joseph nodded, dropping his eyes.

"Why?" demanded Gorba. "He knows nothing about it."

"Keep still," said Mr. Jennings. "Joseph, is there some place we can be in private?"

"Who is Chief in this town?" said Mr. Karima. "We'll use his house."

The Chief, an elderly bent man, was approaching. The visitors were duly presented and upon their request, invited to his house.

"These people are witches," Gorba told the Chief. "Don't let them near you."

Mr. Karima turned to Mr. Jennings. "We shall report this boy's conduct to the Principal on our return."

Gorba said nothing more, but showed signs of accompanying them to the Chief's house.

"We don't wish to see you," said Mr. Johnson. He was such a large, impressive man that Gorba shrank back.

"Let's go, Joseph," said Mr. Jennings.

2

The Chief, by virtue of his office, was expected to entertain guests on occasion, and so his parlor, though small like the others in the town, had a concrete floor and enough chairs to seat the four visitors, Joseph, and himself. Because he spoke no English, however, he moved his chair out of the inner circle and merely looked on.

Mr. Johnson, a muscular, light-complexioned man, who apparently was chairman of the commission, opened the conversation.

"Konda," he said, "the government have appointed Mr. Karima, Mr. Telfa-Cole, and myself to investigate the recent fire at your school. We have brought Mr. Jennings along because he thinks you know something about the cause of the fire and will explain it to him."

"No, sir," said Joseph, his eyes lowered. Mr. Jennings, seated next to him, was watching him closely.

"You won't explain?"

"I don't know anything, sir."

"It will do no good to deny knowledge of the cause of the fire," said Mr. Johnson. "Every boy in the school knew it was coming, and certainly if your dormitory was set on fire, you know how, and why, and who."

"I was sleeping, sir."

"Ah, such ready answers. But Mr. Jennings had been talking with you shortly before."

"It was about an hour before," said Mr. Jennings. "He could have been asleep, I suppose."

"It's not very likely," said Mr. Johnson. "Konda, were your belongings destroyed in the fire?"

"No, sir."

"Of course not. No one's were. Now, when did you take your box out?"

"The sooner the fire started." He remembered this was poor English, but he was too nervous to correct himself. For once Mr. Jennings said nothing.

"You mean to say that after the fire started you took time to pack all your belongings before leaving the building?"

"Yes, sir."

"I'm not prepared to accept that."

Mr. Karima leaned forward. "If I am correct, Mr. Jennings, you said that you were awake when the first alarms were given and that you were on the scene within three minutes."

"That's right."

"And all the boys were already outside with their trunks?" said Mr. Johnson.

"Yes, sir. It might have been more than three minutes, I suppose."

Mr. Johnson laughed—dangerously Joseph thought. "Remarkable courage these boys showed. Consider this, gentlemen: a roaring fire awakens them and they each take time to pack their belongings, carry their trunks outside without panicking or, apparently, stumbling over one another, and stack some of them very neatly in an adjacent dormitory. Remarkable!"

Mr. Karima and the other man, Mr. Telfa-Cole, laughed.

"Am I correct, Mr. Jennings, in thinking that by the time you arrived the fire was already a blazing inferno?"

"Well, I can't be too sure about this boy's particular dormitory, but my general impression of all four fires

was that they were well along."

"You see? Now Konda, may I suggest that we are not fools. Between the moment that the first cry of 'Fire!' was heard and the moment when Mr. Jennings arrived you could have had no time to pack. In fact, at the time of the alarm, the fire must already have been very hot. Gentlemen, I marvel also at how soundly these hard-working schoolboys sleep."

Again Messrs. Karima and Telfa-Cole laughed. Mr. Jennings kept his eyes on Joseph.

"No, sir," said Joseph. "We were shouting 'Fire!' inside the dormitory for many minutes, but we couldn't run outside until we packed our dressings."

"The fact remains that the fire was already too hot when the alarm was given. You couldn't have been in the dormitory."

"Yes, sir. In fact, I didn't leave until after those boys started shouting."

"Who else was still there?"

"Well, I don't remember."

"We are wasting time," said Mr. Johnson. "You are telling falsehoods. We have proved that you could not have had time to pack your belongings after the fire started, and of course it is ridiculously easy to show that the fire was premeditated arson. You cannot fool us. I suggest you answer our questions truthfully."

"Joseph," said Mr. Jennings, "remember the time I asked you always to be frank? I have told the commission what happened that night concerning you, but I've also recommended you as an obedient, intelligent boy who should have a chance to present his side of the story. Please don't disappoint me."

"I am trying, sir."

"Look, Konda," said Mr. Karima,

"this man wants to help you. We all do."

"Yes, sir." Joseph dried his hands on his shorts.

"Let us begin on a new track then," said Mr. Johnson. "When Mr. Jennings made his inspection of the dormitories at ten o'clock that night, he smelled kerosene, and he asked you if you smelled it, correct?"

"Yes, sir."

"And you admitted that you did. Correct?"

Joseph nodded, once.

"You see?" Mr. Johnson said. "Now why did you tell him that it might have been spilled when the lamps were being filled?"

"I said it may be spilled from some lamp, sir."

"Didn't he say, 'When the lamps were filled,' Mr. Jennings?"

"I thought so, but I could be wrong."

Mr. Johnson brushed the reply aside with his hand. "But the lamps are not filled in the dormitories."

"Yes, sir, but I—"

"Go on."

"Well—"

"You knew there was going to be a fire, didn't you?"

Joseph smoothed his palms against each other. "No, sir," he said. "At least, not for sure."

"Were you threatened by other boys, or shall we say, warned to keep quiet?"

"No, sir."

"Then why didn't you report your suspicions when Mr. Jennings asked you about the kerosene?"

"Sir?"

Mr. Johnson repeated the question with unconcealed asperity.

"But I wasn't suspicious," said Joseph.

The Principal of Kurampa School turned to the other men. "You see?" he said. "He has been trapped. If he was not suspicious, why did he lie about the kerosene? If he was suspicious but had not been threatened, why didn't he say something?"

"Tell the truth, Joseph," Mr. Jennings commanded with a scowl.

"I only wished to help, sir. When you asked about the kerosene, I could not explain."

Mr. Jennings looked at Mr. Johnson. "He could be right."

"In this case, Mr. Jennings, we must assume that where there is smoke, there is fire." The other three men smiled. "Or should I say, where there is kerosene, there is fire. And when the same boy is implicated in a dozen different ways, I grow exceedingly suspicious. But never mind; we shall proceed to the next matter. Konda, we are reasonably certain that you are not the firebrand of your own dormitory. Perhaps that is welcome news. Mr. Jennings happened to see this particular young scholar with his torch in his hand. He chased him and he caught him, but he couldn't see the boy's face. Now the reason we know you were not the culprit is because you happened to pull the boy loose."

Joseph shook his head. "No, sir."

"Are you going to deny," said Mr. Jennings, "that you helped pull that boy out of my grasp?"

"I didn't, sir."

"But Joseph, I saw you. I recognized you as soon as we got into the glare from the fire."

"It wasn't me."

"Look, I am familiar with every line of your head. Don't tell me that wasn't you, because I know better."

"Konda," said Mr. Karima, "this man has befriended you in every way. You must not tell him lies."

Joseph wiped his lips on his shirt-sleeve; the little parlor seemed very close. "Yes, sir," he said.

"It was you."

"I was very frightened, sir."

"Because you had pulled that boy from me."

"No, sir. I was putting my trunk in the bush and these boys came running. I didn't know the reason, but I thought I should run too."

The American frowned and shook his head. "No, that story won't work. I was close behind you all the way."

"This boy is an expert at prevarication," said Mr. Johnson. "I think you will agree to that, Mr. Jennings?"

"Well, perhaps, sir. At least he's not telling all the truth."

"Please, sirs, I didn't want to get into trouble."

"Then why didn't you stop when I ordered you to?"

"I don't know. I am sorry."

"Konda," said Mr. Johnson, "you say you didn't want to get into trouble?"

"No, sir."

"And you don't want to be in trouble now, do you?"

"At all, sir."

"But you see—you are."

Joseph licked his lips.

"Serious trouble," said Mr. Telfa-Cole quietly. He was a plump, heavy-jowled man of about forty-five who hadn't spoken before. Joseph had almost forgotten his presence.

"Yet we are inclined to be generous," said Mr. Johnson, "so much so that we are going to turn our other cheek and pray that you will not slap it. Do you hear me, Konda?"

"Sir?"

"Here is the solution to your problems: tell us who organized this fire."

"I don't know, sir."

"Name one boy who was a leader in the conspiracy."

"I can't."

"Who was the boy who had the torch?"

"I don't know."

"Of course you know!" Mr. Jennings said loudly. "If you were packing your clothes you saw who had the torch in the dormitory, even if you didn't see him on the path."

"But I don't remember, sir. It was all very fast."

"Did the ringleaders threaten revenge on the boys if any disclosed their names?"

"No, sir."

"Then why don't you tell us?"

"Well—I can't." Joseph felt his chin quiver. He mopped his face with his shirt-sleeve for a moment, during which time he brought himself under control.

"Who was your dormitory prefect?" said Mr. Karima.

"Michael Museh—2581."

"He set fire to your dorm, didn't he?"

"No, sir."

"How do you know?"

"He was innocent, sir."

"How do you know?"

"He was with me. Outside."

"Who was still inside?"

"I don't know. All the boys were trying to get out."

"Gentlemen," Mr. Johnson broke in, "we are wasting our time. In fact, we have wasted a whole day and a considerable amount of petrol—unless, of course, you consider it worth while that we have now proved what we already suspected, namely, that this boy is at

least an accessory after the fact and a perjurer."

Joseph wasn't quite sure what he meant. "Sir?"

"Don't mind me," Mr. Johnson laughed. "I am only asserting that you are a criminal and that you must be punished severely."

"But I am innocent, sir."

"Oh, perhaps you didn't set the fire, but you helped one of our intellectual young incendiaries to escape. Moreover, you have sometimes told us falsehoods and at all times avoided the truth."

"No, sir. Please—"

"This is your last chance. Name one boy—any boy—who helped to plan or carry out this fire."

He felt the tears in the corners of his eyes and tried vainly to repress them. "I can't, sir," he moaned.

Mr. Johnson stood. "Very well. Gentlemen, let us return to Wayama and make recommendation of the appropriate punishment to Mr. Koblo-Williams."

The others had risen when he did. Joseph knelt at Mr. Jennings' feet. "Please, sir, I beg."

"Stop that! Get up!" Mr. Jennings placed his hands on his hips. "I do no favors for liars."

Joseph got up mutely, his head slumped to his chest. Mr. Jennings wasn't finished with him.

"I'm sure you don't know how much you've disappointed me," he said. "People have said I'm too friendly with the boys, but I thought friendliness was appreciated. Well, I've learned."

"You see?" said Mr. Johnson.

Mr. Karima thanked the Chief in their tribal language and the four men left. Joseph stepped outside to watch them as they walked to their car. For just a moment Mr. Karima paused to say something to Gorba, as well as something about Gorba to the onlookers. Then the four of them got into the car and drove away without a nod or a wave.

3

Joseph walked home with his head held high, determined to permit no one to see his distress. Gorba followed him. When they reached his veranda, where his mother waited for him, he said to Gorba, in English, "They are going to punish me."

"Eh! Why?"

"Because I wouldn't tell them who started the fire."

"But you are innocent. They cannot give you punishments."

"Never mind that. They were too vexed."

His mother meanwhile was watching him patiently; he could tell that she wanted an explanation. "Mama," he said, "those men were asking some questions about a certain matter at school."

"Yes," she said.

"Do you remember the fire I mentioned?"

After a moment, she nodded.

"They wanted to ask me about that."

"But you have behaved well?"

"Yes, ma'am."

"Mother," said Gorba, "he has not done anything wrong."

"And you were respectful to them?"

"Yes."

She seemed pleased. "And they came here just to see you," she said proudly.

"Well, yes. But they wanted some information which I couldn't give."

"But you tried," said Gorba.

"Yes. But Mother, I don't believe they understood."

His mother was puzzled, he himself was shaken; he wanted Gorba to leave. He made motions of going into the parlor. "I shall be coming to you tonight," he told him.

"Very well." Gorba walked away with a pensive air.

"This is strange," his mother said. "Why should they be displeased with an obedient boy?" She sank into one of her low wooden chairs more stiffly than she would have no more than a year ago, he noticed. He took the other chair.

"Mama," he said, "you must believe that I am obedient."

"Then they should be angry with Gorba Konda, not you. They said that he was rude to them."

Joseph resented Gorba for his poor behavior, but didn't want to say so. "You see," he said, "the fire was started by certain boys, and they thought I could name them."

Some of the neighbors were filing into the parlor, while others listened from the veranda. He had to explain the entire matter; it couldn't be helped. He carefully avoided specific details, but fortunately no one tried to trap him. When he had finished, they nodded and waited for his mother to speak.

"But you were obedient," she repeated, "and did not follow the bad boys?"

"No, ma'am." He turned to the crowd. "I only tried hard at my studies. Knowing book is the only thing that is important to me, and I have no time for mischievous behavior."

His mother also spoke to them. "Momo is a serious boy," she said. "He has always been obedient."

"Yes," they all said, nodding, "a serious boy." But some looked doubtful, sensing that he was in trouble.

"Well," said his mother, "what is to be done?"

He hesitated. "It is possible they shall do certain things against me," he said.

Perhaps the others couldn't tell, but he knew that she was worried. The family honor meant considerable to her. She fell silent. One of the big men of the town stepped forward to speak. "I think it would perhaps be best to beg the master of this school for mercy."

"But it is very far away," said someone else.

Most found this a sobering point, but the elder said, "We could ask certain people who live near there to act for us."

Joseph felt Mr. Koblo-Williams would not accept any pleading, but didn't want to say so. Head down, he listened to their words in dejected spirits.

"Perhaps he has had enough schooling," said a younger man. "After all, his father has paid his fees for many years."

Fortunately, the elder cut short this malice from an envious heart. "That is for his father to say."

A period of deliberation ensued, broken finally by a question as to who was the Principal and what sort of man he was. Joseph answered as best he could, confessing that the man wasn't used to the ways of their tribe. They pondered that for another moment.

"Well, what is to be done?" said the elder.

Another of the town's "big men" spoke. "I think we must wait to see what this Principal says."

"But these people from the city cannot be trusted," said a new voice.

"Well," explained several at once, "we can't help that."

Without a decision, then, they brought the meeting to an end and filed out. Joseph's mother seemed hypnotized in her chair. For as long as it took to get the townspeople out of the house, they sat absorbed in their own thoughts, his eyes to the floor, hers riveted on the bush fifty yards away at the edge of the clearing. A breeze brought them to attention; the evening was at hand.

"I must prepare food," said his mother, distractedly. From her bedroom she brought two cigarette-tinfuls of rice which she poured into a flat woven basket. He watched, absently.

The preparation of rice by all but the laziest of wives and mothers took a great deal of work, the first part of which was the winnowing, which his mother now began behind the house. Swinging her basket to and away from her, she cast the rice into the air again and again. It always fell in a cloud right into the basket, as though pulled by a magnet. When she was satisfied that most of the husks had drifted away, she dumped the rice into an empty calabash, adding a little water from a second calabash. For another few minutes she would wash the rice, changing water until it rinsed clear. After that she would pour grain and water all into the black pot, light the fire between the customary three stones, and begin cooking. The sauce would be easier to prepare, but it always took his mother the greater part of her day to trade for the palm oil, to catch an occasional fish, and to collect the greens and peppers.

But he had no interest, however

tender he felt toward his mother, in watching women's work. He saw Hawa walk through the clearing out back toward the stream, an empty bucket on her head, and he decided he would go bathe. Why, he wondered briefly, did he so seldom see Meriema? Even Auntie seemed to avoid him; she hadn't come around this afternoon, which was strange. But he couldn't worry about that just now.

He strolled to the stream, affecting nonchalance. To his surprise, Hawa was bathing alone, and she greeted him amiably. He was excited for a second, for she was very plump and had plaited her hair prettily, tight against her head, but as he sank into the water on his side of the bridge he forgot everything except the fire and Mr. Jennings' voice saying, "I'm sure you don't know how much you've disappointed me." For nothing else in the world mattered but getting back into school and regaining his teacher's confidence.

4

After his mother and he had eaten their supper, exchanging scarcely a dozen words, he put on his robe and walked to his uncle's home, as he knew he was obliged to do. He found Gorba at the court barrie. Ostensibly Gorba was watching a game popular among the men: tops spun into a depressed matting, the winner being the one whose top knocked the others off the matting. Actually, he knew, Gorba had been waiting for him.

"Hello, Gorba."

"Hello." Gorba slipped off the barrie wall; Joseph noted that he moved painfully.

"What's the matter?"

"Our father has flogged me," Gorba answered in English.

"Why?"

"He was angry because those men thought I was rude. I did not wish to let him do it, but I just couldn't help it. Anyway, I didn't cry or beg."

"He was right. You were not polite to those men."

"Eh, bo. I was trying to help you."

"You don't know anything. You did not help at all."

"Well, anyway, I was trying, like a good brother. Don't vex me, please. Speak quietly in our language and tell me what happened in the Chief's house."

Grudgingly Joseph recounted his interrogation. When he had finished, Gorba found trouble in saying anything soothing.

"I shall not forget this," was all he could muster up.

Joseph gave him credit for some fraternal loyalty but felt it had about reached its limit. He looked away. "How is Vandi Tailo'?" he said.

"Well, I don't think he is happy. They have told him you are in trouble."

"What did he say?"

"He said he wanted to see you. I told him you were coming, and then I walked out, for I no longer wished to speak to him."

Joseph folded the sleeves of his robe up onto his shoulders. "I must go," he said. "Perhaps he is angry with me."

"He is a stupid illiterate," Gorba said.

Joseph conveyed his anger by his silence. He loved Vandi Tailo'; even about his own father in Ngolahun he would speak no evil. He said good-bye and walked away.

Vandi Tailo' was in his hammock, clad in his warm European dressing gown and stocking cap to protect himself from the cold night air. He didn't sit up at Joseph's approach.

"Good evening, Father," said Joseph.

"Thank you. Good evening." His younger wife, Jenniba, sat almost invisible in a corner of the veranda. "Momo, good evening," she said. As always, the words, "Yela has left me. Yela has died," came back to him. Fortunately Jenniba had borne more children. Even now she was pregnant.

From greetings Joseph and his uncle moved slowly toward the heart of their concern. Vandi Tailo' at length said,

"Gorba told me those men came to you today about the fire."

"Yes, Father."

"He was very rude to them. For that he received fifty good strokes."

Joseph nodded.

"That boy was never serious," said his uncle. "His mother was too lenient with him."

It was in Joseph's mind to say, "Anyway, he is trying," but he suddenly didn't feel like interceding for his brother. He said nothing.

"He says you had no part in this fire business."

"No, sir. I am innocent."

"Well, I am glad." He hestitated. In the gloom Joseph could see the narrow pointed chin and the small mouth which smiled so much like his mother's. But his uncle wasn't smiling. "Still," he said, "the fact is that they came to see you."

Joseph winced. "You see," he said, "they thought I had witnessed some of the boys starting the fire."

"Why didn't you tell me of this when you first came home?"

"I didn't know."

"But you must have done something, or they wouldn't have come."

"Oh no, sir. Please, Father, have mercy on your son who has always loved you and tried to be worthy."

Vandi Tailo' considered this. "You did not misbehave today as your brother did. That speaks well for you."

"I am always respectful to my elders."

"Yes. So I won't flog you. But I have been thinking for some time that the school fees are too much for me. Soon I wish to send Gorba's brother to school." He sat up in his hammock, swinging his feet to the earth. "You are not my own son, but you have taken my name, and now there is talk you have not used it well."

In despair Joseph turned to the woman in the corner and said, in an unnatural voice, "Mother, he is too harsh."

She said nothing, but he knew she would plead for him later.

"I am tired of paying so much money. Perhaps you have had enough schooling and should find a job. Perhaps you will want to marry."

Joseph bit his lip. Several people, it seemed, were concerned about his neglect of Meriema. "I am young to marry," he said.

"Perhaps. But the mother wants it so, and she has persuaded your own mother. Yes, you are young, but perhaps you can give assurances."

He nodded. "Yes, sir." When his uncle fell silent, he asked to be excused; Vandi's wife would need time to plead for leniency. He walked toward the court barrie where, with the moon coming out, some of the people were dancing and singing. But because Gorba would be there, he skirted the clearing and stole to his home. He wanted to sit alone in his nervousness. "By the grace of God," he thought, "Vandi will have mercy on me."

The next day he walked to his uncle's house feeling a little more hopeful. Vandi Tailo', however, was firmly decided that he could no longer pay his nephew's school fees.

⟳ **Talking it over**

1. *a.* How do the people of Wainke feel about courtesy? Give examples to support your answer.

b. In what ways is Gorba rude to the investigating committee? Why does he act this way?

2. *a.* Why does Joseph lie to the committee? Give examples of his lying.

b. How do the men know he is lying?

c. How does Mr. Jennings react to the meeting with Joseph?

3. *a.* What do you learn about village customs from the way the townspeople learn of Joseph's trouble and the way they react to it?

b. What does Joseph's mother seem most concerned about?

4. Suggest reasons why Vandi Tailo' decides he can no longer pay Joseph's school fees.

Chapter 7

1

CHRISTMAS gave way to Boxing Day;[18] the old year gave way to the new; and still Joseph awaited the news from school. The Harmattan was blowing in earnest, chapping lips and throwing a dusty haze on the sky, but the townspeople, still rejoicing over a good harvest, braved it through the late evening hours, dancing and singing. This was vacation time for the farmers. Before January was gone they would be clearing the brush from a new site in preparation for another planting of rice, but now they could dance, eat their fill, and perhaps even take a trip to visit a relative.

Finally Vandi Tailo' sent for Joseph; a letter concerning him had arrived. Since he was headed to the stream for a bucket of water he couldn't go immediately, as he wanted to do. His nerves, lulled by the long delay, had reawakened, causing him to hurry his pace and spill an inch or two of liquid from the bucket.

"Humph!" said his mother. "These schoolboys don't even know how to carry a full bucket of water."

He scarcely heard her. "Vandi Tailo' wants me," he said. Without waiting for her reply, he walked off. Although many of the townspeople would know of the letter and its meaning, he did not affect nonchalance this time but walked quickly, speaking to no one.

His uncle, Gorba, and other members of the family were waiting for him; at his approach, the neighbors also drifted over. They all entered the parlor, where Jenniba got up from a box so that Joseph might have a seat. Vandi, who held two letters unopened in his hand, and Gorba took the two armchairs.

After greetings had been exchanged, Vandi said, "These two letters came to me today. Gorba says they are from the school. I decided you should read them together."

He gave the letters to Joseph. Gorba came over to look on as Joseph tore them open. The first, a mimeographed form, read:

Dear Sir:

Because of the fire which took place at Wayama School on 12 December, the scheduled terminal examinations were cancelled. Therefore, no terminal report will be issued for 2732—Konda, Gorba.

The new term will start on 7 January. All boys are expected to be in attendance.

R. O. Koblo-Williams
Principal

The second letter looked exactly the same. "Why not?" Joseph wondered excitedly. He wasn't sure yet where he would find his fees, but this he considered a minor problem. He opened the letter, his heart pounding with hope. It was not mimeographed:

Dear Sir:

On 12 December an act of malicious insubordination took place at this school, in which 2733—Konda, Joseph, is suspected of complicity. You are hereby requested to withdraw this boy from school, please.

Failure to comply with this request may lead the administration to take stronger action.

R. O. Koblo-Williams
Principal

---

[18]**Boxing Day,** a British holiday that falls on the first weekday after Christmas. On this day gift boxes are given to postmen and other service people.

After the translation of the second letter, Vandi Tailo' merely said "Um-hum," judiciously. The onlookers turned to one another and nodded. There was a short silence, during which Joseph tried to appear unconcerned.

"They have treated him unfairly," said Gorba. "He is innocent." He seemed about to make a speech, but was interrupted.

"Now is the time for someone to plead for the boy," said one of the on-lookers. Subconsciously Joseph recognized the voice as belonging to Hawa's husband, the blacksmith.

"But the chances do not seem favorable," said someone else, "since the man is from the city and not of our tribe."

"Perhaps the thing to try," said a third, "is another school."

"But who shall pay his fees?" said Vandi Tailo'. "I am tired of it."

They fell to discussing the matter of fees. Although he was educated, Joseph reflected, and considered himself a man, he was still often treated like a small boy.

The assembly got back to the central matter. "At least," said someone, "Gor-ba will be there and can discuss this business with the right people."

"Yes," everyone, including Gorba, agreed. "That is what must be done."

"Of course," said Gorba, "I must help my brother. I shall see what is to be done." It was decided that he should return next day.

Thinking the solution was at hand, the onlookers filed out. But Vandi Tailo' obviously was not enthusiastic about getting Joseph back in school. He said nothing; neither, prudently, did Gorba. After a respectful period, Joseph asked to be excused.

"Withdrawn from school." It was almost synonymous with expulsion, except that it meant he could transfer to another school without the word "expelled" being written on his transfer certificate. As he walked home, maintaining his impassiveness, he realized that unless something could be done soon there was little hope of his becoming a doctor. His mother didn't help his feelings. She was resourceful but also practical, and he was discouraged to realize that his continued education really mattered little to her, or at least not enough to make her swim against a strong current. After he had told her of the letter, she said, "If you say you are innocent, I believe you, for you were always a serious boy. But if these big men are displeased with you, it is not wise to resist."

"Yes, ma'am."

"Vandi Konda has paid your fees so many times. You must now work so that you can help his children."

He nodded. For a moment he watched her as she sliced four great cassava roots into a large wooden mortar and began to beat them with a long pole. Then he said, "Gorba will be returning tomorrow."

"Already? He has been here only a few days."

"But we have a long vacation only during the rainy season. Remember?"

"Oh, yes," she said. "I remember now."

2

Next day Joseph waited by the roadside with Gorba for the Ngolahun Express.

"What will you do," Gorba asked, "if our efforts are not successful?"

Joseph shrugged. "Perhaps another school will be willing."

"But the matter of fees—?"

"Never mind that," said Joseph. "Just help me." He was angry with Gorba, partly because he didn't trust him. But he didn't want to show it too clearly. "If you can plead successfully for me, I will be grateful forever."

"Anyway, I shall try."

"Ask Mr. Jennings. Perhaps he will be merciful."

"I shall try by all means." Gorba seemed weary of the subject. He had on his straw hat, sunglasses, and a bright pink shirt.

"You will write soon?"

"Oh, yes. As soon as I have had some success."

Judging by the position of the sun, Joseph thought the lorry was later than usual. They seated themselves on Gorba's trunk and lost themselves in thought. A few minutes later they saw Meriema behind Auntie's house, pounding rice into flour. Joseph was abruptly reminded that Meriema used to help his mother a great deal, but hadn't once since he had come home. Gorba chuckled.

"She is nice and plump, that girl," he said. "And look how strong. She is meant to have many babies."

"Yes," said Joseph, hiding his annoyance.

"The life here in Wainke would be worth while with her," his brother added, predictably.

Meriema saw them and moved around her mortar until her back was toward them. Gorba tilted his hat to one side and laughed. "But a beautiful back too," he said, loud enough for her to hear. He was, Joseph thought, exceedingly rude.

The lorry came; they flagged it down

and Gorba climbed in back through the open tailgate. His mother, along with the normal crowd of onlookers, walked out to say good-bye. In the confusion, Joseph had time to ask only, again, "Will you write?" The motor-boy closed the tailgate, shouted "Go-go-go!" and his brother was swallowed in the dust. He felt bereft. Gorba hadn't bothered to answer.

3

A few days later Vandi Tailo' asked Joseph to help in the brushing of his new farm, a request he had to meet, however demoralizing he found it. The site lay near the stream, along the bush path to Bandu, a small nearby village. Vandi, he, and the men working nearby plots walked there just after sunrise and labored almost without cease until the morning grew warm. Although the rest of the day would be spent more in talking than in working, they would go home in the evening very tired. Clearing seven years' growth of brush from three acres of land was the hardest step in raising rice. The men generally worked in groups, mitigating their drudgery with companionship—but on the other hand, some would shirk where they could, and this would cause quarrels. Whatever the difficulties, by March the trees would all be down and dry enough to burn. The men would stand around each farm in turn and set the brush afire. The two or three farmers who owned guns would bring them, for the fires would drive out bush babies, civets, all sorts of delicious "beefs."

Near the end of March the first rains could be expected, and thereafter the rice could be planted. Various seeds could be thrown in with it: Guinea corn, benni-seed, cucumber, cassava, pumpkin, China yam, water yam, and so on. Soon the rain would bring them popping from the earth. This was still a time of work, both for the women, who would be weeding, and for the men, who had to build protective fences around their plots. Even small boys were called to duty, to drive away birds and monkeys. Joseph could well remember sitting on a small platform in the middle of a field, armed with his slingshot and a string of tin cans, day after day after day. What a tiresome business was farming, he thought.

As expected, he went back to town tired, sweaty, and unhappy. But a surprise awaited him at home, where he stopped for soap: Meriema was talking with his mother.

"Good evening," he said.

"Yes. Momo?"

"Yes?"

"Good evening. How are you?"

"I am well, thank you." He got his soap and left for the stream. He was pleased that she wasn't angry with him. This, and his bath, revived him; and then too there was the thought that Gorba's letter should arrive soon, and perhaps the news would be good. Several men were washing, also dirty from a day of brushing, and he found himself joining in their jokes and laughter. But he didn't stay long; he hurried back to find, as he had hoped, that Meriema was still there. His mother handed him a pan.

"Meriema has made us some sweets today."

"Eh!" He didn't try to hide his pleasure. This delicacy—groundnuts ground with rice, sugar, and a small touch of ginger—was dear to him. "It's good," he mumbled, munching a large handful. He could see, from Meriema's eyes, that she was pleased. When she left, saying that she had to help her mother, they exchanged warm greetings.

"That girl can prepare food very well," said his mother, adding peppers to her sauce.

"Oh yes," he said, with his mouth full.

"And she is obedient to her mother."

"Yes," he repeated. To forestall further hints he said, "I think I will call on Auntie this evening."

"You should do so," she said.

He mistrusted the way she had almost anticipated him; he was beginning to feel trapped. But he would be thankful to get back in Auntie's good graces, and to be near Meriema again. For too long he had been without her, and this had caused him to look amorously at Hawa. No more of that, he resolved. Meriema was truly the nicest girl he knew. He wanted to be loyal to her. A heavy meal of rice, coming as it did on the heels of a long day of work, fed his determination. He knew he must be careful not to let her think he would give up his schooling for her, but when he called at Auntie's home he was in the highest spirits he had experienced since the fire. For some reason, Auntie too was cheerful. She allowed Meriema—along with her brothers and sisters—to sit with them.

During the talk that followed, he reappraised Meriema's wifely qualities. First, she was young, strong, and healthy, undoubtedly able to work hard and bear many children. She was also obedient. Her face was round and flat, and her complexion was very dark, all of which attributes he admired. She was quiet, and too proper to speak boldly to him, even when they were alone.

Finally, but not the least of her attraction for him, he could expect her to be faithful, for she obviously liked him: whenever he talked she watched him; if he joked, she laughed; if he complained of his treatment in connection with the fire, she let him know, through her remarks to her mother, that she was indignant in his behalf. He appreciated this.

When he left he was quite happy, despite his uncertainty about what he should do. He was going back to school somewhere, sometime, that was definite; but for the moment there was nothing to be done but relax and enjoy himself until he heard from Gorba.

4

Three more days the Ngolahun Express bounced into Wainke, dropping off a passenger or two, a tin of kerosene, or a small bag of foodstuff, but no letter for Joseph Konda. Joseph couldn't contain his disappointment the third day. When he returned from the roadside a group of women were discussing with his mother the possibility of curing a young woman's barrenness, and he announced his predicament to them. They listened respectfully.

"Do not think that Gorba will help you," said his mother. "That boy is not serious."

"Eh! Gorba?" said Hawa, who was among the group. "I was in the primary school with him. He was always being caned."

"Meriema says he has been very brash with her," said Auntie.

"With me, too," said Hawa. "Even after I was married."

Although irked that his grievance had been turned into gossip, Joseph could not help reflecting how much at home Hawa had become among the older women. She had attended school for only four years, but she had shown cleverness, which with her pretty looks allowed her to be more forward than most girls. Joseph had remarked that her husband, the blacksmith, doted on her, and let her do as she pleased; he thought this a mistake, particularly since the blacksmith was currently very busy sharpening the farmers' machetes and hoes.

"Momo is respectful," she was saying, commanding the attention of all six or eight women, most of whom were many years older. "But Gorba? Gorba? I am afraid even to walk by him, the way he looks at me."

She is too pretty and too spoiled, he thought; if he were the blacksmith he would keep her close to home. That's what he would do if he took Meriema as wife. He walked into the house so that he could think quietly about her. He had visited Auntie and Meriema almost every night, and enjoyed being with them, except that they seemed so expectant of something. He had to make a decision. While he was pondering, his mother came to him.

"The ladies have said you must not expect Gorba to help you."

"He is my brother. He must help."

"But why should you want him to? The women say you should stop school now before it makes you brash like him."

He frowned.

His mother seated herself across from him. "Auntie has asked when you will make an offer for Meriema," she said.

"Eh!" he exclaimed, although he wasn't overly surprised. Suddenly he didn't feel like stalling any longer. He would just have to lay out this term while he applied for admission at other schools. If he could work for three months he could get enough to pay his fees and to betroth Meriema. "I will go to Ngolahun and try to get work," he said. "Then, if Vandi Tailo' and my father will help me—well." He preferred to let her interpret what he left unsaid.

"Oh," she said, trying very hard to appear unconcerned. "Vandi Konda will help you. And I too will have a small addition to make."

"You are very kind, Mother. Perhaps tonight I will call on Vandi."

"Of course," she said, "for he has been waiting for you. You must spend the evening with him."

"Yes," he said. While you tell Auntie and Meriema, he thought. Well, he thought with a smile, it is actually a relief. He laughed aloud.

"What is it?" she said.

"Aren't you happy that I am leaving you?"

"Of course I am happy," she said. "It is too much hard work to care for a lazy schoolboy. Look, you." She drew him outside and handed him the bucket. "Bring me water. And be careful you don't spill it."

He carried two pails of water, then returned to the stream to bathe. Preoccupied with his thoughts he paid little attention to his mother's preparation of their meal until, after his bath, he smelled groundnuts. He looked out back and saw chicken feathers and blood strewn about; at that moment his mother was cutting up the chicken and dropping the pieces into the rapidly heating stew—groundnut stew! This was to be a celebration dinner.

"Get me more water," she said, handing him the bucket.

It was all very grand, but somewhat frightening, too, he thought. She poured tin after tin of rice into the big kettle, and he saw that there was more cleaned and ready to cook when this was finished. The neighbors could not help noticing the huge quantities, not to mention the boiling chicken.

"I have plenty," his mother called to them. "You may share with me tonight."

A crowd soon gathered around with bowls. None spoke about the meaning of the occasion, but all knew something was being celebrated. When Joseph's mother said, casually, "Momo is going to Ngolahun for work," most of them got knowing looks in their eyes. Surprisingly, Vandi Tailo' appeared with his family, three of his sons bearing gourds full of palm wine. Auntie and Meriema came, but sat at a discreet distance from him.

The food was ready. First he, then the elders present, were given their choice of the chicken, and afterwards all dug into the rice, which was covered

generously with stew. So that everyone might have a small helping, other women brought rice and palm oil, peppers, and greens to augment the stew. When everything was gone, the men passed the gourds of palm wine among themselves. Joseph was called upon to take several drinks.

After the excitement had abated, Vandi Tailo' beckoned to him. They walked together to the deserted court barrie, talking of this and that, nothing important, until they were quite alone.

"This was a wise decision," his uncle began.

"I want to think so," Joseph replied.

"You will be leaving soon?"

"Perhaps tomorrow, or the next day. It depends on my financial position."

Abruptly his heart jumped. He had a new, frightening idea.

"That can be arranged between the mothers," Vandi replied.

"No," Joseph said nervously, "it's not that. I will need something until I can find work, and the position of my father is in question."

Vandi considered this, removing his stocking cap to rub his bristly scalp. "Well, anyway," he said, "we shall manage."

"Oh," said Joseph, anxious but not wanting to push the matter.

"Come to me tomorrow. We shall make arrangements."

Joseph nodded obediently. They returned then to his house, where some of the people had started dancing. He had no choice but to join in. Meriema was dancing across the way, relishing the sly attention she was receiving from the other women. Fortunately, the effects of palm wine and a day of brushing rendered the men too dull-witted to do anything but dance. They continued their romp until, late in the night, they collapsed from fatigue. The women had long before gone home.

5

It was afternoon when Joseph awoke. His mother was not there; probably, he thought, she is with Auntie and Meriema. He couldn't laugh about it as he had yesterday. Things were happening too quickly, things he could not reconcile with his desire to finish his education.

He got up from his mother's bed, which he now used every night, slipped into his shorts, and washed his face in a calabash. His mother had left him a large portion of cassava in the small pot, which he ate ravenously; ever since he'd begun eating three meals a day, at school, he was always hungry for something the moment he rose. He thought about his friends in Wayama, who would be eating their bread and tea every morning and their heaping bowls of rice at noon and night. Soon, of course, the Moslems would be fasting for Ramadan. It would be a gay time, with everyone building lanterns for the celebration.

He walked to the home of Vandi Tailo', as the latter had asked him to do. When he arrived he found his uncle asleep in his hammock. He didn't disturb him but talked with Gorba's mother for perhaps an hour—without discussing Gorba. Finally his uncle stirred.

"I have come, sir," said Joseph, to prevent his dozing off again.

His uncle looked at him. "Joseph?"

"Yes?"

"Good afternoon. I thank you for coming." After they had talked a few minutes, he said, "I am glad you have made your decision. I want to treat you like my son, so I shall give you a small sum now and more at a future time for your bride-price. It will be a replacement for school fees."

"You are too kind, Father." Was it possible?

Vandi Tailo's small mouth set hard to repress a smile. He was pleased with his own magnanimity. "One day you will help my children," he said.

"By the grace of God," said Joseph, "I shall provide them well." He felt sick, ashamed that he now contemplated being deceitful to this man he loved so much.

Vandi nodded. "You know book," he said. "You will have plenty." He excused himself to get the money. "Here." He handed Joseph a small wad. "This is more than you need. But I am sorry for you, that you weren't able to return to school."

Joseph put the money in his pocket. "I will leave tomorrow," he said.

"God go with you."

"Amen." He excused himself and walked back towards his house. Once out of his uncle's sight he examined the wad of notes: three pounds. He was pleased; it showed that his uncle believed in his innocence of wrongdoing at school and was sorry to have treated him so rashly. But what would his uncle think of him if he used the money for school fees?

When he told his mother he was leaving, she was noncommittal; she said only that he should tell Auntie. He agreed, although he disliked the idea of facing Auntie alone. When he went to bathe he found Meriema at the stream and he told her, after they had exchanged polite greetings, that he would be coming.

"I will inform my mother," she said, quietly. She was much more unassertive than Hawa; he thought that a good sign.

His mother fixed him fu-fu, a thick gum made of cassava roots, which he usually enjoyed, but somehow this evening he felt out of sorts; he ate little and soon excused himself. She noticed and compressed her lips to show that she was amused. To avoid her teasing, he left immediately for Auntie's. It was a cool clear night with a thousand stars spread across a big sky. The small frogs in the grass at the edge of the clearing—as a precaution against snakes no large tracts of grass were permitted in the town—were giving out their huge croaks like drumbeats to the crickets' singing. He found it all very quiet, however; too quiet.

Auntie was seated on her veranda, telling a story to her younger children. It was about a man whose wife died while he was far away; the Chief could get no one to go for him except a little bird, who flew from town to town until, by constantly singing the news, he attracted the man's attention; together they returned home where the bird was awarded a thousand pounds. Joseph listened with half an ear. When Auntie was finished, he drew her into conversation.

"I shall be leaving tomorrow," he said, after a proper time.

"So they told me in the town."

"I don't know," he said, rubbing his hands together, "how long I will be gone."

"I understand."

He was relieved that she did not want to press him. "God keep you well."

"Amen. God go with you."

"Amen. My regards to Meriema."

"She is not here. She is in the town."

"I see." He nodded. "Well, good night."

"Good night, Momo. We shall see each other again."

Feeling that he should talk to Meriema, Joseph walked to the barrie in search of her. She was there, listening to a story recounted by one of the elders. He seated himself beside her. *"Une histoire au coin du feu,"* he thought, remembering a French lesson: a story around the fire. She put her hand near him, making it irresistibly easy for him

to take it. He felt uncomfortable about it, but excited too. A minute later she left; he followed soon after and found her alone by a darkened house.

"Tomorrow I must leave," he whispered.

She nodded. "God go with you."

"I hope I will have money soon. Anyway, I shall try."

"Whatever you say," she said. She seemed pleased.

He embraced her. It was pleasant, and it made everything seem right, until he realized that he was imagining the face against his to be not that of the girl he intended to marry, but Hawa's. He felt sick, and forlorn.

After he had taken her home he lay awake in his own bed for a long time, planning. Some day he would marry her anyway, but not yet. He wanted to go back to school in Wayama, immediately. It was too late to get into another school this term, and if he waited until April no other school was likely to admit him just for the third term. And if he missed both terms he would have to repeat Form III. He fell into a sweat of nervous anticipation. How could he sleep this night?

6

"Momo!" His mother woke him. "Lazy schoolboy, get up."

It was morning. The Ngolahun Express would be coming soon. He packed his trunk in haste and wolfed down leftover fu-fu.

"Why are you taking your trunk?" his mother asked. She had her net out, ready to go fishing with the other women; for the next three months, while the streams grew increasingly shallow and sluggish, she would fish almost every day.

"I may be gone a long time."

"But won't you come home often? The distance is short."

"Well—it depends on my financial position."

"I thought you might walk." She was disappointed, but used enough to his comings and goings, and indifferent enough to matters of time and finance to pass the matter off. "Greet your father for me."

"All right. We shall see each other again, Mother." He picked up his trunk.

"Yes. Momo?"

"Yes?"

"God protect you."

"Amen. I shall be coming as soon as possible."

"Thank you. Good-bye."

He walked to the roadside, put his trunk down, and sat on it. To his relief, his wait was short. He climbed in the back of the big, dilapidated lorry, waved good-bye, and in another minute was dashing perilously toward Ngolahun. He was on his way.

Until this moment he had not made his final decision, and still he hated to face it. He *should* get off at Ngolahun, go to his father's house, and stay there until he found employment. But there were no decent jobs any more for boys who had only a few years of secondary school. It was not like the old days; today every big town had too many half-educated boys looking for work.

He still hadn't made up his mind when they reached the lorry park in Ngolahun. But right beside them stood a lorry bound for Yonima, on the Yargbo road, and the driver, who knew him, beckoned him. "Come, schoolboy. *I go take you.*"

"How soon?"

The driver assured him that they were leaving immediately, but Joseph guessed it would be at least another hour. He would see his father first; perhaps he could still resist his temptation. Nevertheless, before he ran off, he left his trunk in the driver's care.

What happened at his father's home surprised him. The older man had been lolling in the hammock, but the moment he saw Joseph he lumbered into the house. When Joseph entered, his father was waiting with a stick. Once, twice, three times the stick landed on Joseph's shoulder blades before his father sank exhausted into a chair.

"Get out of here," his father wheezed. "Arsonist!"

"I am sorry, sir," said Joseph, startled, and smarting from the pain.

"Don't talk to me. Go on out."

He left without a word. Once he had recovered from his shock he felt relieved, for his decision had been made: he must clear his name and get back into school.

He returned to the lorry park, got on board, and in a few minutes was riding toward Yonima. The moment they left the Ngolahun city limits, however, a terrible sadness descended on him. Not even the fire upset him as much as the thought that he was deceiving Vandi Tailo' and his mother, and Auntie and Meriema. For the first time since he was a small boy he could not restrain himself from weeping.

Talking it over

1. If Joseph is unable to continue his education, what effect will this have on his life?

2. *a.* Do you think Gorba plans to try to help Joseph? Explain your answer by mentioning Gorba's past actions and by referring to the hints in Part 2.

 b. Why does Gorba draw Joseph's attention to Meriema?

3. *a.* Explain what you have learned so far about the marriage customs in Wainke.

 b. How does Joseph's interest in Meriema complicate his problem?

4. *a.* Why does Joseph originally plan to go to Ngolahun?

 b. At what point does he first get the idea to return to Wayama? What finally causes him to make up his mind?

5. *a.* How does his mother interpret his actions? How does she show her approval?

 b. How does Joseph feel about deceiving his mother, Vandi Tailo', Auntie, and Meriema?

Chapter 8

1

THE TRIP to Yonima, for all the driver's reckless speed, was slow. At every town someone wanted to get on or off and sometimes as many as three stops were made in a single small village. As a crowning annoyance, the lorry ran out of gas only four miles from Yonima. Joseph despaired of reaching Yargbo by evening, but another lorry stopped to give a gallon of gas to his driver and he was in Yonima, despite everything, early enough to catch a southbound vehicle.

By the time the wide lavender river came into sight, however, the sun was fading. He was tired, and very hungry; he had had several opportunities along the way to buy food from the flocks of hawkers, but had limited himself to two bananas, for he needed to hold on to every penny. Pa Gulieu took him in without a word, as usual, and fed him.

Only when Joseph had finished eating did his uncle comment briefly. "Well, Gorba Konda said you would be late."

"Yes," Joseph replied casually. "I didn't have the school fees."

The old man—bald, toothless, and taciturn, but nevertheless, in his own way, rather spry—nodded and pulled out his pipe, which he termed his "favorite child." "How did you leave Vandi Konda and your mother?"

"They are well."

"Did they enjoy an abundant harvest?"

"Oh, yes, we have been eating well."

"I prayed to God that you might."

"And you too, Father, are well supplied?"

"By the grace of God." Pa Gulieu was a devout Moslem who still hoped to become an Alhaji by making a pilgrimage to Mecca. "But soon I shall be fasting."

They discussed Ramadan for several minutes, during which time Joseph joked that he too might have to fast because of his financial situation.

"The matter of fees has not been settled?" his uncle inquired, after a proper pause, filled with drawing on his pipe.

Joseph rubbed his hands together. "My father Vandi Tailo' has been kind to me for many years."

"Yes. He is sending his own son to school. Well, he is a good man."

"May God bless him," said Joseph, with more emotion than Pa Gulieu understood.

"Amen." The old man puffed on his pipe. "Something can be arranged," he said at length, as Joseph pretended to watch the women and children of the family eat out back.

"God will provide," said Joseph.

His uncle was going to help him; there was no doubt of that. He hoped only that it would be enough. If he could get three more pounds now he could later send to his brother, or perhaps his sisters, for the rest.

He waited anxiously for his uncle's decision, but he was forced to be patient; it didn't come until morning, when with some ceremony, Pa Gulieu presented him with his contribution. There were, Joseph could tell by feel, only two pounds in his hand, but his uncle indicated that more might be forthcoming at some future date. Joseph was satisfied.

2

Two trains made the run to Wayama, the faster calling at Yargbo about noon and the slower stopping at around 4:00 P.M. Joseph took the latter, arriving in Wayama, as he had planned, as the dusk began to settle. Needing to rid himself of his trunk for the time being, he decided to entrust an acquaintance in the town with the secret of his return and the care of his belongings. Happily, the man was just eating, and he got a few handfuls of rice as well.

In the middle of town stood a clock tower, from which he read the time: 7:10. It was a good hour to slip into the compound, for the boys would be resting and most of the staff would be taking their evening meals. Fortunately the moon was shrouded in clouds; aided by a red shirt in place of his usual white, he could, he thought, go unnoticed.

In fact, it proved very easy. He circled the compound by way of the road leading past the Principal's house without meeting anyone he recognized, and entered the premises near the classroom block. In another minute he was at Mr. Jennings' back step. The American, in white shirt and tight-fitting pants, opened the door and squinted at him.

"What do you want?" he said.

"I have come to you, sir."

"I have eyes. Don't waste my time, what do you want?"

"Please, I want to talk with you."

"About what?"

"About the fire, sir," he said, breathless with nervousness.

Mr. Jennings was slow in replying. "All right," he said. "Come on in."

"Please, sir, I don't want the other boys to know I'm here," said Joseph, hesitating in the pantry when the teacher walked into the brightly-lit front room.

"I'll pull the curtains." A moment later the room was closed to outside view. Joseph took a seat as bidden. "Whatever you have on your mind," said Mr. Jennings, "be quick about it. And don't expect any favors."

"No, sir. It's just about the fire. I am innocent, sir."

"No one ever accused you of starting the fire."

"But this matter of me supporting those boys is not correct, sir."

"Look, Joseph," said Mr. Jennings, jabbing at him with a forefinger from his seat opposite him, "I want no double talk, and no vague, meaningless words. If you want me to listen to you, you must get to the point."

"Yes, sir, I tried to prevent the fire."

The American leaned forward, placing his elbows on his knees. "O.K., go on."

"I did not want those boys to start the fire, and—"

" 'Those boys'? What boys?"

"Well, I don't know their names."

Mr. Jennings shifted back restlessly in his chair. "But Joseph," he said, "you do."

"But I thought you would understand about the kerosene, sir. When I said that of the kerosene that night, I thought you would do an inspection. I wanted you to stop them."

Mr. Jennings shrugged.

"It is true, sir."

"Joseph, I believed too many people too long. I no longer believe. In fact, I don't even care."

"Sir, I even wrote you a note that night, to warn you."

"I didn't receive it."

"No, sir. Those boys stopped me on the path outside." He was breathing hard, but to his relief, the other man seemed interested.

"You mean some boys were guarding the path? Then that's who I heard running up the hill ahead of me."

"Yes, sir, they had closed off all the paths. They sent me back to the dorms."

"Tell me who they were."

Joseph rubbed his palms together. "It was dark, sir."

"Don't expect me to believe you if you won't help me."

"But you see, sir, I tried. When they sent me up, I threw a rock on the roof of one of the dormitories." He hesitated.

"So it *was* you who threw those rocks."

"Yes, sir, but only that night. It was Akinbola dormitory, and you came out on your veranda. You returned back then so I threw another rock."

"Well—you're right there."

"Yes, sir. I wanted that you would do an inspection, for it was almost ten o'clock. That is why I threw another rock on my own dormitory, Nkala."

"You wanted me to *make* an inspection," the English teacher corrected. "Yes, it happened just that way. You must be telling the truth."

"Yes, sir, I threw those rocks."

"But why didn't you tell us when we came to your village?"

He shrugged.

"Answer me!"

"Well—I was afraid."

Mr. Jennings jumped up and paced the room, scratching his pale hair. "Everyone's afraid," he said. "They'd rather give up their education than betray their friends."

"Please, sir," said Joseph, "will you help me get back into school? I promise you my behaviors—my behavior—will be good."

"I don't know that there'll be any school," said Mr. Jennings, absently. "We only called the boys back to continue the investigation. If we don't find the ringleaders, the Ministry will close us down."

Joseph nodded. After a moment, he asked. "Has my brother chanced to see you?"

"No."

Again he nodded, hiding his disappointment. Did such a brother deserve his respect and loyalty at the expense of his own education?

"He's been caned for his insolence," Mr. Jennings added, "and we may take even stronger action." He looked at his watch. "I think the thing to do is for us to call on Mr. Koblo-Williams."

"Please, sir, I don't want the boys to see me."

"But you're not going to get back in school unless you talk to the Principal."

"Well—if he could at all come here—?"

Mr. Jennings thought a moment. "It's not our place to ask that of him," he said. "But perhaps—yes, I'll do it, but I'm going to tell him that you will help us solve this crime." He looked directly into Joseph's eyes.

"Yes, sir." Joseph licked his lips. "I understand."

"I'll be right back." He got a flashlight from his bedroom and walked out.

Joseph retreated to the darkness of the pantry. He had a lot to think about: Gorba, the continued investigation of the fire, his confrontation with the Principal. Uppermost in his mind, however, was the knowledge that, however little Gorba had behaved like a brother to him, he must defend Gorba, and that to cross the oath of fellow society members was to invite revenge by all possible means, even including magic. He decided he might simply have to beg Mr. Koblo-Williams for mercy.

Leaning against the refrigerator, he caught hold of his breath and pulse and subdued them. He was able to relax enough to inspect the pantry in the dim light thrown from the front room. There was a cabinet in front of him; he opened one side of it and saw stacks of canned goods on the shelves. On the table next to him stood a row of bottles containing drinks he had never tasted nor heard of. Then there was the big refrigerator, which he suspected had all sorts of costly foods in it. Some day he wanted a fridge like that.

He peered again into the front room. Mr. Jennings had so many fine things: a radio, record-player, beautiful native carvings. Around the corner, outside his view, was a bookcase full of new and expensive books, he remembered; Mr. Jennings read a great deal, even after working hard all day. On the desk he had a typewriter. Well, he was a wealthy man. This was the way Joseph wanted to live. Some day he would have a car, a big fridge, and a fine phonograph with plenty of records.

The Principal and Mr. Jennings were so long in coming that his nerves had a chance to chafe him anew. At length

he heard footsteps. Instinctively he stepped back into the protective dark of the pantry, but the footsteps belonged to the two men he expected. They entered, and he stood submissively before them.

"Please have a seat, sir," said Mr. Jennings. "This is Joseph Konda."

Mr. Koblo-Williams' suit was as neatly pressed as though the day were just starting. He scarcely glanced at Joseph, who immediately felt apprehensive. "One of our fine little troublemakers," he said, "has found he misses the soft life of the boarding home."

"Sit down, Joseph."

"I would ask that he remain standing, Mr. Jennings. A little discomfort will do him no harm. It's a small price indeed for the discomfort he has caused me."

Joseph shifted from one foot to the other, his eyes on the floor.

"So this is the other Konda boy. Interesting that one family could produce two such miscreants."

Mr. Jennings cleared his throat. "Joseph, perhaps you could tell Mr. Koblo-Williams what you told me."

"By all means, let's hear this protestation of innocence."

Joseph feared the Principal's ridicule, but discovered that he was being allowed to tell his story without interruption. Mr. Koblo-Williams' expression remained scornful, however, and he offered no comment when Joseph had finished.

"I can corroborate many of these statements, sir," said Mr. Jennings.

"No doubt. And it makes a charming bed-time story. But as yet he has given me no names."

"Please, sir, I don't know any."

"Then we're wasting our time."

"Sir, I beg, I beg."

Mr. Jennings broke in. "The boy is at least telling the truth when he says he tried to prevent the fire. Perhaps he should not be punished any more than the other boys."

"Mr. Jennings, I am not here to dispense mercy, but punishment. Have these boys shown me any of the milk of human kindness?"

"Sir, I am innocent," Joseph pleaded.

"You are guilty of withholding information, on two separate occasions."

"Joseph, tell us who set your dormitory on fire. We can't be lenient when you withhold information we know you have."

"I can't."

"Why not?"

"They—they took a society oath."

"Of course they took an oath," said Mr. Koblo-Williams. "That's quite clear. But I don't believe all two hundred and twenty-three boys shared in it."

"Oh, no, sir."

"Did you?"

"No. sir. I didn't want them to burn the dorms."

"Then you are not bound to secrecy."

Joseph shifted his weight again, hiding his emotion. "But, sir, I can't say anything or they will revenge me."

"That is your choice," said Mr. Koblo-Williams, gesticulating angrily. "You must choose between their revenge and mine. As I said immediately after the fire, no boy who is tainted shall escape my wrath. Didn't you hear me?"

"Yes, sir."

"Look," said Mr. Jennings, "you came all this way to school even though you knew you wouldn't be admitted.

Obviously you don't intend to turn around and go back."

Joseph hesitated. For a moment it seemed to him that he really should go directly back home, but then he said, "No, sir. But I am afraid."

"Why? No one needs to know who revealed the names."

"They will know when they see me here."

Mr. Jennings shook his head. "Not necessarily."

"Anyway, they have means."

The American scowled. "Magic? Nonsense."

"I think we must give up, Mr. Jennings." Mr. Koblo-Williams seemed about to rise. "It should be eminently clear to this boy that we shall have no mercy on him unless he names the culprits."

"Sir, I must continue my education."

"I shall be going now. Mr. Jennings, see that he leaves the compound immediately." He stood.

"Joseph, give one name. Sir, you will pardon him if he names just one boy, won't you?"

"In that case I would reconsider." He seemed to lose his temper. "But if he refuses to coöperate, his academic career is finished," he snapped.

"Tell us who led the plot, Joseph. I will protect you from harm."

The tears were now hot on his cheeks. He tried to open his mouth but couldn't. Mr. Koblo-Williams stepped to the doorway.

"Who set fire to your dorm?" asked Mr. Jennings. "Just say 'Yes' or 'No.' Was it Michael Museh?"

"No, sir, he is innocent. I do not say that about the others, but Michael Museh is innocent." He sobbed and hid his face in the cradle of his arms.

"If you want the Principal to believe that," said Mr. Jennings, "then you must say who it was."

Joseph nodded.

"You'll tell us? Good. Which boy?"

"Peter Kaa," he replied, in a choking voice.

4

The two men allowed him to turn away while they reseated themselves and discussed this new development. He listened to them as he dried his eyes.

"I don't think this is a personal vendetta," said Mr. Jennings. "I believe he's telling the truth. Kaa is a troublemaker."

"Of course Kaa is guilty. I've caned him enough times to know he's a scoundrel, and I've known all along that he was one of the conspirators." Mr. Koblo-Williams seemed to be angry yet. "But Kaa undoubtedly will not reveal the others."

"But from what Joseph said, I gathered that all of the expelled prefects were guilty, with the exception of Museh."

Mr. Koblo-Williams scoffed. "He's merely protecting his friend."

Mr. Jennings called Joseph to attention. He faced them again, controlled but more frightened than ever.

"Do you want to tell us who the others are?" said Mr. Jennings.

"No, sir."

"It will mean that school can start again and a lot of innocent boys will be able to continue their education."

"I don't know them all, sir."

"But the prefects who were expelled are guilty, correct?"

"No, sir. Michael Museh was forced by Peter Kaa."

"Was Kaa the ringleader?"

"Yes, sir."

"Very well." Mr. Jennings looked to Mr. Koblo-Williams. "Sir, with all respect, may I say that this boy doesn't deserve expulsion."

The Principal deliberated a moment, then, softly, he began to laugh. "Perhaps, Mr. Jennings," he said, "you now see the efficacy of a little discomfort." He turned to Joseph. "Konda, I am constrained to be more lenient with you than I wish to be. I shall reinstate you on probation. And in addition, I shall recall your friend Museh to allow him the chance to clear himself. Do you understand?"

"Yes, sir. But I am very frightened. I do not want to believe that the society has special powers, but—"

"Mr. Jennings," the Principal interrupted, "did you not tell me that this boy hopes to be a doctor?"

"Yes, sir."

"A man of science who believes in magic? But that is very amusing." He turned again to Joseph. "Konda, I am prepared to expel Kaa and give him the beating of his life if he in any way interferes with this school's business again. Do you think I fear his society oath?"

"No, sir."

"And you are right." Joseph dropped his eyes before Mr. Koblo-Williams' stern gaze. But when the Principal spoke again it was in an almost kindly voice. "You are very young, Konda, and you come from a bush village. We shall not criticize you too harshly for your failings, because we find you are making considerable progress. But in future I shall require two things of you, the first being absolute obedience to school discipline, and the second, your continued high marks in your studies. Is that understood?"

"Yes, sir, I promise." He had never seen the Principal take so much interest in a schoolboy. For a moment he felt grateful, but his conscience seemed to tell him that he didn't deserve it.

"Mr. Jennings," said the Principal, "perhaps we have outsmarted our band of gangsters. I believe I may find means of getting truth from Mr. Kaa and his cronies." He nodded. "Good night."

"Good night, sir." Mr. Jennings watched the Principal a moment in the doorway, then turned back to Joseph. "Our luck has changed at last," he said. "I wish I understood you boys a little better. Think of all the trouble you could have saved yourself and me had you told us everything when we were in Wainke. Look, I've been—let's say, I didn't see much use in my staying here, it was all so discouraging."

Joseph nodded meekly.

"But I guess things are never as good or as bad as they seem. At least, most of my faith in you personally is restored. Now: What am I going to do with you?"

"Please, sir, I am going back to Wainke now."

"To Wainke? But why? Joseph, what's wrong?"

Joseph put a hand over his eyes. "Sir," he said, "I am very wicked."

"Nonsense. What are you saying?"

"I have done a wicked thing to my family. I lied to them and took their money."

"Well." Mr. Jennings sounded concerned. "Let's sit down. You'd better explain."

They took chairs. After a moment Joseph began to talk, and before he was finished he had told Mr. Jennings everything, even about Meriema. Talking about it made him feel a little better.

Mr. Jennings asked a few questions to make sure he had understood. "All right," he said then, "your behavior was not very honorable, but there were mitigating circumstances. I don't know how to advise you about Meriema, but I certainly think you should apologize to your Uncle Vandi and promise to repay his money."

Joseph shrugged. "It is not so easy, sir."

"Perhaps if I write a letter to your Uncle Vandi, he will forgive you. I'll even assume responsibility for your return, if you like."

"No, sir. I must go see him. If he forgives me, perhaps he will help me to return next term. I must also tell Meriema not to wait for me."

Mr. Jennings frowned. "You can't miss another term's work." He stood and paced the floor.

"Well, perhaps my brother Vailo will help me," said Joseph.

Mr. Jennings' thoughts were elsewhere, and he failed to respond.

"Please, sir, I think I should go search for a lorry."

"Wait a minute now," said Mr. Jennings. "Listen to me. You may think that I'm a strange foreigner, but remember that I will always help a boy who tries hard."

"Oh, yes, sir," Joseph exclaimed. "All the boys know you are a good teacher."

"Good." Mr. Jennings didn't smile, but nodded in a satisfied way. Although it was difficult for him to look an elder in the eye, Joseph nodded back to demonstrate to his teacher that he had been sincere.

"Look, Joseph," the teacher continued, "you come back after you've talked to your parents. Try to get your fees. If you can't raise enough, I'll pay the balance."

"No, sir," Joseph exclaimed. "I am not deserving."

"Yes, you are. If it were not for you I'd have no one to teach this term, and frankly, I like teaching."

Joseph looked at his hands. "Sir," he said slowly, "you are too kind."

"Not at all," said Mr. Jennings. "You'll earn whatever you get from me. Since you're a farmer's son, I think in fact that I'll ask you to start a garden for me."

"Thank you, sir, but—"

"But what?"

"I don't think I should return this term in any case. The boys will want to revenge me."

"Revenge themselves; it's reflexive. All right, we'll have to find some way to protect you. But why do you think they'll suspect you? Now, don't tell me 'by magic.'"

"No, sir, they will know because I am back. My brother saw the letter I received from the Principal."

"Can't you trust him to keep your secret?"

"I don't think. I don't think *so*."

Mr. Jennings nodded, his mouth twisted strangely to one side. "Frankly," he said, "your brother is a mischief-maker. But never mind that. The thing to do is to stay in Wainke for a few days, until your uncle receives your letter of reinstatement. By the time you get back, Michael Museh should be here as well. Why should the boys ever know it was you who told us?"

It was not so simple as Mr. Jennings thought, because Gorba would eventually know; even so, it was the only thing to do. He nodded.

"Well, it's all over." Mr. Jennings ran his hand through his hair and sat down again. "Thank goodness you came," he said, with a sigh. "Let's see: lights-out bell will ring in less than five minutes. You should be able to leave then."

"Yes, sir." They waited mutely, a hundred thoughts whirling in Joseph's head. None of his worries seemed very big now. His confessions to Vandi Tailo' and Meriema would be painful, but a relief, too, and if Gorba eventually discovered what had happened, from talking to Vandi—well, no matter. Most surprising of all, he was glad he had betrayed the society oath. It had never occurred to him that the Principal felt no fear of the society, but of course, it was true; and he wouldn't be afraid, either.

A boy rang the gong up the hill, and Mr. Jennings jumped up from his chair. He startled Joseph with his starts and stops. "It's good to have you back, Joseph," he said. "You're going to be first in your class this time, aren't you?"

"I shall try, sir," said Joseph. "I shall do everything possible to stay in school, and I shall finish my education, by the Grace of God."

"Education," said Mr. Jennings, escorting him to the back door. "Very good. You know, you used to say 'educations,' but you've corrected it. Abstract nouns generally don't take plurals, right?"

"No, sir, you are right."

"Good-bye. Come back as soon as you can."

"Yes, sir, and when I am a doctor, sir, I will treat you without cost."

"Thanks." Mr. Jennings laughed, but kindly. "Unfortunately, I may be a long way from your office."

He patted Joseph lightly on the arm and Joseph slipped outside. He felt brave and strong for a moment, but as the dark grew thick around him and he sensed his loneliness, his worries and fears seeped back into his mind. How could he break honorably with Meriema? What would Vandi Tailo' say? His nerves forced him into a trot.

Abruptly he veered off toward the railroad station; perhaps the evening train was late and he could still catch it. Perhaps he would have to leave his trunk behind. That's what he should be worrying about tonight, catching a train, or finding a lorry, or if not that, arranging with his friend to stay for the night. The rest could wait until tomorrow.   THE END

Talking it over

1. *a.* Why does Mr. Jennings receive Joseph as he does?

   b. At what point does Mr. Jennings begin to take a real interest in what Joseph has to say?

2. What is the importance of the scene in which Joseph admires the fine possessions in Mr. Jennings' home?

3. *a.* Despite Joseph's determination to be reinstated, he continues to hold back the names of the conspirators. Why?

   b. How does the Principal's treatment of Joseph differ from the way Mr. Jennings acts? What effect does the Principal's behavior have on Joseph?

   c. Why does the Principal ridicule Joseph's fear of magic?

4. *a.* For the first time Joseph pours out his troubles to another person. Why does he choose Mr. Jennings?

b. What decisions does Joseph make as a result of his conversation with Mr. Jennings?

5. What problems must Joseph still solve? How do you think he will solve them?

A Wind of Change: Views and viewpoints

1. The title of this book comes from a speech by a former British Prime Minister. The complete sentence was: "The winds of change are blowing across Africa." Explain the changes dealt with in the story by answering these questions:

    a. What are Joseph's ambitions? What training must he have in order to fulfill them?

    b. What attitudes do the people in Wainke have about Joseph's plans? Compare this lack of understanding between adults and young people with situations experienced by young people today.

    c. How has Wainke already been influenced by "Europeans"? What other changes may occur that are not necessarily an improvement?

    d. Although Joseph and others like him will probably leave their homes, what responsibilities should they still feel toward their families?

2. Choose a person you like in the story (not Joseph) and one you don't like and explain why you feel as you do.

3. *a.* Choose from the statements below the one you think best expresses the central idea of the novel as a whole:

    (1) In a developing country, education is so important it should come ahead of most other considerations.

    (2) A boy should never tell on his relatives and friends.

    (3) Unless you stand up to people who try to lead you into wrongdoing, you may get into serious trouble.

    (4) When customs are changing, an ambitious young person must make painful decisions between the old and the new.

    (5) It is better to tell the truth than live with a lie.

    (6) A boy who plans to be a doctor should not marry.

    (7) Education does not depend on the condition of buildings.

    (8) A few discontented people have no right to force changes for their own selfish interests.

    (9) Africans should adopt American ways.

    (10) Violent action often defeats its own purpose, for it is almost always met with a violent reaction.

    b. Which of the other ideas listed do you think the author also wanted to bring out in this story? Defend your choices.

Every sound you need in order to pronounce English words is represented by a symbol in the Complete Pronunciation Key.

After each symbol are words containing the sound which the symbol stands for. This is the sound you must produce when you see the symbol in the pronunciation of a word.

a

Most symbols are single letters of the alphabet. Some are printed in the usual way. Some have special marks added.

A vowel letter without markings represents the short sound of the vowel. Special marks added to a vowel letter signal other sounds which that vowel letter may represent.

ā
ä

Some symbols are two letters of the alphabet. One of these symbols has a special mark added: ŦH. Can you hear the difference between the sounds represented by the symbols ŦH and th?

ch
th
ŦH

One symbol is not a letter at all. It is called a schwa, and stands for the vowel sound often heard in a syllable that is not accented. The sound represented by the schwa may be *spelled* with any of the five vowel letters, as in the examples.

ə

Most dictionaries include a few foreign words. These special symbols are used to represent sounds which occur in foreign words but not in English.

Y   N
œ   H

This short key, which appears on each right-hand page of the Glossary, includes the pronunciation symbols you need to refer to most often.

---

hat, āge, fär;   let, bē, tėrm;   it, īce;   hot, gō, ôrder;   oil, out;   cup, pùt, rüle;   ch, child;   ng, long;
th, thin;   ŦH, then;   zh, measure;   ə represents *a* in about, *e* in taken, *i* in April, *o* in lemon, *u* in circus.

GLOSSARY
COMPLETE PRONUNCIATION KEY

The pronunciation of each word is shown just after the word, in this way: **ab- bre vi ate** (ə brē′vē āt). The letters and signs used are pronounced as in the words below. The mark ′ is placed after a syllable with primary or strong accent, as in the example above. The mark ′ after a syllable shows a secondary or lighter accent, as in **ab bre vi a tion** (ə brē′vē ā′shən).

Some words, taken from foreign languages, are spoken with sounds that otherwise do not occur in English. Symbols for these sounds are given at the bottom of the page as "Foreign Sounds."

a	hat, cap	j	jam, enjoy	u	cup, butter
ā	age, face	k	kind, seek	ủ	full, put
ä	father, far	l	land, coal	ü	rule, move
		m	me, am		
		n	no, in		
b	bad, rob	ng	long, bring		
ch	child, much				
d	did, red			v	very, save
		o	hot, rock	w	will, woman
		ō	open, go	y	young, yet
e	let, best	ô	order, all	z	zero, breeze
ē	equal, see	oi	oil, voice	zh	measure, seizure
ėr	term, learn	ou	house, out		
		p	paper, cup		ə represents:
f	fat, if	r	run, try		a in about
g	go, bag	s	say, yes		e in taken
h	he, how	sh	she, rush		i in April
		t	tell, it		o in lemon
i	it, pin	th	thin, both		u in circus
ī	ice, five	ŦH	then, smooth		

foreign sounds

Y as in French *du*. Pronounce ē with the lips rounded as for English ü in **rule**

œ as in French *peu*. Pronounce ā with the lips rounded as for ō.

N as in French *bon*. The N is not pronounced, but shows that the vowel before it is nasal.

H as in German *ach*. Pronounce k without closing the breath passage.

Pronunciation key from the *Thorndike-Barnhart Advanced Junior Dictionary*, copyright © 1968 by Scott, Foresman and Company.

a bate (ə bāt′),　**1.** make less in amount, intensity, etc.; decrease. **2.** become less violent, intense, etc.; diminish: *The storm has abated.* *v.*

a bet (ə bet′),　encourage or help, especially in something wrong. *v.*, **a bet ted, a bet ting.**

ab bre vi ate (ə brē′vē āt),　**1.** make (a word or phrase) shorter so that a part stands for the whole. **2.** make briefer. *v.*

a blaze (ə blāz′),　**1.** on fire. **2.** blazing: *The room was all ablaze with a hundred lights.* *adv.*, *adj.*

a brupt (ə brupt′),　**1.** sudden; hasty; unexpected: *He made an abrupt turn to avoid another car.* **2.** very steep: *The road made an abrupt rise up the hill.* **3.** short or sudden in speech or manner; blunt. *adj.* —**a brupt′ly,** *adv.*

ab sorb ent (ab sôr′bənt),　**1.** taking in, or ready to take in, moisture, light, or heat: *Absorbent paper is used to dry the hands.* **2.** any thing or substance that takes in or sucks up moisture, light, or heat. 1 *adj.*, 2 *n.*

ab stract ed (ab strak′tid),　lost in thought; absent-minded. *adj.* —**ab stract′ed ly,** *adv.*

a bu sive (ə byü′siv),　**1.** scolding severely; using harsh and insulting language. **2.** abusing; treating badly. *adj.* —**a bu′sive ly,** *adv.*

a byss (ə bis′),　**1.** a bottomless depth; a very deep crack in the earth. **2.** lowest depth. *n.*

ac a dem ic (ak′ə dem′ik),　**1.** of or having to do with schools, colleges, and their studies. **2.** *U.S.* concerned with general education rather than commercial, technical, or professional education. **3.** scholarly. *adj.*

ac cu sa tion (ak′yə zā′shən),　**1.** a charge of having done something wrong, of being something bad, or of having broken the law. **2.** the offense charged. *n.*

a cet y lene (ə set′ə lēn),　a colorless gas that burns with a bright light and very hot flame. It is used for lighting and, combined with oxygen, for welding metals. *n.*

ac qui esce (ak′wē es′),　give consent by keeping silent or by not making objections. *v.*

ad ja cent (ə jā′snt),　lying near or close; adjoining: *The house adjacent to ours was sold.* *adj.*

ad mon ish (ad mon′ish),　warn or advise (a person) about his faults in order that he may be guided to improve. *v.*

a dorn (ə dôrn′),　**1.** add beauty to; make greater the splendor or honor of. **2.** put ornaments on; decorate. *v.*

ad vent (ad′vent),　coming; arrival. *n.*

af fect (ə fekt′),　**1.** pretend to have or feel: *He affected ignorance of the fight, but we knew that he had seen it.* **2.** be fond of; like: *She affects old furniture.* *v.*

af fin i ty (ə fin′ə tē),　natural attraction to a person or liking for a thing. *n.*, *pl.* **af fin i ties.**

af front (ə frunt′),　**1.** insult openly; offend purposely: *The boy affronted the teacher by making a face at her.* **2.** a word or act that openly expresses intentional disrespect: *To be called a coward is an affront to a manly boy.* **3.** a slight or injury to one's dignity. 1 *v.*, 2,3 *n.*

aft (aft),　at, near, or toward the back. *adv.*

ag gres sive (ə gres′iv),　**1.** taking the first step in an attack or quarrel; attacking; quarrelsome: *An aggressive country is always ready to start a war.* **2.** *U.S.* active; energetic. *adj.*

ag i tat ed (aj′ə tā′tid),　**1.** moving or shaking. **2.** disturbed; excited: *She was much agitated by the news.* *adj.*

a lac ri ty (ə lak′rə tē),　**1.** brisk and eager action; liveliness. **2.** cheerful willingness. *n.*

al i bi (al′ə bī),　**1.** the plea or fact that a person accused of a certain offense was somewhere else when the offense was committed. **2.** *U.S. Informal.* an excuse. *n.*, *pl.* **al i bis.**

al ien (ā′lyən),　**1.** of another country; foreign: *alien customs.* **2.** entirely different; not in agreement; strange. *adj.*

al lay (ə lā′),　**1.** put at rest; quiet: *His fears were allayed by the news of the safety of his family.* **2.** relieve; check. *v.*

al le giance (ə lē′jəns),　**1.** the loyalty owed by a citizen to his country or by a subject to his ruler: *I pledge allegiance to the flag.* **2.** loyalty; faithfulness to a person, cause, or the like. *n.*

al le vi ate (ə lē′vē āt),　make easier to endure; lessen: *Heat often alleviates pain.* *v.*

a loof (ə lüf′),　**1.** at a distance; withdrawn; apart. **2.** unsympathetic; not interested; reserved: *Because of her shyness Jane seemed aloof.* 1 *adv.*,　2 *adj.*

al ter nate (ôl′tər nāt),　**1.** occur by turns, first one and then the other. **2.** arrange by turns; do by turns: *alternate work and pleasure.* *v.*

a mends (ə mendz′),　payment for loss; satisfaction for an injury; compensation: *If you took more than your share of the money, you should at once make amends by returning the extra amount.* *n. sing. or pl.*

a mi a ble (ā′mē ə bəl),　good-natured and friendly; pleasant and agreeable. *adj.* —**a′ mi a bly,** *adv.*

Roman amphitheater

am phi the a ter or **am phi the a tre** (am′fə thē′ə tər), **1.** a circular or oval building with rows of seats around a central open space. Each row is higher than the one in front of it. **2.** something resembling an amphitheater in shape. *n.*

a nom a lous (ə nom′ə ləs),　departing from the common rule; irregular; abnormal. *adj.*

an tic i pate (an tis′ə pāt),　**1.** look forward to; expect. **2.** do, make, or use in advance. **3.** take care of ahead of time: *The nurse anticipated all the patient's wishes.* **4.** be before (another) in thinking, acting, etc. *v.*

an tique (an tēk′),　**1.** of times long ago; from times long ago; ancient: *This antique chair was made in 1750.* **2.** something made long ago. **3.** old-fashioned; out-of-date. 1,3 *adj.*,　2 *n.*

ap pa ra tus (ap′ə rā′təs or ap′ə rat′əs),　things

---

necessary to carry out a purpose or for a particular use: *apparatus for an experiment in chemistry, gardening apparatus, our digestive apparatus. n., pl.* **ap pa ra tus** or **ap pa ra tus es.**

ap praise (ə prāz′),   **1.** estimate the value, amount, quality, etc., of. **2.** set a price on; fix the value of: *Property is appraised for taxation. v.*

ap pre hen sion (ap′ri hen′shən),   expectation of evil; fear; dread. *n.*

ap pre hen sive (ap′ri hen′siv),   afraid; anxious; worried. *adj.* —**ap′pre hen′sive ly,** *adv.*

ar ro gance (ar′ə gəns),   too great pride; haughtiness. *n.*

as bes tos or **as bes tus** (as bes′təs),   a mineral, a silicate of calcium and magnesium, that does not burn or conduct heat. It usually comes in fibers that can be made into a sort of cloth or felt. Asbestos is used for mats to put under hot dishes. *n.*

as cet ic (ə set′ik),   refraining from pleasures and comforts; self-denying. *adj.*

as pen (as′pən),   **1.** a poplar tree whose leaves tremble in the slightest breeze. **2.** of this tree. 1 *n.,* 2 *adj.*

as per i ty (as per′ə tē),   roughness; harshness; severity. *n., pl.* **as per i ties.**

as sault (ə sôlt′),   **1.** a sudden, vigorous attack; attack. **2.** final phase of a military attack; closing with the enemy in hand-to-hand fighting. **3.** make an assault on; attack. 1,2 *n.,* 3 *v.*

as sert (ə sèrt′),   **1.** state positively; declare. **2.** insist on (a right, a claim, etc.); defend: *assert your independence. v.*

as ser tive (ə sèr′tiv),   too confident and certain; positive. *adj.* —**as ser′tive ly,** *adv.* —**as ser′tive ness,** *n.*

as sur ance (ə shůr′əns),   **1.** a making sure or certain. **2.** positive declaration inspiring confidence: *Mother has given me her assurance that I may go to the circus.* **3.** security; certainty; confidence: *We have the assurance of final victory.* **4.** self-confidence: *Joe's hard studying has given him considerable assurance in school. n.*

as ter (as′tər),   a common flower with white, pink, or purple petals around a yellow center. Some asters are very small; others are large with many petals. *n.*

as ton ish (ə ton′ish),   surprise greatly; amaze: *The gift of ten dollars astonished the little boy. v.*

as ton ish ment (ə ton′ish mənt),   **1.** great surprise; amazement; sudden wonder. **2.** anything that causes great surprise. *n.*

as tro dome (as′trə dōm′),   the clear dome-shaped top of an aircraft. *n.*

a the ist (ā′thē ist),   person who believes that there is no God. *n.*

a troc i ty (ə tros′ə tē),   **1.** very great wickedness or cruelty. **2.** a very cruel or brutal act: *the atrocities of the Nazis. n., pl.* **a troc i ties.**

at ten tive (ə ten′tiv),   **1.** giving attention; observing: *Sally is an attentive pupil.* **2.** courteous; polite: *Children should be attentive to their parents. adj.* —**at ten′tive ly,** *adv.* —**at ten′tive ness,** *n.*

aug ment (ôg ment′),   increase; enlarge: *The king augmented his power by taking over rights that had belonged to the nobles. v.*

au then tic (ô then′tik),   **1.** reliable: *We heard an authentic account of the wreck, given by one of the ship's officers.* **2.** genuine. *adj.*

au to pi lot (ô′tō pī′lət),   an automatic pilot, or device for automatically steering ships and aircraft. *n.*

av a lanche (av′ə lanch),   **1.** a large mass of snow and ice, or of dirt and rocks, sliding or falling down a mountainside. **2.** anything like an avalanche: *an avalanche of questions. n.*

a vert (ə vèrt′),   **1.** prevent; avoid: *He averted the accident by a quick turn of his car.* **2.** turn away; turn aside: *She averted her eyes from the wreck. v.*

awe (ô),   **1.** great fear and wonder; fear and reverence. **2.** cause to feel awe; fill with awe: *The majesty of the mountains awed us.* 1 *n.,* 2 *v.*

ba bel or **Ba bel** (bā′bəl or bab′əl),   **1.** noise; confusion of many different sounds. **2.** place of noise and confusion. *n.*

bale (bāl),   a large bundle of merchandise or material securely wrapped or bound for shipping or storage: *a bale of cotton. n.*

bale ful (bāl′fəl),   evil; harmful. *adj.*

ban is ter (ban′is tər),   railing on a stairway. *n.*

banns (banz),   public notice, given three times in church, that a certain man and woman are to be married. *n.pl.*

ban ter (ban′tər),   **1.** playful teasing; joking. **2.** tease playfully; make fun of. **3.** talk in a joking way. 1 *n.,* 2,3 *v.* —**ban′ter ing ly,** *adv.*

bar rage (bə räzh′ for 1-3; bär′ij for 4),   **1.** barrier of artillery fire to check the enemy or to protect one's own soldiers in advancing or retreating. **2.** constant discharge or shower of missiles or blows. **3.** fire at with artillery; subject to a barrage. **4.** an artificial bar in a river; dam. 1,2,4 *n.,* 3 *v.*

bar ren (bar′ən),   **1.** not producing anything: *A sandy desert is barren.* **2.** not able to bear offspring: *Scientists know that exposure to radioactivity may make animals and plants barren. adj.*

bar ri cade (bar′ə kād′ or bar′ə kād),   **1.** a rough, hastily made barrier for defense. **2.** any barrier or obstruction. **3.** block or obstruct with a barricade: *The road was barricaded with fallen trees.* 1,2 *n.,* 3 *v.*

beam ing (bē′ming),   **1.** shining; bright. **2.** smiling brightly; cheerful. *adj.*

bed lam (bed′ləm),   **1.** uproar; confusion. **2.** insane asylum; madhouse. *n.*

be drag gled (bi drag′əld),   **1.** wet and hanging limp. **2.** dragged in the dirt. *adj.*

be lat ed (bi lā′tid),   **1.** delayed; too late. **2.** overtaken by darkness: *The belated travelers lost their way in the mountains. adj.*

be reft (bi reft′),   **1.** bereaved; deprived: *Bereft of hope and friends, the old man led a wretched life.* **2.** left desolate. *adj.*

---

hat, āge, fär; let, bē, tèrm; it, īce; hot, gō, ôrder; oil, out; cup, pút, rüle; ch, child; ng, long; th, thin; ᵺ, then; zh, measure; ə represents *a* in about, *e* in taken, *i* in April, *o* in lemon, *u* in circus.

be siege (bi sēj′), **1.** make a long-continued attempt to get possession of (a place) by armed force; surround and try to capture. **2.** crowd around: *Hundreds of admirers besieged the famous aviator.* *v.*

be tray (bi trā), **1.** give away to the enemy: *The traitor betrayed his country.* **2.** be unfaithful to. **3.** mislead; deceive. **4.** give away (a secret); disclose unintentionally. **5.** reveal; show. *v.*

be troth (bi trôᴛʜ′ or bi trôth′), promise in marriage; engage. *v.*

bick er (bik′ər), quarrel. *v.*

bide (bīd), *Archaic except in idiom.* **1.** dwell; abide. **2.** continue; wait. **3.** wait for. *v.*

bi ol o gist (bī ol′ə jist), expert in biology, the science of life or living matter in all its forms and phenomena. *n.*

bit (bit), **1.** part of a bridle that goes in a horse's mouth. **2.** the biting or cutting part of a tool. *n.*

bi zarre (bə zär′), odd; queer; fantastic; grotesque. *adj.*

blear (blir), **1.** dim; blurred. **2.** make dim or blurred. 1 *adj.*, 2 *v.*

blem ish (blem′ish), **1.** a stain; spot; scar: *A mole is a blemish on a person's skin.* **2.** injure; mar. 1 *n.*, 2 *v.*
without blemish, perfect.

bloat (blōt), swell up; puff up. *v.*

blun der buss (blun′dər bus), **1.** a short gun with a wide muzzle that fired a quantity of shot, but only for a short distance. It is no longer used. **2.** person who blunders. *n.*

Blunderbuss

bog (bog), **1.** soft, wet, spongy ground; marsh; swamp. **2.** sink or get stuck in a bog. 1 *n.*, 2 *v.*, **bogged, bog ging.**
bog down, get stuck as if in mud.

bo na fi de (bō′nə fī′dē or bō′nə fīd′), in good faith; genuine; without make-believe or fraud.

bow (bou), the forward part of a ship, boat, or airship. *n.*

bow sprit (bou′sprit), pole or spar projecting forward from the bow of a ship. Ropes from it help to steady sails and masts. *n.*

bran dish (bran′dish), **1.** wave or shake threateningly. **2.** a threatening shake; flourish. 1 *v.*, 2 *n.*

brash (brash), **1.** hasty; rash. **2.** impudent; saucy. *adj.*

bra va do (brə vä′dō), a great show of boldness without much real courage; boastful defiance without much real desire to fight. *n.*

breech (brēch), **1.** the lower part; back part. **2.** part of a gun behind the barrel. *n.*

breech es (brich′iz), **1.** short trousers reaching from the waist to the knees. **2.** *Informal.* trousers. *n.pl.*

brig (brig), **1.** a square-rigged ship with two masts. **2.** *U.S.* prison on a warship. *n.*

bro mide (brō′mīd), **1.** compound of bromine with another substance. **2.** *Slang.* a commonplace idea; trite remark. *n.*

brush (brush), **1.** *U.S.* branches broken or cut off. **2.** a thick growth of shrubs, bushes, small

trees, etc. **3.** *U.S.* a thinly settled country; backwoods. *n.*

buff (buf), fan, enthusiast. *n.*

bulk head (bulk′hed′), one of the upright partitions dividing a ship into watertight compartments to prevent sinking. *n.*

bull (bul), **1.** *Slang.* policeman. **2.** *Slang.* foolish talk. *n.*

buoy (boi or bü′ē), **1.** a floating object anchored in a certain place on the water to warn or guide. **2.** a cork belt, ring, or jacket to keep a person from sinking; life buoy. **3.** hold up; sustain; encourage. 1,2 *n.*, 3 *v.*

buoy ant (boi′ənt), `1.** able to float. **2.** lighthearted; hopeful. *adj.* —**buoy′ant ly,** *adv.*

bush (bush), open forest; wild land. *n.*

butt (but), **1.** target. **2.** object of ridicule or scorn: *That boy was the butt of their jokes.* *n.*

buz zard (buz′ərd), any of various heavy, slow-moving birds of prey of the same family as the hawk. *n.*

caf feine or **caf fein** (kaf′ēn), a stimulating drug found in coffee and tea. *n.*

cal a bash (kal′ə bash), **1.** gourd whose dried shell is used to make bottles, bowls, drums, rattles, etc. **2.** the tropical plant or tree that it grows on. **3.** bottle, bowl, etc., made from such a dried shell. *n.*

Decorated calabashes (def. 3)

cal cu late (kal′kyə lāt), **1.** find out by adding, subtracting, multiplying, or dividing. **2.** find out beforehand by any process of reasoning; estimate. **3.** rely; depend; count. **4.** *U.S. Informal.* plan; intend: *That remark was calculated to hurt someone's feelings.* *v.*

cal lous (kal′əs), **1.** hard; hardened. Portions of the skin that are exposed to friction are often callous. **2.** unfeeling; not sensitive: *Only a callous person can see suffering without trying to relieve it.* *adj.* —**cal′lous ly,** *adv.*

cam ou flage (kam′ə fläzh), **1.** disguise; deception. The white fur of a polar bear is a natural camouflage; it prevents the bear's being easily seen against the snow. **2.** in warfare, giving things a false appearance to deceive the enemy. **3.** give a false appearance to in order to conceal; disguise. 1,2 *n.*, 3 *v.*

cane (kān), **1.** a stick to help a person in walking. **2.** beat with a cane. 1 *n.*, 2 *v.*

car bine (kär′bīn), a short rifle or musket. *n.*

ca reen (kə rēn′), **1.** lean to one side; tilt; tip. **2.** sway from side to side. *v.*

car i bou (kar′ə bü), any of several kinds of North American reindeer. *n.*, *pl.* **car i bous** or (*esp. collectively*) **car i bou.**

car niv o rous (kär niv′ə rəs), flesh-eating. Cats, dogs, lions, tigers, and bears are carnivorous animals. *adj.*

Caribou (4 ft. high at the shoulder)

cas cade (kas kād′), **1.** a small waterfall. **2.** anything like this. **3.** fall in a cascade. 1,2 *n.*, 3 *v.*

cas sa va (kə sä′və), a tropical plant with starchy roots. Tapioca is made from cassava. *n.*

cas u al (kazh′u əl), **1.** happening by chance; not planned or expected; accidental: *a casual meeting.* **2.** without plan or method; careless: *a casual answer, a casual glance.* **3.** uncertain; indefinite; indifferent; vague. **4.** designed for informal wear: *We dressed in casual clothes for the picnic. adj.* —**cas′u al ly**, *adv.*

cat a pult (kat′ə pult), **1.** an ancient weapon for shooting stones, arrows, etc. **2.** device for launching an airplane from the deck of a ship. **3.** shoot from a catapult; throw; hurl. **4.** move suddenly or with force. 1,2 *n.*, 3,4 *v.*

cau tious (kô′shəs), very careful; taking care to be safe; never taking chances: *a cautious driver. adj.* —**cau′tious ly**, *adv.*

ca vort (kə vôrt′), *U.S. Informal.* prance about; jump around. *v.*

cen trif u gal (sen trif′yə gəl), moving away from the center. *adj.* —**cen trif′u gal ly**, *adv.*

centrifugal force, inertia of a body revolved around a center, tending to move it away from the center.

cer e mo ni al (ser′ə mō′nē əl), **1.** of or having to do with ceremony: *The ceremonial costumes were beautiful.* **2.** formal actions proper to an occasion. **3.** very formal: *The queen received her guests in a ceremonial way.* 1,3 *adj.*, 2 *n.* —**cer′e mo′ni al ly**, *adv.*

chafe (chāf), **1.** rub to make warm: *She chafed her cold hands.* **2.** wear or be worn away by rubbing. **3.** make or become sore by rubbing: *The stiff collar chafed the man's neck.* **4.** make angry. *v.*

chal lenge (chal′ənj), **1.** call to fight; especially, call to fight in a duel. **2.** call to a game or contest. **3.** call to answer and explain: *A guard challenges all people who come near the fort, asking them who they are and what they are doing.* **4.** question; doubt; dispute: *I challenge your statement; you must prove it before I believe it.* **5.** object to: *The attorney for the defense challenged the juror.* 1-5 *v.*, 1-3 *n.*

chant (chant), **1.** song. **2.** sing. **3.** keep talking about; say over and over again. 1 *n.*, 2,3 *v.*

char ac ter ize (kar′ik tər īz), **1.** describe the special qualities or features of (a person or thing); describe: *I would characterize our teacher as a very friendly person.* **2.** be a characteristic of; distinguish. *v.*

chink (chingk), **1.** a narrow opening; crack; slit: *The chinks between the logs of the cabin let in the wind.* **2.** fill up the chinks in. 1 *n.*, 2 *v.*

cir cum stan tial (sèr′kəm stan′shəl), **1.** depending on circumstances: *circumstantial evidence.* **2.** not essential; not important. *adj.*

civ et (siv′it), civet cat, a small, spotted mammal of Africa, Europe, and Asia which has glands that secrete a yellowish substance with a musky odor. *n.*

clar i ty (klar′ə tē), clearness. *n.*

clinch (klinch), **1.** fasten (a driven nail, a bolt, etc.) firmly by bending over the part that projects. **2.** fasten (things) together in this way. **3.** fix firmly; settle decisively: *A deposit of five dollars clinched the bargain.* **4.** grasp one another tightly in fighting or wrestling; grapple: *When the boxers clinched, the crowd hissed.* **5.** a tight grasp in fighting or wrestling; close grip. 1-4 *v.*, 5 *n.*

clod hop per (klod′hop′ər), **1.** a clumsy boor. **2.** a large, heavy shoe. *n.*

co ag u late (kō ag′yə lāt), change from liquid into a thickened mass; thicken: *Cooking coagulates the white of egg. v.*

co bra (kō′brə), a very poisonous snake of S Asia and Africa. It can dilate the head and neck so that they assume a hoodlike form. *n.*

cock (kok), **1.** a male chicken; rooster. **2.** the male of other birds. **3.** hammer of a gun. **4.** position of the hammer of a gun when it is pulled back ready to fire. **5.** pull back the hammer of (a gun), ready to fire. 1-4 *n.*, 5 *v.*

Cobra (4½ ft. long)

col laps i ble (kə lap′sə bəl), made so that it can be folded or pushed into a smaller space. *adj.*

co ma (kō′mə), a prolonged unconsciousness caused by disease, injury, or poison; stupor. *n., pl.* **co mas.**

com mand ing (kə man′ding), **1.** in command: *a commanding officer.* **2.** controlling; powerful: *commanding influences.* **3.** authoritative; impressive: *a commanding voice.* **4.** having a position of control. *adj.* —**com mand′ing ly**, *adv.*

com mence (kə mens′), begin; start. *v.*

com men da tion (kom′ən dā′shən), **1.** praise; approval. **2.** favorable mention; recommendation. *n.*

com mis sion (kə mish′ən), **1.** a written paper giving certain powers, privileges, and duties. **2.** a written order giving military or naval rank and authority: *A captain in the United States army or navy has a commission signed by the President.* **3.** rank and authority given by such an order. *n.*

com mun ion (kə myün′yən), **1.** act of sharing; a having in common. **2.** exchange of thoughts and feelings; intimate talk; fellowship. **3.** a close spiritual relationship. *n.*

com mu ni ty (kə myü′nə tē), **1.** a number of people having common ties or interests and living in the same place and subject to the same laws; people of any district or town: *This lake provides water for six communities.* **2.** group of animals or plants living together. **3.** likeness; similarity: *Community of interests causes people to work together. n., pl.* **com mu ni ties.**

com par a tive (kəm par′ə tiv), **1.** that com-

hat, āge, fär; let, bē, tèrm; it, īce; hot, gō, ôrder; oil, out; cup, pùt, rüle; ch, child; ng, long; th, thin; ᴛʜ, then; zh, measure; ə represents *a* in about, *e* in taken, *i* in April, *o* in lemon, *u* in circus.

581

pares: *the comparative method of studying.*
2. measured by comparison with something else.
adj.

com par a tive ly (kəm par′ə tiv lē), by comparison; relatively; somewhat. *adv.*

com pe tent (kom′pə tənt), **1.** able; fit: *a competent cook.* **2.** legally qualified: *Two competent witnesses testified. adj.*

com pe ti tion (kom′pə tish′ən), **1.** effort to obtain something wanted by others; rivalry: *There is competition in our class for first place.* **2.** contest. **3.** competitor; rival. *n.*

com pla cent (kəm plā′snt), pleased with oneself; self-satisfied. *adj.* —**com pla′cent ly**, *adv.*

com plic i ty (kəm plis′ə tē), partnership in wrongdoing: *Knowingly receiving stolen goods is complicity in theft. n., pl.* **com plic i ties.**

com po nent (kəm pō′nənt), **1.** constituent; that composes: *Blade and handle are the component parts of a knife.* **2.** an essential part; part: *A chemist can separate a medicine into its components.* 1 *adj.,* 2 *n.*

com posed (kəm pōzd′), calm; quiet; self-controlled; tranquil. *adj.*

com pound[1] (kom′pound or kom pound′ for 1; kom′pound for 2-4; kom pound′ for 5). **1.** having more than one part: *A clover leaf is a compound leaf.* **2.** something made by combining parts; mixture: *A medicine is usually a compound.* **3.** a compound word. **4.** substance formed by chemical combination of two or more substances: *Water is a compound of hydrogen and oxygen.* **5.** mix; combine: *The man in the drugstore compounds medicines and drinks.* 1 *adj.,* 2-4 *v.,* 5 *v.*

compound a felony, accept money not to prosecute a crime, etc.

com pound[2] (kom′pound), an enclosed yard with buildings in it. *n.*

com pre hend (kom′pri hend′), **1.** understand the meaning of: *He comprehends geometry and advanced algebra. If you can use a word correctly and effectively, you comprehend it.* **2.** include; contain. *v.* —**com′pre hend′ing ly,** *adv.*

com prise (kəm prīz′), to make up. *v.*

com rade (kom′rad), **1.** companion and friend; partner. **2.** person who shares in what another is doing; fellow worker. *n.*

com rade ship (kom′rad ship), **1.** condition of being a comrade. **2.** friendship; fellowship. *n.*

con cep tion (kən sep′shən), **1.** act or power of forming in the mind, thinking up, imagining. **2.** thought; idea; impression. **3.** design; plan. *n.*

con cern (kən sėrn′), **1.** whatever has to do with a person or thing; interest; important matter; business; affair. **2.** interest: *We are all concerned about the school play.* **3.** troubled state of mind; worry; anxiety; uneasiness: *The mother's concern over her sick child kept her awake all night.* 1,3 *n.,* 2 *v.*

con ces sion (kən sesh′ən), **1.** a conceding; granting; yielding: *As a concession, Mother let me stay up an hour longer.* **2.** anything conceded or yielded; admission; acknowledgment. *n.*

con clu sive (kən klü′siv), decisive; convincing; final. *adj.* —**con clu′sive ly,** *adv.*

con de scend ing (kon′di sen′ding), **1.** stooping to the level of one's inferiors. **2.** patronizing. *adj.* —**con′de scend′ing ly,** *adv.*

con fes sion al (kən fesh′ən l), **1.** a small booth where a priest hears confessions. **2.** practice of confessing sins to a priest. *n.*

con fine (kən fīn′ for 1-3; kon′fīn for 4), **1.** keep within limits; restrict: *He was confined in prison for two years.* **2.** keep indoors; shut in: *A cold confined him to the house.* **3.** imprison. **4.** boundary; limit: *These people have never been beyond the confines of their own valley.* 1-3 *v.,* 4 *n.*

con fine ment (kən fīn′mənt), **1.** fact or state of being confined. **2.** imprisonment. *n.*

con fron ta tion (kon′frən tā′shən), the act of standing face to face with defiance, opposition, or accusation; a meeting. *n.*

con science (kon′shəns), sense of right and wrong. *Your conscience is the ideas and feelings within you which tell you what is wrong and keep you from doing it, and which tell you what is right and lead you to do it. n.*

con spic u ous (kən spik′yú əs), **1.** easily seen. **2.** worthy of notice; remarkable: *Lincoln is a conspicuous example of a poor boy who succeeded. adj.* —**con spic′u ous ly,** *adv.*

con spir a cy (kən spir′ə sē), secret planning with others to do something wrong, especially a wrong against a government, public personage, etc.; plot. *n., pl.* **con spir a cies.**

con ster nate (kon′stər nāt), to fill with dismay. *v.*

con ster na tion (kon′stər nā′shən), great dismay; paralyzing terror: *To our consternation the train rushed on toward the burning bridge. n.*

con sti tu tion (kon′stə tü′shən or kon′stə tyü′shən), **1.** the way in which a person or thing is organized; nature; make-up: *A person with a good constitution is strong and healthy.* **2.** the system of fundamental principles according to which a nation, state, or group is governed. *n.*

con strained (kən strānd′), **1.** forced. **2.** restrained; stiff; unnatural. *adj.*

con tem plate (kon′təm plāt), **1.** look at for a long time; gaze at. **2.** think about for a long time; study carefully: *I will contemplate your proposal.* **3.** meditate: *All day he did nothing but contemplate.* **4.** have in mind; intend: *She contemplated going to Europe after graduation. She is contemplating a change of work. v.*

con tem pla tion (kon′təm plā′shən), **1.** act of looking at or thinking about something for a long time: *contemplation of the sea.* **2.** deep thought; meditation: *sunk in contemplation.* **3.** expectation; intention: *We are buying tents and other equipment in contemplation of a summer of camping. n.*

con tempt (kən tempt′), **1.** the feeling that a person, act, or thing is mean, low, or worthless; scorn; a despising: *We feel contempt for a liar.* **2.** condition of being scorned or despised; disgrace: *A cowardly traitor is held in contempt.* **3.** disobedience to or open disrespect for the rules or decisions of a law court, a lawmaking body, etc. A person can be put in jail for **contempt of court.** *n.*

con temp tu ous (kən temp′chů əs), showing contempt; scornful: *a contemptuous look. adj.* —**con temp′tu ous ly,** *adv.*

con tend (kən tend′), **1.** fight; struggle: *The first settlers in America had to contend with the Indians, sickness, and lack of food.* **2.** take part in a contest; compete. **3.** argue; dispute. **4.** declare to be a fact; maintain as true: *Columbus contended that the earth was round. v.*

con test ant (kən tes′tənt), **1.** person who contests; person who takes part in a contest. **2.** person who contests election returns, etc. *n.*

con tour (kon′túr), **1.** outline of a figure: *The contour of the Atlantic coast of America is very irregular.* **2.** showing the outlines of hills, valleys, etc.: *a contour map.* 1 *n.,* 2 *adj.*

con trite (kən trīt′ or kon′trīt), **1.** broken in spirit by a sense of guilt; penitent. **2.** showing deep regret and sorrow: *He wrote an apology in contrite words. adj.* —**con trite′ly,** *adv.*

con verge (kən vėrj′), **1.** tend to meet in a point. **2.** turn toward each other: *If you look at the end of your nose, your eyes converge.* **3.** come together; center: *The interest of all the students converged upon the celebration. v.*

con ver sion (kən vėr′zhən), **1.** act of converting; a changing; a turning; change: *Heat causes the conversion of water into steam.* **2.** change from unbelief to faith; change from one religion, party, etc., to another. *n.*

con vert (kən vėrt′), **1.** change; turn: *These machines convert cotton into cloth. One last effort converted victory into defeat.* **2.** change from unbelief to faith; change from one religion, party, etc., to another. *v.*

con vert er (kən vėr′tər), **1.** person or thing that converts. **2.** machine for changing the form of an electric current. *n.*

con vince (kən vins′), make (a person) feel sure; cause to believe; persuade by argument or proof: *The mistakes Nan made convinced me she had not studied her lesson. v.*

con vinc ing (kən vin′sing), that convinces: *a convincing argument. adj.* —**con vinc′ing ly,** *adv.*

con vul sion (kən vul′shən), **1.** a violent, involuntary contracting and relaxing of the muscles; spasm. **2.** a violent disturbance: *The country was undergoing a political convulsion. n.*

con vul sive (kən vul′siv), **1.** violently disturbing. **2.** having convulsions. **3.** producing convulsions. *adj.* —**con vul′sive ly,** *adv.*

cope (kōp), fight with some degree of success; struggle on even terms; deal successfully: *She was too weak to cope with the extra work. v.*

cor nice (kôr′nis), an ornamental molding that projects along the top of a wall, pillar, building, etc. *n.*

cor rob o rate (kə rob′ə rāt), make more certain; confirm: *Witnesses corroborated the policeman's statement. v.*

cor ru gat ed (kôr′ə gā′tid), bent or shaped into a row of wavelike ridges: *corrugated iron. adj.*

cou lee (kü′lē), **1.** in the western United States, a deep ravine or gulch that is usually dry in summer. **2.** stream of lava. *n.*

coun ter (koun′tər), **1.** in the opposite direction; opposed; contrary: *His wild idea runs counter to common sense.* **2.** opposite; contrary: *Your plans are counter to ours.* **3.** go or act counter to; oppose: *She did not like our plan; so she countered it with one of her own.* 1 *adv.,* 2 *adj.,* 3 *v.*

coup (kü), **1.** a sudden, brilliant action; unexpected, clever move. **2.** an act practiced by some American Indians of touching an enemy in warfare in a way that by custom is considered a deed of bravery. *n., pl.* **coups** (küz).

cou ple (kup′əl), **1.** two things of the same kind that go together; pair. **2.** man and woman who are married, engaged, or partners in a dance. **3.** partners in a dance. **4.** join together; join together in pairs: *couple two freight cars.* 1-3 *n.,* 4 *v.*

cow er (kou′ər), **1.** crouch in fear or shame: *The whipped dog cowered under the table.* **2.** draw back tremblingly from another's threats, blows, etc. *v.*

coy (koi), **1.** shy; modest; bashful. **2.** pretending to be shy. *adj.* —**coy′ly,** *adv.* —**coy′ness,** *n.*

coy o te (kī ō′tē or kī′ōt), wolf living on the prairies of W North America. It is noted for loud howling at night. *n., pl.* **coy o tes** or (*esp. collectively*) **coy o te.**

Coyote (total length 4 ft.)

crane (krān), **1.** machine with a long, swinging arm, for lifting and moving heavy weights. **2.** a swinging metal arm in a fireplace, used to hold a kettle over the fire. **3.** a large wading bird with very long legs and a long neck. **4.** stretch (the neck) as a crane does, in order to see better. 1-3 *n.,* 4 *v.*

crank case (krangk′kās′), a heavy, metal case forming the bottom part of an internal-combustion engine. The crankcase of a gasoline engine encloses the crankshaft, connecting rods, etc. *n.*

cra ter (krā′tər), **1.** depression around the opening of a volcano. **2.** a bowl-shaped hole: *The battlefield was full of craters made by exploding shells. n.*

cred it (kred′it), **1.** belief; faith; trust. **2.** believe; have faith in; trust: *I can credit all that you are telling me.* **3.** consider favorably as the performer of an action. **4.** money in a person's bank account, etc. **5.** give credit in a bank account, etc. **6.** reputation in money matters: *If you pay your bills, your credit will be good.* **7.** honor; praise: *The person who does the work should get the credit.* 1,4,6,7 *n.,* 2,3,5 *v.*

crest fall en (krest′fôl′ən), with bowed head; dejected; discouraged: *Nell came home crestfallen because she had a poor report card. adj.*

hat, āge, fär; let, bē, tėrm; it, īce; hot, gō, ôrder; oil, out; cup, pút, rüle; ch, child; ng, long; th, thin; ŦH, then; zh, measure; ə represents *a* in about, *e* in taken, *i* in April, *o* in lemon, *u* in circus.

cre vasse (krə vas′),　a deep crack or crevice in earth, snow, or glacier ice.　*n.*

crev ice (krev′is),　a narrow split or crack: *Tiny ferns grew in crevices in the stone wall.*　*n.*

cringe (krinj),　**1.** shrink from danger or pain; crouch in fear. **2.** bow down timidly; try to get favor or attention by servile behavior: *The courtiers cringed before the king.*　*v.*

cru cial (krü′shəl),　**1.** very important; critical; decisive. **2.** very trying; severe.　*adj.* —**cru′-cial ly,** *adv.*

crys tal (kris′tl),　**1.** a clear, transparent mineral, a kind of quartz, that looks like ice. **2.** piece of crystal cut to form an ornament. Crystals are used as beads, and hung around lights. **3.** made of crystal: *crystal ornaments.* **4.** clear and transparent like crystal. **5.** a very transparent glass. **6.** glass over the face of a watch. **7.** a regularly shaped piece with angles and flat surfaces, into which a substance solidifies. 1,2,5-7 *n.*,　3,4 *adj.*

Crystal shapes (def. 7)

crys tal line (kris′tl in),　**1.** consisting of crystals: *Sugar and salt are crystalline.* **2.** made of crystal. **3.** clear and transparent like crystal. *adj.*

crys tal li za tion (kris′tl ə zā′shən),　**1.** a forming or being formed into crystals. **2.** a forming into a definite shape: *His clear plan was the crystallization of the ideas we suggested.*　*n.*

cu bit (kyü′bit),　an ancient measure of length, about 18 to 22 inches. Once a cubit meant the length of the forearm, from the elbow down.　*n.*

cul pa ble (kul′pə bəl),　deserving blame: *The policeman was dismissed for culpable neglect of duty.*　*adj.*

cul prit (kul′prit),　person guilty of a fault or crime; offender.　*n.*

cul ture (kul′chər),　**1.** fineness of feelings, thoughts, tastes, manners, etc. **2.** civilization of a given race or a nation at a given time. **3.** development of the mind or body by education, training, etc.　*n.*

cul tured (kul′chərd),　having or showing culture; refined.　*adj.*

cu ra tor (kyü rā′tər),　person in charge of all or part of a museum, library, etc.　*n.*

curt (kėrt),　short; rudely brief; abrupt: *His curt way of speaking made him seem rude.*　*adj.*

cus tom ar i ly (kus′təm er′ə lē),　in a customary manner; usually.　*adv.*

cus tom ar y (kus′təm er′ē),　according to custom; as a habit; usual.　*adj.*

dan dy (dan′dē),　**1.** man who is too careful of his dress and appearance. **2.** *Slang.* an excellent or first-rate thing.　*n.*, *pl.* **dan dies.**

dare dev il (der′dev′l or dar′dev′l),　**1.** a reckless person. **2.** reckless. 1 *n.*,　2 *adj.*

daunt (dônt),　frighten; discourage: *Danger did not daunt the hero.*　*v.*

death mask (deth mask),　clay, wax, or plaster likeness of a person's face made from a cast taken after his death.

de bris or **dé bris** (də brē′),　**1.** scattered fragments; ruins; rubbish: *The street was covered with*

debris from the explosion. **2.** a mass of fragments of rock, etc.: *the debris left by a glacier.*　*n.*

de bunk (di bungk′),　to expose false pretenses or remove nonsense or sentimentality from.　*v.*

dec ade (dek′ād),　**1.** ten years: *From 1900 to 1910 was a decade.* **2.** group of ten.　*n.*

de ceit ful (di sēt′fəl),　**1.** ready or willing to deceive or lie. **2.** deceiving; fraudulent. **3.** meant to deceive.　*adj.*

de ci pher (di sī′fər),　**1.** make out the meaning of (bad writing, an unknown language, or anything puzzling). **2.** interpret (secret writing) by using a key; change (a message) from code to ordinary language.　*v.* —**de ci′pher a ble,** *adj.*

de ci sive (di sī′siv),　**1.** having or giving a clear result; settling something beyond question: *a decisive victory.* **2.** having or showing decision: *a decisive answer.*　*adj.* —**de ci′sive ly,**　*adv.*

de cliv i ty (di kliv′ə tē),　a downward slope.　*n.*, *pl.* **de cliv i ties.**

de coy (di koi′ for 1; dē′koi or di koi′ for 2,3),　**1.** lure (wild birds, animals, etc.) into a trap or within gunshot. **2.** place into which wild birds or animals are lured. **3.** any person or thing used to lead or tempt into danger. 1 *v.*,　2,3 *n.*

de cree (di krē′),　**1.** something ordered or settled by authority; official decision. **2.** order or settle by authority: *The government decreed that Washington's birthday should be a holiday.* **3.** decide; determine. 1 *n.*,　2,3 *v.*

de crep it (di krep′it),　broken down or weakened by old age; old and feeble.　*adj.*

de fi ant (di fī′ənt),　showing defiance; challenging; openly resisting.　*adj.*

de fi cien cy (di fish′ən sē),　**1.** lack or absence of something needed or required; incompleteness. **2.** amount by which something falls short or is too small: *If a bill to be paid is $10 and you have only $6, the deficiency is $4.*　*n.*, *pl.* **de fi cien cies.**

de flate (di flāt′),　**1.** let air or gas out of (a balloon, tire, etc.). **2.** reduce the amount of; reduce: *deflate prices, deflate currency.*　*v.*

de form (di fôrm′),　**1.** spoil the form or shape of: *Shoes that are too tight deform the feet.* **2.** make ugly: *Anger deforms the face.*　*v.* —**de form′er,** *n.*

de grade (di grād′),　**1.** reduce to a lower rank; take away a position, an honor, etc., from: *The captain was degraded for disobeying orders.* **2.** make worse; lower; debase: *You degrade yourself when you tell a lie.*　*v.*

de i ty (dē′ə tē),　**1.** god or goddess. **2.** divine nature; being a god: *Christians believe in the deity of Christ.*　*n.*, *pl.* **de i ties.**

de ject ed (di jek′tid),　in low spirits; sad; discouraged.　*adj.* —**de ject′ed ly,** *adv.*

de lib er a tion (di lib′ər ā′shən),　**1.** careful thought. **2.** discussion of reasons for and against something; debate: *the deliberations of Congress.* **3.** slowness and care: *The hunter aimed his gun with great deliberation.*　*n.*

de lir i ous (di lir′ē əs),　**1.** temporarily out of one's senses; wandering in mind; raving. **2.** wildly excited.　*adj.* —**de lir′i ous ly,** *adv.*

de lir i um (di lir′ē əm),　**1.** a temporary disorder of the mind that occurs during fevers, insanity, drunkenness, etc. Delirium is characterized by excitement, irrational talk, and hallucinations. **2.** any wild excitement that cannot be controlled. *n., pl.* **de lir i ums, de lir i a** (-lir′ē ə).

de liv er ance (di liv′ər əns),   act of setting free or state of being set free; rescue. *n.*

del uge (del′yüj),   **1.** a great flood. **2.** a heavy fall of rain. **3.** any overwhelming rush: *Most stores have a deluge of orders just before Christmas.* *n.*

delve (delv),   **1.** search carefully for information. **2.** *Archaic* or *Dialect.* dig. *v.*

de mor al ize (di môr′əl īz),   **1.** corrupt the morals of: *The drug habit demoralizes people.* **2.** weaken the spirit, courage, or discipline of; dishearten: *Lack of food and ammunition demoralized the besieged soldiers.* *v.*

de mount a ble (dē moun′tə bəl),   that can be removed: *a demountable wheel rim.* *adj.*

de mure (di myùr′),   **1.** artificially proper; assuming an air of modesty; coy: *the demure smile of a flirt.* **2.** serious; thoughtful; sober: *The Puritan maid was demure.* *adj.* —**de mure′ly,** *adv.* —**de mure′ness,** *n.*

de pres sion (di presh′ən),   **1.** act of pressing down; a sinking; a lowering: *A rapid depression of the mercury in a barometer usually indicates a storm.* **2.** depressed condition. **3.** a low place; hollow. **4.** sadness; gloominess; low spirits. *n.*

des e crate (des′ə krāt),   treat or use without respect; disregard the sacredness of: *The enemy desecrated the church by using it as a stable.* *v.*

des o la tion (des ə lā′shən),   **1.** act of making desolate. **2.** a ruined, lonely, or deserted condition. **3.** a desolate place. **4.** sadness; lonely sorrow. *n.*

des per ate (des′pər it),   **1.** reckless because of despair; willing to run any risk: *a desperate robber.* **2.** showing recklessness caused by despair; violent: *Suicide is a desperate act.* **3.** with little or no hope of improvement: *a desperate illness.* *adj.* —**des′per ate ly,** *adv.*

des per a tion (des′pər ā′shən),   loss of hope; recklessness caused by despair; willingness to run any risk: *In desperation he jumped out of the window when he saw that the stairs were on fire.* *n.*

des ti na tion (des′tə nā′shən),   place to which a person or thing is going or is being sent. *n.*

des ti ny (des′tə nē),   **1.** what becomes of a person or thing in the end; one's lot or fortune: *It was his destiny to die in battle.* **2.** what will happen in spite of all efforts to change or prevent it. **3.** power that foreordains; overruling necessity; fate. *n., pl.* **des ti nies.**

de tached (di tacht′),   **1.** separate from others; isolated: *A detached house is not in a solid row with others.* **2.** not influenced by others or by one's own interests and prejudices; impartial. *adj.*

dev as tate (dev′əs tāt),   make desolate; destroy: *A long war devastated the border towns.* *v.*

de vi a tion (dē′vē ā′shən),   a turning aside from a way, course, rule, truth, etc.; divergence: *No deviation from the rules will be allowed. The iron in the ship caused a deviation of the magnetic needle of the compass.* *n.*

dex ter i ty (deks ter′ə tē),   **1.** skill in using the hands: *A good surgeon works with dexterity.* **2.** skill in using the mind; cleverness. *n.*

dif fi dent (dif′ə dənt),   lacking in self-confidence; shy. *adj.* —**dif′fi dent ly,** *adv.*

dig ni tar y (dig′nə ter′ē),   person who has a position of honor. *n., pl.* **dig ni tar ies.**

dig ni ty (dig′nə tē),   **1.** proud and self-respecting character or manner; stateliness. **2.** quality of character or ability that wins the respect and high opinion of others. **3.** a high office, rank, or title. **4.** worth; nobleness: *Honest work has dignity; idleness has none.* *n., pl.* **dig ni ties.**

di gres sion (də gresh′ən),   a turning aside; a getting off the main subject in talking or writing. *n.*

di late (dī lāt′),   make or become larger or wider: *The pupil of the eye dilates when the light gets dim.* *v.*

dil i gent (dil′ə jənt),   **1.** hard-working; industrious. **2.** careful and steady. *adj.* —**dil′i gent ly,** *adv.*

di min ish (də min′ish),   make or become smaller in size, amount, or importance; lessen; reduce. *v.*

di min u en do (də min′yü en′dō),   a gradual lessening of loudness. The sign in music for a diminuendo is *dim., dimin.,* or ▭. *n.*

dink y (dingk′ē),   *Slang.* small; insignificant. *adj.,* **dink i er, dink i est.**

dis ci pli nar i an (dis′ə plə ner′ē ən or dis′ə plə nar′ē ən),   person who enforces discipline or who believes in strict discipline. *n.*

dis count (dis′kount or dis kount′ for 1,3; dis′-kount for 2),   **1.** deduct (a certain percentage) of the amount or cost: *The store discounts 3 per cent on all bills paid when due.* **2.** deduction from the amount or cost: *During the sale the dealer allowed a 10 per cent discount on all cash purchases.* **3.** allow for exaggeration, prejudice, or inaccuracy in; believe only part of: *You must discount what Jack tells you, for he is too fond of a good story.* **1,3** *v.,* **2** *n.*

dis creet (dis krēt′),   careful and sensible in speech and action; wisely cautious; showing good sense. *adj.* —**dis creet′ly,** *adv.*

dis dain ful (dis dān′fəl),   contemptuous; scornful. *adj.* —**dis dain′ful ly,** *adv.*

dis em bark (dis′em bärk′),   **1.** go or put ashore from a ship; land from a ship. **2.** get out of any vehicle. *v.*

dis em bod y (dis′em bod′ē),   separate (a soul, spirit, etc.) from the body: *Ghosts are usually thought of as disembodied spirits.* *v.,* **dis em bod ied, dis em bod y ing.**

dis fig ure (dis fig′yər),   spoil the appearance of; mar the beauty of: *Large billboards disfigured the countryside.* *v.*

dis in te grate (dis in′tə grāt),   break up; separate into small parts or bits. *v.*

dis in ter est ed (dis in′tər is tid or dis in′tər-es′tid),   **1.** free from selfish motives; impartial; fair: *A judge should be disinterested.* **2.** uninterested. *adj.*

---

hat, āge, fär; let, bē, tėrm; it, īce; hot, gō, ôrder;   oil, out; cup, pút, rüle;   ch, child; ng, long; th, thin; ŦH, then; zh, measure;   ə represents *a* in about, *e* in taken, *i* in April, *o* in lemon, *u* in circus.

dis may (dis mā′),   **1.** loss of courage because of fear of what is about to happen. **2.** trouble greatly; make afraid.   1 *n.*,   2 *v.*

dis pens er (dis pen′sər),   one in charge of a place where medicines, or medical or dental help, are given out.   *n.*

dis perse (dis pėrs′),   spread in different directions; scatter.   *v.*

dis pos al (dis pō′zəl),   **1.** act of getting rid (of something): *the disposal of garbage.* **2.** an arranging of matters; a settling of affairs: *Mary's disposal of the difficulty pleased everybody.*   *n.*
at or **in one's disposal,** ready for one's use or service at any time; under one's control or management.

dis re spect ful (dis′ri spekt′fəl),   rude; showing no respect; lacking in courtesy to elders or superiors: *The disrespectful boy laughed at his father.*   *adj.*   —**dis′re spect′ful ly,** *adv.*

dis sent (di sent′),   **1.** differ in opinion; disagree. **2.** difference of opinion; disagreement. **3.** refuse to conform to the rules and beliefs of an established church.   1,3 *v.*,   2 *n.*

dis sent er (di sen′tər),   person who dissents.   *n.*

dis taste ful (dis tāst′fəl),   unpleasant; disagreeable; offensive.   *adj.*

dis tin guish a ble (dis ting′gwi shə bəl),   capable of being distinguished; able to be separated or detected.   *adj.*   —**dis tin′guish a bly,** *adv.*

dis tract (dis trakt′),   **1.** draw away (the mind, attention, etc.): *Noise distracts my attention from studying.* **2.** confuse; disturb; bewilder: *Several people talking at once distract a listener.*   *v.*
—**dis tract′ed ly,** *adv.*

dis tress (dis tres′),   **1.** great pain or sorrow; anxiety; trouble. **2.** cause pain, grief, or suffering to; make miserable or troubled.   1 *n.*,   2 *v.*
—**dis tress′ing ly,** *adv.*

ditch (dich),   **1.** a long, narrow place dug in the earth, usually used to carry off water. **2.** dig a ditch in. **3.** run or throw into a ditch: *The careless driver ditched his car.* **4.** land (an airplane not equipped for the purpose) on water. **5.** *Slang.* get rid of.   1 *n.*,   2-5 *v.*

dive (dīv),   **1.** plunge head first into water. **2.** go down or out of sight suddenly: *He dived into an alley.* **3.** of an airplane, plunge downward at a steep angle. **4.** plunge the hand suddenly into anything: *He dived into his pockets and fished out a dollar.*   *v.*

di vert (də vėrt′),   **1.** turn aside: *A ditch diverted water from the stream into the fields.* **2.** amuse; entertain: *Music diverted him after a hard day's work.*   *v.*

dob bin (dob′ən),   a slow, gentle horse.   *n.*

doc ile (dos′əl),   **1.** easily managed; obedient: *a docile dog.* **2.** easily taught; willing to learn: *a docile pupil.*   *adj.*   —**doc′ile ly,** *adv.*

do main (dō mān′),   **1.** territory under the control of one ruler or government. **2.** land owned by one person; estate.   *n.*

do mes tic (də mes′tik),   **1.** of the home, household, or family affairs: *domestic cares, a domestic scene.* **2.** fond of home and family life. **3.** servant in a household. **4.** not wild; tame. Cats, dogs, cows, horses, sheep, and pigs are domestic animals. **5.** of one's own country; not foreign:

This newspaper publishes both domestic and foreign news.   1,2,4,5 *adj.*,   3 *n.*

dom i nate (dom′ə nāt),   **1.** control or rule by strength or power: *A man of strong will often dominates others.* **2.** rise high above; hold a commanding position over: *The mountain dominates the harbor.*   *v.*

door jamb (dôr′jam′),   the upright piece forming the side of a doorway.   *n.*

dor sal (dôr′səl),   of, on, or near the back: *a dorsal fin, a dorsal nerve.*   *adj.*

dote (dōt),   be weak-minded and childish because of old age.   *v.*
dote on or **upon,**   be foolishly fond of; be too fond of.

douse (dous),   **1.** plunge into water or any other liquid. **2.** throw water over; drench. **3.** *Informal.* put out (a light); extinguish.   *v.*

dow ry (dou′rē),   money, property, etc., that a woman brings to her husband when she marries him.   *n., pl.* **dow ries.** Also, **dower.**

drive (drīv),   **1.** make go: *Drive the dog away. Drive the nails into the board. Grief drove her insane.* **2.** force (into or out of some place, condition, act, etc.): *Hunger drove him to steal.* **3.** direct the movement of (an automobile, vehicle drawn by a horse, etc.). **4.** trip in an automobile, carriage, etc. **5.** carry out with vigor; bring about: *drive a bargain.* **6.** vigor; energy. **7.** pressure; impelling force: *The craving for approval is a strong drive in mankind.* 1-3, 5 *v.*, **drove, driv en, driv ing;** 4,6,7 *n.*

eaves (ēvz),   the lower edges of a roof projecting beyond the wall of a building.   *n., pl.*

ec cen tric i ty (ek′sen tris′ə tē),   **1.** something queer or out of the ordinary; oddity; peculiarity. **2.** eccentric condition; being unusual or out of the ordinary.   *n., pl.* **ec cen tric i ties.**

ec sta sy (ek′stə sē),   **1.** state of great joy; thrilling or overwhelming delight; rapture: *Speechless with ecstasy, the little boy gazed at the toys.* **2.** any strong feeling that completely absorbs the mind; uncontrollable emotion.   *n., pl.* **ec sta sies.**

ef fi ca cy (ef′ə kə sē),   power to produce a desired effect or result; effectiveness.   *n., pl.* **ef fi ca cies.**

egg (eg),   urge; encourage (with *on*): *The other boys egged him on to fight.*   *v.*

e ject (i jekt′),   throw out; force out; expel: *The volcano ejected lava and ashes.*   *v.*

e lab o rate (i lab′ə rit for 1; i lab′ə rāt for 2,3),   **1.** worked out with great care; having many details; complicated. **2.** work out with great care; add details to: *The inventor spent months in elaborating his plans for a new engine.* **3.** talk, write, etc., in great detail; give added details: *The witness was asked to elaborate upon one of his statements.* 1 *adj.*,   2,3 *v.*   —**e lab′-o rate ly,** *adv.*

em a nate (em′ə nāt),   come forth: *Light and heat emanate from the sun.*   *v.*

em bark (em bärk′),   **1.** go on board ship: *Many people embark for Europe in New York.* **2.** set out; start: *After leaving college, the young man embarked upon a business career.*   *v.*

em bold en (em bōl′dən), make bold; encourage. *v.*

em broil (em broil′), 1. involve (a person, country, etc.) in a quarrel. 2. throw (affairs, etc.) into a state of confusion. *v.*

e merge (i mèrj′), come out; come up; come into view: *The sun emerged from behind a cloud. New facts emerged as a result of the investigation. v.*

em i nence (em′ə nəns), 1. rank or position above all or most others; high standing; greatness; fame. 2. a high place; lofty hill. *n.*

em pha size (em′fə sīz), 1. give special force to; stress; make important. 2. call attention to. *v.*

en coun ter (en koun′tər), 1. meet unexpectedly: *I encountered an old friend on the train.* 2. a meeting; unexpected meeting. 1 *v.*, 2 *n.*

en dow (en dou′), 1. give money or property to provide an income for: *The rich man endowed the college he had attended.* 2. furnish from birth; provide with some ability, quality, or talent: *Nature endowed her with both beauty and brains. v.*

en gage (en gāj′), 1. bind oneself; promise; pledge: *I will engage to be there on time.* 2. promise or pledge to marry: *John and Mary are engaged. John is engaged to Mary.* 3. keep busy; occupy: *Work engages much of his time.* 4. fit into; lock together. The teeth of one gear engage with the teeth of another. The teeth engage each other. 5. start a battle with; attack: *Our soldiers engaged the enemy. v.*

Cogwheels engaged

en gulf (en gulf′), swallow up; overwhelm; submerge: *A wave engulfed the small boat. v.*

en mi ty (en′mə tē), the feeling that enemies have for each other; hate. *n., pl.* **en mi ties.**

en thrall or **en thral** (en thrôl′), 1. captivate; fascinate; charm: *The explorer enthralled the audience with the story of his exciting adventures.* 2. make a slave of; enslave. *v.,* **enthralled, en thrall ing.**

en to mol o gy (en′tə mol′ə jē), branch of zoology that deals with insects. *n.*

en trance (en trans′), 1. put into a trance. 2. fill with joy; delight; charm. *n.*

e ro sion (i rō′zhən), a gradual eating or wearing away by glaciers, running water, waves, or wind: *Trees help prevent the erosion of soil by running water. n.*

er rat ic (ə rat′ik), 1. not steady; uncertain; irregular: *An erratic mind jumps from one idea to another.* 2. queer; odd: *erratic behavior. adj.*

erst while (èrst′hwīl′), former; past. *adj.*

e rup tion (i rup′shən), 1. a bursting forth. 2. a throwing forth of lava, etc., from a volcano or of hot water from a geyser. 3. a breaking out in a rash. 4. red spots on the skin; rash: *Scarlet fever causes an eruption on the body.* 5. outbreak; outburst. *n.*

es o ter ic (es′ə ter′ik), understood only by the select few; intended for an inner circle of disciples, scholars, etc. *adj.*

e vac u ate (i vak′yu āt), 1. leave empty; withdraw from: *After surrendering, the soldiers evacuated the fort.* 2. withdraw; remove. 3. make empty. *v.*

e vade (i vād′), 1. get away from by trickery; avoid by cleverness: *The thief evaded his pursuers and escaped. The witness tried to evade an embarrassing question.* 2. avoid the truth by indefinite or misleading statements. *v.*

e va sive (i vā′siv), tending or trying to evade: *"Perhaps" is an evasive answer. adj.* —**e va′sive ly,** *adv.* —**e va′sive ness,** *n.*

ev i dence (ev′ə dəns), 1. whatever makes clear the truth or falsehood of something: *The evidence showed that he had not been near the place.* 2. facts established and accepted in a court of law. Before deciding a case, the judge or jury hears all the evidence given by both sides. 3. indication; sign: *A smile gives evidence of pleasure. n.*

ex as per ate (eg zas′pə rāt′), irritate very much; annoy extremely; make angry: *The child's endless questions exasperated her father. v.*

ex clu sion (eks klü′zhən), 1. an excluding. 2. a being excluded: *Amy's exclusion from the club hurt her feelings. n.*

to the exclusion of, so as to shut out or keep out.

ex hil a ra tion (eg zil′ə rā′shən), a being or feeling exhilarated; high spirits; stimulation. *n.*

ex ten sive (eks ten′siv), 1. of great extent; wide; broad; large: *an extensive park.* 2. far-reaching; affecting many things; comprehensive: *extensive changes. adj.* —**ex ten′sive ly,** *adv.*

ex trav a gance (eks trav′ə gəns), 1. careless and lavish spending; wastefulness. 2. a going beyond the bounds of reason; excess: *The extravagance of the salesman's claims caused us to doubt the worth of his product. n.*

ex ude (eg züd′ or ek syüd′), 1. come or send out in drops; ooze: *Sweat exudes from the pores in the skin.* 2. give forth. *v.*

fa ble (fā′bəl), 1. story made up to teach a lesson. Fables are often about animals who can talk. 2. an untrue story; falsehood. 3. legend; myth. *n.*

fab u lous (fab′yə ləs), 1. not believable; amazing: *That antique shop asks fabulous prices.* 2. of or belonging to a fable; imaginary: *The phoenix is a fabulous bird.* 3. like a fable. *adj.*

face (fās), 1. the front part of the head. 2. look; expression. 3. the front part; right side; surface. 4. personal importance; dignity; self-respect: *Face is very important to Oriental peoples. n.*

fa cil i ty (fə sil′ə tē), 1. absence of difficulty; ease. 2. power to do anything easily, quickly, and smoothly. 3. something that serves a special function or makes an action easy; aid; convenience: *Ropes, swings, and sand piles are facilities for play. n., pl.* **fa cil i ties.**

fa kir (fə kir′ or fā′kər), 1. a Moslem holy man who lives by begging. 2. a Hindu ascetic. Some fakirs lie on nails. *n.*

hat, āge, fär; let, bē, tèrm; it, īce; hot, gō, ôrder; oil, out; cup, pùt, rüle; ch, child; ng, long; th, thin; ᴛH, then; zh, measure; ə represents *a* in about, *e* in taken, *i* in April, *o* in lemon, *u* in circus.

false hood (fôls'hůd), 1. quality of being false; falsity. 2. something false. 3. a false statement; lie. *n.*

fal ter (fôl'tər), 1. lose courage; draw back; hesitate; waver: *The soldiers faltered for a moment as their captain fell.* 2. move unsteadily; stumble; totter. 3. speak in hesitating, broken words; stammer. *v.*

fau na (fô'nə), animals of a given region or time: *the fauna of Australia.* *n.*

feign (fān), 1. put on a false appearance of; make believe; pretend: *Some animals feign death when in danger.* 2. make up to deceive; invent falsely: *feign an excuse.* *v.*

feint (fānt), 1. a false appearance; pretense: *The boy made a feint of studying hard, though actually he was listening to the radio.* 2. movement intended to deceive; pretended blow; sham attack. 3. make a pretended blow or sham attack: *The fighter feinted with his right hand and struck with his left.* 1,2 *n.*, 3 *v.*

fer-de-lance (fer'də läNs'), a large, poisonous snake of tropical America. *n.*

fer vor (fer'vər), 1. great warmth of feeling; intense emotion: *The patriot's voice trembled from the fervor of his emotion.* 2. great interest and enthusiasm; zeal. *n.*

feud (fyüd), 1. a long and deadly quarrel between families, tribes, etc., often passed down from generation to generation. 2. continued strife between two persons, groups, etc. *n.*

Fi ber glas (fī'bər glas' or fī'bər gläs'), very fine, flexible threads of glass that can be made into insulating material or fabrics. *n.*

fic ti tious (fik tish'əs), 1. not real; imaginary; made-up: *Characters in novels are usually fictitious.* 2. assumed in order to deceive; false: *The criminal used a fictitious name.* *adj.*

fire brand (fīr'brand'), 1. piece of burning wood. 2. person who arouses angry feelings in others. *n.*

flab ber gast (flab'ər gast), *Informal.* amaze. *v.*

flag (flag), get tired; grow weak; droop: *After you do the same thing for a long time, your interest flags.* *v.*, **flagged, flag ging.**

flange (flanj), a projecting edge, rim, collar, etc., on an object for keeping it in place, attaching it to another object, strengthening it, etc. Railroad cars and locomotives have wheels with flanges to keep them on the track. *n.*

flank (flangk), 1. side of an animal or person between the ribs and the hip. 2. piece of beef cut from this part. 3. side of a mountain, building, etc. 4. be at the side of: *High buildings flanked the dark, narrow alley.* 5. the far right or left side of an army, fleet, etc. 6. get around the far right or left side of. 7. attack from or on the side. 1-3,5 *n.*, 4,6,7 *v.*

flaw (flô), 1. defective place; crack: *A flaw in the dish caused it to break.* 2. fault; defect: *a flaw in a man's character.* *n.*

fledg ling or **fledge ling** (flej'ling), 1. a young bird just able to fly. 2. a young, inexperienced person. *n.*

fleet (flēt), 1. swift; rapid: *a fleet horse.* 2. pass swiftly; move rapidly. 1 *adj.*, 2 *v.*

flinch (flinch), draw back from difficulty, danger, or pain; shrink: *The baby flinched when he touched the radiator.* *v.*

fliv ver (fliv'ər), *Slang.* a small, cheap automobile. *n.*

flog (flog), whip very hard; beat with a whip, stick, etc. *v.*, **flogged, flog ging.**

flour ish (flėr'ish), 1. grow or develop with vigor; thrive; do well. 2. wave (a sword, stick, arm, etc.) in the air. 3. a waving in the air: *The donkey gave a flourish of his heels.* 4. a showy display: *The agent showed us about the house with much flourish.* 5. make a showy display. 1,2,5 *v.*, 3,4 *n.*

flue (flü), tube, pipe, or other enclosed passage for conveying smoke, hot air, etc. A chimney often has several flues. *n.*

flus ter (flus'tər), 1. make nervous and excited; confuse. 2. nervous excitement; confusion. 1 *v.*, 2 *n.*

fo cus (fō'kəs), 1. point where rays of light, heat, etc., meet, appear to meet, or should meet after being bent by a lens, curved mirror, etc. 2. bring (rays of light, heat, etc.) to a point: *The lens focused the sun's rays on a piece of paper and burned a hole in it.* 3. correct adjustment of a lens, the eye, etc., to make a clear image: *If the camera is not brought into focus, the photograph will be blurred.* 4. adjust (a lens, the eye, etc.) to make a clear image. 5. the central point of attention, activity, disturbance, etc. 6. concentrate: *When studying, he focused his mind on his lessons.* 1,3,5 *n., pl.* **fo cus es** or **fo ci;** 2,4,6 *v.*

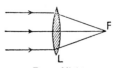

Rays of light brought to a focus at F by the lens, L.

foil (foil), prevent from carrying out (plans, attempts, etc.); get the better of; turn aside or hinder: *The hero foiled the villain.* *v.*

for ay (fôr'ā), 1. a raid for plunder. 2. plunder; lay waste; pillage. 1 *n.*, 2 *v.*

for ceps (fôr'seps), small pincers or tongs used by surgeons, dentists, etc., for seizing, holding, and pulling. *n., pl.* **for ceps.**

fore tell (fôr tel'), tell or show beforehand; predict; prophesy: *Who can foretell what a baby will do next?* *v.*, **fore told, fore tell ing.**

for lorn (fôr lôrn'), 1. left alone; neglected; deserted: *The lost kitten, a forlorn little animal, was wet and dirty.* 2. wretched in feeling or looks; unhappy. 3. hopeless; desperate. *adj.* —**for lorn'ly,** *adv.* —**for lorn'ness,** *n.*

for mal (fôr'məl), 1. with strict attention to outward forms and ceremonies; not familiar and homelike; stiff: *A judge has a formal manner in a law court.* 2. according to set customs or rules. 3. done with the proper forms; clear and definite: *A written contract is a formal agreement to do something.* *adj.* —**for'mal ly,** *adv.*

for mi da ble (fôr'mə də bəl), hard to overcome; hard to deal with; to be dreaded. *adj.*

forth com ing (fôrth'kum'ing), 1. about to appear; approaching: *The forthcoming week will be busy.* 2. ready when wanted: *She needed help, but none was forthcoming.* *adj.*

fort night (fôrt'nīt), two weeks. *n.*

fran tic (fran′tik), very much excited; wild with rage, fear, pain, grief, etc. *adj.* —**fran′-ti cal ly**, *adv.*

fra ter nal (frə tèr′nl), **1.** brotherly. **2.** of twins, coming from two separately fertilized egg cells, as distinguished from identical twins. *adj.*

freight (frāt), **1.** load of goods carried on a train, ship, etc. **2.** the carrying of goods on a train, ship, etc.: *He sent the box by freight.* **3.** carry as freight. **4.** load; burden. **1,2,4** *n.*, **3,4** *v.*

fren zy (fren′zē), brief fury; near madness; very great excitement. *n., pl.* **fren zies.**

fric tion (frik′shən), **1.** a rubbing of one object against another; rubbing: *Matches are lighted by friction.* **2.** resistance to motion of surfaces that touch. **3.** conflict of differing ideas, opinions, etc.; disagreement: *Constant friction between the two nations finally caused a war.* *n.*

frus trate (frus′trāt), **1.** bring to nothing; make useless or worthless; foil; defeat: *Heavy rain frustrated our plans for a picnic.* **2.** thwart; oppose. *v.*

fu gi tive (fyü′jə tiv), **1.** person who is fleeing or who has fled. **2.** fleeing; having fled; runaway: *a fugitive slave.* **1** *n.*, **2** *adj.*

ful fill ment or **ful fil ment** (fúl fil′mənt), a fulfilling; completion; performance; accomplishment. *n.*

fur lough (fèr′lō), leave of absence, especially for a soldier. *n.*

fur tive (fèr′tiv), **1.** done stealthily; secret: *a furtive glance into the forbidden room.* **2.** sly; stealthy; shifty: *The thief had a furtive manner.* *adj.* —**fur′tive ly**, *adv.* —**fur′tive ness**, *n.*

fu ry (fyúr′ē), **1.** wild, fierce anger; rage. **2.** violence; fierceness: *the fury of a hurricane.* **3.** a raging or violent person. *n., pl.* **fu ries.**

fu se lage (fyü′zə läzh or fyü′zə lij), framework of the body of an airplane that holds passengers, cargo, etc. The wings and tail are fastened to it. *n.*

fu tile (fyü′tl), **1.** not successful; useless. **2.** not important; trifling. *adj.*

gale (gāl), **1.** a very strong wind. **2.** wind with a velocity of 25 to 75 miles per hour. **3.** a noisy outburst: *gales of laughter.* *n.*

gall (gôl), **1.** make or become sore by rubbing: *The rough strap galled the horse's skin.* **2.** annoy; irritate. *v.*

gar rote (gə rot′ or gə rōt′), **1.** a Spanish method of executing a person by strangling him with an iron collar. The collar is fastened to a post and tightened by a screw. **2.** execute by garroting. **3.** strangle and rob; strangle. **1** *n.*, **2,3** *v.*

gaunt (gônt), **1.** very thin and bony; with hollow eyes and a starved look: *Hunger and suffering make people gaunt.* **2.** looking bare and gloomy; desolate; forbidding; grim: *the gaunt slopes of a high mountain in winter.* *adj.*

gauze (gôz), **1.** a very thin, light cloth, easily seen through. **2.** a thin haze. *n.*

gear ing (gir′ing), set of gears, chains, etc., for transmitting motion or power; gears. *n.*

gen er a tion (jen′ər ā′shən), **1.** all the people born about the same time. **2.** time from the birth of one generation to the birth of the next generation; about 30 years. **3.** one step or degree in the descent of a family: *The picture showed four generations — great-grandmother, grandmother, mother, and baby.* *n.*

gen er a tor (jen′ər ā′tər), **1.** machine that changes mechanical energy into electrical energy; dynamo. **2.** apparatus for producing gas or steam. **3.** person or thing that generates. *n.*

ges tic u late (jes tik′yə lāt), **1.** make or use gestures. **2.** make or use many vehement gestures: *He gesticulated by raising his arms, pounding the desk, and stamping his foot.* *v.*

ghoul (gül), **1.** a horrible demon in Oriental stories, believed to feed on corpses. **2.** person who robs graves or corpses. **3.** person who enjoys what is revolting, brutal, and horrible. *n.*

ghoul ish (gül′ish), like a ghoul; revolting, brutal, and horrible. *adj.* —**ghoul′ish ly**, *adv.*

gin ger ly (jin′jər lē), with extreme care or caution. *adv., adj.* —**gin′ger li ness**, *n.*

glad i a tor (glad′ē ā′tər), **1.** slave, captive, or paid fighter who fought at the public shows in ancient Rome. **2.** person who argues, fights, wrestles, etc., with great skill. *n.*

glib (glib), **1.** speaking or spoken smoothly and easily: *A glib salesman sold her a set of dishes that she did not want.* **2.** speaking or spoken too smoothly and easily to be sincere: *No one believed his glib excuses.* *adj.* —**glib′ly**, *adv.*

glow er (glou′ər), **1.** stare angrily; scowl: *The fighters glowered at each other.* **2.** an angry or sullen look. **1** *v.*, **2** *n.*

gnarled (närld), covered with knots or hard, rough lumps; knotted; twisted; rugged: *The farmer's gnarled hands grasped the plow firmly.* *adj.*

gouge (gouj), **1.** chisel with a curved blade. Gouges are used for cutting round grooves or holes in wood. **2.** cut with a gouge. **3.** groove or hole made by gouging. **4.** dig out; tear out; force out. **5.** *U.S. Informal.* trick; cheat; swindle. **1,3,5** *n.*, **2,4,5** *v.*

gran ite (gran′it), a hard igneous rock made of grains of other rocks, chiefly quartz and feldspar. Granite is much used for buildings and monuments. *n.*

grat i fy (grat′ə fī), **1.** give pleasure or satisfaction to; please: *Flattery gratifies a vain person.* **2.** satisfy; indulge: *A drunkard gratifies his craving for liquor.* *v.*, **grat i fied, grat i fy ing.**

grave (grāv), **1.** important; weighty; momentous: *grave cares.* **2.** serious; threatening: *grave questions, doubts, symptoms, news.* **3.** dignified; sober; solemn: *a grave face, a grave ceremony.* **4.** somber: *grave colors.* *adj.* —**grave′ly**, *adv.*

griev ance (grē′vəns), a real or imagined wrong; reason for being angry or annoyed; cause for complaint. *n.*

gri mace (grə mās′ or grim′is), **1.** a twisting

---

hat, āge, fär; let, bē, tèrm; it, īce; hot, gō, ôrder; oil, out; cup, pút, rüle; ch, child; ng, long; th, thin; ṭH, then; zh, measure; ə represents *a* in about, *e* in taken, *i* in April, *o* in lemon, *u* in circus.

of the face; ugly or funny smile: *a grimace caused by pain.* **2.** make grimaces. **1** *n.,* **2** *v.*

griz zled (griz′əld), **1.** grayish; gray. **2.** grayhaired. *adj.*

grog (grog), *Esp. Brit.* **1.** drink made of rum or any other strong alcoholic liquor, diluted with water. **2.** any strong alcoholic liquor. *n.*

grog gy (grog′ē), *Informal.* **1.** shaky; unsteady. **2.** drunk; intoxicated. *adj.* —**grog′gi ly,** *adv.*

grope (grōp), **1.** feel about with the hands: *He groped for a flashlight when the lights went out.* **2.** search blindly and uncertainly: *The detectives groped for some clue to the murder.* *v.*

gro tesque (grō tesk′), **1.** odd or unnatural in shape, appearance, manner, etc.; fantastic; queer: *The book had pictures of hideous dragons and other grotesque monsters.* **2.** ridiculous; absurd: *The monkey's grotesque antics made the children laugh. adj.* —**gro tesque′ly,** *adv.*

grot to (grot′ō), **1.** cave. **2.** an artificial cave made for coolness or pleasure. *n., pl.* **grot toes** or **grot tos.**

ground nut (ground′nut′), **1.** any of various plants having edible underground parts, such as the peanut. **2.** the edible tuber, pod, or the like, of such a plant. *n.*

grudg ing ly (gruj′ing lē), unwillingly. *adj.*

gru el ing or **gru el ling** (grü′əl ing), *Informal.* exhausting; very tiring: *a grueling contest. adj.*

guise (gīz), **1.** style of dress; garb: *The soldier went in the guise of a monk and was not recognized.* **2.** external appearance; aspect; semblance: *His theory is nothing but an old idea in a new guise.* **3.** assumed appearance; pretense: *Under the guise of friendship he plotted treachery. n.*

gul ly (gul′ē), **1.** a narrow gorge; small ravine; ditch made by running water. **2.** make gullies in. **1** *n., pl.* **gul lies;** **2** *v.,* **gul lied, gul ly ing.**

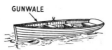
GUNWALE

gun wale (gun′l), the upper edge of a ship's or boat's side. *n.* Also, **gunnel.**

hag gard (hag′ərd), looking worn from pain, fatigue, worry, hunger, etc.; gaunt; careworn. *adj.*

hag gle (hag′l), dispute about a price or the terms of a bargain; wrangle. *v.*

ha lo (hā′lō), **1.** ring of light around the sun, moon, or other shining body. **2.** a golden circle or disk of light represented about the head of a saint, etc., in pictures, etc. *n., pl.* **ha los** or **ha loes.**
Halo about the head of Joan of Arc

ham a dry ad (ham′ə drī′əd), **1.** in Greek mythology, a wood nymph supposed to live and die with the tree she dwelt in; dryad. **2.** king cobra. *n.*

hand out (hand′out′), *U.S. Slang.* portion of food handed out: *The tramp was given a handout.*

hap haz ard (hap′haz′ərd for 1; hap′haz′ərd for 2,3), **1.** chance. **2.** random; not planned: *Haphazard answers are usually wrong.* **3.** by chance; at random. **1** *n.,* **2** *adj.,* **3** *adv.* —**hap′haz′ard ly,** *adv.*

har ass (har′əs or hə ras′), **1.** trouble by repeated attacks; harry: *Pirates harassed the villages along the coast.* **2.** disturb; worry; torment. *v.*

har bin ger (här′bin jər), one that goes ahead to announce another's coming; forerunner: *The robin is a harbinger of spring.* *n.*

har mon i ca (här mon′ə kə), a small, oblong musical instrument with metal reeds, played by the mouth; mouth organ. *n.*

har row (har′ō), **1.** a heavy frame with iron teeth or upright disks. Harrows are drawn over plowed land to break up clods, cover seeds, etc. **2.** draw a harrow over (land, etc.). **3.** hurt; wound. **4.** arouse uncomfortable feelings in; distress; torment: *He harrowed us with a tale of ghosts.* **1** *n.,* **2-4** *v.*

Harmonica

haugh ty (hô′tē), too proud of oneself and too scornful of others: *A haughty girl is always unpopular. adj.* —**haugh′ti ly,** *adv.*

hav oc (hav′ək), very great destruction or injury: *Tornadoes, severe earthquakes, and plagues create widespread havoc. n.*

hawk (hôk), **1.** carry (goods) about for sale as a street peddler does. **2.** spread (a report) around. *v.*

haz ard (haz′ərd), **1.** risk; danger; peril: *The life of an aviator is full of hazards.* **2.** chance. **3.** take a chance with; risk; venture: *I would hazard my life on his honesty.* **4.** any obstruction on a golf course. **1,2,4** *n.,* **3** *v.*

hearth (härth), **1.** floor of a fireplace. **2.** home; fireside: *The soldiers longed for their own hearths. n.*

heave (hēv), **1.** lift with force or effort: *He heaved the heavy box into the wagon.* **2.** lift and throw: *The sailors heaved the anchor overboard.* **3.** act or fact of heaving. **1,2** *v.,* **heaved** or (*esp. Naut.*) **hove, heav ing; 3** *n.*

height en (hīt′n), **1.** make or become higher. **2.** make or become stronger or greater; increase. *v.*

helm (helm), **1.** handle or wheel by which a ship is steered. **2.** position of control or guidance. *n.*

hem i sphere (hem′ə sfir), **1.** half of a sphere or globe. **2.** half of the earth's surface. *n.*

her it age (her′ə tij), what is or may be handed on to a person from his ancestors; inheritance. *n.*

her pe tol o gy (hèr′pə tol′ə jē), branch of zoology dealing with reptiles. *n.*

hes i tant (hez′ə tənt), hesitating; doubtful; undecided. *adj.* —**hes′i tant ly,** *adv.*

hie (hī), hasten; go quickly. *v.*

hitch (hich), **1.** fasten with a hook, ring, rope, strap, etc.: *He hitched his horse to a post.* **2.** harness to a wagon, carriage, etc.: *The farmer hitched up his team and drove to town.* **3.** a fastening; catch: *The hitch joining the plow to the tractor is broken.* **4.** obstacle; hindrance: *A hitch in their plans made them miss the train.* **5.** kind of knot used for temporary fastening. **1,2** *v.,* **3-5** *n.*

hoax (hōks), **1.** a mischievous trick; especially,

a made-up story: *The report of an attack on the earth from Mars was a hoax.* **2.** play a mischievous trick on; deceive in jest or in malice. 1 *n.*, 2 *v.*

hob ble (hob′l), **1.** walk awkwardly; limp: *The wounded man hobbled away.* **2.** tie the legs of (a horse, etc.) together. **3.** hinder. **4.** an awkward or difficult situation. 1-3 *v.*, 4 *n.*

hoist (hoist), raise on high; lift up, often with ropes and pulleys: *hoist sails, hoist blocks of stone. v.*

hom bre (ôm′brā), *Spanish.* man *n.*

hood (hud), **1.** a soft covering for the head and neck, either separate or as part of a coat: *My raincoat has a hood.* **2.** part of the head of an animal that suggests a hood. *n.*

horde (hôrd), crowd; swarm: *hordes of grass-hoppers. n.*

hos tile (hos′tl; sometimes hos′tīl), **1.** of an enemy or enemies: *the hostile army.* **2.** opposed; unfriendly; unfavorable: *a hostile look. adj.*

hulk ing (hul′king), big and clumsy. *adj.*

hum ding er (hum′ding′ər), something extraordinary. *n.*

hu mil i a tion (hyü mil′ē ā′shən), **1.** a lowering of pride, dignity, or self-respect. **2.** state or feeling of being humiliated. *n.*

hu mil i ty (hyü mil′ə tē), humbleness of mind; lack of pride; meekness. *n., pl.* **hu mil i ties.**

hurl (hèrl), throw with much force: *The man hurled his spear at one bear, the dogs hurled themselves at the other. v.*

hur tle (hèr′tl), **1.** dash or drive violently; rush suddenly; come with a crash: *Spears hurtled against shields.* **2.** move with a clatter; rush noisily or violently: *The express train hurtled past. v.*

hys te ri a (his tir′ē ə or his ter′ē ə), **1.** a nervous disorder that causes violent fits of laughing and crying, imaginary illnesses, or general lack of self-control. **2.** senseless excitement. *n.*

hys ter i cal (his ter′ə kəl), **1.** unnaturally excited. **2.** showing an unnatural lack of control; unable to stop laughing, crying, etc.; suffering from hysteria. *adj.* —**hys ter′i cal ly,** *adv.*

il lit er ate (i lit′ər it), **1.** unable to read or write. **2.** person unable to read or write. **3.** person who lacks culture. 1 *adj.*, 2,3 *n.* —**il lit′-er ate ly,** *adv.*

ill re pute (il′ ri pyüt′), bad reputation. *n.*

il lu sion (i lü′zhən), **1.** appearance which is not real; misleading appearance: *an illusion of reality.* **2.** a false impression or perception: *That slender snow-covered bush at the gate produced the illusion of a woman waiting there.* **3.** a false idea, notion, or belief. *n.*

im mi nence (im′ə nəns), **1.** state or fact of being about to occur. **2.** thing that is imminent; evil or danger about to occur. *n.*

im mu ni ty (i myü′nə tē), **1.** resistance to disease, poison, etc.: *One attack of measles usually*

gives a person immunity to that disease for a number of years. **2.** freedom; protection: *The law gives schools and churches immunity from taxation. n., pl.* **im mu ni ties.**

im pact (im′pakt), a striking (of one thing against another); collision: *The impact of the two swords broke both of them. n.*

im pas sive (im pas′iv), **1.** without feeling or emotion; unmoved: *He listened with an impassive face.* **2.** not feeling pain or injury; insensible: *The soldier lay as impassive as if he were dead. adj.*

im pel (im pel′), **1.** drive; force; cause: *Hunger impelled the lazy man to work.* **2.** cause to move, drive forward; push along: *The wind impelled the boat to shore. v.,* **im pelled, im pel ling.**

im per a tive (im per′ə tiv), **1.** not to be avoided; urgent; necessary: *It is imperative that a very sick child stay in bed.* **2.** a command. 1 *adj.,* 2 *n.* —**im per′a tive ly,** *adv.*

im per cep ti ble (im′pər sep′tə bəl), **1.** very slight; gradual. **2.** that cannot be perceived or felt. *adj.* —**im′per cep′ti bly,** *adv.*

im per son ate (im pèr′sə nāt), **1.** act the part of. **2.** pretend to be; mimic the voice, appearance, and manners of: *impersonate a well-known news commentator. v.*

im per ti nence (im pèr′tə nəns), rudeness; impudence; insolence. *n.*

im per turb a ble (im′pər tèr′bə bəl), not easily excited; calm. *adj.* —**im′per turb′a bly,** *adv.*

im pla ca ble (im plā′kə bəl or im plak′ə bəl), that cannot be made calm, quiet, or satisfied; relentless. *adj.* —**im pla′ca bly,** *adv.*

im pli cate (im′plə kāt), **1.** show to have a part or to be connected; involve: *The thief's confession implicated two other men.* **2.** imply. **3.** entangle; fold or twist together. *v.*

im pli ca tion (im′plə kā′shən), **1.** meaning; significance. **2.** indirect suggestion; hint: *There was no implication of dishonesty in his failure in business. n.*

im press (im pres′), **1.** have a strong effect on the mind or feelings of: *A hero impresses us with his courage.* **2.** fix in the mind: *She repeated the words to impress them in her memory. v.*

im pres sion a ble (im presh′ə nə bəl), sensitive to impressions; easily impressed or influenced: *Children are more impressionable than adults. adj.*

im prop er (im prop′ər), **1.** not following accepted standards. **2.** not suitable. **3.** not decent. *adj.* —**im prop′er ly,** *adv.*

im pu ni ty (im pyü′nə tē), freedom from punishment, injury, or other bad consequences: *If laws are not enforced, crimes are committed with impunity. n.*

in ad e quate (in ad′ə kwit), not adequate; not enough; not as much as is required. *adj.* —**in ad′e quate ly,** *adv.*

in cen di ar y (in sen′dē er′ē), **1.** having to do with the setting of property on fire maliciously. **2.** person who maliciously sets fire to property.

---

hat, āge, fär; let, bē, tèrm; it, īce; hot, gō, ôrder; oil, out; cup, pu̇t, rüle; ch, child; ng, long; th, thin; ᴛʜ, then; zh, measure; ə represents *a* in about, *e* in taken, *i* in April, *o* in lemon, *u* in circus.

3. deliberately stirring up strife or rebellion: *The agitator was arrested for making incendiary speeches.* **4.** person who deliberately stirs up strife or rebellion. 1,3 *adj.*, 2,4 *n.*, *pl.* **in cen di ar ies.**

in ces sant (in ses′nt), never stopping; continued or repeated without interruption: *The roar of Niagara Falls is incessant. adj.* —**in ces′sant ly,** *adv.*

in ci sor (in sī′zər), tooth having a sharp edge for cutting; one of the front teeth between the canine teeth in either jaw. *n.*

in co her ent (in′kō hir′ənt), **1.** not sticking together. **2.** disconnected; confused. *adj.* —**in′ co her′ent ly,** *adv.*

in com pre hen si ble (in′kom pri hen′sə bəl), impossible to understand. *adj.* —**in′com pre hen′si bly,** *adv.*

in con gru ous (in kong′grù əs), out of keeping; not appropriate; out of place: *Heavy walking shoes would be incongruous with a party dress. adj.* —**in con′gru ous ly,** *adv.*

in con spic u ous (in′kən spik′yü əs), not conspicuous; attracting little or no attention. *adj.* —**in′con spic′u ous ly,** *adv.*

in cred u lous (in krej′ə ləs), **1.** not ready to believe; doubting. **2.** showing a lack of belief. *adj.* —**in cred′u lous ly,** *adv.*

in di cate (in′də kāt), **1.** point out; point to: *The arrow on the sign indicates the right way to go.* **2.** show; make known: *A thermometer indicates temperature.* **3.** be a sign or hint of: *Fever indicates sickness. v.*

in dif fer ent ly (in dif′ər ənt lē), without distinction; equally. *adv.*

in dig nant (in dig′nənt), angry at something unworthy, unjust, or mean. *adj.* —**in dig′ nant ly,** *adv.*

in dig na tion (in′dig nā′shən), anger at something unworthy, unjust, or mean; anger mixed with scorn; righteous anger: *Cruelty to animals arouses indignation. n.*

in dis put a ble (in′dis pyü′tə bəl or in dis′ pyə tə bəl), not to be disputed; undoubtedly true; unquestionable. *adj.* —**in′dis put′a bly,** *adv.*

in do lent (in′də lənt), lazy; disliking work. *adj.* —**in′do lent ly,** *adv.*

in du bi ta ble (in dü′bə tə bəl or in dyü′bə tə bəl), not to be doubted; certain. *adj.* —**in du′bi ta bly,** *adv.*

in dul gent (in dul′jənt), **1.** indulging; kind; almost too kind: *The indulgent mother bought her boy everything he wanted.* **2.** lenient; making allowances; not critical: *Our indulgent teacher praised every poem we wrote. adj.* —**in dul′ gent ly,** *adv.*

in ert (in ėrt′), **1.** having no power to move or act; lifeless: *A stone is an inert mass of matter.* **2.** inactive; slow; sluggish. *adj.* —**in ert′ly,** *adv.*

in fer no (in fėr′nō), **1.** hell. **2.** a hell-like place or thing: *Firemen fought their way through a roaring inferno of flames. n., pl.* **in fer nos.**

in fest (in fest′), trouble or disturb frequently or in large numbers: *Mosquitoes infest swamps. The mountains were infested by robbers. v.*

in gra ti ate (in grā′shē āt), bring (oneself) into favor: *He tried to ingratiate himself with the teacher by giving her presents. v.*

in her ent (in hir′ənt), existing; abiding; belonging to (a person or thing) as a quality: *In spite of flattery, she kept her inherent modesty. adj.*

i ni ti ate (i nish′ē āt for 1-3; i nish′ē it or i nish′ē āt for 4), **1.** be the one to start; begin: *This year we shall initiate a series of free concerts.* **2.** admit (a person) by special forms or ceremonies (into mysteries, secret knowledge, or a society). **3.** introduce into the knowledge of some art or subject: *initiate a person into business methods.* **4.** person who is initiated. 1-3 *v.*, 4 *n.*

in junc tion (in jungk′shən), command; order: *Injunctions of secrecy did not prevent the news from leaking out. n.*

in no va tion (in′ə vā′shən), **1.** change made in the established way of doing things: *The new teacher made many innovations.* **2.** bringing in new things or new ways of doing things. *n.*

in quis i tive (in kwiz′ə tiv), **1.** curious; asking many questions. **2.** too curious; prying into other people's affairs. *adj.* —**in quis′i tive ly,** *adv.*

in sin u ate (in sin′yü āt), suggest indirectly; hint. *v.*

in so lence (in′sə ləns), bold rudeness; insulting behavior or speech. *n.*

in still or **in stil** (in stil′), put in little by little; impart gradually. *v.*

in stinct (in′stingkt), **1.** natural feeling, knowledge, or power, such as guides animals; unlearned tendency: *An instinct leads birds to fly.* **2.** a natural bent, tendency, or gift; talent: *Dorothy has such an instinct for color that she will study art. n.*

in stinc tive (in stingk′tiv), of or having to do with instinct; caused or done by instinct; born in an animal or person, not learned: *Climbing is instinctive in monkeys. adj.* —**in stinc′ tive ly,** *adv.*

in sub or di na tion (in′sə bôr′də nā′shən), resistance to authority; disobedience; unruly behavior. *n.*

in su late (in′sə lāt), keep from losing or transferring electricity, heat, sound, etc., especially by covering or surrounding with a nonconducting material. Wires are often insulated by a covering of rubber. *v.*

in tact (in takt′), with no part missing; untouched; uninjured; whole: *dishes left intact after a fall. adj.*

in teg ri ty (in teg′rə tē), **1.** honesty; sincerity; uprightness: *A man of integrity is respected.* **2.** wholeness; completeness: *Soldiers defend the integrity of their country against those who want part of it.* **3.** perfect condition; soundness. *n.*

in tel lec tu al (in′tə lek′chü əl), **1.** of the intellect. **2.** needing or using intelligence. **3.** person who is well informed and intelligent. 1,2 *adj.*, 3 *n.*

in tense (in tens′), **1.** very much; very great; very strong: *intense happiness, intense pain, intense light.* **2.** full of vigorous activity, strong feelings, etc.: *An intense life is crowded with action, interests, etc. adj.*

in tent (in tent′),　　1. having the eyes or thoughts earnestly fixed on something; earnest: *an intent look.* 2. earnestly engaged; much interested: *He is intent on making money. adj.* —**in tent′ly,** *adv.*

in ter cede (in′tər sēd′),　　plead or beg in another's behalf: *Friends of the condemned man interceded with the governor for a pardon. v.*

in ter cept (in′tər sept′),　　1. take or seize on the way from one place to another: *intercept a letter or a messenger.* 2. check; stop: *intercept the flight of a criminal. v.*

in te ri or (in tir′ē ər),　　1. inside; inner surface or part: *The interior of the house was beautifully decorated.* 2. part of a region or country away from the coast or border. *n.*

in ter lude (in′tər lüd),　　anything thought of as filling the time between two things; interval. *n.*

in ter po late (in tėr′pə lāt),　　1. alter (a book, passage, etc.) by putting in new words or groups of words. 2. put in (new words, passages, etc.). *v.*

in ter pret er (in tėr′prə tər),　　1. person who interprets. 2. person whose business is translating from a foreign language. *n.*

in ter ro ga tion (in ter′ə gā′shən),　　1. a questioning. The formal examination of a witness by asking questions is an interrogation. *n.*

in ter val (in′tər vəl),　　time or space between: *an interval of a week, intervals of freedom from pain. There are trees at intervals of twenty feet. n.*

in ti mate (in′tə mit),　　1. very familiar; known very well; closely acquainted. 2. close: *an intimate connection, intimate knowledge of a matter.* 3. very personal; most private: *A diary is a very intimate book.* 4. a close friend. 1-3 *adj.,* 4 *n.* —**in′ti mate ly,** *adv.*

in tol er a ble (in tol′ər ə bəl),　　unbearable; too much, too painful, etc., to be endured: *The pain from the toothache was intolerable. adj.*

in trep id (in trep′id),　　fearless; dauntless; courageous; very brave: *A policeman or soldier must be intrepid. adj.* —**in trep′id ly,** *adv.*

in tri cate (in′trə kit),　　1. with many twists and turns; perplexing, entangled, or complicated: *an intricate knot, an intricate maze, an intricate plot.* 2. very hard to understand: *intricate directions. adj.* —**in′tri cate ly,** *adv.* —**in′tri cate ness,** *n.*

in val u a ble (in val′yü ə bəl),　　priceless; very precious; valuable beyond measure. *adj.*

in var i a ble (in ver′ē ə bəl or in var′ē ə bəl), always the same; unchangeable; unchanging. *adj.*

in ves ti ga tion (in ves′tə gā′shən),　　careful search; detailed or careful examination. *n.*

in vol un tar y (in vol′ən ter′ē),　　1. not voluntary; not done of one's own free will; unwilling: *John was threatened until he gave involuntary consent to the plan.* 2. not done on purpose; not intended: *an involuntary injury.* 3. not controlled by the will: *Breathing is mainly involuntary. adj.* —**in vol′un tar′i ly,** *adv.*

in vul ner a ble (in vul′nər ə bəl),　　that cannot be wounded or injured; proof against attack: *Achilles was invulnerable except for his heel. adj.* —**in vul′ner a bly,** *adv.*

i o ta (ī ō′tə),　　a very small quantity: *There is not an iota of truth in the prisoner's story. n.*

irk (ėrk),　　weary; disgust; annoy; trouble; bore: *It irks us to wait for people who are late. v.*

i ron ic (ī ron′ik),　　ironical. *adj.*

i ron i cal (ī ron′ə kəl),　　1. expressing one thing and meaning the opposite: "Speedy" would be an ironical name for a snail. 2. contrary to what would naturally be expected: *It was ironical that the man was run over by his own automobile. adj.* —**i ron′i cal ly,** *adv.*

iron lung′, device to give artificial respiration.

ir re sist i ble (ir′i zis′tə bəl),　　that cannot be resisted; too great to be withstood. *adj.* —**ir′re sist′i bly,** *adv.*

ir rev o ca ble (i rev′ə kə bəl),　　not to be recalled, withdrawn, or annulled: *an irrevocable decision. adj.* —**ir rev′o ca bly,** *adv.*

ir ri ga tion (ir′ə gā′shən),　　supplying (land) with water by using ditches. *n.*

i so la tion (ī′sə lā′shən or is′ə lā′shən),　　1. a place apart. 2. a being separate from others. *n.*

jar (jär),　　1. shake; rattle: *Your heavy footsteps jar my table.* 2. a shake; rattle. 3. a harsh, grating noise. 4. a clash; quarrel. 1 *v.,* **jarred, jar ring;** 2-4 *n.*

jaun ty (jôn′tē),　　1. easy and lively; sprightly; carefree: *The happy boy walked with jaunty steps.* 2. smart; stylish: *She wore a jaunty little hat. adj.,* **jaun ti er, jaun ti est.** —**jaun′ti ly,** *adv.* —**jaun′ti ness,** *n.*

jest er (jes′tər),　　person who jokes or pokes fun (at). *n.*

jet ti son (jet′ə sn),　　1. throw (goods) overboard to lighten a ship in distress. 2. goods thrown overboard; jetsam. 3. throw away; discard. 1,3 *v.,* 2 *n.*

jowl¹ (joul),　　1. part under the jaw; jaw. 2. cheek. *n.*

jowl² (joul),　　fold of flesh hanging from the jaw. *n.*

ju di cial (jü dish′əl),　　1. of or having to do with courts, judges, or the administration of justice. 2. ordered, permitted, or enforced by a judge or a court. 3. impartial; fair: *A judicial mind considers both sides of a dispute fairly before making a decision. adj.* —**ju di′cial ly,** *adv.*

ju di ci ar y (jü dish′ē er′ē),　　1. branch of government that administers justice; system of courts of justice of a country. 2. judges of a country, State, or city. 3. of or having to do with courts, judges, or the administration of justice. 1,2 *n., pl.* **ju di ci ar ies;** 3 *adj.*

ju di cious (jü dish′əs),　　having, using, or showing good judgment; wise; sensible. *adj.* —**ju di′cious ly,** *adv.*

Jug ger naut (jug′ər nôt),　　1. something to which a person blindly devotes himself or is cruelly sacrificed. 2. an object or force that

---

hat, āge, fär; let, bē, tėrm; it, īce; hot, gō, ôrder; oil, out; cup, pùt, rüle; ch, child; ng, long; th, thin; ᴛн, then; zh, measure; ə represents *a* in about, *e* in taken, *i* in April, *o* in lemon, *u* in circus.

moves powerfully forward and crushes whatever is in its way. *n.*

jug u lar (jug′yə lər), **1.** of the neck or throat. **2.** of the jugular vein. *adj.*

jus ti fi a ble (jus′tə fī′ə bəl), capable of being justified; that can be shown to be just and right; defensible. *adj.* —**jus′ti fi′a bly,** *adv.*

jus ti fy (jus′tə fī), **1.** show to be just or right; give a good reason for: *The fine quality of the cloth justifies its high price.* **2.** clear of blame or guilt: *You are justified in shooting a man in self-defense.* *v.,* **jus ti fied, jus ti fy ing.**

ka rait (kə rīt′), a bright-colored, very poisonous snake belonging to the same family as cobras, mambas, and coral snakes, and native to warm parts of E Asia and nearby islands. *n.*

keen (kēn), *Irish.* **1.** a wailing lament for the dead. **2.** wail; lament. 1 *n.,* 2 *v.* —**keen′er,** *n.*

kil o me ter or **kil o me tre** (kil′ə mē tər or kə lom′ə tər), distance equal to 1000 meters, or 3280.8 feet. *n.*

knave (nāv), **1.** a tricky, dishonest person; rogue; rascal. **2.** the jack, a playing card with a picture of a servant or soldier on it. *n.*

lag (lag), move too slowly; fall behind: *The child lagged because he was tired.* *v.,* **lagged, lag ging.**

lance (lans), **1.** a long wooden spear with a sharp iron or steel head. Knights carried lances. **2.** pierce with a lance. **3.** any instrument like a soldier's lance. 1,3 *n.,* 2 *v.*

lash (lash), **1.** the part of a whip that is not the handle. **2.** beat or drive with a whip, etc.: *The driver of the team lashed his horses on.* **3.** pour; rush violently: *The rain lashed against the windows.* 1 *n.,* 2,3 *v.*

lash ing (lash′ing), rope, cord, etc., used in tying or fastening. *n.*

lat er ite (lat′ə rīt′), a reddish soil that is formed by the decay of rocks beneath it and found in hot, humid climates. *n.*

la va (lä′və), **1.** the molten rock flowing from a volcano or fissure in the earth. **2.** rock formed by the cooling of this molten rock. Some lavas are hard and glassy; others are light and porous. *n.*

lead en (led′n), **1.** made of lead: *a leaden coffin.* **2.** heavy; hard to lift or move: *leaden arms tired from working.* **3.** oppressive: *leaden air.* **4.** dull; gloomy. **5.** slow-moving; dragging. *adj.*

leg (leg), **1.** one of the limbs on which men and animals support themselves and walk. **2.** part of a garment that covers a leg. **3.** anything shaped or used like a leg: *a table leg.* **4.** one of the distinct portions or stages of any course: *the last leg of a trip.* *n.*

len ien cy (lēn′yən sē), mildness; gentleness; mercy. *n.*

len ient (lēn′yənt), mild; gentle; merciful: *a lenient conqueror.* *adj.* —**len′ient ly,** *adv.*

le thar gic (lə thär′jik), unnaturally drowsy; sluggish; dull. *adj.*

li a ble (lī′ə bəl), **1.** likely; unpleasantly likely: *Glass is liable to break.* **2.** in danger of having,

doing, etc. **3.** responsible; bound by law to pay: *The Post Office Department is not liable for damage to a parcel sent by mail unless it is insured.* **4.** under obligation; subject: *Citizens are liable to jury duty.* *adj.*

li bel (lī′bəl), **1.** a written or printed statement tending to damage a person's reputation. **2.** write or print a libel about. **3.** make false or damaging statements about. 1 *n.,* 2,3 *v.*

lieu (lū), place; stead. *n.*

in lieu of, in place of; instead of.

lim ou sine (lim′ə zēn′ or lim′ə zēn), a closed automobile, seating from three to five passengers inside, with a driver's seat outside under the same roof. *n.*

lin ger (ling′gər), stay on; go slowly, as if unwilling to leave: *She lingered after the others had left.* *v.*

list (list), tip to one side; tilt. *v.*

lit er al (lit′ər əl), **1.** following the exact words of the original: *a literal translation.* **2.** taking words in their usual meaning, without exaggeration or imagination; matter-of-fact: *the literal meaning of a word, a literal type of mind.* *adj.*

lithe (līth), bending easily; supple. *adj.*

livery stable (liv′ər ē stā′bəl), stable engaged in hiring out horses and carriages.

loathe (lōth), feel strong dislike and disgust for; abhor; hate: *We loathe rotten food.* *v.*

lobe (lōb), a rounded projecting part. The lobe of the ear is the lower rounded end. *n.*

lodge (loj), **1.** live in a place for a time. **2.** provide with a place to live in or sleep in for a time. **3.** place to live in; small or temporary house; house. **4.** put for safekeeping. **5.** put before some authority: *We lodged a complaint with the police.* 1,2,4,5 *v.,* **lodged, lodg ing;** 3 *n.*

log (lôg), **1.** length of wood just as it comes from the tree. **2.** made of logs: *a log house.* **3.** cut down trees, cut them into logs, and get them out of the forest. **4.** the daily record of a ship's voyage. **5.** enter in a ship's log. **6.** record of an airplane trip, performance of an engine, etc. 1,4,6 *n.,* 2 *adj.,* 3,5 *v.,* **logged, log ging.** —**log′like′,** *adj.*

log ic (loj′ik), **1.** science of proof. **2.** reasoning. *n.*

lo gy (lō′gē), *U.S.* heavy; sluggish; dull. *adj.*

loi ter (loi′tər), **1.** linger idly; stop and play along the way: *Mary loitered along the street, looking into all the shopwindows.* *v.* —**loi′ter er,** *n.*

loll (lol), **1.** recline or lean in a lazy manner: *loll on a sofa.* **2.** hang loosely or droop: *A dog's tongue lolls out in hot weather.* *v.*

long shore man (lông′shôr′mən), man whose work is loading and unloading ships. *n.,* *pl.* **long shore men.**

loom (lüm), **1.** appear indistinctly: *A large iceberg loomed through the fog.* **2.** appear in a vague, unusually large, or threatening shape: *War loomed ahead.* *v.*

loon (lün), a large, web-footed diving bird that has a loud wild cry. *n.*

lope (lōp), **1.** run with a long, easy stride. **2.** a long, easy stride. 1 *v.,* 2 *n.* —**lop′er,** *n.*

lu bri cate (lü′brə kāt), **1.** make (machinery) smooth and easy to work by putting on oil,

grease, etc. **2.** make slippery or smooth. *v.*
—**lu′bri ca′tion,** *n.*

lu cra tive (lü′krə tiv), bringing in money; profitable. *adj.* —**lu′cra tive ly,** *adv.*

lu di crous (lü′də krəs), amusingly absurd; ridiculous. *adj.* —**lu′di crous ly,** *adv.*

lull (lul), **1.** hush to sleep: *The mother lulled the crying baby.* **2.** quiet: *lull one's suspicions.* **3.** become calm or more nearly calm: *The wind lulled.* **4.** period of less noise or violence; brief calm: *a lull in a storm.* 1-3 *v.,* 4 *n.*

lunge (lunj), **1.** any sudden forward movement; thrust. **2.** move suddenly forward; thrust. 1 *n.,* 2 *v.,* **lunged, lung ing.**

lurk (lėrk), **1.** stay about without arousing attention; wait out of sight: *A tiger was lurking in the jungle.* **2.** be hidden. *v.*

ma chet e (mə shet′ē or mä chā′tā), a large heavy knife, used as a tool and weapon in South America, Central America, and the West Indies. *n.*

mael strom (māl′strəm), **1.** a great or turbulent whirlpool. **2.** a violent confusion of feelings, ideas, or conditions. *n.*

mag na nim i ty (mag′nə nim′ə tē), **1.** generosity in forgiving; nobility of soul or mind. **2.** a generous or noble act. *n., pl.* **mag na nim i ties.**

mag ne to (mag nē′tō), a small machine for producing electricity. In some gasoline engines, a magneto supplies an electric spark to explode the vapor. *n., pl.* **mag ne tos.**

mag ni tude (mag′nə tüd or mag′nə tyüd), **1.** size. **2.** importance. *n.*

ma lar i a (mə ler′ē ə or mə lar′ē ə), disease characterized by periodic chills followed by fever and sweating. Malaria is caused by minute parasitic animals in the red blood corpuscles, and is transmitted by the bite of anopheles mosquitoes which have bitten infected persons. *n.*

ma lev o lent (mə lev′ə lənt), wishing evil to happen to others; showing ill will; spiteful. *adj.* —**ma lev′o lent ly,** *adv.*

mal ice (mal′is), active ill will; wish to hurt others; spite: *Lincoln asked the people of the North to act "with malice toward none, with charity for all."* *n.*

ma li cious (mə lish′əs), showing active ill will; wishing to hurt others; spiteful: *a malicious tell-tale, malicious gossip.* *adj.* —**ma li′cious ly,** *adv.*

ma lign (mə līn′), **1.** speak evil of; slander: *You malign a generous person when you call him stingy.* **2.** evil; injurious: *Gambling often has a malign influence.* 1 *v.,* 2 *adj.* —**ma lign′er,** *n.*

ma neu ver (mə nü′vər), **1.** a planned movement of troops or warships: *Every year the army and navy hold maneuvers for practice.* **2.** perform maneuvers. **3.** a skillful plan; clever trick: *When we refused to use his idea, he tried to force it on us by a series of maneuvers.* **4.** plan skillfully; use clever tricks: *A scheming person is always maneuvering for some advantage.* 1,3 *n.,* 2,4 *v.*

man han dle (man′han′dl), **1.** treat roughly; pull or push about. **2.** move by human strength without mechanical appliances. *v.*

man i fest (man′ə fest), **1.** apparent to the eye or to the mind; plain; clear. **2.** show plainly; reveal; display. **3.** prove; put beyond doubt. **4.** list of a ship's cargo. 1 *adj.,* 2,3 *v.,* 4 *n.* —**man′i fest′ly,** *adv.*

man i fold (man′ə fōld), **1.** of many kinds; many and various. **2.** having many parts or forms. *adj.*

man u al (man′yü əl), **1.** of the hands; done with the hands: *manual labor.* **2.** a small book that is easy to understand and use. A cookbook is a manual. 1 *adj.,* 2 *n.*

mar a thon (mar′ə thon), **1.** a foot race of 26 miles, 385 yards. **2.** any long race or contest. *n.*

mar quee (mär kē′), **1.** a large tent, often one put up for some outdoor entertainment. **2.** a rooflike shelter over an entrance. *n.*

mar vel (mär′vəl), **1.** something wonderful; astonishing thing: *the marvels of science.* **2.** be filled with wonder; be astonished. 1 *n.,* 2 *v.*

mas sa cre (mas′ə kər), **1.** wholesale, pitiless slaughter of people or animals. **2.** kill (many people or animals) needlessly or cruelly; slaughter in large numbers. 1 *n.,* 2 *v.,* **mas sa cred, mas sa cring.**

mate (māt), **1.** one of a pair: *Where is the mate to this glove?* **2.** join in a pair: *Birds mate in the spring.* **3.** a ship's officer next below captain. 1,3 *n.,* 2 *v.*

Mat ter horn (mat′ər hôrn), a mountain peak in the Alps, between Switzerland and Italy. 14,780 ft. *n.*

ma tu ri ty (mə chúr′ə tē, mə túr′ə tē, or mə-tyúr′ə tē), **1.** full development; ripeness: *He reached maturity at twenty years.* **2.** a being completed or ready. *n.*

maul (môl), **1.** a very heavy hammer or mallet. **2.** beat and pull about; handle roughly: *The lion mauled its keeper badly.* 1 *n.,* 2 *v.*

med i cine (med′ə sn), **1.** substance, drug, or means used to cure disease or improve health. **2.** science of curing disease or improving health; skill in healing; doctor's art; treatment of diseases. **3.** magic power that savages believe certain men have over disease, evil spirits, and other things. *n.*

mel an chol y (mel′ən kol′ē), **1.** sadness; low spirits; tendency to be sad. **2.** sober thoughtfulness. *n., pl.* **mel an chol ies.**

mem brane (mem′brān), a thin, soft sheet or layer of animal tissue lining or covering some part of the body. *n.*

men ace (men′is), **1.** threat: *In dry weather forest fires are a great menace.* **2.** threaten: *Floods menaced the valley with destruction.* 1 *n.,* 2 *v.,* —**men′ac ing ly,** *adv.*

merge (mėrj), swallow up; absorb; combine; gradually blend together. *v.*

miff (mif), *Informal.* **1.** a peevish fit; petty quarrel. **2.** be offended; have a petty quarrel. 1 *n.,* 2 *v.*

---

hat, āge, fär; let, bē, tèrm; it, īce; hot, gō, ôrder; oil, out; cup, pút, rüle; ch, child; ng, long; th, thin; ŦH, then; zh, measure; ə represents *a* in about, *e* in taken, *i* in April, *o* in lemon, *u* in circus.

mil len ni um (mə len′ē əm), period of a thousand years: *The world is many millennia old. n., pl.* **mil len ni ums, mil len ni a** (mə len′ē ə).

mill er (mil′ər), one who owns or runs a mill, especially a flour mill. *n.*

mil li ner (mil′ə nər), person who makes, trims, or sells women's hats. *n.*

mim ic ry (mim′ik rē), a making fun of by imitating. *n., pl.* **mim ic ries.**

mir a cle (mir′ə kəl), **1.** a wonderful happening that is contrary to or independent of the known laws of nature: *It would be a miracle if the sun should stand still in the heavens for an hour.* **2.** something marvelous; a wonder. *n.*

mi rac u lous (mə rak′yə ləs), **1.** contrary to or independent of the known laws of nature. **2.** wonderful; marvelous. *adj.* —**mi rac′u lous ly,** *adv.* —**mi rac′u lous ness,** *n.*

mire (mīr), **1.** soft, deep mud; slush. **2.** bog; swamp. **3.** get stuck in mire: *He mired his horses and had to go for help.* *1,2 n.,* *3 v.*

mis con cep tion (mis′kən sep′shən), a mistaken idea or notion; wrong conception. *n.*

mis cre ant (mis′krē ənt), **1.** having very bad morals; base. **2.** villain. *1 adj.,* *2 n.*

mis shap en (mis shā′pən), **1.** badly shaped; deformed. **2.** a pp. of **misshape.** *1 adj.,* *2 v.*

mit i gate (mit′ə gāt), make or become mild; make or become milder; soften. Anger, grief, pain, punishments, heat, cold, and many other conditions may be mitigated. *v.*

mo bil i ty (mō bil′ə tē), being mobile; ability or readiness to move or be moved. *n.*

mock (mok), **1.** laugh at; make fun of. **2.** make fun of by copying or imitating: *The thoughtless children mocked the queer speech of the new boy.* **3.** imitate; copy. **4.** not real; copying; sham; imitation: *a mock battle. 1-3 v.,* *4 adj.*

mold (mōld), a woolly or furry fungous growth, often greenish in color, that appears on food and other animal or vegetable substances when they are left too long in a warm, moist place. *n.*

mol li fy (mol′ə fī), soften; appease; mitigate: *mollify a person or his wrath. v.,* **mol li fied, mol li fy ing.**

mon i tor (mon′ə tər), **1.** pupil in school with special duties, such as helping to keep order and taking attendance. **2.** person who gives advice or warning. **3.** a low armored warship having one or more turrets for guns. **4.** a receiver used for checking radio or television transmissions. **5.** check (a radio or television transmission) by listening in with a receiver. *1-4 n.,* *5 v.*

mor tal (môr′tl), **1.** sure to die sometime. **2.** a being that is sure to die sometime. All living creatures are mortals. **3.** of man; of mortals: *Mortal flesh has many pains and diseases.* **4.** man; human being: *No mortal should strive against God. 1,3 adj.,* *2,4 n.*

mor tar (môr′tər), **1.** bowl of very hard material, in which substances may be pounded to a powder. **2.** a very short cannon for shooting shells or fireworks at high angles. *n.*

mourn (môrn), **1.** grieve. **2.** feel or show sorrow over: *Mary mourned her lost doll. v.*

mourn ing (môr′ning), **1.** sorrowing; lamentation. **2.** the wearing of black or some other

color (white in the Orient), to show sorrow for a person's death. *n.*

mun dane (mun′dān), **1.** of this world, not of heaven; earthly. **2.** of the universe; of the world. *adj.*

murk y (mėr′kē), dark; gloomy. *adj.* —**murk′i ly,** *adv.* —**murk′i ness,** *n.*

muse (myüz), **1.** think in a dreamy way; think; meditate: *The boy spent the whole afternoon in musing.* **2.** look thoughtfully. **3.** say thoughtfully. *v.*

mus ter (mus′tər), **1.** assemble; gather together; collect. **2.** assembly; collection. **3.** summon: *muster up courage. 1,3 v.,* *2 n.*

mu tant (myü′tənt), a new variety of plant or animal resulting from mutation. *n.*

mute (myüt), **1.** silent; not making any sound: *The little girl stood mute.* **2.** dumb; unable to speak. **3.** person who cannot speak. **4.** clip or pad put on a musical instrument to soften the sound. **5.** soften; muffle. *1,2 adj.,* *3,4 n.,* *5 v.*

mu ti ny (myü′tə nē), **1.** open rebellion against lawful authority, especially by sailors or soldiers against their officers. **2.** take part in a mutiny; rebel. *1 n., pl.* **mu ti nies;** *2 v.,* **mu ti nied, mu ti ny ing.**

myr i ad (mir′ē əd), **1.** ten thousand. **2.** a very great number: *There are myriads of stars.* **3.** countless. *1,2 n.,* *1,3 adj.*

nar rate (na rāt′ or nar′āt), **1.** tell (a story, etc.) of. **2.** tell stories, etc. *v.*

nau sea (nô′shə or nô′sē ə), **1.** the feeling that one has when about to vomit. **2.** seasickness. **3.** extreme disgust; loathing. *n.*

nav i ga ble (nav′ə gə bəl), **1.** that ships can travel on: *The Mississippi River is deep enough to be navigable.* **2.** seaworthy. **3.** that can be steered: *Without a rudder the ship was not navigable. adj.*

nav i ga tion (nav′ə gā′shən), **1.** act or process of navigating. **2.** art or science of finding a ship's or an airship's position and course. *n.*

ne far i ous (ni fer′ē əs or ni far′ē əs), very wicked; villainous. *adj.* —**ne far′i ous ly,** *adv.*

ne phri tis (ni frī′tis), inflammation of the kidneys; especially, Bright's disease. *n.*

net tle (net′l), **1.** kind of plant having sharp leaf hairs that sting the skin when touched. **2.** sting the mind of; irritate; provoke; vex. *1 n.,* *2 v.*

noc tur nal (nok tėr′nl), **1.** of the night. **2.** in the night: *Stars are a nocturnal sight.* **3.** active in the night: *The owl is a nocturnal bird.* **4.** closed by day, open by night: *a nocturnal flower. adj.*

nom i nal ly (nom′ə nl ē), in name; as a matter of form; in a nominal way only. *adv.*

non cha lance (non′shə ləns or non′shə läns′), cool unconcern; indifference: *Eleanor received the prize with pretended nonchalance. n.*

non cha lant (non′shə lənt or non′shə länt′), without enthusiasm; coolly unconcerned; indifferent. *adj.* —**non′cha lant ly,** *adv.*

non com mit tal (non′kə mit′l), not committing oneself; not saying yes or no: *"I will think it over"* is a noncommittal answer. *adj.* —**non′com mit′tal ly,** *adv.*

nos tal gic (nos tal′jik), homesick. *adj.*

not with stand ing (not′wiᴛʜ stan′ding or not′with stan′ding), **1.** in spite of: *He bought it notwithstanding the high price.* **2.** in spite of the fact that: *Notwithstanding there was need for haste, he still delayed.* 1 *prep.*, 2 *conj.*

nov ice (nov′is), one who is new to what he is doing; beginner: *Novices are likely to make some mistakes.* *n.*

nur ture (nèr′chər), rear; bring up; care for; foster; train: *She nurtured the child as if he had been her own.* *v.*

ob li ga tion (ob′lə gā′shən), duty under the law; duty due to a promise or contract; duty on account of social relationship or kindness received: *A wife's first obligation is to her husband and children.* *n.*

o blige (ə blīj′), **1.** bind by a promise, contract, duty, etc.; compel; force: *The law obliges parents to send their children to school.* **2.** put under a debt of thanks for some favor; do a favor: *She obliged us with a song.* *v.*

ob lit er ate (ə blit′ə rāt′), remove all traces of; blot out; destroy: *The heavy rain obliterated the footprints.* *v.*

ob liv i ous (əb liv′ē əs), forgetful; not mindful: *The book was so interesting that I was oblivious of my surroundings.* *adj.*

ob scure (əb skyur′), **1.** not clearly expressed: *an obscure passage in a book.* **2.** not well known; attracting no notice: *an obscure little village.* **3.** not easily discovered; hidden: *an obscure path, an obscure meaning.* **4.** not distinct; not clear: *obscure sounds.* **5.** hide from view; make obscure; dim; darken: *Clouds obscure the sun.* 1-4 *adj.*, 5 *v.*

ob sess (əb ses′), fill the mind of; keep the attention of; haunt: *Fear that someone might steal his money obsessed the old miser.* *v.*

ob vi ous (ob′vē əs), easily seen or understood; clear to the eye or mind; not to be doubted; plain: *It is obvious that two and two make four.* *adj.* —**ob′vi ous ly,** *adv.*

odds (odz), **1.** difference in favor of one and against another; advantage: *The odds are in our favor and we should win.* **2.** in games, an extra allowance given to the weaker side. **3.** things that are odd, uneven, or unequal. **4.** difference: *It makes no odds when he goes.* *n.pl. or sing.*

at odds, quarreling; disagreeing.

off hand (ôf′hand′ for 1; ôf′hand′ for 2, 3), **1.** without previous thought or preparation; at once: *The carpenter could not tell offhand how much the work would cost.* **2.** done or made offhand: *His offhand remarks were sometimes very wise.* **3.** casual; informal. 1 *adv.*, 2,3 *adj.* —**off′hand′ed ly,** *adv.* —**off′hand′ed ness,** *n.*

on slaught (on′slôt′), a vigorous attack: *The Indians made an onslaught on the settlers' fort.* *n.*

op po nent (ə pō′nənt), person who is on the other side in a fight, game, or discussion; person fighting, struggling, or speaking against one: *He defeated his opponent in the election.* *n.*

op ti cal (op′tə kəl), of the eye; visual: *Being nearsighted is an optical defect.* *adj.*

op ti mum (op′tə məm), the best or most favorable point, degree, amount, etc., for the purpose. *n., pl.* **op ti mums, op ti ma** (-mə).

or a tor i cal (ôr′ə tôr′ə kəl), **1.** of oratory; having to do with orators or oratory: *an oratorical contest.* **2.** characteristic of orators or oratory: *an oratorical manner.* *adj.* —**or′a tor′ i cal ly,** *adv.*

or a to ry (ôr′ə tô′rē), **1.** skill in public speaking; fine speaking. **2.** art of public speaking. *n.*

or bit (ôr′bit), **1.** path of the earth or any one of the planets about the sun. **2.** path of any heavenly body about another heavenly body. **3.** the regular course of life or experience. *n.*

or deal (ôr dēl′), **1.** a severe test or experience. **2.** in early times, an effort to decide the guilt or innocence of an accused person by making him do something dangerous like holding fire or taking poison. It was supposed that an innocent person would not be harmed by such danger. *n.*

os ten si bly (os ten′sə blē), apparently; on the face of it; as openly stated or shown. *adv.*

out rage (out′rāj), **1.** act showing no regard for the rights or feelings of others; an overturning of the rights of others by force; act of violence; offense; insult: *Hitler was guilty of many outrages.* **2.** offend greatly; do violence to; insult. 1 *n.*, 2 *v.*

o ver whelm (ō′vər hwelm′), **1.** overcome completely; crush: *overwhelm with grief.* **2.** cover completely as a flood would: *A great wave overwhelmed the boat.* *v.*

o ver wrought (ō′vər rôt′), wearied or exhausted by too much work or excitement; greatly excited: *overwrought nerves.* *adj.*

pa gan (pā′gən), **1.** person who is not a Christian, Jew, or Moslem; one who worships false gods; heathen. The ancient Greeks and Romans were pagans. **2.** having to do with pagans; not Christian, Jewish, or Moslem. **3.** not religious. 1 *n.*, 2,3 *adj.*

pains tak ing (pānz′tāk′ing), very careful; particular; scrupulous: *a painstaking painter.* *adj.* —**pains′tak′ing ly,** *adv.*

pale (pāl), **1.** a long, narrow board, pointed at the top, used for fences. **2.** boundary: *outside the pale of civilized society.* *n.*

pan de mo ni um (pan′də mō′nē əm), **1.** place of wild disorder or lawless confusion. **2.** wild uproar or lawlessness. *n.*

pa pier-mâ ché (pā′pər mə shā′), **1.** a paper pulp mixed with some stiffener and molded when moist. It becomes hard and strong when dry. **2.** made of papier-mâché. 1 *n.*, 2 *adj.*

pa ral y sis (pə ral′ə sis), **1.** a lessening or loss of the power of motion or sensation in any part of the body: *The accident left him with paralysis of the legs.* **2.** condition of powerlessness or helpless inactivity; crippling: *The war caused a paralysis of trade.* *n., pl.* **pa ral y ses** (-sēz).

---

hat, āge, fär; let, bē, tèrm; it, īce; hot, gō, ôrder; oil, out; cup, pût, rüle; ch, child; ng, long; th, thin; ᴛʜ, then; zh, measure; ə represents *a* in about, *e* in taken, *i* in April, *o* in lemon, *u* in circus.

par a lyze (par′ə līz), 1. affect with a lessening or loss of the power of motion or feeling: *His left arm was paralyzed.* 2. make powerless or helplessly inactive; cripple; stun; deaden: *Fear paralyzed my mind. v.*

par a mount (par′ə mount), chief in importance; above others; supreme: *Truth is of paramount importance. adj.*

par a pet (par′ə pet), 1. a low wall or mound of stone, earth, etc., to protect soldiers. 2. a low wall at the edge of a balcony, roof, bridge, etc. *n.*

par a site (par′ə sīt), 1. animal or plant that lives on, with, or in another, from which it gets its food. Lice and tapeworms are parasites. Mistletoe is a parasite on oak trees. 2. person who lives on others without making any useful and fitting return; hanger-on: *Beggars are parasites. n.*

parch ment (pärch′mənt), 1. the skin of sheep, goats, etc., prepared for use as a writing material. 2. a pale yellow-green color, or a grayish yellow color. *n.*

par ox ysm (par′ək siz əm), 1. a severe, sudden attack: *a paroxysm of coughing.* 2. fit; convulsion: *a paroxysm of rage. n.*

pas sion ate (pash′ə nit), 1. having or showing strong feelings: *The fathers of our country were passionate believers in freedom.* 2. easily moved to anger. 3. resulting from strong feeling: *He made a passionate speech. adj.* —**pas′sion ately,** *adv.*

pas sive (pas′iv), 1. not acting in return; being acted on without itself acting: *a passive mind or disposition.* 2. not resisting; yielding or submitting to the will of another. *adj.*

pass port (pas′pôrt), 1. a paper or book giving official permission to travel in a certain country, under the protection of one's own government. 2. anything that gives one admission or acceptance. *n.*

pa ter nal (pə tėr′nl), 1. of or like a father; fatherly. 2. related on the father's side of the family: *Everyone has two paternal grandparents and two maternal grandparents.* 3. received or inherited from one's father. *adj.*

pa thol o gy (pa thol′ə jē), 1. study of the causes and nature of diseases. 2. unhealthy conditions and processes caused by a disease. *n., pl.* **pa thol o gies.**

pa tron ize (pā′trə nīz or pat′rə nīz), 1. be a regular customer of; give regular business to: *We patronize our neighborhood stores.* 2. act as a patron toward; support or protect: *patronize the ballet.* 3. treat in a condescending way: *We dislike to have anyone patronize us. v.* —**pa′tron iz′ing ly,** *adv.*

pawn (pôn), leave (something) with another person as security that borrowed money will be repaid: *He pawned his watch to buy food until he could get work. v.*

pe cu li ar i ty (pi kyü′lē ar′ə tē), 1. a being peculiar; strangeness; oddness; unusualness. 2. some little thing that is strange or odd. *n., pl.* **pe cu li ar i ties.**

pelt (pelt), 1. skin of a sheep, goat, or small fur-bearing animal, before it is tanned. 2. skin. *n.*

pen ance (pen′əns), 1. punishment borne to show sorrow for sin, to make up for a wrong done, and to obtain pardon from the church for sin. 2. any act done to show that one is sorry or repents. 3. sacrament of the Roman Catholic Church that includes contrition, confession, satisfaction, and absolution. *n.*

pend ing (pen′ding), 1. waiting to be decided or settled: *while the agreement was pending.* 2. impending; threatening. *adj.*

pen e trate (pen′ə trāt), 1. get into or through. 2. pierce through: *Our eyes could not penetrate the darkness.* 3. make a way: *Even where the trees were thickest, the sunshine penetrated. v.*

pe nin su la (pə nin′sə lə or pə nin′syə lə), piece of land almost surrounded by water, or extending far out into the water. Florida is a peninsula. *n.*

pen sive (pen′siv), 1. thoughtful in a serious or sad way: *She was in a pensive mood, and sat staring out the window.* 2. melancholy. *adj.* —**pen′sive ly,** *adv.* —**pen′sive ness,** *n.*

pe nul ti mate (pi nul′tə mit), next to the last. *adj.*

per cep tion (pər sep′shən), 1. act of becoming aware of through the senses: *His perception of the change came in a flash.* 2. power of observing: *a keen perception.* 3. the understanding that is the result of perceiving or observation: *Fred had a clear perception of what was wrong, and soon fixed it. n.*

per jur er (pėr′jər ər), person who commits perjury. *n.*

per ju ry (pėr′jər ē), act of swearing that something is true which one knows to be false. *n., pl.* **per ju ries.**

per pe trate (pėr′pə trāt), do or commit (crime, fraud, trick, or anything bad or foolish): *The king's brother perpetrated the cruel murder of the prince. v.*

per pet u al ly (pər pech′ü ə lē), forever. *adv.*

per sist ent (pər sis′tənt), 1. persisting; having lasting qualities, especially in the face of dislike, disapproval, or difficulties: *a persistent worker.* 2. lasting; going on; continuing: *a persistent headache. adj.*

per spec tive (pər spek′tiv), 1. art of picturing objects on a flat surface so as to give the appearance of distance. 2. effect of the distance of events upon the mind: *Many happenings of last year seem less important when viewed in perspective.* 3. view of things or facts in which they are in the right relations. *n.*

per sua sive (pər swā′siv), able, intended, or fitted to persuade: *The salesman had a very persuasive way of talking. adj.* —**per sua′sive ly,** *adv.* —**per sua′sive ness,** *n.*

pes si mism (pes′ə miz əm), 1. tendency to look on the dark side of things or to see difficulties and disadvantages. 2. belief that things naturally tend to evil, or that life is not worth while. *n.*

pet cock (pet′kok′), a small faucet. *n.*

pet ri fy (pet′rə fī), 1. turn into stone; become stone: *There is a petrified forest in Arizona.* 2. paralyze with fear, horror, or surprise. *v.,* **pet ri fied, pet ri fy ing.**

pew ter (pyü′tər),　**1.** alloy of tin with lead, copper, or other metals. **2.** made of pewter: *a pewter mug.* **3.** having the grayish color of pewter. 1 *n.,*　2,3 *adj.*

phe nom e nal (fə nom′ə nl),　extraordinary: *a phenomenal memory. adj.* —**phe nom′e nal ly,** *adv.*

pike staff (pīk′staf′),　**1.** staff or shaft of a pike or spear. **2.** staff with a metal point or spike, used by travelers. *n., pl.* **pike staves** (-stāvz′).

pil grim (pil′grəm),　**1.** person who goes on a journey to a sacred or holy place as an act of religious devotion. **2.** traveler; wanderer. *n.*

pin ion (pin′yən),　a small gear with teeth that fit into those of a larger gear or rack. *n.*

pla cate (plā′kāt),　soothe or satisfy the anger of; make peaceful: *placate a person one has offended. v.*

pla gia rize (plā′jə rīz),　take and use as one's own (the thoughts, writings, inventions, etc., of another); especially, to take and use (a passage, plot, etc., from the work of another writer). *v.*

plain tive (plān′tiv),　mournful; sad: *a plaintive song. adj.* —**plain′tive ly,** *adv.*

plait (plāt or plat for 1, 2; plāt or plēt for 3, 4),　**1.** a braid. **2.** braid: *She plaits her hair.* **3.** a flat, usually narrow, fold made in cloth by doubling it on itself; a pleat. **4.** fold or arrange in plaits; pleat: *a plaited skirt.* 1,3 *n.,*　2,4 *v.*

plane (plān),　**1.** any flat or level surface. **2.** airplane. **3.** glide as an airplane does. **4.** move up or down in water. 1,2 *n.,*　3,4 *v.*

poign ant (poin′ənt or poin′yənt),　**1.** very painful; piercing: *poignant suffering.* **2.** keen; intense: *a subject of poignant interest, a poignant delight. adj.* —**poign′ant ly,** *adv.*

pon der (pon′dər),　consider carefully; think over: *ponder a problem. v.*

pon der ous (pon′dər əs),　**1.** very heavy. **2.** heavy and clumsy. **3.** dull; tiresome. *adj.* —**pon′der ous ly,** *adv.*

por ti co (pôr′tə kō),　roof supported by columns, forming a porch or a covered walk. *n., pl.* **por ti coes** or **por ti cos.**

pos se (pos′ē),　group of men summoned by a sheriff to help him: *The posse pursued the thief. n.*

pre car i ous (pri ker′ē əs　or　pri kar′ē əs),　**1.** dependent on the will or pleasure of another. **2.** not safe or secure; uncertain; dangerous; risky: *A soldier leads a precarious life. adj.* —**pre car′i ous ly,** *adv.* —**pre car′i ous ness,** *n.*

pre cede (pri sēd′),　**1.** go before; come before: *Hoover preceded Roosevelt as President.* **2.** be higher than in rank or importance: *A major precedes a captain. v.*

pre cise (pri sīs′),　**1.** exact; accurate; definite: *The precise sum was 34 cents.* **2.** careful: *Alice is precise in her manners.* **3.** strict; scrupulous. *adj.*

pred i cate (pred′ə kāt),　**1.** found or base (a statement, action, etc.) on something. **2.** declare, assert, or affirm to be real or true: *Most religions predicate life after death. v.*

prej u dice (prej′ə dis),　**1.** opinion formed without taking time and care to judge fairly: *a prejudice against doctors.* **2.** cause a prejudice in; fill with prejudice: *One unfortunate experience prejudiced him against all lawyers.* 1 *n.,*　2 *v.*

pre ma ture ly (prē′mə chúr′lē, prē′mə túr′lē, or prē′mə tyúr′lē),　before the proper time. *adv.*

pre med i tate (prē med′ə tāt),　consider or plan beforehand. *v.*

pre mo ni tion (prē′mə nish′ən),　a forewarning. *n.*

pre oc cu pied (prē ok′yə pīd),　absorbed; engrossed; having all one's attention on something. *adj.*

pre sum a bly (pri züm′ə blē),　as may be reasonably supposed; probably. *adv.*

pre tense (pri tens′ or prē′tens),　**1.** make-believe; pretending: *My anger was all pretense.* **2.** a false appearance. **3.** a false claim. *n.*

pre vail (pri vāl′),　**1.** exist in many places; be in general use: *That custom still prevails.* **2.** be the most usual or strongest: *Sadness prevailed in our minds.* **3.** be the stronger; win the victory; succeed. *v.*
　prevail on, upon, or **with,** persuade: *Can't I prevail upon you to stay for dinner?*

pre var i ca tion (pri var′ə kā′shən),　prevaricating or lying; departure from the truth. *n.*

prime (prīm),　**1.** first in rank; chief: *His prime object was to lower the tax rate.* **2.** first in time or order; fundamental. **3.** first in quality; first-rate; excellent: *prime ribs of beef.* **4.** the best time; best condition: *A man of forty is in the prime of life.* 1-3 *adj.,*　4 *n.*

probe (prōb)　search into; examine thoroughly; investigate: *probe one's thoughts or feelings to find out why one acted as one did. v.*

pro fi cien cy (prə fish′ən sē),　being proficient; knowledge; skill; expertness. *n., pl.* **pro fi cien cies.**

prone (prōn),　**1.** inclined; liable. **2.** lying face down. **3.** lying flat. *adj.*

pro pri e ty (prə prī′ə tē),　**1.** quality of being proper; fitness. **2.** proper behavior. *n., pl.* **pro pri e ties.**

prot es ta tion (prot′is tā′shən),　**1.** a solemn declaration; protesting: *make a protestation of one's innocence.* **2.** a protest. *n.*

prov i dent (prov′ə dənt),　**1.** having or showing foresight; careful in providing for the future: *Provident men lay aside money for their families.* **2.** economical; frugal. *adj.*

prov o ca tion (prov′ə kā′shən),　something that stirs one up; cause of anger: *Their insulting remarks were a provocation. n.*

pru dent (prüd′nt),　planning carefully ahead of time; sensible; discreet: *A prudent man saves part of his wages. adj.* —**pru′dent ly,** *adv.*

ptar mi gan (tär′mə gən),　any of several kinds of grouse that have feathered feet and are found in mountainous and cold regions. *n., pl.* **ptar mi gans** or (*esp. collectively*) **ptar mi gan.**

pug na cious (pug nā′shəs),　having the habit of fighting; fond of fighting; quarrelsome. *adj.* —**pug na′cious ly,** *adv.* —**pug na′cious ness,** *n.*

---

hat, āge, fär; let, bē, tėrm; it, īce; hot, gō, ôrder; oil, out; cup, pùt, rüle; ch, child; ng, long; th, thin; ŦH, then; zh, measure; ə represents *a* in about, *e* in taken, *i* in April, *o* in lemon, *u* in circus.

pum ice (pum′is), a light, spongy stone thrown up from volcanoes, used for cleaning, smoothing, and polishing. *n.*

punc tu al (pungk′chü əl), prompt; on time: *He is punctual to the minute. adj.*

pu ny (pyü′nē), 1. of less than usual size and strength; weak. 2. petty; not important. *adj.*

py thon (pī′thon), 1. any of several large snakes of the Old World that are related to the boas and kill their prey by crushing. Pythons usually live in trees near water. 2. any large boa. *n.*

quadri-, a word element meaning "four." Also, **quadr-.**

quar ry (kwôr′ē), 1. animal chased in a hunt; game; prey. 2. anything hunted or eagerly pursued. *n., pl.* **quar ries.**

quartz (kwôrts), a very hard mineral composed of silica. Common quartz crystals are colorless and transparent, but amethyst, jasper, and many other colored stones are quartz. *n.*

quiz zi cal (kwiz′ə kəl), 1. odd; queer; comical. 2. that suggests making fun of others; teasing: *a quizzical smile. adj.* —**quiz′zi cal ly,** *adv.*

rack (rak), 1. frame with bars, shelves, or pegs to hold, arrange, or keep things on, such as a hat rack, tool rack, or baggage rack. 2. hurt very much: *racked with grief. A toothache racked his jaw.* 1 *n.,* 2 *v.*

raf fi a (raf′ē ə), fiber from the leafstalks of a kind of palm tree growing in Madagascar, used in making baskets, mats, etc. *n.*

rail (rāl), complain bitterly; use violent and reproachful language: *He railed at his hard luck. v.* —**rail′er,** *n.*

rain forest (rān′fôr′ist), a woodland which has very heavy rainfall and broad-leaved trees that remain green throughout the year. *n.*

rake (rāk), 1. a long-handled tool having a bar at one end with teeth in it. 2. make clear, clean, smooth, etc., with a rake, or as if with a rake. 3. search carefully: *He raked the newspapers for descriptions of the accident.* 4. glance over quickly; scan. 1 *n.,* 2-4 *v.*

rak ish (rā′kish), 1. smart; jaunty; dashing: *a hat set at a rakish angle.* 2. suggesting dash and speed: *He owns a rakish boat. adj.*

ral ly (ral′ē), 1. bring together; bring together again; get in order again: *The commander was able to rally the fleeing troops.* 2. come to help a person, party, or cause. 3. recover health and strength. *v.,* **ral lied, ral ly ing.**

ram page (ram′pāj for 1; ram pāj′ or ram′pāj for 2), 1. fit of rushing wildly about; spell of violent behavior; wild outbreak. 2. rush wildly about; behave violently; rage. 1 *n.,* 2 *v.*

ram shack le (ram′shak′əl), loose and shaky; likely to come apart. *adj.*

ran cid (ran′sid), 1. stale; spoiled: *rancid fat.* 2. tasting or smelling like stale fat or butter. *adj.*

ran cor (rang′kər), bitter resentment or ill will; extreme hatred or spite. *n.*

ras cal ly (ras′kə lē), mean; dishonest; bad. *adj.*

rash (rash), too hasty; careless; reckless; taking too much risk. *adj.* —**rash′ly,** *adv.*

rash er (rash′ər), a thin slice of bacon or ham for frying or broiling. *n.*

rav en ous (rav′ə nəs), 1. very hungry. 2. greedy. *adj.* —**rav′en ous ly,** *adv.*

ra vine (rə vēn′), a long, deep, narrow gorge worn by running water. *n.*

re as sure (rē′ə shùr′), restore to confidence: *The captain's confidence during the storm reassured the passengers. v.*

re cede (ri sēd′), 1. go backward; move backward: *Houses and trees seem to recede as you ride past in a train.* 2. withdraw. *v.*

rec on cile (rek′ən sīl), 1. make friends again. 2. make agree; bring into harmony: *It is impossible to reconcile his story with the facts.* 3. make satisfied; make no longer opposed. *v.*

re con nais sance (ri kon′ə səns), examination or survey, especially for military purposes. *n.*

rec ti fi ca tion (rek′tə fə kā′shən), making right. *n.*

re dress (ri dres′), set right; repair; remedy. *v.*

reek (rēk), 1. a strong, unpleasant smell; vapor. 2. send out vapor or a strong, unpleasant smell. 1 *n.,* 2 *v.*

re flec tive (ri flek′tiv), 1. reflecting: *the reflective surface of polished metal.* 2. thoughtful: *reflective look. adj.*

ref uge (ref′yüj), shelter or protection from danger, trouble, etc.; safety; security: *The cat took refuge in a tree. n.*

reg u lar i ty (reg′yə lar′ə tē), order; system; steadiness; being regular. *n.*

re li a bil i ty (ri lī′ə bil′ə tē), quality of being reliable; trustworthiness; dependability: *A machine has perfect reliability if it always does its work. n.*

re luc tance (ri luk′təns), 1. unwillingness. 2. slowness in action because of unwillingness. *n.*

re luc tant (ri luk′tənt), 1. unwilling; showing unwillingness. 2. slow to act because unwilling. *adj.* —**re luc′tant ly,** *adv.*

re mote (ri mōt′), 1. far away; far off: *a remote country.* 2. distant in manner; withdrawn. 3. slight; faint: *I haven't the remotest idea what you mean. adj.* —**re mote′ly,** *adv.*

re press (ri pres′), 1. prevent from acting; check: *She repressed an impulse to cough.* 2. keep down; put down; suppress. *v.*

re pris al (ri prī′zəl), injury done in return for injury, especially by one nation to another. *n.*

rep tile (rep′təl), a cold-blooded animal that creeps or crawls. Snakes, lizards, turtles, alligators, and crocodiles are reptiles. *n.*

re pug nant (ri pug′nənt), distasteful; disagreeable; offensive. *adj.*

re sent (ri zent′), feel injured and angry at; feel indignation at: *Our cat seems to resent having anyone sit in its chair. v.*

re sent ful (ri zent′fəl), feeling resentment; injured and angry; showing resentment. *adj.* —**re sent′ful ly,** *adv.* —**re sent′ful ness,** *n.*

re sent ment (ri zent′mənt), the feeling that one has at being injured or insulted; indignation. *n.*

re sign (ri zīn′), give up: *John resigned his position on the school paper.* *v.*

resign oneself, submit quietly; adapt oneself without complaint: *Jim had to resign himself to a week in bed when he hurt his back.*

re signed (ri zīnd′), accepting what comes without complaint. *adj.*

res o lute (rez′ə lüt), determined; firm; bold. *adj.* —**res′o lute ly,** *adv.*

re source ful (ri sôrs′fəl), good at thinking of ways to do things; quick-witted. *adj.*

re tal i ate (ri tal′ē āt), pay back wrong, injury, etc.; return like for like, usually to return evil for evil. *v.*

re ver ber ate (ri vėr′bər āt), echo back: *His voice reverberates from the high ceiling.* *v.*

rev er ent (rev′ər ənt), feeling reverence, or respect mixed with wonder, awe, and love; showing reverence. *adj.* —**rev′er ent ly,** *adv.*

rheum y (rü′mē), 1. full of mucus. 2. causing rheum; damp and cold. *adj.*

rig id (rij′id), 1. stiff; firm; not bending: *a rigid support.* 2. strict; not changing. *adj.* —**rig′id ly,** *adv.* —**rig′id ness,** *n.*

ro bot (rō′bət), 1. a machine-made man; mechanical device that does some of the work of human beings. 2. person who acts or works in a dull, mechanical way. *n.*

ro guer y (rō′gər ē), 1. conduct of rogues; dishonest trickery; rascality. 2. playful mischief. *n., pl.* **ro guer ies.**

rouse (rouz), arouse; wake up; stir up: *I was roused by the telephone.* *v.*

rout (rout), 1. flight of a defeated army in disorder. 2. put to flight: *Our soldiers routed the enemy.* 3. a complete defeat. 4. defeat completely. 5. a noisy disorderly crowd; mob; rabble. 6. riot; disturbance. 1,3,5,6 *n.,* 2,4 *v.*

rou tine (rü tēn′), 1. a fixed, regular method of doing things; habitual doing of the same things in the same way: *Getting up and going to bed are parts of your daily routine.* 2. using routine: *routine methods, routine workers.* 1 *n.,* 2 *adj.*

sag (sag), 1. sink under weight or pressure; bend down in the middle. 2. become less firm or elastic; yield through weakness, weariness, or lack of effort; droop; sink: *Our courage sagged.* *v.*

sage (sāj), 1. plant whose leaves are used as seasoning and in medicine. 2. its dried leaves. *n.*

sal vage (sal′vij), 1. save from fire, shipwreck, etc. 2. property salvaged: *the salvage from a shipwreck or a fire.* 1 *v.,* 2 *n.*

salve (sav or säv), 1. a soft, greasy substance put on wounds and sores; healing ointment. 2. put salve on. 3. something soothing: *The kind words were a salve to his hurt feelings.* 4. soothe; smooth over: *He salved his conscience by the thought that his lie harmed no one.* 1,3 *n.,* 2,4 *v.*

sap ling (sap′ling), 1. a young tree. 2. a young person. *n.*

sar cas tic (sär kas′tik), using sarcasm; sneering; cutting: *"Don't hurry!" was his sarcastic*

comment as I began to dress at my usual slow rate. *adj.* —**sar cas′ti cal ly,** *adv.*

sav age (sav′ij), 1. wild or rugged: *He likes savage mountain scenery.* 2. not civilized; barbarous: *savage customs.* 3. fierce; cruel; ready to fight; brutal: *a savage dog.* —**sav′age ly,** *adv.*

sav age ry (sav′ij rē), 1. wildness. 2. an uncivilized condition. 3. fierceness; cruelty; brutality. *n., pl.* **sav age ries.**

scan (skan), 1. look at closely; examine with care: *His mother scanned his face to see if he was telling the truth.* 2. *Informal.* glance at; look over hastily. *v.,* **scanned, scan ning.**

scoff (skôf), make fun to show one does not believe something; mock. *v.*

schol ar ly (skol′ər lē), 1. of a scholar; like that of a scholar: *scholarly habits.* 2. having much knowledge; learned. 3. thorough and orderly in methods of study. *adj.*

schoon er (skü′nər), 1. *U.S.* ship with two or more masts and fore-and-aft sails. 2. prairie schooner. *n.*

Schooner (def. 1)

scout (skout), 1. refuse to believe in; reject with scorn: *He scouted the idea of a dog with two tails.* 2. scoff. *v.*

scrag gly (skrag′lē), rough; irregular; ragged. *adj.*

scram ble (skram′bəl), 1. make one's way by climbing, crawling, etc.: *The boys scrambled up the steep, rocky hill.* 2. a climb or walk over rough ground: *It was a long scramble through bushes and over rocks to the top of the hill.* 3. struggle with others for something. 1,3 *v.,* 2 *n.*

scraw ny (skrô′nē), *U.S. Informal.* lean; thin; skinny: *Turkeys have scrawny necks.* *adj.*

scru ti nize (skrüt′n īz), examine closely; inspect carefully. *v.*

scur vy (skėr′vē), disease characterized by swollen and bleeding gums, livid spots on the skin, and prostration, due to lack of vitamin C in the diet. Scurvy used to be common among sailors when they had little to eat except bread and salt meat. *n.*

sear (sir), 1. burn or char the surface of: *The hot iron seared his flesh.* 2. dry up; wither. *v.*

se date (si dāt′), quiet; calm; serious. *adj.* —**se date′ly,** *adv.*

sem blance (sem′bləns), 1. outward appearance: *His story had the semblance of truth but was really false.* 2. likeness. *n.*

sen si bil i ty (sen′sə bil′ə tē), 1. ability to feel or perceive: *Some drugs lessen a person's sensibilities.* 2. fineness of feeling: *She has an unusual sensibility for colors.* 3. awareness; consciousness. *n., pl.* **sen si bil i ties.**

sensibilities, sensitive feelings.

sen ti men tal i ty (sen′tə men tal′ə tē), 1. tendency to be influenced by sentiment rather than reason. 2. feeling expressed too openly or sentimentally. *n., pl.* **sen ti men tal i ties.**

---

hat, āge, fär; let, bē, tèrm; it, īce; hot, gō, ôrder; oil, out; cup, pùt, rüle; ch, child; ng, long; th, thin; ᴛʜ, then; zh, measure; ə represents *a* in about, *e* in taken, *i* in April, *o* in lemon, *u* in circus.

sev er (sev′ər), cut apart; cut off. *v.*

shab by (shab′ē), much worn: *His old suit looks shabby. adj.* —**shab′bi ly,** *adv.* —**shab′bi ness,** *n.*

shaft (shaft), 1. the long, slender stem of an arrow, spear, etc. 2. arrow; spear. 3. something aimed at a person like an arrow or spear: *shafts of ridicule.* 4. one of the two wooden poles between which a horse is harnessed to a carriage, etc. 5. a deep passage sunk in the earth. The entrance to a mine is called a shaft. 6. a well-like passage; long, narrow space: *an elevator shaft. n.* —**shaft′like′,** *adj.*

S, shaft in a mine; T, tunnel.

sham bles (sham′bəlz), 1. slaughter house. 2. place of butchery or of great bloodshed. 3. scene of great destruction. *n.pl. or sing.*

shoat (shōt), a young pig able to feed itself. *n.* Also, **shote.**

shore (shôr), 1. prop placed against or beneath something to support it. 2. prop up or support with shores. 1 *n.,* 2 *v.*

shrew (shrü), 1. a bad-tempered, quarrelsome woman. 2. a mouse-like mammal with a long snout and brownish fur, that eats insects and worms. *n.*

shrewd (shrüd), 1. having a sharp mind; showing a keen wit; clever: *He is a shrewd businessman.* 2. keen; sharp. *adj.* —**shrewd′ly,** *adv.* —**shrewd′ness,** *n.*

shriv el (shriv′əl), 1. dry up; wither; shrink and wrinkle: *The hot sunshine shriveled the grass.* 2. waste away; become useless. *v.*

shroud (shroud), 1. cloth or garment in which a dead person is wrapped for burial. 2. something that covers, conceals, or veils: *The fog was a shroud over the city.* 3. cover; conceal; veil: *The earth is shrouded in darkness.* 1,2 *n.,* 3 *v.*

sim per (sim′pər), 1. smile in a silly, affected way. 2. express by a simper; say with a simper. 3. a silly, affected smile. 1,2 *v.,* 3 *n.*

sin ew (sin′yü), 1. a tough, strong band or cord that joins muscle to bone; tendon. 2. strength; energy. *n.*

sin is ter (sin′is tər), 1. showing ill will; threatening: *a sinister look.* 2. bad; evil; dishonest. 3. disastrous; unfortunate. *adj.*

sin u ous (sin′yü əs), having many curves or turns; winding. *adj.* —**sin′u ous ly,** *adv.*

skep ti cal (skep′tə kəl), 1. inclined to doubt; not believing easily. 2. questioning the truth of theories or apparent facts. *adj.*

skew er (skyü′ər), 1. a long pin of wood or metal stuck through meat to hold it together while it is cooking. 2. something shaped or used like a long pin. *n.*

skimp (skimp), 1. supply in too small an amount: *Don't skimp the butter in making a cake.* 2. be very saving or economical. *v.*

skulk (skulk), 1. keep out of sight to avoid danger, work, duty, etc.; hide or lurk in a cowardly way. 2. move in a stealthy, sneaking way: *The wolf was skulking near the sheep. v.*

slith er (sliŦH′ər), 1. slide down or along a surface, especially unsteadily; go with a sliding motion. 2. a slithering movement; a slide. 1 *v.,* 2 *n.*

slough[1] (slou for 1 and 3; slü for 2), 1. a soft, deep muddy place; mud hole. 2. *U.S.* and *Canada.* a swampy place; slew. 3. hopeless discouragement; degradation. *n.*

slough[2] (sluf), 1. the old skin shed or cast off by a snake. 2. drop off; throw off; shed. 1 *n.,* 2 *v.*

slug gish (slug′ish), 1. slow-moving; not active; lacking energy or vigor: *a sluggish mind.* 2. lazy; idle. *adj.* —**slug′gish ly,** *adv.*

slump (slump), 1. drop heavily; fall suddenly: *The boy's feet slumped repeatedly through the rotting ice.* 2. a heavy or sudden fall. 3. a great or sudden decline in prices, activity, etc.: *a slump in prices.* 4. assume an awkwardly drooping posture. 1,4 *v.,* 2,3 *n.*

smirk (smėrk), 1. smile in an affected, silly, self-satisfied way. 2. an affected, silly, self-satisfied smile. 1 *v.,* 2 *n.*

smug (smug), too pleased with one's own goodness, cleverness, respectability, etc.; self-satisfied; complacent. *adj.* —**smug′ly,** *adv.* —**smug′ness,** *n.*

so ber (sō′bər), 1. not drunk. 2. temperate; moderate: *The Puritans led sober, hard-working lives.* 3. quiet; serious; solemn: *a sober expression.* 4. make sober. 5. become sober. 1-3 *adj.,* 4,5 *v.* —**so′ber ly,** *adv.* —**so′ber ness,** *n.*

sol der (sod′ər), 1. metal or alloy that can be melted and used for joining or mending metal surfaces, parts, etc. 2. fasten, mend, or join with solder. 1 *n.,* 2 *v.*

som ber (som′bər), 1. dark; gloomy: *A cloudy winter day is somber.* 2. melancholy; dismal. *adj.* —**som′ber ly,** *adv.*

sor rel (sôr′əl), 1. reddish brown. 2. a reddish-brown horse with mane and tail of the same or a lighter color. 1 *adj.,* 1,2 *n.*

spas mod ic (spaz mod′ik), 1. having to do with spasms; resembling a spasm: *a spasmodic cough.* 2. sudden and violent, but brief; occurring very irregularly. *adj.* —**spas mod′i cal ly,** *adv.*

spawn (spôn), 1. eggs of fish, frogs, shellfish, etc. 2. young newly hatched from such eggs. 3. bring forth; give birth to. 1,2 *n.,* 3 *v.*

spec ter (spek′tər), 1. ghost. 2. thing causing terror or dread. *n.*

spec tre (spek′tər), *Esp. Brit.* specter. *n.*

spo rad ic (spə rad′ik), appearing or happening at intervals in time: *sporadic outbreaks. adj.*

spry (sprī), active; lively; nimble. *adj.* —**spry′ly,** *adv.* —**spry′ness,** *n.*

squall (skwôl), cry out loudly; scream violently: *The baby squalled. v.*

squal or (skwol′ər), misery and dirt; filth. *n.*

squirm (skwėrm), wriggle; writhe; twist: *The restless boy squirmed in his chair. v., n.*

sta ble (stā′bəl), 1. not likely to move or change; steadfast; firm; steady: *The whole world needs a stable peace.* 2. lasting without change; permanent. *adj.*

stac ca to (stə kä′tō), 1. in music, with breaks between the successive tones; disconnected;

abrupt. **2.** in a staccato manner. 1 *adj.*, 2 *adv.*

stag ger (stag′ər), **1.** sway or reel (from weakness, a heavy load, or drunkenness). **2.** confuse or astonish greatly: *He was staggered by the news of his friend's death.* **3.** arrange in a zigzag order or way. *v.*

sta lac tite (stə lak′tīt), **1.** formation of lime, shaped like an icicle, hanging from the roof of a cave. Stalactites and stalagmites are formed by dripping water that contains lime. **2.** any formation shaped like this. *n.*

sta lag mite (stə lag′mīt), **1.** a formation of lime, shaped like a cone, built up on the floor of a cave. **2.** any formation shaped like this. *n.*

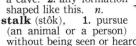

Stalactites and stalagmites

stalk (stôk), **1.** pursue (an animal or a person) without being seen or heard. **2.** walk with slow, stiff, or haughty strides. *v.*

stat ure (stach′ər), **1.** height: *A man six feet tall is above average stature.* **2.** development; physical, mental, or moral growth. **3.** status or position gained by achievement. *n.*

sta tus (stā′təs or stat′əs), **1.** condition; state. **2.** social or professional standing; position; rank: *his status as a doctor.* **3.** legal position. *n.*

stealth y (stel′thē), done in a secret manner; secret; sly: *The cat crept in a stealthy way toward the bird.* *adj.* —**stealth′i ly,** *adv.* —**stealth′i ness,** *n.*

ste nog ra pher (stə nog′rə fər), person whose work is stenography and typewriting. *n.*

ster ile (ster′əl), **1.** free from living germs. **2.** not fertile; not producing crops: *Sterile land does not produce good crops.* **3.** not producing seed or offspring: *a sterile cow.* *adj.* —**ster′ile ly,** *adv.*

stiff-necked (stif′nekt′), **1.** having a stiff neck. **2.** stubborn; obstinate. *adj.*

stim u lant (stim′yə lənt), **1.** food, drug, medicine, etc., that temporarily increases the activity of some part of the body. Tea, coffee, and alcoholic drinks are stimulants. **2.** something that spurs one on or stirs one up: *Hope is a stimulant. n.*

stock y (stok′ē), having a solid or sturdy form or build; thick for its height. *adj.* —**stock′i ly,** *adv.* —**stock′i ness,** *n.*

stol id (stol′id), hard to arouse; not easily excited; showing no emotion; seeming dull. *adj.* —**stol′id ly,** *adv.*

strained (strānd), forced; not natural: *Her greeting was cold and strained. adj.*

stun (stun), **1.** make senseless; knock unconscious: *He was stunned by the fall.* **2.** daze; bewilder; shock; overwhelm: *She was stunned by the news of her friend's death.* *v.*, **stunned, stun ning.**

St. Vi tus's dance (sānt vī′təs iz), a nervous disease, which usually affects children, char-

acterized by involuntary twitching of the muscles. It is often called chorea.

sub due (səb dü′ or səb dyü′), **1.** conquer; overcome. **2.** tone down; soften: *Pulling down the shades subdued the light in the room. v.*

sub mis sive (səb mis′iv), yielding to the power, control, or authority of another; obedient; humble. *adj.* —**sub mis′sive ly,** *adv.* —**sub mis′sive ness,** *n.*

sub side (səb sīd′), **1.** sink to a lower level: *After the rain stopped, the flood waters subsided.* **2.** grow less; die down; become less active; abate; ebb: *The storm finally subsided. v.*

sub ter fuge (sub′tər fyüj), trick or excuse used to escape something unpleasant. *n.*

sub tle (sut′l), **1.** delicate; thin; fine: *a subtle odor of perfume.* **2.** faint; mysterious: *a subtle smile.* **3.** having a keen, quick mind. *adj.*

suf fuse (sə fyüz′), overspread (with a liquid, dye, etc.): *At twilight the sky was suffused with color. Her eyes were suffused with tears. v.*

sul len (sul′ən), **1.** silent because of bad humor or anger: *The sullen child refused to answer my question.* **2.** showing bad humor or anger. **3.** gloomy; dismal: *The sullen skies threatened rain. adj.* —**sul′len ly,** *adv.* —**sul′len ness,** *n.*

sum mons (sum′ənz), **1.** an order to appear at a certain place, especially in a law court: *He received a summons for fast driving.* **2.** a command; message; signal. *n., pl.* **sum mons es.**

su per cil i ous (sü′pər sil′ē əs), haughty, proud, and contemptuous; showing scorn or indifference because of a feeling of superiority. *adj.*

su per im pose (sü′pər im pōz′), put on top of something else. *v.*

swag ger (swag′ər), **1.** walk with a bold, rude, or superior air; strut about or show off in a vain or insolent way: *The bully swaggered into the schoolyard.* **2.** boast or brag noisily. *v.* —**swag′ger er,** *n.*

sward (swôrd), a grassy surface; turf. *n.*

swell (swel), **1.** grow or make bigger: *Bread dough swells as it rises.* **2.** rise or cause to rise above the level: *Rounded hills swell gradually from the village plain.* **3.** piece of higher ground; rounded hill. **4.** a long, unbroken wave or waves: *The boat rocked in the swell.* 1,2 *v.*, **swelled, swelled** or **swol len, swell ing.** 3,4 *n.*

swerve (swèrv), **1.** turn aside: *The car swerved and hit a tree.* **2.** a turning aside: *The swerve of the ball made it hard to hit.* 1 *v.,* 2 *n.*

swirl (swèrl), **1.** move or drive along with a twisting motion; whirl: *dust swirling in the air, a stream swirling over rocks.* **2.** a swirling movement; whirl; eddy. 1 *v.,* 2 *n.*

syn on y mous (si non′ə məs), having the same or nearly the same meaning. *adj.*

ta boo (tə bü′), something forbidden, prohibited, banned: *Eating human flesh is a taboo in all civilized countries. n.*

---

hat, āge, fär; let, bē, tèrm; it, īce; hot, gō, ôrder; oil, out; cup, pút, rüle; ch, child; ng, long; th, thin; ᴛʜ, then; zh, measure; ə represents *a* in about, *e* in taken, *i* in April, *o* in lemon, *u* in circus.

tac i turn (tas′ə tėrn),　speaking very little; not fond of talking. *adj.*

tack (tak),　*U.S. Informal.* shabby, dowdy, or low-class person. *n.*

taint (tānt),　**1.** stain or spot; trace of decay, corruption, or disgrace. **2.** give a taint to; spoil. 1 *n.*,　2 *v.*

taunt (tônt),　**1.** jeer at; mock; reproach: *Some mean girls taunted Jane with being poor.* **2.** a bitter or insulting remark; mocking; jeering. **3.** get or drive by taunts: *They taunted him into taking the dare.* 1,3 *v.*,　2 *n.*

taut (tôt),　**1.** tightly drawn; tense: *a taut rope.* **2.** in neat condition; tidy: *a taut ship. adj.* —**taut′ly,** *adv.* —**taut′ness,** *n.*

te na cious (ti nā′shəs),　**1.** holding fast: *the tenacious jaws of a bulldog, a person tenacious of his rights.* **2.** stubborn; persistent: *a tenacious salesman.* **3.** sticky. *adj.* —**te na′cious ly,** *adv.*

ten ta tive (ten′tə tiv),　done as a trial or experiment; experimental: *a tentative plan. adj.* —**ten′ta tive ly,** *adv.* —**ten′ta tive ness,** *n.*

teth er (teᴛʜ′ər),　**1.** rope or chain for fastening an animal so that it can graze only within certain limits. **2.** fasten with a tether: *The horse is tethered to a stake.* 1 *n.*,　2 *v.*

the o ry (thē′ə rē),　**1.** explanation; explanation based on thought; explanation based on observation and reasoning: *the theory of evolution, Einstein's theory of relativity.* **2.** principles or methods of a science or art rather than its practice: *the theory of music.* **3.** thought or fancy as opposed to fact or practice. *n., pl.* **the o ries.**

thong (thông),　**1.** a narrow strip of leather, etc., especially used as a fastening. **2.** lash of a whip. *n.*

tick (tik),　a tiny insect or spider that lives on animals and sucks their blood. *n.*

Ti tan (tī′tn),　**1.** in Greek mythology, one of a family of giants who ruled the world before the gods of Olympus. Prometheus and Atlas were Titans. **2.** a giant. **3.** of the Titans; gigantic; huge; very powerful. 1,2 *n.*,　3 *adj.*

to pog ra phy (tə pog′rə fē),　the surface features of a place or region. The topography of a region includes hills, valleys, streams, lakes, bridges, tunnels, roads, etc. *n., pl.* **to pog ra phies.**

tor so (tôr′sō),　**1.** the trunk or body of a statue without any head, arms or legs. **2.** the trunk of the human body. *n., pl.* **tor sos.**

tor tu ous (tôr′chü əs),　**1.** full of twists, turns, or bends; twisting; winding; crooked: *a tortuous path.* **2.** mentally or morally crooked; not straightforward: *tortuous reasoning. adj.* —**tor′tu ous ly,** *adv.*

tour ni quet (tur′nə ket or tur′nə kā),　device for stopping bleeding by compressing a blood vessel, such as a bandage tightened by twisting with a stick, or a pad pressed down by a screw. *n.*

tra di tion (trə dish′ən),　**1.** the handing down of beliefs, opinions, customs, stories, etc., from parents to children. **2.** what is handed down in this way. *n.*

trance (trans),　**1.** state or condition of unconsciousness somewhat like sleep. **2.** a dazed or stunned condition. **3.** a dreamy, absorbed, or hypnotic condition that is like a trance: *The old man sat before the fire in a trance, thinking of his past life. n.* —**trance′like′,** *adj.*

treach er ous (trech′ər əs),　**1.** not to be trusted; disloyal: *The treacherous soldier carried reports to the enemy.* **2.** having a false appearance of strength, security, etc.; not reliable; deceiving: *This ice is treacherous. adj.* —**treach′er ous ly,** *adv.*

treach er y (trech′ər ē),　**1.** a breaking of faith; treacherous behavior; deceit. **2.** treason. *n., pl.* **treach er ies.**

trea son (trē′zn),　**1.** betrayal of one's country or ruler. Helping the enemies of one's country is treason. **2.** *Rare.* betrayal of a trust, duty, friend, etc.; treachery. *n.*

trem u lous (trem′yə ləs),　**1.** trembling; quivering: *The child's voice was tremulous with sobs.* **2.** timid; fearful. *adj.* —**trem′u lous ly,** *adv.*

tri um phant (trī um′fənt),　**1.** victorious; successful. **2.** rejoicing because of victory or success: *The winner spoke in triumphant tones to his defeated rival. adj.* —**tri um′phant ly,** *adv.*

trom bone (trom′bōn),　a large brass musical instrument, usually with a sliding piece for varying the length of the tube. *n.*

trous seau (trü sō′ or trü′sō),　a bride's outfit of clothes, linen, etc. *n., pl.* **trous seaux** (trü sōz′ or trü′sōz) or **trous seaus.**

truck (truk),　**1.** *U.S.* vegetables raised for market. **2.** small articles of little value; odds and ends. *n.*

twit (twit),　**1.** jeer at; reproach; taunt; tease. **2.** a reproach; taunt. 1 *v.*,　**twit ted, twit ting;** 2 *n.*

un as sum ing (un′ə süm′ing),　modest; not putting on airs. *adj.* —**un′as sum′ing ly,** *adv.*

un at tend ed (un′ə ten′did),　**1.** without attendants; alone. **2.** not accompanied. **3.** not taken care of; not attended to. *adj.*

un der shot (un′dər shot′),　having the lower jaw projecting beyond the upper. *adj.*

un err ing (un ėr′ing or un er′ing),　making no mistakes; exactly right. *adj.* —**un err′ing ly,** *adv.*

un flinch ing (un flin′ching),　not drawing back from difficulty, danger, or pain; firm; resolute. *adj.* —**un flinch′ing ly,** *adv.*

un kempt (un kempt′),　**1.** not combed. **2.** neglected; untidy. *adj.*

un prec e dent ed (un pres′ə den′tid),　never done before; never known before. *adj.*

un ru ly (un rü′lē),　hard to rule or control; lawless: *an unruly horse, a disobedient and unruly boy. adj.* —**un ru′li ness,** *n.*

un sa vor y (un sā′vər ē),　**1.** tasteless. **2.** unpleasant in taste or smell. **3.** morally unpleasant; offensive. *adj.*

un time ly (un tīm′lē),　**1.** at a wrong time or season: *Snow in May is untimely.* **2.** too early; too soon: *his untimely death.* 1,2 *adj.*,　2 *adv.* —**un time′li ness,** *n.*

val iant (val′yənt),　brave; courageous: *a valiant deed. adj.* —**val′iant ly,** *adv.*

veer (vir),　change in direction; shift; turn:

The wind veered to the south. The talk veered to ghosts. v.

ven det ta (ven det′ə), feud in which a murdered man's relatives try to kill the slayer or his relatives. *n.*

venge ance (ven′jəns), punishment in return for a wrong; revenge. *n.*

ven om (ven′əm), **1.** the poison of snakes, spiders, etc. **2.** spite; malice: *Her enemies dreaded the venom of her tongue. n.*

ven tril o quist (ven tril′ə kwist), person who can make his voice seem to come from some other source. A ventriloquist can talk without any movement of the lips that can be readily observed. *n.*

ven ture (ven′chər), **1.** a risky or daring undertaking: *His courage was equal to any venture.* **2.** expose to risk or danger: *Men venture their lives in war.* **3.** run a risk. **4.** dare: *No one ventured to interrupt the speaker.* 1 *n.,* 2-4 *v.*

ve ran da or **ve ran dah** (və ran′də), a large porch along one or more sides of a house. *n.*

ver nac u lar (vər nak′yə lər), **1.** a native language; language used by the people of a certain country or place. **2.** everyday language; informal speech. *n.*

vex (veks), **1.** anger by trifles; annoy; provoke: *It is vexing to have to wait for anyone.* **2.** disturb; trouble: *Cape Hatteras is much vexed by storms. v.*

vi brant (vī′brənt), alive; vital; responding to things around one. *adj.* —**vi′brant ly,** *adv.*

vi bra tion (vī brā′shən), a movement to and fro; quivering motion; vibrating: *The busses shake the house so much that we feel the vibration. n.*

vi car i ous (vī ker′ē əs or vī kar′ē əs), **1.** done or suffered for others: *vicarious work.* **2.** felt by sharing in others' experience: *The invalid received vicarious pleasure from reading travel stories. adj.* —**vi car′i ous ly,** *adv.*

vi cious (vish′əs), **1.** evil; wicked. **2.** having bad habits or a bad disposition. **3.** spiteful; malicious: *vicious words.* **4.** *Informal.* unpleasantly severe: *a vicious headache. adj.* —**vi′cious ly,** *adv.* —**vi′cious ness,** *n.*

vig il (vij′əl), a staying awake for some purpose; a watching; watch. *n.*

vig i lance (vij′ə ləns), watchfulness; alertness; caution: *Constant vigilance is necessary in order to avoid accidents in driving. n.*

Vi king or **vi king** (vī′king), one of the daring Scandinavian pirates who raided the coasts of Europe from the eighth to tenth centuries A.D. *n.*

vil lain y (vil′ən ē), **1.** great wickedness. **2.** a very wicked act; crime. *pl.* **vil lain ies.**

vi per (vī′pər), **1.** a thick-bodied poisonous snake with a pair of large perforated fangs. **2.** a spiteful, treacherous person. *n.*

vi ril i ty (və ril′ə tē), **1.** manly strength; masculine vigor. **2.** manhood. **3.** vigor; forcefulness. *n., pl.* **vi ril i ties.**

vise (vīs), tool having two jaws moved by a screw, used to hold an object firmly while work is being done on it. *n.*

vis it a tion (viz′ə tā′shən), a punishment or reward sent by God. *n.*

void (void), an empty space: *The death of his dog left an aching void in Bob's heart. n.*

vol un tar i ly (vol′ən ter′ə lē or vol′ən tar′-ə lē), of one's own free will; without force or compulsion. *adv.*

vul ture (vul′chər), **1.** a large bird of prey related to eagles, hawks, etc., that eats the flesh of dead animals. **2.** a greedy, ruthless person. *n.*

wake (wāk), **1.** track left behind a moving ship. **2.** track left behind any moving thing. *n.*
in the wake of, following; behind; after.

watch (woch), **1.** the time of duty of one part of a ship's crew. A watch usually lasts four hours. **2.** the part of a crew on duty at the same time. *n.*

wa ver (wā′vər), **1.** move to and fro; flutter. **2.** vary in intensity; flicker: *a wavering light.* **3.** be undecided; hesitate: *Her choice wavered between the blue dress and the green one.* **4.** become unsteady; begin to give way: *The battle line wavered and broke. v.*

weal (wēl), streak or ridge on the skin made by a stick or whip; welt. *n.*

weath er nap (weŦH′ər nap′), fibrous surface or wood grain raised by rain and sun. *n.*

whee dle (hwē′dl), persuade by flattery, smooth words, caresses, etc.; coax. *v.*

wince (wins), **1.** draw back suddenly; flinch slightly: *The boy winced at the sight of the dentist's drill. v.*

winch (winch), **1.** a machine for lifting or pulling, turned by a crank. **2.** handle of a revolving machine. *n.*

wob ble (wob′əl or wô′bəl), **1.** move unsteadily from side to side; shake; tremble; waver. **2.** a wobbling motion. 1 *v.,* 2 *n.*

wor ry (wèr′ē), **1.** feel anxious or uneasy. **2.** cause to feel anxious or troubled. **3.** anxiety; uneasiness; trouble; care. **4.** annoy; bother: *Don't worry me with so many questions.* **5.** seize and shake with the teeth; bite at; snap at: *A cat will worry a mouse.* 1,2,4,5 *v.,* **wor ried, wor ry ing;** 3 *n., pl.* **wor ries.**

year ling (yir′ling or yèr′ling), **1.** an animal one year old. **2.** one year old: *a yearling colt.* 1 *n.,* 2 *adj.*

zeal ous (zel′əs), full of zeal; eager; earnest; enthusiastic. *adj.* —**zeal′ous ly,** *adv.*

zo o log i cal (zō′ə loj′ə kəl), **1.** of animals and animal life. **2.** having to do with zoology. *adj.* —**zo′o log′i cal ly,** *adv.*

zo ol o gist (zō ol′ə jist), person skilled or trained in zoology. *n.*

zo ol o gy (zō ol′ə jē), the science of animals; the study of animals and animal life. Zoology deals with the form, structure, physiology, development, and classification of animals. It also includes study of special groups, as birds, insects, snakes, mammals, etc. *n.*

---

hat, āge, fär; let, bē, tèrm; it, īce; hot, gō, ôrder; oil, out; cup, pùt, rüle; ch, child; ng, long; th, thin; ŦH, then; zh, measure; ə represents *a* in about, *e* in taken, *i* in April, *o* in lemon, *u* in circus.

INDEX OF AUTHORS AND TITLES

INDEX OF LITERARY TYPES

INDEX OF SKILLS